W9-ACG-738

DISCARDED
URI LIBRARY

Language Arts
Exploring Connections

Third Edition

Karen D'Angelo Bromley

Binghamton University,
State University of New York

Allyn and Bacon

Boston • London • Toronto • Sydney • Tokyo • Singapore

*For the teachers and students
whose work appears here*

*For B. in SC and S. & C.,
who helped with the paper clips*

● ● ● ● ●

Senior Editor: Virginia C. Lanigan
Editorial Assistant: Kris Lamarre
Senior Marketing Manager: Kathy Hunter
Production Administrator: Annette Joseph
Production Coordinator: Susan Freese
Editorial-Production Service: TKM Productions

Text Design/Electronic Composition: Denise Hoffman
Composition Buyer: Linda Cox
Manufacturing Buyer: Suzanne Lareau
Cover Administrator: Linda Knowles
Cover Designer: Studio Nine

Copyright © 1998, 1992, 1988 by Allyn & Bacon
A Viacom Company
160 Gould Street
Needham Heights, MA 02194
Internet: www.abacon.com
America Online: keyword: College Online

All rights reserved. No part of the material protected by this copyright notice may be reproduced or utilized in any form or by any means, electronic or mechanical, including photocopying, recording, or by any information storage and retrieval system, without the written permission of the copyright owner.

Library of Congress Cataloging-in-Publication Data

Bromley, Karen D'Angelo
    Language arts : exploring connections / Karen D'Angelo Bromley. —
3rd ed.
      p. cm.
    Include bibliographical references (p.   ) and indexes.
    ISBN 0–205–26812–9 (alk. paper)
    1. Language arts (Elementary)—United States. 2. English
language—Study and teaching (Elementary)—United States.
I. Title.
LB1576.B76 1997   97–27515
372.6'044—dc21   CIP

Printed in the United States of America

10 9 8 7 6 5 4 3 2 1   02 01 00 99 98 97

Text Credits: p. 188: Excerpt from *Earthdance,* © 1996 by Joanne Ryder. Reprinted by permission of Henry Holt & Co., Inc. p. 188: Excerpt from *The Great Kapok Tree: A Tale of the Amazon Rain Forest,* copyright © 1990 by Lynne Cherry, reprinted by permission of Harcourt Brace & Company. p. 188: Excerpt from *And Still the Turtle Watched* by Sheila MacGill-Callahan, 1991, New York: Penguin USA. pp. 279–280: Excerpt from *Nightjohn* by Gary Paulsen, Copyright © 1993 by Gary Paulsen. Used by permission of Delacorte Press, a division of Bantam Doubleday Dell Publishing Group, Inc. p. 464: Excerpt from *Hush Little Baby* © 1997 by Sylvia Long. Published by Chronicle Books, San Francisco. Reprinted by permission.

Photo Credits: Brian Smith: pp. 1, 132, 138, 208, 267, 297, 329, 404, 417; Will Hart: pp. 5, 57, 91, 109, 220, 264, 279, 309, 335, 377, 385, 395, 451, 480, 501; Will Faller: pp. 10, 33, 41, 51, 67, 81, 117, 127, 154, 169, 191, 199, 203, 214, 235, 254, 291, 317, 347, 382, 409, 431, 446, 475.

Brief Contents

Contents

3 Diversity in the Classroom   57

· · · · ·
Part Two   A Literature Foundation

4 Getting Started with Literature   91

5   Sharing and Responding to Literature   127

· · · · ·
Part Three   Developing Receptive Language

6   Connections: Listening and Reading   169

7 Listening to Learn   203

8 Reading to Learn   235

•••••
Part Four   Developing Expressive Language

9 Connections: Speaking and Writing   279

.....

Part Five   Developing Receptive and Expressive Language Together

12   Language Tools: Spelling, Grammar, and Handwriting   395

13   Connections among the Language Arts   431

Preface

This third edition of *Language Arts: Exploring Connections* blends current research, theory, and practices in integrating the language arts in kindergarten through grade 6 with the content areas and children's literature. It details the connections between and among the receptive language arts—listening, reading, and viewing—and the expressive arts—speaking and writing. This book discusses and gives a variety of examples of thematic instruction in K–6. It presents a balanced view of language arts instruction that focuses on language processes and products. Direct instruction and meaningful, relevant context are advocated as critical to student learning. The text contains colorful stories and examples of teachers and classrooms in which students use language to learn. Many current titles of children's literature and ideas for using them effectively in integrated teaching are included, as well.

Language Arts: Exploring Connections contains several features that make it unique and easy to use:

- A balanced approach is presented to language arts instruction that develops skills and strategies and focuses on processes and products.
- A new chapter discusses the decisions a beginning teacher must make about theory, methods, curriculum, and standards.
- A new chapter is included on diversity in the classroom, and ideas for teaching diverse students are given throughout the book.
- The language tools of spelling, grammar, and handwriting are discussed in a new chapter.
- Two chapters focus on children's literature, and ideas for using children's literature appear in other chapters, along with many bibliographies of special books.
- Language differences are discussed, including the needs of bilingual and English as a Second Language (ESL) students, as well as those with dialects, language delays, and difficulties.
- Standards, rubrics, and portfolios, along with the issues surrounding them, are discussed.
- Viewing and visual literacy are included in several chapters.
- The use of technology and computers in K–6 classrooms is emphasized.
- Discussions of cooperative learning, literature circles and groups, writing workshops, and journals are presented.
- The idea that reading and writing are complementary processes is interwoven throughout the text.

- The text includes a strong theory, research, and information base for each of the language arts.
- Each chapter begins with a *Window on Teaching* that peeks into a classroom and details the life of a real teacher.
- *Stretching Exercises* within chapters invite the reader to think about an issue, read a topical article, or do an activity to extend understanding.
- At the end of each chapter, *Reflections* invite the reader to think about or do something to demonstrate global understanding.
- Each chapter includes an overview, a summary, and a list of current professional resources.
- Many practical strategies for effective classroom teaching and examples of K–6 student and teacher work are included.

This text is written in a friendly, informal style, making it both accessible and engaging to readers. To enhance the descriptions of real classroom situations in the Windows on Teaching and similar sections, actual dialogue from teachers and students is often used. Readers may also note that when single individuals, such as students or teachers, are described in general terms, the use of pronouns alternates between *he* and *she*. This style has been used both to keep the language simple and to avoid any gender bias; it does not mean, however, that the discussion applies only to males or females.

Acknowledgments

I am fortunate to have worked with many fine teachers and their students over the years and I am grateful to them for allowing me to include their work here. The stories of thoughtful and innovative teachers and students from diverse classrooms add meaning and richness to a text like this one.

I especially want to thank Virginia Lanigan, editor at Allyn and Bacon, and Kris Lamarre, editorial assistant, for their support and editorial help throughout this project. I appreciate, also, the thoughtful and positive suggestions from the following reviewers of the manuscript for this book: Helen R. Abadiano, Central Connecticut State University; Cynthia G. Desrochers, California State University, Northridge; Joyce Fiddler, University of Central Arkansas; Danny Fulks, Marshall University; Janet E. McClain, University of Northern Iowa; Bruce A. VanSledright, University of Maryland at College Park; Ruth Ann Williamson, Houston Baptist University; and Phyllis J. Wood, California State University.

About the Author

Dr. Karen Bromley is a member of the School of Education and Human Development at Binghamton University, where she teaches courses in language arts, literacy, and children's literature. Before joining the faculty at Binghamton, she taught third grade in

New York, was a K–6 reading specialist in Maryland, and received her Ph.D. from the University of Maryland. In 1992, she received the Reading Educator Award from the New York State Reading Association. Bromley is also the author of many articles in professional journals and three other books: *Webbing with Literature: Creating Story Maps with Children's Books* (2nd ed.), published by Allyn and Bacon, and *Journaling: Engagements in Reading, Writing and Thinking* and *Graphic Organizers: Visual Strategies for Active Learning* (coauthored), published by Scholastic. Bromley lives with her husband and two Maine coon cats in Vestal, New York.

Becoming a Language Arts Teacher

1

W••••• indow on Teaching

Ann Richardson has a master's degree in elementary education and has been teaching at the elementary level for 12 years. She is in her first year as a third-grade teacher. Ann's advice to beginning teachers is "Discover what you love. Find out all you can and pass it on!" She makes this recommendation to her students, as well. It appears in Ann's room at the center of a bulletin board filled with print and realia about trees, one of her special loves.

Ann has a class of 24 diverse third-graders. Her students speak several languages, represent different social, cultural, and economic groups, and possess varying abilities and interests. Built 70 years ago, Ann's school is located in a neighborhood where most families live close to the poverty level and over two-thirds of the children have only one parent.

Ann firmly believes the literacy curriculum in a diverse classroom should begin with the teacher's own passions. She therefore starts the school year with a theme that is close to her heart because she believes her enthusiasm will be catching. Her classroom contains shelves and baskets full of all sorts of books, green plants, objects and collections, tables (rather than individual desks) where children work together, a bank of computers, and areas where special projects occur. Walls hold children's art and written work as well as lists, questions, and class stories and books, some written by students and others transcribed by Ann. Leaf rubbings, poetry about trees, a painting area, and a mural titled "Our Walk in the Woods—Observations That Illustrate Change" show the fine-arts component of this science-based literacy program. Ann's classroom is planned and arranged for problem solving, investigations, critical thinking, and active learning. It shows her encouragement and support of learners as they gather, analyze, and interpret information to answer the questions they pose.

Why does Ann's philosophy about a teacher's passions and teaching begin this chapter and book? Because a teacher's philosophy guides her in making decisions about curriculum and instruction, and you should be in the process of developing your personal philosophy of teaching as you read this text. Before you read this and ensuing chapters, ask yourself some questions that can help you shape your teaching philosophy. One way to develop prereading questions is to scan chapter headings (e.g., What are the components of an effective language arts program? Who makes curriculum decisions? How can my strengths and interests inform my classroom curriculum? What is integration?). Also ask yourself questions that occur to you as you read and reflect (e.g., What do I do if my philosophy is not shared by the administration? How do I compromise in a meaningful way for my students?). Add to this list of questions as needed and return to these questions with some answers after you finish reading.

·····

Overview

This chapter gives the rationale for integrating listening, speaking, reading, and writing and explains the importance of integrating language arts with content area subjects and children's literature. Curriculum and instruction, language arts standards, and the benefits and criticisms of integration are discussed. The classroom practices of several teachers show you the fundamentals of integration.

The four modes, or forms, of language—listening, speaking, reading, writing—comprise the language arts. As you explore ways to use the language arts in the classroom, you'll discover connections among these modes as well as between language arts and the content areas (science, social studies, and math). Keep these four premises in mind as you read this text:

1. Important connections exist among the four forms of language—listening, speaking, reading, and writing.
2. Both learning and teaching are uniquely individual endeavors. Each child learns in a different way and at a different rate. Each teacher possesses a philosophy, values, and beliefs about teaching. Her language arts program is shaped according to that philosophy as well as her interests and goals and those of the children she teaches.
3. Learning in the content areas of science, social studies, and mathematics provides relevant opportunities for children to use and learn language in authentic ways.
4. Literature that is written for children and youth is a critical ingredient in a language arts program and a natural vehicle for connecting the four language modes.

Next we will explore each premise in relation to the development of effective communication—communication that accomplishes what children want it to and that produces the desired results for them.

The Language Arts

The meaning of *language arts* comes from the definitions of *language,* defined as an ordered system of symbols for transmitting ideas and information, and *art,* defined as the ability to effectively and creatively execute or make something. Together, the two suggest that *language arts* means effective and creative execution of a symbolic system of communication. Language arts includes all the various ways that learners make and share meaning, and an effective language arts program is one that expands the communication potential of all learners (NCTE Elementary Section Steering Committee, 1996).

Language possesses visual symbols—those that a child sees, writes, and reads—and verbal symbols—those that a child speaks and hears. Each child manipulates these visual and verbal symbols in different ways. Basic to each of the language arts is cognitive processing or thinking, which is necessary in order for a child to be an effective listener, speaker, reader, and writer.

All learners receive and express language in their unique ways, but there are some commonalities within the language arts. Together, listening and reading involve language *reception,* whereas speaking and writing involve language *expression* (see Figure 1.1).

When a child listens or reads, she makes meaning from visual or verbal symbols. She constructs meaning based on the knowledge and experience she already possesses and the input she receives from sounds, print, or visual information. The child's affective or emotional response to text influences her meaning-making processes, as well. So, we can think of listening and reading as composing processes that involve the *construction* of meaning. Although viewing and visual literacy do not involve reading print in the traditional sense, they do require a type of reading and are considered part of language reception.

A child also makes meaning from visual and verbal symbols when she speaks or writes. She constructs meaning based on the knowledge and experience she already possesses as she processes ideas and expresses meaning through verbal and visual symbols.

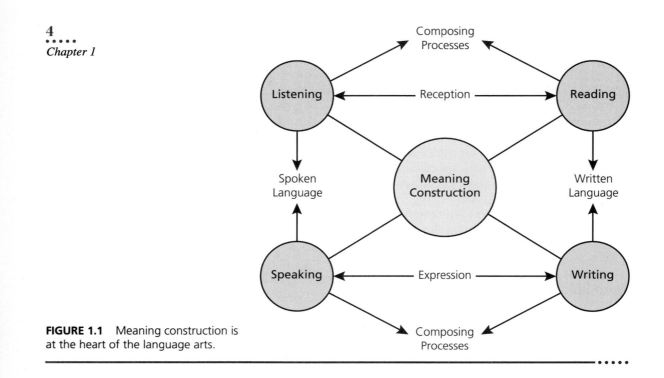

FIGURE 1.1 Meaning construction is at the heart of the language arts.

So, we can also think of speaking and writing as composing processes that involve the *construction* of meaning. Additionally, art, drama, and movement involve the expression of language and thought, even though they may not require speech or writing.

Constructing or composing meaning is basic to learning in general. How children use language helps determine their social, emotional, physical, and cognitive development. Success in content areas such as science, social studies, and mathematics depends on the ability to make meaning with and from language. Thaiss (1985) reports that children understand better and remember more when they have the opportunity to talk, write, sing, draw, and dramatize what they are learning about. He stresses that children learn to read and listen only if they regularly express their own meanings by talking and writing to themselves and others. Thaiss believes that learning occurs only when there is dialogue, such as a conversation between teacher and student, student and student, student and text, or student and the world. He argues that language and learning cannot be separated. The ability to use language effectively is *critical* to a child's general well-being and academic learning. The notion that language and learning are inextricably intertwined is central to this text.

Another fundamental idea in this book is that people must take a broader view of literacy. Certainly, literacy is more than the ability to read and write. Wells and Chang-Wells (1992) believe literacy is a "way of using language for particular intellectual and communicative purposes" (p. 121). They define literate thinking as the use of "mental muscles" to tackle and accomplish intellectual tasks that might otherwise be beyond one's grasp. It is through the use of interrelated language arts that a person is able to employ existing knowledge to create and acquire new knowledge and solve problems. The literate person, then, is a competent user of language to function and improve her life and the lives of others.

Listening, speaking, reading, and writing share the same cognitive process—thinking—and much of the same vocabulary, but they are also strikingly different in several ways:

■ *Language is received and expressed in distinctive and individual ways.* Among these differences, for example, are specific vocabularies, individual pronunciations and distinctive voice inflections, and social registers. *Register* is a level of formality in language use, such as your use of informal language with family members and good friends and more formal language when you give a speech or talk with people you know less well. As a teacher, you should recognize not only the need for effective communication but also the need to respect healthy differences in your students' language use that allow them to be unique individuals. For example, dialect differences and variations in the way children speak, due to children's language differences or difficulties or to their membership in a particular group, need to be honored as long communication is effective. In addition, the first language of students who are learning English as a second language (ESL) needs to be valued and viewed as a strength. You should recognize that since language is a part of a child's culture and identity, rejecting a child's language is, in effect, a rejection of her as a person.

■ *Language reception and expression occur at different rates.* The average adult can handwrite 15 to 25 words a minute. Some adults can type as quickly as 60 or more words a minute on a keyboard or typewriter. The typical third-grader writes from 6 to 15 words a minute when composing stories in class. Writing, then, is a relatively slow act when compared with speaking, which generally occurs at 125 to 150 words a minute, and reading, which generally occurs at about 250 to 350 words a minute. If the cognitive

* * * * *
*These first-graders construct
meaning together as they talk
and listen.*

process of thinking could be measured (which of course it can't), it surely would occur at much higher rates, perhaps as high as 400 to 600 words a minute, because thinking involves associations and images that do not occur in complete sentences and cannot be easily counted.

■ *Language modes differ according to their relative permanence.* Reading and writing involve print that a person can reread or revise and reflect on for longer time periods than when speaking. Listening and speaking are temporary, unless speaking is recorded or videotaped for replay later. Memory limits the retrieval, both in amount and quality, of what was said, read, or written even a few moments ago. People might remember only 10 percent of what they hear, 20 percent of what they read, 30 percent of what they say, and 40 percent of what they write. One version of a Chinese proverb, if one relates it to situations where the learner uses language, is particularly relevant to our discussion: "Tell me—I forget. Show me—I remember. Involve me—I understand." It makes sense, doesn't it? The less people use language to process and manipulate ideas, the less they remember; the more people use language to process and manipulate ideas, the more they remember.

■ *Language modes differ in content and function.* Language used in oral conversation is often quite different from language used in written composition. Word choice is not the same when an individual talks and when she writes, and of course both vary depending on the audience. In addition, facial expressions, gestures, and voice modulations accompany oral language and either enhance or detract from meaning. Written language serves as a more permanent record than oral language, and so it is often more formal than speaking. Depending on the function or reason for language, the syntax of a person's written language may also be more precise than the syntax of her oral language. In talking, people often interrupt themselves with a new idea, get sidetracked and never finish a sentence, or speak in one long, run-on sentence.

STRETCHING EXERCISE

Compare a teacher's spoken directions for completing a task with her written directions for the same task. How might one mode be more effective? Why? To be most effective, how would you present directions? Do factors such as the type of directions and the length of directions affect your decision? Why would it help to have students paraphrase your directions?

• • • • •

Integrating the Language Arts

In many schools, separate blocks of time are spent on teaching the skills of listening, spelling, handwriting, reading, speaking, writing, and grammar. When this occurs, language learning is not typically integrated with the subject areas, and thus learning, in general, becomes fragmented. Children might learn how to spell a list of words but they do not necessarily learn how to use these words in their writing. They may learn how to write but not necessarily how to write about what they are learning in science or social studies. When language lessons are separated from other subjects, learning is disconnected and often lacks meaning.

Teaching the language arts together and integrating literature and content learning with language learning makes sense for several reasons:

- Listening, speaking, reading, and writing use the same sound-symbol system, so learning in one mode reinforces learning in the others.
- Listening and reading are receptive processes and speaking and writing are expressive processes that share the common cognitive process of thinking, which is basic to learning.
- Children use listening, speaking, reading, and writing together naturally as they interact with others to communicate and learn.

From the beginning, a child depends on these similarities among the language arts. A child first understands the world by receiving and constructing meaning from incoming information through listening. She develops a *listening* vocabulary—those words that she hears and understands but does not use in speech—long before she composes meaning by speaking. A child's *speaking* vocabulary is the words she understands through listening and expresses through speech. This vocabulary develops from words in the listening vocabulary, with the addition of new words and phrases that a child tries out as she experiences the world and gains command over the rules of language. The *reading* vocabulary—those words a child recognizes and understands in print—and the *writing* vocabulary—those words the child uses in composing written language—both require more sophisticated skills and develop most easily once listening and speaking vocabularies are in place.

Traditionally, the acquisition of listening, speaking, reading, and writing competence was thought to occur in that order, which perhaps explains the practice of teaching discrete skills sequentially. However, research suggests that the four language arts develop concurrently and reinforce each other as they grow. For instance, research in writing indicates that a child does not need to have a large reading vocabulary before a writing vocabulary begins to develop. In fact, some children learn to write words first and then learn to read what they write (Chomsky, 1971). Oral language research shows that facility with the spoken word does not always precede the written word, and it is not always necessary to learn to read first (Myers, 1987). Children with no oral language—for example, children who are deaf or have hearing impairments—do learn to read. However, facility with spoken language does contribute to the development of reading and writing competence.

So, it should not be difficult to understand that the typical child in the early elementary grades possesses four overlapping vocabularies. Figure 1.2 shows the relative sizes of these vocabularies and how they intersect with one another. In the upper-elementary grades, as a child becomes more fluent in the use of language, vocabulary sizes change. For example, as a child learns to use syntax, semantics, graphophonemics, and pictures that accompany text to recognize unknown words and as that child's experiences broaden over time, her reading vocabulary becomes larger than the other vocabularies. Sizes of the typical literate adult's vocabularies vary among individuals and are quite different from that of children. An adult's career, hobbies, and interests will shape the relative sizes of her vocabularies.

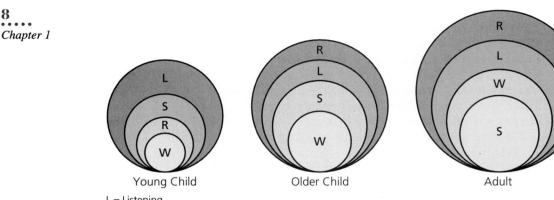

L = Listening
S = Speaking
R = Reading
W = Writing

FIGURE 1.2   The overlapping vocabularies of a young child, older child, and adult.

STRETCHING EXERCISE

Talk with a friend about possible reasons for the developmental shifts in vocabulary sizes. What are your smallest and largest vocabularies? Why? Which vocabularies would you like to expand? How could you develop each?

• • • • •

From the previous discussion of vocabulary, you can see that a child uses listening, speaking, reading, and writing together naturally. When a child listens to spoken language, it is normal to respond in turn with spoken language, in the form of a question, answer, paraphrase, or elaboration of what was heard. When a child reads or is read to, she may respond orally or in writing. When a child writes, rereading the written language to revise or share is natural also. Since the forms of language are interrelated and used together in learning, it makes sense to teach them together.

Differences in Teaching and Learning

Teaching and learning are uniquely individual endeavors. As a teacher, you do not necessarily use the same curriculum, methods, and strategies your fellow teachers use, nor do you always use the same curriculum, methods, and strategies yourself. For instance, a teacher who is a talented musician, an avid environmentalist, or a breeder of golden retrievers may incorporate these passions and skills in a variety of ways into a language arts program. Like Ann Richardson, the third-grade teacher mentioned at the beginning of this chapter, your own personality is reflected in your classroom organization and atmosphere, the curriculum and projects you plan and implement, the instructional strategies you use, and the feedback and reinforcement you provide children. What works well in someone else's classroom may not work for you in your classroom.

In general, though, successful teachers demystify the unknown for children and interact with them in ways that enable them to learn (Comber, 1987). Comber's study of successful teachers identified some common characteristics they possess. She found that successful teachers have high expectations for children, help children identify their own goals, show children the hows and whys of tasks, interact with children in positive ways to promote success, and let children help each other learn. Successful teachers plan meaningful classroom interactions that are related to the real world, and they watch, listen to, and talk with children as they monitor their own teaching and the children's learning.

Monitoring your teaching and your students' learning will allow you to grow as a teacher. You will learn from observing the children you teach, reflecting on your mistakes and successes, talking with and observing your fellow teachers, reading and studying professional literature, participating in inservice workshops provided by your school or district, and taking college or university courses. From all of this, your philosophy, teaching style, and the strategies and methods you use will vary and change over time.

What are your passions and skills? What do you feel strongly about and know a lot about that could become of part of your classroom curriculum? Make a list. • • • • •	**STRETCHING EXERCISE**

Children also bring their own special strengths and needs to the classroom and the learning situation. They come with various backgrounds of experience, expectations, and ways of learning. For instance, children who have lived in other countries, speak other languages, or have knowledge of special topics, such as dinosaurs or robots, bring wonderful diversities to the classroom. As well, there are often many similarities between English and other languages (e.g., Spanish) that an alert teacher can build on to help validate bilingual students. As the teacher, it is your job to discover what these special strengths and abilities are, especially with children who are bilingual and/or possess language difficulties or delays and may not be able to communicate easily. You can help all your children understand and use the valuable resources they have in each other within their classroom.

Along with differences in interests and/or culture, children develop and learn differently. Theories about learning and the brain suggest that people's traditional conceptions of intelligence—as comprising primarily linguistic and logical abilities—is too narrow, and that all human beings actually have seven distinct intelligences that work together, not in isolation (Armstrong, 1994; Gardner, 1983). Explanations of the seven areas of intelligence and vocations that evidence a high degree of each intelligence follow:

1. *Spatial.* The ability to perceive the visual-spatial world accurately and to transform these perceptions (e.g., hunters, guides, interior designers, architects, artists, and inventors)
2. *Bodily-kinesthetic.* The ability to use the entire body to express ideas and feelings and to use the hands to produce things (e.g., actors, mimes, athletes, dancers, craftpersons, mechanics, and surgeons)

• • • • •

Opportunities for movement and dance allow children to use their bodies to express ideas and feelings.

3. *Musical.* The capacity to perceive, discriminate, transform, and express musical forms (e.g., singers, composers, and musicans)
4. *Linguistic.* The capacity to use words effectively, either orally or in writing (e.g., storytellers, orators, politicians, poets, writers, playwrights, editors, and journalists)
5. *Logical-mathematical.* The ability to use numbers effectively and to reason well (e.g., mathematicians, accountants, statisticians, scientists, and computer programmers)
6. *Interpersonal.* The ability to perceive and make distinctions in the intentions, moods, motivations, and feelings of other people; to be sensitive to voice, gesture, and facial expressions; and to respond effectively to such cues and influence other people (e.g., psychologists, psychiatrists, and clergy)
7. *Intrapersonal.* Self-knowledge and the ability to act and adapt on that knowledge; having an accurate picture of one's strengths and limitations, awareness of one's moods and motivations, and the capacity for self-discipline (e.g., a highly trained specialist like a Green Beret soldier)

More recently, Gardner (1997) has identified an eighth intelligence, *naturalist* intelligence, that allows a person to recognize and distinguish among flora and fauna, and other things in the world such as rocks and clouds. Naturalists, botanists, zoologists, and biologists are examples. Gardner also posits a ninth intelligence, *existential* intelligence, which is the ability to ask fundamental questions such as Who are we? and Why are we here? Philosophers and leaders possess this type of intelligence.

It is important to remember that neither adults nor children possess intelligence that is "fixed" in one area. People depend on different areas of their brains in different ways and in different situations. It is risky and limiting to assume, for example, that a child lacks linguistic potential (and then ignore this aspect of her learning) because she has logical/mathematical strengths on which it might seem more natural to focus, or to provide a musical child with many more opportunities to develop in this area and exclude the interpersonal area because the child seems to be shy. To function successfully in most situations, a child must possess and be able to use ability in several areas. However, one area, intrapersonal intelligence, seems critical to all other intelligences.

As well, many children need active involvement in order to learn. Reflective children, who are slow to answer but often correct, respond and learn differently than impulsive children, who may be quick but inaccurate. As content becomes more difficult and concepts more abstract, children who learn easily by listening may need both to hear and see written language and to process it by speaking and writing. Just as your teaching style, strategies, and methods may change over time, so do children's ways of learning change and evolve as they grow. Just as you learn from others, from experience, and from reading and study, so do children.

Since teaching and learning are both highly individual in nature and changeable over time, this text does not outline a specific language arts program that is right for every teacher and every group of children. Instead, it provides theory, research, and practical support for several components that you can incorporate into your own integrated language arts program. Teaching and learning styles evolve, and the planning and implementation of your language arts program will evolve, as well, depending on you and the children you teach.

> Interview an experienced language arts teacher to find out how his or her instructional practices and program have changed over time. Before you talk with the teacher, make a list of questions (e.g., How do you describe yourself as a beginning language arts teacher? How have you grown/changed as a teacher of writing [spelling, reading, etc.]? How does technology support your language arts program?).
> ••••• **STRETCHING EXERCISE**

Theories, Methods, Strategies, and Skills

In this text, you will see several terms used to discuss and describe language arts classrooms where teaching and learning occur. Terms such as *theories, methods, models, strategies, skills, processes,* and *activities* appear throughout this book and are not all used synonymously. Since these are the "tools of your trade," you should understand them and be prepared to use them appropriately with students, parents, administrators, and other teachers. Before we go further, a brief review of the definitions for these teaching terms may be helpful.

■ *Theory.* A theory is a philosophy, hypothesis, or belief that explains something. For example, there are several theories of learning that explain integration as an effective way of creating curriculum. Dewey's (1938) theories include the notions that to be sound, curriculum should be relevant to children's everyday lives and include learning through firsthand experiences. Vygotsky's (1978) theories suggest that learning occurs as a result of scaffolding, which he describes as the guidance and support provided to children as they learn, and the creation of a child's zone of proximal development, which is the distance between a child's actual learning level and her potential level. Vygotsky believes that language mediates learning and that interaction and collaboration are two critical keys to learning. Throughout this text, you will be introduced to theories of learning and teaching that will help you develop your own philosophy or theory of teaching.

■ *Method.* A method is a recognized procedure or way of teaching that has certain unique characteristics. *Method, approach,* and *procedure* are often used interchangeably. Examples are the basal reader method of teaching reading that includes carefully planned lessons and sequenced books and other materials, and the Language Experience Approach (LEA) that uses the learner's own transcribed language about an experience to teach reading and writing (Stauffer, 1970). Whole Language (Goodman, 1986) is sometimes erroneously called a method, but in reality it is a philosophy, theory, or outlook about how children learn.

■ *Model.* A model is a paradigm or design that represents a process. Models usually possess identifiable components that are represented graphically. For example, Figure 1.1 is a model that explains the interrelationships among the language arts and Figure 1.2 is a model that shows vocabulary differences among a younger child, an older child, and an adult.

■ *Strategy.* A strategy is a flexible plan that is used consciously (Dole, Brown, & Trathen, 1996), often to improve comprehension. Strategies can be teacher directed or student centered. Good readers possess many flexible, adaptable strategies that they use before, during, and after reading to increase their comprehension. An example is Think Aloud, a strategy that is often modeled by good teachers as a way of showing students how the teacher deals with problems she encounters while reading a text (Davey, 1983).

■ *Skill.* A skill is an automatic behavior that is routine and unconscious. Examples are the recognition of letter clusters or blends such as *bl* or *str* at the beginning of a word, and the appropriate use of capital letters and punctuation marks in writing. A skill is so routine that it is ingrained in one's behavior; the learner doesn't have to consciously think about it when she applies it.

■ *Process.* A process is the skills and strategies used in listening, speaking, reading, and writing. It is the way the learner uses language or the procedure she follows to construct meaning with language. An example is the writing process, which involves planning, drafting, revising, editing, and sharing or publishing. This text proposes a balanced view of learning that includes direct instruction in strategies and skills with opportunities to use and develop the language processes.

■ *Activity.* An activity is an event that involves doing something, either spontaneously or planned. Activities can be unrelated or related in some way. Good teachers often use activities that are planned and related and sometimes call them *projects* because they take longer to complete than an activity. Examples of projects that may be composed of several activities are a Storytelling Celebration in which students learn, practice, and then tell stories (e.g., telling Native American tales or fables to an audience) and a Mock-Caldecott Book Award Ceremony that culminates the research children have done on their favorite books that exhibit quality in illustrations and story.

Knowing the distinctions among these terms will make reading and understanding this text easier. Now, let's look at the components of an effective language arts program.

Components of an Effective Program

As Goodman (1986) explains, keeping language whole rather than teaching it in fragmented blocks, and involving children in using language functionally and purposefully to meet their own needs will make language learning easier for children. A balanced language arts program includes the direct, intentional teaching of skills and strategies within the context of meaningful content. An effective language arts program has several key components; among them are the following:

1. *Curricular integration.* The language arts can be connected and taught together. Listening, speaking, reading, and writing develop together naturally and mesh with content in other subject areas. Successful teachers integrate language with content learning.

2. *Children's literature.* Language arts and other subject areas are taught more effectively when quality literature that is written for and about children is used to develop subject area content. Literature possesses a special appeal for children, and its use enhances the school curriculum, in general, as well as the growth of the total child. Successful teachers use literature to develop and extend language and content learning.

3. *Learner interaction and involvement.* Children learn language and content best when they are actively using and manipulating language in real and meaningful situations. Children also learn from each other as well as from teachers. They need many opportunities to interact with other children of varying backgrounds, abilities, and interests to develop to their full potentials. Successful teachers observe children and interact with them so they know each child individually.

4. *Direct instruction and authentic experiences.* Children need a balance of direct, intentional instruction that challenges them to learn new things. Opportunities should be provided to children to set their own goals and pursue learning that they identify as important. Successful teachers model behaviors children should acquire, demonstrate and supply examples of what they expect children to produce, help children set their own goals, and guide children carefully through tasks and activities that will lead to competence and independence.

5. *An environment that fosters integrated learning.* An integrated learning environment is:
  —Literate and stimulating with plenty of printed material, realia, and technology that relates to what is being learned
  —Flexible as opposed to static in terms of classroom arrangements, scheduling, grouping, and instructional time
  —Supportive and safe so every child will take risks and one in which self-esteem is valued
  —Cooperative, collaborative (not necessarily quiet), and orderly

6. *Teachers with values and children who feel valued.* Successful teachers hold values and beliefs about the positive contributions made by all children as well as their capabilities and inherent goodness. These teachers hold a philosophy of teaching that accepts all children as individuals to be treated with respect. When children feel valued because of their individuality—regardless of differences in cognitive and physical abilities, language, culture, race, or ethnicity—they can more easily become capable learners who achieve in school.

The teacher who plans and implements an effective program is able to weave together literature, language, science, social studies, math, art, music, health, and physical education in ways that make sense and allow children to explore their own questions. This teacher promotes literacy in every subject. She helps all children become effective listeners, speakers, readers, writers, thinkers, and learners and does so with the help of books, stories, and poems written especially for children. This teacher accepts children regardless of their backgrounds and language. She models for children what and how she wants them to learn. She makes decisions and takes risks because she knows the difference a good teacher makes in a child's life. She is exhilarated and excited about her role.

The effective language arts teacher must make important decisions about curriculum, as well. Next, we'll examine some of the factors that may influence her decisions.

Curriculum Models

Curriculum decisions traditionally have followed a unidirectional model. Curriculum has been something that experts outside the classroom develop, teachers implement, and students receive (Short & Burke, 1996). Figure 1.3 shows four models for making curriculum decisions. In Model A, teachers, students, parents, and the community are left out of the process of curriculum development. However, the direction of curriculum decisions can be reversed (see Model B), with curriculum originating with students, parents, and the community, implemented by teachers, and then received by experts. This model is unidirectional, as well, but it puts students in charge of their own learning. Curriculum decisions can also originate with teachers, who then consult with outside experts, leaving students as the recipients again (see Model C). The major shortcoming of these three models is that only one party makes the important decisions.

It makes sense that teachers, students, and outside experts should be part of the curriculum development process (students because they will learn from the curriculum,

Models for Curriculum Decisions

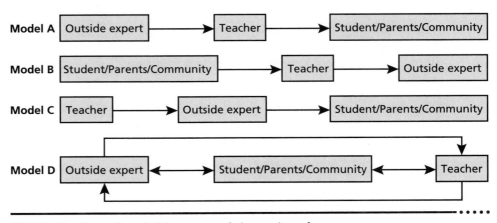

FIGURE 1.3 Curriculum decisions are made in a variety of ways.

teachers because it is they who will teach the curriculum, and outside experts because they offer a broader view and extended range of vision about what the curriculum might be). Short and Burke (1996) tell us, "As teachers, we are also experts along with our students on learning, teaching, and research in our community of learners" (p. 7). They remind us that the knowledge of outside experts should not automatically dictate what a teacher does in her classroom, but rather be an important part of what she considers in forging her own beliefs.

A fourth model, which is tridirectional and includes collaboration among the three partners, can also help in making curriculum decisions (see Model D in Figure 1.3). In this model, the experience and knowledge of teachers and outside experts with parents, the community, and students have an equally important place in what and how curriculum decisions are made.

Perhaps some curriculum decisions are best made in collaboration with all the important players having a voice. The biggest danger may lie in decisions that continually follow one model to the exclusion of the others. At times, however, it is best to make decisions yourself, as sixth-grade teacher Laura Schiller (1996) did in her Coming to America unit. At other times, the benefits of curriculum negotiated with students, as Manning, Manning, and Long (1994) suggest, make this model atttractive. Throughout this text, you will read about curriculum decisions that follow all of these models.

Read "Coming to America: Community from Diversity" by Laura Schiller in the January 1996 issue of *Language Arts,* Volume 73, pages 46–51. Why do you think the model Laura chose for curriculum development was the best fit for her students and classroom community?

STRETCHING EXERCISE

• • • • •

Curriculum Decisions

Often, a big question for beginning and experienced teachers is How do I decide on my classroom curriculum?

Some teachers consult and follow published curriculum guides mandated by the nation, state, or district. One problem with this is that separate curriculum guides exist for each subject area and there is not enough time in a crowded day to cover everything adequately. One advantage to published curriculum guides is that a sequenced and well-planned set of learning experiences is provided and accompanied by suggested materials.

Other teachers follow the topics included in their textbooks or basals. One problem with this is that textbooks are not necessarily interesting, well written, grade-level appropriate, or current. An advantage of textbook teaching is that it provides basic information and structure to a subject area and it is easy to use for this reason.

Still other teachers follow their own instincts and interests when planning curriculum, often including what their students are interested in as well. One problem is that students at one grade level may develop gaps and fail to learn what teachers in later grades assume they have learned. An advantage is that both teachers and students are engaged in what they are studying.

In making decisions about your classroom curriculum, a moderate position makes sense—one that strikes a balance among curriculum mandates, standards, available textbooks, your students and your own knowledge and interests. For example, teaching fifth-grade social studies using only the textbook could be a very dry experience for both you and your students. Teaching that integrates a content area and language arts around a theme or organizing idea and strikes a balance among curriculum mandates and textbooks yields meaningful and rich experiences.

English Language Arts Standards

What are *standards* and why are they important for teaching and learning? Standards are content goals and objectives for K–12 students that align curriculum, instruction, and assessment. Many experts believe that by creating national standards, society will raise its academic expectations for all students. Several states, such as Michigan and New York, have developed standards for teaching the English language arts. In Michigan, the creation of standards is an attempt to bring together state goals and objectives in the areas of listening, speaking, reading, writing, and literature into a unified framework that is useful for teachers and students (Wixson, Peters, & Potter, 1996). The Michigan standards project focuses on the development of content, performance, and opportunity-to-learn standards that integrate listening, speaking, reading, and writing.

The *Learning Standards for English Language Arts* (1996) (see Figure 1.4) reflect the goal of changing curriculum and instruction in the state of New York. Creators of the framework state, "Many of our students do not achieve proficiency as readers, writers, listeners or speakers, not because of a lack of ability or interest on their parts, but because not all the important uses of language are included in their programs or measured by the tests they are required to pass" (p. iii). These standards were developed so that all students would "have experiences that allow them to develop all of these important language abilities as fully as they can, and to develop some of them to a higher degree of excellence according to their talents and interests" (p. iii). In New York, the measures used to assess learning in language arts are in the process of changing, as well. The standards require that the curriculum provide opportunities for students to encounter and demonstrate five qualities:

1. *Range.* Number, variety, and complexity in the forms, genres, structures, and texts students use and create
2. *Flexibility.* Facility in adapting to purpose, audience, and context with quality in performance
3. *Independence.* Personal control and responsibility in strategies used and work accomplished
4. *Connections.* Links among texts, ideas, and experiences that connect the new and known to uncover similarities and relationships
5. *Conventions.* Etiquette of English discourse; spelling, mechanics, and usage conventions of standard written and spoken English

Following the lead of the National Council of Teachers of Mathematics (NCTM), who created widely praised standards a few years ago, the International Reading Association (IRA) and the National Council of Teachers of English (NCTE) together established national standards for the English language arts (*Standards for the English Lan-*

FIGURE 1.4 New York State developed these performance standards for the English language arts (1996) at three levels: elementary, intermediate, and commencement.

Learning Standards for English Language Arts

1. *Language for information and understanding.* Students will read, write, listen, and speak for information and understanding.

   As listeners and readers, students will collect data, facts, and ideas; discover relationships, concepts, and generalizations; and use knowledge generated from oral, written, and electronically produced texts. As speakers and writers, they will use oral and written language to acquire, interpret, apply, and transmit information.

2. *Language for literary response and expression.* Students will read, write, listen, and speak for literary response.

   Students will read and listen to oral, written, and electronically produced texts and performances; relate texts and performances to their own lives; and develop an understanding of the diverse social, historical, and cultural dimensions the texts and performances represent. As speakers and writers, students will use oral and written language for self-expression and artistic creation.

3. *Language for critical analysis and evaluation.* Students will read, write, listen, and speak for critical analysis and evaluation.

   As listeners and readers, students will analyze experiences, ideas, information, and issues presented by others using a variety of established criteria. As speakers and writers, they will present, in oral and written language and from a variety of perspectives, their opinions and judgments on experiences, ideas, information, and issues.

4. *Language for social interaction.* Students will read, write, listen, and speak for social interaction.

   Students will use oral and written language for effective social communication with a wide variety of people. As readers and listeners, they will use the social communications of others to enrich their understanding of people and their views.

—•••••

Source: Adapted from *Learning Standards for English Language Arts,* 1996, Albany, NY: State Education Department.

guage Arts, 1996). Figure 1.5 lists these 12 standards and the qualities they identify. IRA and NCTE propose these standards as a guide and a place to begin conversations about curriculum, teaching, and learning in language arts.

Examine the IRA/NCTE Learning Standards in Figure 1.5. What observations and interpretations can you make? What is missing from them? How would you strengthen them? Why do you think the subject of spelling does not appear?
• • • • •

STRETCHING EXERCISE

Where do viewing and visual literacy fit within these standards? Children and adults must construct meaning not only from printed materials and traditional textbooks

FIGURE 1.5 These national standards provide teachers and curriculum planners with a set of guiding principles for language arts teaching and learning.

Standards for the English Language Arts

The International Reading Association (IRA) and the National Council of Teachers of English (NCTE) have established voluntary national standards for English language arts (1996). These standards call for students to:

1. Read a range of print and nonprint texts to build an understanding of texts, of themselves, and of the culture of the United States and the world.
2. Read a range of literature from many periods in many genres to build an understanding of the many dimensions of the human experience.
3. Apply a range of strategies to comprehend, interpret, evaluate, and appreciate texts.
4. Adjust their use of spoken, written, and visual language to communicate effectively with a variety of audiences and for different purposes.
5. Employ a range of strategies as they write and use different writing-process elements appropriately to communicate with different audiences.
6. Apply knowledge of language structure, language conventions, media techniques, figurative language, and genre to create, critique, and discuss print and nonprint texts.
7. Conduct research on issues and interests by generating ideas and questions and by posing problems.
8. Use a variety of technological and informational resources to gather and synthesize information and to create and communicate knowledge.
9. Develop an understanding of and respect for diversity in language use, patterns, and dialects across cultures, ethnic groups, geographic regions, and social roles.
10. For students whose first language is not English, make use of their first language to develop competency in English language arts and develop understanding of content across the curriculum.
11. Participate as knowledgeable, reflective, creative, and critical members of a variety of literacy communities.
12. Use spoken, written, and visual language to accomplish their own purposes (learning, enjoyment, persuasion, and exchange of information).

• • • • •

Source: Adapted from *Learning Standards for English Language Arts,* 1996, Albany, NY: State Education Department.

but also from nonprint visual representations that carry messages. Thus, the term *text* has taken on a broader meaning than in the past. Some examples of the nonprint texts people view almost daily are pictures, television images, films, videos, art, performances and media. In future chapters of this book, you will learn more about the role of viewing and visual literacy in effective communication and how to teach your students to be literate consumers of visual texts.

The development of standards is, of course, controversial. Some experts see them as disempowering for teachers, promoting mediocrity and minimizing the individuality of students (Goodman, 1994). Others see them as creating a forum for conversations about what educators value in teaching and learning (Casteel, Roop, & Schiller, 1996; Wixson, Peters, & Potter, 1996). Standards may provide several benefits because they:

- Establish common targets for learning.
- Provide teachers with guidance and allow for local interpretation.
- Promote involvement of parents and other members of local communities in the process of curriculum development.
- Provide a forum for discussion of curriculum and changes in teaching practices.
- Honor the cultural and linguistic variations found in the United States by promoting the use of diverse texts and languages.
- Encourage teachers to be responsible, accountable, and successful professionals.

There are just as many concerns about standards, however. Standards are said to:

- Restrict learning.
- Provide technical guidelines that narrow teaching.
- Ignore differences in students and encourage conformity to one set of predetermined notions.
- Take curriculum decisions out of the hands of teachers and students.
- Result in control and disempowerment of teachers.
- Maintain the status quo in the United States.

Read Patrick Shannon's "Mad as Hell" in the January 1996 issue of *Language Arts,* Volume 73, pages 14–19. How do you feel about his belief that the standards are "part of a coordinated effort by corporations in America to discredit public schools in order to reduce the costs of social services in the United States and, thereby, significantly reduce the tax burden on businesses"?

● ● ● ● ●

STRETCHING EXERCISE

Integrating Language Arts and Content

A common synonym for *integrate* is *combine.* The first thought that may come to mind when you think of integration in language arts is teaching that combines listening, speaking, reading, and writing. Another kind of integration involves combining language arts with curriculum areas such as science, social studies, or math. This kind of integration or integrated instruction is sometimes used interchangeably with the terms *integrated thematic instruction* and *interdisciplinary instruction.* Integration or integrated instruction that combines language arts with curriculum areas also characterizes good teaching. It is this integration about which you will learn more as you read this text.

Integration means using books, stories, poems, and other materials written for children to help them become effective listeners, speakers, readers, and writers as they learn in science, social studies, math, art, music, health, and physical education. Integration involves natural learning with real purposes and real audiences. It means weaving literature and language into the science or math curriculum to invite, excite, and challenge children to become successful language users and lifelong learners.

Including Literature

Children's literature is a critical ingredient and tool in a language arts program for teaching effective communication. Literature naturally promotes all aspects of language learning:

- Children enjoy and appreciate the beauty and magic of print as they learn.
- Learning difficult concepts is easier.
- Children's knowledge is enriched and extended.
- Children are better able to understand themselves, others, and other places and situations.
- A variety of models of excellent language are provided.
- Dreaming, fantasizing, and wondering are fostered as conceptual knowledge grows.
- Learning is balanced as it invites, excites, and challenges children to learn.

Children's literature is an excellent way to personalize content. For example, a fifth-grade social studies class studying the concept of identity might read *Bridge to Terabithia* by Katherine Paterson (1977) and *Maniac Magee* by Jerry Spinelli (1990), both winners of the Newbery Medal. These books can help develop understanding of how children find out who they are. *Bridge to Terabithia* gives children insights into how two fifth-graders from different family cultures learn from each other and care for each other yet remain individuals. You can draw appropriate parallels for children in your classroom who are from different cultures. *Maniac Magee* includes reverse stereotyping of Black and White families to give children insights into the formation of prejudice. Reading Spinelli's book may promote classroom discussions about other kinds of stereotyping (e.g., people with learning disabilities, such as Albert Einstein, who are ostracized because they appear different or strange, but actually have much to offer).

You can read these stories orally or silently to reinforce and develop children's listening and reading competence. Children may discuss their opinions and feelings about character development and events and the special friendships between Leslie and Jess in *Bridge to Terabithia* and Maniac and Mars in *Maniac Magee.* In turn, the children's speech will develop and improve. When children read their favorite parts of a story orally or when they read their own or each other's written responses, they practice and reinforce reading for a purpose. These books can inspire children to write about a special friendship they have known, a special hideaway they have made their very own, or the death of someone close to them. An invitation to children to write about a personal connection to a book builds confidence and competence because you can honor each individual response.

Here is another example of using children's literature to personalize content. A third-grade class studying electricity might read *Ben and Me* by Robert Lawson (1939) and *What's the Big Idea, Benjamin Franklin?* by Jean Fritz (1976). This literature can make science come alive for students. *Ben and Me* is a story about Benjamin Franklin's life told from the perspective of a mouse named Amos, who lived in Ben's coonskin cap. Amos takes credit for all of Franklin's noteworthy scientific accomplishments. *What's the Big Idea, Benjamin Franklin?* is based on biographical information and historical facts. Franklin is portrayed as a curious man who has many ideas and follows them through to fruition. His biggest idea, of course, was that lightning and electricity were the same thing, and he was able to prove the truth of this idea.

What a wonderful way to introduce young children to Benjamin Franklin and to teach them that he was a statesman, politician, writer, editor, publisher, scientist, humorist, shaper of democracy, and discoverer of electricity, yet, at times, a bit vain, arrogant, and headstrong. These books provide personal glimpses into Franklin's life that social studies and science texts often lack. When you give children opportunities to listen, speak, read, and write about what they learn from their social studies texts and from literature, then you give them richer possibilities for growth and learning.

Maria Moy, a fourth-grade teacher, found that using Lois Lowry's Newbery Award–winning book, *Number the Stars* (1990), in a unit on World War II helped personalize learning because the story is written from a girl's point of view and tells the story of what it was like to live in a Nazi-controlled country. Annemarie befriends a Jewish girl and her family, thereby betraying the unwanted Nazi rulers but supporting the Danish Resistance movement. Readers build a relationship with the characters, thus becoming emotionally involved in the events that took place in a turbulent, complex era in history. Parallels between the discrimination in this story and the discrimination in this country against Blacks, Mormons, and other groups can be discussed, as well. A wealth of children's literature like *Number the Stars* is available for teachers who want to promote literacy through integrated content area learning.

How do you integrate language, content, and literature? Here are some guidelines:

- Identify content first.
- Focus on exploring questions and researching topics.
- Plan for different ways of understanding content through listening, speaking, reading, and writing.
- Encourage language use for real purposes and real audiences.
- Provide an environment rich with literature and resources for learning and making connections.
- Foster personal responses to literature and content through art, music, and drama.
- Set aside large blocks of time, be flexible, and encourage interaction and cooperation among learners.

Criticisms of Integration

There have been some justifiable criticisms of integrated instruction. To help you avoid some of the pitfalls in your teaching, a discussion of three of those criticisms follows.

Curriculum Is Trivialized. The content of integrated units often does not focus on powerful ideas or organizing concepts. Too many teachers select a topic such as *Apples, Bears,* or *Dinosaurs* in an attempt to connect curriculum areas. Actually, these topics often lack significance and become more of a "placeholder" that functions as a name only.

When you realize the danger in this and consciously choose a substantial topic that represents an important issue, question, or problem such as *Environmental Pollution* or you choose a theme or organizing idea such as *We Are What We Throw Away* or *What Is a Worthwhile Life?* you accomplish two things. First, you focus on a significant idea that characterizes the entire unit. Second, you focus on understandings that are at the heart of student learning rather than facts that are often forgotten.

Manning, Manning, and Long (1994) talk about "theme immersion" (TI) and suggest the theme be *important* to the classroom community and society. In addition, they say it should be *broad* enough in scope to help students become aware of the interconnectedness of the world. A theme immersion should provide opportunities for nurturing and understanding cultural diversity and should have the potential for disagreement. In these ways, a TI reflects the real world and is not gimmicky or glitzy.

Curriculum Is Lost. When a teacher integrates curriculum areas, there is often not enough time for one area to be explored in the same depth as another. Learning in one subject area often takes a backseat to learning in another subject area. So, at the risk of being inclusive and extensive in the coverage of content, the teacher actually does only surface coverage in another content area.

As a fifth-grade science teacher involved in an integrated science and social studies unit called *1492: Seeds of Change,* Roth (1994) felt frustrated with the constraints placed on her students' science learning by the needs of the social studies concepts. She said, "It is very difficult to work within an integrated theme without in some way distorting or diminishing one or another of the disciplines involved" (p. 46). She felt that there was not sufficient time for her to develop meaningful understandings about diversity, interdependence, and ecosystems within the theme. She believed her students needed time just to focus on the biology of plants, interactions within ecosystems, and scientific ways of thinking. Roth felt her teaching was compromised and diluted with the need to fit with the theme. Immersion in disciplinary study is necessary, and, according to Roth, teachers need to make sure the kinds of integration they do are "compelling, meaningful and powerful for children."

Connections Are Forced. Overenthusiasm for a theme sometimes results in connections that are not meaningful. At times, teachers include activities in integrated units that lack substance and purpose but are cute or fun. Unfortunatley, these are the wrong criteria to use in making instructional decisions.

Roth (1994) talks about an elementary school teacher whose unit theme was *Teddy Bears.* The children "read stories about teddy bears, everything they did in writing class was written on paper cut in the shape of a teddy bear, they wrote their own teddy bear stories, brought in teddy bears from home, did math problems with 'Gummy Bear' candy, explored different kinds of 'real' bears in science and on and on" (p. 45). The teacher was so enthusiastic about making everything fit the theme that she lost sight of her curriculum content and the goals she had for her students. Roth calls these connections "forced" rather than "natural" and reminds teachers to focus on how children integrate knowledge, rather than on how teachers can make connections. So, a good rule of thumb for curriculum integration is: If it feels unnatural or superficial, avoid it.

STRETCHING EXERCISE

Read "Avoiding Some of the Pitfalls of Thematic Units" by Tim Shanahan, Bonita Robinson, and Mary Schneider in the May 1995 issue of *The Reading Teacher,* Volume 48, Number 8, pages 718–719. Why do these authors say "themes . . . allow for a deeper examination of ideas"? How do you feel about this?

• • • • •

As you plan for integrated instruction, here are some ideas to consider in light of the reservations just discussed. First, when you integrate curriculum, you may want to include only one content area. There is nothing wrong with integrating just science and the language arts. In fact, it may be a more effective vehicle for doing meaningful and deep study.

Two fourth-grade teachers, Diane Mannix and Sandra Whitehouse, provide an example. They chose *Let's Eat a Sunbeam* as the theme and organizing idea for their integrated science and language arts unit called *The Web of Life*. As a language arts teacher, Diane's goal was to develop competence in language arts skills and processes as well as help Sandy achieve her goal of building student understanding in science. So, the two teachers collaborated to focus on the writing process and the food chain. They used learning logs as one way to document thinking and integrate reading and writing that was purposeful. They did not explain the meaning of the unit's theme, *Let's Eat a Sunbeam;* rather, they challenged students to figure it out for themselves as the unit progressed. Every day following science class, students wrote in their learning logs. They summarized what they learned that day and explored what they thought the theme meant. The students were always eager to see what the teachers had written in response to the information in the learning logs (see Figure 1.6). Both teachers felt the math their students needed to learn required in-depth instruction beyond the scope of this unit and so they kept math a separate subject.

Second, you may need to alternate curriculum integration with brief focuses on a specific, individual curriculum area. Here are some examples. Perhaps you feel your

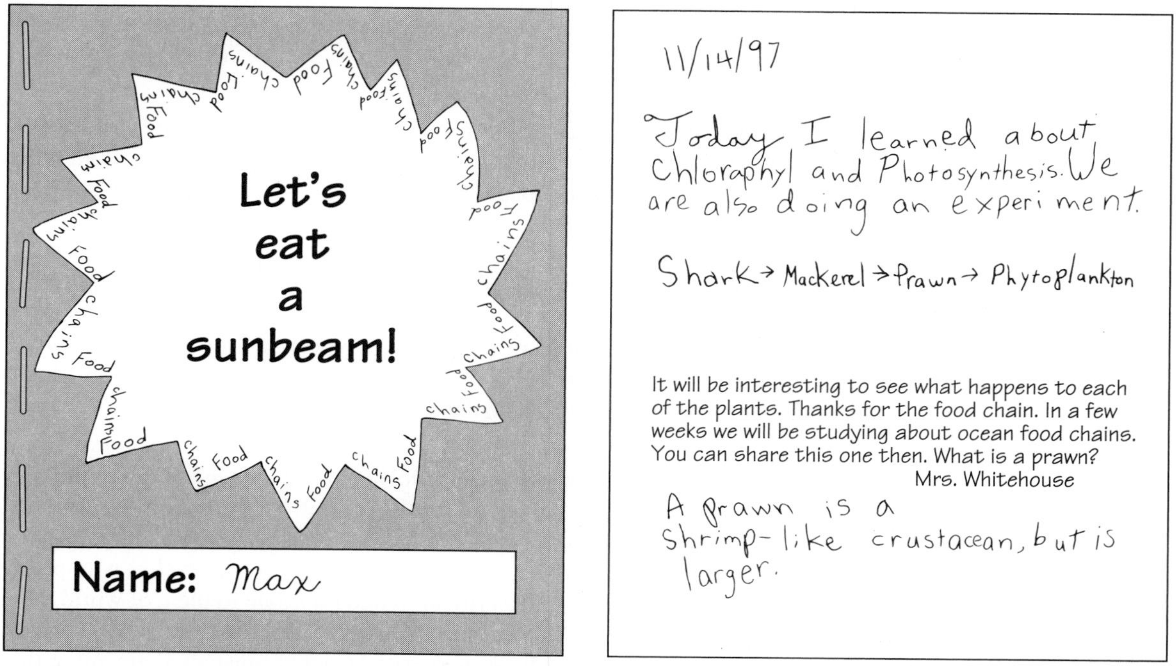

FIGURE 1.6 The cover and first page of a fourth-grader's learning log in science.

third-grade students need in-depth, direct instruction in researching, notetaking, and organizing and writing reports before report writing is part of an integrated unit. So, you do a brief mini-unit focused solely on research and expository writing before integration with social studies. Another example is fifth-grade students who may need intensive, focused opportunities to become adept at problem solving in math that is not easily possible with the limited math opportunities you have imbedded in your integrated unit in social studies and language arts. Your unit may include opportunities for students to graph demographic statistics related to their community but may not provide in-depth work on problem solving. So, in addition, you will need to do a mini-unit devoted to problem solving with these students. It makes sense to isolate what you and your students feel needs direct, intensive instruction and do that teaching separately from the integrated unit.

Quilting as a Metaphor for Integration

Quilting provides a metaphor for language arts teaching. Just as there are different ways to make quilts, there are different ways to teach integrated language arts. In general, there are two types of quilts: crazy quilts and pieced quilts (see Figure 1.7). A *crazy quilt* is made of random scraps of leftover material that vary in size, color, and texture. It has no overall plan or design except that it is unplanned. A *pieced quilt* has an intentional and symbolic overall design or motif. It is carefully planned and created from fabrics that are specifically chosen to blend colors, patterns, and shapes. A pieced quilt, such as those called Fence and Rail, Corn and Beans, or Trail of the Covered Wagons, (actual names of quilts), is a metaphor for integrated instruction. The following sections address some of the similarities that characterize both integrated instruction and a pieced quilt.

A Theme or Organizing Idea.   To make a pieced quilt, one must first choose the overall design or motif. An integrated unit also has an overall design or motif. Both quilt and unit possess a theme or organizing idea that communicates a message. Two teacher-selected units are:

- The theme or organizing idea for Karen Wassell's integrated unit in kindergarten was *Eat Smart—Be Smart.*
- The theme for an integrated unit in Elizabeth Pylypciw's fifth grade was *Small Towns Really Are BIG in Many Ways.* Figure 1.8 shows the planning web Elizabeth put on her bulletin board to guide this unit study.

Goals and/or Outcomes.   Goals or outcomes revolve around the *why* of the project. A quilter first considers why she is making the quilt. Will it be used as a blanket for warmth on a bed in a particular room, or will it decorate a wall in a particular room? Next, she considers *what* she wants to accomplish and *when*. For the teacher who plans an integrated thematic unit, the *why* is also critical. It should relate to the real world. For example, Why will you engage your students in this study? What do you want them to be able to do or understand as a result? Both quilter and teacher must also remember the time frame involved in their projects. They must allow for adequate time to accomplish everything their projects entail.

For example, Karen's goals in the *Eat Smart—Be Smart* theme were for kindergartners to understand that when they eat well and take care of their bodies, their minds can concentrate on the job of learning. She also wanted her students to become "smart" in literacy, mathematical, and social development. Elizabeth's goal in the *Small Towns Really Are BIG in Many Ways* theme was for her students to understand that their hometown has made many lasting contributions to the growth and development of the central part of their state, even though it is a small, rural town.

Carefully Chosen Components. To make a pieced quilt, one must next decide on the colors and patterns of fabric to use. Aside from the fabric and thread, special tools are needed, such as a rotary blade, cutting board, scissors, needles, pins, and perhaps a

Crazy Quilt   **Crossed Canoes Quilt**

FIGURE 1.7 A crazy quilt and a pieced quilt called Crossed Canoes.
Source: Reprinted by permission of Karen Wassell.

thimble. An integrated thematic unit requires carefully chosen components, too. Integration includes and connects content area learning with language arts and children's literature in meaningful ways. Other components include, for example, multicultural literature, cooperative learning strategies, and a range of projects for diverse students. Special tools such as a computer, CD-ROMs, videos, an overhead projector, and field trips may also help effectively achieve unit goals.

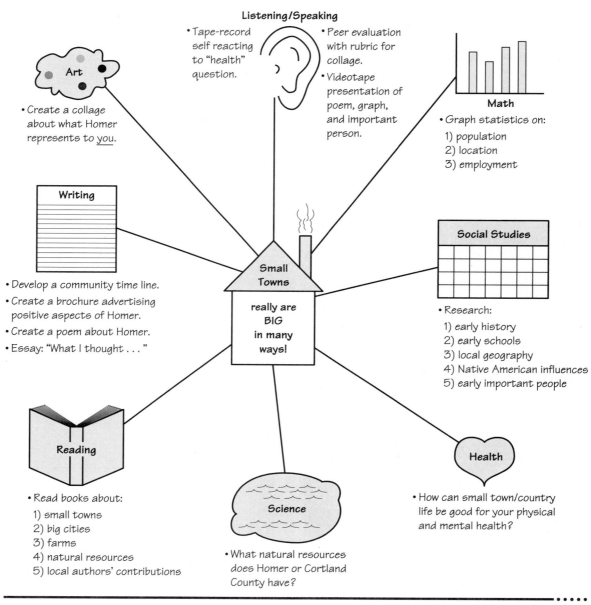

Listening/Speaking
• Tape-record self reacting to "health" question.
• Peer evaluation with rubric for collage.
• Videotape presentation of poem, graph, and important person.

Art
• Create a collage about what Homer represents to you.

Math
• Graph statistics on:
1) population
2) location
3) employment

Writing
• Develop a community time line.
• Create a brochure advertising positive aspects of Homer.
• Create a poem about Homer.
• Essay: "What I thought . . ."

Small Towns really are BIG in many ways!

Social Studies
• Research:
1) early history
2) early schools
3) local geography
4) Native American influences
5) early important people

Reading
• Read books about:
1) small towns
2) big cities
3) farms
4) natural resources
5) local authors' contributions

Science
• What natural resources does Homer or Cortland County have?

Health
• How can small town/country life be good for your physical and mental health?

FIGURE 1.8 Elizabeth Pylypciw's web for a unit called *Small Towns Really Are BIG in Many Ways.*
Source: Reprinted by permission of Elizabeth Pylypciw, sixth-grade Resource Room teacher.

Karen's unit included topics from science, language arts, and math that she related to knowledge of healthy foods. She wanted to develop her students' social skills and literacy through this study. Elizabeth's unit spanned social studies, science, langauge arts, and math (see Figure 1.8). She wanted to connect her students with their hometown and develop their pride in it as they learned about the geography and natural resources of the area. Elizabeth wanted her students to develop their reading, writing, and graphing skills, as well.

Intentional Planning and Teaching.   A pieced quilt is the result of intentional planning and teaching that uses fabrics cut in specific shapes and from certain colors. The interlocking pieces will complement each other as they form one overall prearranged pattern. Just as with a quilt, planning and teaching are a huge part of the success of an integrated thematic unit.

Both Karen and Elizabeth planned lessons, projects, and activities to include individual, small-group, and whole-class instruction. They each used a calendar to plan and contain unit activities. Both teachers sought the help of other teachers, their library media specialists, and art, music, and physical education teachers to plan for teaching that supported and coincided with each units.

Implementation That Responds to Successes and Failures.   To make a pieced quilt, one sews fabric pieces together to form a repeating visual pattern or an overall motif. As the quilt is created, one looks for places where pieces were mistakenly sewn in the wrong position. An alert quilter corrects a misplaced piece before sewing too many other pieces in place. Just like the alert quilter, an alert teacher observes her students at work and modifies her plans and teaching based on what she sees.

As Karen and Elizabeth taught, they constantly monitored their students' progress. They watched students use the language processes, they examined the products their students created, and they talked with their students to discover what the students understood about those language arts processes and products. With this kind of assessment, as they noted individual student needs, they retaught or redirected experiences and opportunities. They provided mini-lessons to small groups and individuals as well as whole-group instruction. They were flexible and ready to adapt their goals and sometimes the direction of the unit to the interests and abilities of their students. In other words, their daily instruction involved assessment and immediate response to how their students were doing.

Pride in the Finished Product.   Upon completion of the quilt, one undoubtedly feels satisfaction and pride in the accomplishment. The individual probably enjoys looking at the quilt and may even show it to friends and family. The completion of an integrated thematic unit should feel much the same.

As a culminating activity, the kindergartners created a class "big book" called *The Very Hungry Children,* patterned after Eric Carle's (1969) *The Very Hungry Caterpillar.* They made butter and biscuits one day and then enjoyed them at a "Storytime Picnic" where they read their big book together and each child shared a favorite storybook from the unit.

At the conclusion of the fifth-graders' unit, Elizabeth videotaped the students' presentations and explanations of the collages they made to represent their hometown, their graph of statistics on their town, and their essay on an important person from their town's history. The class invited another fifth-grade class as well as the principal, media specialist, art teacher, reading teacher, physical education teacher, and their parents to watch the video with them.

Both groups of students excitedly participated in the culminating activities at the end of the units. The sharing of their work gave these learners a sense of self-worth, pride, and satisfaction that is critical.

Teacher- or Student-Selected Units?

Elizabeth's and Karen's units were teacher selected because both teachers followed the suggested curriculums of their state and their local school district. However, both teachers encouraged student input and allowed students to shape the direction their research and study might take and how they would share it with their classmates. For teachers who have favorite topics and special knowledge that may be the result of an individual passion (e.g., a hobby or travel), selecting unit topics themselves makes sense. However, many teachers have discovered that student-selected units also have advantages. Students are often interested and excited about a unit they have chosen. The unit may be relevant and more contemporary than one selected by the teacher that mirrors mandated curriculum or a textbook and it may concern an issue affecting the world today. Studying a current topic may lead students to social actions that can cause change and have an impact on their world.

STRETCHING EXERCISE

How might you deal with this "caught in a vise" condition related to curriculum planning that many teachers experience? For example, how could you mesh your love of a topic with national and state standards, student ideas, parental and community input, and the textbook?

· · · · ·

Debby Griesinger, a fourth-grade teacher, alternates teacher-selected units with student-selected units. To decide on their next four- to six-week unit, Debby had her students brainstorm a list that included unemployment, racial conflict, pollution, the environment, waste management, chemical warfare, gun control, poverty and hunger, astronomy, global warming, toxic waste disposal, endangered species, careers, drug abuse, climate control, and assisted suicide. A class vote showed most students were interested in pollution, the environment, toxic waste disposal, and endangered species. With Debby's help, they decided that the topic *Environmental Awareness* would include all their interests. When students can't agree on a topic, some experienced teachers solve the problem by launching two different units at the same time.

Both webs in Figures 1.9 and 1.10 represent initial ideas Debby and her students supplemented and modified as the unit progressed. They show Debby's plan, prior to teaching the unit, for integrating literature with content and the language arts. For Debby, integrating the language arts and children's literature with content area subjects makes sense because it helps her students develop and use language naturally as they learn.

Including the students' voice and choice in a unit makes sense because it builds ownership and helps students become self-directed learners. An example of a unit that blends teacher and student choice in a fifth-grade social studies class includes study of a state-mandated topic—*The Industrial Revolution in the United States*—and the student-chosen topic of *Technology*. Students learn about the topic in a variety of ways: by reading their texts and/or a variety of library books about industrialization on farms, the growth of railroads in the West, and steel making in Pittsburgh. They listen to the teacher and their peers talk about the topic. They also listen to a special guest speaker, a farmer who talks about how his farm has changed dramatically over the last 40 years and how he uses computers to help him. They ask and answer questions. They take part in discussions. They watch filmstrips and movies about other economies. They use CD-ROMs and explore aspects of industrialization on the Internet. They write notes, outlines, summaries, reports, and answers to questions by using a word processor and desktop publishing on the computer. They also make presentations to the class about their independent research topics.

The unit includes teacher-selected and student-selected topics, which makes it a blend of "must-dos" with "want-to-dos." This gives the unit the added benefit of student interest, which can inspire participation from those students who do not seem to be as easily engaged in school. If you are interested in guiding your students in choosing unit

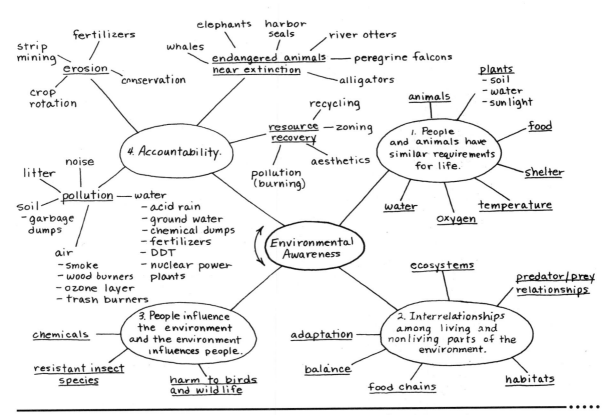

FIGURE 1.9   Debby Griesinger and her students planned the objectives for a science unit titled *Environmental Awareness*.

Source: Courtesy of Deborah Possemato Griesinger.

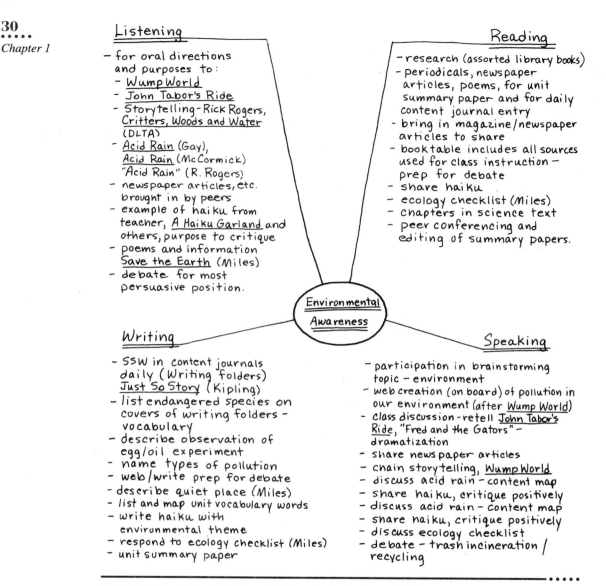

Listening

- for oral directions
  and purposes to:
  - Wump World
  - John Tabor's Ride
  - Storytelling-Rick Rogers,
    Critters, Woods and Water
    (DLTA)
  - Acid Rain (Gay),
    Acid Rain (McCormick)
    "Acid Rain" (R. Rogers)
- newspaper articles, etc.
  brought in by peers
- example of haiku from
  teacher, A Haiku Garland and
  others, purpose to critique
- poems and information
  Save the Earth (Miles)
- debate for most
  persuasive position.

Reading

- research (assorted library books)
- periodicals, newspaper
  articles, poems, for unit
  summary paper and for daily
  content journal entry
- bring in magazine/newspaper
  articles to share
- booktable includes all sources
  used for class instruction —
  prep. for debate
- share haiku
- ecology checklist (Miles)
- chapters in science text
- peer conferencing and
  editing of summary papers.

Environmental
Awareness

Writing

- SSW in content journals
  daily (Writing folders)
  Just So Story (Kipling)
- list endangered species on
  covers of writing folders —
  vocabulary
- describe observation of
  egg/oil experiment
- name types of pollution
- web/write prep for debate
- describe quiet place (Miles)
- list and map unit vocabulary words
- write haiku with
  environmental theme
- respond to ecology checklist (Miles)
- unit summary paper

Speaking

- participation in brainstorming
  topic — environment
- web creation (on board) of pollution in
  our environment (after Wump World)
- class discussion-retell John Tabor's
  Ride, "Fred and the Gators" —
  dramatization
- share newspaper articles
- chain storytelling, Wump World
- discuss acid rain — content map
- share haiku, critique positively
- discuss acid rain — content map
- share haiku, critique positively
- discuss ecology checklist
- debate — trash incineration /
  recycling

FIGURE 1.10 Debby Griesinger and her students planned the language arts process objectives for a unit called *Environmental Awareness*.

Source: Courtesy of Deborah Possemato Griesinger.

topics, Manning, Manning, and Long (1994) suggest these sources that teachers and students can refer to in searching out topics that intrigue them:

- World events
- Local events
- Local history
- Family history

When you integrate content area subjects, the language arts, and children's literature, you help children develop and use language in real and personal ways. Then, language and literature have solid reasons for being part of the content curriculum because they help develop your students' competence as thinkers and learners.

The rest of this book explores the components of an effective program more fully, as it provides you with practical suggestions for planning and implementing your own language arts program. As you read this text, you can add other features to this list of components of a successful language arts program.

Summary

Learners develop effective communication more easily when the teacher integrates the language arts—listening, speaking, reading, and writing—with a content area and children's literature. This promotes the natural and meaningful use of language to learn. Planning for integrated instruction includes attention to standards, curriculum, and student interests.

R.....eflections

1. What is your philosophy of teaching? What do you value and believe are the most important things about being an effective teacher? Find a metaphor for good teaching or a good teacher (similar to the quilt metaphor) and identify the components.

2. How important are viewing and visual literacy in today's world? Do either the state or national standards in Figures 1.4 and 1.5 include viewing or nonprint texts? Where, how, and why do they fit?

Professional Resources

Bingham, A. A. (1995). *Exploring the multiage classroom.* York, ME: Stenhouse. This handbook, written by a teacher with wide classroom experience, provides a treasury of practical advice and ideas for moving from a conventional classroom to multiage teaching.

Canfield, J., & Wells, H. C. (1994). *100 ways to enhance self-concept in the classroom* (2nd ed.). Boston: Allyn and Bacon. These practical, classroom-tested activities are appropriate for today's diverse classrooms that need to provide supportive environments that help students discover and build on their strengths.

Dudley-Marling, C. (1997). *Living with uncertainty: The messy reality of classroom practice.* Portsmouth, NH: Heinemann. A university professor documents his year-long return to an elementary school classroom with his experiences and reflections. This book looks at complex and critical issues, including student ownership, discipline, gender, building community, and teaching struggling students.

Temple, C., Martinez, M., Yokota, J., & Naylor, A. (1998). *Children's books in children's hands: An introduction to their literature.* Boston: Allyn and Bacon. This is a comprehensive children's literature resource with guidelines and issues to consider when making decisions about using all types of literature as well as multicultural books.

References

Armstrong, T. (1994). *Multiple intelligence in the classroom.* Alexandria, VA: Association for Supervision and Curriculum and Development.

Casteel, L., Roop, L., & Schiller, L. (1996). No such thing as an expert: Learning to live with standards in the classroom. *Language Arts, 73,* 30–35.

Chomsky, C. (1971). Write first, read later. *Childhood Education, 47,* 296–299.

Comber, B. (1987). Celebrating and analyzing successful teaching. *Language Arts, 64,* 182–195.

Davey, B. (1983). Think aloud: Modeling the cognitive processes of reading comprehension. *Journal of Reading, 27* (1), 44–47.

Dewey, J. (1938). *Experience and education.* New York: Macmillan.

Dole, J. A., Brown, K. J., & Trathen, W. (1996). The effects of strategy instruction on the comprehension performance of at-risk students. *Reading Research Quarterly, 31,* 62–89.

Gardner, H. (1997). Speech to General Session of Association for Supervision and Curriculum Development. Baltimore: 52nd Annual Conference.

Gardner, H. (1983). *Frames of mind: The theory of multiple intelligences.* New York: Basic.

Goodman, K. (1994). Standards, not! *Education Week, 14,* 39.

Goodman, K. (1986). *What's whole in whole language?* Portsmouth, NH: Heinemann.

Learning standards for English language arts. (1996). Albany: State Education Department.

Manning, M., Manning, G., & Long, R. (1994). *Theme immersion: Inquiry-based curriculum in elementary and middle school.* Portsmouth, NH: Heinemann.

Myers, M. (1987). The shared structure of oral and written language and the implications for teaching writing, reading and literature. In J. R. Squire (Ed.), *Dynamics of language learning: Research in reading and English* (pp. 121–146). Urbana, IL: ERIC CLearinghouse.

NCTE Elementary Section Steering Committee. (1996). Exploring language arts standards within a cycle of learning. *Language Arts, 73,* 10–13.

Roth, K. J. (1994). Second thoughts about interdisciplinary studies. *American Educator, 18,* 44–62.

Schiller, L. (1996). Coming to America: Community from diversity. *Language Arts, 73,* 46–53.

Short, K. G., Burke, C. (1996). Examining our beliefs and practices through inquiry. *Language Arts, 73,* 97–104.

Standards for the English language arts. (1996). Newark, DE: International Reading Association.

Stauffer, R. G. (1970). *The language experience approach to the teaching of reading.* New York: Harper and Row.

Thaiss, C. (1985). *Language across the curriculum in the elementary grades.* Urbana, IL: National Council of Teachers of English, ERIC Clearinghouse.

Vygotsky, L. (1978). *Mind in society: The development of higher order psychological processes.* Cambridge, MA: Harvard University Press.

Wells, G., & Chang-Wells, G. L. (1992). *Constructing knowledge together: Classrooms as centers of inquiry and literacy.* Portsmouth, NH: Heinemann.

Wixson, K. K., Peters, C. W., & Potter, S. A. (1996). The case for integrated standards in English language arts. *Language Arts, 73,* 20–29.

Children's Book References

Carle, E. (1969). *The very hungry caterpillar.* New York: Philomel.

Fritz, J. (1976). *What's the big idea, Benjamin Franklin?* New York: Coward-McCann.

Lawson, R. (1939). *Ben and me.* Boston: Little, Brown.

Lowry, L. (1989). *Number the stars.* New York: Doubleday.

Paterson, K. (1977). *Bridge to Terabithia.* New York: Crowell.

Spinelli, J. (1990). *Maniac Magee.* Boston: Little, Brown.

The Beginnings of Language

2

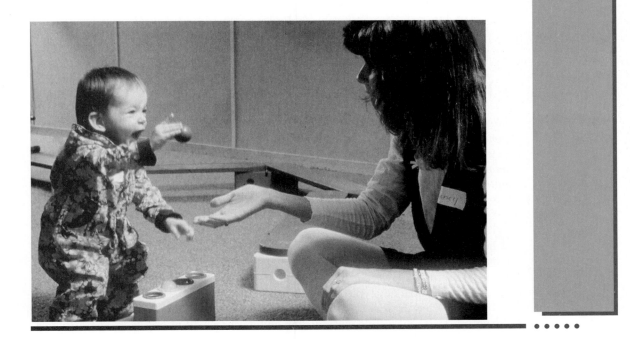

W••••• indow on Teaching

Henry Bouchard, a prospective teacher in his last year of college, has kept a journal for the past three years, expressing his thoughts and feelings regarding teaching. Here is one of his latest entries:

> I've never really thought much about how I learned language. It was just some-thing that happened for me. My mother says she remembers how I imitated her when she said, "I can't believe it," except I would say, "I can't believe about it." Apparently, I used the phrase often and we still say it in our family today.
>
> Recently, I've been wondering just how language develops and why it grows in different ways and at different rates in different kids. Ryan, my 3½-year-old

nephew, still doesn't talk much and other kids his age talk a blue streak. He didn't even really babble or make any sounds or repeat sounds when he was a baby. But we know he's smart. He can put puzzles together that I have a hard time with. He listens and follows directions—like, you can tell him to get a book and put it on the shelf. He watches cartoons and TV shows and laughs at the funny parts. But what's going on in his head and why isn't he using words?

I would like to better understand why and how language develops in young children. I'd like to understand what makes the human brain comprehend language and what makes humans able to create their own language. Where did English come from, anyway? Why are there different forms of it? I'd like to know how language creates bonds among people and how a child's language develops.

· · · · ·

O·····verview

This chapter discusses language acquisition and development, the functions and components of language, the factors affecting language development, and emergent literacy. You will see that, to become effective and fluent language users, children need many rich opportunities, unstructured as well as planned, to construct meaning as they initiate and produce language.

The learning of language is one of the great natural wonders of civilization. It is indeed a marvel that a child easily and effortlessly learns so intricate and sophisticated a system for making meaning. What's more, most children become fluent and effective oral language users without any type of formal instruction.

Have you ever wondered why and how this learning of language occurs? Is there a connection between a child's acquisition and development of oral language before entering school and the acquisition and development of written language while in school? There actually are significant parallels between oral and written language learning that language researchers are just beginning to discover. These parallels have important implications for your teaching. We'll explore some possible answers to these questions in the rest of this chapter.

Language and Communication

Before we examine how a child acquires and develops language, let's first look at the difference between language and communication

- *Communication* is the transmission of meaning through sounds, signals, gestures, or symbols.
- *Language* is an ordered system of symbols for transmitting meaning. (For example, the English language uses 26 symbols [letters] to compose hundreds of thou-

sands of words. The Russian language uses 32 symbols, the German language uses 28 symbols, and the Chinese language uses approximately 3,000 symbols to transmit meaning.)

Language, then, is a refined type of communication that involves a specific symbol system that is recognized and used by a certain group to communicate ideas and information.

Both humans and animals have signal systems. In fact, some animals are thought to possess a language of their own. Research with dolphins and gorillas, for instance, suggests these animals can use sounds, sign language, gestures, and computer pictures to communicate with humans. They do not possess the physical mechanisms to produce speech, but they do learn to manipulate language. Some gorillas have learned signs for more than 1,000 words—the level of development seen in many 2- and 3 year-old humans.

Three things distinguish human language from animal language:

1. Human language is productive. New messages with new meanings are constantly created.
2. Human language is independent of context. Conversations, telephone calls, and writing can communicate meanings unrelated to the situation or environment in which they occur.
3. Human language can be written.

Language researchers are trying to better understand how language evolves in animals and humans so that educators can more effectively teach language to children with language delays, language and cultural differences, brain damage, and autism.

Functions of Language

For young children, language is acquired and learned quite naturally to fulfill needs within the environment. Language changes and controls not only the child's behavior, but the behavior of others. As a social tool, language becomes a way of reacting to others. It facilitates and is responsible for cognitive growth. From the beginning, language also is a social tool. It allows for the development of fuller interactions with others and permits people to express their own uniqueness as individuals.

Halliday's (1996) analysis of how beginning language develops for a child includes seven functions that involve interactions with others:

1. Instrumental language *(I need . . . or I want . . .)*
2. Regulatory language *(Let me go or Give it to me)*
3. Interactional language *(You and I . . . or Take me with you)*
4. Personal language *(I like the puppy or I think . . .)*
5. Heuristic language *(Why? or How does it work?)*
6. Imaginative language *(Let's pretend or Once . . .)*
7. Representational language *(I have something to tell you)*

For example, when a child says "juice" and holds up an empty cup, he realizes that language can be used to request and receive something from someone.

A discussion of the functions or roles language plays in one's everyday life will enable you to better understand the unique characteristics of language.

STRETCHING EXERCISE

Observe a young child in a preschool or kindergarten and jot down specific things the child says that accomplish Halliday's functions of language. How does language create fuller interactions with others for the child?

• • • • •

Language Identifies Wants and Needs. From the very beginning of a child's life, learning to use language results in acquisition of, among other things, water, food, a certain toy, or a dry diaper. The young child soon learns words that satisfy primary wants and needs. Attainment of fulfilled desires reinforces using these words. For example, the child who is thirsty and says "wa-wa" receives water more quickly than the child who merely cries because he is thirsty. Similarly, when a child receives a drink after saying "wa-wa," the water itself reinforces the learning and use of the word.

Language Changes and Controls Behavior. Children learn that they can effect change in their environment and control or direct behavior of adults around them by using language. Toddlers use language to shape adult and peer behavior, greet others, get attention, challenge, contradict, and agree. For example, the young child who says "peek" or "peek-a-boo" knows the response these words elicit from an adult. The adult and child then enjoy the consequences of the resulting change in behavior. The older child who attempts to respond to a teacher's question knows that a partially correct answer elicits a more desirable response from that teacher than silence or a refusal to answer. So the child who seeks approval or wants to avoid disapproval responds with, "I'm not sure, but I think . . ." rather than no response or "I dunno." At other times, a language user may attempt to control behavior and the environment with the use of intentionally inappropriate language, as when a child swears to gain attention.

Language Facilitates Cognitive Growth. Language symbolically identifies both the tangible and the intangible. It allows people to retrieve from memory and make connections with newly acquired information. It also permits individuals to speculate and form generalizations about the past, present, and future. Language is the system by which people add to the store of knowledge that they accumulate through experiences and learning. It allows people to store and sort information that is later used to explore and solve problems. Language also helps individuals know information better. When writing or speaking about a topic, people clarify their ideas as well as generate new knowledge.

For babies, the relationship between cognition and language seems to be strongest at the earliest stages of language development. At first, they draw heavily on concepts as a way to master language; later, they use language to learn new concepts (Rice, 1996). At around 18 months, toddlers begin to name things with words. When they start to combine words, their vocabularies grow very quickly. In the preschool years, young children learn to comprehend more than 14,000 words, or about 9 new words a day (Templin, 1957).

Language Allows for Fuller Interactions with Others. Language permits people to establish and maintain relationships with others. They can define and explore personal thoughts, feelings, and actions with others through the use of language. People use language to communicate within their own group and participate in a social structure. Language plays just as central a role in the successful social functioning of a child as it does in that of an adult. In dramatic play, for example, young children use language as they begin to make stories and establish interpersonal relationships with their peers. Language allows children to interact and connect with adults during the shared reading of books. It also allows children and adults to get to know each other better.

Language Expresses the Uniqueness of the Individual. Knowing how to use language allows people to establish their own individuality. Personal opinions and feelings are shared in ways that are distinctive and special for each individual. This is readily apparent in young children who often communicate knowledge, understanding, and opinions of their work in uniquely different ways that are reflective of the development of their individual personalities. For example, with a twinkle in his eye and a teasing expression, a child who has created a rainbow with fingerpaints may tell an adult about the "up-down mouth" in his picture. The association of an upside-down mouth with the rainbow, as well as the child's name for it, suggests an imagination and sense of humor in this young child.

An understanding of these developmental functions is important to the teacher of young children because a huge part of his responsibility is to provide learners with opportunities to grow in the full range of language functions. It is the role of the knowledgeable teacher to help young children discover and explore the power of language within their environments, both at home and at school. Children need to learn how language allows them to construct meaning through listening, speaking, reading, and writing.

List three people you talked to today. How did they use language? Jot down the role or function language played for each of them. How does language function differently for the class bully, an evangelist, a radio disc jockey, and an elementary school teacher?

STRETCHING EXERCISE

• • • • •

Characteristics of Language

How are the functions and characteristics of language related? Can the roles language plays shed light on why language is the way it is? Let's look now at the characteristics that identify language as a unique form of communication. The following discussion explains this distinction and identifies several characteristics of language to share with your students.

Language Is Systematic. Language is an orderly, regular, and uniform means of putting sounds and/or graphics together in ways that recur. The English language possesses a far greater number of consistent patterns than inconsistent patterns, although critics often emphasize its inconsistencies. For example, consonant clusters such as *fl-, sl-,* and *str-* and letter patterns such as *-ame, -ipe,* and *-ot* consistently represent the same basic sounds. When certain clusters and patterns are put together—*fl-ame, sl-ot,* and *str-ipe,* for example—they consistently communicate the same basic meanings. Every language possesses its own individual type of order.

English is not only regular and systematic but within its orderliness it is also precise. It possesses a great number of synonyms with nearly the same dictionary meanings but different connotations, which allows its speakers different levels of formality and great precision in communicating shades of meaning (Parshall, 1995). For example, English speakers may *end, finish,* or *conclude* their remarks. A girl can be *fair, beautiful,* or *attractive.* A bully may cause *fear, terror,* or *trepidation.* It's easy to understand what Mark Twain meant when he said, "The difference between a word and the right word, is like the difference between a lightning bug and lightning."

Language Is Arbitrary. English is composed of arbitrary connections between sounds and/or visual graphics and the objects and ideas they represent. For example, every language has different words to symbolize the numbers 1 to 10. The English word *two* and the Spanish word *dos* are symbols for the same concept. Every language establishes meanings for certain patterns of graphics and sounds in whatever way seems most appropriate and useful. The English language is alphabetic, having 26 letters; the Chinese language is a system of approximately 3,000 characters. For every language, an arbitrary decision determines how the language is read. For example, Japanese and Chinese are read in columns from the top of the page to the bottom and from the right side of the page to the left, whereas Hebrew is read row by row from right to left.

Language Is Flexible. Languages change according to the need for change. For instance, the English vocabulary has experienced fantastic growth with the addition of thousands of words related to science and technology (e.g., *cyberspace, virtual reality, quark, byte,* and *web*) as well as acronyms (e.g., *AIDS, CD-ROM, VCR,* and *VDT).* Besides generating new words, a language changes in the meanings its users give words. For example, for many, *chill* means relax or calm down, obviously a new twist on its meaning. *Rad,* a shortened form of *radical,* is used by some teens, along with *phat* and *cool,* to describe something that impresses them in a very positive way. Colloquial expressions or slang—such as *bug off, out of my face, step off,* and *gross*—popular for a time with a particular group are a constantly changing part of language.

Parshall (1995) presents some interesting facts about the English language. He says the *Oxford English Dictionary* lists more than 600,000 words, and half the books being published in the world are in English. He maintains that English grammar and syntax are relatively simple, that the English sound system is flexible and user-friendly, and that foreign words are pronounced in the United States the same as in their original tongues. Parshall says, "Its depth and precision have helped make English the foremost language of science, diplomacy, and international business" (p. 48).

Language Is Variable. Languages have various dialects or different ways of being spoken by different groups. For example, in Russia, there are over 200 languages spoken and well over 1,000 variations or dialects. In India, there are more than 20 languages and 80 dialects spoken. Dialects initially represented divergent geographic origins, but today they also represent different social groups within a community.

Dialect differences in the United States occur in pronunciation, vocabulary, and syntax. Examples of pronunciation differences are the Texan who might say " You cain't go" and the New Yorker who might say "Youse can't go"; a Californian who might refer to a "park" while a New Englander might say "pahk"; and a midwesterner might say "warsh" while a Floridian might say "wash." Examples of vocabulary and syntax differences are the Pennsylvania Dutch phrase "spritz a plant" and the more widely accepted phrase "water a plant." There are also differences in syntax according to different regions. A Marylander might say "The house needs painted" while an Arizonian might say "The house needs to be painted." A southerner might say "I might could" and a northerner might say "Maybe I can."

Black English is a dialect that possesses its own syntax, pronunciation, and vocabulary (Cazden, 1981)—for example, "he bin" (he has been), "Who dat?" (Who is that?), "She be here" (She is here) "wif" (with), and "he don't got no" (he hasn't got any). Called *Ebonics,* from *eb*ony and ph*onics*, some believe it derives from *Pidgin English* and West African speech, with similarities to the English of the early Pilgrims. Other dialects heard in the United States are *Gullah,* spoken on some East Coast islands; *Creole,* a combination of French, African American, and English spoken in Louisana; and *Appalachian,* spoken in the mountains of the South. An idiolect, another variation of language, is a person's own individual and unique language style. For example, some people frequently preface comments with "anyway" or "you know."

Language Is a Composite.   English is a composite, or *smorgasbord* (Swedish), of words borrowed from foreign tongues. In fact, three out of four words in English dictionaries are foreign born (Parshall, 1995). Many of these words are so familiar that one does not realize their origins. "Ask your *pal* (Romany) to go to the *opera* (Italian), and he may prefer instead to go hunting in the *boondocks* (Tagalog), to play *polo* (Tibetan) or to visit the *zoo* (Greek) to test his *skill* (Danish) at milking a *camel* (Hebrew), after which he may need a *shampoo* (Hindi)" (p. 48).

As well as words taken from hundreds of other languages, Americans have happily coined their own phrases—*groundhog*, *lightning rod*, *belittle*, and *seaboard*—as well as adopting many Native American terms as place names and welcoming useful words brought by immigrants (Parshall, 1995). For example, the Dutch gave the Americans *pit* (the one found in fruit) and *boss* (the one found in the front office), *sleigh*, *snoop*, and *spook*. *Filibuster* and *bonanza* originated from Spanish, and *kibitz* and *schmaltz* originated from Yiddish.

English is a huge and unique collection of words. Lederer (1991) says, "We have the most cheerfully democratic and hospitable language that ever existed. Other people recognize their language in ours" (p. 142). The *Oxford English Dictionary* lists more than 600,000 English words, whereas the German language has only one-third that number and the French has only one-sixth that number (Parshall, 1995).

Choose a language other than English (e.g., French, Spanish, Russian, or Hawaiian) and make a list of English words that come from that language.
• • • • •

**STRETCHING
EXERCISE**

Language Is Cognitive.   The distinct but related forms of listening, speaking, reading, and writing make up language. Basic to these modes of language is cognitive processing that results in thinking and reasoning. The ability to think and reason depends partially on the ability to use language that identifies concepts, ideas, or relationships that can be manipulated during a person's thinking and reasoning. However, language may not be a prerequisite for all thinking. Although children between birth and age 2 do not yet possess fully developed language abilities, they do demonstrate the ability to reason. Nevertheless, language does facilitate thinking as the two develop together. Language is used and manipulated to create knowledge and concepts.

STRETCHING EXERCISE	Think of an idea that occurred to you of which you were not conscious until you said or wrote it.
	• • • • •

Nonverbal language, including viewing and visual literacy (which will be discussed in later chapters), is also a part of language. Gestures, facial expressions, body movement, and special aspects of graphics all convey different messages to the language receiver. Certain nonverbal and body language cues enhance or confuse messages communicated through listening, speaking, reading, and writing. The weak scribble on a note from a 70-year-old woman who professes her quick return to perfect health after a stroke tells more than the actual words she used.

Body language meshes with spoken language to strengthen the messages sent. You can strengthen your positive verbal message to a child about a task he has accomplished well with a smile, extended eye contact, a pat on his arm, or a handshake. Body language also conveys messages that conflict with spoken messages. The child who says that a trip to the bathroom is not necessary yet stands with his legs crossed, tensely rocking from toe to heel, may cause you to guess a meaning different than the spoken message.

The six characteristics you've just read about describe what language is and what it does. Now, how do children *acquire* language?

Cultural, Social, and Physical Factors

Overall, research shows that there is quite a similarity in the general acquisition sequence for language skills across language and cultures, although there is much individual variability in individual learning strategies and the rate of language acquisition for individuals (Rice, 1996). Across languages and cultures, children acquire language at generally the same rate and in the same sequence. Some of the factors that affect language development and use are gender, age, ethnicity, social class, social status, and changing customs and values of people communicating with each other.

Sociolinguistics, the study of language as a social behavior, has added much to the knowledge of how and why language develops. For example, typically, you would not say to one of your professors, "Pick me up a ham sandwich and coffee while you're at the snack bar," nor normally would you ask a sick friend, "Does my little pumpkin-face feel better today?" The language you use in a formal research paper on acid rain is probably different from the language you use in a letter to the editor of your local newspaper

.....
*Social interaction stimulates and
shapes children's language growth.*

or a letter to your parents. So you can see that social status and social roles define how a person uses language.

It is important to realize that the child who uses nonstandard English or has a dialect, a language delay, or difficulty learning language may not have limited intelligence. What a child produces orally is not necessarily representative of what goes on in his head. The 3-year-old who does not say any words may not need to if parents or caregivers anticipate his needs and provide for those needs without inviting his spoken language. Sometimes parents inadvertently do not provide the language stimulation, questions and answers, modeling, and repetition that encourages language use. Often, an older sibling will talk for the younger one, thus making it unnecessary for the younger one to learn to speak right away. Some evidence suggests that children who are gifted and who speak late may do so because they have so much going on in their heads as they make associations and connections that they cannot deal with oral language processing at the same time. Of course, a relaxed environment that encourages and rewards attempts to produce language is critical to its development in young children.

Equally important is the realization that second-language learners who have difficulty trying to learn English do not necessarily have cognitive or conceptual problems. Many English language difficulties for second-language learners result from efforts to teach skills directly—to develop speaking skills through practice and grammatical accuracy that occurs via drill and error correction rather than through meaningful language interactions (Krashen, 1985). As well, some second-language learners have difficulty with English because they are not literate in their own language. Knowing the rules of one language enhances learning a second langauge.

For example, through conversations with an English-speaking tutor about her everyday life, Suh Hee, a Korean immigrant student, wanted to develop and refine her vocabulary. She understood concepts and could explain them but wanted to learn specific vocabulary. For example, she decribed how she felt before a 5K race as "some tense" and learned she could use the word *nervous*. When she struggled to explain her place of finish in the race, she said she was "almost top of the end" and learned that *almost last* was the more accepted way of saying it.

Research indicates that *comprehensible language input,* language used in meaningful situations that accomplishes things for the user and often is obtained indirectly, is critical in second-language learning (Krashen, 1985). The best way to develop competence in second-language speaking, writing, and grammatical accuracy is to listen, talk, read, and write in natural situations (e.g., doing a science experiment or conversing in the cafeteria or on a fieldtrip) rather than memorizing rules or words that do not have meaningful associations.

Age is a factor that does not appreciably affect language development if opportunities for exposure and use of language are provided for the learner. There seems to be no critical period for learning oral or written language. Research with children who have not heard, spoken, or written language until well past puberty, because of isolation and neglect, supports this idea (DeVilliers & DeVilliers, 1979). When these children are placed in a normal environment and given opportunities to interact with language users, they learn to use language.

However, the human brain seems best suited to language learning before puberty (Moskowitz, 1978). Second languages are certainly learned more easily in childhood, and adults who learn more than one language in childhood have an easier time learning additional languages in later years. In fact, both native and second-language learning are enhanced when they occur together, especially if both languages possess similar patterns.

There is no evidence, though, that learning a second language is more difficult for an adult than for a child. The critical factors are exposure to language and opportunities to speak and write it in meaningful situations. It may be that children learning a second language are immersed in it and so it comes more easily to them. Adults, on the other hand, tend to learn a second language via a brief class, which may not provide them with similar opportunities. In fact, adults make the same kinds of errors of omission and overgeneralization a child does in learning a new language (DeVilliers & DeVilliers, 1979). If they have opportunities to practice the new language in meaningful situations (e.g., order food in a restaurant or take a trip to Mexico), adults may learn more quickly because they already know a language and its rules, and they are more experienced learners than children.

Language Acquisition

Controversy exists among linguists as to whether language is an innate ability present at birth, whether language growth depends on the processing of external factors, or whether language acquisition is a composite of both. It is amazing that a baby's cooing and babbling eventually develop into a meaningful sound-symbol system. Without any type of formal instruction, children acquire knowledge of phonology (sound units), morphology (meaning units), syntax (rules of grammar), semantics (variations in meanings), and pragmatics (use) of language. Several theories try to explain the origin and development of phonology, morphology, syntax, and semantics (McCormick & Schiefelbusch, 1984).

Behavior Theory

Behaviorists propose that language is learned through environmental conditioning and imitation of adult models (Skinner, 1957). Imitation, reward, reinforcement, and frequency of these behaviors are important factors in learning language. According to Skinner, thinking is the internal process of language, and both thought and language are initiated through interactions in the environment. The behaviorist view is incomplete, however. Children who are surrounded by rich language begin to imitate and use the language they hear, even though their imitation is often not accompanied by comprehension. Also, this theory does not account for rapid increases in children's language nor does it account for new and different utterances made by children, such as "I playded outside" or "Daddy allgone's car." Young children seem to have many notions of what language is and they use these rules to create new words and sentences. Much of the language children produce is not purely imitation but often an overgeneralization of certain rules.

Native Theory

Nativists suggest that language is native, innate, or natural to children, and that all children have a built-in *language acquisition device (LAD)* and discover how language works (Chomsky, 1974). Language learning is independent of intelligence or experiences. Lenneberg (1967) also suggests that language learning is based on biologically determined preknowledge. Nativists believe that children are born with internal mechanisms or capacities that allow them to organize the environment and learn language. Additionally, nativists believe that children internalize the rules of grammar and thus can make an infinite number of sentences, and that they do so without the practice, reinforcement, and modeling offered by adult language. Nativism holds that language depends on maturation; so as children grow, their language grows. This theory attempts to separate language learning from cognitive development, but linguists have clearly identified the relationship between knowledge and language.

Cognitive Theory

Cognitivists suggest that language is learned as a result of the active role that children take in that learning. This theory proposes that a child is born with a propensity to act on the environment, process information, and reach conclusions about the structure of language. According to Piaget (1962), thinking is a prerequisite of language, which develops as a result of experiencing and reasoning. Language growth is progressive and occurs in stages. Children's early language and their general development relate to actions, objects, and events they have experienced through touching, hearing, seeing, tasting, and smelling. This theory suggests that language has little effect on cognition, yet it is known that, through talking and writing, new knowledge can be generated.

Pragmatic Theory

Pragmatists believe that children learn language in order to socialize and direct the behavior of others (Bruner, 1974). This theory assumes that besides learning the meaning and form of language, children are motivated to learn language because of the functions it performs for them. Language begins with single words that often represent whole sentences of meaning. Halliday (1996) says, "We are still very ignorant of many aspects of the part language plays in our lives. But it is clear that language serves a wide range of human needs, and the richness and variety of its functions are reflected in the nature of language itself, in its organization as a system" (p. 40). Pragmatists study speech acts, the context within which they are performed, and the intentions of the speaker, yet they lack answers about how children learn syntax.

Interaction Theory

Interactionists propose that language is a product of both genetic and environmental factors. Children are born with the ability to produce and learn language, and interactions with the environment—which include imitation, reinforcement, reward, and social function—shape language. Cognition and language acquisition are thought to occur together, with a good deal of language stimulating thought and a good deal of concept development stimulating language. Although each of the previous theories provide valuable insights into how language is acquired and developed, interactionist theory presents a balanced, or eclectic, view that borrows from the other theories.

Vygotsky's (1978) theories suggest that social interactions affect language growth and that language stimulates cognitive development. Specifically, he believes that interactions with adults and teachers guide a child's movement into his *zone of proximal development*, which is between his independent level and his potential level. Your goal as a teacher is to help students move into this zone and become all they are capable of becoming.

Interactionists assume that many factors (social, linguistic, maturational, biological, cognitive) affect the course of development and that these factors depend on, interact with, and modify one another (Bohannon & Warren-Luebecker, 1989). The growing knowledge of human cognition and how information is processed helps educators better understand language development and how social interactions shape and drive language acquisition. The eclectic nature of this theory seems to explain language acquisition most fully. As a teacher, you need to understand the unique mixture of biological, psychological, social, and environmental factors that affect children's learning and use of language inside and outside the classroom.

Language Development

To initiate and produce oral and written language effectively, young children need many rich unstructured and planned opportunities in an environment where interactions with adults and other children are possible. To provide appropriate language experiences that will meet the needs of individual children, to deal more effectively with language problems or language delays, and to promote smooth transitions in development for all children, you need to understand the natural development of spoken and written language from birth onward. Figure 2.1 gives the general characteristics of language from birth to 6 years of age.

It is important to realize that some children develop language more quickly and some more slowly than others. Children with language delays or difficulties first need their language accepted as it is. The meaning of what children communicate needs to be reinforced rather than constantly corrected. While doing these things, you need to provide a model of standard language yourself. Children with language delays or difficulties often have problems hearing language, so this is the first avenue you might explore. Your school nurse can give an audiometric screening test that will identify many problems. Children who quickly develop a facility for language need reinforcement and re-

FIGURE 2.1   General characteristics of language from birth to age 6.

Typical Language Growth
(Birth–6 years)

0–6 months   Child turns eyes and head to sound sources. Makes all possible language sounds but eliminates those not used in the environment.

6 months–1 year   Responds to own name, voices of others, and environmental sounds. Speaks with single words that express thoughts and entire sentences (e.g., *dada* and *doggie*). Imitates simple words and sounds.

1–2 years   Uses two- or three-word phrases (e.g., *See truck*). Follows simple spoken directions. Points to or looks at familiar objects or people when asked (e.g., *Where's the ball?*). Possesses 300- to 500-word spoken vocabulary.

2–3 years   Child develops own rule systems. Uses simple and compound sentences. Begins to use plurals, pronouns, prepositions, and concepts such as *big* and *little, many* and *few.* Enjoys being read to. Points to objects in pictures. Puts several words together to convey a message (e.g., *Milk all gone.*). Possesses 800- to 1,000-word spoken vocabulary.

3–4 years   Uses verb past tenses. Overgeneralizes *-ed* and *-s* endings. Understands number concepts (e.g., *one, two,* and *three.*) Uses more complex complete sentences, including adjectives and adverbs. Enjoys being read to. Begins scribbling and drawing. Possesses 1,000- to 2,000-word spoken vocabulary.

4–5 years   Tells stories about recent events. Follows sequence of two directions. Language is becoming more abstract. Produces sentences using standard grammar with most words pronounced correctly. Enjoys being read to and talking about pictures in storybooks. Continues to scribble and draw. Begins to recognize some printed letters and words and to write letters to represent words. Possesses most basic rules of language and 3,000- to 5,000-word spoken vocabulary.

5–6 years   Uses complex sentences most of the time and can carry on a conversation. Syntax is established. Uses *I* rather than *me.* Correctly uses most pronouns and verbs in present and past tenses. Enjoys stories, participates in shared reading, and recognizes printed letters and words. Draws pictures and writes letters and words using invented spellings. Follows sequence of several directions. Possesses spoken vocabulary of approximately 10,000 to 15,000 words.

•••••

ward, too, but they also need stimulation and good models so that their language skills will grow.

Dialect speakers also need your support and acceptance. A *dialect* is a variation of English that is characteristic of a region or social group. Most people tend to think that the way they speak is the "correct" way and they sometimes look down on others who do not speak their way, but there is no evidence that one dialect is better than another. Each expresses the thoughts of the speaker as well as another. However, some dialects are more socially acceptable than others, and to be accepted by a group, an individual must often change his dialect to match that of the group. Because of the mobility of today's society, a person often develops his own *idiolect*—that is, a unique dialect composed of a blend of different dialects the person has spoken in his lifetime.

Second-language learning in children is also important to understand in that it may occur slowly, with the bilingual learner using nonstandard language forms and switching back and forth between his native tongue and English (Wallace & Goodman, 1989). This should be seen as evidence of growth, as it is a necessary prerequisite of learning English as a second language. Difficulties with English do not go hand in hand with cognitive or conceptual problems. In fact, bilingual children often bring strengths to school that children who speak only English do not possess. Moreover, multilingual classrooms offer rich opportunities for linguistic growth of all children. Whether language grows quickly or slowly, the components of language are the same. The following discussion includes the terms linguists use to describe these components.

Components of Language

What are the components of language? How is language constituted? Why is it important for you, as a teacher, to be knowledgeable of these components? The following sections explain the makeup of the English language.

Phonology. *Phonological development* is the growth and production of the sound system of language. From birth to 1 year of age, children produce cooing and babbling sounds called *phonemes.* These are the smallest, distinguishable speech sounds produced. Vowel phonemes are uttered before consonant phonemes, which appear when a child is about 4 to 6 months old. When a child babbles, he combines phonemes such as *b* and *u* to produce a *bu-bu-bu* sound.

There are 18 consonants, most representing one consistent sound, and five vowels, each representing more than one sound. The generally consistent nature of the English language helps make learning these phonemes easier. By about the age of 6 months, without first hearing them, a child produces all of the hundreds of sounds that are possible to make in any language. A child drops many of these sounds if they are not heard or repeated in the environment. Intonation (pitch or highness or lowness of the voice), juncture (pauses or interruptions or suspensions in the flow of sound), and stress (accent or the amount of emphasis given to a syllable or word) are also a part of phonology.

Morphology. *Morphological development* is the growth and production of meaning in language. The smallest distinguishable unit of meaning a child produces is called a *morpheme.* For example, to a young child, *ta* is a morpheme and could mean "table." To illustrate further, *cat* is one morpheme and *cats* is two morphemes; *sing* is one morpheme and *singer* is two. The inflectional endings *-s, -er, -ed,* and *-ing* are examples of morphemes, since they change the meanings of base words. From 9 to 12 months of age, a child produces distinguishable words composed of one or more morphemes and several phonemes. During this stage of development, single-word utterances, called *holophrases,* express complete thoughts. For example, the child produces a one-word sentence such as *Milk* that means "I want a drink" or *Ball* that means "Roll the ball to me." Holophrases representing many ideas are prevalent up to 1 to 1½ years of age.

Syntax.   *Syntax* refers to the rules of language that determine word order and function. Syntactic development, then, is the production of a number of words in a meaningful order that results in a complete thought or sentence. During the first six years of life, a child experiments with syntax. From age 1 to 1½ years, a child uses syntax when single words are combined into telegraphic speech. The child produces two-word sentences similar to messages sent by telegraph such as "See truck," "Drink milk," or "Bread all-gone." Articles, adjectives, and adverbs, in many cases, do not appear until later. As a child develops linguistically, more morphemes and phonemes per utterance appear; he begins to make three- and four-word sentences.

As sentences become longer, a child uses intonation to ask questions by raising the pitch at the end of an utterance to signal a question and a request for an answer, such as "Kitty eat?" or "Book done?" As the child's syntax and vocabulary grow, questions requiring more detailed explanations appear. For example, "who," "what," "why," "when," "where," and "how" questions appear at about the age of 1½ to 2 years. By about the age of 6 years, the child masters a major portion of the syntax of language, although there is evidence that some of the complex syntactic structures used by adults develop in the child after the age of 6 (Chomsky, 1974). However, the growth of semantics, another aspect of language development, continues throughout a person's entire lifetime.

Semantics.   *Semantic development,* the ability to distinguish the various meanings for words, occurs at a slower rate and over a longer period of time than do phonology, morphology, or syntax. Both adults and children learn and use words in new and different ways every day, so semantic development can be considered ongoing. The growth of semantics begins when children are 9 to 12 months old and first begin to use nouns, then verbs, and finally adjectives and adverbs. Prepositions, conjunctions, and words representing more abstract concepts appear later. Of the language cuing systems, semantic growth is strongest during the elementary years.

It is interesting to note that children's selective speech initially includes only concrete words. They concurrently use a knowledge of syntax (word endings, word order, and function), phonology (sounds, intonation, juncture, and stress), and morphology (smallest units of meaning), as well as the social context of a situation to aid in semantic growth. It is through the interdependence of these four aspects and the broader social context that language develops.

Vocabulary development is rapid in the first six years of life as a child's lexicon, or personal dictionary, expands. Children gradually become aware of the various functions a word performs and the variety of meanings it possesses in different situations. For example, the word *toast* functions as a noun when the child hears "Eat your toast" or when an adult says "A toast to happiness." It also functions as a verb when one says "I toasted the bread." Understanding various functions and producing a variety of meanings for words signals growth in semantics. Here are some interesting statistics related to words and word meanings:

- By the age of 5 or 6, some children understand approximately 8,000 words (Harris & Sipay, 1980).
- The typical child adds more than 3,000 words a year, or about 16 words per school day, to his recognition vocabulary (Miller & Gildea, 1987).
- The average fifth-grader may encounter between 16,000 and 24,000 unknown words per year in the course of reading (Anderson & Freebody, 1983).

Of course, not all these words are *taught* to students. Many words are learned through use during reading, talking, and listening.

Pragmatics.   *Pragmatics* refers to the use of language to express one's intentions and to get things done in the world. Even young children use one-word utterances to accomplish various pragmatic ends. Adult pragmatics may include functions such as refusing, blaming, flattering, and offering condolences. There are rules for using language appropriately in various social situations, and when these rules are followed, an individual is said to possess communicative competence. In both overt and covert ways, adults provide children with guidance in the use of pragmatics. Successful conversations, for example, are characterized by appropriateness in quantity, quality, relevance, and manner of speaking (Gleason, 1989). Specifically, topics that are appropriate to talk about at a wedding may not be appropriate at a funeral, and the way one express oneself in one-to-one conversations is different from the way one might address a large group. As well, what a person writes is often very different from the way he might express himself in speaking.

Which of these components of language explains dialect? Dialect differences can be related to phonology, with differences in pronunciation (e.g., *river* and *rivuh).* Dialect variations can reflect lexical differences (a *lexicon* is a fund of possible words an individual uses to describe or name something), which are variations in words used to name the same thing (e.g., *creek, crick, brook, branch, gutter,* or *bayou* for a small river). Dialects can also be related to syntax, with differences in word order (e.g., *He no go with us* or *In restaurant we eat).*

Children who use a dialect different from yours need your support and acceptance of their language. In order to develop a standard dialect, one that is more universally understood and accepted, it is also important not to negate the language or dialect children speak at home, but rather help them develop patterns that are acceptable in particular situations.

Models of Language and Literacy Learning

As mentioned earlier, there is evidence that children learn to talk without direct instruction or intentional teaching of sounds, meanings, or grammar. Most children easily learn the rules of language and become proficient in language use. How do they do this and, for most of them, do it so effortlessly?

Two models of learning help explain how language and literacy may unfold for young children. Both Holdaway (1986) and Cambourne (1988) propose paradigms for how a child constructs knowledge, unconsciously, as in language and literacy learning, and consciously, in more formal kinds of learning. Both models are constructivist in nature. That is, both models place the child at the center of his own learning as he constructs meanings, often unconsciously, about language and literacy, and as he practices and learns it in natural situations. These models are built on the wholistic philosophy of learning that is found in many elementary classrooms today.

Holdaway (1986) believes natural learning is composed of:

- Observation of demonstrations
- Guided participation
- Unsupervised role-playing practice
- Performance: Sharing and celebration of accomplishment

If you think about how a child learns to tie his sneaker laces, for example, these four aspects make sense. First, the child likely watches as a parent ties the laces of his sneakers or shoes. When the child is ready, with an adult's or sibling's help, he is shown how to hold the laces and weave them together to make a knot and tie a bow. Once he has the basics down, the child tries to tie the lace by himself. If he is unsuccessful, he may need more guided help and so he returns to someone for help. When he can tie a lace on his own, the child shares this event with his parents and siblings, who happily celebrate the child's accomplishment.

This model of natural learning helps explain how language and literacy are learned. In learning how to talk and how to read and write, the child first watches demonstrations of language and has many opportunities to participate with the help and guidance of other language users. Then, the child tries to use language on his own, usually moving and back and forth between guided use and independent attempts until he masters a particular word, phrase, or sentence type. This usage is then affirmed, reinforced, and celebrated by others.

Cambourne (1988) proposes another model of natural learning that can be applied to language and literacy (see Figure 2.2). If Cambourne's model is used to understand literacy learning, immersion in texts of all kinds and demonstrations of how texts are created and used are critical. For example, the child must see adults using and creating print naturally for a variety of reasons and in a range of ways in order for the child's willing engagement in literacy. The probability of the child's engagement is increased if those close to the child show him that they expect him to engage with literacy. It is also important for the child to have the responsibility and power to make decisions about his own involvement in the learning. Next, the child needs opportunities to use and practice his knowledge in natural situations and ways. The environment should be free from risks so that the child can make mistakes or approximations as he attempts to master the learning. Last, the child needs feedback from exchanges with those who are literate to continue his attempts at becoming literate.

As you can see, there are important similarities between learning to talk and learning to read and write. Halliday's seven functions of language and the components of

Holdaway's and Cambourne's models all imply that interactions with others and use for real reasons in natural situations are at the heart of language and literacy learning. Let's look now at how and when early literate behaviors begin to emerge in young children.

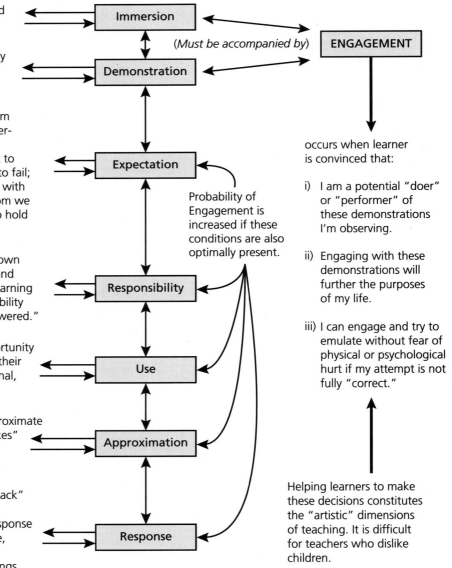

Learners need to be immersed in text of all kinds.

Learners need to receive many demonstrations of how texts are constructed and used.

Expectations of those to whom learners are bonded are powerful coercers of behaviour. "We achieve what we expect to achieve; we fail if we expect to fail; we are more likely to engage with demonstrations of those whom we regard as significant and who hold high expectations for us."

Learners need to make their own decisions about when, how and what "bits" to learn in any learning task. Learners who lose the ability to make decisions are "depowered."

Learners need time and opportunity to use, employ, and practise their developing control in functional, realistic, non-artificial ways.

Learners must be free to approximate the desired model — "mistakes" are essential for learning to occur.

Learners must receive "feedback" from exchanges with more knowledgeable "others." Response must be relevant, appropriate, timely, readily available, non-threatening, with no strings attached.

Immersion

(Must be accompanied by)   **ENGAGEMENT**

Demonstration

Expectation

Probability of Engagement is increased if these conditions are also optimally present.

Responsibility

Use

Approximation

Response

occurs when learner is convinced that:

i) I am a potential "doer" or "performer" of these demonstrations I'm observing.

ii) Engaging with these demonstrations will further the purposes of my life.

iii) I can engage and try to emulate without fear of physical or psychological hurt if my attempt is not fully "correct."

Helping learners to make these decisions constitutes the "artistic" dimensions of teaching. It is difficult for teachers who dislike children.

FIGURE 2.2 Learning to read results from immersion in texts of all kinds and demonstrations of how texts are constructed and used.

Source: Reprinted by permission of Brian Cambourne, Faculty of Education, University of Wollongong, New South Wales, Australia.

So far, we have explored the growth of spoken language, which initially precedes the growth of written language. What about the child's growing knowledge of reading and writing? How and when does this begin to develop? A child of age 2 or 3 who identifies a box of cereal, a stop sign, the McDonald's logo, or the printed title *Sesame Street* at the start of the television show demonstrates awareness of written language. This behavior is one of the initial signs that a child understands that print communicates meaning and has a function. This example of early print awareness is called *emergent literacy.*

Emergent literacy has become a well-known term only recently (Teale & Sulzby, 1989). Why only recently? Because recently researchers began to study children of 14 months and younger, whereas in the past, the focus of attention was on older children. For the past two decades, children's developing senses of reading and writing at home and in the community, as well as the social aspects of literacy, have been studied. Also, partly as a result of that research, one realizes there is a synergistic relationship between reading and writing. That is, researchers today know that reading and writing develop simultaneously and, in fact, each contributes to the growth of the other. So, rather than thinking of readiness for reading as a prerequisite for beginning reading instruction, teachers consider a child's emergent literacy development and use reading and writing together to support literacy and learning.

Many children come to school exhibiting readinglike behavior (Holdaway, 1986) in which they imitate pleasurable book experiences they have had at home. As children "pretend read," they attempt to reconstruct text that has been read to them or to imitate a situation in which they have enjoyed an interaction with someone concerning the print and pictures of a storybook. Some children can tell a book's story by reading the pictures and remembering what an adult read to them previously.

There is strong evidence that story reading and the level and type of conversations between parents and children are probably two of the most important environmental factors affecting language acquisition. Wells (1986) found striking differences in the lan-

·····
*Emergent literacy develops as
young children see literacy in use
at home and as they hear and talk
about books themselves.*

guage and achievement of Jonathan, age 7, who had about 6,000 stories read to him before entering school, and Rosie, age 7, who had heard none. He concludes that in homes where print is an important and valued medium for learning and sharing ideas and knowledge, a young child's language grows quickly. When parents and siblings share enjoyable books and a child hears books read, both spoken and written language awareness and facility develop naturally.

Many children come to school able to recognize a number of words they have learned from their daily environment. Some kindergarten children recognize and can write letters of the alphabet and a few words. Others recognize that written language often matches spoken language and will point to print and ask "What does this say?" or write an unintelligible string of letterlike shapes and tell you what it says.

Most children, such as 3-year-old Emily, begin to write by drawing and scribbling (see Figure 2.3) and eventually start to experiment with shapes and letters (see Figure 2.4). As phonology, morphology, and semantics develop, children begin to represent words with letters, as 4-year-old Erin does in Figure 2.5. Five-year-old Richie invents spellings of words in his speaking vocabulary and begins to compose entire thoughts (see Figure 2.6). Growth in syntax and semantics of written language shows in 8-year-old Melinda's sophisticated Halloween story containing an introduction, problem, resolution, and conclusion (see Figure 2.7). Four-year-old David's picture and demand (see Figure 2.8) demonstrate his use of language to accomplish a pragmatic end.

Just as with the development of spoken language, all children do not learn written language at the same rate or in the same ways. Some children become proficient writers much more quickly and easily than others. For most young children, however, listening and speaking vocabularies develop first and are much larger than their reading and writing vocabularies, at least until fourth or fifth grade. As language develops, the sizes of older children's spoken and written vocabularies become more nearly the same.

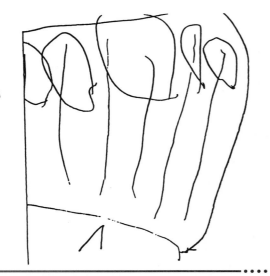

FIGURE 2.3 Three-year-old Emily's drawing and scribbling signal the beginnings of writing.

FIGURE 2.4 Six months later, Emily reproduces several capital letters.

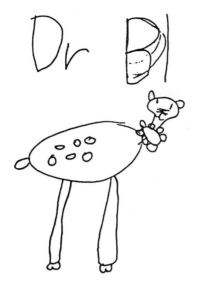

FIGURE 2.5 Four-year-old Erin represents a *deer* and a *bell* with initial and final letters.

FIGURE 2.6 Richie uses invented spelling to write *I'm scared of lions* after a visit to the zoo.

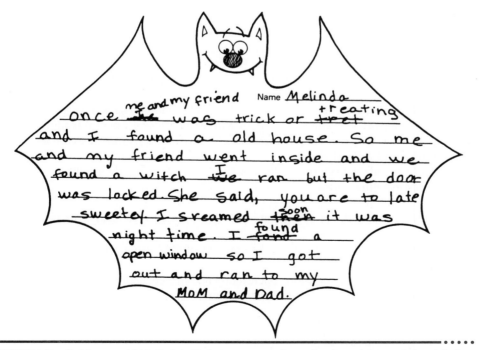

Name __Melinda__

once me and my friend was trick or treating and I found a old house. So me and my friend went inside and we found a witch I ran but the door was locked. She said, you are to late sweetey I sreamed soon then it was night time. I found a open window so I got out and ran to my MoM and Dad.

FIGURE 2.7 Eight-year-old Melinda's Halloween story shows her broad semantic knowledge.

FIGURE 2.8 Four-year-old David demonstrates the pragmatic use of language by writing *Go give a present to me.*

Although spoken and written language differ in many ways, they share a similarity in the way they begin. The beginnings of writing are evident in children's drawings, scribbles, letter strings, and invented spellings, and the onset of speaking is evident in children's babbling, word approximations, and telegraphic speech. Just as adults encourage the young child to experiment with speech (most children do not begin with properly composed and grammatical sentences), adults must encourage young children to experiment with reading and writing. Richie's invented spellings in Figure 2.6 and Melinda's nonstandard syntax in Figure 2.7 indicate growth and should not necessarily be corrected or discouraged. Teachers and parents need to be careful about correcting the child who makes miscues as he attempts to match print with spoken language during reading. Both a child's invented spelling in writing and miscues in oral reading present valuable information about the processes the child uses to construct meaning and make sense of his world with language.

Teale and Sulzby (1989) provide a picture of the young child as a literacy learner that includes five dimensions:

1. For almost all children in a literate society, learning to read and write begins very early in life.
2. The functions of literacy are an integral part of the learning process that is taking place.
3. Reading and writing develop concurrently and interrelatedly in young children.
4. Literacy learners learn through active engagement, constructing their understanding of how written language works.
5. Even more important than demonstrations of literacy is the time parents and children spend interacting around print.

This perspective on young childen's literacy learning has implications for teaching reading and writing and the language arts in the elementary school classroom. Research on emergent literacy has shown that children learn through storybook reading; talk and discussion; responding to stories; writing and experimenting with drawings, letters, sounds, words, and word order; dramatic activities; and shared language experiences. Just as in learning to talk, children learn to read and write through immersion and demonstration that results in engagement with books and stories as well as other readers and writers.

Summary

Language is an ordered system of symbols for transmitting information and ideas that are systematic, arbitrary, flexible, and variable. English, which is a composite of many languages, shapes and forms the user's world. It is cognitively based and composed of the distinct modes of listening, speaking, reading, and writing. Various theories give insights into the acquisition and development of phonology, morphology, syntax, semantics, and pragmatics. Young children's emergent literacy develops with the help of language immersion and demonstration.

R•••••
Reflections

1. As a first-grade teacher, you will host Curriculum Night for parents one evening in September. How will you explain to parents the nature of the development of children's spoken and written language? Briefly outline your talk and share it with a friend who can play the role of a parent and ask questions so you have the experience of explaining yourself.

2. Which theory/theories of language development make the most sense to you? Why? What questions do you still have about language acquisition and learning?

Professional Resources

Durkin, D. B. (Ed.) (1995). *Language issues: Reading for teachers.* New York: Longman. This is a collection of essays for teachers concerned with first- and second-language acquisition, nonstandard English, the teaching of grammar, language change, and attaining literacy.

Power, B. M., & Hubbard, R. S. (Eds.) (1996). *Language development: A reader for teachers.* Englewood Cliffs, NJ: Prentice Hall. This collection of work by educators, linguists, anthropologists, and classroom teacher-researchers challenges readers to rethink their beliefs about language, learning, and culture. Extensions at the end of each section help teachers analyze language in their own classrooms.

Spangenberg-Urbschat, K., & Pritchard, R. (1994). *Kids come in all languages: Reading instruction for ESL students.* Newark, DE: International Reading Association. This practical text includes background information on reading, ESL instruction, and ESL learners, as well as specific strategies that are effective with ESL students.

References

Anderson, R. C., & Freebody, P. (1983). Reading comprehension and the assessment and acquisition of word knowledge. In B. Hutson (Ed.), *Advances in reading/language research* (pp. 231–256). Greenwich, CT: JAI Press.

Bohannon, J. N., & Warren-Luebecker, A. (1989). Theoretical approaches to language acquisition. In J. B. Gleason (Ed.), *The development of language* (pp. 167–224). Columbus, OH: Merrill.

Bruner, J. (1974). The organization of early skilled action. In M. P. M. Richards (Ed.), *The integration of a child into a social world* (pp. 375–403). London: Cambridge University Press.

Cambourne, B. (1988). *The whole story: Natural learning and the acquisition of literacy in the classroom.* Auckland, New Zealand: Scholastic.

Cazden, C. (1981). *Child language and education.* New York: Holt, Rinehart and Winston.

Chomsky, N. (1974). *Aspects of the theory of syntax.* Cambridge, MA: MIT Press.

DeVilliers, P. A., & DeVilliers, J. G. (1979). *Early language.* Cambridge, MA: Harvard University Press.

Gleason, J. B. (1989). Studying language development. In J. B. Gleason (Ed.), *The development of language* (pp. 1–34). Columbus, OH: Merrill.

Halliday, M. A. K. (1996). Relevant models of language. In B. M. Power & R. S. Hubbard (Eds.), *Language development: A reader for teachers* (pp. 36–41). Englewood Cliffs, NJ: Prentice Hall.

Harris, A. J., & Sipay, E. R. (1980). *How to increase reading ability.* New York: Longman.

Holdaway, D. (1986). *The foundations of literacy.* Auckland, New Zealand: Scholastic.

Krashen, S. (1985). *The input hypothesis: Issues and implications.* New York: Longman.

Lederer, R. (1991). *The miracle of language.* New York: Pocket Books.

Lenneberg, E. (1967). *Biological foundations of language.* New York: Wiley.

McCormick, L., & Schiefelbusch, R. L. (1984). *Early language intervention.* Columbus, OH: Merrill.

Miller, G. A., & Gildea, P. M. (1987). How children learn words. *Scientific American, 257* (93), 94–99.

Moskowitz, B. A. (1978). Acquisition of language. *Scientific American, 239,* 90–110.

Parshall, G. (1995). A "glorious mongrel." *U.S. News & World Report*, September 25, p. 48.

Piaget, J. (1962). *The language and thought of the child.* New York: Humanities Press.

Rice, M. L. (1996). Children's language acquisition. In B. M. Power and R. S. Hubbard (Eds.), *Language development: A reader for teachers* (pp. 3–12). Englewood Cliffs, NJ: Prentice Hall.

Skinner, B. F. (1957). *Verbal behavior.* Englewood Cliffs, NJ: Prentice Hall.

Teale, W. H., & Sulzby, E. (1989). Emergent literacy: New perspectives. In D. S. Strickland & L. M. Morrow (Eds.), *Emerging literacy: Young children learn to read and write* (pp. 1–15). Newark, DE: International Reading Association.

Templin, M. C. (1957). *Certain language skills in children.* Minneapolis, MN: University of Minnesota Press.

Vygotsky, L. S. (1978). *Mind in society: The development of psychological processes.* Cambridge, MA: Harvard University Press.

Wallace, C., & Goodman, Y. (1989). Research currents: Language and literacy development of multilingual learners. *Language Arts, 66,* 542–551.

Wells, G. (1986). *The meaning makers: Children learning language and using language to learn.* Portsmouth, NH: Heinemann.

Diversity in
the Classroom

W•••••indow on Teaching

Karen Wassell is a first-year teacher with a diverse group of fifth-grade students. Recently, her community had an influx of immigrant families from Russia, Bosnia, Somalia, and Laos, who join a population that is already quite diverse. Karen says:

> I have such a mix of kids in my class that it scares me. My students range in reading levels from grades 2 through 8, some don't speak or write English, they represent many different racial and ethnic backgrounds, many are on the free-lunch program because their family incomes fall below the poverty level, and several

have learning disabilities. Here is a sampling of the more obvious differences in my class:

- *Kevin is classified with a learning disability in reading and writing. He receives free lunch.*
- *Sharam, whose first language is Kurdish, has just come to the United States from Turkey. His family is living in poverty.*
- *Shamiko is an African American who has a learning disability. She lives with her mother, who does not work.*
- *Jason is a Euro-American who is reading on grade level and loves science and social studies.*
- *Vu is a recent immigrant from China. She has a hearing impairment and has difficulty with English.*
- *Bryan was born to an unmarried drug-addicted teenager who gave him up for adoption. He is not working up to his potential and is hyperactive and a behavior problem.*
- *Dillon has cerebral palsy and wears a leg brace. Previously, he received physical therapy and speech therapy, and this year he is working on grade level. He lives with his Euro-American mother and does not see his African American father.*
- *Kristen is easily distracted, seems disinterested, and does not finish her work. Her Japanese mother is ill with leukemia.*
- *Steven is a gifted student who is reading on a eighth-grade level and plays four different musical instruments.*
- *Maria does well in school. She is the oldest of five siblings who live with their mother, who does not work.*

Surely there are other factors that are equally as important as those I have mentioned—many that I don't know about—that will affect the way these kids learn. For many of them, my classroom is a safe haven where they can be accepted, supported, and protected. But how will I ever be able to meet all their needs and to challenge them? Will my White, middle-class, Euro-American background prevent me from reaching those from other cultures? How can I teach a child when I don't speak her language? Will we be able to come together as a group that knows, cares, and trusts each other? How can I make this happen? What curriculum and which strategies will allow them all to achieve at grade level or beyond?

Karen is certified in elementary education with a master's degree and K–12 certification as a reading specialist. She pursued this master's degree because, as she says:

Unless kids possess the ability to read and write, it's impossible for them to do well in school. I believe literacy is critical to achievement in every academic area and success in the world of work. Being illiterate not only limits learning; it can negatively affect self-concept and behavior, the chances that kids will finish school, the ability to hold a job and function in society, and so much else.

Karen is better prepared than many first-year teachers, yet she is uncertain about the best course to follow with this group of students. She says:

*On the one hand, I'm nervous and unsure. With these kids being so diverse in so
many ways, there can easily be conflict and behavior problems. Plus, I just don't
know enough about how to teach kids who are so different from one another.
But on the other hand, I am excited about the diversity in my class. I think we have
a rich pool of experiences and knowledge to draw on. The makeup of this class
should extend our possibilities for learning because the children possess such neat
differences. The key will be to build understanding, respect, and cooperation first,
and then to get them feeling like a commmunity that cares about each other. But
I sure don't want any of them to feel inadequate or apologetic about being different from their classmates.*

O· · · · ·verview

*This chapter examines diversity (cognitive, physical, cultural, and linguistic) and the
makeup of today's classrooms. You will read about the beliefs several teachers hold
about pluralistic classrooms and their units and lessons for diverse students. You will
also be introduced to guidelines for teaching diverse learners effectively and presented
with specific ways to meet their needs.*

The motto of the United States, "E pluribus unum," was adopted in 1777 and appears
on the country's seal and currency. It means "Out of many, one" or "In diversity, unity."
Today, this motto seems even more appropriate than it was over 200 years ago.

The meaning of *diversity* varies considerably within the educational community.
Today, *multicultural, diverse,* and *pluralistic* are used interchangeably to describe classrooms, schools, and U.S. society. Teachers, administrators, and policymakers generally
agree that diversity in the classroom means that students come from a variety of groups,
each of which is characterized by marked differences.

Today's students are diverse in cognitive and physical ability, language, culture,
race, ethnicity, learning style, and socioeconomic level, to name some of the major
groups represented. The two primary categories of diversity we will consider in this
chapter are *cognitive and physical diversity* and *cultural and linguistic diversity.* In
other chapters of this book, you will also find discussions about diverse students and descriptions of ideas for teaching them effectively. Now, let's look briefly at some statistics that will set the stage for the rest of this chapter.

Cognitive and Physical Diversity

Federal legislation called the Education for All Handicapped Children Act, PL 94–142,
was passed by Congress in 1975. This law allocated funding for schools to provide education for students identified as having special needs. PL 94–142 requires that children

who are handicapped must, "to the maximum extent appropriate," be educated "with children who are not handicapped." This legislation means children who have mild disabilities who can benefit from being in regular classrooms will be mainstreamed; that is, they will spend part or all of each school day in the regular clasroom. Thus, it is likely that you, like Karen, will have one or more of these students (e.g., those with specific learning disabilities (LD), speech impairments, mental retardation (MR), serious emotional disturbance (ED), or other disabilities such as physical-motor) in your classroom (see Figure 3.1).

Numbers of students in the cognitive and physical category of diversity served by special education teachers and teacher aides are significant and they have increased surprisingly in recent years (Meyen, Vergason, & Whelan, 1996):

- The most dramatic increase is for students with learning disabilities—a group that has more than doubled since 1977.
- The number of students with serious emotional disturbances has increased slightly.
- Students in other groups have declined (mental retardation, speech and language impairments, visual and hearing impairments, orthopedic impairments, deafblindness, autism, and other health impairments).

Schools across the country have experienced huge increases in the number of students with learning disabilities. Why such dramatic increases? Several things may contribute. Since labeling a child as learning disabled does not carry the stigma of the mental retardation label, many otherwise MR students may be labeled LD in order to receive services. Also, funding for special education services continues as funding for other supplemental services is cut. In addition, as numbers of special education students increase, schools and families are eligible for increased aid, which is a powerful incentive to label students.

What Is a Learning Disability?

Learning disabilites are referred to as the "hidden handicap," with some estimates indicating that about 15 percent of the population is affected (Ellis & Cramer, 1995). The legal definition of *learning disability (LD)* is "a disorder in one or more of the basic psychological processes involved in understanding or in using language, spoken or written, which may manifest itself in an imperfect ability to listen, think, speak, read, write, spell, or do mathematical calculations" (Meyan et al., 1996, p. 8).

A learning disability interferes with the ability to store, process, or produce information, and is usually found in individuals such as Kevin, Shamiko, and Bryan (described earlier), who usually have at least average levels of ability. To be considered learning disabled, a student must be functioning at least two years below grade level and there must be a significant discrepancy between intelligence and achievement. Kevin, Shamiko, and Bryan are reading and writing on a second-grade level yet have average intelligence, which should enable them to function at fifth-grade level.

Despite the legal statement just given, professionals cannot agree on a common definition (Mather & Roberts, 1994); indeed, some special educators would rather avoid

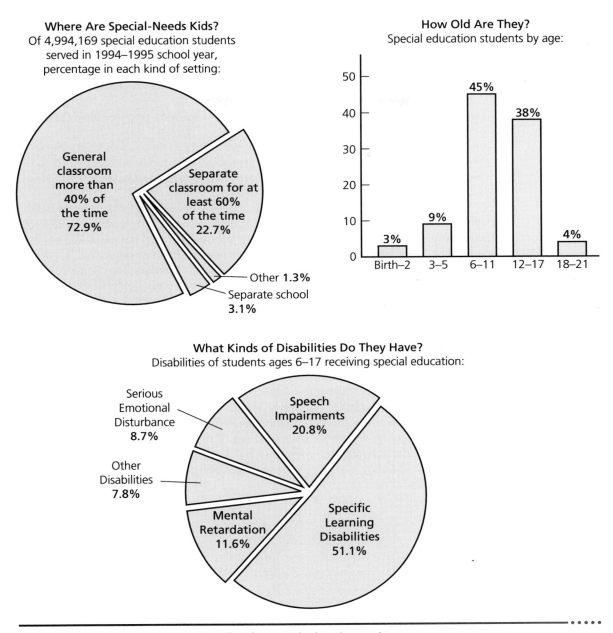

Where Are Special-Needs Kids?
Of 4,994,169 special education students served in 1994–1995 school year, percentage in each kind of setting:

General classroom more than 40% of the time 72.9%

Separate classroom for at least 60% of the time 22.7%

Other 1.3%
Separate school 3.1%

How Old Are They?
Special education students by age:

Birth–2 3%
3–5 9%
6–11 45%
12–17 38%
18–21 4%

What Kinds of Disabilities Do They Have?
Disabilities of students ages 6–17 receiving special education:

Serious Emotional Disturbance 8.7%

Speech Impairments 20.8%

Other Disabilities 7.8%

Mental Retardation 11.6%

Specific Learning Disabilities 51.1%

FIGURE 3.1 Statistics on students identified for special education services.

Source: U.S. Department of Education, Office of Special Education Programs. 18th Annual Report to Congress, 1996.

the term altogether. Heward and Orlansky (1995) report that a national task force identified 99 separate characteristics of children with LD, who have average IQs and do not have hearing or vision problems. Statistics on LD are startling (Ellis & Cramer, 1995):

- Some 2.25 million children, or 50 percent of all students in special education in public schools, have learning disabilities.
- From 75 to 80 percent of students identified as learning disabled have their basic deficits in language and reading.
- More than one-third (35 percent) of students with LD drop out of high school.
- Half (50 percent) of juvenile delinquents tested had undetected LD.
- Some 62 percent of students with LD are unemployed one year after graduating.

So, how and why do these language and reading deficits occur? Educators believe environmental factors, individual factors, or a combination of both cause LD. The home, community, school, and classroom must share responsibility for not providing environments that foster academic success in these students. Relationships among parents, home, and school, as well as among peers, can influence learning, too. Some educators believe students with LD have brain damage or "minimal brain dysfunction" due to an injury that may have occurred before, during, or after birth (Heward & Orlansky, 1995). Others believe that chemical imbalances or neurological anomalies cause learning disabilities. At any rate, for Karen and you and other teachers, the challenge is to find these students' strengths and work from them to develop the skills and understandings they need to work on grade level.

Today, students with learning disabilities often remain in the regular classroom setting. In Karen's school, the special education teacher consults and collaborates with Karen to provide supportive instruction in the classroom for Kevin, Shamiko, and Bryan. In other schools, students with mild disabilities (those who are LD, mentally retarded, or emotionally disturbed) are pulled out of their regular classes for separate instruction. In some schools, these students are placed in separate settings or resource rooms. The trend today, however, is for students who are mildly disabled to remain in the classroom with their peers.

STRETCHING EXERCISE Special education teacher Marilyn Scala collaborated with three teachers to form three entirely different working relationships that are described in "What Whole Language in the Mainstream Means for Children with Learning Disabilities" in *The Reading Teacher*, Volume 47, Number 3, pages 222–229. How do you think these students with LD might benefit from from some *pull-out* instruction? What is/or should be the role of the reading specialist in this school?

• • • • •

Special education teachers and teaching assistants provide the supportive instruction for students identified as learning disabled. Proponents of the in-class support model, or *push-in* model, believe it has many advantages over *pull-out* instruction (Allington, 1993). With proper training and time to develop collaborative relationships, push-in support programs

- Reduce instructional time lost in transition from one classroom to another.
- Minimize curricular fragmentation.
- Reduce potential stigma for students who work with both the special education teacher and classroom teacher as a team.
- Foster professional learning by classroom and special education teachers when they work side by side.

Many students, however, still need the kind of individual instruction that is best provided outside the classroom where there are fewer distractions. A number of special education teachers and reading specialists who use both pull-out and push-in instruction with their students say this balanced approach provides many advantages.

There are many current sources to consult on the topic of students with special needs. Professional journals include:

Teaching Exceptional Children   *Reading and Writing Quarterly*
Journal of Special Education   *Topics in Language Disorders*
Learning Disabilities: Research and Practice   *Perceptual and Motor Skills*
Remedial and Special Education

Cultural and Linguistic Diversity

Although immigration has increased in some states (e.g., California, Florida, and Texas), today it is the lowest it has ever been in this country's history. Overall, however, the nation's population continues to become more diverse despite lower immigration and declining fertility rates for Anglo-Americans. However, the United States Census Bureau predicts the following population increases from 1990 to 2030 (Cortes, 1990):

- White Americans up by 25 percent
- African Americans up by 68 percent
- Asian Americans, Pacific Islander Americans, and Native Americans up by 79 percent
- Hispanic Americans up by 187 percent

At the beginning of the twenty-first century, demographers believe nearly one-third of all school-age children will be from minority populations (DeVita, 1989). In many traditionally White middle-class schools, demographics are changing quickly as communities experience economic transformations and population shifts. Even in rural and private schools, where populations may not be very diverse nor have changed much over time, appreciation and understanding of diversity is critical since students will one day enter a workplace that reflects the diversity in the United States.

Student diversity often encompasses more than one aspect of difference. For example, many students with physical impairments, such as Dillon in Karen's class, also have cognitive deficits. Poverty most often accompanies other aspects of diversity and can magnify or mask them. For instance, students such as Vu, who has a language deficit, frequently come from poor homes. Others, such as Sharam, who is an immigrant living in poverty, possess adequate ability but do not have the language, world experiences, literacy models, or financial resources that allow them to achieve as easily and quickly as some students from more financially secure homes. You can see, then, that diversity frequently has a direct impact on achievement in school. It is important for you to remember that although some of your students possess obvious aspects of diversity, others (such as Kristen and Maria) possess differences that may be more subtle, but no less important, than the more easily identified and visible aspects of diversity that affect learning.

So, large numbers of students who are different in culture and language, including race and ethnicity, make up today's classrooms. As well, mainstreaming or inclusion of students with learning disabilities and students with physical disabilities and behavioral disorders in regular classrooms further explains today's diverse classroom populations. Also, students who are diverse in more than one way help to richly texture classroom populations.

Students with Limited English Proficiency

The number of migrant, immigrant, and refugee children in the United States who have little knowledge of English is increasing at a tremendous rate. As many as one in three students in some of this nation's largest school districts have limited English proficiency, and the number of these students in smaller school districts is growing daily (Fitzgerald, 1993). There are also many nonstandard speakers of English (e.g., Native Americans who speak the language of their tribe, African Americans who speak Ebonics [African American English], and dialect speakers such as those who speak Appalachian or Spanglish [a combination of Spanish and English]).

Limited English proficient (LEP) students and other English learners have much to offer monolingual, mainstream classrooms. They bring rich cultural and ethnic histories, varied family traditions and experiences, assorted languages, different ways of thinking, and unique views of the world. In a diverse classroom environment, all students can learn to celebrate their own uniqueness and expand their perspectives. When students from various backgrounds work and learn together in school, they prepare to work and live together in an increasingly multicultural world.

STRETCHING EXERCISE

What happens when you honor both English and Spanish in the classooom? How do children view bilingualism? For answers, read the December 1993 issue of *Language Arts,* Volume 70, pages 659–668, "Emerging Biliteracy and Cross-Cultural Sensitivity in a Language Arts Classroom" by M. D. Reyes, E. A. Laliberty, and J. M. Orbanosky.

· · · · ·

Success in school and the workplace for students from diverse backgrounds depends, to a large degree, on their English literacy. Several things can potentially make students at risk for reading and writing failure in school. Many students never attended school in their native countries or were not there long enough to become literate in their own languages, and so learning a new language is even more difficult. Other students have been in U.S. communities and schools all their lives, but the language spoken in their homes and communities is nonstandard English. Fortunately, English-speaking students can help classroom teachers and special teachers (ESL teachers, reading teachers, resource room teachers) develop the English literacy of these diverse learners. Conversely, these English learners can teach their monolingual peers much about their native cultures and languages.

Fitzgerald (1993) reviewed the research on programs for language-minority students and concludes that many of these programs are based on outdated models of literacy learning. In general, these programs minimize the interrelationships among listening, speaking, reading, and writing; focus on spoken language proficiency; and specify the teaching of grammar but ignore the functional and social aspects of literacy. In her review of the research, Fitzgerald found that although reading and writing processes in a first and second language tend to be similar, for second-language learners, reading and writing in English may be slower because of a lack of fluency and limited background knowledge for specific content and vocabulary. This is important information for Karen and teachers like her who will need to put extra effort into developing students' background knowledge and specific vocabulary.

ESL and Bilingual Programs

English as a second language (ESL) programs teach English to students for whom English is not their first language. These programs, taught by ESL teachers who speak English but not necessarily the native language of their students, are found in schools where English is the primary language but other languages are also spoken. For example, consider this scenario: Caroline is an ESL teacher in an upstate New York school where 35 percent of the students are recent immigrants who speak 16 different languages. Caroline often works in a Resource Center outside the classroom with small groups of students who speak the same language. She also supports her students in the classroom as they learn English and content. In schools such as Caroline's, native adult speakers of other languages often volunteer for home/school communications, translating and tutoring English learners and acting as resources for teachers.

Bilingual programs operate in schools where large numbers of English learners speak the same language. In these programs, teachers who are proficient in the students' native language and English provide classroom instruction in both languages to students who are grouped by their home language. In this example, Carlos, a bilingual teacher in California, teaches his first-grade class in Spanish for the content areas of science, social studies, and math, and spends one period a day teaching ESL. Over the next two years, his students will make the transition into English as they develop the cognitive and academic language proficiency necessary for school success. In this way, Carlos's students learn grade-level content as they learn English.

Controversy exists around bilingual education, though. One part of the debate is the cost of employing teachers in bilingual programs who speak the native language and have bilingual teaching certification that most states mandate. There is also a question of whether to support another language in U.S. schools where English is the native language. Many parents and students believe that teaching in the native language not only slows English learning but also slows cultural assimilation.

How might a bilingual program help or hinder a child who hears and speaks only Spanish (or a dialect) at home? How might bilingualism be extended into the home to encourage English learners to use English beyond school?

. . . . .

STRETCHING EXERCISE

Children with cultural and linguistic differences must learn to read and write from textbooks written in an unfamiliar language about topics that may not be relevant for them. The same is often true for children whose language is slow to develop and for children with problems in processing or expressing language. It is more likely that these children will learn to write if they can first attain some facility with oral language.

In schools where ESL and bilingual teachers work with immigrant children or where speech and language specialists and reading teachers work with students who speak nonstandard English or have language difficulties, remedial instruction that occurs outside the classroom is often not enough. As the classroom teacher, you play an important role in the literacy development of these students. Your beliefs, your language program, how children participate in it, and, in particular, how they make the connection between oral and written language are critical.

It is important for you to view the first-language abilities of LEP children and non-standard English speakers as strengths and resources for your classroom (Smolkin & Suina, 1996). English learners should experience the same language arts environments as English-speaking children because it is through the social aspects of interaction and responding in meaningful situations that children learn English. It should be no surprise that speaking is the key language art for these students and classroom talk is of prime importance to learning English.

Listening to Immigrant Children

Immigrant children have stories to tell that can give Karen and other teachers a new lens for viewing these students and themselves as they gain a better understanding of how to teach immigrant children. Igoa (1995), an immigrant herself and an ESL teacher in California, documents the personal stories of immigrant children who have been uprooted and find themselves in a new and unfamiliar country. In her book, she shares her view of the central place literacy has in learning and the child's sense of self-empowerment.

Igoa (1995) shares the thoughts of Cindy, an immigrant student from Hong Kong who Americanized her Chinese name. One easily discovers that listening to children is one of the most basic ways to learn about them and begin to teach with what Cortes (1996) calls a "multicultural attitude." Cindy hints at the importance of the teacher's demeanor and personal interactions with students that provide understanding, hope, and support essential to her and students like her who have been uprooted and inserted into a foreign culture. Cindy says:

> *I think that if I were an elementary school teacher and I had kids coming in from other countries, I would try really hard to understand their background first and somehow . . . realize that it's . . . a lot different here than in their old country. . . . I think . . . it's really important for them [kids] to know that everybody makes mistakes, because when you first arrive, you get discouraged from your mistakes. Children don't express what they feel verbally and so would be upset or real quiet. If teachers can tell something is bothering them . . . they [should] try to get it out of them. I went through a stage where I was thinking I don't understand what they are saying to me, when am I going to be able to communicate back to them? [It] kinda made me confused and unsure exactly whether I'm going to be able to reach that point. So I think it's little talks that help [them] realize that if [they] put enough into it, that you reach that something. I did have a counselor. Everything that first year went from my teacher to Linda to me. I think the teacher would basically have to tell me, not the counselor, that I was going to make it. (p. 101)*

What else do immigrant students believe teachers should know? From interviews with many students, Igoa (1995) makes the italicized suggestions:

- *Teachers need to understand other cultures' attitudes toward teachers.* Many immigrant children bring a deeply ingrained attitude of respect for and obedience to teachers. When teachers are rushed, irritated, or overloaded, they may unconsciously communicate an attitude of not caring.

- *Teachers need to understand how the educational system discriminates.* Schools often treat immigrant children separately and differently because of their language alone and ignore the psychological trauma they experience.

- *Teachers need to understand the cultural backgrounds of immigrant students.* Every culture has its own traditions, holidays, and accepted ways of behaving. Not knowing that a certain behavior is offensive to a particular culture can be mistaken for not caring or antagonism.

- *Teachers need to understand the education the students received in their own home countries.* When students are accustomed to a style of teacher lecture, working independently, and being silent, but are expected in U.S. schools to take part in discussions and work in cooperative groups, this can cause silence and conflict. Also, some immigrant students can read and write in their own langauges; others have never attended school or attended only for brief periods and cannot read or write but have good oral facility. When teachers know these details, how and what they expect and teach can have a huge impact on student success.

- *Immigrant students need to feel valued and accepted.* "More than anything else, the immigrant child needs friendship, companions, warmth, and continued renewal and connection to his or her roots" (p. 103). These students do not need to feel rushed. They need patience and encouragement and they need to be given assignments in which they can experience success.

• • • • •
Student-led conferences with parents are one way for teachers to better understand their students and their students' cultures and traditions.

▬ *Immmigrant students need teachers who are models and "educational parents" they can trust.* Many immigrant students believe that teachers should be people who the students can admire and emulate and who help the students develop "good personalities."

STRETCHING EXERCISE

Which of Igoa's (1995) suggestions also are appropriate for students who are cognitively and physically diverse? Add some suggestions to this list so it is appropriate for these students, as well.

•••••

Teaching Diverse Learners

Since literacy is the most fundamental challenge of students in the cognitively and physically diverse group (Ellis & Cramer, 1995) and students in the linguistically and culturally diverse group (Goldenberg, 1996), it will undoubtedly be the focus of your attention with these diverse learners. First, it is important that you, like Karen Wassell, who was introduced at the beginning of this chapter, have an appreciation for diverse learners, an attitude about differences that allows you to accept and celebrate them.

Cortes (1996) warns that this is not enough, however. He believes teaching with a "multiculutral attitude" involves "a way of doing things that brings people together by using their similarities and differences to bridge people beyond themselves." In your curriculum, you must stretch beyond the limits of your classroom to provide your students with information and understanding of groups not represented there. How do you adopt an appreciation for diversity and multicultural attitude like this? Knowledge and understanding are basic prerequisites that you are in the process of developing and will develop as you read the remainder of this text, take other courses, and grow professionally throughout your career as a teacher. Cortes reminds educators how important it is to continually widen their views of the world as they examine their "blind spots."

Rather than provide a discussion of specific strategies for building the literacy of diverse learners, which you will find in later chapters, a discussion of principles to guide your teaching and brief descriptions of suggested strategies seem most relevant here.

Guidelines for Literacy Teaching

The following guidelines are based on research, theory, and exemplary practices (Fitzgerald, 1993):

▬ *Understand the role of cultural and societal contexts in second-language learning.* Different families and cultures have different expectations for learning and schooling and the potential benefits of schooling. If children come from countries where there are no schools or where schooling is not required, they may not understand its importance in U.S. culture. Some parents may believe "skill and drill" instruction is what their children need and so may not appreciate other methods. Communication with parents and families about the importance of school, classroom rules, routines, interactions, and methods is critical. Family nights at school and home visits by teachers can be helpful.

■ *Immerse students in reading and writing situations as apprentices.* Authentic reading and writing engagements that allow children to learn about the functions and meaning of literacy with other literacy users can begin immediately. Two kinds of journals work well because students use language for real purposes: dialogue journals, in which the teacher and student write back and forth to each other, and buddy journals, in which two students write to each other. Literature groups and group reading conferences allow English learners and speakers to participate together.

■ *Capitalize on the interrelatedness of orality and literacy.* Instead of focusing primarily on listening and speaking, teachers should also incorporate writing and reading into literacy lessons, since all four modes support each other. The Language Experience Approach (LEA) and process writing are two approaches that integrate the language arts.

■ *Immerse students in literacy situations at the earliest possible time.* Even infants who are exposed to literacy before they are able to read or write develop concepts of the purposes of literacy and what print and stories are. As soon as ESL students come into the classroom, the teacher can begin introducing them to reading and writing English.

■ *Focus on the "big picture" first.* Teachers might want to ignore incorrect grammar, nonstandard punctuation, and misspelling at first and instead focus on keeping students interested and able to comprehend. Getting main ideas, making inferences, developing metacognitive strategies, and locating information make the "big picture."

■ *Immerse learners in reading and writing across the curriculum.* When students learn social studies or science content, they are motivated and focused, and literacy learning has a purpose and is meaningful. ESL students must be included in regular instruction and integrated units of study. Flexible groups and cooperative learning may be used.

■ *Create classroom communities conducive to risk taking.* Literacy develops through social interactions when relationships are established between English learners and English speakers. These social interactions require an atmosphere that is safe for making mistakes, and ESL learners will make many. The teacher should downplay mistakes, reward efforts, and encourage experimentation.

As you read the remainder of this chapter, be aware of ways in which the classrooms and teaching you read about are built on these guidelines. Also, think about how to modify the following approaches and situations to better meet Fitzgerald's guidelines.

Thematic Instruction

Thematic instruction that emphasizes social interaction is an excellent vehicle for literacy development and learning for students with linguistic diversity. For second-language learning, the integration of English and content area instruction (such as social studies, science, or math) through thematic teaching can build on students' personal and educational experiences. A three-year research study by Wells and Chang-Wells (1992) with children in inner-city elementary schools from a wide variety of ethnic and cultural backgrounds supports this notion. These researchers found that through thematic, inquiry-driven curriculum, students become literate as they use their literacy to learn about topics that interest them and as they share their understandings with each other. Collaborative discussion—oriented toward tasks and problem solving—requires and encourages children to engage in literate thinking. In classrooms like those studied by Wells and Chang-Wells, students take an active problem-solving approach to learning, and the classroom environment is flexible and supportive of linguistically diverse students.

Teachers who use thematic instruction create an environment that focuses on the learner. They promote conversations and sharing to connect old knowledge with new knowledge as they develop a community of learners. They use partner work, often matching students according to language proficiency (sometimes called *language twins*), and arrange desks in clusters so students can talk, listen, read, write, and learn together. This approach seems appropriate not only for second language learners but also for students with language delays and difficulties.

Perez (1996) reports that instructional conversations focused on concepts and content serve as catalysts to the acquisition of second language for children whose native language is other than English. Perez shows how the making of bubbles in a third-grade bilingual class's science lesson permitted the children to use new vocabulary—*experiment, measure, solution, observe,* and *results*—contextually as they worked with the activity. The teacher did not directly teach the new words, but told the children they were the words she wanted to hear as they talked. Children of varying linguistic abilities added their own experiences to the discussion to control the interactive conversation and make sense out of a topic.

Effective classrooms should provide language-minority children with the following:

- A context and activities for making meaning with language
- Situations that allow a range of ways to use language in purposeful ways
- Predictable and repetitive language patterns
- Interactions with others who reinforce, prompt, and respond to language

Social Interaction

To learn another language, it is important for children to use that language to function in real situations. As well, the social aspect of language use is critical in learning a new language. In their three-year research study in four schools serving inner-city multilingual communities, Wells and Chang-Wells (1992) studied this social aspect of language learning. They found that when teachers created classrooms where children used literacy not only as a tool for learning about topics that interested them but also for sharing their understanding with others, the result was communities of literate thinkers, with teachers and children learning with and from each other. They also found that collaborative talk with each other around classroom inquiry projects helped Vietnamese, Chinese, Portuguese, Indian, and Caribbean students learn English. The researchers concluded that "whether in monolingual or multilingual classrooms, equal outcomes for all children can best be maximized, regardless of cultutral and linguistic background, by providing collaborative learning opportunities that integrate a wide range of uses of oral and written language with action and reflection" (p. 120). When teachers conceptualize learning in this way, children develop thinking and language together.

The Wells and Chang-Wells (1992) study reminds us that one of the richest resources of teachers is *children*. Adults often overlook the potential children have for teaching each other. As a teacher in a bilingual or multilingual classroom, what are some ways you can encourage children to develop their thinking and language together? How can a teacher foster the learning of English and, at the same time, validate a learner's first language? The following sections describe classrooms where teachers are building English proficiency as well as validating other languages.

Cooperative Learning

I like cooperative learning. Instead of one brain you have a lot of brains.

—Bryan

You learn how to get along and everybody participate.

—Maria

You get to tell other people what you think and you get to hear what other people think.

—Shamiko

It helps me to learn and it is fun.

—Steven

We work in teams. We work together to do things.

—Sharam

These diverse learners, whose names you will recognize from the beginning of this chapter, view cooperative learning positively. They were involved in cooperative learning during their year in fourth grade when they learned to work in groups during social studies and science.

What is *cooperative learning?* It is the instructional use of small groups that work together to maximize learning. Although there are different models of cooperative learning (Kagan, 1994; Johnson, Johnson, & Holubec, 1994; Slavin, 1986), this definition is generally accepted. You will find specific ideas for using cooperative learning with diverse learners in the remainder of this text.

Reviews of research in elementary and secondary schools explain that cooperative learning that includes group goals and individual accountability increases student achievement and has positive effects on intergroup relations (Slavin, 1990). When you use this approach in language arts, you will discover the following about cooperative learning:

- *Increases motivation for literacy learning.* As students work in teams to achieve mutual goals, they are positive and enthusiastic about learning.
- *Increases sharing of metacognitive strategies for thinking and learning.* Students talk about how they find answers, examine the processes they use, and develop awareness of how to learn.

- *Builds effective communication skills.* Students use listening, speaking, reading, and writing together to achieve common goals. Individual students become accountable since their performance affects group outcomes.
- *Improves social skills.* Students become active language users and learn to accept and respect each other's opinions.

STRETCHING EXERCISE

What are some disadvantages of cooperative learning (e.g., for students who are English learners)? Do these drawbacks warrant a balance among individual, small-group, and whole-class instruction to most effectively help all students become academically successful?

• • • • •

Next, we will discuss three cooperative learning strategies that build social interaction and help students get to know one another as they develop literacy.

Buddy Journals.   Students in an elementary school and a middle school were introduced to buddy journals as a way to help them build peer relationships and develop writing fluency (Bromley, 1995). Their teachers also hoped to establish respect and understanding among cultures, create enthusiasm for writing, and develop audience awareness. English-speaking students were paired with students who did not speak English or who had limited proficiency. Using journals, the students wrote back and forth to each other in a nonthreatening context about things that were important to them. They shared feelings, described activities, asked and answered questions, made requests, explored ideas, and solved problems together (see Figures 3.2, 3.3, and 3.4).

HI Autumn Howareyo
Doyou like dog
I like.littledogs.
  AutumnDo you like rabbits
I like small white rabbits.
  AutumnDo you liketoread book S?
I like books about birds.

                    Vu

Dear Vu,
  yes i do like dogs. I like a germing shepard. What is your favorite food. Mine is pizza from Puggies and pizza hut.
              sincerly autumn

FIGURE 3.2   Ten-year-old Vu's drawing and journal entry and Autumn's response.

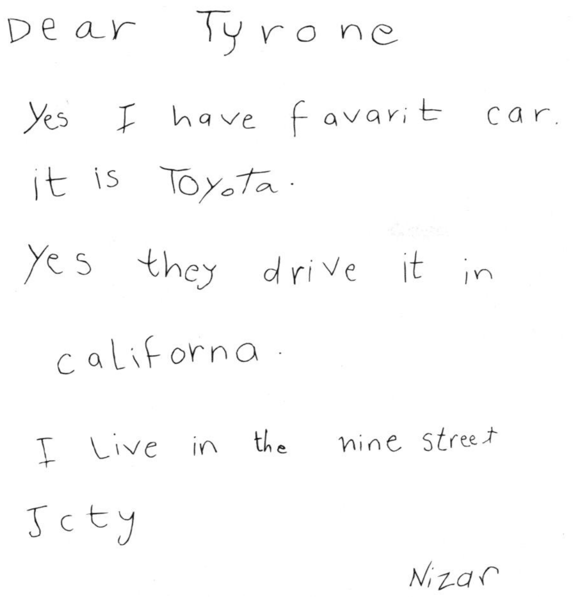

Dear Tyrone

Yes I have favarit car.
it is Toyota.
Yes they drive it in
californa.
I live in the nine street
Jcty

Nizar

• • • • •

FIGURE 3.3 Nizar told his ESL teacher what to write and she drew dots, which he connected to write this entry.

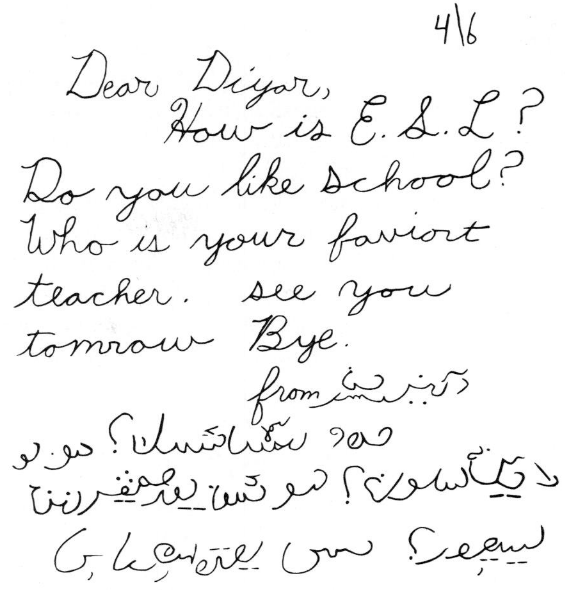

4\6

Dear Diyar,
How is E.S.L?
Do you like school?
Who is your faviort
teacher. see you
tomrow Bye.
from کیث

سۆ شوانیسکان؟ دە وە
دێکانیشکاتی دەسک شفیرن؟
سەیین؟ من چۆنیک لا گ

• • • • •

FIGURE 3.4 Keith's journal entry to Diyar in both English and Kurdish.

Keith, an 11-year-old student with an identified learning disability in reading and written expression, and Diyar, an 11-year-old Kurdish student newly immigrated to the United States who is beginning to learn English, had an unusually positive experience as a result of their buddy journal. They became close friends outside school and spent considerable time together. As Keith helped Diyar learn to speak and write in English, Diyar taught Keith the Kurdish alphabet.

First Friends. Carol's fifth-grade students came from homes in which the first language spoken is Kurdish, Russian, Lao, Vietnamese, or English. In April, Carol and her class prepared to welcome two new students who speak Russian and one who speaks Kurdish. In anticipation of their arrival and following an established schoolwide practice, Carol has talked with her class about their soon-to-be new classmates. They talked about how it feels to be in a totally foreign environment. They discussed why and how they can make the new students feel welcome and relaxed.

Three students volunteered to be a First Friend, or buddy, to each of the newcomers. As First Friends, these students get to know the new students and introduce them to their friends, the school, classroom schedules, special class teachers, lunchtime procedures, and school routines and traditions. It is the responsibility of each First Friend to help make the school and classroom a welcoming place for the newcomer. The First Friend accompanies his or her buddy to lunch and they eat together. Their desks are side by side and they help with all the things that make a new place unfriendly and undecipherable. Children's picture books (discussed in a later section of this chapter) can be read together by First Friends.

Peer Tutoring.   Three other students in Carol's class volunteered to be peer tutors. For one month, each peer tutor spends 30 to 45 minutes a day with his or her new student in a one-on-one tutoring situation. In September, Carol and her students created a Language Survival Kit for peer tutoring, which is a cloth bag containing a collection of things the class brought in that can help the newcomers learn about the community as they learn English. Carol and her students brainstormed ways to use things (e.g., a local and a world map, a driver's handbook, *TV Guide,* restaurant menus, a deck of cards, a calculator, a calendar, and a telephone book) to develop concepts and language with English learners. The new students were invited to add items to the kit, and before long, a Kurdish calendar and postcards from Russia appeared. Working together, these English speakers support the literacy development of the English learners and each discovers new insights about the other's culture.

Teaching Idioms

Idioms make up about two-thirds of the English language (Morris & Morris, 1971) and are one of the major obstacles to learning English. Since they add confusion and difficulty to the learning of the language, they occupy a special place in the teaching of literacy. *Idioms* are phrases or expressions that mean something other than what they say. They are figurative expressions representing one concept in terms of another that may be thought of as analogous. Idioms are often based on highly specialized local customs or habits.

If one interprets an idiom literally, the picture one gets is often a funny one. For example, *the spitting image* literally means that someone or something is expelling saliva from its mouth. The literal interpretation is what often confuses second-language learners. The teacher needs to help these learners understand the real meaning of the idiom. The real, but not literal, meaning of *the spitting image* is that someone actually looks a lot like someone else. Is it enough for English learners to ignore the literal interpretation of an idiom and learn its real meaning? No. This is just the first step in building an understanding of English that will result in its use by the second-language learner.

The teacher can take the instruction of idioms one step further to help English learners understand, remember, and use idiomatic expressions themselves. Every idiom has its own origin, and when the history of an idiom is known, its real meaning makes sense. For example, *the spitting image* originated many years ago in the South where *spit* probably was shortened from *spirit* and people said "He's the very spirit and image of his father." Today, people say "spitting image" when they mean that someone looks like someone else. Knowing the origin or history of an idiom builds one's appreciation for English and increases the likelihood that one will understand, remember, and use that idiom correctly in speech and writing. The same holds true for ESL learners. So, whenever you can, it is a good idea to help your students understand the origin of idiomatic phrases. Several common idioms and their definitions and origins (Morris & Morris, 1971; Nevins & Nevins, 1977; Rogers, 1985) appear in Figure 3.5.

How does one teach idioms effectively? Because an idiom's meaning cannot always be inferred grammatically or from context, an ESL student needs to study its origin or have the meaning taught by someone who is familiar with it. Since many English-speaking students know the meaning for many idioms, but do not know the history or

FIGURE 3.5   Understanding the meanings and origins of idioms helps English learners overcome a major language obstacle.

75
• • • • •
Diversity

Some Common Idioms

Idiom: *Bury the hatchet*

Definition: To stop arguing or fighting

Origin: In pre–Revolutionary War times, Native Americans in New England made peace with White men by performing a ceremony in which they dug a hole in the ground and buried their tomahawks as a symbol of peace.

Idiom: *Happy as a clam*

Definition: To be satisfied, content, or cheerful

Origin: In the Northeast, clams, which were a popular food for early colonists, could only be dug at low tide when a person could get to the mud banks where the clams live. Thus, the saying *Happy as a clam at high tide* came to be.

Idiom: *Make both ends meet*

Definition: To be careful with money

Origin: In the 1800s, a bookkeeper in Boston or New York made certain that assets (cash income) and liabilities (cash outflow) equaled each other. So the bookkeeper made "both ends meet" by getting liabilities to equal assets.

Idiom: *Bite the bullet*

Definition: To be brave and take what is coming gracefully

Origin: On Civil War battlefields, when doctors did surgery without anesthesia, patients were often given a bullet on which to bite hard to dull the pain of the surgery.

Idiom: *Grind to a halt*

Definition: To stop slowly

Origin: When railroads first crossed the plains, steam-powered locomotives pulled heavy trains that stopped to avoid hitting buffalo on the tracks. As brakes were applied, the train stopped slowly, with harsh sounds of rubbing steel.

Idiom: *Blue chip*

Definition: Something of high quality

Origin: In Western frontier saloons, the poker chips used for gambling were red (cheapest), white (moderately cheap), and blue (most valuable). Today, this means high-quality stock that grows steadily and is a good investment.

Idiom: *Fly off the handle*

Definition: To lose your temper without warning

Origin: While a frontiersman was chopping wood, if the head flew off the ax handle, it happened unexpectedly and quickly, like a sudden outburst or explosion of anger.

Idiom: *Low man on the totem pole*

Definition: The person with the least important job

Origin: The bottom carving on a Northwestern Native American totem pole appears to hold the weight of the carvings above it. This low job was one that a servant or unimportant person held.

• • • • •

Source: Morris and Morris (1971); Nevins and Nevins (1977); and Rogers (1985).

origin, learning about idioms can be useful for both populations of students. Here are three steps to use in teaching an idiom (Bromley, 1984):

1. *Define*. Define and explain idioms when they are encountered in context or teach them directly. You could introduce and teach an *Idiom of the Day* or an *Idiom of the Week*. Some teachers classify idioms into those involving colors, food, animals, actions, the body, and so on, and teach them in categories.

2. *Use*. Give your students oral and written opportunities to use the idioms you have taught. When your students dramatize idioms, this builds their comprehension and reinforces meanings. Another popular activity is to illustrate idioms and compile a class book or an idiom dictionary.

3. *Apply*. Your class might compile a running list of idioms they hear as they listen to TV, radio, or conversations among people. Your students can add idioms they come across in their own reading, too. Or you can have them write creatively about the origin of a particular idiom. Another vehicle for helping students use their knowledge of idioms is children's literature. For example, Peggy Parish's (1988) *Amelia Bedelia's Family Album* and others in the series are about a maid who translates idioms literally and has hilarious things happen to her. *Mad as a Wet Hen! and Other Funny Idioms* (1987) and *Punching the Clock* (1990), written by Marvin Terban, include idioms with their real and humorous meanings.

Picture Books for Diverse Learners

For many English learners, practice in speaking and using English in real situations is not enough. These students, and students with delayed language or for whom learning is difficult, may lack concepts that may easily be learned and reinforced through children's picture books. There are many alphabet, counting, concept, poetry, and easy-to-read books written in English with illustrations that support and extend text. Pictures in these books reinforce concepts and vocabulary in both spoken and written English. You will find specific titles in Chapter 4.

Bilingual Literature.   Many writers and publishers of children's books are working to make English language learning easier for those whose first language is not English by publishing books written in the dialect of a particular ethnicity in both English and another language. Battle (1996) explains that these books contribute to the sense of validation that results when children recognize themselves in books. These books also stir interest in learning about people who are new and different. Language-minority children delight in reading literature written in both their first and second languages (Hudelson, Fournier, Espinosa, & Bachman, 1994).

There are many picture books printed in both English and another language that you can use in your classroom (Battle, 1996). In these books, the English text usually appears with the translation above or below it. *Table Chair Bear* (1995) by Jane Feder presents several languages. In this book, familiar objects from a child's bedroom are introduced in 13 languages and illustrated with colorful paintings in the style of folk art. Feder includes phonetic spellings with each word that is translated into Korean, French, Arabic, Vietnamese, Japanese, Portuguese (Brazilian), Lao, Spanish (Mexican), Chinese (Mandarin), Tagalog, Cambodian, and Navajo. Children can say the words in their own language or learn to pronounce them in the other 12. To help with pronunciation, Feder provides a guide to the symbols she uses in the phonetic spellings. Children can see the difference between alphabetic languages (English, French, Vietnamese, Portuguese, Spanish, Tagalog, and Navajo) and ideographic languages (Korean, Arabic, Japanese, Lao, Chinese, and Cambodian).

Bilingual literature facilitates the learning of English for non-English speakers by providing a bridge to English. Using bilingual literature with your students is an excellent way to acknowledge and validate the cultures and languages of your ESL students and to broaden the understandings of your English-speaking students. Hearing or reading stories that deal with the trauma and joy of learning English and how the main character deals with feelings of ambivalence between disparate cultures can be helpful for English learners. When English speakers read or hear these stories, they come to understand and appreciate the difficulties involved in learning a second language. The following books, written in English, include characters who experience intercultural conflict (also see the Annotated Bibliography of Children's Books at the end of this book):

> *I Am Here. Yo Estoy Aqui* by Rose Blue (New York: Watts, 1971). A 5-year-old Puerto Rican girl is ambivalent.
>
> *I Hate English!* by Ellen Levine (New York: Scholastic, 1992). A Chinese girl struggles with language and culture.
>
> *Heroes* by Ken Mochizuki (New York: Low, 1995). A Japanese American boy is teased by his classmates.
>
> *Yang the Third and Her Impossible Family* by Lensey Namioka (Boston: Little, Brown, 1995). A Chinese girl living in Seattle struggles with traditions.
>
> *White Bead Ceremony* by Sherrin Watkins (Tulsa: Council Oak Books, 1994). A Shawnee girl is caught between her Native American and contemporary American cultures.
>
> *Maria Luisa* by Winifred Madison (Philadelphia: Lippincott, 1971). Spanish-speaking children move from Arizona to San Francisco.
>
> *Angel Child, Dragon Child* by Michele Maria Surat (New York: Carnival, 1983). A Vietnamese girl has trouble in her new American school.

Folktales from Other Cultures. You can also promote the learning of English by using the English translation of a familiar folktale from the child's own culture as a text for teaching her to read English. It makes sense that when a story contains familiar concepts, learning to read it in English is easier.

Red Riding Hood Tales. Many cultures have their own version of the Little Red Riding Hood story. For example, consider the following:

> *Little Red Riding Hood* by Trina Schart Hyman (German) (New York: Holiday House, 1983).
>
> *The Talking Eggs* by San Soucci (Southern USA—Creole) (New York: Scholastic, 1989).
>
> *Lon Po Po* by Ed Young (China) (New York: Scholastic, 1989).
>
> *Liza Lou and the Yeller Belly Swamp* by Mercer Mayer (African American) (New York: Parents Press, 1976).

Flossie and the Fox by Patricia McKissock (African American) (New York: Scholastic, 1986).

Little Red Riding Hood by Charles Perrault (French) (New York: Doubleday, 1991).

The Gunniwolf by Wilhelmina Harper (German) (New York: Dutton, 1967).

The Little Wolf and the Giant by Sue Porter (English) (New York: Simon & Schuster, 1990).

Little Red Riding Hood: A New-Fangled Prairie Tale by Lisa Campbell Ernst (Early Midwest) (New York: Simon & Schuster, 1995).

Tara, a kindergarten teacher, chose several of these folktales and others to represent the culture or country of each of her students. She said, "My kindergarten class looks like a five-year-old's version of the United Nations. Among my students, there are Chinese, Korean, Russian, Italian, Laotian, Japanese, and African American children, as well as one in a wheelchair." Tara wanted to create an environment in which to celebrate the diversity in language, physical attributes, culture, race, and ethnicity in her classroom. She wanted her children to be proud of their individual heritages and to learn more about each other. She also wanted to develop the oral language skills of some of her students who were not yet talking easily with each other or her. Tara wanted to introduce books to a few children who were not read to at home and she wanted to begin to make the spoken/written language connection for them with Draw and Tell Journals (Bromley, 1993).

Tara read a different folktale every day and her students drew pictures in their journals about the story. As the children told her about their pictures, Tara transcribed their oral language onto each picture. See Figure 3.6 for the picture drawn by Tom, an

FIGURE 3.6 Tom wrote *Lon PoPo,* a character's name *Shang,* and dictated his favorite part for the teacher to write.

Americanized name for Tong in Chinese. After reading each caption together, Tara invited each child to share her picture with the class. She found that this is a good way to build her students' awareness and appreciation of each other's backgrounds and develop their confidence and competence in oral language use.

Cinderella around the World.   Around the world there are over 1,500 versions of the Cinderella tale. The following list contains several of these titles and the country or people where the story originates:

> *Ashpet: An Appalachin Tale* by Joanne Compton (southern USA) (New York: Holiday House, 1995).
> *Moss Gown* by William Hooks (southern USA) (New York: Clarion, 1987).
> *The Rough-Faced Girl* by Rafe Martin (Algonquin Tribe) (New York: Putnam, 1992).
> *Yeh-Shen* by Ai Ling Louis (China) (New York: Philomel, 1982).
> *Mufaro's Beautiful Daughters* by John Steptoe (Africa) (New York: Lothrop, 1987).
> *The Egyptian Cinderella* by Shirley Climo (Egypt) (New York: Crowell, 1989).
> *Vasilisa the Beautiful* by Thomas Whitney (Russia) (New York: Crowell, 1989).
> *Princess Furball* by Charlotte Huck (Europe) (New York: Greenwillow, 1989).
> *The Korean Cinderella* by Shirley Climo (Korean) (New York: HarperCollins, 1993).

Robert, a sixth-grade teacher, used these books with his class of self-contained special education students in a language arts unit they called *Cinderella around the World*. These students all had severe problems in reading and writing. Robert's main goals were for them to develop familiarity with literary elements, build skill in writing summaries and descriptions, develop critical thinking skills, learn about other cultures, and learn to appreciate illustrations and their importance to stories. Through this unit, Robert coincidentally validated the ethnic origins of some of his students and helped them learn to appreciate different cultures' versions of the same story.

A Unit for Diverse Students: Piecing Together America

Karen Wassell intentionally planned a unit to bring her class together and promote acceptance of differences. The unit integrated social studies and language arts for the class of diverse fifth-grade students described at the beginning of this chapter. Karen's goal was to create an atmosphere in her classroom that supports students with cognitive, physical, linguistic, and cultural differences. Karen's rationale and a description of her first three lessons follow.

Planning the Unit.   As Karen designed this unit on pioneers and westward expansion in the United States, she sifted through a variety of texts and found information on two families mentioned in the fifth-grade social studies textbook. (Karen uses the term *text* broadly to include more than books. For example, she consulted videos, historical fiction for children, song lyrics, poetry, computer software such as *The Oregon Trail* on CD-ROM, and historical documents on the Internet.) Karen said:

> One thing that struck me about the social studies text was how it gave a partial account of the lives of two families and left the reader with the impression that all ended happily. After reading a variety of other sources, I discovered that these two families endured many hardships as they traveled to Oregon in the 1830s and 40s. When they were finally settled, the Cayuse Indians attacked and killed most of them. Half the Cayuse tribe had died after catching measles from passing pioneers, and the rest of the tribe was seeking revenge. The other thing that struck me was the similarity between the lives of these pioneers and immigrant families in our community—what drove them to uproot and relocate, the hardships they endured, and their single-minded commitment to succeed. I thought the unit could help my class come together and better understand the history of our country.

One of the primary sources Karen consulted first was *Women's Diaries of the Westward Journey* by Lillian Schlissel, which contains actual diary entries of women who lived through the experience of uprooting their family, leaving home, and traveling across America on the rough trails that led to the western territories. After reading this book, Karen decided to use historical fiction and other literature to bring the pioneer experience to life. Some of the books she used and made available to her students were:

> *The Quilt-Block History of Pioneer Days: With Projects Kids Can Make* by Mary Cobb (Brookfield, CT: Millbrook Press, 1995).
> *A Journal, Giving the Incidents of a Trip to California in the Summer of 1859 by the Overland Trail* by M. Casler (Fairfield, WA: Ye Galleon Press, 1969).
> *New Guide for the Overland Route to California* by Andrew Child, 1852. Reproduced by Lyle H. Wright (Los Angeles: N. A. Kovatch, 1946).
> *The Quilt Story* by Tony Johnston and Tomie dePaola (New York: Putnam, 1985).
> *Joshua's Westward Journey* by James Anderson (New York: Morrow, 1987).
> *The Story of Gold at Sutter's Mill* by R. C. Stein (Chicago: Children's Press, 1981).
> *The Story of Women Who Shaped the West* by M. V. Fox (Chicago: Children's Press, 1991).
> *Cassie's Journey: Going West in the 1860's* by Brett Harvey (New York: Holiday House, 1988).
> *Women's Diaries of the Westward Journey* by Lillian Schlissel (New York: Schoken, 1987).

Another source Karen consulted was the World Wide Web. Using the Internet, she searched for information under the topic History. Among other historical documents, she found The Treaty of Greenville, a treaty of peace between several Native American tribes in the Ohio Valley and the U.S. government signed in 1795. Karen thought this would be an interesting document for her students to examine that would also make the conflict between pioneers and Native Americans real.

With the help of the school library's media specialist, Karen collected and immersed herself in reading a wide array of sources. After doing her own research, she said:

I decided it was important for children to learn how to research and dig up facts as they "piece together" American history. I wanted my students to see that they are all a part of the quilt that is the United States of America. So "Piecing Together America" became the organizing idea for my unit.

As she read about this era of American history, Karen also examined her state's social studies syllabus and language arts standards to identify unit objectives. The content area goals Karen decided on were for students to:

- Understand when and how the United States acquired the land west of the Mississippi River.
- Understand how the Gold Rush and land opportunities led pioneers to move west.
- Appreciate and understand the hardships pioneers faced on their journeys on the Overland Trail.
- Discover what life was like for the pioneers living on the frontier in the 1800s.
- Reflect on and make connections with their own lives as they learn about the pioneers.

After introducing the unit, Karen planned to have students identify things they wondered about and wanted to learn. She decided to involve students in inquiry-oriented learning because she knew how much more interested and committed students are when they pose the questions and search for answers.

Along with using a variety of texts to enrich learning, Karen believes students learn best when they have opportunities to use the language arts in the construction of meaning. So, Karen involved her students in individual, paired, small-group, and whole-class activities that included reading, writing, listening, and speaking.

• • • • •
These middle-school students work in pairs to use a CD-ROM and the Internet to research a topic.

Karen used New York's *Learning Standards for English Language Arts* (1996, p. 1) to guide her in identifying appropriate language arts objectives. She wanted her students to have opportunities to achieve all four of the following standards. Following each Standard are examples of activities she planned.

> *"Standard 1. Read, write, listen, and speak for information and understanding."*
> - Students read and discuss information from a variety of sources (textbooks, historical fiction, nonfiction, biographies, computer, etc.) as they learn about events and people in history.
> - Students use what is learned to write research reports and record important information on a time line and map.
>
> *"Standard 2. Read, write, listen, and speak for literary response and expression."*
> - Students read historical fiction and express what they think and feel in a character journal, share their responses with the class, and create an artistic impression of what they have read."
>
> *"Standard 3. Read, write, listen, and speak for critical analysis and evaluation."*
> - Students participate in a variety of reading, writing, listening, and speaking activities where they will need to think critically and share their opinions and ideas. (For example, students create a Venn diagram comparing the characters in *The Quilt Story* and work in a group as a "pioneer family" to use *The Overland Guide* to pack a covered wagon to weigh no more than 1 ton.)
>
> *"Standard 4. Read, write, listen, and speak for social interaction."*
> - Students engage in a variety of activities that involve pairs, small groups, and the whole class, such as share individual projects with others. (For example, students choose a person who had an important role in the U.S. westward expansion and, with a partner, research this person and prepare an oral and written report for the class; as a class, add to a graphic organizer chart as the unit progresses; and listen to *Cassie's Journey Westward* and write a response in literature journals to be shared in small groups as discussion starters.)

Do the New York State English Language Arts Standards overlap? Yes. Note that many of the learning experiences Karen planned involved students in work that achieved more than one of the standards simultaneously. For example, as students read and gathered information for writing the reports (Standard 1), they talked with each other to share and clarify ideas and information (Standard 4) and they read critically to analyze and evaluate information (Standard 3).

So, Karen used the state's curriculum guides and standards to help her plan rich learning experiences for her students. She was aware that an integrated unit is more than a collection of activities. Karen intentionally planned learning experiences for her students that used a variety of sources for learning and that involved them in using all the language modes. She wanted to engage students in meaningful learning events that would provide factual information and opportunities to develop literacy as well as build affective understandings that many textbooks omit. Karen created a tentative time line (see Figure 3.7) to help manage unit activities.

Karen wanted to give her students opportunities to use artistic expression to enhance and demonstrate their learning. To help with this aspect of the unit, she collaborated with the art, music, and physical education teachers. She asked the music teacher to teach her students to sing American folksongs of that era, she asked the physical education teacher to teach her students folk dances of that era, and she asked the art teacher to help her students explore the medium of pencil and charcoal sketching used in *Cassie's Journey: Going West in the 1860's* by Brett Harvey (1988). Karen felt the artistic renditions in this children's book, which is based on the diaries of real women who made the westward trek in covered wagons, spoke more powerfully than words about the hard existence these travelers suffered.

Tentative Time Line

M	T	W	Th	F
Intro to Unit Elicit Prior Knowledge Create Web Historical Fiction Character Journal	Intro to Research Class Time Line	Begin Research	"Louisiana Purchase"	"Lewis & Clark"
"The Mexican Cession"	"California" "Cassie's Journey; Supplies"	"California Gold Fever" "The High Cost of Gold"	Begin Writing Process	"A Letter from Father"
"Westward to the Mountains" "A Letter to a Loved One"	"The Quilt History of Pioneer Days"	"Fifty-Niners"	"Homesteaders"	"Finally Settled" Polish Research Projects
Sharing Unit Projects and Eating Ice Cream				

FIGURE 3.7   Karen created a time line to help manage the unit.

Source: Reprinted by permission of Karen Wassell.

Three Lessons. Karen introduced this unit with three whole-group lessons. In the first lesson, she wanted to elicit her students' prior knowledge about moving and resettlement. She chose a strategy called *Think-Pair-Share* that requires students to think individually, talk with partners, and share with the class. Karen added writing to the strategy and followed these steps:

■ *Think.* Karen began with a class discussion of reasons her students may have moved and then reasons others may have left home, family, friends, and a familiar community to resettle somewhere else. She posed these questions:

> Where were you born?
> Have you ever moved? When? Where? Why?
> How did you feel about moving?
> Why do you live/stay here?
> Do you know anyone leaving our community today?
> Where is he or she going? Why?
> How does he or she feel about moving?

■ *Pair.* Karen then she had each student work with a partner to talk about answers to the questions and to create a list of reasons why people move or stay where they are.

■ *Share.* Last, Karen had the class share their ideas and she recorded a comprehensive list on a tagboard chart that students would use later to compare the similarities and differences between people of the past and present.

Karen's objective for the second lesson was to determine what students knew about pioneers and establish what they wanted to learn. For this lesson, Karen used the *K-W-H-L* strategy (Ogle, 1986; Carr & Ogle, 1987). On a large piece of butcher paper that covered an entire bulletin board, Karen and her students created a column with the heading *K—What we know.* Under this category, Karen wrote all the factual knowledge her students possessed about pioneers. If there were things the students weren't sure of, Karen placed a question mark after the item. Next, she created the heading *W—What we want to know.* In this column, Karen listed all the questions her students had about pioneers. She then headed a column with *H—How we'll find out.* In this column, Karen transcribed all the ways her students brainstormed to find answers and learn more about the topic. Karen headed the last column with *L—What we learned*—and told her students they would come back to the chart periodically to fill in the things they were learning, add new resources and ways to find answers, and add new questions or refine old ones. By putting this K-W-H-L chart on public display, it became a graphic organizer for the direction of the unit and a place to document students' questions and their learning.

In the third lesson, Karen's objective was to help students compare and contrast the experiences, settings, and feelings of American pioneers of long ago and Americans who relocate today. Karen read *The Quilt Story* by Tony Johnston and Tomie dePaola (1985) to the class, showing students the illustrations often so they could compare the different eras represented in the story. Karen encouraged discussion by asking students what they noticed in the story. This practice is one she often uses because it allows for divergent opinions and encourages careful listening and viewing. Karen guided a discussion of similarities and differences in the two girls' lives using a Venn diagram.

Then, Karen felt her students were ready to read the first chapter independently from *Joshua's Westward Journey* by James Anderson (1987) and, on their own, identify the similarities and differences between Joshua and themselves if they were traveling the same route today. She had students work in pairs to document their ideas on a Venn diagram and she encouraged each pair to draw pictures depicting both boys in the story. Student pairs then shared their work in small groups and Karen displayed the written work on a bulletin board in the room.

Karen felt these lessons were particularly important for her students since their community was in the midst of huge industrial layoffs and economic change due to drastic downsizing in U.S. defense-related businesses following the fall of the Iron Curtain and end of the Cold War. For many of these students and their families, moving was a reality, and talking about the issues related to resettlement can often make it easier to understand and accept.

When she came across a list of supplies and prices in the *New Guide for the Overland Route to California*, Karen decided to include problem solving in math as part of the unit, as well. She wanted her students to read, think critically, and use their math skills to prepare for a journey like that of the early pioneers. Although math was not an original focus or content area for integration, it made sense to Karen to include this opportunity to develop analytic and critical thinking through problem solving.

Why did Karen choose these three lessons to introduce her unit? Could you introduce a unit like this one with Barbara Cohen's *Molly's Pilgrim* (1983) or *Make a Wish, Molly* (1994) or with Eve Bunting's *How Many Days to America?* (1993). Read one of these books and decide on questions to ask to prompt student discussion.

STRETCHING EXERCISE

Bridging the "Diversity Gap"

As classrooms become increasingly diverse, you may face a "diversity gap" or a "culture clash" that can affect your relationships with both students and parents and have a negative effect on student learning. How can you learn to bridge this gap? Some ideas follow (Cortes, 1996; Ross, 1995):

- Examine your own assumptions and then find new ways to reach out to those who are different. First, take a quiz about your assumptions (see Figure 3.8) and reflect on your responses.
- Have an outsider observe you in your classroom and give you feedback about your behavior. Without realizing it, you may respond in special ways to certain students because of implicit assumptions you hold.
- Be aware of cultural differences. For example, although eye contact is most often considered critical for good communication, "people from many cultures, including some Asians, Native Americans, Africans, and Hispanics/Latinos, don't make eye contact like Caucasian Americans do—in some cultures, in fact, making eye contact is considered an insult!" (Ross, 1995, p. 52).
- Be sensitive to the culture shock that new students experience. It can be exciting to move to a new place, but it also can be frightening and depressing when you do not fit in or understand new ways.

FIGURE 3.8 Examine your own assumptions and biases with this self-assessment quiz.

Diversity: Self-Assessment

1. How do I define the term *diversity?*
2. What diverse populations are there in my school and classroom?
3. How do I perceive students who are racially or ethnically diverse? Have special needs? Have different language or dialects from me? Have different cognitive abilities? Are mentally or physically challenged?
4. Where did these impressions come from (family, peers, media, religion)? How reliable are my sources?
5. What stereotypes do I hold?
6. How do I treat students/people based on these stereotypes?
7. When did someone make assumptions about me based on a group I belong to? How did it make me feel?
8. How can I learn more about the diverse students in my school?
9. How frequently do friendships occur between diverse student populations in my school?
10. How have I made my curriculum and instruction more inclusive and culturally responsive to the needs of all my students?
11. What attitudes, knowledge, and skills do I need to develop so I can effectively teach all students from a multicultural perspective?
12. Do I routinely collaborate with other teachers to plan curriculum and instruction for diverse students?

Source: Adapted from Ross (1995).

FIGURE 3.9 Using a letter similar to this, invite parents to participate in your classroom.

Date

Dear Parents, Caregivers, and/or Siblings,

The children and I invite you to be part of our new unit that integrates listening, speaking, reading, and writing with the content area ————————————— .

The theme of our unit is:—————————————————————

Your child and I will be pleased and proud to have you participate in some way. I look forward to hearing from you and hope you can join your child in learning about this exciting new unit!

Please check the item(s) that interest you from the following list and return it to me.

Sincerely,

————————————————————

- Learn about all the holidays and traditions your students celebrate. Record these important dates on a year-long class calendar. Highlight everyone's special days and check the calendar before you schedule class events.
- Build positive communication with parents. Send home a newsletter or regular letters in which you share your expectations, curriculum goals, and school and classroom routines. Invite parents to participate (see Figure 3.9) and tell them how to get in touch with you. Use jargon-free language all parents can understand and have your messages translated by volunteers into parents' native languages, if necessary.
- Show parents you care about their child and give them ways they can help their child succeed in school. Help them find community resources that will assist them, such as childcare facilities.
- Publicize diversity in your classroom by making sure that various groups are reflected in books in your library; pictures on bulletin boards; and the curriculum, materials, and literature (including folktales, biographies, information books, realistic fiction and historical fiction) you use in reading, social studies, and science.
- Avoid rigidity and be proactive. Deal constructively with diversity and speak out against racism, bigotry, and prejudice. Help develop and strengthen support mechanisms in your school.
- Help arrange for ongoing multicultural inservice education for your faculty, staff, students, and parents. Knowledge will help everyone deal positively with issues of diversity.
- Learn about programs at other schools. Examine, adapt, and modify them to meet your own school's uniqueness.

FIGURE 3.9   Continued

As a Parent/Caregiver/Sibling . . .

_____ I can share a hobby or interest that relates to the unit by talking with the children for 20 to 30 minutes.

_____ I can read a children's book to the class that is related to the unit.

_____ I can help in the classroom with a writing project or other activity.

_____ I can provide food or a snack related to the unit.

_____ I can write a letter to the class about their unit or their projects.

_____ I can _____

_____

(If there is something you can do that is not listed, please add it here).

(I can suggest a children's book for you to read or arrange a time for you to come into the classroom. **If you can accept our invitation, please call me to arrange a time and date.**)

Signed _____
             (Parent/Caregiver/Sibling)

Telephone _____

— Be open to new learning and experiences and continue to grow in your knowledge and understanding of others. In this way, your outlook broadens and you are a good model for others.

In conclusion, it is important that teachers avoid stereotyping as they learn more about their diverse students. All educators must be careful when talking about cognitively, physically, culturally, or linguistically diverse groups so that they do not develop unfair or inaccurate expectations of these individuals. People within a group vary in characteristics, beliefs, and behaviors, and certainly a host of variables affect how they respond. Teachers should avoid the mentality that is characterized by a statement such as "If you're working with Russian (or LD, deaf, Hispanic, Laotian, etc.) students, you should do this."

Summary

Today's classrooms are becoming increasingly pluralistic, with more learners representing cognitive, physical, linguistic, and cultural diversity. In this chapter, you have learned about the importance of a teacher's appreciation and knowledge of diversity, pluralism, or multiculturalism in the classroom and you have learned ways to make your classroom environment and curriculum diverse.

R•••••eflections

1. How do Cristina Igoa's (1995) suggestions for teachers of immigrant children apply to you as a prospective teacher of students with special needs? Interview a student who is cognitively or physically diverse to determine what advice this student might have for teachers. What else would you add to Igoa's list related to students with special needs? Why?

2. What lessons and activities would you include in Karen's unit to follow the first three lessons outlined here? What are your goals and why did you choose them? How would you make a better classroom environment for diverse students?

Professional Resources

Banks, J. A., & Banks, C. A. (1997). *Multicultural education: Issues and perspectives* (3rd ed.). Boston: Allyn and Bacon. This comprehensive overview of multicultural education prepares preservice and inservice teachers to address the needs of both gender groups as well as various social classes, religions, and cultures.

Beaty, J. J. (1997). *Building bridges with multicultural picture books for children 3–5*. Upper Saddle River, NJ: Prentice Hall. This book for early childhood teachers provides ideas for engaging children with multicultural book characters through dance and movement, music, food, arts-and crafts, language, family, and caring about the earth.

Bridges, L. (1996). *Creating your classroom community*. York, ME: Stenhouse. Ideas from the classrooms of 21 elementary school teachers help you create a classroom environment that supports each student as an individual while drawing the class together as a thriving community.

Dyson, A. H. (1997). *What difference does difference make? Teacher reflections on diversity, literacy, and the urban primary school.* Urbana, IL: National Council of Teachers of English. This book reports on conversations in which dedicated elementary school teachers with an average of 20 years' experience talk about their frustrations, celebrations, and day-to-day life in the classroom. It includes portraits of diverse students becoming literate in urban classrooms.

Freeman, D. E., & Freeman, Y. S. (1994). *Between worlds: Access to second language acquisition.* Portsmouth, NH: Heinemann. An explanation of second-language acquisition theory and social and cultural factors that affect school performance of language-minority students. Classroom examples put second-language acquisition theory into practice and promote cultural sensitivity.

Parker, D. (1997). *Jamie: A literacy story.* York, ME: Stenhouse. This is the story of Jamie, a child with spinal muscular atrophy, and her K–3 classroom years, told by her teacher, that touches many critical educational issues—parent involvment, inclusion, assesment, equity, and curriculum reform.

References

Allington, R. (1993). Michael doesn't go down the hall anymore. *The Reading Teacher, 46* (97), 602–604.

Battle, J. (1996). Bookalogues: Celebrating language variety. *Language Arts, 73,* 204–211.

Bromley, K. (1995). Buddy journals for ESL and Native-English-speaking students. *TESOL Journal, 4,* 7–11.

Bromley, K. (1993). *Journaling: Engagements in reading, writing and thinking.* New York: Scholastic.

Bromley, K. (1984). Teaching idioms. *The Reading Teacher, 38,* 272–276.

Carr, E., & Ogle, D. (1987). KWL Plus: A strategy for comprehension and summarization. *Journal of Reading, 30,* 626–631.

Cortes, C. (1996). *Teaching with a multicultural attitude.* Presentation at Board of Cooperative Educational Services, Binghamton, NY.

Cortes, C. (1990). Multicultural education: A curricular basic for our multiethnic future. *Doubts & Certainties: Newsletter of the NEA Mastery in Learning Project, IV* (7/8), 1–5.

DeVita, C. J. (Ed.) (1989). *America in the 21st century: A demographic overview.* Washington, DC: Population Reference Bureau.

Ellis, W., & Cramer, S. C. (1995). *Learning disabilities: A national responsibility.* Report of the Summit on Learning Disabilities. Washington, DC: National Center for Learning Disabilities.

Fitzgerald, J. (1995). English-as-a-second-language reading instruction in the United States: A research review. *Journal of Reading Behavior, 27,* 115–152.

Fitzgerald, J. (1993). Literacy and students who are learning English as a second language. *The Reading Teacher, 46,* 638–647.

Goldenberg, C. (1996). The education of language-minority students: Where are we, and where do we need to go? *Language Arts, 96* (1), 353–361.

Heward, W. L., & Orlansky, M. D. (1995). *Exceptional children* (5th ed.). New York: Merrill.

Hudelson, S., Fournier, J., Espinosa, C., & Bachman, R. (1994). Chasing windmills: Confronting the obstacles to literature-based programs in Spanish. *Language Arts, 70,* 164–171.

Igoa, C. (1995). *The inner world of the immigrant child.* New York: St. Martin's Press.

Johnson, D. W., Johnson, R. T., & Holubec, E. J. (1994). *The new circles of learning: Cooperation in the classroom and school.* Alexandria, VA: Association for Supervision and Curriculum Development.

Kagan, S. (1994). *Cooperative learning.* San Juan Capistrano, CA: Resources for Teachers.

Learning Standards for the English Language Arts (1996). Albany, NY: State Education Department.

Mather, N., & Roberts, R. (1994). Learning disabilities: A field in danger of extinction. *Learning Disabilities Research and Practice, 9* (1), 49–58.

Meyen, E. L., Vergason, G. A., & Whelan, R. J. (1996). *Strategies for teaching exceptional children in inclusive settings.* Denver: Love.

Morris, W., & Morris, M. (1971). *Morris dictionary of word and phrase origins.* New York: Harper and Row.

Nevins, A., & Nevins, D. (1977). *From the horse's mouth*. Englewood Cliffs, NJ: Prentice Hall.

Ogle, D. (1986). K-W-L: A teaching model that develops active reading of expository text. *The Reading Teacher, 39*, 564–570.

Perez, B. (1996). Instructional conversations as opportunities for English language acquisition for culturally and linguistically diverse students. *Language Arts, 73*, 173–181.

Rogers, J. (1985). *The dictionary of cliches*. New York: Facts on File Publications.

Ross, L. (1995, July/August). Connect with kids and parents of different cultures. *Instructor*, 51–53.

Slavin, R. E. (1990). Research on cooperative learning: Consensus and controversy. *Educational Leadership*, 52–54.

Slavin, R. E. (1986). *Using student team learning* (3rd ed.). Baltimore, MD: Center for Research on Elementary and Middle Schools, Johns Hopkins University.

Smolkin, L. B., & Suina, J. H. (1996). Lost in language and language lost: Considering native language in classrooms. *Language Arts, 73*, 166–172.

Special Needs Kids (1996). Washington, DC: U.S. Department of Education, Office of Special Education Programs.

Wells, G., & Chang-Wells, G. L. (1992). *Constructing knowledge together: Classrooms as centers of inquiry and literacy*. Portsmouth, NH: Heinemann.

Children's Book References

Anderson, J. (1987). *Joshua's westward journey*. New York: Morrow.

Bunting, E. (1993). *How many days to America?* New York: Clarion.

Cohen, B. (1994). *Make a wish, Molly*. New York: Bantam.

Cohen, B. (1983). *Molly's pilgrim*. New York: Bantam.

Feder, J. (1995). *Table chair bear*. New York: Ticknor & Fields.

Harvey, B. (1988). *Cassie's journey: Going west in the 1860's*. New York: Holiday House.

Johnston, T., & dePaola, T. (1985). *The quilt story*. New York: Putnam.

Parish, P. (1988). *Amelia Bedelia's family album*. New York: Greenwillow.

Schlissel, L. (1987). *Women's diaries of the westward journey*. New York: Schoken.

Terban, M. (1990). *Punching the clock*. New York: Clarion.

Terban, M. (1987). *Mad as a wet hen! and other funny idioms*. New York: Clarion.

Wright, L. (1946). *New guide for the Overland Route to California*. Los Angeles: N. A. Kovatch. (Originally by Andrew Child, published in 1852).

Getting Started
with Literature

W ••••• indow on Teaching

Matthew Rick, a student teacher, had read several of R. L. Stine's "Goosebumps" books as well as an article by Diana West, titled "The Horror of R. L. Stine." Matthew told his cooperating teacher, Diane Connors:

> *After reading the books, I wondered if they should have a place in the classroom library and I wanted to find out what third-graders see in them. I found rude characters who talk back to parents and strangers and who are disrespectful to each other and disobey authority. I wondered if other school libraries had Stine's work, so I inquired. Of the 11 library media specialists I spoke with, 7 told me they had more than 10 Stine titles on their shelves but none had even read one of the books. The librarians said they include the books because of their popularity with students.*

Matthew's view of these books was different from the article's view which called Stine's work "shock fiction" and compared it to pornography. Matthew said:

> *Horror is not the argument I have against Stine, for even I like a good scare once in awhile. What I have against Stine is the disloyalty and disobedience of his main characters who don't respect others or themselves. It also frightens me to think that this cheap, transparent writing is the only literature some kids read.*

Several times over the next few days, Diane returned to her conversation with Matthew. His observations resonated with ideas she found in Barbara Kiefer's *The Potential of Picture Books: From Visual Literacy to Aesthetic Understanding*. Kiefer believes children can recognize and analyze quality literature. Diane agreed:

> *I want my students to be able to make informed choices as readers. I want them to develop their own criteria for evaluating and critiquing literature and so I decided to talk with them about holding an "Academy Awards for Books." They quickly warmed to the idea and decided to critique "pond" books for two nearby first-grade classrooms studying pond life and then share the critiques with the first-graders to motivate them to read the books.*

Later, Diane told Matthew how he had unknowingly helped her initiate a classroom project for her children. She described the project:

> *First, we learned about the origin and history of the Caldecott Award. The children read and examined several Caldecott Medal and Honor books, considered aspects of art, compared illustrators' styles, and created their own list of important criteria for a good book. Then, we used the computer in the library to search for "pond" books. They separated the books into three genres: fantasy, realistic fiction, and information books. We then examined one genre each day. In small groups, the children read and evaluated the books, filling out a scoring sheet that included their criteria. We shared books and chose class favorites based on scores. We then charted and tallied the preferences, made award ribbons for the top three choices in each genre, and shared our ideas about what made each book outstanding.*

Through this project, Diane also developed her students' writing and presentation skills. She told Matthew:

> *Each child chose a book to share with one of the first-grade classes. Each wrote a critique, practiced it first with peers, then presented it to the first-graders and left the book with them to read and enjoy. At the end of the project, we also applied the students' criteria to the books they are reading. I was thrilled to see that my students were able to identify a lack of quality in some of these books. For example, Tamika said although she liked Stine's scarey surprises, in comparison with Stine's characters, "Jess and Leslie in* Bridge to Terabithia *(Paterson, 1977) are more like real kids I know" and Tom remarked "*Bridge to Terabithia *took my heart and stretched it for kids who are different and lonely" and about Stine's work, "It's just fantasy, anyway." So, I have a strong sense that they can now talk about what makes a good book and they sense genre differences. In addition, I was able to*

negotiate and co-construct the mock-awards project with them, and integrate language arts into it. My opinion of what should constitute my own clasroom library changed quite a bit as a result.

93
• • • • •
Getting Started

O_{verview}

This chapter contains background information about quality literature written especially for children and youth to help you and your students select and evaluate literature for use in the curriculum. It details books from each genre that can be critical ingredients in integrated language arts instruction.

Good literature possesses unique language that truly delights the senses and develops the knowledge of children who read it or hear it read to them. Literature shows children how others live and have lived, developing within them a better understanding of themselves and others. Well-known experts in the fields of literature and literacy explain its special and important nature:

> *Literature entices, motivates and instructs. It opens doors to discovery and provides endless hours of adventure and enjoyment.* (Norton, 1995, p. 4)

> *Literature at its best gives both pleasure and understanding. It explores the nature of human beings, the condition of humankind.* (Lukens, 1995, p. 8)

> *The most important thing about literature is that it presents to us the memorable things and the things worthy of reflection in life.* (Holdaway, 1983, p. 3)

> *Readers are made in childhood; the models we provide and the books we select influence children in lasting ways.* (Cullinan, 1994, p. 1)

Learning to appreciate and love literature should be a positive and enriching part of a child's school experience. It can be the start of a lifelong habit that brings pleasure and knowledge. Although home is where reading habits begin, many children do not receive encouragement or experience the joy of reading at home. School for these children, then, is critical. The reading beliefs and behaviors you exhibit, as well as your use of literature in the curriculum, will help set good reading habits for these children.

Children's Literature

Children's literature is the entire body of printed material written specifically for children and sometimes for adults. It is often adapted and used in magazines, comic books, records, filmstrips, movies, and TV shows. It includes the literary genres of picture books, folktales, fantasy, poetry, realistic fiction, historical fiction, biography, and information books. Although individual characteristics distinguish each genre, some books are not readily classified and fit into more than one category. For example, biography and historical fiction are often indistinguishable. There are also many books that cross genres and include characteristics of each in the same book; for example, *The Magic Schoolbus inside a Hurricane* by Joanna Cole (1995) is a blend of nonfiction and fantasy.

At present, approximately 3,000 new books (Lukens, 1995) and dozens of magazines are published each year for children. Many more magazines, hardcover books, and paperbacks are published than were 5 or 10 years ago. Increases in printing and sales of paperbacks are due to increased publication costs of hardcover books, bigger markets, and expediency. Today, more children and parents buy books for home use than librarians or media specialists for school libraries and media centers. Evidence of the growing market and demand for children's books is seen in mall bookstores, department store book sections, and drugstore and supermarket book displays. These books are easily obtainable and affordable but are often not of high quality. As a teacher, one of your tasks is to help children locate and appreciate *quality* children's literature not readily obtainable in the usual store displays.

Today, the study of children's literature is recognized as a serious college and university subject, with all the merits and characteristics of literature for adults. These courses examine and evaluate children's literature in terms of plot, setting, characters, theme, point of view, style, tone, and mood. Children's literature enjoys the attention of scholars and academicians and has changed its "kiddie lit" image of the past. Part of the reason for this newly earned but long-deserved respectability is the recognition that many children's books are of high quality. Another reason may be the trend toward realism in today's books, which some view as more respectable and more useful to children than fantasy. There is an increase in nonfiction books and books on topics such as death, divorce, disabilities, nuclear warfare, drugs, and sexuality.

Integrating Children's Literature

Both theory and practice support the use of children's literature throughout the school curriculum. It is a natural base from which learning can occur. Many experts see literature helping children of all ages to learn about spoken and written language and guiding them toward becoming effective language users (Cullinan, 1994; Norton, 1995). Harwayne (1992) shows how literature promotes children's writing by providing models of good writing and inspiring children to write. Holdaway (1979) explains that "more than ever before there is a need to introduce children to a satisfying literature, to use such materials as the center of instruction, and to develop methods of teaching which bring to children the sustained and special joy from the written word that they can experience from no other activity" (p. 191). Bettelheim (1977) contends that, in general, the folk literature of fairy tales children listen to and read reflects and develops their growth to maturity and self-knowledge.

Specifically, literature can enrich content learning; almost any professional journal provides ideas. Pierce and Short (1994) discuss children's books that introduce complex, contemporary, social and political issues such as family conflict, homelessness, leaders, social challenges, and political conflict. Freeman, Lehman, and Scharer (1996) propose titles for teaching about cycles (seasons, life cycles, daily cycles, generations, etc.). Galda (1992) presents books for the social studies curriculum and Galda and MacGregor (1992) discuss books for the science curriculum. Norton (1993) suggests the teaching of geography and Columbus's travels with children's literature. Whitin and Wilde (1995) provide ideas for using children's books to teach such math concepts as geometric shapes, ordinal numbers, counting, addition, money, fractions, and the history of the number system. Norton (1995) discusses literature about the history of language, word play, and vocabulary extension activities that are useful for developing children's knowledge and appreciation of language.

So you can see that both theory and practice support the use of children's literature to develop literacy and learning. But the existence of the material is only one side of using literature. It is also important that you know and understand which books fit which children and how best to use these books. In addition, you need be able to advise parents about the merits of children's literature in general and suggest specific books for their use with their children.

One of your most important tasks as a language arts teacher is to get children hooked on good books that will promote connections among the four language arts—listening, speaking, reading, and writing.

Characteristics of Quality Literature

Each of us has a different definition of what constitutes quality literature, but excellence and permanence are integral to most definitions. *Excellence* is the degree to which a book is outstanding or exceptional. *Permanence* refers to a book's endurance as a well-loved piece of literature over time. Books that are lasting favorites with children are quality books. With new books, perhaps it makes more sense to ask "How memorable is it?" since they haven't withstood the test of time. However, a quality book allows readers to experience it and be changed by it because of that experience.

Recall a favorite childhood book and answer the questions in Figure 4.1. How do the terms *excellence* and *permanence* fit your book?

• • • • •

STRETCHING EXERCISE

FIGURE 4.1 Ask these questions to determine a book's quality.

Quality: Self-Assessment

1. Why do I like it?
2. What makes it an excellent or special story?
3. Why is it believable?
4. What strengths or weaknesses make the characters seem real?
5. What characters seem like real people with strengths and weaknesses?
6. How does the main character overcome the problem?
7. What makes the setting "right" for the story?
8. What is the theme(s)? Is it important?
9. Why would others like, understand, or appreciate the story?

• • • • •

Literary Elements

You can encourage children to judge the quality of texts by teaching them to identify the literary elements of books. Frequent discussion of books in terms of their literary elements instills a critical way of thinking and gives students a vocabulary to use as they evaluate books. Questions about specific literary elements appear in Figure 4.2. Even young children can use terms such as *setting, characters,* and *problem* effectively as they talk about a book. Lukens (1995) explains these literary elements:

— *Setting.* The setting is the "when and where" of the story, or the time, place, and situation in which the story occurs. Setting can be integral to the story or a backdrop that is relatively unimportant to the story.

— *Characters.* The characters are the "beings," either people or animate objects, that carry the action. Main characters are called "round" because they are well developed and they grow and change during the story. Secondary characters are called "flat" since they are undeveloped and the reader does not know them well.

— *Plot.* The plot is the "skeleton" of the story. It is the sequence of events or episodes that occur as the characters find solutions to problems or achieve goals. A basic view of plot is that a story has a beginning, middle, and end. Usually, there is a conflict in the plot (e.g., person vs. self, person vs. person, person vs. nature, or person vs. society).

— *Theme.* The theme is the "heart" of the story or the "glue" that holds it together. It is often the most difficult for children to grasp. Theme can be explicit (stated literally) or implicit (unstated but understood). Children often grasp theme more easily when it is stated as a thought or sentence rather than as a word (e.g., *Friends can be found in unexpected places* rather than *friendship*).

— *Point of view.* The point of view is the storyteller or narrator of the story. When the story is told with *he* or *she* and the narrator is all-knowing about details, thought,

FIGURE 4.2   Ask these questions to build understanding of literary elements.

Literary Elements: Self-Assessment

Setting	Where and when does the story take place? What makes the setting appropriate?
Characters	Who are they? Do they seem real? How are they developed? How do they grow and change?
Plot	What are the events in the story? What is the conflict or problem? Does the solution make sense?
Theme	What is the message, or "heart," of the story?
Point of View	Who tells the story? How effectively?
Style	How is the writing special?
Mood	What is the author's attitude? How does the story make you feel?

.....

and actions, the pont of view is omniscient. Limited omniscient is when the story is told with *he* or *she* and the thoughts of one or two characters are known. When the story is told in the voice of the first person, the pronoun *I* is used and the thoughts of only one character are revealed. The objective point of view uses the third-person voice, which allows readers to interpret and draw their own conclusions.

- *Style.* The style is the "form" an author uses, or "how" something is said rather than what is said. It can involve word choice and usage that convey ideas in distinctive ways (e.g., imagery, figurative language [personification, simile, metaphor], hyperbole, metaphor, understatement, allusion, symbol, puns, wordplay, and devices of sound [onomatopoeia, alliteration, assonance, consonance, rhythm]).

- *Mood.* The mood is the "attitude" or stance an author takes toward the subject and/or readers communicated by word choice and usage. Mood or tone can change or be consistent throughout a story. It can be humorous, sentimental, condescending, didactic, reminiscent, resigned, cynical, reflective, straightforward, and so on.

Obtain a copy of Andrew Ward's (1980) *Baby Bear and the Long Sleep* and a newer paperback book found on a grocery or drugstore shelf. With a friend, read and evaluate both books, using the questions from Figure 4.2.

STRETCHING EXERCISE

• • • • •

Visual Literacy

Four-year-old Ryan loves Jan Brett's stories. In the unique borders of *Town Mouse Country Mouse* (1994), Ryan finds small versions of the animals and objects that appear in the illustrations. In fact, he soon discovers that Brett's distinctive sidebars tell a story in themselves. Is Ryan developing visual literacy? Kiefer (1995) defines *visual literacy* as the ability to discriminate and interpret what is seen. She says the process involves attention, recognition, and, finally, understanding. Another factor in becoming visually literate is the ability to recognize representations in pictures. Visual literacy, then, is the reading and analysis of images. Kiefer says this begins to occur at about age 2 and is easily learned. So, Ryan's enjoyment in scanning pictures and seeing small details signals the beginning of visual literacy for him. Moving from identification and analysis of the concrete to identification and analysis of the abstract can signal further growth for Ryan.

Kiefer (1995) believes early interactions between parents and children during shared reading of picture books develops the child's ability to understand representations in pictures and language. "This early experience with pictures in the meaningful and supportive context of picturebook reading may be necessary to lay the foundation for visual literacy as well as literary and aesthetic understanding" (p. 9). Difficulties in comprehending come when the child must interpret relationships and activities in pictures. Kiefer as well as Short (1993) believe that adults have overlooked the potential of picture books to develop children's visual literacy.

Today, a child's world is visually complex. Few teachers spend time helping children sort, recognize, and understand visual information. Visual literacy skills can apply to the "reading" of all visual media (e.g., road signs, ads, TV, computers, film, video, picturebooks, etc.). Children need to be taught how to analyze and think critically about the visual messages they are bombarded with daily. Jacobs and Tunnell (1996) state, "As teachers and parents we have the opportunity to help our children become visually literate through fine picture books, to curb the numbing effects of mindless television viewing. Our charge is to offer our children the best in pictures and in words, to give them an arsenal for making judgments and developing taste" (p. 41).

So, understanding and analyzing quality illustrations in picture books can offer children a unique opportunity to develop visual literacy. In analyzing illustrations, the most important question is whether the pictures fit the story and communicate something to the reader. Remember: The reason for looking at pictures, in general, is that they provide information—some do this better than others. You can teach your students how to evaluate pictures by modeling the process.

To begin, choose two books with different illustrative styles. For example, use *Monster Mama* (1993), written by Liz Rosenberg and illustrated by Stephen Gammell, done in intense, spatter-painted colors, and Janell Cannon's (1993) *Stellaluna*, illustrated in soft-colored pencils and acrylic paints. Would the story of Stellaluna, the baby fruit bat who is separated from its mother, be as effective if it were done in the bright, spatter-painted style used to tell about the relationship between a boy and his seemingly unique mother (see Figures 4.3 and 4.4)? Read each story and then discuss the pictures using the questions from Figure 4.5. Together, you can help your children see these elements in pictures, talk about them, and identify quality in illustration. Caldecott Medal and Honor books are especially good to use for lessons like this one, since they represent quality in various illustrative styles.

FIGURE 4.3 Stephen Gammell used intense spatter-painting in *Monster Mama* by Liz Rosenberg. (Painting by Aksel Pederson.)

FIGURE 4.4   Janell Cannon used colored pencils and soft acrylic paints in *Stellaluna*.
(Drawing by Rachel Daddezio.)

FIGURE 4.5   Ask these questions to develop visual literacy as you analyze the illustrations in
picture books.

Illustrations: Self-Assessment

Color	What colors are used? Are they bright? Soft? Do they match the mood or content of the story?
Line	Where are the lines? How are they arranged? Are they thick or thin? Dark or light? What purpose do they serve?
Shape	What shapes are used? Are they distinct or subtle? Simple or ornate? Free flowing or rigid? Do they match the story?
Texture	Do objects seem rough/smooth? Furry/jagged? Heavy/light? What makes the objects look this way?
Arrangement	Where is the print? Where are the pictures? Do they go together in a special way?
Effect	How do pictures, print, type, endpapers, and cover go together? How do they create a special design or composition?

Once your students have had experience comparing and contrasting different media and styles in two books, you can help them establish their own criteria and evaluate books accordingly. Figure 4.6 shows the evaluation tool Gloria (the teacher mentioned at the beginning of this chapter) and her students developed and how one student completed it.

STRETCHING EXERCISE	Many awards are given annually for quality children's books. The Caldecott Medal is given to a picture book for excellence in pictures and the Newbery Medal is given for excellence in story. Choose a Caldecott winner or runner-up and evaluate it by using the questions from Figure 4.5. • • • • •

How do you find good literature to use in planning your curriculum? Which books should you share with your students and have in the classroom for them to read? Professional Resources at the end of this chapter includes references that contain titles of children's books in print, award-winning books, and books on specific subjects. Journals that publish reviews of new books include the following:

The Horn Book Magazine
*Bulletin of the Center for Children's
    Books (BCCB)*
School Library Journal (SLJ)
Booklist

Language Arts
Booklinks
The New Advocate
The Web: Wonderfully Exciting Books
The Reading Teacher

Children's Literary Genres

Descriptions of eight genres of literature for children and youth follow, with examples of quality literature given in each genre. Knowing genre characteristics is important in developing children's understanding of a book or story. Knowing the traits of fables, for example, allows children to see how they are constructed and, in turn, write their own. All genres possess most, but not always all, literary elements. For example, poetry may not always include a conflict or characters.

Picture Books

The term *picture book* is commonly used to describe a book that tells a story through both text and illustrations. An *illustrated book,* however, is one that is primarily text, containing only a few drawings to illustrate the story, and is mainly for the older reader. In a picture book, the story can often be told from the pictures alone, but usually pictures and text support each other.

Art in picture books can involve a wide range of media, techniques, and styles (Cullinan, 1994). The *medium* is the material used to produce the work, such as watercolors, oils, acrylics, ink, pencil, charcoal, photographs, tissue paper, acetate sheet, or

Picture-Book Rubric

Genre: _Fantasy_

Title of Book: _Little Beaver and the Echo_

Author: _Amy McDonald (1990)_

Illustrator (if different): _Sarah Fox-Davies_

The medium that the illustrator used (if known): _water colors_

	Strongly Agree 5	Agree 4	Maybe 3	Disagree 2	Strongly Disagree 1
I think the pictures in this book are outstanding.	✓				
I think children would like this book.		✓			
I think this book was written with children in mind.			✓		
I think the pictures match the story theme. (Think about Smoky Night vs. Officer Buckle and Gloria.)	✓				
I think the pictures make the written part of the story even better.		✓			
I think this book is educational or teaches something, even if it's in a funny way.			✓		
I think this is an excellent book.	✓				

Total Score _29_

What, if anything, about the illustrations in this book did you think was outstanding?
the way that she blended the water colors in with the other colors. The beaver looks cute, fuzzy and reel!

What would you tell kids about this book to encourage them to read it? _I liked it because he didin't have a friend and then he found a ton of friends. The pictures are pretty and detailed._

FIGURE 4.6 Amy, a third-grader, evaluated a book's pictures and story.

fabric. Peter Spier (1977) uses watercolor in *Noah's Ark* (Caldecott Medal winner), Russell Freedman (1988) uses photographs in *Lincoln: A Photobiography* (Newbery Medal winner), and David Macaulay (1993) uses ink drawings in *Ship*. The *technique* could be painting, woodcut, linoleum cut, air brush, or collage. Ed Emberley (1968) uses woodcuts in *Drummer Hoff*, written by Barbara Emberley (Caldecott Medal winner), and Ezra Jack Keats (1962) uses collage in *The Snowy Day* (Caldecott Medal winner), as does Faith Ringgold (1991) in *Tar Beach* (Caldecott Honor Book). *Style* is the way the artist uses the medium, such as the way Leo and Diane Dillon use an air brush with pastels in *Why Mosquitoes Buzz in People's Ears* by Verna Aardema (1995) (Caldecott Medal winner).

Five special types of picture books are worth noting because of their appropriateness for young children and English learners:

1. *Poem picture books* contain an illustrated poem, such as *Birches* by Robert Frost (1988), *Heartland* by Diane Siebert (1989), and the rap in *Twist with a Burger, Jitter with a Bug* by Linda Lowery (1995).
2. *Pop-up books* contain stand-up, fold-out, or movable pages, such as *The Jolly Postman and Other People's Letters* by Janet Ahlberg (1986).
3. *Predictable books* contain a pattern of repetition, rhyme, rhythm, or style that allows children to predict language or actions to follow, such as Eric Carle's (1990) *The Very Quiet Cricket* and Jonathan London's (1996) *I See the Moon and the Moon Sees Me*.
4. *Song-picture books* contain lyrics and pictures, such as *Crocodile Smile* by Sarah Weeks (1994).
5. *Wordless picture books* contain pictures but no text, such as Mercer Mayer's *Frog Goes to Dinner*, or little text as in David Wiesner's (1987) *Tuesday* (Caldecott Medal winner).

Some other special types of picture books that appeal to young children and English learners because they focus on specific vocabulary and concepts are alphabet books, counting books, concept books, and easy-to-read books (see Figure 4.7). Since these books invite oral interactions, using them with students who speak English as a second language, who are language delayed, or who are cognitively challenged helps them learn concepts and build English vocabulary. These special picture books, however, hold rich potential for developing the literacy of *every* child in your classroom. When your students read these books as models from which to write and illustrate their own books, they learn English as they create and read their own language.

Bilingual Picture Books. Another group of picture books is special because they are written in more than one language (see Figures 4.8 and 4.9). Bilingual literature aids the learning of English for non–English speakers by providing a bridge to English. It is an excellent way to acknowledge and validate the cultures and langauges of your ESL learners and make learning English easier for them. Additionally, books like these sensitize English speakers to other languages and broaden their understandings of English learners.

Are all these picture books and those described in the genres that follow just meant for young children? No. Although most picture books are written for children

FIGURE 4.7 Some special picture books for young English learners.

103
· · · · ·
Getting Started

Alphabet Books

Ehlert, L. (1989). *Eating the alphabet: Fruits and vegetables from A to Z.* San Diego: Harcourt Brace.
Johnson, S. T. (1995). *Alphabet city.* New York: Viking.
Kitchen, B. (1984). *Animal alphabet.* New York: Dial.
MacDonald, S. (1986). *Alphabetics.* New York: Bradbury.
Onyefulu, I. (1993). *A is for Africa.* New York: Cobblehill.
Van Allsburg, C. (1987). *The Z was zapped.* Boston: Houghton Mifflin.

Counting Books

Bang, M. (1983). *Ten, nine, eight.* New York: Greenwillow.
Chandra, D. (1994). *Miss Mabel's table.* San Diego: Browndeer.
Giganti, P. (1992). *Each orange had eight slices.* New York: Greenwillow.
Onyefulu, I. (1995). *Emeka's gift: An African counting story.* New York: Cobblestone.
Sloat, T. (1991). *From one to one hundred.* New York: Dutton.

Concept Books

Cisneros, S. (1994). *Hairs/pelitos.* New York: Knopf.
Emberly, R. (1990). *My house/mi casa: A book in two languages.* Boston: Little, Brown.
Heller, R. (1995). *Behind the mask: A book about prepositions.* New York: Grossett.
MacKinnon, D. (1995). *What am I?* New York: Dial.
McGuire, R. (1994). *Night becomes day.* New York: Viking.
McMillan, B. (1989). *Super, super, superwords.* New York: Lothrop.
Miller, M. (1993). *Can you guess?* New York: Greenwillow.

Poem-Picture Books

Adoff, A. (1973). *Black is brown is tan.* New York: Harper.
Carlstrom, N. (1986). *Jesse bear, what will you wear?* New York: Macmillan.
Hopkins, L. B. (1984). *Surprises.* New York: Harper and Row.
Lenski, L. (1987). *Sing a song of people.* Boston: Little, Brown.
McMillan, B. (1994). *Play day: A book of terse verse.* New York: Holiday House.
Mora, P. (1994). *The desert is my mother/El desierto es mi madre.* Alameda, CA: Pinata Books.

Song-Picture Books

Carle, E. (1993). *Today is Monday.* New York: Philomel.
Child, L. M. (1993). *Over the river and through the woods.* New York: North-South.
Hurd, T. (1984). *Mama don't allow.* New York: Harper.
Peek, M. (1987). *The balancing act: A counting song.* New York: Clarion.
Trapani, I. (1993). *The itsy bitsy spider.* New York: Whispering Coyote.

Predictable Books

Carle, E. (1990). *The very quiet cricket.* New York: Philomel.
Cole, J. (1995). *Jack's garden.* New York: Greenwillow.
Fox, M. (1988). *Hattie and the fox.* New York: Bradbury.
Hawkins, C., & Hawkins, J. (1987). *I know an old lady who swallowed a fly.* New York: Putnam.
Neitzel, S. (1995). *The bag I'm taking to grandma's.* New York: Greenwillow.
Shaw, N. (1992). *Sheep eat out.* New York: Houghton Mifflin.

Easy-to-Read Books

Bennett, J., & dePaola, T. (1985). *Teeny tiny.* New York: Trumpet.
Cowley, J. (1995). *The mouse bride.* New York: Scholastic.
Giff, P. (1992). *Look out, Washington, D.C.!* New York: Dell.
Lobel, A. (1976). *Frog and toad all year.* New York: Harper and Row.
Minarik, E. (1957). *Little bear.* New York: Harper.
Sharmat, M. W. (1992). *Nate the Great and the stolen base.* New York: Coward.
Turner, A. (1995). *Dust for dinner.* New York: HarperCollins.

· · · · ·

FIGURE 4.8   Books printed in English and a second language can aid English learners.

Chinese and English
Lee, H. V. (1994). *At the beach.* New York: Henry Holt.
Lee, J. M. (1995). *The song of MuLan.* Arden, NC: Front Street.

French, Chinese, and English
Dabcovich, L. (1992). *The keys to my kingdom: A poem in three languages.* New York:
   Lee & Shepard.

Hebrew and English
Bogot, H. I., & Orkand, R. J. (1994). *A children's Haggadah.* New York: Central Conference
   of American Rabbis (CCAR Press).

Korean and English
Paek, M. (1990). *Aekyung's dream.* San Francisco: Children's Book Press.

Japanese and English
Tompert, A. (1993). *Bamboo hats and rice cakes.* New York: Crown.

Spanish and English
Winter, J. (1991). *Diego.* New York: Knopf.
Garza, C. L. (1990). *Family pictures.* San Francisco: Children's Book Press.
Emberley, R. (1993). *Let's go: Vamos.* Boston: Little, Brown.
Rohmer, H. (Adaptor) (1989). *Uncle Nacho's hat: El sombrero del Tio Nacho.* San Francisco:
   Children's Book Press.
Eversole, R. (1995). *La flautista/The flute player.* New York: Orchard.

Vietnamese and English
Tuyet, T. K. (1987). *The little weaver of Thai-Yen village: Co be tho-det lang Thai-Yen.* San
   Francisco: Children's Book Press.

• • • • •

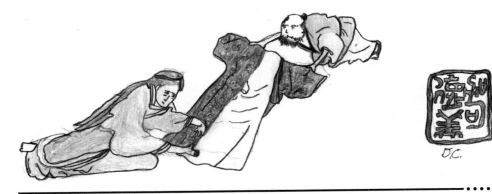

FIGURE 4.9   Ann Tompert's *Bamboo Hats and Rice Cakes* includes Japanese characters and
English text. (Drawing by David Caramore.)

ages 2 to 8, many are enjoyed by older readers, too, since they contain stories with sophisticated concepts and vocabulary. In each of the following genres, you will find examples of books for both young and older readers.

Folktales

Folktales deal with the legends, superstitions, customs, and beliefs of ordinary people. They are timeless in their appeal, reflecting universal human feelings and desires. Tales such as "The Three Billy Goats Gruff" and "The Three Bears" were told originally by one generation and passed on to the next in this way. The Grimm brothers were first to write down some of these oral tales. Most folktales contain a brief introduction that identifies the setting, characters, and problem. Characters are one dimensional (flat) with one obvious trait (e.g., good, evil, kind, wise). The action is fast paced, often with three attempts to solve the problem, and the conclusion quickly follows the climax. Folktales often include the number *3* (e.g., 3 sons, 3 wishes, 3 trials) and almost always contain a lesson. The universal appeal of folktales can be attributed to their simplicity and the lessons they teach. They use the vocabulary and folkways of the common people.

Some folktales have circular plots, beginning in one place and continuing until the story ends where it began. Others are cumulative tales, in which objects are added as a character goes on a journey. There are trickster tales in which a wise animal is the central character, such as Anansi the spider in African tales and Br'er Rabbit in tales of southern United States.

Folktales include five special kinds of stories:

1. *Fairy tales* usually contain magic or an imaginary being with special powers, such as the godmother in "Cinderella."
2. *Fables* are brief stories that illustrate a lesson (often a one-sentence moral) and include animals or inanimate objects that are personified with human traits, such as Arnold Lobel's (1980) *Fables* (Caldecott Medal winner). Fables are popular with both children and adults, perhaps because they are concise lessons on human behavior.
3. *Myths* answer questions about something people cannot explain, such as a cosmic phenomenon, a strange natural happening, the start of civilization, or the origins of a custom. Myths often have gods, goddesses, mystical forces, and magic. Older children enjoy Greek, Roman, and Norse myths not only because of the beauty and imaginative quality of these stories but also because they are the source for much of the children's language and thinking (Sutherland, 1997).
4. *Epics* are long collections of tales about legendary heroes who personify the best human traits and the ideals of a nation. *Robin Hood,* for instance, is an English epic that was originally a series of ballads.
5. *Tall tales* have a regional setting and dialect with heroes and heroines who are brave, witty, and often have exaggerated size or strength, such as *John Henry* by Julius Lester (1994) (Caldecott Honor Book). Both epics and tall tales help children understand heroism.

Folktales help children see that good often wins out over evil, that cleverness triumphs over strength and might, and that the plain and simple are often rewarded for

their honesty and goodness. Folktales let children experience fast-paced action, sometimes violent and horrible acts, but all in the guise of stories that often contain the elements of magic or fantasy and that happened long ago. Through folktales, children can
learn about human problems, solutions, morals, and values. Folktales show children
what different cultures have contributed to U.S. society.

Fantasy

Fantasy is fiction that contains an element of unreality. It twists or manipulates reality,
often using fast-paced action, humor, magic, and imaginary events or characters. Maurice Sendak's (1963) *Where the Wild Things Are* (Caldecott Medal winner) is one of the
most popular examples of fantasy for young readers (see Figure 4.10). Lois Lowry's
(1993) *The Giver* (Newbery Medal winner) and all of Chris Van Allsburg's works are
other examples.

Science fiction is a special type of fantasy that is set in other worlds and deals with
the future. Based on scientific facts, science fiction explores the technology of the future
as it raises questions about the future of humanity. Madeleine L'Engle's (1962) *A Wrinkle in Time* (Newbery Medal winner) is created around the concept of the *tesseract*, a
scientific term that means "fifth dimension." The three children in the story travel by
tessering through time to a far off planet with the help of three imaginary characters—
Mrs. Who, Mrs. Whatsit, and Mrs. Which—who have supernatural powers.

Good fantasy appeals to children's imaginations. It must be believable within the
context of a logical and consistent story framework. Fantasy provides adventures into
new and exciting worlds for children. It allows children to use their imaginations and
explore with characters who often have special powers. Fantasy can help children understand the difference between fiction and fact. Often humorous and entertaining, it is one
of the most popular genres for these many reasons.

Poetry

Poetry is the expression of a writer's inner thoughts and feelings and the writer's relationship to the world and to others. A poet often uses images, rhyme, metaphor, simile,
and other techniques to give the reader a particular thought or feeling (see Figure 4.11).

FIGURE 4.10 Sendak's monsters are
perennial favorites with young children.
(Drawing by Melissa Salisbury.)

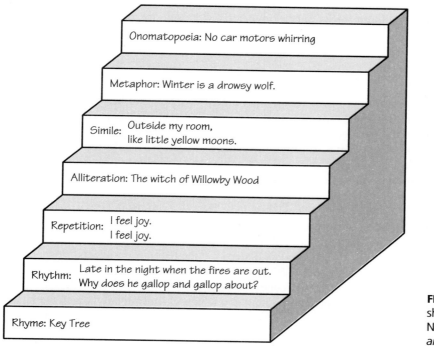

Onomatopoeia: No car motors whirring

Metaphor: Winter is a drowsy wolf.

Simile: Outside my room,
like little yellow moons.

Alliteration: The witch of Willowby Wood

Repetition: I feel joy.
I feel joy.

Rhythm: Late in the night when the fires are out.
Why does he gallop and gallop about?

Rhyme: Key Tree

FIGURE 4.11 A "stairway" showing the stylistic devices in Nancy Larrick's *To the Moon and Back*.

Source: Reprinted by permission of Pat Turner-Massey.

Poets, perhaps more often than other writers, build sensory images through the use of simile (*shrill as a whistle*), metaphor (*the sun was an egg yolk*), alliteration (*leaping lizards lured me*), onomatopoeia (*slushing and slurping her slops*), and other techniques. The sensuous and concise language of poetry appeals to children's intellects and their emotions by giving new meaning to everyday events, people, or places.

Because poems often contain rhyme, rhythm, and repetition that enhance their message and impact, they should be read aloud to be best enjoyed. Paul Fleischman's (1988) *Joyful Noise: Poems for Two Voices* is a collection of poetry about insects that can be read aloud chorally by two individuals or groups.

A poetry anthology, such as Beatrice de Regniers's (1988) *Sing a Song of Popcorn: Every Child's Book of Poems,* should be on your desk for reading to children at free moments. Poetry by Jack Prelutsky (e.g., *For Laughing Out Loud: Poems to Tickle Your Funny Bone* [1991]) or Shel Silverstein (e.g., *Falling Up* [1996]) delights children of all ages. Books such as *I Hear America Singing* by Walt Whitman (1991), *To the Moon and Back* by Nancy Larrick (1991), *The Dream Keeper and Other Poems* by Langston Hughes (1994), and *Street Rhymes around the World* by Jane Yolen (1992) are other examples of poetry children love.

Poetry allows children to hear, see, and live in the everyday world with new insights. Through poetry, they can explore the world of the unknown, exercise their imaginations, and learn to appreciate the rhyme and rhythm of language. Poetry should be shared with children for its pure enjoyment, for its sensory stimulation, and for its language.

Realistic Fiction

Realistic fiction is true-to-life stories set in a time period that children know and understand. This genre includes mysteries, adventures, and realistic stories about animals, sports, and people involved in the dilemmas and social issues of today's world. Topics include divorce, death, drugs, disabilities, peer relationships, family problems, school failure, and survival. *Smoky Night* by Eve Bunting (1994) (Caldecott Medal winner), for example, portrays a young boy's experience in the riots in Los Angeles after an earthquake.

Realistic fiction shows students they have the power to change their lives. These stories help children know and learn about their world. They show children that people are more alike than different. As they read this genre, children can gain insights into their own problems and at the same time understand the feelings of others. For example, *Walk Two Moons* by Sharon Creech (1994) (Newbery Medal winner) helps middle-grade readers see how a young girl copes with the loss of her mother. In *Park's Quest*, Katherine Paterson (1989) portrays a young boy who seeks information about his father who was killed in Vietnam. Realistic fiction also helps students rehearse roles they may have in the future.

Historical Fiction

Historical fiction is based on facts and set in the past, but is not restricted by the past. It is realistic for the time period depicted and contains convincing dialogue and accurate descriptions of settings and happenings that further children's knowledge of other times and places. When integrated into subject areas, this literature not only supports learning the facts of history but it also makes history more real and relevant.

Historical fiction can make the past come alive for students. It can also build your students' awareness of their heritages. It can make content area learning more interesting by providing related knowledge about people, places, and events in history. Older readers enjoy Lois Lowry's (1992) *Number the Stars* (Newbery Medal winner), the story of a young Jewish girl and her family who were hidden from the Nazis by heroic

Danish people during World War II. Joan Blos's (1979) *A Gathering of Days* (Newbery Medal winner) is an account of the hardships and tranquility of a young girl's life on a small New Hampshire farm in the 1830s.

Biography

Biography is nonfiction that deals with the history of a person's life. Autobiographies are written by a person about her own life. Biographers must research and read about their subjects to accurately and interestingly portray their lives. To be realistic, a biography should represent both a person's strengths and weaknesses so that the person is a believable human. Among the most accurate and entertaining biographies are those written by Jean Fritz. Her work is carefully researched and contains realistic, believable dialogue and accurate, factual information. Recently, more biographies are available of women and minorities, such as *My First Book of Biographies: Great Men and Women Every Child Should Know* by Jean Marzollo (1996).

Questions to ask in evaluating both biography and historical fiction follow:

- How authentic is the setting?
- Are characters/dialogues realistic for the time period?
- Is the account objective? Are all sides of the conflict or person described?
- How important is the story? Is it worth telling?
- How believable is the story? How is it documented?

Biography, like historical fiction, not only teaches children about other times and other places but it also provides them with role models with whom to identify and from

• • • • •
Biographies can inspire students to read about famous people and stimulate studies in science and social studies.

whom to learn. This genre may help students think about setting personal goals and aspirations. Biography relates real happenings and experiences of real people to children, and thus it has a special allure and place in the curriculum.

Information Books

Information books are nonfiction books primarily written to inform and explain. For young children, there are alphabet books, counting books, and concept books that teach or reinforce language concepts. Information books for older children are written about all sorts of topics, from cats and molecules to drugs and the management of wildlife. Ask yourself these three questions when evaluating and choosing an information book:

- How accurate is the information?
- How recently was the book written?
- Do credentials or experiences qualify the author to write about the subject?

Often, older books are not up to date in the facts and concepts they contain, especially if the topics are science, technology, and other areas where knowledge grows so quickly that recent changes and developments make the books inaccurate. Read several books on the topic to check for accuracy, and compare the information and concepts they contain for similarities and differences that could indicate accuracy or authenticity.

Information books provide children with knowledge and quench their thirst for answers to questions. Nonfiction supports content learning in science and social studies by providing specific facts and information often not found in content texts, and by providing more current information. Photographs, such as the excellent ones in *Snakes* by Seymour Simon (1992), are often used in information books.

The brief overview of genres included here is not considered to be a thorough discussion of the characteristics of literature or all the authors of quality children's books. Consult comprehensive children's literature resources such as *Children's Literature in the Elementary School* (Huck, Hepler, Hickman, & Kiefer, 1997) for some of the hundreds of authors and thousands of titles of books in print today.

In addition to these eight genres, there are dozens of fiction and nonfiction magazines for children (Stoll, 1997). These magazines cover many topics or focus on a specific one, such as science and nature, computers, literature, games, sports, or crafts. They range from preschool to adult in difficulty level, and many contain original children's work as well as quality adult writing. Many children like magazines because they are current, are usually colorful, include short stories and articles of high interest, and are similar to adult reading material.

| **STRETCHING EXERCISE** | Choose two books from each of the genres just described to integrate into an upcoming content unit in a classroom. Begin a card file or add to one you already started. On each card, list the book's title, author, reading level, and year of publication. Include a summary and a strategy that integrates reading and writing. |

••••••

Finding the "Isms" in Children's Books

Racism, sexism, and *ageism* are just some of the terms for attitudes about particular groups that result in negative stereotypes. A *stereotype* is an oversimplified generalization about a particular group, race, or gender that usually carries derogatory implications. You may be aware of stereotypical images that demean an individual and are inaccurate ways to see a particular group.

Both in and out of school, students are exposed in the media and in books to notions about groups of people that are not necessarily accurate. When one allows stereotypes to develop and perpetuate, there is a danger that because of these inaccurate images one will treat minority groups unfairly and in ways that make them less than one's equals. Perhaps if a child can see how to detect racism and sexism in a book, then the child can transfer that perception to life beyond the book. So, it is important to select stereotype-free books to use with your students. Or, if a book does portray a stereotypical image but has other redeeming qualities, you need to be ready to discuss the issues it raises. Ten guidelines, still relevant today despite their publication dates, can help you choose stereotype-free literature follow (Council on Interracial Books for Children, 1974):

1. *Examine the illustrations.* Look for images that demean characters because of race or gender. Be aware of *tokenism,* or the inclusion of minorities that look like Whites except for tinted skin or who all look alike and are not depicted as individuals with unique features. Do minority characters have active roles and leadership positions?
2. *Examine the storyline.* The story should be a sensitive portrayal of real people with real problems that can be solved through initiative and intelligence. Do female characters achieve as a result of their looks or relationships with males? Are minorities "the problem" or shown as passive and accepting?
3. *Look at the life-styles.* The story should give genuine insights into another culture, not oversimplify it. Negative value judgments should not be implied, even though minorities are depicted as different.
4. *Weigh the relationships among people.* Does a certain group of people possess the power, make the important decisions, or provide the leadership? Which are the supporting characters and which are the main characters?
5. *Note the "heros."* Minority heros may be involved in conflict with the "White establishment." Do the actions of minorities benefit their cultures or the culture of White people?
6. *Consider the effects on a child's self-image.* Characters in the story must possess positive and constructive models so as not to limit the readers' aspirations and self-concepts.
7. *Consider the author's or illustrator's background.* What qualifies the author to write about a minority theme? Is the author or illustrator a minority, or has travel, study, or life given the author (and/or illustrator) credentials to create the story?
8. *Consider the author's pespective.* Examine the author's perspective to determine if it is biased toward or against a group. Is the story patriarchal or feminist? Eurocentric or minority?

9. *Watch for loaded words.* Be on the lookout for words that have insulting overtones, sexist language, and adjectives that exclude minorities.
10. *Look at the copyright date.* Diversity was first reflected in the 1970s, but this date is a not a guarantee of stereotype-free literature.

Stereotypical images are said to exist in *Ten Little Rabbits* by Virginia Grossman and Sylvia Long (1991) because Native Americans are depicted as animals that all look alike but "wear different blankets" even though differences among the 10 tribes portrayed are documented at the end of the book (McCarty, 1995). As well, *The Five Chinese Brothers* by Claire Bishop (1938) portrays the five brothers as look-alike cartoon-style characters. But a new version by Margaret Mahy (1990) replaces the older version with more realistically drawn brothers. Temple, Martinez, Yokota, and Naylor (1997) discuss these and other stereotypical images in children's literature and identify authentic multicultural authors and books for classroom use.

Using Diverse Literature

"The study of multicultural literature is a powerful means for literacy educators to help students develop an appreciation and understanding of their literary and cultural heritage" (Norton, 1991, p. 38). As well, it makes the study of content areas more lively and interesting. Literature also builds awareness of diversity. Since the world is becoming increasingly diverse, you and your students need to understand and appreciate one another's similarities and differences. Using literature about diverse students or literature that includes characters with different cultural, racial, or ethnic backgrounds has a variety of benefits. Using multicultural literature

- Increases cultural awareness
- Helps children understand themselves and others better
- Develops awareness of different languages
- Allows children to identify with the people who created the stories
- Helps children discover themes and values important to people today
- Expands knowledge of geography and natural history, and develops knowledge of history and social changes
- Builds appreciation of literary techniques

How do students react to the use of diverse literature that is integrated with language arts and a content area subject? They react in positive ways, as you can see from the following excerpts from letters of sixth- and seventh-grade students who have learning disabilities to Jan, their teacher. Their statements demonstrate how the reading of novels and the use of response journals enlivened their integrated unit on World War II.

Jan's students read *Number the Stars* by Lois Lowry (1992) (Newbery Medal–winner), a story of a Danish family who helped Jewish friends escape to Sweden, and *Baa, Baa, Black Sheep* by Pappy Boyington (1989), a story of how Pappy Boyington survived torture in a Japanese prisoner-of-war camp and became a hero of the Pacific

Fleet Squadron named the "Black Sheep." They wrote responses to each chapter in journals and they also role-played, wrote poetry, and made books, which helped them become authors. Their interest and excitement about the unit is clear:

> Reading about the Danes and Jews made me think your friends can be real different from you and that is OK. You're all still people with hearts. When you care about them you'll do anything to protect them.
>
> *—Adam*

> Writing on the computer to you was a RIP!! You should always have a project to encourage reading novels. I can hardly wait to go buy more books with you. Bet you can't believe Rob and me are on the second time around to reading five novels.
>
> *—Alex*

> Reading the novels was the best idea. At first I did not think I was going to like it. . . . They made everything come alive. They relate to the lives of kids our age.
>
> *—Katrina*

> What I think we should do is make a short play after reading the novel to make sure we really understand it. Please always do the poems after reading the books, as that makes you put it in your heart. Publishing the book was a fun way to see all that we had written in our journals.
>
> *—Ruth*

> I like writing from historical fiction because you can become immersed in the history of the moment by becoming the character. It was a different perspective to become Annemarie and be interviewed.
>
> *—Antonia*

It is possible to teach, enrich, and make every subject more interesting with children's literature. Children gain much when the connections you make between new and known information involve literature written for them. Using children's books makes teaching comprehension and composition easier and more fun.

Literacy Role Models

The power of reading to influence and change attitudes is well recognized. Zimet (1976) even contends that the content of material read modifies attitudes and behaviors. Gibson and Levin (1975) indicate that when children identify with a model who commands respect, they adopt and internalize the motives of the model. When children imitate a model's behavior, both their attitudes and learning change. Many role models that shape attitudes and behaviors are found in children's books.

Through the actions of main characters, the actual processes, functions, and satisfactions of effectively using language are seen. There are a number of books for children that depict listening, speaking, reading, and writing as valuable and important activities. Main characters use their language skills for enjoyment, for gaining and sharing new knowledge, and even for survival. Fictional and nonfictional characters who read and write serve as reading and writing models for children (D'Angelo, 1982).

There are many books in which main characters use and enjoy their literacy. Reading is a major interest of the main character in stories such as *Aunt Chip and the Great Triple Creek Dam Affair* by Patricia Polacco (1996). In this story, Aunt Chip saves the town of Triple Creek, where everyone has forgotten how to read because of the invasion of television. In *Dear Benjamin Banneker*, by Andrea Pinkney (1994), Benjamin writes an almanac that he has trouble publishing. His letter to then Secretary of State, Thomas Jefferson, and Jefferson's reply are included. Other stories, such as *The Other Way to Listen* by Byrd Baylor (1978) and *Aunt Flossie's Hats (and Crab Cakes Later)* by Elizabeth Howard (1991), depict listening in a positive way. In *The Other Way to Listen*, a young boy and old man learn to listen to nature together. In *Aunt Flossie's Hats (and Crab Cakes Later),* two African American sisters, Sarah and Susan, visit their favorite aunt and share tea, cookies, crab cakes, and stories about hats. *Stage Fright* by Ann Martin (1984) tells about a young girl's shyness over her part in a play and the rewards she earns when speaking before an audience.

Following this book's chapters on listening, speaking, reading, and writing are annotated bibliographies of books for children in which that particular language art is a main theme, a critical aspect, or related in some important way to plot or characterization. These are books to read aloud to your class, perhaps a chapter a day at a specified time, or to make available in your classroom library for children to borrow and read themselves. These books promote the affective as well as the cognitive dimensions of literacy. From them, children learn to value the ability to use language well and to develop into language users throughout their lives.

Determining Interests

Like adults, children enjoy reading what their peers are reading. This accounts for the fact that many characters and books children say are their favorites come from classroom book club orders. This is a source of concern for many teachers like Matthew (mentioned at the beginning of this chapter), who read several R. L. Stine books and was disappointed in their quality. We know that children's interests often differ from adult notions of what constitutes quality in children's literature.

What can you do to bridge the gap between children's interests and quality literature? How can you positively influence children's reading habits? One way to help determine children's interests is with an inventory that can be given orally to children who are too young to read or write their answers. Older students enjoy administering the inventory and transcribing younger children's responses. The survey might include starters like the following:

My hobbies are . . .
On the weekend I like to . . .
My favorite sports are . . .
My pet is . . .
In school I am good at . . .
My favorite television shows are . . .
My favorite book is . . .

My favorite author is . . .
Right now I am reading . . .
A book I want to read is . . .
When I grow up I want to be a . . .
I would like to learn more about . . .
If I could be anyone it would be . . .
If I could travel anywhere it would be . . .
My wish for the world is . . .

You can help a class book committee administer and analyze results of a survey like this to discover the students' own reading interests. If the committee administers the survey several times a year, the children will see that their interests change. Your students can use results of the survey and the criteria discussed earlier in this chapter to help find quality literature for the classroom library that will interest class members. Chapter 5 includes many other ideas for sharing quality literature with your students.

When children read quality literature, they relate to it and enjoy it. In a study of fifth- and sixth-grade students and classic books, Wilson and Abrahamson (1988) encouraged students to choose and read three or more books from a list of classics that had survived at least one generation. Students were asked what their favorite book was and why. The most common favorites were *Charlotte's Web* by E. B. White (1952), *The Borrowers* by Mary Norton (1953), *The Lion, the Witch, and the Wardrobe* by C. S. Lewis (1950), and *Little House in the Big Woods* by Laura Ingalls Wilder (1953). Comments made by students about their reasons for selecting *Charlotte's Web* follow:

- *"I liked the story because it is not possible for something like that to happen, yet it seems so real."*
- *"I loved the story because it touched me. It made me sad in parts and happy in others."*
- *"I like the book because the animals could talk."*
- *"It was well written. The author made me feel like I was there with Charlotte and Wilbur."* (Wilson & Abrahamson, 1988, p. 410)

These comments suggest that these students could identify some aspects of quality literature. But when students are not exposed to quality literature, do they recognize and seek it out themselves? Experience shows that many of them do not. Children need more guidance and direction in differentiating between popular and quality literature than one realizes.

Besides identifying children's interests, you also need to help children determine whether they can read a book once they have chosen it. One method to use with easy-to-read books is the five-finger readability test. Have the child choose a page in the middle of the book to read orally. The child should hold down one finger each time he encounters an unrecognizable word. If he reads an entire page missing fewer than five words, he can probably read the book. If the child misses more words, a parent or sibling may need to read the book to him or help him read it, or the child needs to find a book that is easier to read. For older children reading more difficult books, the two-fist test works the same way. With two pages of text, the child can miss twice as many words and the book is still readable.

These and other readability methods are only guides, however. A motivated child or one with background in a particular topic can read a more difficult book than a less motivated child or one who lacks appropriate background experiences. To determine whether a child can read a book, predictability is also important, whether in rhyme, rhythm, repetition, language patterns, or illustrations. Children thereby derive clues that help them read and comprehend. For example, a book that contains the same phrase repeated on every other page exhibits one element of predictability that makes it easier for a new reader to read.

To provide you with books children choose to read, the International Reading Association (IRA) publishes (yearly since 1975) a graded and annotated bibliography called Children's Choices in the October issue of *The Reading Teacher*. These are the favorite 100 titles selected from a list of 500 books that the IRA and Children's Book Council (CBC) selects from the 3,000 or so books published yearly for children. The 500 books, selected as examples of good books for recreational reading and teaching reading, are tested in five school districts around the country. Children vote for their favorites, and a bibliography of these top 100 books is published every year.

STRETCHING EXERCISE

Administer the interest survey (on pages 114–115) to a child, adding any other appropriate questions. Then take the child to the library, and, using the information from the survey, use the five-finger or two-fist method to help the child find appropriate books to read.

• • • • •

Monitoring Reading

Teachers need to know if their students are reading, what they are reading, whether they enjoy the books, and whether they read different genres and experience a wide range of print. With a system for monitoring and record keeping, you can effectively guide your students toward the most rewarding reading experiences. For example, Andrew, a second-grade teacher, knows that Lakiesha likes humor. So, Andrew can suggest Peggy Parish's books, such as *Come Back, Amelia Bedelia* (1995), or riddle books such as *Home on the Range: Ranch-Style Riddles* by Diane and Andy Burns (1995).

To monitor reading progress, some teachers have students keep response journals in which the children write personal responses to what they read. Other teachers have students write brief summaries and feelings they experience as they read. Atwell (1987) had her students keep a dialogue journal in which they wrote her at least one letter a week about what they were reading. She wrote back to every student in response to their entries. She felt that this strategy helped her keep in touch with what her students were reading and how they were personally connecting with their reading.

When children keep their own records of their reading, they begin to take responsibility for their reading. Atwell (1987) had her students keep a simple log at the end of their journals where they listed three items: the title of each book they finished, the author, and the date they finished it. Logs like these are valuable because they provide a ready reference for you, the students, and the parents that not only shows what each child has read but also shows trends and cycles in reading. Whether you have students keep response journals, dialogue journals, literature logs, or some combination of the three, having students write is an excellent way to involve them in monitoring their own progress.

There are other ways to keep track of books the entire class has read. Some teachers use a bookworm on a wall or bulletin board, with a body section added to the worm by each child as a book is read. A variation of this idea is a tree with a leaf added for each book read. Some classes keep a file box of reactions to books read. Children record their reactions as they read books and also read others' reactions before choosing a new book. Children also like to use the computer to keep records of what they have read. Periodic printouts and comparisons with earlier printouts encourage and surprise children when they realize how their reading lists have grown.

Be aware of the competition that may result from some of these public record-keeping activities, however. Remind children that the important thing is to enjoy reading. Encourage them to share their responses to favorite books and deemphasize competition as you emphasize sharing and enjoyment.

Growing a Classroom Library

Although you and your students borrow books from the school library, this supply is often limited and may not provide the titles you feel you need to supplement the topics your children are studying. In this case, there are several ways to "grow your own classroom library." The most obvious way is to borrow books from your public library. Most libraries will lend you a large number of books that you can keep in your classroom for

. . . . .
There are many ways to build your own classroom library to supplement your school's library holdings.

a month at a time. Plan well in advance when you need books for a special unit of study. Most librarians are happy to locate and save them for you.

Another way to acquire books is to buy them yourself from book outlets that sell at reduced prices because they are slightly damaged or there is some defect in print. Always ask for a teacher's discount when you shop at retail stores, even when you buy books on sale. Attend professional conferences where publishers often sell books at lower prices. Shop at local public libraries when used-books sales occur. (In the case of nonfiction, however, check to be sure the information is still accurate.)

Many Parent/Teacher Associations (PTA) sponsor book fairs during the school year where you can buy paperback books. With profits from the sale, additional books are often purchased and donated to the school library. In addition, PTAs often sponsor used books sales to benefit the library collection. Garage sales also offer a cheap way to grow your library.

Another source of children's books is companies that publish inexpensive paperbacks and deal directly with classroom teachers. Each month, these companies send brochures and order forms advertising their books, which you distribute to your class. When your students order books, you collect completed order forms and money to send to the company. You receive bonus credits for the books ordered by your class, which you can use to obtain free books, cassettes, and CD-ROMs for your library. Here are the names of some book clubs:

The Trumpet Club, P.O. #604, Holmes, PA 19043
Troll Book Clubs, Mahwah, NJ 07430
Scholastic Book Clubs, Jefferson City, MO 65102
Weekly Reader Paperbacks, P.O. #3750, Jefferson City, MO 65102
Alfonsi News and Book Services, 380 Brooks Drive, Suite 106, Hazelwood, MO 63042

These companies will also send free materials, such as author biographies, posters, book covers, and letters from authors. Keeping files on your favorite authors and illustrators of these materials gives you ready access to information for an author or illustrator study. To pique interest in a particular author and encourage reading, some teachers create an Author Corner with a bulletin board and display of books that changes every month.

When you establish a classroom library, be sure to take precautions to preserve it. Have children sign books out and return them regularly, just as they do with books from the school or public library. Stamping books that belong in your classroom library helps ensure their return if they are misplaced or lost. With a little attention to acquiring a classroom library, you'll discover that it will grow quickly.

Chayet (1994) proposes a number of other ideas for growing your classroom library. She suggests collecting restaurant menus, travel brocures, discarded phone books, user's manuals, clothing catalogs, and newspapers. You can bind student-created work, make class recipe books, encourage student hand-me-downs, and print and bind on-line information. The information department of your state government and your state or local historical society or museum are also good sources of materials for your classroom library.

Write to a company that sponsors book fairs and request a catalog and information so you can find out about holding a book fair.

• • • • •

STRETCHING
EXERCISE

Using Bibliotherapy

The term *bibliotherapy* comes from *biblion,* which means "book," and *therapeia,* which means "treatment." Bibliotherapy is the practice of using books to promote mental health, solve personal problems, and become aware of societal concerns (Lenhowsky, 1987; Rudman, 1995). The medical profession was the first to recognize the value of bibliotherapy when medical practitioners used it as part of a hospital patient's treatment in the early nineteenth century. Today, bibliotherapy means "everything from literature used in counseling prisoners to sharing a picture book on peer acceptance with a preschooler" (Jalongo, 1983).

Bibliotherapy involves interaction between the personality of the listener or reader and the content of a particular piece of literature. The three interdependent stages of bibliotherapy are identification, catharsis, and insight (Russell & Shrodes, 1950). First, the child senses a common bond with the character or situation described in the book. Second, the child shares the character's feelings surrounding the resolution of the story's conflict. Third, the child gains insight into dealing with or solving his own problems.

Controversy exists over the degree to which a teacher should use a bibliotherapeutic approach in helping a child with a problem. Of course, you should avoid rashly defining a child's problem and then suggesting a particular book. Unless you are trained in psychology or counseling, it is best to limit your role to that of making certain books available for children and reading appropriate books to children as part of your regular reading-aloud program.

Remember, you should be comfortable with the subject and any possible discussion associated with it. Be aware of your knowledge, or lack of it, and learn more if necessary. Whether or not you subscribe to bibliotherapy, don't overlook the potential value of books for sensitizing children to problems and for affirming that they are not alone in their experiences. Children need reassurance and the knowledge that they are not the only ones faced with a problem. The bibliography in Figure 4.12 contains some potentially stressful experiences and examples of books that can help children understand and deal with each problem.

Stressful experiences or issues for children include alcoholism, stepfamilies, self-reliance, absent parents, drugs, disabilities, illnesses, abuse, growing up, and peer acceptance. Choose three of these issues and locate and read at least two books on each. Make cards to add to your card file.

• • • • •

STRETCHING
EXERCISE

FIGURE 4.12 Some books to share with children about difficult issues.

Books about Stressful Experiences

Adoption

Banish, R., & Jordan-Wong, J. A. (1992). *A forever family*. New York: Harper. A girl reflects on her biracial adoption. (Gr. K–3)

Bunting, E. (1993). *Sharing Susan*. New York: Harper. Based on a real story about a baby who goes home from the hospital with the wrong parents. (Gr. 4–7)

Caines, J. (1973). *Abby*. New York: Harper. Adoption in an African American family is explored. (Gr. K–3)

Fowler, S. G. (1993). *When Joel comes home*. New York: Greenwillow. A young girl experiences a new adopted baby. (Gr. K–3)

Rosenberg, M. (1984). *Being adopted*. New York: Lothrop. Explores the feelings and concerns of three children involved in a multiracial adoption. (Gr. 2–6)

Aggression

Caseley, J. (1988). *Silly baby*. New York: Greenwillow. A young girl, unhappy about a new baby, resolves her conflict. (Gr. K–3)

Cole, B. (1987). *The goats*. New York: Farrar. Laura and Howie are outcast and bullied by fellow campers. (Gr. 4–7)

Dragonwagon, C. (1983). *I hate my brother Harry*. New York: Harper. A story about a girl and the caring and rivalry between two siblings. (Gr. K–3)

Viorst, J. (1982). *I'll fix Anthony*. New York: Atheneum. Sibling rivalry between brothers is explored. (Gr. K–3)

Aging

Arkin, A. (1995). *Some fine grandpa!* New York: HarperCollins. A girl and her parents find that grandpa's life was amazing. (Gr. 1–3)

Buckley, H. (1994). *Grandfather and I*. New York: Lothrop. A celebration of the relationship between the oldest and youngest family members. (Gr. K–3)

Bunting, E. (1994). *Sunshine home*. New York: Clarion. A look at how three generations cope with Gram's move to a nursing home. (Gr. 1–3)

Dexter, A. (1992). *Grandma*. New York: Harper. A girl's energetic grandmother defies stereotypes. (Gr. K–3)

Gray, L. (1993). *Miss Tizzy*. New York: Simon & Schuster. An elder, African American woman is a model for children. (Gr. K–3)

Griffith, H. V. (1990). *Georgia music*. New York: Greenwillow. A girl and her grandfather show each other affection. (Gr. K–3)

Say, A. (1995). *Stranger in the mirror*. New York: Houghton Mifflin. A boy ages prematurely in this fantasy that encourages discussion of attitudes and stereotypes (Gr. 1–4)

Death

Adler, C. S. (1993). *Daddy's climbing tree*. A girl acknowledges her father's death with a visit to their previous home. (Gr. 3–6)

Little, J. (1985). *Mama's going to buy you a mockingbird*. New York: Viking. A family adjusts to a father's death from cancer. (Gr. 3–6)

• • • • •

FIGURE 4.12 Continued

121
• • • • •
Getting Started

Maclachlan, P. (1993). *Baby*. New York: Delacourt. A family deals with their newborn's death by caring for a foster toddler. (Gr. 4 and up)

Paterson, K. (1977). *Bridge to Terabithia*. New York: Crowell. Explores a boy and girl's friendship and her death. (Gr. 4–6)

Smith, D. (1973). *A taste of blackberries*. New York: Crowell. A boy deals with a friend's bee sting death. (Gr. 3–6)

Viorst, J. (1971). *The tenth good thing about Barney*. New York: Atheneum. A young boy's cat dies. (Gr. 1–3)

Yolen, J. (1994). *Grandad Bill's song*. New York: Philomel. A boy tries to make sense of his grandfather's death. (Gr. K–3)

Divorce

Mann, P. (1973). *My Dad lives in a downtown hotel*. Garden City, NY: Doubleday. A boy learns he is not to blame for his parents' divorce. (Gr. 3–6)

Park, B. (1989). *My mother got married (And other disasters)*. New York: Knopf. A boy resents his new stepfather and two stepsiblings. (Gr. 2–6)

Pfeffer, S. B. (1993). *Make believe*. New York: Holt. Discusses the roles of friends in helping children understand divorce. (Gr. 2–6)

Rofes, E. (1981). *The kids' book of divorce*. Lexington, MA: Lewis. Twenty children discuss aspects of divorce. (Gr. 3–6)

Vigna, J. (1987). *Mommy and me by ourselves again*. Niles, IL: Whitman. A girl is upset when her mother and boyfriend break up. (Gr. 1–4)

Moving

Aliki (1984). *We are best friends*. New York: Crowell. Two boys learn about friendship when one moves away. (Gr. K–3)

Danziger, P. (1995). *Amber Brown goes forth*. New York: Putnam. A girl's best friend moves away. (Gr. 3–5)

Namioka, L. (1995). *Yang the third and her impossible family*. New York: Little, Brown. An Asian American girl moves to a new school in Seattle. (Gr. 4–6)

Paterson, K. (1996). *Flip-flop girl*. New York: Lodestar. A girl copes with her father's death, moves in with her grandmother, and attends a new school. (Gr. 4–6)

Viorst, J. (1995). *Alexander, who's not (Do you hear me? I mean it!) going to move*. New York: Atheneum. Alexander refuses to move if it means losing his friends. (Gr. K–3)

Unemployment

Alda, A. (1983). *Matthew and his dad*. New York: Simon & Schuster. A family copes with the father's job loss. (Gr. K–3)

Goldwasser, A. (1979). *No job for mom*. New York: McGraw-Hill. Two children learn to adjust to a limited budget. (Gr. 2–6)

Marks, K. D. (1982). *God, why did dad lose his job?* A girl faces a new lifestyle when her father loses his job. (Gr. 4–6)

• • • • •

Many books are appropriate for all ages of children on a variety of potentially stressful experiences. Rudman (1995) and Sutton (1997) provide annotations of quality literature on a range of topics that can help children learn about themselves and how to deal more effectively with the complexities of their lives. Kobrin (1995) provides teaching tips and annotations of over 500 nonfiction books for children that you can integrate with your curriculum. In addition, Professional Resources at the end of this chapter as well as your library media specialist can provide other appropriate resources.

Before suggesting a book for a child to read or making a book available in the classroom library, you should be aware of the intent and content of the book. Since many books deal with sensitive issues, it is always a good idea to be sure the author handles the topic humanely, tastefully, and realistically.

When children hear or read and respond to books that are personally important to them, they have many opportunities for learning. These books encourage effective language use by children who often will not read or respond to other books. Your enjoyment of reading is contagious, so remember to show daily that books are important in your life.

Summary

Quality children's literature from all genres is critical to an integrated language arts program. It is a vehicle for teaching effective communication, since it naturally promotes all aspects of language learning. You can help children select and appreciate literature by knowing their interests and needs and by making appropriate books available. You can model reading behaviors for children, help them monitor and record their progress, and help them enjoy and learn to love reading.

R•••••eflections

1. Diane, the teacher mentioned at the beginning of this chapter, has several R. L. Stine books in her classroom library. Her policy is that children can borrow them but must read them at home. Do you agree with this policy? How else might you handle this dilemma to permit and encourage the reading of quality literature, but not stifle the reading tastes of your students?

2. List your three favorite books and the three most recent books you have read. Is there a genre that appeals to you? Identify a book you want to read and a time during each day to read a chapter. Buy or borrow the book and begin to read it, writing your response in a journal after each chapter.

3. Read "The Line and Texture of Aesthetic Response: Primary Children Study Authors and Illustrators" by Sandra Madura in *The Reading Teacher*, Volume 49, Number 2, pages 110–118. Choose an author or illustrator with a considerable body of work and plan an Author/Illustrator Study for students of a specific age.

Professional Resources

Burke, E. M., & Glazer, S. M. (1994). *Using nonfiction in the classroom.* New York: Scholastic Professional Books. This practical guide discusses reasons for using nonfiction books in the curriculum, guidelines for selection, environments that support nonfiction, and how to use specific titles across the curriculum.

Harris, V. J. (Ed.) (1997). *Using multiethnic literature in the K–8 classroom.* Norwood, MA: Christopher-Gordon. This is a collection of information and ideas for creating, publishing, and using multicultural/multiethnic literature in the classroom, including specific criteria and guidelines for selecting quality, authentic literature.

Mazer, A. (1993). *America street: A multicultural anthology of stories.* New York: Persea. A collection of stories to read aloud, written by well-known adults from diverse backgrounds about incidents from their own childhoods.

Short, K. G. (Ed.) (1995). *Research and professional resources in children's literature: Piecing a patchwork quilt.* Newark, DE: International Reading Association. This book includes annotations of recent research, practical strategies, and resources related to locating and using literature in the classroom.

References in the Children's Section of Most Libraries

Bishop, R. S. (1994). *Kaleidoscope: A multicultural booklist for Grades K–8.* Urbana, IL: NCTE.

Bowker, R. R. (1998). *Children's books in print.* New Providence, NJ: Reed.

Dreyer, S. S. (Ed.) (1992). *Best of bookfinder: A guide to children's literature about interests and concerns of youth.* Circle Pines, MN: American Guidance Service.

Dreyer, S. S. (Ed.) (1990). *The bookfinder* (Vol. 5). Circle Pines, MN: American Guidance Service.

Freeman, E. B., & Goetz, D. (1992). *Using nonfiction tradebooks in the elementary classroom: From ants to zeppelins.* Urbana, IL: NCTE.

Gillespie, J. T., & Naden, C. T. (1994). *Best books for children preschool through grade 6* (5th ed.). New York: Bowker.

Lima, C. W. (Ed.) (1997). *A to zoo: Subject access to children's picture books* (5th ed.). New York: Bowker.

Newbery and Caldecott Awards: A guide to the medal and honor books (1977). Alabama: Association of Library Services to Children's Staffs.

Rasinski, T., & Gillespie, C. S. (1992). *Sensitive issues: An annotated guide to children's literature, K–6.* Phoenix: Oryx.

Samuels, B. G., & Beers, G. K. (1995–96). *An annotated booklist for middle school and junior high.* Urbana, IL: NCTE.

Sutton, W. K. (1997). *Adventuring with books: A booklist for pre K–grade 6* (11th ed.). Urbana, IL: National Council of Teachers of English.

Video and Audio Media

Children's Literature in the Audiovisual Media. Weston Woods. Weston, CT 06883-1199. Tel. (800) 243-5020. A catalog of movies, sound filmstrips, records, bookcassettes, and videocassettes of selected children's literature.

Internet Sources

Gopher. Using the Information Highway, select Gopher from the Internet Resources menu. Then choose Academic Resources by Discipline, then Education, then Children's Literature: Electronic Resources. You will find author information, awards, bibliographies, indexes, and library guides.

Mosaic. Using the Information Highway, select Mosaic from the Internet Resources menu. Then URL http://www.ucalgary.ca/kbrown/index.html#wru tubgs:Children's Literature Web Guide.

Listservs. For discussin on relevant topics, try KIDLIT-L@BINGVMB.CC.BINGHAMTON.EDU and CHILDLIT@RUTVM1.RUTGERS.EDU

References

Atwell, N. (1987). *In the middle: Writing, reading, and learning with adolescents.* Portsmouth, NH: Heinemann.

Bettelheim, B. (1977). *The uses of enchantment: The meaning and importance of fairy tales.* New York: Random House.

Chayet, B. (1994). 20 penny-pinching ways to double your classroom library. *Instructor,* July/August, 51–53.

Council on Interracial Books for Children (1974). *Ten quick way to analyze books for racism and sexism.* Bulletin *5* (3).

Cullinan, B. E. (1994). *Literature and the child.* (3rd ed.). New York: Harcourt Brace Jovanovich.

D'Angelo, K. (1982). Biblio-power: Promoting reading and writing with books. *Reading Psychology, 3* (4), 347–354.

Freeman, E. B., Lehman, B. A., & Scharer, P. L. (1996). Cycles. *The Reading Teacher, 49* (7), 564–572.

Galda, L. (1992). Stories of our past: Books for the social studies. *The Reading Teacher, 47* (4), 330–336.

Galda, L., & MacGregor, P. (1992). Nature's wonders: Books for a science curriculum. *The Reading Teacher, 46* (3), 236–240.

Gibson, E., & Levin, H. (1975). *The psychology of reading.* Cambridge, MA: MIT Press.

Harwayne, S. (1992). *Lasting impressions: Weaving literature into the writing workshop.* Portsmouth, NH: Heinemann.

Holdaway, D. (1983). Quoted in *What's a good book?* Weston, CT: Weston Woods.

Holdaway, D. (1979). *The foundations of literacy.* New York: Ashton Scholastic.

Huck, C. S., Hepler, S., Hickman, J., & Kiefer, B. Z. (1997). *Children's literature in the elementary school* (6th ed.). Madison, WI: Brown & Benchmark.

Jacobs, J. S., & Tunnell, M. O. (1996). *Children's literature, briefly.* Englewood Cliffs, NJ: Merrill.

Jalongo, M. (1983). Bibliotherapy: Literature to promote socioemotional growth. *The Reading Teacher, 36* (8), 796–803.

Kiefer, B. (1995). *The potential of picturebooks:From visual literacy to aesthetic understanding.* Englewood Cliffs, NJ: Merrill.

Kobrin, B. (1995). *Eyeopeners II: Children's books to answer children's questions about the world around them.* New York: Viking.

Lenhowsky, R. (1987). Bibliotherapy: A review and analysis of the literature. *Journal of Special Education, 21,* 123–132.

Lukens, R. J. (1995). *A critical handbook of children's literature* (5th ed.). Glenview, IL: Scott, Foresman.

McCarty, T. L. (1995). What's wrong with *Ten little rabbits? The New Advocate, 8* (2), 97–98.

Norton, D. E. (1995). *Through the eyes of a child* (4th ed.). Englewood Cliffs, NJ: Prentice Hall.

Norton, D. E. (1993). Circa 1492 and the integration of literature, reading and geography. *The Reading Teacher, 47* (7), 610–615.

Norton, D. E. (1991). Teaching multicultural literature in the reading curriculum. *The Reading Teacher, 44* (1), 28–39.

Pierce, K. M., & Short, K. G. (1995). Journeying through books: A potpourri. *The Reading Teacher, 48* (8), 708–715.

Pierce, K. M., & Short, K .G. (1994). Contemporary social and political issues. *The Reading Teacher, 47* (8), 148–157.

Rudman, M. K. (1995). *Children's literature—An issues approach* (3rd ed.). New York: Longman.

Russell, D., & Shrodes, C. (1950). Contributions of research in bibliotherapy to the language arts program. *School Review, 58,* 335–342.

Short, K. G. (1993). Visual literacy: Exploring art and illustration in children's books. *The Reading Teacher, 46* (6), 506–516.

Stoll, D. R. (1997). *Magazines for kids and teens* (rev. ed.). Newark, DE: International Reading Association.

Sutherland, Z. (1997). *Children and books* (9th ed.). New York: Longman.

Sutton, W. K. (1997) *Adventuring with books: A booklist for pre K–grade 6* (11th ed.). Urbana, IL: National Council of Teachers of English.

Temple, C., Martinez, M., Yokota, J., & Naylor, A. (1998). *Children's books in children's hands: An introduction to their literature.* Boston: Allyn and Bacon.

West, D. (1995). The horror of R. L. Stine. *American Educator, 19* (3), 39–41.

What's a good book? (1983). Weston, CT: Weston Woods.

Whitin, D. J., & Wilde, S. (1995). *It's the story that counts: More children's books for mathematical learning.* Portsmouth, NH: Heinemann.

Wilson, P. J., & Abrahamson, R. F. (1988). What children's literature classes do children really enjoy? *The Reading Teacher, 41*, 406–411.

Zimet, S. G. (1976). *Print and prejudice*. London: Hodder & Stoughton.

Children's Book References

Aardema, V. (1975). *Why mosquitoes buzz in people's ears*. New York: Dial.

Ahlberg, J. (1986). *The jolly postman and other people's letters*. Boston: Little, Brown.

Baylor, B. (1978). *The other way to listen*. New York: Scribner.

Bishop, C. H. (1938). *The five Chinese brothers*. New York: Coward.

Blos, J. (1979). *A gathering of days*. New York: Scribner.

Boyington, P. (1989). *Baa, baa, black sheep*. Blue Ridge, PA: TAB.

Brett, J. (1994). *Town mouse country mouse*. New York: Putnam.

Bunting, E. (1994). *Smoky night*. San Diego: Harcourt.

Burns, D., & Burns, A. (1995). *Home on the range: Ranch-style riddles*. New York: Lerner.

Cannon, J. (1993). *Stellaluna*. San Diego: Harcourt.

Carle, E. (1990). *The very quiet cricket*. New York: Philomel.

Cole, J. (1995). *The magic schoolbus inside a hurricane*. New York: Scholastic.

Colman, H. (1978). *Tell me no lies*. New York: Crown.

Creech, S. (1994). *Walk two moons*. New York: HarperCollins.

de Regniers, B. S. (Ed.) (1988). *Sing a song of popcorn: Every child's book of poems*. New York: Scholastic.

Emberley, B. (1986). *Drummer Hoff*. Englewood Cliffs, NJ: Prentice Hall.

Fleischman, P. (1988). *Joyful noise: Poems for two voices*. New York: Harper and Row.

Freedman, R. (1988). *Lincoln: A photobiography*. New York: Clarion.

Fritz, J. (1981). *Where do you think you're going, Christopher Columbus?* New York: Coward-McCann.

Frost, R. (1988). *Birches*. New York: Holt.

Grossman, V., & Long, S. (1991). *Ten little rabbits*. New York: Chronicle.

Howard, E. F. (1991). *Aunt Flossie's hats (and crab cakes later)*. New York: Clarion.

Hughes, L. (1994). *The dream keeper and other poems*. New York: Knopf.

Keats, E. J. (1962). *The snowy day*. New York: Viking.

Larrick, N. (1991). *To the moon and back*. New York: Delacourte.

L'Engle, M. (1962). *A wrinkle in time*. New York: Farrar.

Lester, J. (1994). *John Henry*. New York: Dial.

Lewis, C. S. (1950). *The lion, the witch, and the wardrobe*. New York: Macmillan.

Lobel, A. (1980). *Fables*. New York: Harper and Row.

London, J. (1996). *I see the moon and the moon sees me*. New York: Viking.

Lowery, L. (1995). *Twist with a burger, jitter with a bug*. New York: Houghton Mifflin.

Lowry, L. (1992). *Number the stars*. Boston: Houghton Mifflin.

Lowry, L. (1993). *The giver*. Boston: Houghton Mifflin.

Macaulay, D. (1993). *Ship*. Boston: Houghton Mifflin.

Mahy, M. (1990). *The seven Chinese brothers*. New York: Chronicle.

Martin, A. M. (1984). *Stage fright*. New York: Holiday House.

Marzollo, J. (1996). *My first book of biographies: Great men and women every child should know*. New York: Scholastic.

Mayer, M. (1974). *Frog goes to dinner*. New York: Dial.

Norton, M. (1953). *The borrowers*. New York: Harcourt.

Parish, P. (1995). *Come back, Amelia Bedelia*. New York: Houghton Mifflin.

Paterson, K. (1989). *Park's quest*. New York: Dutton.

Paterson, K. (1977). *Bridge to Terabithia*. New York: Crowell.

Pinkney, A. D. (1994). *Dear Benjamin Banneker*. San Diego: Harcourt.

Polacco, P. (1996). *Aunt Chip and the great Triple Creek Dam affair*. New York: Putnam.

Prelutsky, J. (1991). *For laughing out loud: Poems to tickle your funny bone*. New York: Knopf.

Ringgold, F. (1991). *Tar beach*. New York: Crown.

Rosenberg, L. (1993). *Monster mama*. New York: Philomel.

Sendak, M. (1963). *Where the wild things are.* New York: Harper.

Siebert, D. (1989). *Heartland.* New York: Crowell.

Silverstein, S. (1996). *Falling up.* New York: Harper.

Simon, S. (1992). *Snakes.* New York: HarperCollins.

Spier, P. (1977). *Noah's ark.* New York: Doubleday.

Tompert, A. (1993). *Bamboo hats and rice cakes.* New York: Crown.

Van Allsburg, C. (1981). *Jumanji.* Boston: Houghton Mifflin.

Ward, A. (1980). *Baby bear and the long sleep.* Boston: Little, Brown.

Weeks, S. (1994). *Crocodile smile.* New York: HarperCollins.

White, E. B. (1952). *Charlotte's web.* New York: Harper and Row.

Whitman, W. (1991). *I hear America singing.* New York: Philomel.

Wiesner, D. (1987). *Tuesday.* New York: Lothrop.

Wilder, L. I. (1953). *Little house in the big woods.* New York: Harper.

Yolen, J. (Ed.) (1992). *Street rhymes around the world.* Honesdale, PA: Wordsong.

Sharing and Responding to Literature

5

Window on Teaching

indow on Teaching

Josh: Look! It's the same praying mantis as in *The Very Quiet Cricket*. (while looking at *The Grouchy Ladybug*)

Tasha: Can I read *Draw Me a Star* to the class. Please?

Megan: Oh look at the designs at the beginning of this book! (*A House for Hermit Crab*)

Tasha: Look! They're at the back, too!

Chris: The designs are the same at the front and end of this book, too. (*The Honey Bear and the Cricket*)

Chris: He uses tissue paper and lots of colors.

Skye:	He does designs and in *The Greedy Python* he didn't learn a lesson.
Tasha:	There's a sun and moon in every story.
David:	Eric Carle uses lots of numbers and months in his stories.
Megan:	He uses the same animals in all his books.
Marcus:	This is still a good book even though it isn't in color. (*Now One Foot, Now the Other*)
Chris:	I think Tom is the same in *The Art Lesson, Nana Upstairs,* and *Now One Foot.*
Tasha:	*Clown of God* looks like *Strega Nona.*
Josh:	People die in *Clown of God* like they do in *Nana Upstairs.*
Skye:	Oh look at the heart! It's here and here and on a lot of pages.
Josh:	Yeah, and look at them here in *Strega Nona.* Tomie dePaola likes to use hearts in his pictures.
Marcus:	And they're in this book everywhere, too.
David:	Let's find them all!
Sherry:	He probably uses markers, crayons, and watercolors maybe. The watercolors remind me of tissue-paper colors.
Josh:	The characters are the same in *Strega Nona* and in *Big Anthony and the Magic Ring.*

This dialogue among students took place in Julie Van Atta's first-grade classroom. Julie's anecdotal records show how immersion in an author/illustrator study helped her first-graders develop visual literacy. She says:

My goal for the project was to develop visual and verbal awareness that leads to aesthetic response and expression through the use of visual arts. I wanted the children to become familiar with an author/illustrator's style and be able to identify particular qualities of that style in several examples of his or her work.

Julie and her class chose Eric Carle and Tomie dePaola and spent three weeks on each. Julie says:

I gathered as many copies as I could find of their books. For the first three weeks, we focused on Carle, and the second three weeks, dePaola. I displayed the books on a special table and the class spent one week just reading and discussing the stories. Then, the second week, we returned to the books to examine and discuss the artistic style and the repeated themes and patterns used in the artwork and writing. The third week, we immersed ourselves in the artwork, using the medium the illustrator used.

For Carle, we fingerpainted many sheets of paper in the primary colors. Then, once they dried, I cut them into various sizes with a paper cutter. The next day, each table had a big supply of fingerpaint scraps, scissors, glue, pencils, and crayons. They could create anything they wanted. Most of the children chose to imitate one of Carle's books.

For Tomie dePaola, I gave the children a basic lesson on using watercolors. I showed them the different ways to achieve a look using tissue paper to blot and putting water on before the color to keep the color from spreading. They practiced and then each child did a final project with many imitating dePaola's style.

Julie was pleased with the results. She continues:

Providing my class with exposure to the books for two weeks prior to the art experience enabled them to be comfortable with Eric Carle and Tomie dePaola. The children noticed many themes and patterns in the artwork that I had not picked up on. Once it came time for the art lesson, these two people were part of our classroom lives.

Using the fingerpaint scraps for collage was a visually effective way for the children to appreciate Eric Carle because their pictures came out looking like his. The watercolors we used for the dePaola pictures didn't look like Tomie's pictures, but that was not my goal. Watercolors are a more difficult and less forgiving medium. My first-graders have had minimal experience with them, but they told me they liked them better than their Eric Carle artwork. So, that tells me to give them the opportunity to make their own decisions about what they want to work with.

I learned the importance of repeated readings and discussion. The children began to recognize aspects of an illustrator's style and use the appropriate vocabulary to talk about it. In a way, they became little art critics. Using the artistic medium of a particuar artist lends itself to further discovery and findings that help to enrich the entire reading process. My class is asking me when the next author/illustrator is coming and they are giving me suggestions!

O••••• verview

This chapter addresses ways to share children's literature as you develop receptive and expressive language. By choosing quality literature that you like, effectively sharing it with children and promoting a variety of responses, you build appreciation and enjoyment of literature. Additionally, you develop children's use of effective language and enrich your curriculum.

As children hear or read a story, they have some comprehension of it. As they retell, talk, or write about it, they construct ideas about the story. As children examine, reread or listen to something again, their understanding can deepen, and what they say and write will possibly be different, more complete, and insightful. As children talk about what they have read and listen to others talk, they co-construct new meanings. Through the shared meaning construction that occurs during social interactions, understandings are clarified, change, or grow.

While 8-year-old Aaron listens to *Charlotte's Web*, he grimaces at some of Templeton's nasty comments, sits in quiet wonderment as Wilbur reads the messages in the spider web, cries when Charlotte dies, and says, "Charlotte was a friend to Wilbur" at the end of the story. Aaron responds with understanding and emotion. Some of his responses are obvious and overt; others are not visible. Aaron can talk about the book, identify with the farm setting, love Wilbur's bright personality, or retell a sequence of events to a peer. He can draw a picture and write a story of his own that contains similar characters or plot. He can role-play and dramatize a favorite scene. Each of these responses develops and extends Aaron's ability to think and his competence in listening, speaking, reading, and writing.

The Nature of Response

Research and theory have shown that response to literature grows from the personal interactions we have with print and that interactions are different for everyone (Purves, Rogers, & Soter, 1990; Rosenblatt, 1995). Both children and adults bring different experiences, values, beliefs, and knowledge to print. As we read, we make different meanings when we interact with print at different times and even in different places. Rosenblatt (1995) suggests that there are two predominant ways of responding to literature. She believes that the reader's attitude of mind includes both cognitive and affective elements. If your purpose in reading is to acquire and remember information, you read from an *efferent* (from the Latin for "carry away") stance. If you pay attention to what you are thinking, feeling, and experiencing as you read, then you have adopted an *aesthetic* stance toward print.

Rosenblatt (1995) thinks of these two transactions with print as occurring on a continuum. In every reading there is a "mix" of both types of responses—sometimes from a predominantly efferent stance and sometimes from a more aesthetic stance. For example, you might read *All the Places to Love* by Patricia MacLachlan (1994), and from an aesthetic stance, relate strongly to the beauty, comfort, and serenity of nature. But you also may read it from an efferent stance, in that you recognize the places visited in the story (e.g., plowed fields, river, blueberry barren, barn, and marsh). Both the text and your predetermined purpose for reading help determine how you read a book.

But what about reading nonfiction and textbooks? How does this theory of response fit in integrated content area learning? Spink (1996) says that an aesthetic response is not limited to fiction. He encourages an emotional and intellectual response toward all literature, nonfiction as well as fiction. He describes his sixth-graders as able to experience informational reading about sea life, both aesthetically and efferently, as they had emotional involvements in their factual research.

Like adults, children identify with, feel, and remember differently. For children, too, both text and purpose for reading affect the transaction with print. Each child brings her own special background and experiences to literature and has a different literary transaction and response to a story or poem (see Figure 5.1). Rapt attention, a question, an observation, a comment, an opinion, a recalled memory, or a demand to hear a story or poem again are all evidence of response to literature. As children talk, draw, write, dramatize, dance, or retell a story or poem, it can be recaptured, relived, and then discussed and analyzed.

Included on the continuum of response to literature are the interpretive, critical, and evaluative responses. These stances toward print require the reader to examine, analyze, infer, and evaluate both what and how the author says things and helps the reader make meaning. You can help your children engage in these forms of response by drawing their attention to themes and issues, character development, relationships, cause/effect patterns, the effect of setting on mood and message, use of stylistic devices, similarity in themes across books, and so on.

FIGURE 5.1 Turn this page upside down to see the princess become someone else when examined from a different perspective.

•••••

Rosenblatt (1991) warns us not to use literature simply for the efferent purpose of teaching information. For example, she says when American history is studied, a novel about colonial life is valuable, but primarily it is seen as an aesthetic experience—a sharing of what it would have been like to live in those days—rather than a way to teach incidental information. She says only *after* a book is read and an aesthetic response is elicited, is it appropriate or effective to examine the story critically for information and understanding. Zarillo (1991) believes that rather than reduce literature to a teaching tool, we should use it to elevate the role of the reader, celebrate the joy of reading, and realize the full potential of literature in the lives of our students.

How do Rosenblatt's ideas work for you? Choose a picture book, read it, and then analyze your response and interpretation of the story. In what ways do an efferent and asethetic stance inform your response?

•••••

**STRETCHING
EXERCISE**

Mikkelsen (1984) reports that what mattered to a group of children about Maurice Sendak's (1981) *Outside Over There* was related to their place in the family as older or younger siblings and their feelings and needs. Older siblings variously believed the story was about a stolen horn, flying, another planet, and the responsibility of saving someone. Two younger siblings thought it was about seeing goblins and a kidnapped baby.

Although many children respond to literature in immediate and observable ways, some responses are difficult or impossible to gauge or are not evident at all because children have trouble articulating them. In interviews with children who read a book that gave them a special feeling for a long time afterward, Cramer (1984) reports that the magic of special books is sometimes hard to express and difficult to relate to others, but it was definitely there for each child. So keep in mind that you may not be aware of every response a child has to literature.

Roles of Peers and Teacher

A child's response to literature will be essentially an individual and personal one, but there are other factors—namely, the child's environment and the people in it, that influence her reading and her responses. Children inspire each other's reading and responding, as does the teacher. Not only do children influence book choices by recommending good books to each other but they also model responses for each other. They spontaneously share good parts and appealing passages of their books with each other, talk about their reactions to books, draw pictures, make puppet plays, design game boards, and otherwise rethink and represent stories in different ways for each other. In short, children in a class form a community of readers and show each other how to act like readers who respond personally to the books they read.

You play a critical role in developing your students' responses to literature (Hickman, 1995). The teacher who reads, enjoys the experience, and shares it with children is a model for children to imitate. She models how a reader acts by telling the students about the books she is reading and showing this literature to them. She suggests special books for specific students. She regularly reads aloud to children and reads children's

•••••
Children inspire each other's reading and responding, as does the teacher.

books independently, as well. She asks children for their opinions of certain characters or authors and tells children why a certain book is a favorite. She arranges time in the daily schedule for reading, provides a variety of materials within the classroom environment, and invites children to read orally and share their responses. She provides comfortable and inviting places where children can browse, read, or gather to hear readings. She acts as a discussion leader and skillfully guides talk about a book or character to help children arrive at new meanings. She values the children's perspectives.

Your role is also one of encouraging diverse responses to a wide variety of literature. As a teacher, you can help students respond in many ways—role-playing, improvisational drama, storytelling, audio- and videotaping, choral speaking, art activities, and flannel-board retellings are but a few. Also, students can respond by performing skits and plays, making dioramas, keeping journals, and writing reviews and creative stories. In all of these ways, you foster children's responses to literature.

Integrating the Curriculum

Response to literature should be interwoven throughout the curriculum. You can use literature to enhance the language arts program and integrate it into science, social studies, and math, as well. Additionally, you can give your students opportunities to respond to literature as a separate part of the curriculum or as part of the school library program.

Science and social studies typically use information books, but books from other genres are also appropriate. For example, studying a topic such as the Revolutionary War is more interesting when it is supplemented with historical fiction or biography. Ann McGovern's (1979) biography *The Secret Soldier: The Story of Deborah Sampson*, the story of the only woman to serve in the Revolutionary War, for instance, makes historical facts about the war come alive. Chris Van Allsburg's (1990) *Just a Dream* similarly enlivens a unit on Protecting Our Natural Resources/Environment. The addition of science fiction, such as Madeleine L'Engle's (1978) *A Swiftly Tilting Planet,* and biographies of people like Robert Oppenhiemer, who made space exploration possible, enliven a study of the solar system. Poetry such as *Navajo: Vision and Voices across the Mesa* by Shonto Begay (1995) supports a unit on the Southwest and Navajos. Biographies of mathematicians and contemporary realistic fiction about characters who use math in their everyday lives add interest to the study of math. Magazines such as *3-2-1 Contact: A Science Magazine, Ranger Rick, National Geographic World*, and others provide excellent pictures and information to supplement many units of study for various age levels.

Sharing Literature

One of the most common ways to use literature in the classroom and to promote comprehension through listening is to read to children and involve them in shared reading. Storytelling is another natural way to foster children's comprehension through listening. Additionally, booktalks allow you to introduce books to students in ways that entice them to read and "hook" them on various books and authors.

Reading Aloud

No matter what age level or grade you teach, you should establish a fixed time each day for reading to your class. Sharing stories orally with middle-grade students is just as important as it is with young children. You can read first thing in the morning to set the tone for the day, before or after lunch, or at the end of the day for a pleasant finale. You can also read during transition times during the day. For example, when children line up to leave for lunch, a short poem or two may fit perfectly into the available time. Another suggestion is to read to your class when you are frazzled and you know your children also need a relaxing break.

Story reading is especially important for English learners. It helps them acquire English and guides them toward reading books in this language. English learners benefit from listening frequently to stories in small groups because it gives them the opportunity to interact with each other, with children who speak English, and with you. This also gives them an opportunity to see pictures and print together. Hough, Nurss, and Enright (1986) suggest using well-illustrated and predictable books, rereading favorite stories, and asking children questions appropriate to their language-acquisition levels as you engage them in discussion. English-speaking children benefit from these methods, as well.

Don't overlook the chance to introduce children to genres they might not normally choose to read themselves during your regular reading-aloud times. When you read historical fiction or biography, for instance, you expose children to books from a genre they might usually pass up. Just as children learn to appreciate and value literature from you, they can also learn to appreciate and value the kinds of books you do.

Reading aloud to children has many benefits. Perhaps most important, you provide a model of good reading for your students to imitate. Some helpful hints for sharing books with students of all ages appear in Figure 5.2. Besides being pleasurable, enjoyable, soothing, and energizing, reading aloud promotes the following:

- Builds general knowledge
- Expands vocabulary
- Develops concepts of print
- Reveals different language patterns
- Reveals different writing styles
- Encourages visual imagery
- Boosts comprehension
- Extends knowledge of literary elements
- Broadens genre knowledge
- Improves listening skills
- Fosters curiosity and imagination
- Promotes motivation to read and learn
- Builds ease with the English language
- Inspires writing
- Increases achievement

Research evidence is strongly in favor of reading aloud to children. It has been cited as the single-most important activity for building the knowledge required for later literacy (Anderson, Hiebert, Scott, & Wilkinson, 1985). In a longitudinal study, story-

FIGURE 5.2 Hints for sharing books with students of all ages.

135
• • • • •
*Sharing and
Responding*

Before Reading
- Show the cover of the book to the children. Ask them to predict what the book will be about.
- Introduce the author and illustrator. Point out their credentials, experiences, or other titles by them.
- Connect the children's experiences to those in the book.
- Discuss the genre of literature to be read (folktale, fantasy, realistic fiction, etc.).
- Introduce the main characters and setting.
- Help the children set a purpose for listening or reading.

During Reading
- Encourage reactions and comments as the children listen.
- Show pictures and ask the children to analyze them.
- Explain the text when necessary to help the children understand the written language and the literary elements.
- Pose questions occasionally to monitor the children's comprehension.
- Have the children rephrase the text when they do not understand the ideas.
- Reread parts of the story that may be unclear.
- At appropriate points, have the children predict what might happen next.
- Prompt the children to interpret the story.

After Reading
- Review the literary elements (characters, setting, problem, etc.).
- Help the children connect the main character to themselves.
- Point out distinctive style, use of setting, character growth, and so on that makes the story special.
- Have the children take turns retelling the story in their own words.
- Help the children identify a variety of themes in the story.
- Draw a picture or graphic representation of the story.
- Help the children connect this story to others that are similar in theme, setting, and so forth.
- Engage the children in a follow-up activity that involves thinking about the story.

• • • • •

Source: Adapted from "Reading to Kindergarten Children" by Jana M. Mason et al., in Strickland and Morrow (eds.), *Emerging Literacy,* 1989, Newark, DE: International Reading Association.

book reading by parents to their young children before beginning school was the most significant factor leading to the children's later success in school (Wells, 1986). It seems common sense, then, that teachers at all grade levels should set aside time for reading aloud.

In a survey of 537 teachers of kindergartners through sixth-graders, the most frequently occurring read-aloud practices showed a teacher who reads for 10 to 20 minutes a day from a tradebook that is not connected to a unit of study and spends less than 5 minutes in discussion, including talk before and after the reading (Hoffman, Roser, & Battle, 1993). This is a troubling picture in light of what is known about the benefits of reading aloud. These researchers also looked at model read-aloud programs and make the following suggestions to teachers:

- Set aside a special time and place for a daily read-aloud.
- Select quality literature.
- Share literature related to other literature.
- Discuss literature in lively, invitational, thought-provoking ways.
- Group children in ways that maximize their responses.
- Offer a variety of opportunities for response and extension.
- Reread selected pieces.

**STRETCHING
EXERCISE**

Read Barbara Moss's 1995 article, "Using Nonfiction Tradebooks as Read-Alouds" in *Language Arts*, Volume 72, Number 2, pages 122–127. How do nonfiction read-alouds have, in Moss's words, "the ever-widening effect of a pebble thrown into a pond"?

• • • • •

Tips for Read-Alouds.   During your daily read-aloud, you can do several things to promote your students' enjoyment, appreciation, and learning:

1. *Choose well-written literature you enjoy.* When you relish a story or poem, you communicate your enjoyment of it to the children you read to. When you select literature you enjoy, your oral reading is also probably fueled by genuine feeling, smoother, and more animated than when you read a story you do not especially like. Sharing your enthusiasm and love of literature through good oral reading also provides a role model for children to emulate.

Be sure to seek new stories and poems so that your repertoire grows and is current. Share new books along with your old favorites and read a range of selections from every genre. A blend of old and new titles representing all types of literature is a treat for both you and your children.

Talk with your library media specialist when you need books on special topics. References such as the following also yield titles and descriptions of good books and poems to read aloud:

The Read-Aloud Handbook (4th ed.) by J. Trelease (New York: Penguin, 1995).

The Latest and Greatest Read-Alouds by S. L. McElmeel (Englewood, CO: Libraries Unlimited, 1994).

A Jar of Tiny Stars: Poems by NCTE Award-Winning Poets by B. Cullinan (Ed.) (Urbana, IL: NCTE, 1996).

2. *Read the story or the poem before presenting it to the children.* By becoming familiar with the story and language before sharing it with children, you avoid surprise or embarrassment over a concept or word that is offensive. If you are uncomfortable with language or ideas in a book, either omit those particular sections or do not read the book at all. If you can justify using questionable material, then inquire about your school's policy on censorship and obtain parental permission before sharing the material.

3. *Practice orally.* Especially if oral reading is new for you, practice before reading to a group is a must. Using inappropriate phrasing or stumbling over words creates po-

tential comprehension problems for the children and also dampens their interest. Fluent reading is not only more comfortable to hear but it also demonstrates a model of good oral reading for children. Practice in front of a mirror to discover how to use your eyes, voice, and facial expressions effectively. To create mood, heighten suspense, and generally read with better expression, you should vary your intonation, juncture, stress, and pacing.

Familiarity with a story ensures its enjoyment by all. Orally reading a book or story first helps you determine an author's style and tone, make mental note of how to interpret various characters, and identify critical points in the story so you know where to stop and start for best effect. As you gain experience and confidence in reading orally, you may find that skimming or previewing suffices. An exception to this is poetry, which you should *always* practice beforehand since it is written for the ear and the mind.

4. *Be sure the children can see and hear you.* Position yourself front and center so that the children face you or can comfortably turn to see and hear you. Stand or sit on a chair or desk so you are comfortable and can enjoy the reading. When you read to a small group, sit on a low chair and hold the book close to or at the children's eye level. Minimize distractions so that every child enjoys and appreciates what you read.

5. *Share the story pictures.* If you read a picture book, master the art of reading from the side so that children can see pictures at all times, or read the text first and then show the pictures. You can also show the pictures first to prepare for the text and show no pictures while you read. Then let the children look at the pictures later as they reread the book. A combination of methods can also be used. Since so much of a picture book's appeal is the pictures, sit or stand close to children so they can see the illustrations. Even older children enjoy seeing the few illustrations in books written for them. Walk the book around the room for everyone to see these smaller drawings, since this additional visual input enriches and broadens responses. Remember, though, audience and story determine how best to share text and pictures.

6. *Watch for the children's responses.* Be attuned to the audience as you read orally to them, watching for signs that the children are involved or do not understand. Look for spontaneous responses such as a smile, grimace, rapt attention, or other changes in facial expression that coincide with the characters' actions, story mood, or plot. These responses signal emotional involvement with the story and are the basis for interpreting and evaluating literature. Accept, encourage, and extend these observed responses with questions and discussion when the situation is right. An observed response or remark a child makes, such as a comment about a setting that sounds like her grandmother's house or a value judgment about how one should act in the real world compared to a character's actions, often triggers discussion. The responses you note and extend are often critical to developing deeper responses.

7. *Review the story.* Both during and following the reading, be sure to allow time for discussion to encourage children's responses to what they have heard and to extend comprehension. Ask questions and invite the children to ask and answer each other's questions. Time for discussion and talk allows children to share their interpretations, analyze the story, and construct story meanings together. Discussion can help clarify concepts, vocabulary, and issues your students are not familiar with or do not understand.

After you read a book, most children enjoy rereading it, even though they have just heard it. Let them examine pictures closely. Working with some books in depth and reading the same story aloud on several occasions broadens and deepens student response. Just as adults reread favorite poems or novels, so do children enjoy hearing stories read to them more than once. Deeper insights into characters and events develop when children are already familiar with plot structure. Also, elements of style are sometimes not evident or appreciated until the second or third reading.

Give children opportunities to retell the story. By paraphrasing and putting it into their own words, they will remember it better. Also, make the book available by including it in a display with other books by the same author and illustrator or other books on the same topic.

If children are not listening or are disruptive while you read, ask yourself some questions: Do you like the story? Is it well written, interesting, and fast paced enough to maintain attention? Can children understand it? Were you familiar with the story before you read it? Did you practice it? Is your voice well modulated and do you use appropriate facial expressions? Are conditions in the classroom conducive to listening? It may help to talk with children about how to listen effectively, or place disruptive children close to you.

Shared Reading

Shared reading is a social activity in which children share with other readers or listeners in the reading of meaningful, predictable texts (Holdaway, 1979; Short, Harste, & Burke, 1995; Slaughter, 1993). It is based on the belief that children learn to read by reading, and that reading is learned in much the same way as speech is learned. Reading and rereading familiar and predictable stories with others provides successful and enjoyable experiences with books. Repetition helps children learn vocabulary, rhythm and pattern, story structure, and concepts in stories. As children actively participate in rereading stories, they can attend to different aspects of the story and thus develop confidence in their knowledge of the story and of themselves as readers.

•••••
Reading and rereading familiar and predictable stories with others provides positive experiences with books.

Typically, shared reading is done with a "big book"—an enlarged version of a storybook—so that everyone can see and read it. Shared reading is helpful for all readers, but particularly for emergent readers, less fluent readers, and those learning English as a second language, because it shows them *how* to read. These children need a supportive, nonthreatening atmosphere so that they can take risks and make predictions based on meaning and structure, not exact word-for-word decoding. Klesius and Griffith (1996) describe a form of shared reading called *interactive storybook reading* for children who begin school with limited reading experiences. Interactive reading is done in small groups and with small books and is focused on meaning and conversational dialogue, as opposed to shared reading, which is often done in a larger group with a big book and is focused on literacy. Both shared reading and interactive storybook reading, however, allow you to demonstrate literacy for your students and to act as a model.

In a shared reading experience, children participate in the reading of a book. Morrow (1997) explains that shared-book experiences should be relaxed, cooperative, and enjoyable read-aloud events. Predictable books or "big books" (oversized books that can sit on an easel or chalkboard ledge and are designed so that everyone in a group can see the pictures and words) are often used in shared-book experiences. Big books are available from many publishers or can be made by a class or the teacher. The teacher usually reads a story first. Then, during repeated readings, or when the story is familiar to children, the teacher stops at predictable parts in the story and asks children to participate. The students are encouraged to add sound effects, fill in words and phrases, supply repetitive lines, dramatize a story, or take part in other types of story-extension activities.

Choose a book you love and read it with a child, using the ideas for shared-book reading in Figure 5.2. Note the child's reactions, verbal comments, body language, attention span, involvement, and so on. What techniques did you use before, during, and after reading to keep the child involved?

• • • • •

**STRETCHING
EXERCISE**

Poetry makes good material for shared readings because of its predictable nature. The rhyme and rhythm of most poems, as well as their length, which is shorter than most stories, make them good vehicles for shared readings. Wicklund (1989) suggests that shared poetry reading can be highly motivating for remedial readers. She also provides ideas for extending the shared reading to shared writing of poetry.

Storytelling

Some teachers who enjoy reading and read often to children are afraid of storytelling. Contrary to popular belief, however, one does not need to possess special skills to be storyteller. If you stop to think about it, you practice storytelling every day when you tell someone about something you have seen or done. Storytelling is just retelling a story, whether an actual event or a tale once told by someone else.

Storytelling provides a different forum for sharing literature than does reading aloud. When telling a story, you can use your hands and body in ways that are not possible if you are holding a book. Storytellers can also use drama and props to add interest and power to a story and, unlike story readers, can hold the audience's attention with uninterrupted eye contact. Storytellers make print come alive for children by removing print from the interacation that occurs between story readers and stories. For these reasons, telling stories has a special place in the sharing of literature as an alluring avenue to explore with your students.

Storytelling shares many of the same benefits of reading aloud. Perhaps most important among these is that storytelling stimulates the imagination, instills a love of language, improves listening skills, inspires writing, develops vocabulary, promotes comprehension, and motivates reading. Looking back at the list of reading-aloud benefits reveals that there is only one benefit—builds concepts of print—that is not a direct result of storytelling.

When you give your students opportunities to retell stories they have heard or to search for their own stories to tell, the benefits of storytelling are accentuated (Hamilton & Weiss, 1990). Children who tell stories reap many rewards, among which are the following:

- Self-esteem improves.
- Confidence and poise in speaking to a group increase.
- Inventive thinking and improvisation occur.
- Expressive language skills improve.
- Class cooperation increases.
- Learning, in general, improves.

When children tell folktales and fairy tales, the easiest kind of stories to tell, they learn about the world and build an appreciation of other cultures. They develop literary knowledge and a frame of reference for their own moral and ethical development.

You will learn a great deal about your students from listening to them tell and retell stories. Their storytelling will give you insights into their personalities, language development, thinking, creativity, learning styles, and interpersonal relationships, both inside and outside school. When shy or usually quiet children tell stories or use props and puppets in their storytelling, they can become characters and temporarily step into other personalities. Many teachers see children bloom through storytelling and discover their students' otherwise hidden qualities.

Many teachers find that telling a story from the pictures in a book helps them feel more comfortable as a storyteller. For example, a prekindergarten teacher strongly believed in daily read-aloud periods and began to read to her class on the first day of school in September. But she found that the children were not ready, interested, or able to sit still and listen to even the simplest of books. So she began by telling the story in her own words and using the illustrations to support her storytelling. She found that this method was successful and used it to prepare the children for listening to formal read-aloud sessions.

Traditionally, storytelling has been the privilege of professionals and some brave teachers, but the story-creating process is a meaning-making strategy in which children should also be involved. Family and classroom storytelling is less intimidating than the more theatrical variety (Cooper & Collins, 1992). Indeed, Buchoff (1995) explains that the telling of family stories encourages students to learn more about their heritage, to acquire and refine literacy skills, and to develop greater repect for the multicultural differences that make them unique.

When children tell personal anecdotes, share recollections, and make up creative stories, they verbalize personal experiences, communicate feelings, and construct meaning. Storytelling is also a way of enhancing mathematics learning. Since some stories allow students to see aspects of math that are not part of the curriculum, they help children take a more creative and critical role in learning mathematics (Borasi, Sheedy, & Siegel, 1990). In social studies, hearing and sharing personal stories allows students a familiar context for exploring social studies issues such as democratic ideals, cultural diversity, economic development, and global perspectives (Combs & Beach, 1994). In science, storytelling can bring scientific knowledge to life for children, and it can prompt observation, which is a basic scientific tool (Martin & Miller, 1988).

Interactive storytelling is a strategy some teachers use to invite children to participate in storytelling (Trousdale, 1990). You can encourage children to supply sound effects or dialogue, and, as they become more confident, to take turns with you in telling the story. This strategy will help children feel comfortable enough in storytelling to be confident of their own emerging narrative ability. Kindergartners usually need only two tellings of a folktale before they know it sufficiently to take part in interactive storytelling with you. Interactive storytelling is just as appropriate for older students because of its power to help them learn as they construct meaning through narration.

Every family has its own special stories that children can collect. To help children interview family members who may have trouble recalling a specific memory or anneccdote, give them a list of "Tell me about . . ." prompts such as these from Davis (1993) and help them add their own:

- "Tell me about a time when I got lost."
- "Tell me about your favorite relative when you were a child."
- "Tell me about the neighborhood where you lived when you were a child."
- "Tell me about someone who used to come and visit at your house when you were growing up."

After hearing *Tell Me Again about the Night I Was Born* by J. L. Curtis (1995), about a girl who retells a favorite family story, and other books about families, such as *The Canada Geese Quilt* by Natalie Kinsey-Warnock (1989) and *Sarah, Plain and Tall* by Patricia MacLachlan (1995), each of Tonya Dauphin's third-graders interviewed a family member about a story from his or her past. The children retold these stories in class in preparation for writing them down. They conferenced with each other and Tonya as they wrote their stories, and then Tonya collected them in a class book called "A Patchwork of Stories" in which everyone's story was included in a different font style to reflect the diversity of stories. She put many other books about families and grandparents in the classroom library for children to read during this Family Story Project. A few of the books Tonya collected follow:

Cousins Are Special by S. Goldman (New York: Whitman, 1978).
Homeplace by C. Dragonwagon (New York: Macmillan, 1990).
My Rotten Red-Headed Brother by P. Polacco (New York: Philomel, 1994).
Picnic at Mudsock Meadow by P. Polacco (New York: Bantam, 1992).

The Mother's Day Sandwich by J. Wynot (New York: Orchard, 1990).
Sunshine Home by E. Bunting (New York: Clarion, 1994).
Grandma's Promise by E. Moore (New York: Lothrop, 1988).
The Memory Box by M. Bahr (New York: Whitman, 1992).
Anna, Grandpa and the Big Storm by C. Stevens (New York: Clarion, 1982).
Knots on a Counting Rope by B. Martin (New York: Holt, 1987).
Halmoni and the Picnic by S. Choi (New York: Houghton Mifflin, 1993).
A Very Important Day by M. Herold (New York: Morrow, 1995).
My Mama Had a Dancing Heart by L. Moore (New York: Orchard, 1995).

STRETCHING EXERCISE   Choose a family story you enjoyed as a child. Using the guidelines given here, pre-pare your story and tell it to a group of children for whom it is appropriate. Evaluate yourself. Did the children enjoy it? Were you comfortable and prepared? Were the children attentive and responsive? Would you do anything differently next time?

• • • • •

Hamilton and Weiss's handbook *Children Tell Stories: A Teaching Guide* (1990) is filled with practical ideas for classroom storytelling. They also suggest simple folk-tales and fables from around the world for children who are beginning storytellers and provide 25 stories. These stories are each a page or less in length and are arranged in order of difficulty, beginning with the most simple. A few of the titles and places of ori-gin follow:

"How the Rabbit Lost His Tail" (Native American)
"The Rat Princess" (Japan)
"The Miser" (Middle East)
"The Country Mouse and the City Mouse" (Greek)
"How Brother Rabbit Fooled Whale and Elephant" (African American)
"The Baker's Daughter" (England)

The guide includes plans for a six-week unit on storytelling that is adaptable to all grade levels. Hints and handouts for replication are provided, such as suggestions for learning a story, techniques for telling a story, interview questions for families, ideas for parents, and self-evaluation sheets for students. It is a wonderful resource for your intro-duction to storytelling.

Besides folktales, wordless picture books and predictable books with repetitive language or cumulative story events are easy stories for children to tell.

Booktalks

Booktalks are another way to share literature with your students. A *booktalk* is a sales pitch or short promotion for a book that you can plan in advance or do impromptu. It is designed to help students learn about a book and be inspired to read it, but it is not a re-view of a book. A good booktalk is entertaining and it involves the listener. You may or may not have read the books you talk about and introduce to your class. Of course, the most successful booktalks are those done on books you have read and genuinely like.

The rationale for booktalks is twofold. First, many children are immediately interested in a book their teacher suggests or has read and likes. Second, you can share many books quickly with a class through booktalks and can pique student interest in reading with this tool.

Bodart (1986) reports a study conducted with adolescents in which library circulation figures for titles that were discussed in booktalks dramatically increased, even though the students' attitudes about reading did not change. But Julie Conklin found that booktalks paid dividends in increasing her 12- to 14-year-olds' interest in reading and the amount of reading they did to support their content area study. Part way through eight booktalks she did one morning, several times she heard "I want that one!" and one student said, "So far, you've made me want to read all of these books!" Julie gives several hints, based on Barban (1991):

- Don't talk about books you haven't read.
- Talk about books you like.
- Show copies of the books as you talk.
- Start with a short introduction.
- The first and last titles should be your strongest.
- Limit each booktalk to 3 to 6 minutes.
- Use logical transitions between titles.
- Involve the listener. Ask questions.
- Don't give away the ending of the story.

To introduce books related to a thematic unit, you may want to ask your school library media specialist to identify titles. You can spend several minutes each day introducing a few of these books to your class in short booktalks. First, skim, survey, or read an entire book. Next, plan your booktalk to bring out the aspect of the book you see as most important—for example, plot, character description, and so on. Last, choose one of the following ideas for a booktalk that best suits the book:

- Introduce the main character and the conflict.
- Share information from the book's flap.
- Describe the setting and locate it on a map.
- Read a first paragraph or an interesting part.
- Share a picture or an object and tell how it relates to the book.
- Tell about the author's credentials, experiences, or other books the author has written.
- Use a theme and share several books on a topic.
- Introduce the literary elements of the story.
- Create an acrostic with the title or a main character's name.
- Role-play one of the characters.

Once you have modeled booktalks, students can do their own. When students give a booktalk, it should be done on a book they have read and want to endorse. Children will know these books well and be able to talk about them easily.

Whether listening to stories read aloud or told to them, sharing in a book-reading experience, telling their own stories, or hearing booktalks, children's comprehension of language develops when you share quality literature with them. Sharing stories, if it is done well, allows children to respond emotionally as they comprehend. Just as important, children learn to enjoy and appreciate good literature.

Experiences like these help children become and remain bookworms throughout their lives. Furthermore, children learn to attune their ears to the way well-crafted language sounds. When children hear fluent oral reading and speaking, they have a model from which to develop their own fluency in both speaking and writing. Finally, when children listen to stories they are unable to read on their own, they gain an understanding of new concepts, relationships, and vocabulary, as well as a better sense of who they are.

Responding to Literature

What does *response to literature* mean? Rosenblatt (1995) identifies the efferent and aesthetic responses that result from the interactions a reader has with print. Students who read *Bridge to Terabithia* by Katherine Paterson (1977) may have efferent responses, identifying Jess and Leslie as the two main characters, realizing that the story is set in the countryside outside Washington, DC, and observing that Terabithia is a fantasy hideaway. They may also have aesthetic responses. Recognizing their own loneliness and longing for a special friend, they may feel the events in the story and the loss of Leslie in such a way that they experience or live through the story and are touched by it emotionally. In responding to *Bridge to Terabithia*, the literature becomes real for these students and they experience it in unique ways. Responding to literature has to do with how readers personalize what they read, how it becomes real for them, and how it makes them feel.

Personal style, reading preferences, cognitive development, and other factors influence and contribute to each reader's response to literature (Galda, 1988). All students bring their own individual backgrounds of experiences, values, beliefs, and knowledge to the reading of literature, and each story or text possesses unique elements that encourage response, such as genre, style, structure, and characterization. The context within which literature is read can also impact response, with teacher expectation and behavior, classroom atmosphere, and peers also contributing to that response. So, it should be clear that each student will have a different literary response to a story.

You can use the Response Inventory in Figure 5.3 to help determine how a child responds to literature. This tool includes a range of behaviors that occur on a response continuum from efferent to aesthetic. You can expand the inventory by adding other responses, or the inventory can become a self-check for students by prefacing the responses with the statement "When I read or listen I . . . " Be sure to reassess regularly, since a child's ability to respond changes and develops over time as a result of exposure, practice, and various other factors.

Teachers create opportunities to respond to literature in many ways. Hickman (1995) reminds us to allow time to think, offer choices of response modes and materials, recognize and encourage the beginnings of good ideas, and offer support for further response. Discussion, creative dramatics, and writing are three common response modes discussed later in this book. This section describes four types of book-response activities

FIGURE 5.3 Use this Literature Response Inventory regularly to document growth in response to literature.

145
· · · · ·
Sharing and
Responding

Literature Response Inventory

Date

				Enjoys stories and books
				Enjoys pictures in books
				Chooses reading as an independent activity
				Shares reading experiences with others
				Takes part in drama related to stories
				Communicates ideas in writing about stories
				Reads a variety of genres
				Names favorite author/s
				Names favorite illustrator/s
				Prefers certain types of books
				Responds with smiles, laughter, or other emotions
				Relates personal experience to stories
				Uses both pictures and print to make meaning
				Makes meaning from a sequence of events or actions
				Asks questions and seeks meaning related to stories
				Retells stories just read
				Makes predictions about story events
				Changes predictions based on new information
				Interprets an author's meaning
				Compares story with similar stories or book by same author
				Searches information to clarify or verify an idea
				Participates in whole-class discussions about books
				Participates in small-group discussions about books
				States an opinion and supports it with ideas
				Modifies an opinion in light of new information
				Listens and values other opinions or alternate views
				Uses literary elements in discussing stories
				Setting
				Characters
				Plot
				Theme
				Point of view
				Style
				Mood
				Identifies multiple themes in stories
				Understands symbolism and metaphor in appropriate stories
				Identifies special uses of language and stylistic devices

(*E* = Emerging, *D* = Developing, *I* = Independent)

Comments:

Date: _____
Date: _____
Date: _____

that promote both speaking and writing: retelling, visual literacy and picture reading, journal writing, and book sharing. In each of these activities, you can encourage children to develop their interpretations and evaluations of literature. Even young children, whose verbal responses seem most often to be retellings, are capable of more subjective responses to literature with your guidance.

Retelling

A *retelling* is an oral or written reconstruction of a book or story after a child has read or listened to it. Morrow (1990) says, "Both as an instructional strategy and an assessment tool, retelling helps move teachers away from the view that reading is a set of isolated skills to a view of reading as a process for conveying and recreating meaning" (p. 138). Retelling is a more natural way of responding to a story than answering questions. It gives a wholistic, rather than fragmented, notion of a child's comprehension. This easy-to-use strategy works with one child or a group and any genre. Retelling has the following characteristics:

- Requires active involvement as the story is recreated
- Reflects comprehension authentically
- Develops a sense of story structure
- Provides a self-checking procedure
- Improves comprehension
- Makes the child an expert (if you have not read the story)
- Allows for shared interactions

Johnston (1997) cautions that retelling is an unusual social situation when the reader and teacher have both just read the story. When a child recounts a story she has just read that you do not know, this provides a natural and effective way for her to relate this knowledge. In situations where you know the story, a child may omit details and tell it much differently than she might if she thought she had something to say that you didn't already know.

Weaver (1994) believes that retelling and miscue analysis should be an integral part of literacy assessment. She says it is important not to interrupt or ask questions during the initial retelling. She believes in encouraging without confirming or disconfirming accuracy, and, if the child remembers little, having the child reread and try again. If she still has trouble comprehending, let the child read silently. When you do ask questions, ask those that elicit the child's response to the story, those that stimulate further thinking about the story, and those that encourage the child to reflect on her own reading process (e.g., Where did it go well? Where did you have trouble? etc.). Avoid yes or no questions and supplying information or insights the child has not already given. Weaver suggests recording the retelling for later playback to ensure accurate transcription.

As with any strategy, there are some cautions to keep in mind with retelling.

1. Shy and nonverbal students may not participate fully.
2. Retelling may not accurately reflect comprehension when a story is told to someone who already knows it.

3. Interest in the selection or a story can affect the retelling.
4. Retelling can be time consuming.

Despite these cautions, teachers who use retelling as a formal assessment twice a year with their entire class find it valuable when they couple it with a miscue analysis of oral reading. You can use a shared retelling as a way of helping your students better understand a story or as an assessment tool. Figure 5.4 gives tips for encouraging retelling and the form in Figure 5.5 presents a way to record a student's or group's retelling.

Knowledge of the story elements, the components or grammar of a story (e.g., characters, setting, problems, events, resolutions, etc.), aids comprehension and memory of traditional stories. This knowledge is probably developmental, with older children and adults possessing a more elaborate concept of what constitutes a story than younger children. The elements of a story or a story grammar typically occur in folktales and fairy tales, but are often found in stories from other genres as well. See Figure 5.6 for one example using "The People Could Fly," an African American folktale by Virginia Hamilton (1985) based on Mandler and Johnson's (1977) story grammar.

You can use a chart to present the elements of a story to the children, using an overhead projector or the blackboard. Keep the elements in view so the students can use them after reading as a guide for retelling. Or you can map the elements of the story in flowchart form as the children retell the story. When children use story components and reconstruct the story within this framework, three important things happen. First, mem-

---

FIGURE 5.4   Retelling should begin with a personal response.

1. Ask the child for her response to the story with questions like:
   —"Did you enjoy the story/selection? Why? Why not?"
   —"What did it remind you of or make you think about?"
   —"What did you learn from it?"

2. Ask the child to retell the story/selection by saying:
   —"Tell me about (name of selection)." (Add ". . . as if you were telling it to someone who has never heard it before" if you know the story.)

3. Use the following prompts *only* when necessary.
   —"What comes next?"
   —"Then what happened?"
   If the child does not respond, ask a question based on the point in the story where she paused (e.g., "What did the wolf do after he drank the water?").

4. When a child cannot retell the selection, or if the retelling lacks sequence and detail, prompt in a step-by-step fashion with:
   —"Who was the story/selection about?"
   —"When did the story/selection happen?"
   —"Where did it happen?"
   —"What was the main character's problem?"
   —"How did the main character try to solve the problem?"
   —"How was the problem solved?"
   —"How did the story/selection end?"

•••••

Source: Adapted from Morrow (1990).

FIGURE 5.5 Record a student's retelling on this form.

Retelling Assessment

+	gives answer on own
√	prompted
L	looked back
−	No

Name _____

Date _____ /_____ /_____

Title:	Author:

Opinion (what I liked or didn't like about this book):

Characters:

Setting:	Theme (author's message or big idea):

Plot
(problem, events,
solution):

Illustrations:	Awards:

Favorite part:

What did I do well?	What do I want to do better?

ory improves and the chances for successful retellings increase. Second, children develop a sense of story when they see how stories are constructed (see Figure 5.7). Third, retelling a story according to standard story elements familiarizes children with these elements so they can then include them in their own story writing. Children who use the elements or grammar of a good story as a guide when they write usually produce better stories than those who do not.

STRETCHING EXERCISE

Ask a child to share a book she has just read with you (one you haven't read). Use the retelling tips and record in Figures 5.4 and 5.5 to guide and document the retelling. Afterward, analyze the retelling with the child, focusing on what she did well and clarifying any misunderstandings.

•••••

THE PEOPLE COULD FLY
told by Virginia Hamilton

SETTING: A land where harsh masters made slaves like old Toby and young Sara work hard in the fields and the hot sun.

BEGINNING: The slaves had come from Africa where some of them knew magic and could fly.

REACTION: An old man named Toby said the magic words to make a slave, Sara, and her baby fly away from the fields.

ATTEMPT: Toby gave the magic words to other slaves working in the fields.

OUTCOME: The slaves who had the magic flew away to Free-dom.

ENDING: Toby flew away with his people, leaving some in the fields who he didn't have time to teach to fly.

FIGURE 5.6 An example of Mandler and Johnson's (1977) story grammar used with an American Black folktale.

·····

Retelling can also be informal and done by a group for presentation to an audience of younger children, parents, or peers. Here are three ideas for group retelling:

■ A second-grade teacher involves several children in "yarn tug stories." She cuts some 6-foot pieces of yarn and ties them all together at one end. One child holds the knot and everyone takes the end of a piece of yarn and sits in a semi-circle around the

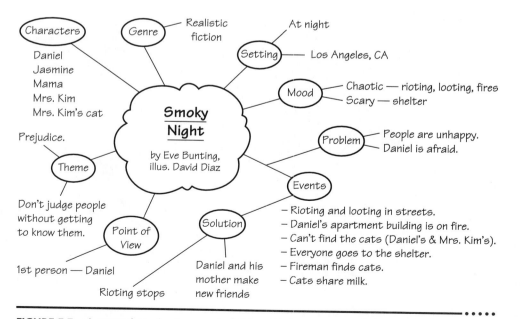

FIGURE 5.7 A second-grade class created this web showing story elements in *Smoky Night* by Eve Bunting (1994).

child who holds the knot. This child begins the retelling of a story they have just heard and gently pulls someone's piece of yarn to signal that child to continue the story. The retelling continues until everyone has had a turn and the story is complete.

▬ A third-grade teacher reports success with a ball to aid the retelling of a story the class is reading. He seats children in a circle and tosses a soft rubbery "koosh" ball to a child to signal his or her turn to continue the story he has begun. The child can then toss the ball back to the teacher or to someone else to continue the story.

▬ A first-grade teacher drew the picture web in Figure 5.8 on chart paper as the children retold the story after she read it to them. She reports that children eagerly used the web as an aid to retelling the northwestern folktale *Whale in the Sky* by Anne Siberell (1982), a story about the origin of totem poles. She posted the web on an art easel in the corner of the room and put the book on the easel so the children could revisit the book and retell the story to a friend.

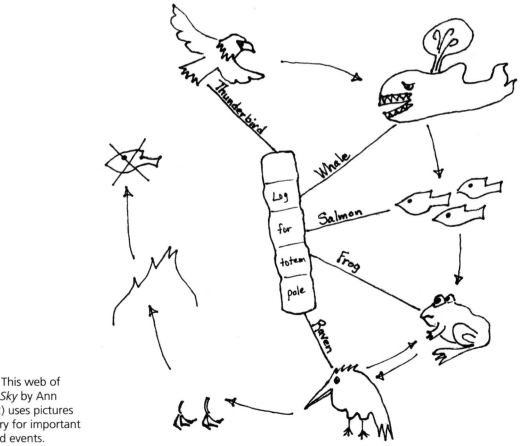

FIGURE 5.8 This web of *Whale in the Sky* by Ann Siberell (1982) uses pictures and vocabulary for important characters and events.

Puppetry.   Children of all ages enjoy retelling stories with the help of puppets. Even the simplest puppets give shy children a vehicle for self-expression and allow all children to be creative in responding and interpreting stories. Whether used by you or your students as an aid to storytelling, puppets are highly motivating for the listener because they add an air of mystery and another dimension to the spoken word.

Puppets made from paper bags, socks, cardboard cylinders, boxes, tagboard, construction paper, straws, sticks, gloves, mittens, or fabric (see Figure 5.9) are easy projects for your class to make with or without the art teacher's help. Add clothing, hair, facial features, and other details to puppets with colored markers, buttons, beads, yarn, fabric swatches, and other materials. Finger puppets, hand puppets, stick puppets, mask puppets, and humanette puppets are easier for children to make and manipulate than marionnettes, but older children may enjoy the challenge of making and manipulating the wire- or string-controlled puppets for a retelling.

A puppet stage can be as simple as a blanket held in place by two children while the puppeteers stand or crouch behind (Ross, 1980). A rope strung through the hem of a sheet and tied between two points in the classroom, or over which a blanket is hung, is just as effective. Advantages of the blanket or sheet are many: It is always the proper height for the children no matter how short, since it can be raised or lowered; it hides 6 to 10 children for a story having many characters; it is portable; and it requires little storage space. For a smaller puppet show with one to three characters, turn a table on its side and seat children on the floor behind the table, remembering that holding puppets up is tiring.

Suggestions for successful puppet shows follow (Ross, 1980):

1. Keep the production short, since puppets have limited actions and voices are sometimes hard to hear.
2. Tie the performance together with music, which can create effects, too.
3. Observe the ceremonies appropriate to a play. Darken the room and light the stage area, introduce the play and players, have puppets take curtain calls at the end, and so on.
4. Have the children improvise their lines, and don't record speaking parts (they make a performance stilted).
5. Use a narrator to help move the action along, describe the setting, explain the passage of time, and so on.

As well as responding to literature by speaking through their puppets, several meaningful writing activities grow naturally from a puppet show. Older children enjoy making handbills or programs that include a brief synopsis of the show (perhaps using the elements of story grammar, discussed earlier), a list of puppets and puppeteers, and other important information about the show. Copies can be reproduced for performers and the audience. Children can also write letters inviting other classes, parents, and the principal to attend the production.

Children enjoy writing and producing scripts for their own puppet shows to accompany science, social studies, or math units. In a fourth-grade social studies class where children were studying local history, small groups wrote reports about different topics they had read about and researched. They had read historical fiction and biographies of local figures. Each group then made puppets, wrote scripts based on their re-ports, and gave a puppet show to the third grade (see Figures 5.10, 5.11, and 5.12). Their puppets were so popular that the third-graders requested directions for making them. Writing the directions was more challenging for the fourth-graders than writing their own scripts.

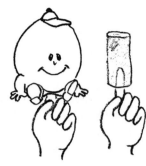

1. Finger Puppet   2. Glove Puppet   3. Stick Puppet

4. Styrofoam Ball Puppet   5. Box Puppet   6. Sock Puppet

7. Shadow Puppet   8. Rubber Ball Puppet   9. Human Board Puppet
•••••

FIGURE 5.9   Your students can make different types of puppets from a variety of materials.

Rana & Val?
The Big Fire

The fire of 1849 was very big. The fire burned down 104 buildings only three buildings were left standing. The fire burned down so many buildings that they had to pay over 300,000 dollars.

The fire was in the Hall of Sons of Temperance. It started at 3:00 in the morning on September 27, 1849.

When the engines had to be changed the fire went out of control because it took so long for the engines to be changed. This fire was the biggest fire in the history of Owego.

Rana Hurry up! were trying to get to a fire.
Val This is the biggest fire we have ever had.
Rana Yeah I know
Val The engines have to be changed Hurry help me so the fire doesn't go out of control
Rana It did already
Val Oh, shoot!
Rana How can we get it out then
Val Just hurry with the engine and we can manage it. Don't worry!

The End

FIGURE 5.10 Script for a puppet show based on the report "The Big Fire."

---

abbey Karen Emily
Mrs Belva Lockwood

Mrs Belva A Lockwood was born in Royalton Ny. June 1857. She started teaching when she was fourteen She was married a few times, her madin name was McNall. She was head of a school called The Owego Seminary she came in the fall of 1863 because she was head of that school. She left Owego in 1865. She got refused from a law school because the head of the school thought she would distract act the men and they wouldn't do there studying. She finaly got admited into the National Univarse of Law. She was fanos because she was the first woman to practise for the suprem court. She ran for President of the U.S.A. in 1884 as the woman rights canadet. She was important person to the community.

FIGURE 5.11 Introduction to the script for a puppet show based on the report "Mrs. Belva Lockwood."

Belva A. Lockwood

Karen Martha – Hello Im martha Grady.

Belva – Hello Im Belva Lockwood

Karen Martha Im going to vote for you.

Abbey Belva – Im very glad your voting for me. I need the vote.

Emily Grover – What am I hearing? a woman running for President!

Abbey Belva – Yes, that's very true. I would like to become president. I promise to try to make peace with others and Im very fair. Thank you for lisening.

Emily Grover – all I would like to say is ill try to be very hard and I do what is right for our country. Thank you!

Littman The votes have been at Desk counted and mr. Grover Oreviand has won.

FIGURE 5.12 The script for the puppet show in Figure 5.11.

153

• • • • •
Shy children often enjoy puppetry because they can speak through their puppets.

Flannel-Board Stories. Flannel boards have been a staple in classrooms for many years. Young children enjoy watching a flannel-board story unfold as it is told. Using this medium and only a few figures, they can easily retell the stories they hear. Just as with puppets, the flannel board often frees shy children from their inhibitions and allows the composition of creative oral language.

A flannel board is a small cork bulletin board, a piece of plywood, or other wood about 18 inches by 24 inches covered with flannel or felt that is glued down. Some teachers use the type of indoor-outdoor carpet to which Velcro adheres. A one-foot-square board is excellent for storytelling with a small group of children or when children share stories in pairs.

Figures do not need to be elaborate. Characters can be shapes of various sizes, colors, or symbols (e.g., a dagger for a villain or jagged teeth for a shark) or they can resemble the actual character. Those cut from colored felt cling to felt, flannel, or carpet. For figures made of other materials, glue a small piece of Velcro onto the back. Figures cut from Pellon, the soft white interlining fabric available in fabric stores, can be drawn on with colored chalk-crayons and sprayed with hair spray to set the colors. Adding color and detail makes figures look more real (e.g., simple figures can be torn from colored paper or made from photocopied and colored book illustrations).

When telling the story, place the flannel board on an easel or on the seat of a chair and lean it against the back of the chair. You can sit or stand beside the board and arrange figures on a surface nearby for quick access or keep them in a hinged-lid box to add mystery.

You can make mini-flannel boards from a shoe box, cigar box, or hinged-lid box by gluing flannel or felt inside the box lid, which is propped up to provide a stage for the display of small figures. Draw these characters on paper or cut them from magazines or books. Glue a small piece of sandpaper to the back of each, which makes them cling easily to the felt stage. Cover figures on the facing side with clear adhesive plastic or laminate them so they last longer.

Children enjoy making their own mini-flannel boards to use alone or with a partner at their desks, in the hallway, or in a corner of the classroom for frequent storytelling practice. Because of their size, these mini-boards are best used by two to three children at most. A few small boxes are enough for a classroom, but many sets of story characters made by children to accompany favorite books and kept in individual self-seal plastic bags make multiple storytelling experiences possible.

Three types of stories lend themselves to the flannel board (Ross, 1980):

1. *Folktales.* Limited characters and settings and more talk than action make these simple stories perfect.
2. *Scientific accounts.* Explanations of phenomena, the functioning of an object or organism, and many other science and social studies concepts are explained well in this way.
3. *Cumulative tales.* Adding figures to the board as you add details to the story make these stories easy for retelling.

Leave the figures and board in place after the story is told. Children love to handle the figures, retell the story, and make up sequels, alternate endings, or new stories. As you or your students create figures for a story, keep the items together in self-seal plastic bags or manila envelopes labeled with the title of the story. Staple to each bag a piece of tagboard or a 5" × 8" card that lists the elements of the story to help a child in retelling. Your collection of flannel-board stories will grow quickly and you should keep it available for ready use by the students.

Projected Visuals.   Children enjoy using visuals that project onto a screen, sheet, or light-colored wall. This is a good way to share the art in nonfiction or information books, which is often photographs. You can project selected pictures from a book by using an opaque projector while the child retells the text. Older children enjoy making their own slides and filmstrips. Use a blank filmstrip material on which children create images by writing and drawing on the blank plastic with colored markers. Produce slides by using colored tissue paper to create pictures to put into cardboard slide frames or just take pictures with a camera and have slides developed.

The overhead projector is also useful for retelling. Cut pieces of paper into desired shapes or forms for a retelling, lay them on the overhead screen as the story is told and project them as silhouettes whose movements accompany the retelling.

Children like to make their own transparencies. One way to do this is to draw the story on a transparency, using permanent or nonpermanent felt-tip markers, as the story unfolds. Draw simple symbols and/or stick figures. Drawing the main events of the story before the retelling speeds the process along. The transparency is entirely covered as the retelling begins and slowly revealed, part by part, as the story progresses. Or draw figures from colored acetate sheets, cut them out, and the resulting figures can be moved around on the screen of the overhead projector as the retelling progresses.

Children can also be the projected visuals. Hang a sheet from the ceiling, put the overhead projector at the back of a darkened room with the projector light shining on the sheet, and as children dramatize a retelling between the sheet and the projector, their images will appear on the sheet. The audience, seated on the other side of the sheet, sees the silhouettes on the sheet as the children move. Students can have speaking parts and a narrator who supplements their lines, or one child can narrate the entire story with no speaking parts, or all action can be silently mimed.

Visual Literacy and Picture Reading

Pictures cut from magazines, calendars, or children's book illustrations offer plentiful and interesting material to use in developing oral and written composition skills. Asking children to read pictures—that is, examine them and extract their meaning—promotes interactions and responses that strengthen comprehension, as well. Stewig (1995) says that book illustrations can be used to develop skills in describing, comparing, and valuing.

Visual literacy is important in today's world, where we are bombarded with visual images and must be able to identify and analyze them. But visual literacy is also a precursor to reading. The ability to read pictures is one aspect of readiness to read print. When a child speaks coherently about a picture, she soon learns to match this oral language with print. Reading pictures is also an important ingredient in vocabulary development and comprehension. The child who notices and interprets pictures probably comprehends more fully the accompanying print than the child who ignores clues found in pictures.

You can develop your students' visual-verbal literacy with the art in children's picture books. Caldecott Award books are especially good for developing visual-verbal literacy since these books have quality illustrations. Other children's books, basal readers, content texts, advertisements, and television also provide material for developing visual literacy. Although many books appear appropriate only for younger children, the thinking skills involved in this kind of literacy make these pictures challenging for older students, too. The following sequence is suggested for teaching these skills:

1. *Teach children to describe.* Help children study a picture and learn to describe it clearly, concisely, and concretely. It helps to have children think of themselves as cameras with zoom lenses, seeing exactly what is there but not interpreting it. Illustrations from books such as *Round Trip* (Jonas, 1983) work especially well since turning the pages upside down reveals a completely different scene. Viewed upright, pages 6 and 7 of Jonas's book show a farm, but when the book is turned upside down, the same lines depict factories. However, children can learn to describe any picture, whether or not it is reversible. Ask questions such as the following to help children describe:

Who do you see in the picture?
What is happening?
Where is this taking place? How do you know?
What colors did the artist use?
How is line used?
What shapes are used?
What textures do you see?
How are print and pictures arranged?

Be sure to give children lots of practice in orally describing pictures before they describe pictures in writing. You may need to help young children make a list of what they see, whereas older children who know how to write can compose their own, more elaborate descriptions. Children enjoy trading written descriptions of pictures in different books and finding the picture that matches the description. These descriptions and illustrations also make good bulletin board displays that highlight children's observational skills.

2. *Provide opportunities to compare.* Comparing pictures is more difficult than describing them, because it involves finding similarities and differences. Encourage your students to become good picture detectives by having them compare pictures of the same story done by two different illustrators. Two examples are Burkert's medieval *Snow White and the Seven Dwarfs* (Jarrell, 1972) and Hyman's *Snow White* (Heins, 1974). Ask children to look for what is the same and what is different in the depictions of Snow White, the dwarfs, and the background details. Most library shelves contain different versions of "Cinderella" or "Little Red Riding Hood" and other folktales they can compare (see Chapter 4 for these lists).

Have the children make comparisons within the same book. For example, have them compare pictures of Miss Nelson and Viola Swamp in *Miss Nelson Has a Field Day* (Allard, 1985). Ask questions such as the following:

How are the pictures alike?
What is the same?
How are the pictures different?
What things are not the same?
How are colors (line, shape, texture, and arrangement) used differently?

You can also help younger as well as older children make comparisons of the content of stories. Have children describe and compare both orally and in writing the content of different versions of stories such as *Stone Soup* (Brown, 1947) and *Nail Soup* (Zemach, 1964) or *Tom Tit Tot* (Ness, 1965) and *Duffy and the Devil* (Zemach & Zemach, 1973).

As with describing, when children orally analyze and compare illustrations easily, you can then take them on to composing written comparisons. These comparisons, featuring the two different versions of the book, make good displays for the library corner. Many children enjoy reading what their friends have to say about literature. Composing in oral and written activities as described here builds children's readiness for more formal report writing.

3. *Encourage evaluation.* The most important and sophisticated of the three visual-verbal skills is the ability to evaluate or state a preference and reasons for it. The act of stating a preference or opinion is what sets us apart as individuals. Children of all ages should be encouraged to express their opinions and verbalize the reasons they hold them.

Though many children easily choose a preferred picture, most have difficulty expressing why they like it. Stewig (1995) compares this to the adult who says "I don't know anything about art, but I know what I like." A lack of background upon which to make evaluations and a lack of language with which to express preferences handicap children and adults alike. However, children and adults can learn to describe, compare, and evaluate pictures if they have opportunities to practice these skills.

You can help children examine illustrations to see how the artist uses color, line, shape, texture, arrangement, and total effect to articulate whether they feel these aspects enhance or detract from the picture and the story's meaning. The following questions may help students form their opinions:

Why do you like the picture?

Do you like the way colors (line, shape, texture, or arrangement) are used? Why?

Does color (line, shape, texture, or arrangement) enhance or detract from the picture's effect? Why?

Determining reasons for a visual judgment leads naturally to identifying reasons for verbal judgments orally and in writing. Teaching children visual-verbal literacy assures that they can take a position and then provide support for their point of view.

In your classroom, display several artists' interpretations of the same character, object, or scene for children to examine for a few days. Lead discussions in which children describe, compare, and evaluate the illustrations. Encourage similar evaluations when children voice a preference for a particular story or character so they learn to feel comfortable verbalizing the reasons for their opinions. Have children write down their preferences for a picture. These can accompany a book, perhaps taped inside the fly leaf as a review for prospective readers before they read the book.

Picture reading that involves describing, comparing, and valuing requires children to construct meaning using both new and known information. It is closely related to reading print, which involves understanding, interpreting, and evaluating. Comparing two pictures is slightly more difficult and is similar to interpreting what the literal facts mean. Valuing is the most difficult skill and is similar to an evaluation of writing in that both picture reader and print reader make personal judgments that they support with their own reasons. Describing, comparing, and valuing involve the use of meaningful oral and written language. In these activities, children verbalize for a purpose that results in critical thinking. The writing they do is also purposeful and is done for their peers to read, which results in more meaningful composition. When activities make sense and have a purpose that is real and tangible, they move children toward using language effectively.

STRETCHING EXERCISE

Read a Caldecott Award book. How well do the pictures fit the story? What do they communicate? Analyze them according to color, line, shape, texture, arrangement, and effect. Read the story to a group of children. Help them orally describe, compare, and evaluate the pictures. Encourage them to share their views and justify their value statements.

• • • • •

Journal Writing

Writing in a journal allows children to respond freely to what they have read. They learn to connect a story—its characters, themes, setting, and so on—to their own lives. Journal writing also provides a place for children to interpret and analyze a story. Reading and writing are connected in a meaningful and nonthreatening way, since the children can write about what they think and how a story makes them feel without fear of being right or wrong and usually without a grade. If you have not tried journals yet or want some basic information about a variety of journal formats, Bromley (1993) gives descriptions of classrooms where 15 different types of journals are used.

Atwell (1987) has her students keep response journals in which they write their personal response to books they are reading. She asks them to write her at least one letter a week in their journal about their reading and she writes back to them in a dialogue journal format. At other times, they may write to peers and swap journals with each other.

To begin journal writing, you might first want to introduce prompts such as the following as an oral activity and then as a written activity:

> It makes me think of . . .
> I felt . . .
> I noticed . . .
> I predict . . .
> I wonder . . .
> I learned . . .
> I think . . .
> A "key word" is . . . because . . .
> It's about . . .
> Dear _____,
> I liked . . .
> I disagreed with . . .

This is often helpful for younger students, English learners, and students who have trouble with writing. Middle-grade teachers report their students eagerly "get into" characters and stories and relate to them freely after using prompts briefly, especially when the teacher models her own response to a book or when students role-play characters. However, you will probably want to pose questions occasionally that focus students on a writer's style or a character's actions, like the following, used by fifth-grade teacher Deb Pease:

- Think about how the story might change if pages 18–24 were written from the rabbit's point of view.
- Write about how the rabbit would tell the story. What would he think of Harold? The other characters? His new name? His new home?

One strategy that keeps journal writing alive is a time for voluntary sharing of entries when students read themselves or you read anonymously to the class. Sharing journal entries gives students the opportunity to see that there are many perspectives from which to view literature and that books and stories can be interpreted and responded to in various ways. Among other benefits, sharing and discussing journal-writing responses deepens comprehension and gives students confidence in the validity of their own personal response.

For young children, drawing a picture may form the basis of their response to literature. Drawing is a precursor to writing and often a stimulus to the creation of oral and spoken language. As children are able, they will add letterlike symbols to their drawings, or they may want you to write a phrase or sentence for them on their picture, which they can then read.

STRETCHING EXERCISE

Read "Book Buddies: Creating Enthusiasm for Literacy Learning" in *The Reading Teacher* (1994), Volume 47, Number 5, pages 392–403 by K. Bromley, D. Winters, and K. Schlimmer. What are the benefits and problems of writing to a real audience? What other real audiences can you think of for third-graders?

• • • • •

Book Sharing

Book sharing is frequently used to encourage students' responses to literature. The processes of listening, speaking, reading, and writing can develop naturally when children respond to and share literature they read. Book-sharing activities foster comprehension and promote effective oral and written composition skills. Consistently offering choices of response modes and materials shows students that you value literature and their perspectives (Hickman, 1995).

Although a book report a child writes for you to read and grade serves a valid purpose, it is only one way to respond to a book. When children write a report, they often summarize or retell the story, failing to include their personal feelings or to interpret, analyze, or evaluate what they have read. There are many other ways to respond to literature (e.g., creatively through art, music, drama, etc.) that require other ways of knowing and making meaning. Sometimes drawing a picture is the easiest way for a child to begin a response to a book (see Figure 5.13). Following are two ways to develop children's book-sharing skills:

1. *Establish criteria.* Talk with children about the purpose of book sharing. Give them some ideas and then brainstorm together so the class list represents everyone's ideas. If the children are to give a booktalk, then present or review the criteria for a booktalk. If they are to write a report or create some other project to share their book, then help them generate criteria for writing or presenting a good book report. Post the criteria in the classroom for ready reference so the children can refer to them when preparing their reports. Encourage the students to compose a draft of an oral or written report, with peers reacting to the draft before it is shared with the entire class. Stress at the draft stage that reports should meet the criteria.

2. *Share models.* Save various examples of reports done by children and share these with them. Of course, as children have opportunities to compose and share, their book-sharing skills will improve. Also, when book sharing in varied formats becomes a regular but informal part of the classroom routine, then the occasional graded book report makes sense.

If you vary the type of book sharing, both presenter and audience are apt to be more interested. For example, a regular rotation of spoken and written activities allows for each child to experience both. Divide your class in half, with each half responsible for one type of book sharing. In this way, when children share, there is variety for the ear and the eye, and every child can engage in regular speaking and writing activities.

Mr. Popper's Penguins by Richard and Florence Atwater

FIGURE 5.13 A picture of *Mr. Popper's Penguins* drawn by a fifth-grader provides rich material for either a spoken or written sharing of the book.

Posters or lists describing and listing different types of book-sharing activities provide children with choices. Giving children alternatives from which to choose builds the ability to make decisions and direct their own learning. The following activities for sharing books interrelate the four language modes. These may be done in pairs, small groups, or by individuals, and they are adaptable to your students and their needs. The labels *spoken* and *written* represent the main kind of composition necessary for the activity, although each activity requires listening and reading, as well. The directions are written for the student and may have to be altered, depending on the grade level.

Spoken Book Sharing

- Give a *booktalk.* On paper, identify the setting, characters, a little bit of the plot, and an anecdote. Practice by tape-recording your booktalk. Listen to yourself and make changes to improve your talk before presenting it.
- Do a *chalk talk.* Use colored chalk to draw a picture or web with labels on the chalkboard and tell the class or a small group about the book. Plan it on paper first. Choose an important part of the story, draw a picture of it, and add labels or a caption. Practice by explaining your picture to a friend first, then share it on the board.
- Do an *oral reading* for younger children. Choose a favorite picture book. Practice by reading it into a tape recorder, listen to hear how you sound, and then read it again before you present it. Write an announcement for the reading and read it to the class as an introduction.

- Take part in *role-playing and interview* an author or character. Write a script of questions to ask and the answers. You may need to do some library work to find out more about the author or book. Ask a friend to interview you as the author or character and practice together before you make a presentation.

- Do a *character study*. Write a speech for the main character of your book. Explain his or her opinion of the world today and include reasons for the opinion. Dress as the character and give your speech to the class.

- Present a formal *book report* orally to the class. Include the story elements of setting, character, point of view, plot, style, tone, and theme. (Choose those that are appropriate for the age level you teach.) Practice the report with someone or tape-record it and make necessary changes before you present it.

- Create a *skit* to depict briefly one of the important incidents in the story. Include the main characters. Have a friend help you present the skit. You can use stick or torn-paper puppets.

- Tape a *radio talk show*. Interview a character or author from the story, or tape two characters having a conversation that relates to a key part of the story.

- Compare two *biographies* of the same person or two information books on the same topic. Prepare a chart of the similarities and differences you discovered to use during your booktalk.

- Tell a *flannel-board story*. Make the props to go with the book, and practice your story with a friend before you tell it to the class.

- Use an *opaque projector* to show a few illustrations from the story you read. Explain how the pictures helped or hindered your enjoyment of the story.

- Dramatize a *scene* from a book. Use props and costumes the characters might have used and worn.

- Plan a *storytelling session* for younger children. First, tell them a story, using the pictures from a book or a few props. Then tell the story again, stopping to let the children supply information or take turns telling part of the story.

- Read some *key entries* from your response journal. Show the other students how you personally responded to the story.

Written Book Sharing

- Make a *study guide* to help someone find the most important information in the book. Have a friend use the guide and suggest improvements. Revise and share it.

- Write an *obituary* for a character (perhaps one you didn't like). Read some obituaries from the newspaper first, then write your own to include the necessary information. Proofread it and revise so it looks like a newspaper obituary.

- Compose an *advertisement* to interest your classmates in reading the book. Write it the way a publisher would to sell the book. Look on the back of book covers for what publishers say about their books. Include what you liked about the book and what impressed you. Proofread it and revise it at least once.

- Write a *travelogue* to convince the reader to take a vacation in the book's setting. Describe the setting in which the action occurs. Have a friend read it aloud to you, and then make changes.

- Make a *book jacket*. Include a short summary or an interesting part on one flap, and something about the author on the other flap. Put the title, author, and pictures of characters or the theme on the cover. Have a friend proofread it. Make changes.

- Make a *mobile* of vocabulary words and a picture of each word with the definition on the back of the picture, and explain it to the class.
- Make a *diorama* of an important scene from the book with a written description to accompany it, and read it to the class.
- Write a formal *book report* that includes the story elements of setting, characters, point of view, plot, style, tone, and theme. Have a friend read it orally to you and revise it so that it sounds the way you want it to.
- Compose a *book blurb,* or a brief advertisement, for a book you own and like. Post it on a bulletin board in your classroom, and include the title, author, and your name so that a classmate can borrow the book from you to read.
- Write an *annotation* for a book you have read (see Figure 5.14). Illustrate it or have a friend illustrate it. (These can be printed on heavy tagboard and used as bookmarks.)

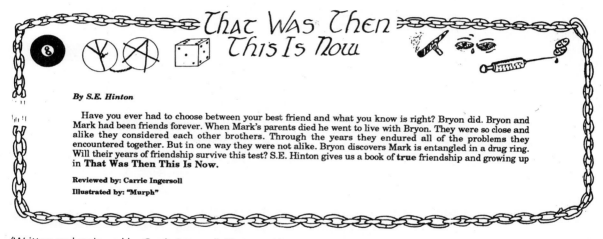

That Was Then This Is Now

By S.E. Hinton

Have you ever had to choose between your best friend and what you know is right? Bryon did. Bryon and Mark had been friends forever. When Mark's parents died he went to live with Bryon. They were so close and alike they considered each other brothers. Through the years they endured all of the problems they encountered together. But in one way they were not alike. Bryon discovers Mark is entangled in a drug ring. Will their years of friendship survive this test? S.E. Hinton gives us a book of **true** friendship and growing up in **That Was Then This Is Now.**

Reviewed by: Carrie Ingersoll
Illustrated by: "Murph"

(Written and reviewed by Carrie Ingersoll, illustrated by Sean Murphy.)

HARLEM SUMMER

Author: Mary Vrooman
Written & reviewed by: Mark Hills
Illustrated by: Guy C. Allis VII

In the novel **Harlem Summer** John Brown learns to deal with the many problems of growing up. When he moves from Montgomery, Alabama to Harlem, New York to live with his aunt and uncle, his problems begin. John was a very curious boy and in Montgomery when you are curious you are picked on, but when you live in Harlem you are beaten up. John was not very independent, but when he moves to Harlem he has to learn how to become independent because he cannot trust anyone. John has many problems when he moves to Harlem, and he must learn to adjust to them or he will not be around much longer.

(Written and reviewed by Mark Hills, illustrated by Guy. C. Allis VII.)

·····

FIGURE 5.14 Seventh-graders wrote annotations for their favorite books, and friends illustrated them on tagboard for use as bookmarks.

- Keep a *response journal and log* of the books you read during the year. As you read, write about the thoughts and feelings each book stirs in you.
- Create *new titles* for the chapters in your book. Be creative (see Figure 5.15).
- Make an *illustrated time line* of important events in the story. Post it on a bulletin board for classmates who may want to read the book.
- Using a *song* you already know, create new lyrics to accompany the story. Sing and tape-record your song, and share it with the class.
- Write a *letter to a publisher,* and share your evaluation of a book and its author. Send the letter and wait for a reply.
- Create a *crossword puzzle* with a computer program and vocabulary from the story you read. Give the puzzle to someone who is currently reading the book.
- Create a *rating scale* for your favorite kind of book (for example, historical fiction or fantasy). Let a friend use it with a book she has read. Compare notes, then revise your scale for others to use it.
- Write an *imaginary journal* by pretending you are one of the characters in the story. Take on the role that character plays in the book.

Chapter Titles for __Weasel__

1. Knock Knock Knock
2. Into the Night
3. A dark eerie journey...
4. Is weasel Real?
5. The Silent finding...
6. Ezra: Gentle Healing
7. Preparing for the Journey Home
8. The burial
9. Who goes there in the night?
10. Weasel's Web...
11. moment of truth!
12. I am proud of you son.
13. Good-bye -- the bond of hatred!
14. The Secret Wall
15. Gettin' Revenge
16. Weasel will get what he deserves
17. Changes
18. I want to learn to fiddle.
19. Awakening Buds of Spring

Other possible book titles:
- Dark Journey
- Night Stalker

FIGURE 5.15 Roberto created these new chapter names and book titles for *Weasel* by Cynthia DeFelice (1987).

- Write a *new ending* for a story that had an ending you did not particularly like. Share it with your class, and be ready to tell your classmates why your ending is better than the author's.
- Write a *poem* to express how a book makes you feel. Your poem may or may not rhyme, depending on how you decide to compose it.
- Create an *acrostic* (see Figure 5.16) using the title of the book. Write the title vertically down the left side of a piece of paper. Then find words about the books that begin with each letter of the title. Choose the best word for each letter of the title, and post your acronym.

Of course, storytelling, puppets, the flannel board, visuals, and picture reading, as well as creative dramatics (discussed in Chapter 8), are other possibilities for book sharing. These and various other activities give children several ways to respond to literature, add interest to reports, and aid the shy child. The addition of objects or artifacts related to the book also serves the same purposes. You will find that the books you share and that children share will be the books that everyone can't wait to read.

In general, encouraging children to choose the books they will read and share, rather than assigning them, keeps interest high. If children have trouble finding or deciding on an appropriate book, you can provide a few titles from which they can choose. To make sure her first-grade students read books that are challenging as well as easy for them, Denise French chooses every third book her students will read. The students choose the other two books. For a first sharing, encourage children to select a book they have already read and for which they have strong positive or negative feelings. In preparation for the sharing, rereading helps recall the finer points. Encourage the children to include valid reasons to support their evaluation of the book.

Book-response activities allow children to demonstrate their comprehension of works of literature through a variety of creative activities. Some activities focus on specific aspects of literature, whereas others require children to draw on their understanding of the entire work. All the activities help children refine their interpretations, analyses,

D iary
e ntries
a nd
r eal + not-so-real letters

M other + father separated
r. oad – trucker

H enshaw (Boyd)
e ventually Leigh finds the lunchbox invader
n o-account dog "Bandit"
S ixth grader
h ome – Bakersfield, CA
a uthor
W riter

FIGURE 5.16 An acrostic for *Dear Mr. Henshaw* by Beverly Cleary (1983), which uses the first letter of each word in the title.

and evaluations of literature because they require thoughtful interactions with it. Sharing their responses to books with other children, whether in small- or large-group situations or in classroom or library displays, are important ways to encourage children to read and develop confidence in their own responses.

Summary

Reading aloud, shared reading, storytelling, and booktalks give children opportunities to interact with literature and form a personal emotional response to it. Sharing literature effectively with children enhances comprehension and enriches response. Choices in oral and written response activities build ownership and develop composition abilities. Retelling, picture reading, journal writing, and book sharing extend comprehension and allow for practice and development of speaking and writing as they enrich content learning.

R•••••eflections

1. Think back to Julie's author/illustrator study at the beginning of this chapter. Choose an author/illustrator who has a distinctive style and one whose work correlates with your curriculum in either language or a subject area. Plan a unit that includes a summary of information about the author, a bibliography of the books you will use, your objectives for developing literacy with the author's books, and your lesson plans. Which of the strategies discussed in this chapter could you incorporate and why?

2. You have arranged with your principal to have a storyteller visit. How will you prepare your class for this event and why? What kind of follow-up activity might make sense, such as a storytelling festival?

Professional Resources

Beck, I. L., McKeown, M. G., Hamilton, R. L., & Kucan, L. (1997). *Questioning the author: An approach for enhancing student engagement with text.* Newark, DE: International Reading Association. This resource for elementary teachers describes an interactive teaching strategy and contains transcripts of it in use that shows how students learn to think critically as they question the ideas presented in the texts.

Bromley, K. (1995). *Webbing with literature: Creating story maps with children's books* (2nd ed.). Boston: Allyn and Bacon. A book about the use of webbing with children's literature to enhance children's enjoyment and learning. It contains webs for 125 books and many ideas for promoting response.

McClure, A. A., & Kristo, J. V. (Eds.) (1996). *Books that invite talk, wonder, and play.* Urbana, IL: NCTE. Many of today's best writers share their thoughts and ideas with teachers on the creative writing process, literary language, literary genres, and developing appreciation for language diversity with students.

Roser, N. L., & Martinez, M. G. (1995). *Booktalk and beyond: Children and teachers respond to literature.* Newark, DE: International Reading Association. This collection of articles by well-known educators contains practical ideas and classroom scenarios of ways to encourage student talk and learning through interactions with literature.

References

Anderson, R. C., Hiebert, E. H., Scott, J. A., & Wilkinson, I. A. G. (1985). *Becoming a nation of readers: The report of the commission on reading*. Washington, DC: National Institute of Education.

Atwell, N. (1987). *In the middle: Writing, reading, and learning with adolescents*. Portsmouth, NH: Heinemann.

Barban, L. (1991). Booktalking: The art of the deal! *School Library Journal, 37* (8), 106.

Bodart, J. (1986). Booktalks do work! The effects of booktalking on attitude and circulation. *Illinois Libraries, 68,* 378–381.

Borasi, R., Sheedy, J. R., & Siegel, M. (1990). The power of stories in learning mathematics. *Language Arts, 67,* 174–189.

Bromley, K. (1993). *Journaling: Engagements in reading, writing and thinking*. New York: Scholastic.

Bromley, K., Winters, D., & Schlimmer, K. (1994). Book buddies: Creating enthusiasm for literacy learning. *The Reading Teacher, 47* (5), 392–403.

Buchoff, R. (1995). Family stories. *The Reading Teacher, 49* (3), 230–233.

Combs, M., & Beach, J. D. (1994). Stories and storytelling: Personalizing the social studies. *The Reading Teacher, 47* (6), 464–471.

Cooper, P. J., & Collins, R. (1992). *Look what happened to frog: Storytelling in education*. Scottsdale, AZ: Gorsuch Scarisbrick.

Cramer, B. B. (1984). Bequest of wings: Three readers and special books. *Language Arts, 61* (3), 253–260.

Cullinan, B., Jaggar, A., & Strickland, D. (1974). Language expansion for black children in the primary grades: A research report. *Young Children, 29,* 98–112.

Davis, D. (1993). *Telling your own stories*. Little Rock, AR: August House.

Galda, L. (1988). Readers, texts, and contexts: A response-based view of literature in the classroom. *The New Advocate, 1,* 84–91.

Hamilton, M., & Weiss, M. (1990). *Children tell stories: A teaching guide*. Katonah, NY: Richard C. Owen.

Hickman, J. (1995). Not by chance: Creating classrooms that invite responses to literature. In N. L. Roser & M. G. Martinez (Eds.), *Booktalk and beyond: Children and teachers respond to literature* (pp. 3–9). Newark, DE: International Reading Association.

Hoffman, J. V., Roser, N. L., & Battle, J. (1993). Reading aloud in classrooms: From the modal toward a "model." *The Reading Teacher, 46* (6), 496–503.

Holdaway, D. (1979). *The foundations of literacy*. Sydney, Australia: Ashton Scholastic.

Hough, R. A., Nurss, J. R., & Enright, D. S. (1986). Story reading with LES children in the regular classroom. *The Reading Teacher, 39* (6), 510–514.

Johnston, P. H. (1997). *Knowing literacy: Constructive literacy assessment*. York, ME: Stenhouse.

Klesius, J. P., & Griffith, P. L. (1996). Interactive storybook reading for at-risk learners. *The Reading Teacher, 49* (7), 552–560.

Mandler, J., & Johnson, N. (1977). Remembrance of things parsed: Story structure and recall. *Cognitive Psychology, 9,* 111–151.

Martin, K., & Miller, E. (1988). Storytelling and science. *Language Arts, 65,* 255–259.

Mikkelsen, N. (1984). Talking and telling: The child as storymaker. *Language Arts, 61* (3), 229–239.

Morrow, L. M. (1997). *Literacy development in the early years: Helping children read and write* (3rd ed.). Englewood Cliffs, NJ: Prentice Hall.

Morrow, L. M. (1990). Retelling stories as a diagnostic tool. In S. M. Glazer, L. W. Searfoss, & L. M. Gentile (Eds.), *Reexamining reading diagnosis: New trends and procedures*. Newark, DE: International Reading Association.

Purves, A., Rogers, T., & Soter, A. (1990). *How porcupines make love II: Teaching a response centered literature curriculum*. New York: Longman.

Rosenblatt, L. M. (1995). Continuing the conversation: A clarification. *Research in the Teaching of English, 29* (3), 349–354.

Rosenblatt, L. (1991). Literature—S.O.S.! *Language Arts, 68* (6), 444–448.

Ross, R. R. (1980). *Storyteller* (2nd ed.). Columbus, OH: Merrill.

Short, K. G., Harste, J. C. & Burke, C. (1995). *Creating classrooms for authors and inquirers* (2nd ed.). Portsmouth, NH: Heinemann.

Slaughter, J. P. (1993). *Beyond storybooks: Young children and the shared book experience*. Newark, DE: International Reading Association.

Spink, J. K. (1996). The aesthetics of informational reading. *The New Advocate, 9* (2), 135–149.

Stewig, J. W. (1995). *Looking at picture books*. Fort Atkinson, WI: Highsmith.

Trousdale, A. (1990). Interactive storytelling: Scaffolding children's early narratives. *Language Arts, 67*, 164–173.

Weaver, C. (1994). *Reading process and practice: From socio-psycholinguistics to whole language.* Portsmouth, NH: Heinemann.

Wells, G. (1986). *The meaning makers: Children learning language and using language to learn.* Portsmouth, NH: Heinemann.

Wicklund, L. K. (1989). Shared poetry: A whole language experience adapted for remedial readers. *The Reading Teacher, 42*, 478–481.

Zarillo, J. (1991). Theory becomes practice: Aesthetic teaching with literature. *The New Advocate, 4* (4), 221–234.

Children's Book References

Allard, H. (1985). *Miss Nelson has a field day.* New York: Doubleday.

Atwater, R., & Atwater, F. (1938). *Mr. Popper's penguins.* Boston: Little, Brown.

Begay, S. (1995). *Navajo: Visions and voices across the mesa.* New York: Scholastic.

Boyington, G. (1989). *Baa, baa black sheep.* Blue Ridge Summit, PA: TAB.

Brown, M. (1947). *Stone soup.* New York: Scribner.

Bunting, E. (1994). *Smoky night.* San Diego: Harcourt.

Cleary, B. (1983). *Dear Mr. Henshaw.* New York: Morrow.

Curtis, J. L. (1995). *Tell me again about the night I was born.* New York: HarperCollins.

DeFelice, C. (1987). *Weasel.* New York: Avon.

Hamilton, V. (1985). *The people could fly: American black folktales.* New York: Knopf.

Heins, P. (1974). *Snow White.* Boston: Little, Brown.

Hogrogian, N. (1971). *One fine day.* New York: Macmillan.

Jarrell, R. (1972). *Snow White and the seven dwarfs.* New York: Farrar, Straus & Giroux.

Jonas, A. (1983). *Round trip.* New York: Greenwillow.

Joslin, S. (1958). *What do you say dear?* Reading, MA: Addison-Wesley.

Kinsey-Warnock, N. (1989). *The Canada geese quilt.* New York: Cobblehill.

L'Engle, M. (1978). *A swiftly tilting planet.* New York: Farrar, Straus & Giroux.

Lowry, L. (1989). *Number the stars.* Boston: Houghton Mifflin.

MacLachlan, P. (1994). *All the places to love.* New York: HarperCollins.

MacLachlan, P. (1985). *Sarah, plain and tall.* New York: Harper.

McGovern, A. (1979). *The secret soldier: The story of Deborah Sampson.* New York: Scholastic.

Ness, E. (1965). *Tom tit tot.* New York: Scribner.

Paterson, K. (1977). *Bridge to Terabithia.* New York: Crowell.

Prelutsky, J. (1985). *My parents think I'm sleeping.* New York: Greenwillow.

Sendak, M. (1981). *Outside over there.* New York: Harper and Row.

Siberell, A. (1982). *Whale in the sky.* New York: Dutton.

Van Allsburg, C. (1990). *Just a dream.* Boston: Houghton Mifflin.

White, E. B. (1952). *Charlotte's web.* New York: Harper and Row.

Yolen, J. (1985). *Commander toad and the disasteroid.* New York: Coward-McCann.

Zemach, H. (1964). *Nail soup.* Chicago: Follett.

Zemach, H., & Zemach, M. (1973). *Duffy and the devil.* New York: Farrar, Straus & Giroux.

Connections:
Listening and
Reading

6

Window on Teaching

Mark Casey is a first-grade teacher who believes in the importance of parental involvement in a child's schooling. He says:

> It's a dilemma, trying to decide what and how much to say to parents in the letters I send home to them. For example, I struggled with the one I just sent home. I had another first-grade teacher read it, and, of course, my principal. They thought it was too long and difficult for many parents to understand. My colleague thought

I shouldn't bother sending it; the principal thought I should water it down. I won't NOT send it because I want to communicate with these parents about their roles.

Mark did make the letter easier to read by using short sentences and a numbered list. He said:

There are many parents who will read and understand this letter. If it makes a difference for even a few children, I think it's worth sending, even if some can't or won't read it.

He had the letter translated into Spanish by a high school student for several families who speak only Spanish. When he met with the other parents—some Lao, Russian, and Chinese who are also non–English speaking—he took an older student who spoke their language and suggested that an English-speaking sibling or neighbor could interpret it for them. Here is the letter Mark sent home:

September 10th

Dear First-Grade Parents,

Welcome to the world of first grade at Cedarhurst School! I'm looking forward to teaching your child this year and talking with you about the best ways we can help your child be a successful learner. During the year, I'll send home a letter to let you know what we are doing and to give you some ideas for things you can do at home to help your child in school. One of the things you should know is that you play a big role in your child's education. You are your child's first and most important teacher. What you do at home can have a huge impact on your child's ability to learn.

In first grade, one of our main goals is to become good listeners and readers. You can help by regularly taking your child to the library to choose books, reading with your child, and talking and listening to him or her about what you read. How do you choose books for your child? Here are some tips:

1. *Let your child lead the way.* Pick books that appeal to your child. What are his special interests? Does she have a pet? Try books that match your child.
2. *Share favorite books from your childhood.* If you loved a book, chances are it's worth sharing with your child.
3. *Choose a challenging book.* If you read the book to your child, it can be more difficult than one he would read by himself because you can explain things to him.
4. *Reread books.* Your child will get more out of a book each time you reread it together. Your child can begin to "read" with you if she already knows the story.

5. *Look for pictures with detail.* Your child will enjoy discovering new things in the pictures when you reread the book.
6. *Choose books with predictable lines, rhymes, and repetition.* These books invite your child to chime in as you read.
7. *Aim for variety.* Choose a wide variety of books. Read information books, poetry, fantasy, realistic fiction, and so on.
8. *Ask your librarian.* Ask what the most checked-out books are in your library or have the librarian suggest titles your child will enjoy.

I hope these ideas will help as you choose books for your child. If you can make story reading a regular part of each afternoon or evening, you will do much to help your child become a successful reader and listener!

If you have questions or want to talk with me, please call school (555-1244) and leave a message so I can call you back. I will call this week to arrange a time to come to your home for a brief visit.

Sincerely,

Mr. Casey

Mark believes in the critical role of parents in helping their children succeed in school. Some of his beliefs are grounded in what he learned in his education courses. Mark says:

I remember reading research in one of my courses about parents who made sure their kids did their homework. Those kids did well in school, and the kids whose parents didn't follow through on the homework didn't do well or dropped out of school. It wasn't that the parents helped the kids do the homework, but they made sure there was a place for the child to work, they turned the TV off, and they were right there often in the same room while the kids did their homework. They supported what was going on in school.

I also remember reading about the importance of parental support in kids' schooling in another class when we read Growing Up Literate: Learning from Inner-City Families *by Denny Taylor and Catherine Dorsey-Gaines. It was a study of 10 inner-city kids who lived in poverty and whose lives were characterized by all the risks that normally result in school failure and dropping out. But the kids succeeded, and part of it was due to the value the parents placed on education and the way they supported learning at home. I've never forgotten that message and I communicate directly with my kids' parents about their roles. Even if some parents dropped out of school or can't read, supporting their kids in lots of ways makes a huge difference in whether or not the kids succeed in school.*

Mark's dilemmas about communicating with parents to enlist their help in their child's education are not unlike those you will face as a teacher. In this instance, Mark views language reception (listening and reading) as basic skills that parents can help develop at home, and he gave them some good ideas for doing this. Undoubtedly, some of your students will be at risk for failure, and how you collaborate with parents to help them build their child's receptive language can be a deciding factor in how these children learn.

O•••••verview

The processes of listening and reading involve receptive language and the construction of meaning. In both processes, children receive messages for which they must make meaning. This chapter discusses common elements and differences, as well as details strategies to develop children's comprehension of both spoken and written language. These understandings will prepare you for Chapters 7 and 8.

Listening and reading are indeed related. Research indicates a continuing interdependence up to at least age 14 (Hedrick, 1995). A study of 166 fourth-, sixth-, and eighth-grade students found a correlation of .52 between listening and reading and a significant relationship (Carlisle & Felbinger, 1991). This study also showed that the two modes are not identical, even though about 25 percent of their traits are common. From this research, it is also known that some students can benefit from direct instruction in comprehension as listeners and readers.

Models of listening (Pearson & Fielding, 1982) and reading (Weaver, 1994) propose that listening and reading are active cognitive processes. To comprehend or construct meaning, the language receiver interacts with either spoken or text-based information and monitors comprehension in a search for meaning. Both processes involve critical thinking and actively associating what is new with what is known. Listeners and readers monitor or check information as it is processed to determine whether it makes sense to them.

Important linkages between listening and reading exist for both learning in English and other langauges. In a study of 122 English-speaking fourth-grade students, Hedrick (1995) reports that higher levels of wide reading are associated with stronger listening comprehension abilities. Krashen (1995) recognizes the relationship for learning a second language. He suggests language programs use a reading/listening library where students can choose nonacademic reading material and audiotapes to promote interest and understanding of the target language.

Aside from their common traits, listening and reading each possess their own, distinctly different elements. Listening adds spoken language elements that contribute to the process of comprehending. Nonverbal language (the speaker's facial expressions and gestures), as well as the speaker's intonation (pitch), juncture (pauses), and stress (accent) all provide additional clues to meaning and can sometimes make what is heard more memorable than what is read. There are, however, limitations to listening. A speaker's dialect may not match the listener's. In such a case, the listener must stop the speaker to verify what is being said. Listeners also have the disadvantage that memory

places on listening. Most people are limited by how much and how accurately they remember. Some figures indicate that individuals forget up to 80 percent of what they hear
15 minutes after hearing it.

Printed text provides certain advantages to readers. One is permanence. If readers
can't remember what they read, they can reread the text. Visuals such as pictures, illustrations, graphs, diagrams, and maps can increase comprehension if readers know how
to use these aids. Readers also have the advantages of print variations, page layout, and
design. For instance, bold type, font variations, or colored print highlight important information, as do underlining, lists, or numbered sequences (such as what you saw in
Mark's letter at the beginning of this chapter). Proper use of space and margins also
makes the printed page more readable. In addition, readers may also use the context surrounding an unknown word to figure it out. As with listening, the distinctive elements
that reading possesses are also sometimes impediments to comprehension. If the text is
poorly organized or not clearly written or if the graphics are not explained well, a reader
cannot ask the author what was intended.

Young children learn that spoken and printed words have meaning and that these
meanings can be the same. They learn that printed words are visible symbols for spoken
words. The child who understands this correspondence between listening and reading
learns to read more easily and quickly than the child who does not. Likewise, the child
who reads but does not listen effectively may be able to translate the process of comprehension in reading to listening if he understands how the two connect.

Theoretical Models

There are many explanations about how comprehension occurs, and theorists in the field
of reading propose several models or ways of explaining these theories (Weaver, 1994).
The following discussion applies these theories to comprehension and the way the mind
processes language in general. For further reading, Ruddell, Ruddell, and Singer (1994)
present a comprehensive collection of work about theories and models of reading comprehension. Before continuing, three terms need to be defined:

> *Graphophonemics:* sounds and print that represent meaning
> *Syntax:* grammar or rules of oral and written language
> *Semantics:* meanings attached to words

Bottom-Up Model

Some theorists represent comprehension with a text-based, stimuli-driven, or bottom-up
model Weaver (1994) calls the *commonsense model.* In this model, the language process
occurs in an orderly sequence, beginning with the recognition of sounds in spoken language (consonants, vowels, digraphs, dipthongs, and word patterns) or graphics in written language (letter features, letter clusters, spelling patterns, and words). Semantic associations are then attached to words and the listener or reader comprehends phrases,
sentences, paragraphs, chapters, and entire texts.

In this model, initial emphasis is on perception, discrimination, and recognition of
letters and words and the sounds they represent as a prerequisite to understanding and

meaning. This theory suggests that semantics and syntax reside in oral and written language. A person can comprehend the message by decoding the graphophonemics. Thus, comprehension begins with sound and visual input and proceeds from there.

Top-Down Model

A second explanation for how comprehension occurs depends on a knowledge-based, concept-driven, or top-down model. Critical to this model are schemata or the background knowledge, experiences, conceptual understandings, attitudes, values, skills, and procedures people possess (Vacca & Vacca, 1995). The semantic system of language stores the schemata that one brings to listening and reading. For example, your mind contains organized chunks of information such as a schema for "cat," which is different in some ways and similar in others to your schema for "dog."

This model suggests that when people listen or read, they have their own schemata that they attempt to match to spoken or written language. Aspects of the immediate situation and of a person's broader sociocultural background play an important role also in what that person understands as he processes language. People use semantic knowledge to immediately recognize and associate meanings with words. As people read or listen, they sample text and seek the familiar as they predict what will come. A child may hear or read "the enigmatic gymnast" as "the energetic gymnast" because his mother is a physical education teacher, because he has a background in sports, specifically gymnastics, or because his concept of a gymnast is a person who is full of energy. Only when there is a syntactic or semantic mismatch does a person attend more closely to letter features, letter clusters, or spelling patterns. This theory suggests that semantics and syntax exist in people's schemata, not in spoken sounds or written graphics.

Transactional Model

A transactional language processing model, which Weaver (1994) calls *socio-psycholinguistic,* represents elements of both the bottom-up and top-down models. In this model, comprehension is based on schemata, semantics, syntax, and the graphophonemics of spoken or written language. As in the top-down model, a person's sociocultural background, as well as the situation in which the language processing occurs, affect comprehension. The three cuing systems interact simultaneously as the reader or listener relates to print or spoken language. Thus, he uses this transaction between his mind and the oral or written language to construct her own personal meaning.

Comprehension occurs when people bring meaning to language in order to get meaning from it. They rely on syntax to provide clues and help construct meaning. In this transactional model, comprehension is an active process that keeps the listener or reader engaged in constructing meaning (see Figure 6.1).

In a top-down model, people may have mismatches since they are not necessarily attending closely to the spellings or sounds of words or the grammar of sentences. When people read, they may substitute words that make more sense to them than those actually appearing in print. For example, the sentence *The couch was lumpy and springs protruded from it* might be read *The couch had lumps and the springs stuck out of it.* As people listen, they may anticipate certain spoken words, supply them in their own minds, and not hear what is actually said. Comprehension occurs for each person at

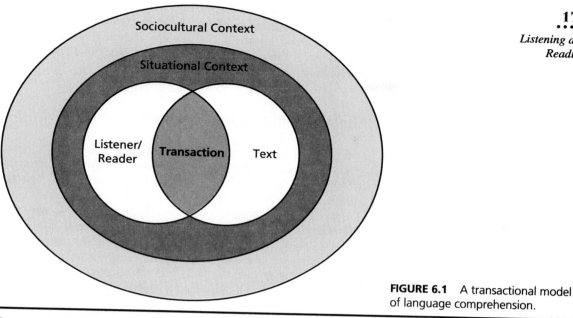

FIGURE 6.1 A transactional model of language comprehension.

Source: Adapted from Weaver (1994).

some level. However, there is not always a one-to-one correspondence between what is spoken and what is written.

In the bottom-up model, people may be excellent at word recognition or remembering exact wording because they attend more to pronunciation than to understanding. A reader might read the sentence as *The couch was lumpy and strings perturbed from it* in an attempt to closely match his oral language with the print. Or a reader might read the sentence perfectly and still not comprehend what he read because he focused on pronunciation. A listener might be able to repeat an exact quote but may not understand what it means or how it applies to the speech.

In the transactional model, people hypothesize about what is heard or read using their own schemata, including semantic and syntactic knowledge and based on the situation and sociocultural context. They then use the graphophonemics and syntax to verify or disprove these hypotheses. In this model, a reader may be sitting at the beach looking at the ocean and read the sentence as *The conch was lumpy and strings protruded,* thinking of a particular kind of shell with seaweed covering it. But if this doesn't fit the text that follows, he may reread and correct himself. The reader may even use his knowledge of the meaning for *protrude* to go back and change *strings* to *springs*. If the sentence was spoken, the listener might stop the speaker to ask questions or request that a word or idea be repeated so that he can better comprehend what he hears.

It may be that beginning listeners and readers use a bottom-up approach as they start to read, and then as they become proficient, they may use the top-down model. As listeners or readers mature in their awareness of the situational context and broader sociocultural context, the transactional model seems to best reflect what occurs in expert language comprehension. It is your task as a teacher to apply this current knowledge to help children interact with language as they use their schemata and the available semantic, syntactic, and graphophonemic information for comprehension. Understanding these models is important if you are to deal effectively with the range of differences in your students' comprehension abilities.

Types of Listening and Reading Comprehension

Comprehension is a complex process of meaning construction that involves prior knowledge about the world and language, the use of various strategies for meaning making, and personal interaction with text. Clearly, many factors can enhance or detract from the transaction with text that results in comprehension.

There are many hierarchies or taxonomies for different types of comprehension. In the past, basal readers often defined three types of comprehension that range from a narrow to a more broadly based construction of meaning: literal, interpretive, and evaluative (see Figure 6.2). To comprehend literally, we recognize, recall, or locate information that is specifically stated orally or found in text. Interpreting requires listening or reading critically to determine what is meant or implied but not explicitly said. When we evaluate, we think creatively, solve a problem, or make a generalization that extends beyond the text. These three types of comprehension can occur during listening or reading as the child makes sense of text.

Another way to think about comprehension is that it involves making meaning by reading what is found "in the lines," "between the lines," and "beyond the lines" (Pearson & Johnson, 1978). For the listener, this is hearing what is said, understanding what is not directly said but implied, and understanding how what is heard relates to the larger world.

There are problems with both of these ways of categorizing comprehension, however. Think about the difficulty involved in identifying any one of these discrete types of comprehension as you consider the nebulous and personal way we construct meaning and interpret sounds and symbols. For instance, authors aren't always clear in their intent and don't always know what their intentions are when they create a text. Let's use the simple comparison of a text to an onion. The beauty of good writing and literature lies in the multiple layers of meaning that we peel away and the multiple perspectives the text represents when diverse people read or hear it. Think also about the fine line be-

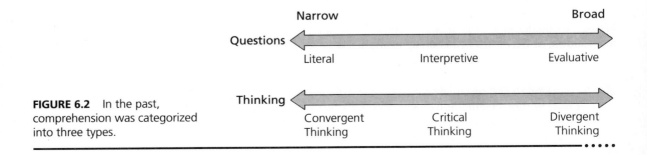

FIGURE 6.2 In the past, comprehension was categorized into three types.

tween what might be considered an interpretation and an evaluation or reading between and beyond the lines.

You can determine a child's comprehension of spoken or written language in many ways. The ability to discuss, retell, ask and answer questions, respond to statements, summarize, draw, dramatize, write, perform, and make or do something demonstrate comprehension. When assessing comprehension, though, remember that many things can confound it. For example, when children write a response, spelling ease and handwriting fluency can affect a demonstration of comprehension. Also, answering questions may confine a child's comprehension because he may respond only to the questions and not to issues that may be broader than the questions. The child may comprehend differently from what the writing or question calls for. Also, a child may comprehend the text but not understand the question and so appear not to comprehend. In addition, many times, questions measure prior knowledge, or what the child knew before he heard or read something, so comprehension isn't accurately measured. Asking a child to react or respond personally to what was heard or read, or to retell it by recalling freely or with prompts or clues from you, may result in a richer picture of comprehension than writing or asking questions.

Shanklin and Rhodes (1989) suggest enhancing comprehension by encouraging children to share their personal interpretations with each other. They believe that through social interaction, children extend their understanding of text. When children talk with each other about something they have just read or heard, each child shares an interpretation that is shaped by his unique background. By alerting them to the different ways in which a text or spoken message can be understood, you extend children's comprehension. Shanklin and Rhodes suggest the use of open-ended questions that encourage divergent thinking to develop comprehension.

Factors Affecting Comprehension

No matter how you determine comprehension, a multitude of factors influence the meaning a child constructs from spoken or written language. Separating these factors into four categories—individual, text, context, and instructional—is a helpful way to think about them.

1. *Individual factors.* Individual factors include a child's purpose for listening or reading; his schemata or experiences and prior knowledge about the subject; his language knowledge; his concept of himself as a listener, reader, and learner; his attitude and motivation; his sociocultural experiences; and his involvement with the speaker, writer, or subject. Facility with language—including dialects and knowledge of a language other than English, and a child's listening vocabulary specifically—affect his comprehension, since listening is the primary base for vocabulary development in the other language modes. Memory and intelligence also affect comprehension, although even children with low IQs can learn to comprehend reasonably well through listening or reading. A child's social and emotional intelligences also affect his comprehension.

2. *Text factors.* Text factors include the special characteristics of spoken or written texts that set them apart from each other and the social aspects of a situation in which

comprehension occurs. In reading printed material, certain graphic elements are important: size and style of type, clarity of the print, pictures or diagrams, color, underlining, italics, and so on. In listening, the way in which the speaker uses tone, juncture, stress, nonverbal language, and eye contact are important. There are also features of content that affect comprehension: style of writing or speaking, organization, use of examples, and vocabulary choices are a few of these. Such things as syntax or grammar, concept density, and the length of words and sentences also affect comprehension. Content texts are especially difficult because they are written in expository style that uses a variety of organizational patterns and technical vocabulary as well as charts, tables, maps, and other graphic aids.

3. *Context factors.* Context factors include the "here-and-now" situation and the broader sociocultural context in which the listening or reading occurs. One here-and-now factor is the rate of speaking or reading that can dampen interest if it is too slow or that can negatively affect comprehension if it is so fast that concepts can't be understood. Environmental elements such as noise, light, and audience affect comprehension, as does the place in which the language reception occurs. Sociocultural factors include relationships with other children or adults, status within a group, and the cultural beliefs or attitudes the child may hold that are similar or different from what she hears or reads. Every language reception event occurs in a social and cultural context that can affect it.

4. *Instructional factors.* Clearly, a teacher's philosophy of language arts instruction can affect how he teaches and how children develop receptive language comprehension. These factors include all of the things you can do as a teacher to help make a child's transaction with text meaningful. Among some of the most important are setting a purpose, previewing, brainstorming, developing vocabulary, predicting, self-monitoring, thinking aloud, and assessing and organizing prior knowledge. Questions, discussion, modeling, visual imagery, think-alouds, and wait-time are also strategies that are useful comprehension builders.

To be successful in promoting receptive language comprehension, remember first to consider the child's language, current knowledge, and experience (see Figure 6.1). Then consider the text and context within which the language reception occurs. Always consider the multiplicity of factors that affect comprehension before you make a judgment about a child's seeming lack of understanding. Since there are so many factors influencing comprehension, you should not be surprised to learn that there are many strategies for developing children's comprehension that take these factors into account.

STRETCHING EXERCISE

Read *The River Ran Wild* by Lynne Cherry (1992). Identify the possible factors that could affect the comprehension of a child who reads this story as part of a science unit in your classroom. Also identify the factors affecting the same child hearing the same story read to him by his father at home. Determine where your factors fit in the four categories used here. Did you identify any not discussed here? Where does each fit?

• • • • •

Inviting and Extending Comprehension

You can direct children's comprehension and critical thinking at various times during the listening or reading process. Comprehension strategies work for all children but are particularly important for students who lack background experiences or knowledge, are English learners, have language delays or difficulties, are from other cultures, or have learning disabilities.

An important role for you, as a teacher, is to invite and extend children's comprehension at three key points in the reading process: before, during, and after reading.

■ *Before* children listen or read, assess their knowledge, attitudes, and understanding to determine whether comprehension will be difficult for them. Prepare for a particular listening or reading activity first. Establish what they already know, provide background information, introduce them to new vocabulary words or concepts they will meet, and show how you might approach the material. Share what you want to learn from the listening or reading or tell them the questions you have about the topic. Then help children establish their own purposes.

■ *During* listening or reading, ask questions to evaluate purposes that you set initially, ask other questions or lead discussion to help children check what they learned or did not learn, encourage children to ask and answer each other's questions, and show children the processes you use to comprehend. Create a drawing or graphic organizer to show organization of content and key vocabulary to help better understand it.

■ *After* listening or reading, do more of the same things you did during the activity and discuss reactions and responses to the entire text. Extend the children's thinking by discussing other texts that are similar to the one just read. Invite the children to hypothesize about why the author wrote what he or she did, how accurate it is, and what it means in light of what is known today. Discuss ideas or issues that are related, help children hypothesize about connections, and encourage judgments about how ideas fit together.

These are only a few of the ways you can invite and extend children's comprehension and help them to direct their own comprehension through sharing and taking ownership for it themselves. You will discover additional and more specific ways to direct children's comprehension as you read the remainder of this chapter and text and as you work with children in the classroom.

Directed Listening/Reading Activty

Before expecting children to comprehend spoken or written information, it is important for them to have a clear purpose that is both relevant and compelling to them. They must be interested and have a real reason for listening or reading. For example, will they need to respond personally to relate what they read to their own lives, identify a main idea, verify a prediction, answer a question they have, make or do something, find a fact or detail, or compare and contrast two things? When children have a genuine interest and clear purpose in mind that is relevant and important, they are motivated to listen or read. They are also more apt to have better comprehension. As a teacher, you can help children establish meaningful purposes for listening and reading, and then help them monitor their comprehension in light of the purposes they set.

Most reading lessons in the basal reader follow the format of a Directed Reading Activity (DRA) (Betts, 1946). The DRA is based on sound principles of learning theory, and teachers have traditionally used it to teach reading. You can use the following steps to teach reading or as a Directed Listening Activity (DLA) to invite and extend children's listening comprehension:

1. *Readiness and motivation.* Prepare for reading by building on the children's experiential backgrounds and introducing new concepts.
2. *Vocabulary introduction.* Preteach new words that appear in the selection in a meaningful context such as a sentence.
3. *Purpose setting.* Establish the reason(s) for reading the selection, perhaps by posing a question(s).
4. *Guided silent reading.* Stop the reading at appropriate points to ask questions and discuss the selection. This establishes new purposes for reading when the silent reading resumes. Usually, children read a selection in parts, with discussion and new purposes set several times.
5. *Oral rereading.* Have the children read selected parts orally to share them for enjoyment, answer questions, or develop expression for an audience.
6. *Skill development.* Introduce or reinforce word analysis, vocabulary, or comprehension skills.
7. *Extension.* Follow up with activities related to the selection such as writing letters or stories, reading related stories and materials, viewing filmstrips or videos, listening to recordings, or using the computer.

You can see that the DRA/DLA provides opportunities to develop all four language arts. However, if you use it exclusively, children may not become strategic, independent, and flexible listeners and readers. This strategy divides a story into many segments that are read sequentially. Although chopping up a story helps promote comprehension, it also frustrates impatient children who intently read for meaning and want to find out how the story ends. Another problem with the DRA/DLA is that typically you, rather than the learner, set the purpose for reading or listening. When children are not individually involved in purpose setting, they can become bored or complete the activity only to please you. The DRA/DLA makes no special provision for helping children vary their rate or develop flexibility. It requires only that children read silently, usually to answer a question. Nor does the DRA provide opportunities to take risks by meeting unknown words in context and using word analysis skills independently.

Directed Listening/Reading-Thinking Activity

A strategy developed with the shortcomings of the DRA in mind is the Directed Reading-Thinking Activity (DRTA) (Stauffer, 1981). Like the DRA, it is an exemplary and widely used instructional activity for developing comprehension and critical thinking. The Directed Listening-Thinking Activity (DLTA) is an adaptation for listening. The DRTA/DLTA helps students establish their own purposes for listening or reading by making predictions (see Figure 6.3). In this strategy, children use the title of the selection and/or a picture to predict what a story will be about. When children predict in this way, they often use the story vocabulary orally before they hear or read it. Children use

FIGURE 6.3 A plan for a DLTA or DRTA.

181
•••••

Listening and
Reading

Prelistening/Reading

1. Help the children set purposes by making predictions.
   A. Locate the title (table of contents or first page of story) and picture (cover or first page).
   B. Ask: What do you think this story is about? and Why do you think that?
   C. Involve as many children as possible in the discussion and interact without imposing your own ideas.

During Listening/Reading

2. Have the children look at pictures and listen to or read the text.
   A. Stop or have the children stop at an appropriate point (perhaps after one page).
   B. Give help with unfamiliar words when needed by telling the children the word and/or its meaning.
3. Have the children verify or reject predictions and then refine and adjust them.
   A. Ask: Which prediction was right? or Which were close? and Can you prove it?
   B. Have the children reread orally or retell the parts that verify their prediction.
   C. Encourage the children to revise or adjust predictions in light of new information.
4. Continue with steps 2 and 3.
   A. Stop at appropriate points in the story and have the children verify their predictions and make further ones (provide at least three or four opportunities for this).
   B. Once or twice during the lesson, have the children skim quickly (or look ahead) to confirm or reject a prediction, and then go back to read (or listen) at their normal rate.

Postlistening/Reading

5. Extend comprehension/develop skills.
   A. Reinforce important vocabulary and main concepts.
   B. Follow up with focus on areas of need.

•••••

context and word analysis skills to figure out unfamiliar words since new vocabulary is not pretaught in a DRTA/DLTA.

Research supports the idea that predicting before reading facilitates comprehension (Weaver, 1994). Perhaps this is because children process information differently when they establish their own predictions for reading, rather than when you set purposes that may not have meaning for them. Learning to make predictions and then listening or reading with the intention of verifying them fosters independence because children are not listening or reading to determine a purpose set by the teacher. They are personally involved; they have made their own predictions and thus set their own purposes.

You can use the DRTA or DLTA with one child or a group of children of any age to increase listening or reading comprehension. To develop the essential elements of prediction and evaluation, encourage children throughout the lesson to make educated guesses or predictions about a story. Their predictions will be based on the information they have heard or read so far in the story, pictures that accompany the text, and their own knowledge and experience.

Following is a detailed explanation of how to engage children in a DLTA. As young children listen to a story either read or told, you can use this sequence. First, the title and cover picture of the book provide information from which you can ask children to make initial predictions. Then, as the children listen to the story and look at the pictures, stop at appropriate points and have them evaluate their predictions. Two critical questions to ask at each stopping point in the story are:

What do you think is going to happen?
Why do you think that?

Based on information from pictures and what they hear, children can decide whether their predictions are or are not on target. They can accept and verify a previously made prediction, reject it and make a new prediction, or refine and adjust the original one. As they engage in this process, they may want you to reread parts of the story or show them certain pictures a second time so they can look more carefully at them. Encourage this behavior, since it is a rehearsal for rereading and locating important information in printed text when children read to themselves or engage in a DRTA.

When you use a DLTA or DRTA, it is a good idea to write the children's predictions on a chalkboard or a chart. Put their names or initials beside their own words, so when they discuss what they have heard or read, they do not forget the predictions they made or who made them. This promotes the ownership of opinions, and as long as you accept plausible predictions, you foster prediction making and risk taking—not just being correct.

In order for children to make good predictions, the material must be potentially meaningful and interesting. Students must feel confident in making predictions and they must not be afraid to make mistakes. Books with surprise endings make good sources for beginning DLTA or DRTA lessons (see Figure 6.4). Stories with an unexpected twist or unusual ending lend themselves to DLTAs or DRTAs with older students. But any material children can make predictions about is usable, even nonfiction selections. By accepting all reasonable predictions, you encourage sensible guesses and eliminate anx-

---

FIGURE 6.4 Use these books with surprise endings for DLTA or DRTA lessons.

Younger Readers
Allard, H. (1985). *Miss Nelson has a field day*. Boston: Houghton Mifflin.
Amstutz, A. (1994). *Mystery tour*. New York: Mulberry.
LeMieux, A. (1995). *Super snoop Sam Snout and the case of the missing marble*. New York: Avon.
Miller, M. (1985). *Oscar mouse finds a house*. New York: Dial.
Montgomery, P. (1983). *The frog who drank the waters of the world*. New York: Atheneum.
Shafner, R. L. (1994). *Belly's deli*. New York: Lerner.

Older Readers
Adler, D. A. (1985). *The fourth floor twins and the fish snitch mystery*. New York: Viking.
Arden, W. (1984). *The mystery of the smashing glass*. New York: Random House.
Craighead-George, J. (1996). *The case of the missing cutthroat: An ecological mystery*. New York: HarperCollins.
Ecke, W. (1983). *The castle of the red gorillas*. Englewood Cliffs, NJ: Prentice Hall.
Howe, J. (1985). *What Eric knew: A Sebastian Barth mystery*. New York: Atheneum.
Seabrooke, B. (1995). *The haunting of Holroyd Hill*. New York: Dutton.

•••••

iety. Be sure students agree not to read ahead, since this spoils the prediction aspect of the lesson.

183
· · · · ·
Listening and Reading

Find a picture book appropriate for a DLTA or DRTA. Read the story with a child or group of children following the steps in Figure 6.4. Use Figure 6.5 to evaluate yourself.

· · · · ·

STRETCHING EXERCISE

You can develop children's critical thinking with the DRTA or DLTA because the strategy requires children to speculate, predict, and answer questions as they draw conclusions and provide support for them. In a DRTA, children can use a blank piece of paper as a "cover sheet" to cover everything on the first page except the title. Discourage reading ahead by having children cover up remaining sections of the story before they make new predictions concerning what they are about to read.

However, overuse of either the DRTA or DLTA can be a death knell. So, adapt these strategies and don't use them everyday. For example, Tricia Morgan varies the DRTA with writing. Her third-grade students occasionally write predictions based on careful examination of the pictures. These written predictions form their purposes for reading and are the basis for discussion afterwards. Randall Sawyer adapts the DRTA to a written format after his sixth-graders are familiar with the strategy. When they have used the DRTA orally with his guidance several times, each child uses the DRTA format with a book he is reading indpendently (see Figure 6.6). Randall's purpose is to integrate writing into a reading lesson. He feels that when children write complete thoughts, not just one-word responses, as most workbook activities require, this reinforces comprehension and gives them writing practice.

FIGURE 6.5   Evaluate your DLTA or DRTA with these questions.

1. **Prelistening/Reading**
   A. What information did I use to stimulate initial predictions?
   B. Did this lead children to predict story type, setting, and characters?
   C. Did all children make a prediction?
   D. Was the discussion full enough to develop children's interests?

2. **During Listening/Reading**
   A. Were three to four different predictions made at each stopping point?
   B. Did all children make a prediction?
   C. Were predictions evaluated periodically and verified by the text?
   D. Was good thinking reinforced rather than correct answers?
   E. Was pacing rapid enough to maintain interest and not so fast that children failed to develop ideas?

3. **Postlistening/Reading**
   A. Were important concepts reinforced?
   B. Was follow-up appropriate?

· · · · ·

Source: Reprinted by permission of Donna Ogle, Chicago Literacy Development Project, 1997.

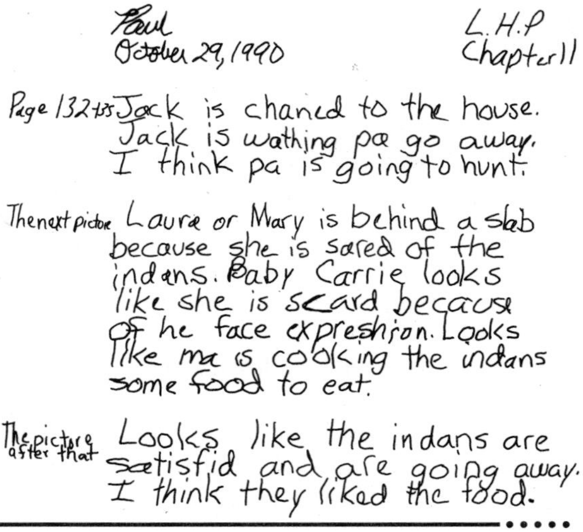

Paul
October 29, 1990

L.H.P
Chapter 11

Page 132 to Jack is chained to the house.
Jack is watching pa go away.
I think pa is going to hunt.

The next picture Laura or Mary is behind a slab
because she is scared of the
indans. Baby Carrie looks
like she is scard because
of he face expreshion. Looks
like ma is cooking the indans
some food to eat.

The picture
after that Looks like the indans are
satisfid and are going away.
I think they liked the food.

FIGURE 6.6 Paul's written
predictions for Chapter 11 from
Little House on the Prairie.

•••••

Along with establishing a purpose for listening and reading, it is also important to consider the material. Comprehension is easier if the language in the story makes sense to children and if they are interested in the topic. Books or stories with predictable language patterns and repeated or cumulative story elements make sense to children and give them a chance to predict and practice what they know. When older children read or listen to books or stories that have predictable directions or outcomes, their comprehension improves.

Upper-elementary-grade students can take your place as the teacher in directing a DLTA or DRTA lesson (Bear & Invernizzi, 1984). Have pairs of children work with you ahead of time to choose material and learn how to lead the group. With your guidance, these students will plan the strategy they will use, decide what the important issues are in the story, determine where the natural breaks occur, and perhaps write out questions to ask at these breaks. Then the children, with your guidance, will teach the lesson to you and a group of children. This role reversal promotes comprehension and independent thinking and is highly motivating for children.

Another similar strategy that involves children in directing their own learning is called *reciprocal teaching* (Palincsar & Brown, 1988). Just as with the student-directed DRTA, children take responsibility for their own learning. In the reciprocal teaching strategy, children and teacher take turns assuming the role of teacher and work together to comprehend the text. They engage in dialogues or conversations about a story or selection. The teacher may lead the dialogue, but both teacher and children make predictions, ask questions, summarize, and clarify comprehension. Reciprocal teaching can be used with a story that children hear or read themselves.

**STRETCHING
EXERCISE**

Read "Colonel Bouquet's Lullaby" by Robert Duffey (see Figure 6.7) and the lesson outline following it (see Figure 6.8). How does this lesson combine attributes of both the DRA and the DRTA? What are the advantages of blending these two strategies?

•••••

FIGURE 6.7 "Colonel Bouquet's Lullaby," written by Bob Duffey, is from a true historical event.

185
•••••
Listening and
Reading

Colonel Bouquet's Lullaby
by Robert Duffey

The time was the year 1764, and the place was Carlisle, Pennsylvania. The Indians and the settlers had signed a treaty. A professional soldier who was hired by the king of England had brought peace to this part of the frontier. The soldier's name was Colonel Henry Bouquet and, as you will see, he was a very wise man.

In the treaty, the Indians promised to bring back all the women and children they had captured, some long ago, some recently. On the day agreed upon, all the captives were brought to the town square. Also in the square were the white folks hoping to find their children and relatives.

Many settlers and captives found each other quickly; others had to study each other and talk a bit to be sure. Some of the girls had grown up and had married Indian men; a number of these young wives chose to return to the Indian camps with their husbands and children.

Of course this was a very happy time. The historian wrote, "Many affecting scenes were enacted as mutual recognition between brothers and sisters, parents and children, separated for years, took place."

But not everyone was happy. Among the settlers was an older woman who was crying, heartsick because she could not find her daughter. Her little girl had been kidnapped at the age of three or four; by this time, she had become twelve or thirteen years old.

Think about the problem. The daughter has grown. She no longer has a little girl's round face. Her skin has been darkened by living out of doors and by the smoke of many campfires. She is dressed as an Indian, her hair braided, and so on. For years she has heard little or no English spoken. The mother may look much as she did when the girl last saw her, but the girl has forgotten her mother's appearance. When she was taken, the young child cried for her mother, but gradually the memory of that beloved face faded and passed away. Neither mother nor child can identify the other.

Colonel Bouquet saw the mother's distress. How could he help her? He thought and thought. Finally, he told an aide to group all the unclaimed girls off to one side. Then he said to the woman, "Madam, please sing a song to our girls. Sing a song you sang to your little girl at bedtime."

The mother nodded, wiped away her tears, and in a clear, quiet voice began to sing an old lullaby:

"Hush my dear, lie still and slumber;
Holy angels guard thy bed."

As she began to sing the next line,

"Heavenly blessings without number,"

a voice from the gathered girls joined hers, haltingly at first, then surely and strongly,

"Gently falling 'round thy head.
Sleep, my babe . . ."

Did the two singers finish the lullaby? We aren't told. The historian wrote simply,

"And her long lost child rushed into her arms."

Surely, Colonel Bouquet allowed himself a smile of satisfaction.

•••••

Source: Reprinted by permission of Robert Duffey. This true story is based on Wing (1789).

FIGURE 6.8   A lesson that combines aspects of the DRA and DRTA.

**Lesson Outline for "Colonel Bouquet's Lullaby"
by Robert Duffey**

1. Introduce new words in meaningful context.
   treaty: a written agreement to end fighting
   frontier: a border between settled and unsettled land
   distress: great unhappiness
   aide: helper; assistant
   slumber: sleep
   identify: pick out; recognize

2. Make predictions. From the title and the new words, what do you think this story will be about?

3. Silently read the story.

4. Check on predictions.

5. Retell the story.

6. Discuss the story. Some questions to initiate discussion:
   —Why, originally, were Native Americans called Indians?
   —Why did Indians fight settlers?
   —Colonel Bouquet, not an Englishman, was in England's army. Why? What does *mercenary* mean? Use the dictionary.
   —Some of the young white wives decided to remain with the Indians. How do you explain this?
   —In what way was Colonel Bouquet wise? What did he know about childhood memories?
   —What is your earliest memory of your mother or the person who raised you?
   —Describe your visual image of the Colonel, the mother, the little girl, the grown girl.
   —Imagine that you are the grown girl. How do you feel as you bid your Indian "mother" good-bye? Your Indian friends? What do you say to them?
   —On the way home what questions do you ask your mother?
   —What will you do at home right away? Later?
   —Which adjustments will be easiest? Most difficult?
   —Name some new things that will come into your life. Think of people, the calendar, stores, church, customs, money.
   —What BIG problems do you face in school?
   —Will you ever visit your Indian family? If not, why not?

7. Tell or write a sequel to this story.

•••••

Source: Reprinted by permission of Robert Duffey.

There are many other strategies that are equally effective for promoting comprehension of spoken and written language. Whatever strategy you use, remember to motivate children, guide them in establishing a background for understanding the selection, and help them set purposes for listening or reading. In doing so, you will actively involve learners in listening and reading, and you will augment their comprehension.

Modeling

Children learn through imitation. Their first models are parents from whom they learn about how to respond and deal with their environment. Siblings and peers also serve as models. As a teacher, you, too, are an important model for children. In fact, Weaver (1994) says, "In order to foster students' development of literacy and learning, teachers must demonstrate that they themselves are pasionate readers, writers and learners. Teachers also need to demonstrate what it means to be risk takers and decision makers" (p. 336). Children use you and your behavior as a basis for learning and developing their own behavior. So what you do in your teaching to show children how you process information has an influence on children's learning.

Some children comprehend language easily and naturally, yet others have difficulties with comprehension. Often, children learn how to comprehend only when you give them a model by sharing with them what you do and how you think as you listen or read. Through visual imagery, metacognition and comprehension monitoring, thinking aloud, questioning, and wait-time, you can model comprehension for children.

Visual Imagery

Visual imagery is a nonverbal personal representation of a concept or experience (Konopak, Williams, & Jampole, 1996). It is the creation of pictures in the mind that enhance comprehension. This powerful yet simple strategy can reduce blood pressure, lessen anxiety, allow for relaxation, and release pent-up feelings. In a study of fourth- and fifth-graders with reading difficulties, those who were taught to use imagery had better comprehension than a control group of students (Gambrell & Bales, 1986). In another study, use of imagery and illustrations independently enhanced the reading performance of fourth-graders (Gambrell & Jawitz, 1993). Visualization actively involved these students in reading because it required them to picture the content of what they were reading. You can help children learn to use visual imagery in a number of ways (Irwin-DeVitis, 1990):

■ Give children opportunities to create images of concrete objects. For instance, show a stuffed lion and let them examine it carefully. Then put it away and ask them to close their eyes and visualize a picture in their minds of what they just saw. Ask them to draw their "picture" and encourage them to talk about what they saw.

■ Have children remember and then visualize, with their eyes closed, familiar objects, scenes, or past experiences outside the classroom, such as their bedroom at home, the bed, playing on the floor with their toys, and so on.

■ Read stories to children that are rich with images. For example, read aloud daily from books with descriptive scenes and action, and have children close their eyes and imagine the scenes they hear about. Then encourage them to share their images so that they will begin to see that everyone's image is somewhat different, depending on background, knowledge, and experiences.

■ Encourage children to begin to create their own visual images as they listen and read stories by themselves. By modeling imagery for children and letting them model it for each other, you increase the possibility that they will use mental imagery.

To help children "get into" stories, read stories that are written from a character's perspective. Joanne Ryder's (1996) *Earthdance* asks children to "imagine you standing tall in an empty space." *Pedro's Journal* by Pam Conrad (1991), told from the perspective of a cabin boy on the *Santa Maria,* and *Encounter* by Jane Yolen (1992), narrated by a young Taino boy who tells about Columbus's arrival in the New World, are also excellent sources to involve children personally with characters. Or read *Working Cotton* by Sherley Williams (1992), in which a little girl tells how her migrant family picks cotton from dawn to dusk in California.

Stories with descriptions that create rich visual images are also great ways to involve children. For instance, *The Great Kapok Tree* by Lynne Cherry (1993) is set in the South American jungle: "A jaguar had been sleeping along a branch in the middle of the tree. Because his spotted coat blended into the dappled light and shadows of the understory, no one had noticed him. Now he leapt down and padded silently over to the sleeping man." *And Still the Turtle Watched*, written by Sheila MacGill-Callahan (1991), is a story about the significance of the turtle to the Delaware Indians: "The rains washed him, the winds blew him, countless snows chilled him, blowing dust rubbed him."

As you guide children through these steps, model for them by sharing the pictures you conjure up in your own mind. The children will imitate your behavior. Also, help children share their images, for this validates their own experiences and adds richness to their interpretations of print and spoken language.

Metacognition and Comprehension Monitoring

Metacognition is the conscious knowledge we have about how we learn (Weaver, 1994). *Comprehension monitoring* is the ability to detect problems, use strategies, and judge the quality of what we understand (Garner, 1987). The comprehension monitoring strategies we use in listening and reading help us check and evaluate our understanding of language and take action when comprehension doesn't occur. Effective listeners and readers actively construct meaning and monitor their comprehension. Research has shown that strategic readers use the following comprehension monitoring strategies that you can model for children:

■ *Ignore disruptions.* Temporarily ignore a disruption in meaning. In other words, continue to listen or read until the remaining text of the message clarifies the disruption. For example, a set of directions may include a statement such as *Then you will see a fork in the road.* A child who is not familiar with the meaning of *fork* in this context might visualize a piece of silverware on a highway. If the child temporarily ignores this disruption, the information that follows (e.g., *Take the road on the right and go about a mile until you come to the church*) may restore meaning.

■ *Adjust rate.* If a meaning disruption occurs for the listener, adjust the rate of information received by interrupting and asking the speaker to stop or slow down. The reader adjusts rate by slowing down or scanning ahead. Although it is not always possible or a good idea to teach children to interrupt a speaker with questions, you can encourage them to ask questions when the speaker finishes and to ask the speaker to slow down.

■ *Relisten or reread.* The only way the listener can relisten, unless the message is played back from a tape recorder, is to have something repeated or explained. The reader, however, can reread an entire section if it causes a problem or reread a part to locate the specific information in question. Readers with good comprehension look back or reread parts of the text without being directed to when they encounter obstacles. Poor readers do not seem to spontaneously engage in looking back, but they can be taught this technique and become better readers (Reis & Leone, 1985).

■ *Paraphrase.* Another way to clarify information is to have listeners or readers put it into their own words either mentally, verbally, or in writing. Research supports the notion that the active cognitive processing involved in retelling, paraphrasing, or summarizing aids children's comprehension and learning. So, encourage children to explain in their own words what they heard or read. This repetition also allows for a rehearing by everyone and gives the speaker practice using oral language.

■ *Ask questions.* Both effective listeners and readers ask questions. You can teach children to ask Does this make sense? and Do I understand what I have heard or read? Asking questions about content allows children to keep track of ongoing comprehension. A widely used study strategy called *SQ3R (Survey-Question-Read-Recite-Review)* involves self-questioning that improves comprehension and learning.

■ *Make predictions.* Making predictions ensures accurate comprehension because the listener or reader is personally involved. Help children not only make predictions but also evaluate them by verifying whether they are correct and modifying them based on new information. The discussion of predictions and evaluations actively involves children in comprehending.

■ *Verify understanding.* Effective listeners and readers check to make sure their predictions are accurate. They find answers to the questions they posed as they evaluate their ongoing comprehension processes. They consciously locate information to confirm their predictions.

Good readers are strategic readers. In other words, they use some or all of these strategies for successful comprehension. Children with difficulties in processing language often do not use these strategies. Through instruction, however, these strategies can be taught to poor readers.

Thinking Aloud

Another comprehension enhancing strategy for good listeners and readers is thinking aloud. When people think aloud, they verbalize their thoughts as they read (Davey, 1983). You can model a *think-aloud* by reading aloud a text or watching a video, filmstrip, or movie and pointing out what you do to understand it. Through think-alouds, you can model the comprehension monitoring strategies previously discussed.

For example, after reading the cover and first page of *Galimoto* by Karen Williams (1990), you might say something like this: "At first, I thought the boy's name was Galimoto because of his picture on the cover. But then the first sentence said his name was Kondi. As I read on, I wondered where he got the shoe box, since none of the kids had shoes on. But I knew it was like my special box where I keep my fossil. It's where he keeps his treasures. It said he made a knife from a piece of tin. I wonder what the handle was made from. He had a dancing man made from corn stalks—that must be like the cornstalk dolls my sister used to make."

Some children are not aware of how to keep track of or judge their own comprehension. They need to see and hear how someone else does it so they can imitate these strategies. Davey (1983) identifies five behaviors to model for children.

1. Make predictions.
2. Describe the visual image you have.
3. Share an analogy to link prior knowledge with new information.
4. Verbalize a confusing point.
5. Show how you fix your comprehension problem.

You will find that as you practice these five behaviors with children, it is unnecessary to include all five with every story or in every lesson. With younger children, especially, it is best to use only two or three of the behaviors at a time; otherwise, they may be overwhelmed. But do use these think-aloud behaviors with a variety of materials and genres so children become comfortable using them in any situation where their comprehension breaks down.

STRETCHING EXERCISE Which of Davey's five strategies are used in the think-aloud for the cover and first page of *Galimoto*? Choose a book and try to pause and think aloud as you read. Which strategies do you use?

• • • • •

Baumann, Jones, and Siefert-Kessell (1993) call these strategies *fix-up strategies* since they allow students to correct a comprehension problem. They found that having students share and discuss their own think-alouds together was helpful. Participating in the social construction of think-alouds gave these students control over their own comprehension.

The strategies of modeling, visual imagery, comprehension monitoring, and thinking aloud help both the listener and reader detect problems with comprehension and restore meaning when things they hear or read don't make sense.

Questioning

Another important way to invite and extend comprehension is through questioning. Asking questions is a form of predicting that is critical to comprehension. Children naturally ask questions and the most often asked by them when they are young is Why? Teachers would do well to use children as models in this instance, since Why? questions are often at the heart of learning, with other types of questions also important (e.g., Could? What? How? I wonder? Would? Do you think? When? Who? Should? What if? Where? Is it? etc.). Avoiding yes/no or one-word answers and using questions that require reflection fosters critical thinking, divergent responses, and sound reasoning.

In planning lessons, constantly ask yourself: Why am I doing this? and How does it benefit this child's (or these children's) learning? If you were teaching a lesson on visual imagery with a science text to second-graders, what would your response to these two questions be?

● ● ● ● ●

In the past, teachers often asked questions predominantly to check students' literal comprehension of facts and details. The role of questions has changed today, but Langer (1994) says they are still "at the heart of critical thinking in literature" (p. 208). She says techers' reasons for asking questions are different than they were in the past. Questions should be asked not to guide students toward a predetermined interpretation of a story, but to discover the author's work in their own ways. Langer says that sharing ideas and interpretations from different perspectives allows students to explore multiple meanings—"a horizon of possibilities." Since no person knows exactly what the author intended, this makes sense. Langer suggests that a lesson's questions that accompany it include inviting initial understandings, developing interpretations, and taking a critical stance

Probing with questions such as Do you think? How do you know? What's your hunch? Why did the author . . . ? What if . . . ? I wonder . . . ? How did that happen? Why was it important? How does that conflict with . . . ? allows you to invite and extend personal meaning construction, and to model questioning and curiosity.

Busching and Slesinger (1995) write, "Whether a question is about facts or concepts is less important than whether a question is part of something significant. The outward form of the question may have little to do with the level, the depth, or the importance of thinking that has occurred" (p. 344). In their World War II Holocaust study with seventh-graders, they created a learning environment that stimulated students "to raise

● ● ● ● ●
Children need opportunities to look back, locate, and reread information to confirm and verify their ideas.

and pursue their real questions" that were guided by their own curiosity and emotional involvement. These included questions about information seeking, connected understanding, psychological and moral reconstruction, historical specualtion, literary imagination, style, personal issues, and emotional isssues.

Although nearly 30 percent of the questions the students in Busching and Slesinger's study asked were Why? questions, they believe teachers must rethink their notions that so-called higher-order questions are superior to factual ones. They explain, "In real inquiry, facts offer power and control. The search for an additional fact may be integral to constructing a theory or testing a belief. Facts are both the basis for beliefs and theories and the means for testing them" (p. 344). These researchers remind us of the importance of literal comprehension of text.

Do remember that comprehension and memory are not necessarily the same. Be sure to give children opportunities to look back and reread or locate information to answer questions. This is how adults naturally use print, and it shifts the focus from memory to understanding. Locating information gives children practice in confirming or verifying information, a skill which, if used, improves scores on standardized tests considerably.

How important *are* student questions? Shanklin and Rhodes (1989) believe that when teachers ask questions, they may inadvertently test children's comprehension of the teacher's interpretation of text. So, they suggest teachers turn over the role of asking questions before or after their silent reading of a passage to students. They report that with the teacher as a facilitator and model, children respond to each other's questions, thereby enhancing their comprehension as they arrive at collective meanings for stories. Similarly, Helfeldt and Henk (1990) found that involving middle- and upper-grade students who are considered at risk for failure in self-questioning and reciprocal questioning is an effective way to direct their comprehension.

You can also have children write questions that occur to them as they hear or read a story. These questions can then become the heart of a group discussion in which children interact with each other to answer questions and determine meaning. Some teachers use literature response journals as a place where students can write questions they have about a story as they read it. Students then bring their journals to the literature group and these questions drive discussion.

Carol Hogan, a third-grade teacher, supplied each student in one of her reading groups with a few Post-it notes. As they read the Japanese folktale about the fisherman and his wife, the children wrote their questions on these notes and stuck each note on the page of the story where the question occurred. Figure 6.9 shows some of the questions children posed. Notice many of the questions are Why? questions and involve interpretations of text. The group discussion that followed was lively and student directed because the children took turns asking and answering their own questions. The children returned to the story occasionally to verify information and interpretations.

For students who have trouble writing questions, a list of words that begin questions can help. You can make a bulletin board or bookmarks for young children with question starter words such as the *5 Ws, H and I* (Why? When? Where? What? Who? How? and If?). This straightforward approach provides a prompt for young children and children with language difficulties and differences. Remember to pose your own questions for students to consider after they have read, especially if there are different ways to interpret the material or if students seem to have overlooked an important aspect of the selection.

When children learn to ask and answer their own questions you involve them actively and directly in learning. You help them see that they have much to learn from each other, and you transfer ownership of comprehension and learning to them. What's more, you can learn much about your children by the questions they ask.

Why does she want the Power of the moon and sun?	how come the fishedman let the fish go when he wanted a fish	why does the wife keep saying we will see about that?
Why wasn't the wife happy?	how come the sea changed collers	Why won't the husband, stand up to his wife and tell her no
Why does she want to be King?	What is a larder?	How did the wife know he granted him a wish?
Why does she want to be a Emperor?	why does the wife always change her mind on what she wants	how come the water changes colors?
Was the wife ever happy?	why dose the water keep changing colors	I wonder why she dosent go get them
how come she keeps ayincg that?		Why was the sea green and yellow insted of blue?

FIGURE 6.9 Third-graders wrote these questions on Post-it notes as they read, and the questions fueled their discussion.

STRETCHING
EXERCISE

Read "Circle of Questions" by M. B. Sampson, M. R. Sampson, and W. Linek in the 1995 issue of *The Reading Teacher*, Volume 48, Number 4, pages 364–365. Try this strategy with a group of students. Could they brainstorm, predict, generate questions, and categorize with your help? How would you describe the questions they asked?

● ● ● ● ●

Of course, the classroom environment you create greatly affects your students' questions. You can establish a supportive environment of trust, caring, and respect by accepting every question as valid, accepting all answers and probing for clarification, offering verbal and nonverbal reinforcement, and providing enough wait-time.

Wait-Time and Think-Time

Good teachers ask questions that require interpreting and evaluating written or spoken language. Effective teachers also allow enough time for children to reflect and think before answering questions. *Wait-time* is the length of time teachers wait for answers from students after asking a question. It is used in science and social studies teaching (Atwood, 1991; Rowe, 1987). *Think-time* is essentially the same strategy but used in reading instruction (Gambrell, 1980) (see Figure 6.10).

Research indicates that teachers allow about one second after asking a question before they repeat or rephrase the question, give a clue, call on someone else, or answer the question themselves (Gambrell, 1983). By extending wait-time to three to five seconds, teachers invite children's comprehension and reflective thinking. When the time teachers wait after asking a question and before accepting an answer increases, more children participate and several changes occur in children's responses (Rowe, 1987):

- Length of response increases.
- Responses are more appropriate.
- Speculative thinking increases.
- Quality improves.
- Clarifications and extensions increase.
- Confidence increases.

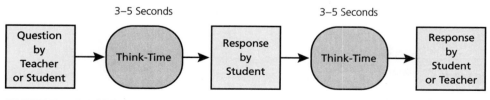

FIGURE 6.10   You can invite and extend comprehension when you increase your think-time to three to five seconds.

Teachers also show changes in their behaviors. The type of questions they ask changes. Teachers ask more reflective questions, and their perceptions of students change. Teachers begin to view students who were perceived as less capable as being more able.

The following is an example of changes in response length and quality due to increased wait-time. After Joseph read the first few pages in *The Armadillo from Amarillo* by Lynne Cherry (1994), his teacher asked him each of the following questions twice. In the A responses, Joseph had one second to think; in the B responses, he had five seconds to think.

1. Why were you smiling as you read these pages?
   A. They were funny.
   B. The postcards on the bottom of the pages were funny. His name was Sasparillo and he sent postcards back to his friend Brillo. He used "tooth and claw" to get up the tower.
2. Why was the armadillo unhappy?
   A. He wanted to know what was out there.
   B. He wanted to explore the world and see what he was missing by staying home.
3. How did he travel?
   A. He walked.
   B. He walked with a stick on his shoulder and a red cloth tied to it with all his belongings in it.

Joseph's answers were longer and more varied when he had more time to think before he spoke. His responses held less information when he responded quickly. Reading his B answers, you get a fuller picture of why Joseph enjoyed the story and how he comprehended it.

Think-time enhances comprehension for both listeners and readers. Both receive information and need time to process it, access their own background information, mesh the two, and formulate a response to the question or to the answer. When you ask children to listen or read and make any type of response at all, be aware of the importance of extending the think-time you allow. Increases in think-time stimulate deeper thinking, expand participation, and improve the quality of children's responses.

Media Literacy

Cortes (1990) states, "For everyone, school learning will come to an end, but media learning will continue, so learning to learn critically from the media should become an integral part of the curriculum" (p. 5). Developing the ability to view the media critically is an important aspect of literacy. Teaching students to identify propaganda and advertisement techniques makes them informed citizens who can make rational decisions and choices. Discriminating viewers of television, magazines, and advertising in general are not as gullible or liable to be swayed by various propaganda techniques used to sell products today. It is also easier for discriminating viewers to reject subtle messages sent by the media to sell products.

Television and Video Viewing.   Here are some provoking statistics:

- The average U.S. household has 2.24 TV sets.
- Two-thirds (66 percent) of Americans regularly watch TV while eating dinner.
- Some 6 million videos are rented daily.
- Approximately 3 million public library items are borrowed daily.
- The average child watches television 1,680 minutes per week.
- The average child spends 38.5 minutes a week in meaningful conversation with parents.
- Half (50 percent) of children ages 6 to 17 have TVs in their bedrooms.
- Some 70 percent of daycare centers use TV during a typical day.
- Of the 10 best-selling toys in 1985, 100 percent were tied to TV shows.
- Some 73 percent of parents would like to limit their children's TV viewing.

These statistics from *TV Free America* (1995) suggest that for many U.S. children and adults, television is a pervasive element in daily life. How do TV and video viewing influence *illiteracy,* which is the inability to read, and *aliteracy,* which is the ability to read but avoidance of reading? Some experts believe TV viewing is at the root of both illiteracy and aliteracy. As a teacher, you can capitalize on this relationship and use television and videos in positive ways to support literacy growth.

You might provide parents with statistics like the ones just given here as well as information on advertisement and propaganda techniques. To develop media literacy, suggest the following ideas to parents:

- Pay special attention to educational shows and those geared toward literacy.
- Limit TV viewing to shows agreed on by the family.
- Plan ahead by marking these shows for the upcoming week in a guide to television shows.
- Turn the TV off until it is time for these shows.
- Watch TV together and talk about the issues and questions the shows raise.
- Define new vocabulary and use these words as you discuss the shows in which they occur.
- Watch TV commercials together and develop *media literacy,* or the notion that many shows exist to provide an audience for advertisers.
- Talk about the relationship between shows and ads. Consider questions such as:
  —Who is that commercial aimed at?
  —Which propaganda technique does this ad use?
  —Why does this company advertise during this show?

Becoming Informed Viewers.   As a teacher, there is much you can do with your students to develop their literacy through TV viewing. You can integrate purposeful TV viewing into your curriculum and encourage the reporting and analysis of TV data in the classroom. You and your students can become "TV-nauts" or "Info-nauts" as you become informed and selective users of television. Here are some ideas:

- Invite students to watch and report on TV shows that relate to topics you are studying in science and social studies.

- Encourage students to watch TV versions of books and compare the two presentations.
- Critique new TV shows and comment on their educational value.
- Teach students to identify propaganda techniques.
- Have students keep a log of TV shows and ads they watch. Ask them to analyze their TV viewing habits and suggest ideas about why advertisers support certain shows.
- As a class, create criteria for watching TV shows and have cooperative groups use the criteria. Ask each group to watch one night's TV, rate the shows, and report their analysis to the class. Then create a guide for TV watching for parents and kids.
- Invite older students to focus on violence in TV shows and explore the ramifications in people's daily lives.
- Have students watch and analyze various TV news shows. Help students explore the terms *shock appeal* and *viewer appeal* and how they relate to what is reported as news.
- Read and discuss magazine and newspaper reviews of TV coverage such as the one in *U.S. News and World Report* (September 11, 1995, p. 67).

Pipher (1994), a psychologist, explains that young girls today are living in a new world with higher levels of violence and sexism than in the past. She believes the crises of adolescence—dropping out of school, suicides, attempted suicides, running away from home, drug use and addiction, eating disorders, and teenage pregnancies—are not the result of dysfunctional families or incorrect messages sent to their daughters by parents.

Rather, Pipher's research suggests that the "media-saturating, lookist, girl-destroying culture" is the culprit. She believes that society needs to make adolescence safe for girls so they can experiment with being girls rather than trying to be the female objects depicted by advertisers in order to sell products. One of the things Pipher suggests is for girls to keep journals where they have a safe place for their own voices to be heard.

Teaching your students to identify advertisement and propaganda techniques is also important. This knowledge may help students understand themselves better as they perceive the stereotypes established by society that are not necessarily good. Such stereotypes contribute to making adolescence difficult for many children and their parents.

Propaganda Detection. During two hours of watching television, children see as many as 50 commercials. If children watch two hours of television a day, and this is a low estimate, they may see as many as 36,500 commercials in one year. Although children don't read magazines and newspapers as often as they watch television, it is important to note that the content of magazines and newspapers is over 50 percent advertising. Both hearing and reading these advertisements in the media provides children with opportunities for interpretation, evaluation, and critical thinking. As educated consumers, children should learn to detect the various techniques often employed to sell products.

Even children in first grade can become critical listeners and readers (Allen, Wright, & Laminack, 1988). They can detect words such as *tasty, tender, softer,* and *longer-lasting* that persuade the viewer to buy products. They can then test the products against these claims and evaluate the accuracy of ads. You can have older students bring in advertisements from magazines and newspapers and display them on a bulletin board. Help them analyze these ads for the following propaganda devices:

- *Endorsement.* A popular and respected person supports or approves a product.
- *Bandwagon.* Everyone is doing a certain thing or using a certain product.
- *Plain folks talk.* A person, product, or program is linked to the common people.
- *Card stacking.* Information on one side of an argument or story is given, and the opposing view is omitted.
- *Glittering generalities.* Vague words are used to shape an opinion without being specific.
- *Derogatory words.* Scare words or negative labels are used to influence.
- *Statistics.* Numbers are erroneously used to impress.
- *Slogans.* Catchy phrases or tunes are attached to a product.
- *Snob appeal.* The rich, famous, or popular who are smart or classy use the product.
- *Humor.* A funny incident is associated with a product.

These techniques for selling products are called *propaganda devices* because they attempt to distort the truth or deceive the viewer and influence opinion to sell a certain product. First, teach children to identify a propaganda device, then help them see how the device affects the listener or reader. Have them compare the ad to the product and form their own opinions. Every informed consumer should possess this critical, functional skill.

STRETCHING EXERCISE   Watch television for one hour and use the preceding list to identify the propaganda device in each commercial. What conclusions can you draw? Students of what age group might benefit from this activity and learning?

● ● ● ● ●

Listening/Reading Transfer

Although listening and reading differ in many ways, they also possess several similarities, one of which is the construction of meaning by the receiver. Most elementary-school-age children can understand more when a story or selection is read to them than when they read it themselves. These children have large listening vocabularies and knowledge of the world but have not yet developed word identification strategies or large sight-word vocabularies. A child's listening vocabulary is the first to develop and it remains larger than speaking, reading, or writing vocabularies until well into the upper-elementary grades.

Cunningham and Allington (1994) suggest the listening-reading transfer lesson as one way to achieve better comprehension. In this lesson, children learn that the kinds of things they do during and after listening to construct meaning are the same as the kinds of things they do during and after reading.

·····
*A child's reading vocabulary
usually develops from his listening
vocabulary, which is the basis for
his speaking, reading, and writing
vocabularies.*

To teach a transfer lesson, you need to plan two parallel activities. In the first, have the children listen and respond in certain ways, and in the second, have them read and respond in the same ways. After the children listen to a story and respond to it, you can tell them what they just did during the listening lesson is exactly the thing you will ask them to do during reading. For example, the children might write a response in a journal or draw a picture or ask a question about the story. Three things are basic to the success of a transfer lesson:

1. Ask the children to read like they listen.
2. Set specific purposes for listening and reading.
3. Have the children explain how they arrived at meaning.

When children engage in the same activities during and after reading that they used during and after listening, they have a better chance of realizing how the two are similar. Of course, your observations about this similarity are important reinforcement. When you help children set purposes for listening and reading, then they have a reason to listen and read and they have confidence that they will comprehend. When a child thinks aloud or explains how he arrived at a conclusion, you provide opportunities for other children to see the thinking that results in meaning construction. In this way, children become models for each other, showing each other how to make sense and comprehend both oral and written text. You, of course, can be a constant model for them, too.

As you invite and extend children's comprehension, keep three things in mind:

1. Comprehension is a personal process of constructing meaning that is influenced by many factors.
2. Each child constructs meaning, interprets, and evaluates information differently.
3. There are a myriad of strategies for enhancing comprehension. What works for one child may not necessarily work for another.

Summary

Both listening and reading involve the construction of meaning from incoming data and what is already known. You can invite and extend comprehension and enhance reflective thinking by helping children establish their own purposes for listening and reading. Promote children's comprehension by being a good model and teaching them to use visual imagery, comprehension monitoring, and think-aloud strategies. Promote comprehension and reflective thinking through questioning, think-time, media literacy, knowledge of propaganda techniques, and listening/reading transfer lessons.

R•••••eflections

1. Interview an experienced K–6 teacher about the connections between listening and reading. First, make a list of questions to ask (e.g., Are the good listeners in your class the good readers? Why or why not? Do you emphasize the similarities between listening and reading in your teaching? Why or why not?). Compare your findings with others. Do you see any patterns across or within grade levels?

2. Examine the language arts curriculum guides for reading and listening in your school. What similarities or differences are there in the way they develop comprehension? What are some possible explanations? Write a letter (like Mark's at the beginning of this chapter) to first-grade parents about why and how you intend to teach the two together.

Professional Resources

Gallas, K. (1994). *The languages of learning how children talk, write, dance, draw, and sing their understanding of the world.* New York: Teachers College Press. With classroom examples and anecdotes, a teacher talks about the many types of communication children use to express their thoughts in a new kind of learning community.

Glazer, S. M. (1992). *Reading comprehension: Self-monitoring strategies to develop independent readers.* New York: Scholastic. This book gives classroom-tested strategies for teaching children how to monitor and improve comprehension as they read a variety of texts.

Manning, B. H., & Payne, B. D. (1996). *Self-talk for teachers and students: Metacognitive strategies for personal and classroom use.* Boston: Allyn and Bacon. Full of classroom examples, this book explains the use of metacognitive strategies you can use to improve planning, organization, and classroom management while you improve students' study skills and achievement.

References

Allen, E. G., Wright, J. P., & Laminack, L. L. (1988). Using language experience to ALERT pupils: Critical thinking skills. *The Reading Teacher, 41,* 904–910.

Atwood, V. A. (1991). Wait time and effective social studies instruction: What can research in science education tell us? *Social Education, 55* (3), 179–181.

Baumann, J. F., Jones, L. A., & Seifert-Kessell, N. (1993). Using think alouds to enhance children's comprehension monitoring abilities. *The Reading Teacher, 47* (3), 184–193.

Bear, D. R., & Invernizzi, M. (1984). Student directed reading groups. *Journal of Reading, 28* (3), 248–257.

Betts, E. (1946). *Foundations of reading instruction.* New York: American.

Busching, B. A., & Slesinger, B. A. (1995). Authentic questions "What do they look like? Where do they lead?" *Language Arts, 72* (5), 341–351.

Carlisle, J. F., & Felbinger, L. (1991). Profiles of listening and reading comprehension. *Journal of Educational Research, 84* (6), 345–354.

Cortes, C. E. (1990). A curricular basic for our multi-ethnic future. *Doubts and certainties; Newsletter of the NEA Mastery in Learning Project, 4* (7/8), 1–5.

Cunningham, P. M., & Allington, R. L. (1994). *Classrooms that work: They can all read and write.* New York: HarperCollins.

Davey, B. (1983). Think aloud: Modeling the cognitive processes of reading comprehension. *Journal of Reading, 27* (l), 44–47.

Gambrell, L. B. (1983). The occurrence of thinktime during reading comprehension instruction. *Journal of Educational Research, 77* (3), 77–80.

Gambrell, L. B. (1980). Think-time: Implications for reading instruction. *The Reading Teacher, 34* (2), 143–146.

Gambrell, L. B., & Bales, R. J. (1986). Mental imagery and the comprehension-monitoring performance of fourth- and fifth-grade poor readers. *Reading Research Quarterly, 21,* 454–464.

Gambrell, L. B., & Jawitz, P. B. (1993). Mental imagery, text illustrations, and children's story comprehension and recall. *Reading Research and Instruction, 28* (3), 264–273.

Garner, R. (1987). *Metacognition and reading comprehension.* Norwood, NJ: Ablex.

Hedrick, W. B. (1995). The relationship between wide reading and listening comprehension of written language. *Journal of Reading Behavior, 27* (3), 425–438.

Helfeldt, J. P., & Henk, W. A. (1990). Reciprocal question-answer relationships: An instructional technique for at-risk readers. *Journal of Reading, 33,* 509–515.

Irwin-DeVitis, L. (1990). *Imaging: A strategy for improving reading, listening, and writing.* Presentation to Binghamton Area Reading Council, Binghamton, NY.

Konopak, B. C., Williams, N. L., & Jampole, E. S. (1996). Students' use of imagery for understanding in individual and shared readings of a short story. *The Language and Literacy Spectrum, 6,* 58–63.

Krashen, S. D. (1995). The reading/listening library. *Mosaic, 24,* 20.

Langer, J. A. (1994). A response-based approach to reading literature. *Language Arts, 71* (3), 203–211.

Ogle, D. (1997). *DLTA/DRTA evaluation.* Evanston, IL: National College.

Palincsar, A. S., & Brown, A. L. (1988). Teaching and practicing thinking skills to promote comprehension in the context of group problem solving. *Remedial and Special Education, 9,* 53–59.

Pearson, P. D., & Fielding, L. (1982). Research update: Listening comprehension. *Language Arts, 59* (6), 617–629.

Pearson, P. D., & Johnson, D. D. (1978). *Teaching reading comprehension.* New York: Holt, Rinehart and Winston.

Pipher, M. (1994). *Reviving Ophelia: Saving the selves of adolescent girls.* New York: Putnam.

Reis, R., & Leone, P. E. (1985). Teaching text lookbacks to mildly handicapped students. *Journal of Reading, 28* (5), 416–421.

Rowe, M. B. (1987). Wait time: Slowing down may be a way of speeding up. *American Educator, 11* (l), 38–43, 47.

Ruddell, R. B., Ruddell, M. R., & Singer, H. (Eds.) (1994). *Theoretical models and processes of reading* (4th ed.). Newark, DE: International Reading Association.

Sampson, M. B., Sampson, M. R., & Linek, W. (1995). Circle of questions. *The Reading Teacher, 48* (4), 364–365.

Shanklin, N. L., & Rhodes, L. K. (1989). Comprehension instruction as sharing and extending. *The Reading Teacher, 42,* 496–500.

Stauffer, R. (1981). *Directing the reading-thinking process.* New York: HarperRow.

Taylor, D., & Dorsey-Gaines, C. (1988). *Growing up literate: Learning from inner-city families.* Portsmouth, NH: Heinemann.

TV Free America (1995, March). Government publication. 1322 18th St. NW, Suite 300, Washington, DC 20036.

Vacca, R. T., & Vacca, J. L. (1995). *Reading and learning to read* (3rd ed.). New York: Addison Wesley-Collins.

Weaver, C. (1994). *Reading process and practice: From socio-psycholinguistics to whole language.* Portsmouth, NH: Heinemann.

Wing, C. P. (1879). *History of Cumberland County, Pennsylvania 1731–1789.* Philadelphia: J. D. Scott.

Children's Book References

Cherry, L. (1994). *The armadillo from Amarillo.* San Diego: Harcourt.

Cherry, L. (1992). *A river ran wild.* San Diego: Harcourt.

Cherry, L. (1993). *The great Kapok tree.* New York: Trumpet.

Conrad, P. (1991). *Pedro's journal.* New York: Scholastic.

MacGill-Callahan, S. (1991). *And still the turtle watched.* New York: Trumpet.

Ryder, J. (1996). *Earthdance.* New York: Holt.

Williams, K. L. (1990). *Galimoto.* New York: Mulberry.

Williams, S. A. (1992). *Working cotton.* San Diego: Harcourt.

Yolen, J. (1992). *Encounter.* San Diego: Harcourt.

Listening
to Learn

7

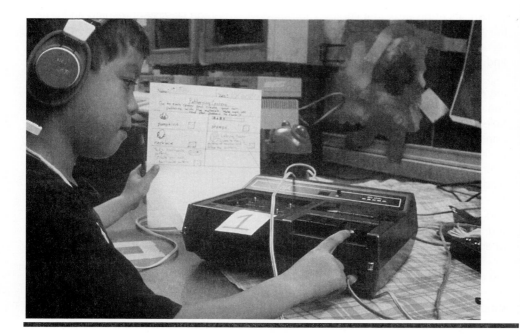

W•••••
indow on Teaching

Brandon stands in a circle with his kindergarten peers. They are singing "Hokey Pokey" and doing the movements that accompany it. At first, Brandon can't decide which is his right and left, but he watches Shelly beside him and imitates her movements.

Across the hall in a first-grade classroom, Tori and her classmates stand behind their desks and carry out the verbal directions their teacher gives them, such as:

"Point to the front of the room."
"Take two steps away from me."
"Take one step to your right."

"Point up . . . point down."

"Take three steps toward me."

A few doors down in a second grade, Samantha sits alone in a small red chair, looking out the window. At first glance, she is so still one might think she is in a trance. A closer look shows that she is wearing headphones connected to a small tape recorder. A sign above the table says "Listening Lab." There is an unopened copy of *Wilfred Gordon McDonald Partridge* by Mem Fox (1990), the story of a small boy who helps an old woman find her memory, on the table in front of Samantha and she listens intently to the story on tape.

In another part of this school, wearing earphones connected to a tape recorder, Shawn sits at his desk in a combination third/fourth-grade classroom reading and listening to a student-created book titled *Adventure with an Adirondack Bear*, written and recorded by his classmate, Chris. Shawn intently examines the hand-drawn illustrations and photographs in the book as he reads the handprinted text on each page.

What do these snapshots have in common? Each shows children actively constructing meaning as they listen. How do these snapshots differ? Brandon, Tori, and Shawn can use available visual input to aid their listening. Their teachers know the value of multiple cues and reinforcement, and so they encourage this kind of active listening. Brandon's and Tori's teachers are beginning to develop the geographic concept of *location* by having the children respond physically to oral directions. Samantha is following the instructions printed at her listening center: "1. Listen and imagine. 2. Listen, look, and read." To promote comprehension, Samantha's teacher has the children listen to stories twice, making their own visual images first without any visual stimulation, and then read and listen to the story again. Shawn is reading and hearing a peer's story. Shawn's posture and attention to what he is doing suggest his interest and enthusiasm for the work of an author he knows.

In September, the teachers in this K–4 elementary school identified improved listening as one of their goals for students. In October, they invited their curriculum coordinator to work with them on the topic of listening. Some of their comments after the workshop follow:

It was an excellent review of the importance of listening. In this day and age when computers and computer literacy seem to have caught everyone's attention, I was glad to be reminded how much of what we do and how children learn still involves listening. The examples she gave and our brainstorming about how listening is required in our everyday jobs were sobering.

—Brandon's teacher

What was the most fun for me was seeing how, with a little bit of attention, I can include opportunities for purposeful listening in my everyday lessons, like social studies for example. When we participated in the role-playing activity, I was reminded again of how to be an active listener. I think I interrupt too much and I allow too much of it in my classroom. We're always in such a rush that we don't give kids the time they need to talk, and so we show them how to be terrible listeners.

—Tori's teacher

When we were asked to take the listening comprehension test required in this state in twelfth grade, it was a challenge for me. It was two long selections that we had to understand and compare. A lot of teachers missed several questions, but I got them all right. I pride myself on my listening skills. I think they're pretty good because I listen to books on tape every day when I walk. I thought about it and decided part of the reason I have good listening skills is these tapes. They force me to listen hard and I've learned to make visual images of what I hear. So, I decided to teach this strategy to my kids and I incorporated it into our classroom Listening Lab.

—Samantha's teacher

The idea of "Dialing 'D' for Doctor" was a surprise to me. We learned that medical schools are now adding courses in "telephone medicine" to their curriculums. Diagnosis and doctoring by telephone require careful listening, good questioning, data collecting, and tactful responses, not to mention accurate replies. I learned that it's important to know the message giver because it helps you understand and care about the message. These are real-life skills we can help our kids develop right here in school."

—Shawn's teacher

These teachers have made a commitment to learning more about listening and the development of good listeners. They are learning how to listen themselves and how to embed listening opportunities in their regular curriculum. These four students and the others in their classes are becoming active listeners.

· · · · ·

Overview

Listening is a receptive language process and is the first of the language arts to develop in young children. It involves the construction of meaning from the listener's schemata as well as what is heard and often seen. Good listening is best developed when it is embedded in authentic classroom learning. As you read this chapter, remember that listening and speaking are interactive processes that directly affect each other.

The ability to listen develops early, but exactly how early has yet to be determined. Research with unborn babies suggests that sounds and voices are perceived even in the uterus. A newborn baby who hears her father talk and read to her before birth turns her head toward her father's voice at birth and shows little response to the voice of an unfamiliar male. Likewise, a baby also has a decided preference for her mother's voice compared to an unknown female. A good example of this is witnessing a child who stops crying at the sound of her mother's voice. Listening continues to develop and function in specific ways for children as they grow and become more aware of the environment. Careful and effective listening:

- Allows children to appreciate and enjoy their world
- Helps children make their wants and needs known
- Changes and controls speakers' voices
- Aids learning because it involves information processing
- Permits fuller interaction with others
- Is a social tool that is basic to communication
- Helps children express their uniqueness

Meaning Construction and the Listener

Sound is "an onrushing, cresting, and withdrawing wave of air molecules that begins with the movement of any object, however large or small, and ripples out in all directions" (Ackerman, 1990, p. 177). *Hearing* involves the reception of sound. *Listening,* however, is the interpretation of sound into meaning. It is "the process by which spoken language is converted to meaning in the mind" (Lundsteen, 1979, p. 1). Listening is an active, cognitive process that requires conscious attention to relate sound to meaning. The listener interacts with incoming information and monitors her comprehension to obtain meaning. Most young children and many older students can listen to and understand more sophisticated language than they can read. Listening, a receptive language skill, involves acuity, auditory discrimination, and auding (Buttery & Anderson 1980).

- *Acuity* is the ability to hear (e.g., a pencil sharpener in use, paper torn from a notebook, a person's voice, a helicopter, wind in the trees, etc.).
- *Auditory discrimination* is the ability to distinguish among sounds (e.g., a typewriter vs. a telephone, a question vs. a statement, *hot* vs. *hat, same* vs. *name,* and *bed* vs. *dead*). The phonological aspects of pitch, stress, intonation, and juncture also affect auditory discrimination.
- *Auding* is the ability to link meaning with a spoken message (e.g., understanding the content and intention of speech by using semantics [word meanings] and syntax [word order and function]).

Listening is often called the *neglected language art* because it is assumed that students can listen well and can learn by listening. However, that is not the case. Listening is a receptive language process that involves the listener's schemata as well as what is heard and often seen. Some children are not effective listeners, but strategies for good listening can be taught.

On average, adults gain 80 percent of what they know by listening; however, most adults operate below a 25 percent listening efficiency level (Hunsaker, 1990). Most students spend more than 50 percent of each school day engaged in listening (Wolvin & Coakley, 1988), and one can assume that their listening efficiency levels are probably similar. So, it seems that merely practicing listening does not result in effective listening. But you can incorporate listening instruction into your classroom in natural ways through both indirect and direct instruction (Brent & Anderson, 1993).

Effective Listening

Effective listening occurs when a listener uses auditory acuity and discrimination to identify sounds and words and simultaneously translates these words into meaning by auding or comprehending. Meaning construction does not occur when a speaker's message is merely decoded. In order for meaning construction to occur, the listener must be an active participant in the transaction as she hears, identifies, and associates meaning with the sounds of language.

As language develops, "the infant in the crib furnishes a ready example of a child learning to listen; the fact that the infant soon eliminates all but the sounds of the language she is learning from her repertoire of noises suggests that she differentiates among sounds and chooses to reproduce only the meaningful ones" (Bauman, 1987, pp. 56–57). Older children and adult listeners are also active participants in the listening process. As effective listeners, they actively comprehend spoken messages by creating meaning and predicting what a speaker will say next, choosing from a whole variety of possibilities.

Effective listeners concentrate on what is said. They are usually silent and attentive. They watch a speaker for nonverbal cues to meaning that might be evident in facial expressions or body gestures. They monitor their comprehension and realize that when there is a mismatch between what they hear and what they think, they can check or verify the mismatch in some way and "fix" their comprehension. They may ask questions, request that a word or idea be repeated, or take notes. Effective listeners actively process incoming information as they construct meaning.

Factors Affecting Listening

You can categorize the factors that affect listening in the same way as the factors that affect meaning construction (Chapter 6). The slight differences between the two involve the specific characteristics of an oral interaction.

1. *Listener factors*

▬ *Purpose.* If there is no reason to listen, children will often have a comprehension problem. So, make sure that before listening, there is a reason or purpose for it. This increases the chances that the children will be able to make sense out of what they hear. Providing a purpose for listening is perhaps the single most important thing you can do as a teacher, and probably one of the most neglected (Funk & Funk, 1989).

▬ *Schemata.* Children with a fund of knowledge from both firsthand and vicarious experiences have the required concepts and meanings to associate with spoken language. Children with limited experiences, such as English learners or those from other cultures, may have trouble and will need you to fill in the gaps in their schema.

▬ *Physical characteristics.* Clearly, acuity is an important aspect of good listening and keenness of hearing can affect what is heard. Children who are deaf or have hearing difficulties should sit near you or close to the front of the room. When you and students speak, these children need to be able to see the speakers' faces because lipreading and body language can give clues to what is said.

2. *Situation or context factors*

▬ *Environment.* For children who are deaf or have hearing difficulties, when an oral event occurs, the environment should be free of distractions and noise. Arrange the classroom so children can concentrate on the verbal message. Certainly, learning isn't always quiet, but a relatively silent classroom is more conducive to comprehending a story or oral report than a classroom with loud or distracting noise.

▬ *Visual reinforcement.* The concrete visual stimuli you give can increase listening comprehension. For example, if you want children to learn about the countries of the Western Hemisphere, use a map or globe to reinforce your oral explanation. Use the chalkboard or overhead projector to draw diagrams or write notes to give children the benefit of visual reinforcement.

3. *Speaker factors*

▬ *Redundancy.* Communicating a message in several ways (e.g., through gestures, facial expressions, and nonverbal language) is important. The more redundant you make a message, the better its chance of being understood, especially by those with hearing and language difficulties.

▬ *Content organization and clarity.* When you speak, organization, logically sequenced ideas, examples, and paraphrasing help your message be more easily understood.

▬ *Pronunciation.* Clear and distinct articulation, pitch, stress, and juncture affect listening comprehension.

▬ *Eye contact.* Children are more apt to hear, understand, and appreciate a message delivered by a speaker who makes eye contact than one who looks away.

▬ *Speed of delivery.* Speaking too quickly can make it difficult for many children to process concepts and ideas.

•••••
Dressing as book characters to give a report heightens audience interest and gives these shy speakers confidence.

4. Instructional factors

■ *Classroom environment.* You can create an interesting, rich, and supportive classroom environment that reinforces good listening in many ways. Most important, initially, is to help learners establish a purpose for listening.

■ *Comprehension monitoring.* You can model strategies such as checking and adjusting understanding, associating new information with what is already known, questioning, paraphrasing, and stopping the speaker to request the message be repeated or explained.

■ *Active listening.* You can model the characteristics of an active listener and teach your students to listen actively.

To what extent do listening and thinking overlap? Studies comparing children's performances on listening tests with their performances on IQ tests, which measure cognitive processing and thinking, show that listening and IQ have a correlation as high as .82 (Devine, 1978). This rather high correlation means that about 67 percent of the tests measure the same thing, not necessarily that one causes the other. The remaining 33 percent of the differences in test scores depends on other factors.

Make a list of other factors that tests of listening and IQ may measure. How else are listening and IQ related? Are poor listeners usually poor readers? Why? Are reading and writing easy for all good listeners? Explain your answer.

● ● ● ● ●

STRETCHING EXERCISE

Modeling Active Listening

Active listeners are alert to all of the messages conveyed by a speaker, and they process information as they receive it. The minds of active listeners are as energetic, vigorous, and agile as the body of a gymnast at work on a balance beam.

Paley (1986), a kindergarten teacher, writes that if we are to help children learn in our classrooms, which have "all the elements of theater," then "We must listen with curiosity and great care to the main characters who are, of course, the children" (p. 300). In her work, Paley documents the teaching and learning that occur in her classroom because she listens actively and makes careful observations. You, too, can engage in active listening and praise children who are active listeners so your classroom has good models to emulate. Here are some suggestions to help you:

■ *Be quiet.* Practice think-time. Don't supply a hesitant child with a word or two when she pauses. This disrupts her thoughts and tells her you lack confidence in her ability to find the right language. The best way to convey to children that you value what they say is to remain silent, absorb their message, and wait so you have time to form a response. Encourage children to practice think-time, too.

▬ *Make eye contact.* Avoid looking away from a child. Gazing around the room or working on a bulletin board tells the child that you have something else on your mind or that her message is unimportant. For some Native Americans, eye contact denotes disrespect or arrogance. So, don't always mistake a lack of eye contact as rudeness or inability to listen; it may be a cultural behavior.

▬ *Note nonverbal language.* Watch the child's gestures, facial expressions, and body movements, all of which convey a variety of messages. These nonverbal cues can clarify the message of an English learner, an ESL student, or a child with a hearing loss. When nonverbal cues don't match a verbal message, they often communicate something unsaid. As an alert listener, you should actively process all the messages a child conveys, watching for her feelings and *how* she says something.

▬ *Monitor comprehension.* Make associations between what you know and what you hear. When you can't make sense of what you hear, find an appropriate time to ask a question or paraphrase what you heard. A verbal summary or paraphrase is a good way to process information, and it lets the child know you comprehended what she said.

▬ *Share visual images.* Create visual images for what the child says and share them. The child can then confirm or correct you if you misinterpreted.

▬ *Encourage the speaker.* Give a shy or tense child encouragement as she speaks (e.g., nod your head, raise your eyebrows, smile, give a quizzical look, or ask a question to clarify a point or obtain more information) (see Table 7.1). Many children have little

TABLE 7.1   Use these prompts to help you listen actively.

Verbal Prompts for Active Listening

Type of Prompt	Purpose	How to	Example
Clarifying	▬ To get more information ▬ To introduce other points of view	▬ Ask questions ▬ Avoid yes/no questions	▬ What do you mean? ▬ Why did this happen?
Encouraging	▬ To show interest ▬ To prompt more talk	▬ Neither agree nor disagree ▬ Use neutral words	▬ Tell me more . . . ▬ Go on . . .
Restating	▬ To check your understanding ▬ To acknowledge what you heard	▬ Restate what is said	▬ You said . . . ▬ This means . . .
Summarizing	▬ To review ▬ To establish basic ideas and information	▬ Restate main ideas	▬ You said . . . ▬ This means . . .

opportunity to speak or be heard at home, and so need a good listener at school. When you listen intently to a child, you provide her with practice and confidence in speaking as well as a model to emulate.

■ *Share reflections.* Take time to think about the child's message, and make associations between what you know and don't know. Respond personally to the message.

A practical application of these guidelines follows.

Teleconferencing

Kisten Schroeder, a fourth-grade teacher in a rural school, uses teleconferencing to enrich her curriculum and demonstrate the critical nature of active listening. The kind of teleconferencing she uses includes a telephone conversation performed with a standard telephone and a speaker system owned by her school. She has used two types of teleconferences. In the first, an informational teleconference, she and her class spoke with a naturalist at a nature center to learn more about what he did and what resources the center had. In the second type, an author interview, she and her class spoke with James Howe, who wrote *Hot Fudge* (1990), the story of a vampire rabbit named Bunnicula, among many other humorous stories. Teleconferences allow students to speak directly with the personal representative of a company, a governmental figure, an author, or an illustrator, for example.

Kisten cautions that teleconferencing involves planning and collaboration with students. Because Kisten uses a literature approach to reading instruction and a writing process approach, she feels that talking to a published author gives authenticity to what she hopes to teach her students. Kisten began the project by asking the library media specialist in her school for a list of authors available for a teleconference. She chose James Howe because some of her students were reading his books. She obtained copies of all his books and the class spent several days reading and discussing his work. In small groups, students brainstormed questions to ask Howe about his books and the writing process he uses. As a class, they omitted duplicate questions and practiced on the equipment the day before with a friend of Kisten's who role-played James Howe.

From this teleconferencing experience with an author, students modeled quiet and attentive listening and learned the importance of taking turns, speaking slowly and clearly, cooperating, and preplanning. They had firsthand experience finding out how and why an author writes and even discovered that Howe was once a fourth-grader, like themselves, who liked to write "gross tales." The students also learned that Howe writes from three to five drafts of a story before it ever goes to his publisher.

Chance (1993) says teleconferencing is an overlooked approach to learning and gives specific ideas on how to do it. Gorton (1989) shows how writing skills, as well as listening and speaking skills, can be sharpened by teleconferencing. She recommends the following preconferencing activities: Write letters to parents and invite them to attend, write a sequel to the author's book, draw a portrait and write a description of what you think the author looks like and where he or she may live, and list the questions to ask the author. Gorton then suggests activities for after the conference: Write and send a thank-you note to the author, compose a description of what you and the author have in common, and write a story for the school or local newspaper or class newsletter about the teleconference. You can undoubtedly think of many more reading and writing connections.

Kisten believes teleconferencing is truly an integrative activity that can provide role models for students, increase self-esteem, broaden cultural awareness, provide career information, and foster cooperation. At the same time, teleconferencing is strongly rooted in the curriculum.

STRETCHING EXERCISE

Read "Communications Technology for Literacy Work with Isolated Learners" by Diane Taylor, Peter Skippington, and Lloyd Lacey in the 1989 issue of *Journal of Reading,* Volume 32, pages 634–639. In what other settings besides rural schools can teleconferencing be useful? How?

• • • • •

Developing Listening with Literature

Listening to literature read orally functions in special ways for children. Results of several studies show reading achievement—measured in terms of comprehension, vocabulary, decoding abilities, and readiness—improves as a result of listening to literature read orally. Dennis (1995) reports that first-graders who listened to multiple read-alouds of the same story increased their story comprehension. Cullinan, Jaggar, and Strickland (1974) report that when 20 classes of African American 7-year-olds were read to for 20 minutes a day for one school year, they showed significantly higher gains in vocabulary and comprehension than a group that had not been read to. Kimmel and Segel (1983) report that first-, second-, fourth-, and sixth-graders read to on a regular basis over a period of months showed significant gains in reading comprehension, decoding skills, and vocabulary over control groups who were read to only occasionally or not at all.

Listening to literature read aloud also develops language and learning, in general. It stimulates children's language and the desire to want to read. Martinez and Teale (1988) studied a kindergarten classroom where a teacher read some books repeatedly and other books less often. They found that not only did children choose the more familiar books three times as often, they also imitated the teacher in the ways they "read" them. A review of literature dealing with parents reading aloud to children shows that the single most important factor in developing children's interest in reading and becoming readers themselves may well be regular exposure to books at home as a natural and enjoyable part of everyday life.

When young African American children with language difficulties were read to daily and took part in related oral activities, their general facility with language was significantly increased over children in a control group who merely listened to stories (Strickland, 1973). Storytelling and oral reading to upper-elementary school students also improves both language and learning (Frick, 1986). There are other benefits as well, such as increased motivation for both reading and writing and an opportunity for the imagination to roam. Listening to stories read orally is a pleasurable and relaxing experience for all students—no matter what the ability or age.

Listening to quality literature can affect writing as well. Dressel (1990) reports that fifth-grade students who heard and discussed quality literature had richer retellings and wrote stories that differed significantly on traits related to literary quality than those who heard and talked about literature that was not considered quality by a panel of experts. The richness and characteristics of the three mysteries they heard were reflected in the richness of the narratives these children wrote. There were no differences between good and poor readers; both did equally well. The richer stories included well-developed characters who came alive through dialogue, thought, and action, and they created unique plots developed with appropriate details.

Besides these measurable benefits from listening to literature read aloud, there are others not as easily measured but still evident. Mendoza (1985) reports that both primary-grade (94 percent) and intermediate-grade (73 percent) children overwhelmingly enjoy being read to. She concludes that listening to stories read orally

- Promotes a desire to read
- Enhances independent reading skills
- Broadens reading experiences and interests
- Exposes children to books they might not otherwise read
- Provides a model of reading for enjoyment that children can emulate

Trelease (1989) writes convincingly about how a teacher can instill a desire for books and reading in an entire family or class. He reports that the attitudes of sixth-grade remedial students changed considerably when their teacher read them *Where the Red Fern Grows* by Wilson Rawls (1974). At first, the children were insulted when she read aloud to them, but they quickly became eager to hear each morning's chapter. One boy even got a library card, took the book out, and finished it himself.

As important as these benefits are, however, children's learning is the major concern of most teachers. Approximately 75 percent of the information a child receives through language comes through listening (Lundsteen, 1974), and teachers estimate that children spend over half their time in the classroom listening. Despite its basic role in classroom learning, teachers have concentrated on reading and writing and have largely ignored listening (Funk & Funk, 1989). So, although listening is a critical language process, and teachers, for the most part, recognize its importance, we know less about listening than the other language arts.

Listening Models in Literature

Children's literature provides children with important models of good and poor listeners, children who have problems listening, and the consequences of different listening behaviors. There are many books that include situations where listening is a main theme or critical component of the story.

Young children relate to Mary Ann and Louie, who learn from their grandfather how wonderful it can be to listen to a good storyteller in *There's Nothing to Do* by James Stevenson (1986), and to a young girl who hears sounds in *I Thought I Heard* by Alan Baker (1996), as she tries to go to sleep at night. In *The Conversation Club* by Diane Stanley (1983), a mouse starts his own listening club when he discovers that everyone talking at once doesn't work.

• • • • •
Children's literature provides children with models of good listeners and the results of different listening behaviors.

Older children enjoy such stories as *The Harvest Birds/Los Pajaros de la Cosecha* by B. L. De Mariscal (1995), a story in English and Spanish about a young Hispanic who realizes his dream by listening to the voices of nature; *Carolina Shout!* by Alan Schroeder (1995), about the street sounds an African American girl hears in the Charleston of a bygone era; *Keeping It Secret* by Penny Pollock (1982), a story about the determination of a young girl named Wisconsin who hides her hearing problem from classmates in a new school; and *Your Silent Language* by Evelyn McGough (1974), about the science of kinesics or body language and how it affects what one hears and perceives. In *The Kidnapping of Aunt Elizabeth* by Betty Parte (1985), a girl learns the importance of listening as she interviews her relatives. Annotations of these and other books appear in Children's Books about Listening at the end of this chapter.

Teaching Listening

Listening instruction receives little attention in the professional literature, as compared to reading and writing, for example. But recent attention on listening instruction gives teachers valuable ideas to consider when planning their curricula and teaching (Brent & Anderson, 1993; Winkle, 1991).

There are three important reasons for teaching children how to listen. First, listening is the principal way children get directions and information from the teacher and peers in the classroom. Second, children spend enormous amounts of time outside the classroom each day listening. Third, the ability to be an effective listener is critical for learning in the classroom and for survival in the everyday world. Television, radio, and video affect nearly all people in some way daily. Listening to a news report, speech, or conversation for information contained in each message is a skill that is used constantly. Critical listening to political and consumer messages is almost a daily necessity for an adult and should be for children, as well. In addition, the ability to listen for appreciation and enjoyment makes life fuller and more satisfying for all.

Considerable evidence exists supporting the notion that there is a direct relationship between listening and learning (Strother, 1987) and that listening is a skill that can be taught. Reviews of research (Devine, 1978; Pearson & Fielding, 1982) cite evidence that children who get direct training through systematic instruction show improvement in listening comprehension. Most of the training methods and tests employed in this research use reading comprehension skills such as identifying the main idea, sequencing, summarizing, and remembering facts as they apply to listening. Findings suggest that when some type of active involvement—such as establishing purposes or providing follow-up experiences to a spoken or written response—accompanies listening, the listener processes the information received and better understands and remembers it.

There many things to consider when teaching listening to all students, and especially to those with learning difficulties, with hearing problems, or who are English learners. Among them are the following:

- *Music* is pleasurable for children, whether they listen to music they have created themselves or hear it live or recorded. Knowing the special beauty of music should be a part of every child's experience. The music teacher in your school can suggest records and tapes, as well as provide your students with instruction in music appreciation.
- *Rhythmic language* in literature includes everything from nursery rhymes to poetry and prose. Reading aloud to children and encouraging them to read aloud to each other helps them understand and savor the cadence and rhythm of language.
- *Visual imagery* is an excellent way to develop listening. Visual images are a special tool for helping children understand and remember what they hear with rich detail.
- *Metacognitive strategies* allow children to think for themselves and give them control over their own comprehension. You can teach these strategies to K–6 students and then provide them with a Fix-Up Checklist, like the one in Figure 7.1 to use when they have a problem with comprehension.

FIGURE 7.1 Teach children how to use this self-assessment checklist when they experience a problem with comprehension.

"Fix-Up" Checklist

When I don't understand something, do I:

_____ Have a purpose?

_____ Keep going? (reading or listening for clues)

_____ Slow down? (or ask the speaker to slow down)

_____ Reread or ask for a repeat?

_____ Say it my own way?

_____ Ask questions?

_____ Make predictions?

_____ Check my predictions?

·····

■ *Cooperative group work* is another way to develop careful and effective listening. As children work together in pairs or small groups or as buddies to accomplish goals and specific tasks, they learn the importance of listening to each other.

Teaching listening in situations that are unrelated to content is useless, since there must be a purpose for listening. An effective listening program is one that is integrated with children's literature and the content areas. You need to plan activities that develop listening naturally within the context of science, social studies, and mathematics. As Winn (1988) says, "The activities that enhance listening skills are readily available in the existing curriculum and are just waiting for identification" (p. 145). So, be flexible in adapting the strategies in this chapter to content units. There are opportunities to promote effective listening in every subject, and wise teachers teach listening directly by incorporating it into the rest of their curriculum.

Listening can be taught and with positive results (Funk & Funk, 1989; Winn, 1988). Often, though, there is no established curriculum for teaching listening, but the similarities between reading and listening provide a common foundation for listening instruction. Comprehending in listening and comprehending in reading appear to be very closely related, as you will remember from the discussion in Chapter 6.

Standards for Listening

The *Learning Standards for English Language Arts* (1996) in New York state consider listening and reading as complementary processes. These standards for teaching and student performance suggest that K–6 students will *read, write, listen,* and *speak*

1. For information and understanding
2. For literary response and expression
3. For critical analysis and evaluation
4. For social interaction

These standards overlap, and in good teaching, probably some aspect of each standard is present. For example, the difference between Standard 2, which involves comprehending, interpreting, and critiquing, and Standard 3, which involves analyzing and evaluating, is difficult to identify exactly. How is critiquing different from evaluating? Nevertheless, these standards do give teachers a criteria or gauge to guide their teaching. Also, the existence of standards that attempt to delineate performance will probably drive improved student performance in the long run.

The following ideas for teaching listening are presented within the four standards just discussed. On first glance, each should fit the category under which you will find it because the activity predominantly helps to develop that standard. But remember that the lines separating these standards are often fuzzy, and so some activities fall in more than one standard. Think of these suggestions as ideas to embed in your curriculum whenever possible. When you incorporate them into your students' everyday classroom study in science, social studies, math, and language, your students' learning will be authentic.

Information and Understanding

Listening for information and understanding involves collecting data, facts, and ideas; discovering relationships, concepts, and generalizations; and using knowledge from oral sources. People listen for these purposes to identify and remember facts, ideas, and relationships. Informational listening involves children in comprehending information as data are processed.

There are many ways to develop children's listening for information and understanding. All depend on establishing a purpose for listening. An effective listener knows what to listen for, focuses her attention on what is said, and comprehends better than the listener who listens vaguely without purpose. By incorporating the following activities into your teaching of subjects across the curriculum and adapting them to meet the needs of diverse children, you develop informational listening:

▬ Play "Blind Man's Bluff" to give children opportunities to identify sounds. Have them keep their eyes closed as you (or a child) provide sounds to identify (sharpen a pencil, drop a book, open a door, turn on a faucet, use a typewriter or computer keyboard, etc.). Use the same format to identify voices. Cover the eyes of one or two children and ask them to guess the voices of other children who say only a word or phrase.

▬ Read books such as *Train* by Charles Temple (1996), *Night Sounds* by Louise Grambling (1996), *The Ear Book* by Al Perkins (1995), and *Storm in the Night* by Mary Stolz (1988), and have the children provide sound effects. Tape record the sound effects and put the book and tape in a listening center for the children to listen to later. (These books are found in Children's Books about Listening at the end of this chapter.)

▬ Make a collection of the various gifts the boy receives in Lily Hong's (1993) *Two of Everything*, a Japanese story about a man who discovers a magic pot that makes two of everything he puts in. Read it to a group of young children and, as you read, have them identify and remove each gift as it appears in the story.

▬ In math, read sequences of digits for children to write down what they hear. Begin with three- or four-digit numbers and gradually increase the number of digits as children acquire the ability to do this.

▬ Read sequenced directions for children to follow. Make items simple or more difficult and coordinate the activity to a content area (e.g., by changing the underlined words to match the topic of study). Directions can involve physically moving around the room or drawing, such as the following:

1. If <u>New York</u> is a <u>city</u>, write a *z* beside number 3.
2. If your teacher is a female, write your middle name.
3. Write the first three letters of the <u>alphabet</u>.

4. Draw a circle. Draw a triangle inside the circle.
5. If <u>fish</u> can <u>talk</u>, write the number 13.
6. Write three things you might find at the end of a *sentence*.
7. Write the word that tells how old <u>you</u> are.
8. If the date today is odd, write a *y* beside number 8.
9. Draw a box around each word you have written on your paper and write the number of boxes you have drawn.
10. Write the numbers of the items you left blank.

Depending on the age and ability of your children, you can begin with 5 to 10 items and increase to 20 or more.

■ Read short paragraphs from science or social studies selections or news stories. Ask the children Who? What? Why? When? Where? How? and If? questions.

■ Read rhymed verses or stories, occasionally omitting a word at the end of a line or sentence so the children can supply them. This develops the ability to use rhyming words and context clues.

■ During regular read-aloud time, have the children make visual images of what they hear as you read from a collection such as *Animal Crackers: A Delectable Collection of Pictures, Poems, and Lullabies for the Very Young* by Jane Dyer (1996), which depicts children from many cultures. Encourage them to share their pictures and discuss how they create them.

■ Draw the outline of an object or animal on lined graph paper, using the squares to make a rectilinear drawing. Have the children label north, south, east, and west sides of a blank sheet of graph paper. Establish a starting point and give step-by-step directions for drawing the object. For instance, "Go north three squares, west two squares" and so on.

■ As part of your current social studies unit, give teams of two children a map and a three-by-five-inch card with the names of two cities printed on it. Have children write directions to get from one city to another (or one country to another), then read to the class the name of the first city and the directions so the class can guess the destination.

■ Use every pupil response (EPR) techniques to allow everyone to simultaneously answer questions after listening to a short content area selection or fictional story. Heward (1996) reports that the participation, learning, and on-task behavior of students with special needs increases when teachers use these response techniques. Give each child a set of cards on which various responses are printed, or have children make their own EPR cards (see Figure 7.2). Print *yes* on one side or *no* on the other side, or print other words, numbers, faces, or symbols on them. Punch holes in each card so the children can keep them together on a metal shower curtain ring, or keep them in envelopes. You can use the EPR technique by giving every child an erasable slate and chalk, which allows for longer answers.

Some creative teachers use a variety of other EPR techniques, such as hand signals like thumbs up and thumbs down; touching the nose, ear, or elbow; facial expressions such as smile, scowl, or questioning; and individual chalk or magic slates on which students can write responses. Let your imagination be your guide in defining the method and use of EPR in your classroom.

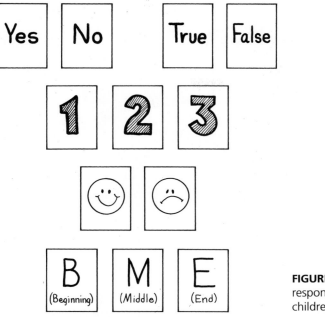

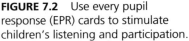

FIGURE 7.2 Use every pupil response (EPR) cards to stimulate children's listening and participation.
.....

Choose a story to read to a group of children. Read it yourself and create 10 EPR statements. Read the book to the children and have them use EPR to respond to the statements. Then have the children write some statements to use with EPR. How can EPR both promote and inhibit critical listening?

STRETCHING EXERCISE

● ● ● ● ●

Literary Response and Expression

Listening for literary response and expression involves comprehending, interpreting, and critiquing spoken texts; drawing on personal experiences and knowledge to understand the text; and recognizing the social, historical, and cultural features of the text. It requires more than identifying and remembering facts, ideas, and relationships. It requires the ability to understand and make an interpretation about what is heard. Just as with listening for information and understanding, children must have a purpose for effective literary listening to occur. Consider the following activities:

▬ Ask the children to bring in newspaper or magazine stories related to your science or social studies unit. Have some of them share the gist of their stories and ask the audience to retell the most important idea they heard. Help the children understand that it is natural for individuals to differ in what they consider most important, and that judgments are acceptable as long as there are valid, text-based reasons for the judgments.

•••••
Students watch a videotape and listen with headphones in their classroom's Listening Lab.

■ Select a corner of the room and set up a Listening Center or Listening Lab with tape recorders, earphones, tapes, and books. Most libraries have a collection of children's book-cassette packages that contain a hardcover book and a taped version of the text that children of all ages enjoy listening to and reading. Include taped versions of student-written books so children can listen to each other's works.

■ Read riddles to the children and encourage them to guess a variety of answers. K–6 students enjoy *Riddle City, USA! A Book of Geography Riddles* by Marco Maestro and Giulio Maestro (1995) and Laura Kvasnosky's (1995) *See You Later, Alligator*. Second- and third-grade children enjoy creating their own riddles, and when they accompany a content area unit of study, children demonstrate understanding of the subject. An easy way to teach riddling to children is to brainstorm hink-pinks, hinky-pinkys, and hinkety-pinketies. A *hink-pink* contains two one-syllable words that rhyme, a *hinky-pinky* contains two two-syllable words that rhyme, and a *hinkety-pinkety* contains two three-syllable rhyming words. Children begin by thinking of a rhymed answer to their riddle and then supplying the question. Marilyn Burns's (1981) *The Hink Pink Book* is a collection of these fun riddles. Some examples follow:

fat-bat	What do you call a blind, overweight, flying animal?
sad-dad	What do you call an unhappy father?
cooler-ruler	What do you get if you put a measuring stick in the freezer?
chubby-hubby	What do you call a plump husband?
sinister-minister	What do you call a dishonest clergyman?
vanilla-gorilla	What's an ice cream flavored ape?

Thaler (1985), in *Funny Side Up*, describes four simple steps to make another type of riddle:

1. Pick a subject (such as *pigs*).
2. Make a list of words that mean the same or are closely related (*hog, boar, swine, oink, mud*).

3. Pick a famous person, place, or thing. Divide into syllables (*Al/bert Ein/stein*). Substitute rhyming words from the list (*Al/boar Swine/stein*).
4. Make up the riddle question from the most important fact about the person, place, or thing. (*What pig was a great twentieth-century physicist?*)

When pairs or teams of children generate their own riddles, they can then read them to other teams or the class to guess the answers. These riddles can then be bound together in a book of riddles to which the entire class contributes.

Critical Analysis and Evaluation

Listening for critical analysis and evaluation involves using experiences, ideas, information, and issues, along with criteria from a variety of perspectives, and recognizing the difference in evaluation based on different sets of criteria. Again, when possible, incorporate the following suggestions into content area study:

■ Read brainteasers to children when a few extra minutes permit. Problem solving like this extends conceptual understanding in math. Encourage careful listening and creative thinking to help children come up with answers. Here are a few examples:

—How many birthdays does the average person have?
—If you live in a four-sided house, each side faces south, and a bear approaches your house, what color is the bear?
—How far can you run into the woods?
—If a farmer has 19 cows and all but 9 die, how many does he have left?
—Why can't a man marry his widow's sister?
—What do you have if you take four oranges from five oranges?

Books such as *Mind Twisters* by Godfrey Hall (1993) and *The Book of Think (Or How to Solve a Problem Twice Your Size)* by Marilyn Burns (1976) contain problems and brainteasers for a range of abilities.

■ Share song-picture books with children, which you either read as poetry or augment with music. Or find songs from a particular time period or geographic area to accompany your social studies unit. Children enjoy hearing rhymed song lyrics, and they will often join in on a familiar chorus or refrain, sometimes even learning all verses of the song. There are tapes and compact discs (CDs) to accompany Louis Armstrong's *What a Wonderful World* by George Weiss and Bob Thiele (1995) and Sandra De Cotreau Orie's (1995) *Did You Hear the Wind Sing Your Name? An Oneida Song of Spring.* Children can easily learn to accompany many song-picture books, such as Aliki's (1968) *Hush Little Baby*, on the autoharp using a few chords. Encourage them to write their own song lyrics for songs they already know.

■ Allow children to create visual images as they listen. This can be especially helpful in content areas when places and concepts are foreign to children. The image gives children a point of reference and helps make text "come alive." Have them make mental images as you read sentences that are at first simple, containing few main elements, then becoming more complex—for example:

—The squirrel buried a nut.
—The boy threw a stone into the lake.
—The camel walked slowly across the desert toward the palm trees and the oasis.

Discuss the children's visual images and then show them a picture of each sentence for comparison. Encourage the children to engage their imaginations with all types of listening, since it actively involves them and facilitates rich comprehension.

- Have a specially painted or decorated Author's Chair in which individual children sit to read their own written work to their peers. The audience can give support and feedback for revisions and later hear the finished piece.

- Read books such as *Knots on a Counting Rope* by Bill Martin and John Archambault (1990), and *The Other Way to Listen* by Byrd Baylor (1978). Help children compare each child's behavior to their own. Other books in which main characters listen purposefully are found in the Children's Books about Listening bibliography at the end of the chapter.

- Help the children distinguish fact from opinion. This activity can be one way to evaluate learning in science or social studies. Even young children should learn this critical listening skill. First, teach the children that a fact is something that has actually happened or is true. An opinion is a personal thought or idea that may be based on fact. Prepare statements of each type to accompany the following and read them to the children:

—Chocolate is the best kind of candy.
—The Empire State Building is a skyscraper.
—The president is the most important person in the United States.
—Always say "Thank you" when someone gives you something.
—NASA will send astronauts to Pluto next year.

Be sure to discuss the reasons each statement is considered the type it is and the reasons for possible differences of opinion.

- Use printed advertisements in magazines, newspapers, or taped television ads to help children learn to listen critically when evaluating various advertising techniques and detecting the propaganda devices discussed in Chapter 6. Read statements such as the following and discuss them with the children:

—This is 100% cheese. Some aren't. We believe good cooks care.   (Cheese)
—Top Banana Pudding has one-third less calories—finally, a fruit filling that isn't filling.   (Pie filling)
—Warm and cozy in winter, cool and refreshing in the summer. Lambsleeps live up to their promises.   (Wool mattress overlay)
—Designed to charge your engine even before you turn the key.   (Car)
—Look at other brands, then decide. We stand up to comparisons.   (Apple juice)
—Even a five-year-old can run it.   (Software program)
—Absorbant. Nothing soaks it up like sponge towels. Try a roll.   (Paper towels)
—The sign of a rare man.   (Watch)

Encourage the children to analyze each ad for fact and opinion, to interpret the language used, and to evaluate the effect of the ad before making a judgment about its appeal or effectiveness. Teach older children the various types of propaganda devices and help them analyze ads for the specific device each one uses. Children will soon become adept at spotting misleading ads.

- Another good way to build children's critical listening skills and vocabulary is to supply an omitted word in an analogy. This particular activity lends itself well to subject area study, too. Here's one complete example: *hair : mammal : : feathers : bird.* You finish the rest:

    —gravy : potatoes : : frosting: ?
    —biology : biologist : : psychology: ?
    —gun : bullet : : arrow: ?
    —Blue Jay : bird : : bee: ?
    —second : minute : : minute: ?
    —in : out : : up: ?
    —listening : reading : : speaking: ?

Middle- and upper-elementary-grade children enjoy creating their own analogies and reading them to each other. Many standardized tests use this format, so, analogies are not only fun but they can also prepare children for this form of test item.

■ Read sentences containing malapropisms (the misuse of words) that are similar in sound to properly used words, and ask the children to identify the confused word and supply the correct one. Middle- and upper-grade children enjoy creating their own malapropisms and reading them to the class. A few examples follow:

    —May I have the vanilla folder?
    —Ann was absent because she had the chicken pops.
    —The word *big* is a cinnamon for *large.*
    —At the museum we saw the Egyptian mommy.
    —Conversation experts fight forest fires.
    —Harold's father couched the baseball team.
    —Hurry and distinguish the fire before it spreads.
    —The cantelopes ran across the field.
    —The alphabet contains vowels and constants.
    —I hope the catsup I spilled won't strain the rug.

■ Have the children sit with their backs to the television to listen to and compare two similar television shows. Before listening to the shows, have the class help you design a listening guide—a list of things to be aware of during the shows. The guide might include these and other elements listed on the left side of a sheet of paper with space for writing impressions on the right side: setting, characters and characterization, plot or action, language, relationships among family members, mood or tone, and purpose or theme.

For young children, a parent, older sibling, or friend can help with this activity by writing down the child's opinions. The next day in class, use the elements just listed to discuss the children's impressions. Have your students repeat the activity a week later, but this time, have them watch the show while listening. Discuss the visual effects of each show and the differences that emerge as a result of seeing as well as hearing stories.

■ To give firsthand experience in critical listening, ask volunteers to wear blindfolds for part or all of a school day, assigning each a buddy or helper to assist the blindfolded children when help is needed.

■ Obtain a record or tape of an old radio show, such as *The Shadow* or *Sky King,* and have the students listen to it, comparing it to a modern detective or adventure show on television. Discuss characteristics of the main characters, the use of slang, words that have changed their meaning or new words that have evolved, and fads and fashions in both shows.

■ Read orally the same news event reported in different newspapers or magazines and compare them for differences and similarities in facts conveyed, bias or political beliefs held, language used, and important ideas communicated. Children gain interesting insights about topics related to their science or social studies learning by comparing stories covered in first and second editions of a newspaper or stories written by people in two different magazines (e.g., *Newsweek* and *U.S. News & World Report*). Or compare eyewitness accounts of an actual happening reported in the newspaper. Children need to be aware that everything they read in print or hear on the radio or television must be evaluated for its factual content and emotional content.

■ Listen to a recording of "Peter and the Wolf" by Prokofiev. Talk about how the music intensifies the images, characters, and drama in the story. Have the children listen to the recording a second time, and again talk about their impressions of the music. Discuss the visual images the flute suggests and compare these to visual images suggested by the French horn. Do the same with the bassoon, kettle drums, and the stringed instruments. Encourage the children to share their impressions and the reasons for them.

■ Listen to parts of Dvorak's "The New World Symphony," the impressions of a homesick Czechoslovakian musician's stay in the United States. "A Night on Bald Mountain," by Mussorgsky, is a Russian legend about a witch's celebration. Perhaps the music teacher may suggest other recordings. Talk about the mood of the music, perhaps listing words that describe the feelings the music evokes. Help the children relate the mood they feel to other times in their lives when they have felt the same way.

■ Read to young children from a collection such as *Sing a Song of Popcorn: Every Child's Book of Poems* by Beatrice Schenk de Regniers (1988) to introduce rhyme and alliteration (letter and sound repetition, as in "Sing a song of sixpence . . ."). Read books such as Joanna Cole's (1989) *Anna Banana: 101 Jump-Rope Rhymes* and Wilson Gage's (1977) *Down in the Boondocks* to introduce children to repetition and refrain. Talk about feelings, moods, or images that these stories evoke.

■ Read quality literature to children, such as E. B. White's (1952) *Charlotte's Web*, bringing their attention to the use of onomatopoeia (words that sound like their meanings), as in the slushy sounds of Wilbur's "swishing and swooshing" as he eats his slops. Discuss the feelings, moods, or images the story evokes.

■ Read all types of poetry to children and help them repond to the sensory content of poems by visualizing and feeling. Use the senses of seeing, hearing, tasting, smelling, and touching to do this. Repeat favorite poems and encourage children to join in as you read them so that they experience the feeling of poetry on their tongues. Help them verbalize their impressions. Here are a few suggestions:

Falling Up: Poems and Drawings, by Shel Silverstein (1996), contains rhymed and unrhymed poetry about humorous everyday things.

Celebrating America, by Laura Whipple (1994), contains poems about the American spirit.

If I Were in Charge of the World and Other Worries, by Judith Viorst (1981), is a collection of her humorous, contemporary poetry.

Joyful Noise: Poems for Two Voices and *I Am Phoenix: Poems for Two Voices*, both by Paul Fleischman (1985), are poems about insects and birds, respectively, that sound like a musical duet when they are read aloud by two readers at once.

Snuffles and Snouts are poems selected by Laura Robb (1995) about pigs.

Mother Earth, Father Sky is a collection of poems by Jane Yolen (1996) celebrating the earth's blessings and sacrifices.

I Am Wings: Poems about Love, by Ralph Fletcher (1995), contains poetry about the nature of love.

■ Share poem-picture books or picture-book editions of single poems with students of all grade levels. Glazer and Lamme (1990) write that beautifully illustrated, quality poetry has double the artistic impact of quality poetry without illustrations. They report that older as well as younger readers enjoy poems such as *Stopping by Woods on a Snowy Evening* by Robert Frost (1978).

■ Encourage children to consult each other during writer's workshop when they are working on their own writing. Listening and supplying feedback, helping each other clarify topics and getting advice require critical listening for a purpose.

Social Interaction

Listening for social interaction involves listening to presentations by people of different ages, genders, and cultures. Possessing effective social communication skills is important in school today and in the world outside school. Again, be alert to ways you can adapt the following ideas and incorporate them into your curriculum:

■ Invite a storyteller to visit your classroom so that children can learn to enjoy this special art form. McCord (1996) describes the beneficial impact storytelling can have on literacy. She shows how listening and reading comprehension, as well as oral and written expression, can grow from storytelling. Hold a storytelling fest at which children tell family stories.

■ Children of all ages love draw-and-tell stories in which the storyteller draws a picture on the chalkboard or overhead projector while telling a story. Figure 7.3 is an example of one of these stories. *Draw and Tell* by Richard Thompson (1986) and *Chalk in Hand: The Draw and Tell Book* by Phyllis Noe Pflomm (1986) contain short stories with simple story outlines. Encourage your students to relate their own experiences by telling and drawing their own stories.

■ Encourage group problem solving in all subjects. At all grade levels, word problems in mathematics are an excellent means of developing critical listening skills. Children must listen to the problem as it is read, make interpretations about what they hear, then listen to each other as solutions are suggested. This activity stimulates children to cooperate to solve the problem.

■ Involve the children in story building by starting a story yourself with a few sentences to establish setting and characters. Then ask for volunteers to add a sentence or two until everyone has participated, and you (or a child) end the story. Some starters are:

Two Very "Special Friends"

A long time ago, the world was very young. In this world, there was Sun and Water. *(Draw sun and water.)* There had never been two friends that were closer.

Once a day Sun would visit her friend Water. This, the two would lovingly call morning because this was when they could be together.

Sun loved Water and wished with all her heart that Water would come and visit her, too. One day, Sun said, "Water, here I am visiting you every day. I wish you could visit me and see where I live."

Water replied, "Sun, I would love to come and visit you more than anything in the world, but there is no place for me to stay. I need a space of my own where I can rest. If I have my own space, I will visit you again and again.

Sun set to work right away. For there was nothing more that Sun wanted than for Water to come and visit. Sun built many beautiful spaces for Water. These spaces took many different sizes and shapes.

(Draw clouds.) Sun named these spaces clouds. Clouds only came out when Water visited Sun.

When the clouds were complete, Sun once again invited Water up to visit. This time Water accepted the invitation. Sun was so happy. She usually is when she's with Water. She beckoned all the clouds to come out so Water had a place to rest. Water then secretly went into the sky to visit Sun and both were very happy. *(Draw arrows going up to represent evaporation.)*

After three days, it was time for Water to return home. Although it was impossible to see Water visit Sun, one cannot miss Water's journey back. *(Draw raindrops.)* This is what humans call rain.

Humans sometimes compare rain to tears. This is because rain is the sad time when Water is leaving and can no longer be with Sun. Since the beginning of time, Water has been able to visit Sun. However, she must always return home. There is no need to worry, though, Water always finds a way to visit Sun so they can be happy once again. This is why every so often, rain falls to the Earth.

FIGURE 7.3 This Native American how-and-why tale easily becomes a draw-and-tell story.

Source: Adapted by Dawnmarie DeMatteo from "Sun, Moon and Water" in *Legends of the Sun and Moon*, 1989, New York: Cambridge University Press. Reprinted by permission of Dawnmarie DeMatteo.

—One day a clever little field mouse saw an evil-looking fox watching a family of ducks swimming in a pond . . .

—He did not know what to do. There was a mystery to be solved. His new bicycle was missing . . .

—Once upon a time when magic was an everyday happening, a strange looking giraffe who had no spots met a . . .

—She would always remember the first time she climbed a mountain because . . .

You can create story starters from your science or social studies unit. This kind of storytelling gives children opportunities to weave content area learning into their stories.

▬ Encourage the children to share the stories, reports, and projects they create for science or social studies with each other by reading or presenting them orally. Children are often their own best judges of each other's work, and when they know how to respond appropriately, they can serve as valuable audiences for each other. Having children read each other's work orally sometimes gives them a better sense of what they've said than if they read it silently.

▬ In pairs, have the children discuss and write out directions from one location in school to another. Supply them with a floor plan of the school. Then have each pair read their directions slowly to the class so that they can guess where the destination is. Repeat the same activity using a map of the community. Figure 7.4 suggests a similar activity.

FIGURE 7.4 You can adapt this activity to a science or social studies unit by using a specific geographic location.

Sample Listening Activity

Name:	LET'S GO
Purpose:	To develop informational listening, the ability to follow directions, and sequential order
Group:	Small groups or with whole class
Age Level:	Grades 2–4
Directions:	The teacher or a child gives directions to a certain place in the school, community, or city. Specific directions are given regarding direction, landmarks, turns, and approximate distances. Children follow these verbal directions in their minds and try to figure out where they would be when they arrive at the destination.
Suggestions:	Children must be familiar with the school building, their immediate community, and the city. For older students, expand the geographic area and increase the number of directions.

•••••

Source: Adapted from "Guidelines for Developing Listening Skills" by H. D. Funk and G. Funk, May 1989, *The Reading Teacher*, page 661.

— Teach the children how to take accurate telephone messages. Role-play several typical telephone messages and show the children how to record important information on a form such as the one in Figure 7.5. Reproduce enough copies for each child to take some home. Encourage the children to take messages as they answer the telephone at home. Call your local telephone office to borrow a packet of educational materials to use in a unit on the telephone.

— Play "I'm Going on a Trip . . ." and embed it in your social studies unit. Have the children choose objects to correspond with letters of the alphabet. Each child repeats the things chosen previously and takes something herself by identifying a word to correspond with the next letter of the alphabet and includes this object in her travel trunk or suitcase. For instance, the fourth child to play the game (about Texas) might say, "I'm going on a trip, and I'm going to take Jeff's *Alamo*, Laurie's *Blue Bonnet*, Kyle's *Cows,* and my *Dallas Cowboys.*"

The four standards for listening that you have just read about don't consider a type of listening that we all do every day. *Marginal listening,* the hearing that goes on at the fringes of our consciousness and that we are sometimes not quite aware of, is an important type of listening. This type of listening does not warrant direct teaching, but children need to be aware that it exists and that they have the ability to tune out and tune in to environmental noise as necessary.

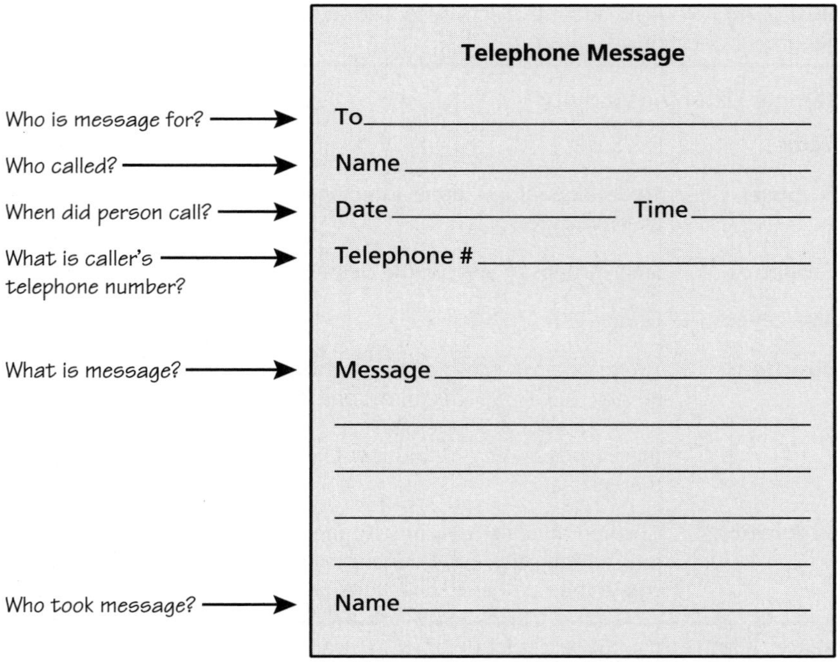

Telephone Message

Who is message for? → To_____

Who called? → Name_____

When did person call? → Date_____ Time_____

What is caller's telephone number? → Telephone #_____

What is message? → Message_____

Who took message? → Name_____

FIGURE 7.5 Taking an accurate telephone message is an important skill for both children and adults.

Separating listening into categories and then suggesting appropriate activities to develop each is actually more difficult than it seems here. During nearly all listening, besides identifying information, the listener comprehends, interprets, evaluates, and is critical of what she hears. Listeners often engage in different types of listening concurrently. So, remember that as the listener constructs meaning, she probably engages in some aspects of each listening standard.

Assessing Listening

Listening is the most difficult aspect of the language arts to assess. There are several reasons for this, but the most critical is the huge variety of ways a listener can demonstrate comprehension. In contrast to listening, writing results in a visible and concrete written product you can assess. A formal or informal listening assessment should

- Correspond closely to the purpose for listening.
- Use listening in a familiar situation.
- Be practical, simple, and suitable for the child.

Whether you are formally or informally evaluating listening, it is important to remember that if you ask children to respond orally or with paper and pencil, then you are also measuring writing, reading, and speaking, which can affect the results of your assessment. So, when you ask children to listen to a selection and write a summary of the content, if the summary is not accurate or does not contain the most important idea, it may be that spelling problems, inept handwriting, or poor organization of ideas are to blame. Similarly, if you ask children to respond by reading and answering questions, you may not get a true measure of listening. Likewise, an oral response requires a process different from listening. When assessing listening, remember to allow children to demonstrate comprehension as they listen, while you make every attempt to separate writing, reading, and speaking from listening.

As you should remember from the beginning of this chapter, there is a high correlation between listening and intelligence. When you evaluate listening, you also evaluate the child's ability to think. Be sure to keep in mind, though, that children who are poor listeners may be good thinkers, and the reverse is also true.

Since there are so many factors that confound the evaluation of effective listening, it is not surprising that there are few reliable or valid formal tests for it. An informal reading inventory, discussed in greater detail in Chapter 8, can provide information on a child's listening comprehension if you read selections orally and then have the child retell it or answer questions. In scoring, what is a good rule of thumb for adequate listening? If a child can give a pretty accurate retelling or answer about 70 percent of the questions, she probably has satisfactory listening comprehension.

Although there are several formal measures of listening available, many of them require the use of reading and writing. Therefore, the best way to evaluate listening is with informal measures that include your observation of the child's listening behavior as well as self-assessment on the part of the child in a variety of situations. Your observations and a child's self-evaluation of her own behavior during and after listening are

When I listen do I:

_____ Hear what people say?

_____ Listen carefully?

_____ Tune out the speaker?

_____ Watch the speaker?

_____ Make pictures in my mind?

_____ Have a purpose for listening?

_____ Think about what I hear?

_____ Connect what I hear to what I know?

_____ Answer questions?

_____ Summarize what I hear?

_____ Retell it or put it in my own words?

_____ Talk about what I hear with others?

NAME _____

GRADE _____

DATE _____

GOOD LISTENER
★ AWARD ★

FIGURE 7.6   Adapt this sample checklist to fit your students.

FIGURE 7.7   A Good Listener Award is one way to promote listening.

quickly and easily recorded on prepared checklists. Given directions, children of all age levels can take part in class discussions and brainstorming sessions to identify the characteristics of an effective listener. You can phrase these characteristics or behaviors as questions and create your own checklist (see Figure 7.6).

Use checklists regularly during the year, and encourage children to chart their own progress. Don't forget the Literature Response Inventory in Chapter 5, which is another way of assessing how children listen. Also, give awards (such as the one in Figure 7.7) and make them a part of your ongoing assessment of children's listening development. You may want the class to help in decisions about recipients of these awards. When children evaluate their own listening behaviors, they become actively involved and thus more responsible for their own learning.

Summary

Listening, the first of the four language arts to develop, is an active comprehension process that requires conscious attention to sounds to associate meanings with them. You and your students act as models of effective listening for each other. Various factors affect listening comprehension, which can be improved with direct instruction. You can develop standards for listening and teach it through a variety of activities integrated within the teaching of content area subjects. Listening is probably best assessed by both you and the students through informal observations and self-assessment checklists.

Reflections

1. A child in your second-grade classroom has a hearing problem. Describe the things you might do in the classroom to provide a good listening environment for this child. List three suggestions for the child's parents to promote a positive listening environment at home.

2. Observe a classroom for a morning or an afternoon to determine how much and what types of listening are required of children and how the teacher reinforces good listening. Relate what you saw and heard to your own beliefs about listening and teaching.

Professional Resources

Chatton, B. (1993). *Using poetry across the curriculum: A whole language approach.* Pheonix: Onyx. This is a practical resource of ideas for teaching with all kinds of poems.

Jalongo, M. R. (1991). *Strategies for developing children's listening skills.* (Phi Delta Kappa Fastback Series #314). Bloomington, IN: Phi Delta Kappa Educational Foundation. This small book contains practical classroom-tested suggestions.

Miscallef, M. (1984). *Listening: The basic connection.* Carthage, IL: Good Apple. This guide takes a metacognitive approach to improving listening, as it helps students focus on what and how they learn. It includes self-evaluation checklists for third- to eighth-graders.

References

Ackerman, D. (1990). *A natural history of the senses.* New York: Random House.

Bauman, M. L. (1987). Literature, repetition, and meaning. *Language Arts, 64* (1), 54–60.

Brent, R., & Anderson, P. (1993). Developing children's classroom listening strategies. *The Reading Teacher, 47* (2), 122–126.

Buttery, T. J., & Anderson, P. J. (1980). Listen and learn! *Curriculum Review, 19* (4), 319–322.

Chance, R. (1993). Teleconferencing: An overlooked technological approach to learning. *Reading Motivation, 21* (2), 20–23.

Cullinan, B., Jaggar, A., & Strickland, D. (1974). Language expansion for black children in the primary grades: A research report. *Young Children, 29,* 98–112.

Dennis, G. (1995). The effects of repreated read-alouds on story comprehension as assessed through story retellings. *Reading Improvement, 32* (30), 140–153.

Devine, T. (1978). Listening: What do we know after 50 years of research and theorizing? *Journal of Reading, 21* (4), 296–303.

Dressel, J. H. (1990). The effects of listening to and discussing different qualities of children's literature on the narrative writing of fifth graders. *Research in the Teaching of English, 24* (4), 397–414.

Frick, H. A. (1986). The value of sharing stories orally with middle grade students. *Journal of Reading, 29* (4), 300–303.

Funk, H. D., & Funk, G. D. (1989). Guidelines for developing listening skills. *The Reading Teacher, 42,* 660–663.

Glazer, J. I., & Lamme, L. L. (1990). Poem picture books and their uses in the classroom. *The Reading Teacher, 44,* 102–109.

Gorton, L. (1989). The electronic field trip. *The Writing Notebook, 44,* 9.

Heward, W. L. (1996). Everyone participates in this class: Using response cards to increase active student response. *Teaching Exceptional Chidlren, 28* (2), 4–10.

Hunsaker, R. A. (1990). *Understanding and developing the skills of oral communication: Speaking and listening* (2nd ed.). Englewood, CO: Morton.

Kimmel, M. M., & Segel, E. (1983). *For reading out loud!* New York: Delacorte.

Learning Standards for English Language Arts (1996). Albany, NY: State Education Department.

Lundsteen, S. W. (1974). Procedures for teaching critical reading and listening. In J. Stefano & S. E. Fox (Eds.), *Language and the language arts* (pp. 87–99). Boston: Little, Brown.

Lundsteen, S. W. (1979). *Listening: Its impact on reading and the other language arts* (2nd ed.). Urbana, IL: National Council of Teachers of English.

Martinez, M., & Teale, W. H. (1988). Reading in a kindergarten classroom library. *The Reading Teacher, 41*, 568–572.

McCord, S. (1996). *The storybook journey: Pathways to literacy through story and play.* Englewood Cliffs, NJ: Merrill.

Mendoza, A. (1985). Reading to children: Their preferences. *The Reading Teacher, 38* (6), 522–527.

Paley, V. G. (1986). On listening to what the children say. *Harvard Educational Review, 56*, 122–131.

Pearson, P. D., & Fielding, L. (1982). Research update: Listening comprehension. *Language Arts, 59* (6), 617–629.

Strickland, D. (1973). A program for linguistically different black children. *Research in the Teaching of English, 7*, 79–86.

Strother, D. B. (1987). Practical applications of research on listening. *Phi Delta Kappan, 68*, 625–628.

Trelease, J. (1989). Jim Trelease speaks on reading aloud to children. *The Reading Teacher, 43*, 200–206.

Trelease, J. (1995). *The read-aloud handbook* (4th ed.). New York: Penguin.

Winkle, A. M. (1991). Listen my children: Strategies for listening instruction. *Ohio Reading Teacher, 25* (4), 14–20.

Winn, D. D. (1988). Develop listening skills as a part of the curriculum. *The Reading Teacher, 42*, 144–146.

Wolvin, A., & Coakley, G. (1988). *Listening* (3rd ed.). Dubuque, IA: William Brown.

Children's Book References

Aliki (1968). *Hush little baby.* Englewood Cliffs, NJ: Prentice Hall.

Baylor, B. (1978). *The other way to listen.* New York: Scribner.

Burns, M. (1976). *The book of think (or how to solve a problem twice your size).* Boston: Little, Brown.

Burns, M. (1981). *The hink pink book.* Boston: Little, Brown.

Cole, J. (1989). *Anna Banana: 101 jump-rope rhymes.* New York: Morrow.

De Cotreau Orie, S. (1995). *Did you hear the wind sing your name? An Oneida song of spring.* New York: Walker.

de Regniers, B. S. (1988). *Sing a song of popcorn: Every child's book of poems.* New York: Scholastic.

Dyer, J. (1996). *Animal crackers: A delectable collection of pictures, poems, and lullabies for the very young.* Boston: Little, Brown.

Fleischman, P. (1985). *I am phoenix: Poems for two voices.* New York: Harper and Row.

Fleischman, P. (1985). *Joyful noise: Poems for two voices.* New York: Harper and Row.

Fletcher, R. (1995). *I am wings: Poems about love.* New York: Bradbury.

Fox, M. (1990). *Wilfred Gordon McDonald Partridge.* New York: Scholastic.

Frost, R. (1978). *Stopping by woods on a snowy evening.* Illus. by Susan Jeffers. New York: Dutton.

Gage, W. (1977). *Down in the boondocks.* New York: Morrow.

Hall, G. (1993). *Mind twisters.* New York: Random House.

Hong, L. T. (1993). *Two of everything.* New York: Whitman.

Howe, J. (1990). *Hot fudge.* New York: Morrow.

Kvasnosky, L. M. (1995). *See you later, alligator.* San Diego: Red Wagon/Harcourt.

Maestro, M., & Maestro, G. (1995). *Riddle city, USA! A book of geography riddles.* New York: HarperCollins.

Martin, B., & Archambault, J. (1990). *Knots on a counting rope.* New York: Trumpet.

Pflomm, P. N. (1986). *Chalk in hand: The draw and tell book.* Metuchen, NJ: Scarecrow.

Rawls, W. (1974). *Where the red fern grows*. New York: Bantam.

Robb, L. (1995). *Snuffles and snouts*. New York: Dial.

Silverstein, S. (1996). *Falling up: Poems and drawings*. New York: HarperCollins.

Thaler, M. (1985). *Funny side up*. New York: Scholastic.

Thompson, R. (1986). *Draw and tell*. Willowdale, Ontario: Firefly.

Viorst, J. (1981). *If I were in charge of the world and other worries*. New York: Aladdin.

Weiss, G., & Theile, B. (1995). *What a wonderful world*. New York: Atheneum.

Whipple, L. (1994). *Celebrating America: A collection of poems and images of the American spirit*. New York: Philomel.

White, E. B. (1952). *Charlotte's web*. New York: Harper and Row.

Yolen, J. (1996). *Mother earth, father sky: Poems of our planet*. Homesdale, PA: Boyd's Mill Press.

Children's Books about Listening

Aseltine, L., Mueller, E., & Tait, N. (1986). *I'm deaf and it's okay*. Niles, IL: Whitman. (Gr. K–5). A young boy who is angry and frustrated by his own deafness finds solace in the friendship of a young man who is also deaf.

Baker, A. (1996). *I thought I heard*. Brookfield, CT: Millbrook/Copper Beech Books. (Gr. K–2). Night sounds keep a young girl from going to sleep.

Baylor, B. (1978). *The other way to listen*. New York: Scribner. (Gr. K–4). A young boy and an old man learn to listen to nature together.

Breitner, S. (1981). *The bookseller's advice*. New York: Viking. (Gr. K–3). Because he is hard of hearing, the old bookseller gives some strange advice. After some humorous mistakes, the advice turns out just right for the surprise ending.

Carle, E. (1990). *The very quiet cricket*. New York: Philomel. (Gr. K–3). As a quiet cricket searches for his own voice, he meets one insect after another who greets him with the special hello of its species.

Cole, J. (1989). *It's too noisy!* New York: Crowell. (Gr. K–3). A poor farmer lives in a very small house with many people, where there is too much noise. He yearns for quiet and goes to the village wise man for help.

De Mariscal, B. L. (1995). *The harvest birds/Los pajaros de la cosecha*. Emeryville, CA: Children's Book Press. (Gr. 2–6). A young Hispanic realizes his dream by listening to the voice of nature.

Denslow, S. P. (1990). *Night owls*. New York: Bradbury. (Gr. K–3). An aunt and her nephew share a midsummer visit and all the sights and sounds of a night noise picnic.

Dinardo, J. (1986). *Timothy and the night noises*. Englewood Cliffs, NJ: Prentice Hall. (Gr. 1–3). Timothy the frog finds a way to deal with the ghosts, monsters, and other scary things that make noises in the night.

Duke, K. (1992). *Aunt Isabel tells a good one*. New York: Dutton. (Gr. K–3). Aunt Isabel shares the art of storytelling with her young niece Penelope, and together they spin an enchanted tale.

Gibbons, G. (1993). *Puff . . . Flash . . . Bang!* New York: Morrow. This book describes ways people communicate without using spoken or written words through sounds and actions with whistles, sirens, bells, horns, guns, beacon fires, hand signals, sign language, lights, and flags.

Grambling, L. (1996). *Night sounds*. Windsor, CA: Rayve Productions. (Gr. 1–3). A boy lies in bed listening to night sounds. He thinks about where they are coming from and wonders if they will still be there after he falls asleep.

Lemieux, M. (1985). *What's that noise?* New York: Morrow. (Gr. K–3). Brown bear searches through the springtime forest for a mysterious sound and finds out it is his heart.

Lester, H. (1995). *Listen Buddy*. New York: Houghton Mifflin. (Gr. K–3). A rabbit goes for a long hop but doesn't listen to directions and hops into trouble, until he learns to listen to get out of this predicament.

Lindbergh, R. (1990). *The midnight farm*. New York: Dial. (Gr. K–3). A mother and a child tour their farm at night, when there is no moon or sun to guide them. The story is told with a counting rhyme.

Martin, B., & Archambault, J. (1990). *Knots on a counting rope*. New York: Trumpet. (Gr. 2–6). A Native American tells the story of his birth and life to his grandson who is blind. They share the storytelling and put another knot on a rope to represent one more time that the story has been told.

McGough, E. (1974). *Your silent language*. New York: Morrow. (Gr. 4–6). This book is about the science of kinesics, or body language, as it affects the lives of adolescents.

Myller, R. (1981). *A very noisy day*. New York: Atheneum. (Gr. 1–5). A dog named Fred experiences many sounds throughout one day. Each sound is presented visually and in a variety of typefaces, type sizes, and colors.

Numeroff, L. J. (1981). *Beatrice doesn't want to*. New York: Watts. (Gr. K–3). Beatrice learns from listening that a book can be fun.

Parte, B. A. (1985). *The kidnapping of Aunt Elizabeth*. New York: Greenwillow. (Gr. 3–6). A girl collects material for a social studies report as relatives tell her tales of their youth.

Perkins, A. (1985). *The ear book*. New York: Bantam. (Gr. K–3). A boy and his dog listen to the world around them.

Peterson, J. W. (1994). *My mama sings*. New York: HarperCollins. (Gr. K–3). A boy listens as his mama sings cricket songs, sunshine chants, and soft blues. When things go wrong for her at work, he makes up his own song to cheer her.

Pollock, P. (1982). *Keeping it secret*. New York: Putnam. (Gr. 3–6). A young girl adjusts poorly to a new school and hides her hearing aid and her feelings from everyone. Her family finally helps her change her attitude.

Rylant, C. (1986). *Night in the country*. New York: Bradbury. (Gr. K–3). This book is about the various sounds of the night.

Sattler, H. R. (1985). *Train whistles*. New York: Lothrop, Lee & Shepard. (Gr. K–3). This book about train whistles explains their fascinating language in code.

Schroeder, A. (1995). *Carolina shout!* New York: Dial. (Gr. 1–6). Delia, an African American girl, relates the sounds of Charleston's streets in a bygone era.

Scott V. M. (1986). *Belonging*. Washington, DC: Kendall Green. (Gr. 6–up). A teenage girl loses her hearing and finds she must start her life over. However, she finds a lack of support and understanding from the people around her.

Sharmat, M. (1984). *My mother never listens to me*. Niles, IL: Whitman. (Gr. K–3). Jerome seeks his mother's attention by telling her shocking things.

Sheldon, D. (1991). *The whale's song*. New York: Dial. (Gr. K–3). A young girl listens to her grandmother's story of the whales she loved as a child and the beautiful songs they sang.

Stanley, D. (1983). *The conversation club*. New York: Macmillan. (Gr. 1–3). Peter Fieldmouse moves to a new neighborhood and joins a club where he finds that everyone talks at once, so he becomes a listening expert and establishes a listening club.

Stevenson, J. (1986). *There's nothing to do*. New York: Morrow. (Gr. K–3). When Mary Ann and Louie are bored, Grandpa tells them what he did one day when he and his brother were bored.

Stolz, M. (1988). *Storm in the night*. New York: Harper and Row. (Gr. 1–4). As a young boy named Thomas sits through a thunderstorm, he listens to a story of his grandfather's boyhood and the sounds of the stormy night.

Sturges, P. (1996). *What's that sound Woolly Bear?* New York: Little, Brown. (Gr. K–2). Woolly Bear quietly wanders among the other noisy insects as she looks for a place to spin her cocoon.

Temple, C. (1996). *Train*. Boston: Houghton Mifflin. (Gr. K–2). Everyone along the way enjoys the sights and sounds of the C&O train.

Zolotow, C. (1983). *The song*. New York: Greenwillow. (Gr. K–3). Through every season, Nancy hears a bird singing different songs that no one else can hear. She makes a special friend who shares the bird's song with her.

Reading
to Learn

Even with four years of teaching experience, Denise McAllister feels frustrated. She says:

> My reading program wasn't meeting the needs of my diverse third-graders, who
> are multiethnic and multiracial with many receiving free or reduced-cost breakfast
> and lunch. Reading levels range from prefirst to fourth grade. There are 5 students
> reading on grade level and 2 students labeled gifted reading above grade level. I
> have 19 students reading below grade level and of these, 5 have learning disabili-
> ties, 6 are ESL students, and 8 are remedial readers.

So, after reading, studying, and consulting with the reading teacher, Denise created a program she calls Reader's Choice. She explains:

> *I used Pamela Haack and Nancy Madden's works as models for my program. I want each child to achieve success in reading by being challenged, not frustrated. I want to give each child choices and promote a habit of lifetime reading. I want to move away from total reliance on the basal, integrate the language arts with a strong reading and writing base, and use cooperative learning. I hope to help these kids, many of whom aren't read to at home and don't have access to books, enter a literary world. The program includes a variety of literature on various levels.*

Denise and the reading teacher planned several three-week thematic units to use alternately with the basal. They chose themes related to the science and social studies curriculum (e.g., interdependence and Native American cultures). For each theme, they identified at least eight children's books on reading levels from grade 1 through 4 and obtained 3 to 5 copies of each from their school district and public library. They identified the most difficult vocabulary from each book and wrote several questions to foster response, intensive reading, and comprehension of the story. They put the vocabulary and questions on tagboard cards in a pizza box in alphabetical order by author. Denise continues:

> *Every morning, the special education teacher and reading teacher are with us for an hour. On Monday, we introduce the books with brief booktalks and each child chooses a book that would be "just right" for him or her, not too hard and not too easy. Then we meet with children individually to have each read the vocabulary and a page or two to make sure the book is on his or her instructional level. At first, some of the children couldn't gauge what they could handle, and so we made suggestions. But they soon were able to find books on their levels. To ensure that students are challenged and read a variety of genres, we identify one book and each child chooses two, with three the minimum number they must read.*

Briefly, the components of Denise's reading program are the following:

■ *Vocabulary.* The words for each book appear in a list, with 3 or 4 words noted with an asterisk. Each student uses a dictionary to look up the asterisked words and write the definitions or put the words in sentences. The children work in pairs or triads to do this and are encouraged to be creative. Some groups chant, sing, or group the words according to meaning. Then each child's recognition is checked in context and isolation.

■ *Reading.* Next, students read the story and think about the BIG QUESTION, a universal question that all the members of the class can answer about their books, which is posted on a big question mark hanging from the ceiling. This question involves predicting, problem/solution, feelings about characters and events, or story elements. Children monitor their comprehension as they read by using a series of questions they each have on a bookmark, but they are allowed to ask for help if they get stuck. At the beginning of the year, the rule "Three before me" helps children learn to use each other as resources and lets Denise work uninterrupted with individuals or small groups. (The children must ask three peers before they ask the teacher for help.)

■ *Writing.* Writing has two parts: *Your Thoughts,* which is their answer to the BIG QUESTION, and *Comprehension,* which is the answers to each book's set of questions, which they write in complete sentences. Work goes in an envelope marked with the story title, and it is checked.

■ *Skill.* Skills are selected according to individual needs and are taught in mini-lessons to small groups of children. For example, the lesson might focus on digraphs for those having trouble with them. The children then list words from the story related to that skill (e.g., parts of speech, contractions, compound words, endings, making a concept web for the story, finding cause/effect or problem-solution patterns, or listing other characters or books that are similar).

■ *Share project.* In pairs or triads, students choose a project from a list, or create their own, that combines reading and writing with the fine arts. Some of the projects are: Make an ad to convince someone to read or not read the book, create a diorama and poem about the story, and write the author a letter and draw a picture to go with it. The child first shares his project with a teacher and then with a small group or the class. The project might even be put on the hall bulletin board or in a hall display case.

■ *Evaluation.* Students who read the same story meet with a teacher to discuss it and read a favorite section aloud. Then they "buddy read" the story aloud to another child who has read it. At this point, teachers do "running records" of oral reading and make notes on comprehension. Students are graded on the quality of their work, with 5 points given for each of the program's components. Comprehension has two sections, and the total points a child can receive is 35. If a score is 28 or better, the child gets a Reader's Choice Certificate and a package of candy. The child's name, the date, and the book's title go on a star that is added to a "Shining Stars" bulletin board.

At the end of the first year, Denise was pleased with the results. She says:

Although it took time for students to get used to the routine, before long they were begging us to spend more than our allotted two hours a day. I took care to explain the routine well to parents, since they were used to having their children read the basal cover to cover and we were reading it selectively and alternating with Reader's Choice every three weeks. During the year, several parents noted their children's growing enthusiasm for reading. The best part is four students tested out of remedial reading and one student tested out of ESL in June. Of course, we have some changes planned for the program for next year, based on how it worked this year, and some new ideas we've been reading about.

Denise has adapted her reading program in a special way to meet the needs of diverse students in her classroom. As you read this chapter, think about how Denise's individualized program that incorporates self-selection measures up to current research and theory about reading.

• • • • •

O• • • • •verview

Reading is a receptive language process involving the construction of meaning using both the reader's prior knowledge and print as the reader actively uses strategies to comprehend an author's message. Reading and writing are interactive processes that directly affect each other. Various approaches to reading instruction develop proficient readers who are strategic, engaged, fluent, and independent. This chapter supplements, but should not replace, a reading methods course.

Students define *reading* in a variety of ways:

Opening a book, seeing words and you read.

—Rheana, age 6 (poor reader)

You look at the words and you make pictures and stories in your mind.

—Roberto, age 7 (good reader)

Learning. It teaches you how to write too. You get ideas about making books.

—Brenda, age 7 (good reader)

It's something that helps you go farther into your mind and use your imagination.

—Emily, age 8 (good reader)

It's reading class . . . I don't know.

—Sharma, age 10 (poor reader)

It feeds your brain.

—Joseph, age 10 (good reader)

These definitions of reading by children of various ages and reading proficiencies suggest the complex nature of the reading process. Perhaps the definitions suggest, too, the importance of having an accurate definition of reading. The less proficient readers seem to have simpler definitions than the better readers. How worthwhile would it be to discuss the definition of reading with children? Perhaps poor readers do not understand what reading is about or how good readers think as they read. Sharing definitions and discussing the reading process and strategies one uses may help problem readers better understand what good reading is all about.

Reading is an active, cognitive process of meaning construction using one's prior knowledge and print to arrive at an author's message. Meaning does not result from the precise identification of every word in a sentence, but from the interplay between the mind of the reader and the language of the text (Weaver, 1994). Reading is the instantaneous recognition of various written symbols, simultaneous association of these symbols with existing knowledge, and comprehension of the information and ideas communicated. Readers react and interpret print from their own knowledge base. The following note illustrates this and the difficulty of establishing meaning when there is a mismatch between an author's and a reader's schemata:

> Mary,
>
> You should have seen the cancer under that roach that mooch brought in for trade. The guts were frayed and the skins were bald. I told him to buzz.
>
> Brent

Schema theory can help one better understand the personal aspect of reading and comprehension. As you read the preceding note, you recognize words and phrases and search your schemata to associate meanings with words. You may stop to reread or question your definition of a word. For instance, you know that *cancer* is a disease, a *roach* is a bug, and *frayed* means worn out. But unless you are familiar with the language of used-car sales, you probably can't understand the message. Used in this context, some of these words don't match your schemata for them. The message involves a rusted car in poor condition with a worn interior and bald tires that was brought in for trade by an opportunistic customer with whom Brent wouldn't do business.

We bring our prior knowledge and schemata to print and make inferences about what the author means based on what we know and what we read. Your schema or cognitive structure for *cancer, roach,* and *frayed* doesn't match Brent's. We each have different schemata that hold both events and actions as well as objects. A child's schema for *dog* may include several types of dogs, his experience with dogs (being bitten last summer), and such characteristics as a furry, four-legged animal that barks and growls. You may have other meanings in your schema for the term, depending on your experiences.

Emergent Literacy

Researchers today know that very young children's schemata for reading and writing develop earlier and to a greater degree than was realized in the past. The term *emergent literacy* is used today in place of *reading readiness. Emergent literacy* is the appearance of the ability to receive and express language to accomplish goals, or the first indications of a child's awareness that print communicates meaning and has a function. *Reading readiness* was defined as being ready to learn to read and was characterized by letter and word knowledge that appeared around age 6.

Literacy includes oral language, reading, and writing, not just reading that begins at home where children have their first experiences with print. Early literate activities form the foundation for literacy growth (e.g., seeing parents reading and writing, being read to, looking at pictures, turning pages of books and magazines, talking about stories, and scribbling and drawing). As children hear stories, talk about pictures, "write" notes and letters, supply words, and tell stories themselves, they begin to associate oral language and meaning with print.

Wells (1986) documented the importance of early story experiences for later school achievement of 32 English children in his nine-year study from just after their first birthdays to the end of their primary school years. Jonathan, who had the highest achievement on the literacy tests administered throughout the study, had "something in the order of six thousand book and story experiences before starting school." Rosie, the child who had the lowest score on all the tests, "was not read to once before starting school" (p. 158). For 90 percent of the sample, Wells found no relationship between family background and level of language development. Other researchers (Morrow, 1993; Teale & Sulzby, 1989) confirm the importance of parents providing early literacy experiences for children's later school success.

Children develop concepts about print from their first experiences at home and at school. Awareness of written language develops as they learn that words are groups of letters separated by spaces, that written language moves from left to right on a page, and that oral language can match printed language (Butler & Clay, 1982). As you begin to teach children to read, you should focus not on whether they are ready in terms of possessing a list of prerequisite skills, but on whether they are ready for the type and quality of instruction you will provide.

Teale and Sulzby (1989) provide a portrait of the young child as a literacy learner. From their research with very young children, they have found the following:

- For almost all children in a literate society, learning to read and write begins early in life. Even children as young as 1 year old can process and use written language.
- The functions of literacy are an integral part of the learning process that is taking place. For example, reading a recipe is an integral part of helping to bake cookies.
- Reading and writing are interrelated and develop concurrently in young children. Oral language is part of the literacy development process, as well.
- Children construct their understanding of how written language works through active engagement. They learn by experiencing reading and writing as purposeful and goal-directed everyday activities.

Today, in many kindergarten and first-grade classrooms, print-rich environments encourage literacy development. Many children are involved in very different activities than they were in the past. Teachers model real uses of language for children, and immerse children in activities that promote literacy development, such as dramatic play in theme areas (doctor's office, restaurant, grocery store); shared-book experiences; storybook reading; writing stories, keeping journals and learning logs; and art, music, and scribbling and drawing (Morrow, 1997). Teachers accept and encourage invented spelling and creative reading and work with parents to promote these literacy behaviors at home.

Candy Stroud, a kindergarten teacher, has several areas in her room where small groups of children spend time each day (e.g., a listening center, areas devoted to reading and writing, and the dramatic play centers [housekeeping and doctor's office]). In the housekeeping center, Candy encourages dramatic play in which the children use reading and writing in natural ways. She includes literacy tools for the children's use, such as newspapers, magazines, note pads, pens, pencils, cookbooks, a telephone, a calendar, and empty food boxes that contain print.

As you examine reading and reading instruction, don't overlook the pivotal role that writing and oral language play. The language arts are inextricably interwoven. While examining reading and reading instruction, remember that in the real world, reading is not separated from listening, speaking, or writing, nor should it be in the classroom.

As well as in school, literacy activities that occur at home should include opportunities for children and parents to use oral and written language together. Different families use print in different ways at home and these practices can support or ignore children's early literacy development. The importance of family literacy, especially for families with few financial resources and for children who are at risk for failure in school, is not disputed. There are many ideas and activities for developing the literacy learning of both children and parents at home (Come & Fredericks, 1995; Purcell-Gates, L'Allier, & Smith, 1995).

What else besides rich literacy environments and experiences at school and home help prepare young children to be successful readers? There is substantial evidence that phonemic awareness is related to success in reading, as is the ability to spell.

Phonemic Awareness

Phonemic awareness is the knowledge that speech consists of a series of sounds or phonemes. For example, when you hear the word *cat* spoken, you should be able to hear three separate sounds, /c/-a/-t/. Phonemic awareness involves the ability to attend to a sound in the context of the other sounds in a word. It is critical because it seems to precede the knowledge that printed letters represent sounds in words. In fact, phonemic awareness tasks are believed to be "the best predictors of the ease of early reading acquisition—better than anything else we know of, including IQ" (Stanovitch, 1994).

By the end of first grade, most children have gained this awareness and can manipulate phonemes in their speech (Yopp, 1995). They can

- Break spoken words into their constituent sounds, saying /d/-i/-g/ for *dig*.
- Remove a sound from a spoken word, saying *rake* when asked to remove the /b/ from the beginning of *break*.
- Isolate sounds at the beginning, middle, or end of a word. Use sound boxes (see Figure 8.1) to separate sounds and to help children see and hear the breaks.

The Yopp-Singer Test of Phonemic Segmentation (Yopp, 1995) is used by kindergarten and first-grade teachers to identify English-speaking children who may benefit most from phonemic awareness activities (see Figure 8.2). But phonemic awareness may be a problem for some ESL students, since some English speech sounds may not exist in their first language and some languauges are not phonetic. For example, some Native American languages do not follow a phonological system. But students of Hispanic heritage often respond well to phonemic awareness activities, since Spanish is a

FIGURE 8.1 An example of sound boxes used to segment the phonemes in a word.

· · · · ·

phonetic language. With children who lack phonemic awareness, activities within the context of reading books and writing stories will develop their phonemic knowlege. Imbed the following activities within the connected text of real stories and poetry:

- Read nursery rhymes and note rhyming words.
- Identify phoneme segments (e.g., What sounds do you hear in *bat*?).
- Develop auditory discrimination (e.g., Which last sound is different in *ball, bat,* and *rat?*).
- Play sound-to-word matching games (e.g., Is there a /d/ in *dog?*).
- Isolate sounds (e.g., What is the first sound in *farm?*).
- Blend sounds to make words (e.g., What word do the sounds /c/a/t/ make?).

FIGURE 8.2 Use this test of phonemic awareness with English-speaking children to determine their strengths and needs.

Yopp-Singer Test of Phoneme Segmentation

Student's Name _____ Date _____

Score (number correct) _____

Directions: Today we're going to play a word game. I'm going to say a word and I want you to break the word apart. You are going to tell me each sound in the word in order. For example, if I say "old," you should say /o/-/l/-/d/." *(Administrator: Be sure to say the sounds, not the letters, in the word.)* Let's try a few together.

Practice items: (Assist the child in segmenting these items as necessary.) ride, go, man

Test items: (Circle those items that the student correctly segments; incorrect responses may be recorded on the blank line following the item.)

1. dog	_____		12. lay	_____
2. keep	_____		13. race	_____
3. fine	_____		14. zoo	_____
4. no	_____		15. three	_____
5. she	_____		16. job	_____
6. wave	_____		17. in	_____
7. grew	_____		18. ice	_____
8. that	_____		19. at	_____
9. red	_____		20. top	_____
10. me	_____		21. by	_____
11. sat	_____		22. do	_____

Source: The author, Hallie Kay Yopp, California State University, Fullerton, grants permission for this test to be reproduced. The author acknowledges the contribution of the late Harry Singer to the development of this test.

- Create rhyming words (e.g., What word rhymes with *same?* Change the /c/ in *cat* to /p/.).
- Tap out the syllables in multisyllabic words or the phonemes in one-syllable words.
- Use chips, markers, and boxes to represent syllables or sounds in words.

Activities like these—including rhyming, blending phonemes, segmenting sounds, splitting words into syllables, and making new words—allow children to use letter-sound correspondence to read and spell words. Yopp (1992) suggests a host of other suggestions for enhancing students' phonemic awareness.

Effective Early Reading Programs

It should be no surprise to you that phonemic awareness activities within the context of real reading and writing experiences are central to effective early reading programs. But what other components of successful programs should you include in your instruction of early readers? Also, what components will be most beneficial for building the literacy of young children who are at risk for school failure?

Pikulski (1994) reviewed five early intervention programs in communities across the United States that were designed for implementation early in a child's school career, primarily in first grade. He chose programs that were effective according to published data for students likely to make limited progress in reading. The critical features common to these programs follow:

- *Coordination between compensatory program and classroom instruction.* High-quality classroom instruction coordinated with the special program is important.
- *Small groups and one-on-one instruction.* Smaller teacher/student ratios and individual tutoring for children who are the most at risk seem to increase success.
- *Increased time spent in literacy activities.* Students spend more time reading and writing than students not at risk.
- *Interventions that are early and of various durations depending on student needs.* Programs that serve preschool children and those who still have difficulty beyond first grade are most effective for students who need intense support.
- *Variety of readable texts.* Predictable, easy-to-read, and other motivating children's books were most prevalent with an absence of traditional workbooks and isolated skill practice.
- *Orientation toward reading as a meaning-constructing process* and *instruction in word identification strategies.* Repeated reading was the most common activity; word-level strategies with deliberate instruction in phonemic awareness and word recognition was also part of all programs.
- *Writing activities.* Focus writing opportunities, from brief to more extended, on reinforcing word recognition.
- *Regular ongoing assessment.* Regular monitoring of oral reading, the use of writing portfolios and teacher observation to assess progress, and direct teaching were important components.
- *Connections with the home.* Parent support for homework, at-home reading, and parent support teams were common components.
- *Experienced, certified teachers.* Professionally prepared, accomplished teachers are the mainstay of successful early intervention programs.

Pikulski (1994) concludes that these components ought to be part of early intervention programs. It is important to note that he found in these programs a balance between meaning making and word-level activities. In fact, he says, "There is a firm research base for the position that a *balance* between the reading of meaningful, connected texts and systematic word identification instruction results in superior achievement" (p. 36).

Reading Recovery (Clay, 1985; Lyons, Pinnell, & DeFord, 1993), a popular early intervention program with impressive results, was one of the programs Pikulski reviewed. It involves a daily, 30-minute, one-on-one lesson in which a trained teacher and a first-grader work together on a variety of reading and writing activities. During the entire lesson, the teacher observes and records the strategies used so he knows what to reinforce or redirect. A lesson consists of five components: (1) the child rereads a familiar book; (2) the teacher keeps a running record of oral reading that he analyzes to determine the reading strategies the child is using; (3) the child works with movable plastic letters to construct and analyze words; (4) the child writes a sentence or two that can become a story over a period of days; and (5) the child and the teacher preview a new book together, looking at new vocabulary and illustrations, and predicting the story line.

Reading Recovery has been criticized because of its high cost, a lack of emphasis on comprehension and the prescribed routine that doesn't allow children to select the books they read. However, as a program to support classroom instruction (where comprehension and choice can be integral parts of reading), Reading Recovery has transformed many children from nonreaders or struggling readers into learners capable of reading on grade level. Many schools use adaptations of Reading Recovery and/or programs that include the components Pikulski identified to intervene early to prevent later reading failure.

STRETCHING EXERCISE

Why do traditional remedial reading programs have a marginal impact on children's reading? Read Dixie Lee Spiegel's "A Comparison of Traditional Remedial Programs and Reading Recovery: Guidelines for Success for All Programs" in *The Reading Teacher*, Volume 49, Number 2, pages 86–96. How do her suggestions differ from Pikulski's?

• • • • •

Proficient Reading

It is important that you include comprehension in your definition of reading because your teaching will then reflect this. How and what you do when you teach reading grows directly from your beliefs and knowledge. If you define reading as primarily a decoding process, as in a bottom-up model, then you will emphasize word recognition and perfect oral reading and deemphasize comprehension. If you define reading as primarily a comprehending process, as in the top-down model, then you are not overly troubled when a child mispronounces words, adds or leaves out words, or occasionally repeats words in oral reading, as long as the child understands what he reads.

As well as a definition of reading as a meaning construction process, it is also important that you have in mind ultimate goals to guide your everyday teaching. No matter what the age of the students you teach, reading should be an enjoyable activity that students engage in voluntarily, and from which they gain insights and understandings into their own lives. Reading, both silently and aloud, is a means of communicating with others and a way of learning.

Proficient readers possess several characteristics that you can help your students develop (see Figure 8.3), such as the following:

- *Strategic*. Strategic readers use various strategies to help them monitor comprehension. For example, they predict, verify, preview, set purposes, self-question, draw from background knowledge, paraphrase, vary their rates, summarize, reread, visualize, suspend judgments, and continue to read to make sense out of text.
- *Engaged*. Engaged readers are motivated to read and enjoy and learn from what they read. They are involved with what they read and interact with others about it.
- *Fluent*. Fluent readers possess huge sight-word vocabularies with multiple meanings for words. Their minds make quick associations between print and their schemata. They read easily and smoothly at a comfortably well-paced rate, probably not reading every word but sampling text and predicting meaning.
- *Independent*. Independent readers are self-reliant and self-directed. They are strategic, engaged, and fluent; they read without the direction or help of others; and they choose to read independently when they have free time. They use strategies appropriate to the print they read and read easily.

No matter what your approach to reading instruction, your long-range goals should be to develop proficient readers who possess these characteristics. Your modeling of proficient reading behaviors and positive reinforcement *before, during,* and *after reading* are pivotal in helping students adopt these characteristics.

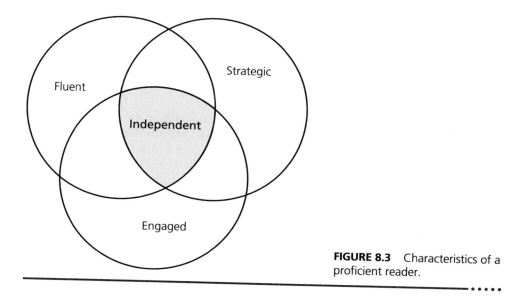

FIGURE 8.3 Characteristics of a proficient reader.

Students with Special Needs

Students who read below grade level and have special needs are found in almost every heterogeneously grouped classroom. Struggling readers who exhibit problems learning how to read need literacy instruction that is not necessarily different from literacy instruction for typical learners, but is more intense and deliberate. It needs to be meaning based, rather than skill based, and more explicit than instruction for typical learners (Sears, Carpenter, & Burstein, 1994). Consider the following facts:

- Students labeled gifted also have special needs. They master the basic curriculum easily and quickly, and differentiated reading programs are often suggested for them (Dooley, 1993).
- Children with severe disabilities often find success in learning to read with the assistance of technology (Erickson & Koppenhaver, 1995).
- Second-language learners need intense, explicit, and direct instruction that supports their first language. They may seem to have short attention spans or low intelligence, but may just behave in ways related to the fatigue of trying to make sense out of a new language and the confusion of a new culture (Freeman & Freeman, 1993).

Clearly, there are many students with special literacy needs who want and need teachers who are caring and committed to treat them as worthy and respected individuals regardless of their differences. Throughout this text, there are suggestions for teaching diverse students, thus the reason for the brief discussion here.

STRETCHING EXERCISE   Read "A Case Study of Middle School Reading Disability" by D. Morris, C. Ervin, and K. Conrad in *The Reading Teacher*, Volume 49, Number 5, pages 368–377. How meaning centered, direct, and intense was Ervin's instruction?

• • • • •

Basal Reader Approach

Many teachers in the United States rely on basal readers either as the mainstay of their reading program or as an adjunct to it. Older basals have been criticized for controlled vocabulary, emphasis on isolated skills, and stories that lack authenticity. Often, stories in older basals either were contrived to teach certain skills or they were adaptations of children's books in which content was omitted or changed, characters were renamed, or stories were rewritten to make them less offensive to censorship and more palatable to a wider audience (Goodman, 1988).

The basal approach is structured and uses basal readers or graded books that span kindergarten to sixth or ninth grade. Basal readers are usually accompanied by teacher manuals, student workbooks, activity sheets, placement and progress tests, and other materials. Although the introduction of reading skills and vocabulary is carefully controlled within each, wide variations exist among the various published series. Not only are there differences in *when* skills are introduced but also in *what* skills are emphasized and reinforced. In addition, the basal approach was often criticized because of the following:

- The basal approach assumed that reading was the acquisition of an arbitrary sequence of skills that every child needs in order to learn to read. It involved children in skill development activities that represented fragmented, abstract language use (Goodman, 1986).
- The basal approach assumed that there are only three levels of reading ability in a class, and thus three reading groups, and each child in a group would progress at the same rate to the next basal level. Educators now know that static grouping has many problems, since children learn at different rates with spurts and delays in growth experienced at different times in their development.
- Little time was left for independent reading or practice in the skills of reading with relevant material.

However, according to a study of five first-grade basals published in 1986 and five in 1993, the newer basals are different (McCarthey & Hoffman, 1995) in the following ways:

- The total number of words is considerably less in newer basals than in the older ones, but newer programs hold substantially more unique words.
- Vocabulary control and repetition are significantly reduced, if not eliminated.
- Format, organization, and genres are more diverse (e.g., they now include anthologies, big books, tradebooks, and poetry).
- Literary quality is higher. There are fewer adaptations, selections have more complex plots and well-developed characters, and selections require more interpretation on the reader's part.
- Language is more colloquial and idiomatic.
- Artwork is more engaging.
- More predictable text features appear (e.g., familiar concepts, cumulative patterns, repetition, rhyme, rhythm, and familiar sequences).
- Decoding demands placed on the reader are far greater in the new series than in the old.

In the teacher's editions, McCarthey and Hoffman (1995) found a shared reading model rather than a teacher-directed model. Vocabulary is introduced in the context of the stories, fewer comprehension questions are offered, and more higher-level questions are asked. Although skills are still prevalent, they tend to be more integrated. The teachers who took part in the study indicated wide variation in the way they use the basal.

So, preliminary evidence suggests that, at least at the first-grade level, the newer basals seem to have overcome many prior criticisms. Certainly, this discussion of basal readers suggests why the approach is so popular. Basals are well organized, sequential, and easy to use because of carefully planned teachers' manuals that not only tell the teacher what to do but also when, where, and how to do it. Written expression ranges from plays and poetry to newspaper stories and science fiction. Publishers include entire children's books and excerpts, as well. Minorities, ethnic groups, rural and urban settings, older people, and males and females in nonstereotypical roles are found in today's basals, making them more relevant for diverse student populations. Also, the artwork in newer basals is often breathtaking.

Wisely, McCallum (1988) reminds us that basals play a critical role in reading instruction. He says they partially fill the gap between research and practice, offer a coordinated package designed for a wide range of skills and attitudes, provide a management system for coordinating instruction, and provide on-the-job training for new teachers. As well, most teachers do not have the time, energy, or expertise to develop materials that meet parents' and schools' goals. McCallum cautions, however, that how teachers apply the instructional suggestions in basals is critical to their effectiveness or ineffectiveness.

Literature-Based Reading Instruction

Literature-based reading instruction is an approach to teaching reading that primarily uses "real" books to develop literacy (Norton, 1992). This approach evolved partly as a response to reports such as *Becoming a Nation of Readers* (Anderson, Hiebert, Scott, & Wilkinson, 1985), which criticized the state of reading materials and instruction. Literature-based reading instruction also grew from the whole-language movement that advocates the use of children's books by teachers who want to make their own decisions about instruction (Zarrillo, 1989).

Enthusiasm for literature-based reading instruction is high, and preliminary research evidence in favor of this approach is positive (Stahl & Miller, 1989; Tunnell & Jacobs, 1989). However, definitive conclusions are difficult because of the lack of long-term studies of children beyond the third grade, and differences between traditional basal reading instruction and whole-language instruction, which includes the development of writing, are often minor (Schickedanz, 1990).

In place of the skills-oriented, teacher-directed basal programs of the 1970s, many classroom reading programs now have a very different look. Some programs use children's literature or tradebooks exclusively, while others use basal texts in which the amount and quality of literature has increased dramatically in recent years. Some use content textbooks and tradebooks, or both the basal and children's literature, and some use sustained, silent reading periods. Some classroom teachers, such as Denise, mentioned at the beginning of this chapter, use a variety of these components in different combinations. In many classrooms, student choice, student/student interactions, and shared meaning construction are the norm. Teachers are guides and facilitators, with students taking the lead in their own learning much more than they did in the past.

Effective Instruction

When planning your reading program, the key word is *balance.* You want to provide students with whole-group instruction, small-group interactions, and time for independent reading. If you use one pattern exclusively, problems arise. For example, if you focus only on independent reading of student-chosen material, you may rob students of expert direction and guidance that can help them become proficient readers. When you focus only on teacher-led instruction, you inhibit student ownership of reading development and independence. A rich reading program should contain various combinations of teacher and student interaction and literature selection to develop proficient readers.

It is important to note here, however, that basal publishers have responded to the criticisms raised earlier in this chapter. Basals are revised regularly with the aid of literacy experts who help translate the latest research findings. In addition, the materials that accompany basal readers provide teachers and students with options for personal responses to literature, a variety of writing activities, literature extension projects, and flexible grouping suggestions. They also include research-based strategies for developing fluent and proficient readers. The important role that basal readers play in reading instruction, whether as the sole text used or as one of several materials used in a literature-based program, cannot be discounted.

No matter what classroom approach to teaching reading you adopt or what strategies you use in a given lesson, several aspects of instruction will help you develop proficient readers. These will be discussed next.

Motivation and Interest

Motivation and interest in what is read are important whether one is age 4 or 44. The student who is motivated, interested, curious, and involved is ready to read and will probably have better comprehension and learn more than one who is not.

A good way to ensure that students are motivated is to give them choices. Let your students choose from a number of quality books so they have real reasons to read. Of course, as the teacher, you also choose some of the books to be read. Another way to ensure motivation and interest is to connect with the students' background experiences first. Help them establish what they already know so that new information will more easily fit with old. Another important part of motivation is understanding the purpose for reading and what you expect after reading. When you attend to content, assess prior knowledge, and help students relate to print, while ensuring that they have a purpose for reading, you enhance the possibility that your students will be motivated to read. You are a catalyst and model for your students, so share your enthusiasm for a selection, story, or book, and watch it spread.

Students bring a variety of motivations to reading, but you can distinguish between two main types (Sweet & Guthrie, 1996):

- *Intrinsic motivation.* These goals are internal to the learner and come from personal experiences and interests that develop into reasons for reading.
- *Extrinsic motivation.* These goals originate outside the learner, perhaps with a teacher or parent who gives stars, recognition, praise, or good grades.

It seems that both types of motivation need to be present to build proficient readers (Sweet & Guthrie, 1996). Intrinsic motivation drives self-directed learners and controls long-term reading behavior. Extrinsic motivation temporarily controls reading behavior and often drives skill development. Many students need the teacher to provide reasons for learning—for example, an explanation of why the learning of a particular strategy or skill will benefit the student.

Comprehension

Comprehension is an active cognitive process that requires the construction of meaning from incoming information and prior knowledge. The single, most often overlooked factor in poor comprehension is the difficulty level of text. When children read material in which they recognize and know the majority of words, their chances of successful comprehension greatly increase. Of course, interest, knowledge, the use of strategies that aid comprehension, and the ability to monitor comprehension are also critical, as are purposes for reading and background knowledge.

In the past, questioning was considered to be one of the best practices teachers could use to develop comprehension, but now, educators know that asking questions is often merely one way to assess memory and test comprehension. Discussion that centers on personal responses to what is read fosters richer comprehension, as it allows students to interact and build on each other's reactions and interpretations. Less teacher direction (not the absence of it) and a judicious amount of teacher questioning and commenting, coupled with student/student interactions, promotes effective comprehension.

If you use questions to foster comprehension and discussion, you should model interpretive- and evaluative-type questions and encourage children to pose these kinds of divergent questions that involve critical thinking. Of course, children can demonstrate their comprehension in many other ways, such as retelling a story, writing in a response journal, dramatizing, drawing or creating an artistic representation, or writing a poem, among a number of options. Most of all, remember that comprehension is a personal process of making sense out of print, and all people comprehend what they read somewhat differently.

Word Analysis

Primary teachers (first, second, and third grade) spend a good deal of time teaching strategies for word analysis. After students read on a fourth-grade level, teachers spend less time on word analysis, since, by then, students have likely learned most of the strategies. Word analysis relies on using the three cue systems—context, phonics, and structure—of written language to figure out unknown words and make sense out of print. They are:

Context. Words, phrases, and sentences, as well as illustrations, surrounding an unknown word give clues to pronunciaton and meaning. A good way to use context is to continue reading to the end of the sentence or paragraph to obtain clues to the word.

As she reads orally to her first-graders, Margaret occasionally omits a word but continues to read to the end of the sentence or paragraph. She does this to model for her students how context can help them make sensible guesses about unknown words. Rhymed poetry can also be used in the same way to teach this skill. Context is a powerful word analysis strategy and an integral part of comprehension, since many words in the English language have more than one meaning.

Phonics. Phonics is the set of relationships between the sound system of oral language and the letter system of written language (Goodman, 1986). The sounds that letters and letter clusters represent give clues to meaning and pronunciation. In order for children to use phonics successfully, they must have good phonemic awareness that involves auditory acuity and discrimination.

Research with phonics and spelling rules suggests few rules hold true often enough to warrant time spent teaching them (Weaver, 1994). Phonics is probably best taught when it is integrated into meaningful reading and writing instruction across the curriculum. Some children need explicit instruction and short lessons focused on a specific skill. Routman and Butler (1995) suggest beginning by working with whole texts. Nursery rhymes and poetry are especially good for developing knowledge of rudimentary phonics skills and the ability to identify and produce rhyming words and words that begin and end the same. Reading books aloud, shared reading, and writing activities will help the teacher focus student attention first on sentences, then on words, and last on letters. Students will then be able to manipulate syllables and phonemes to make new words. For example, nearly 500 one-syllable words can be created by using *onsets* or initial letter(s), with the following rimes (rhymes) (Adams, 1990):

-ack	-all	-ain	-ake	-ale	-ame	-an	-and	-ap	-ash
-at	-ate	-aw	-ay	-eat	-ell	-est	-ice	-ick	-ide
-ight	-ill	-in	-ine	-ing	-ink	-ip	-ir	-ock	-oke
-op	-ore	-or	-uck	-ug	-ump	-unk			

Although phonics is a necessary tool, especially for beginning readers, it may be a problem for children with hearing difficulties and for some ESL students. However, knowledge of context and initial consonants, consonant blends, consonant digraphs, and rhyming words, at the very least, is critical. Remember, though, phonics is only one tool for figuring out unknown words. Once children possess proficiency in other word analysis skills and a growing sight vocabulary, there is little need for phonics.

Structure.   Analyzing word parts (e.g., prefixes, suffixes, root words, or inflectional endings and the special structure of compound words, contractions, and multisyllabic words) gives children clues to meaning and pronunciation. For example, examine the structure of the word *divaricate*. The prefix */di/* means "two" (a dialogue is a conversation between two people), */vari/* means "many" (from various), and the suffix */cate/* is like that in *locate*. By analyzing structure, children can guess the meaning and pronunciation of a word. Context (e.g., when a child reads, "The main trunk of the tree began to divaricate five feet above the ground") can help children confirm or revise their guess if it doesn't provide the initial clue to meaning.

Besides direct instruction in word structure, there are many indirect ways to build children's awareness of word parts. Reading poetry and nonsense verse focuses children's attention on word structure. For example, George Shanon's (1996) *Spring: A Haiku Story* is a collection of three-line, 5-7-5-syllable poetry, and Eve Merriam's (1960) *The Inner City Mother Goose* is a collection of poetry about inner-city living. Writing their own haiku or traditional poetry helps students learn about the syllabic structure of words. Nonsense such as *The Pelican Chorus and Other Nonsense* by Edward Lear (1995), rap in *Bein' with You This Way* by Nikola-Lisa (1994), and word play such as *Prowlpuss* by Gina Wilson (1994) focuses attention on word structure.

Consulting a peer, sibling, parent, teacher, the dictionary, or a glossary provides help with meaning and pronunciation. But this takes time and the result is not always satisfying, since another child may not know the word and the dictionary usually gives several definitions and pronunciations from which to choose. Teach children to use this method last.

A Combined Strategy.   Children of all ages need a useful method of figuring out unknown words that results in the least disruption to the natural flow of reading. Good readers unconsciously use context, phonics, and structure in different combinations.

Children who stop at unfamiliar words or use only one strategy, such as sounding words out letter by letter, need to improve fluency by using a combination of strategies.

Have a discussion with your class to determine what strategies they use. Then, together, create a list of things to do. Reproduce the list on tagboard as a bookmark for individual children or post it in a prominent place in your classroom. The first list here was created by a group of first-graders and the second by fourth-graders:

If the Picture Won't Help
1. Skip it and read on.
2. Look at the first letter(s).
3. Sound it out.
4. Ask.
5. Look it up.

What to Do When You Come to a Word You Don't Know
1. Read to the end of the sentence or paragraph.
2. Look at the first letter(s).
3. Look at the way the word is put together.
4. Sound out the word.
5. Ask or look it up.

STRETCHING EXERCISE Talk with a group of children to find out what they do when they meet unknown words. Help them identify a sequential strategy. Transcribe and revise the ideas together until they are useful and brief. Have each child put the list on a bookmark to use during reading.

• • • • •

Vocabulary and Word Study

For both children and adults, vocabulary is probably best increased through extensive independent reading. But direct instruction also results in vocabulary growth. Vocabulary knowledge is a principal contributor to reading comprehension, perhaps comprising as much as 50 to 80 percent of what children comprehend, and this is especially true in subject areas where vocabulary is technical.

One has only to look at a randomly chosen page in any dictionary to discover that most of the words have more than one meaning. Some estimates are that more than 70 percent of the English language has multiple meanings. For this reason, direct instruction in the multimeanings of words, including dictionary usage, is critical.

Children learn words in several ways but primarily through association rather than repetition. Research has not established the number of repetitions necessary before a word becomes part of sight vocabulary. It is known that meaningful associations with words establishes them in memory. It is also known that good vocabulary instruction involves contextual as well as definitional instruction (Stahl & Fairbanks, 1986). So, the following steps are recommended for teaching vocabulary:

1. See, hear, and say the word printed and spoken (in isolation and context) and look at a picture.
2. Talk about the word connecting with what is already known.
3. Use the word in a sentence and suggest synonyms.
4. Define the word. Explain it or look it up in the dictionary.
5. Write the word in isolation and context (have students do this in their own dictionaries).

This approach to vocabulary learning involves the use of all four language modes. It gives children opportunities to hear, see, say, and write words, both in and out of context, and to talk about meaning and usage. Captioned television and video also use both visual and audio to build vocabulary and comprehension for problem readers and for those children difficult to reach with traditional methods (Koskinen, Wilson, Gambrell, & Neuman, 1993).

Studying words and their component patterns to determine structure, spelling, and meaning also builds vocabulary (Bear, Invernizzi, Templeton, & Johnston, 1996). Students may be asked to create *word trees* like the one in Figure 8.4 for the Latin root */struct/*, which means "to build." Bear and colleagues provide over 300 word-study mini-lessons or activities to use with students from the emergent literacy stage to more advanced readers and writers.

Linda, a reading teacher, often uses *word webs* because she wants to develop her students' understanding that words have multiple meanings. After reading *Everett Anderson's Year* by Lucille Clifton (1992) with a group of second-graders, Linda realized the children knew that spring was a season, but they did not know other meanings for the word. After discussing the story, the children identified other words they were unsure of and Linda had them work in pairs with dictionaries to look the words up. Then, each pair of children shared their findings and Linda created word webs like the one in Figure 8.5.

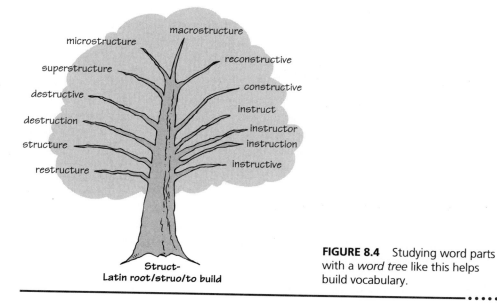

FIGURE 8.4 Studying word parts with a *word tree* like this helps build vocabulary.

•••••
Opportunities to create words and sentences help children understand word structure and build vocabulary.

Jack, a fourth-grade teacher, uses a strategy he calls *List-Group-Label* to help students expand their vocabulary. For example, the children created a vocabulary web to represent the things they saw and learned about a visit to a local museum (see Figure 8.6). First, they remembered all the things they could and Jack listed them on the blackboard. Next, they found words in the list that went together (e.g., *dagger, swords,* and *muskets*), and then they identified a name for the group or category (e.g., *weapons*). This kind of visual representation organizes vocabulary into appropriate categories and provides one kind of association for children.

There are many aspects of words to be learned; the aspects children learn depend on how words are used or practiced. Ehri and Wilce (1980) report that first-grade children who learned target words in sentences learned more about the semantic and syntactic identities of the words than children who learned words in lists. First-graders who learned words in lists remembered graphic and phonic identities of words and could pronounce words faster and more accurately in isolation than the sentence learners. Thus, when instruction includes experiences with a word in isolation and context, the children make many different associations and enlarge their vocabularies.

Along with extensive reading and direct instruction, students learn many words incidentally through casual contact (e.g., hearing books read aloud and words used in spoken language). After he heard his teacher read *A Wrinkle in Time* by Madeline L'Engle (1962) to the class, one fifth-grader used the word *tesseract,* which means "to travel back in time," in a different context. He said, "First, I added the two numbers, and then I just used my head and, uh, *tesseracted* to get the answer." The child was describing how he arrived intuitively at the answer to a math problem. A second-grade teacher, surprised to hear a child refer to a group of children standing at a drinking fountain as "a gaggle of kids," remembered reading the class *A Gaggle of Geese* by Eve Merriam (1960), a book about different ways to say *group*.

Other books, such as *A Snake Is Totally Tail* by Judi Barrett (1983), introduce unexpected and unique words that describe "specifically stripes," "conspicuously claws,"

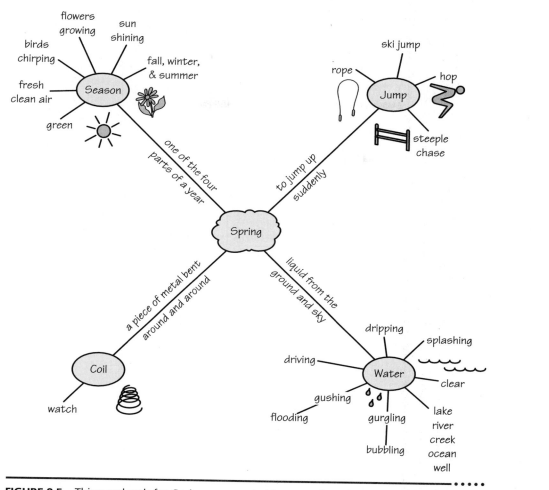

FIGURE 8.5   This word web for *Spring* was created by second-graders doing a word study.

and "essentially ears." *Naming Colors*, written by Ariane Dewey (1995), gives the origin of color words. Children learn many words in just these ways, by hearing them read or spoken and using them themselves. When words become part of children's listening and speaking vocabularies, they are more easily identified in reading and become part of the sight vocabulary. The words also then transfer more naturally to writing.

Read Pat and Jim Cunningham's "Making Words: Enhancing the Invented Spelling-Decoding Connection" in *The Reading Teacher*, Volume 46, Number 3, pages 106–107. Choose a "big word" from a story the children are currently reading and make a set of cards for it. Try the activity with the children.

STRETCHING EXERCISE

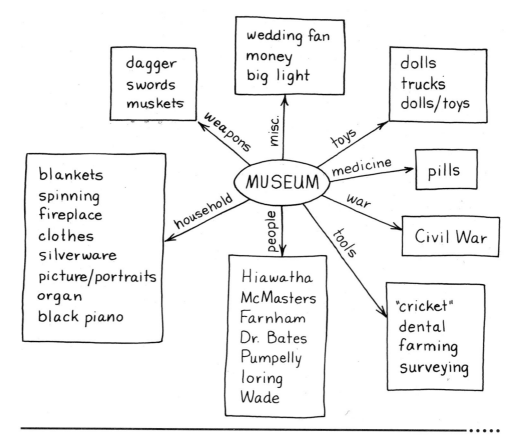

FIGURE 8.6 A vocabulary web makes word learning easier because words are organized into categories.

Study Strategies

Strategies needed to read, locate, and remember facts and important ideas in nonfiction materials are called *study strategies*. These strategies are usually introduced in grades 4 through 6, when students begin to read more expository text (information books and content texts laden with information and technical vocabulary). Flood and Lapp (1986) emphasize the need to provide adequate instruction in how to read and comprehend expository text because most basal manuals are deficient in this area.

Expository text that is written to *explain* is quite different from the traditional narrative of stories. An expository text may contain one of the following organizational patterns: cause/effect, time order or sequence of events, comparison/contrast, analogies, or simple listing of facts. Expository text often contains technical vocabulary, a heavy concept load, and special graphic features. Typical study strategies that students do not learn on their own and should learn include the abilities to:

- Interpret graphic aids.
- Locate information by varying reading rates.

- Locate and understand the function of various book parts.
- Use the library.
- Use reference materials.
- Study and remember information.
- Organize information.
- Take notes.
- Create outlines, webs, or maps.
- Write reports and research papers.

Today, many more nonfiction selections are found in basal readers, and many more information books are published for and read by younger students. Therefore, teaching study strategies earlier makes sense.

Guided Reading

When you vary the strategies used in your reading instruction depending on the strengths and goals of your students (e.g., by both allowing children time to read independently and at other times guiding their reading), you maintain interest and ensure that students will become proficient readers. By varying and adapting your reading instruction, you can increase the chances for children in your classroom to succeed, whether they are learning disabled, linguistically or culturally diverse, second-language learners, gifted, or in other ways diverse.

The strategies you use should be appropriate in terms of your students' interests, needs, and personal goals, as well as the material they will read. Involving children at different times in small-group, large-group, and individual instruction will probably provide the most valuable results. Teaching mini-lessons to only those children who need a particular skill makes sense.

The following three wholistic strategies are only a few of the many available strategies for developing comprehension through guided reading. The Directed Reading Activity (DRA) and Directed Reading/Thinking Activity (DRTA) and other ideas from Chapter 6 are mainstays of teachers who use a repertoire of wholistic strategies for teaching reading. Descriptions of other strategies appear throughout this book and in professional journals such as *Language Arts* and *The Reading Teacher*.

Interview a K–6 teacher who uses the basal reader. Beforehand, examine the basal and make a list of questions to ask. Find out how the teacher uses the basal and adapts it to fit his or her students' interests and needs.

• • • • •

STRETCHING EXERCISE

Read-a-Book-in-an-Hour

Read-a-book-in-an-hour is a strategy in which a group of older children read a story or book with a sequential plot (Childrey, 1980; Porter, 1988). It is a dramatic alternative to the DRA, since it allows students with differing language and reading abilities to work cooperatively to read an entire story in a short amount of time. The strategy motivates reluctant or problem readers who have never read an entire book or have trouble completing books.

To use this jigsaw strategy, either obtain multiple copies of a chapter book, tear out the chapters of a paperback book, or photocopy chapters. Read the first chapter orally to the class to establish characters, setting, and plot. Then introduce vocabulary and help students make predictions so that they have a reason for reading. Then give each child or pair of children a chapter to read silently or orally together and then to retell to the group. Before retelling, let the students rehearse with each other what they will tell the group. Both reading and retelling occur in about 15 to 20 minutes for reading and 3 to 5 minutes for retelling. With this strategy, each child makes a meaningful contribution, and in an hour, an entire book is read, summarized, analyzed, and discussed.

This strategy works best with books with a strong story line and few main characters (e.g., *Stone Fox* by John Gardiner [1980] and *Weasel* by Cynthia DeFelice [1989]). Two cautions help ensure success:

1. A book written at an easy enough reading level for all students is important. A student's *independent level* is the level where he comprehends successfully, recognizes almost every word, and reads alone comfortably without teacher help. The *instructional level* is the level where a child comprehends about 85 percent of what he reads, recognizes 95 percent of the words he meets, and needs some teacher help. If material is even more difficult, then it is at the child's *frustration level,* since the child knows so few words and comprehends so little that he is frustrated.

2. Keep to the hour limit or students may lose interest. You may need to keep retellings focused with appropriate questions to keep a reasonable pace. Childrey (1980) suggests that retellings focus on character development, style of writing, or theme.

You can adapt this strategy in many ways. Barbara, a fifth-grade teacher, discovered that her students liked to write predictions and/or questions about the parts of the book they had not read. As they finished reading and were waiting for the rest of the class to finish, she encouraged students to jot down their guesses and wonderings, which then helped focus their listening on the retellings and encouraged critical response and interpretations of the story.

Graphic Organizers and Webbing

Graphic organizers and webbing are also options for guided reading. A graphic organizer is a visual representation of knowledge, a way of structuring information or arranging important aspects of a concept or topic into a pattern using labels (see Figure 8.7) (Bromley, Irwin-DeVitis, & Modlo, 1995). Visual displays like these enhance comprehension and promote learning by helping students structure ideas and actively engage with print. Visual displays focus on key elements and details in text and show how they mesh to create a story or represent ideas. The addition of pictures or drawings to graphic organizers makes them that much more interesting and memorable.

Webs are one type of graphic organizer (Heimlich & Pittelman, 1986). A close look at webbing reveals its potential for sharing and responding to literature. Webbing

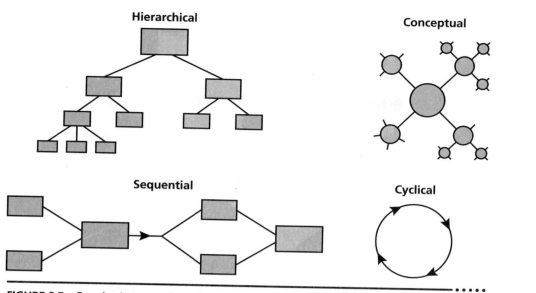

FIGURE 8.7 Four basic types of graphic organizers.

enhances understanding, enjoyment, and appreciation of books and stories children read, but it is also a springboard for discussion and response through retelling and writing. Webs are an excellent collaborative strategy to use with students of diverse backgrounds and varying abilities, as the children can help and support each other.

The basic structure of a web consists of a core concept or idea at the center and web strands at various points beyond the core to represent related categories of information (see Figure 8.8) (Freedman & Reynolds, 1980). Each web strand is connected to the core by a strand tie, which represents relationships among web strands and contains supporting details or facts. Of course, not all webs look exactly like Figure 8.8; the exact nature of a web is determined by the content of the story.

Make a web with your name as the core concept and your characteristics or the various roles you play in the outer strands (e.g., student, jogger, musician, cook, athlete, parent, sibling, etc.). Add facts to support each strand. How could a web like this be used to write a character sketch?

● ● ● ● ●

STRETCHING EXERCISE

When you generate webs *before reading,* students share experiences related to some aspect of the story, which prepares them to understand and respond to the text. This organizes prior knowledge and establishes purposes for reading. Using webs *during reading* helps identify important information and relationships. Creating webs *after reading* allows for summarizing, promotes comprehension, and becomes the raw material for writing. When you think aloud while modeling webbing, children see how to use

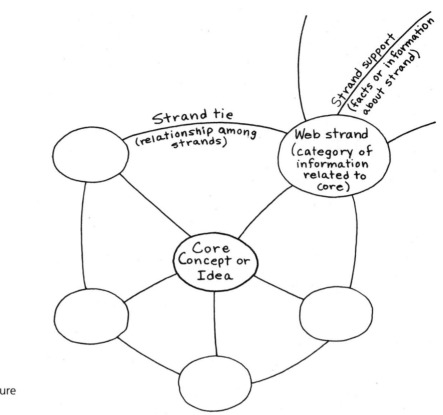

Strand tie
(relationship among strands)

Web strand
(category of information related to core)

Strand support
(facts or information about strand)

Core Concept or Idea

FIGURE 8.8 The basic structure of a web.

it themselves. You can create many kinds of webs to represent a story (e.g., literary elements, vocabulary, other possible conclusions, events in the plot, etc.). Different books and stories provide a variety of possibilities for webs.

Webbing allows children to share and discuss their personal responses and develop a richer understanding and appreciation for what they have read or heard. They begin to see the variety of interpretations and inferences others have for a story because of their different experiences and backgrounds. In addition, as children talk together about a story and share story-related experiences, they develop facility with oral language. When you draw a web on chart paper or on the blackboard and leave it for children to review, young children or students with language delays or disabilities can use it to retell the story.

K-W-L Plus

K-W-L Plus is a simple strategy to use with selections at all grade levels that assumes prior knowledge about a topic is essential to learning more about that topic (Carr & Ogle, 1987; Ogle, 1986). Discussion at each of the four steps required in KWL Plus is critical for group meaning construction. A strategy sheet like the one in Figure 8.9 facilitates group discussion and the reading/thinking process because it makes KWL concrete.

- *What I know (K).* First, have the students brainstorm what they know about the topic (e.g., if the topic is *loons,* ask students "What do you know about loons?" not "What do you know about birds?"). Second, have the students think about general categories of information they might find when they read (e.g., "Before we read this article on loons, let's think about the kinds of information the author probably includes. Look at this list of things we already know. Do some of them fit together to form a general category of information?"). You may need to model one or two categories so students see how to do this.

- *What do I want to learn (W)?* Help the students form questions as they think about what they already know and the general categories of information to expect. Here, students' personal reasons for reading emerge and you are critical because you help students identify gaps in their understanding and raises questions to be answered. Have the students write their own questions before reading.

- *What I learned (L).* After reading the article, discuss what students learned from reading and then have them write what they learned. Have them check their questions to see if the selection gave answers, and if not, suggest further reading to find answers. Readers' questions should be addressed in this step so that they feel in charge of their own learning and capable of pursuing further learning.

- *Plus.* Have the students write a summary or draw a graphic organizer to represent what they learned.

This strategy is effective with students of diverse backgrounds and reading abilities because it allows for shared meaning construction. Pairing students with different abilities to work cooperatively is one suggestion for adapting KWL Plus.

FIGURE 8.9   A strategy sheet for KWL Plus.

K–W–L Strategy Sheet

1. **K**—What we know   **W**—What we want to   **L**—What we learned and
                                      find out   still need to learn

2. Categories of information we expect to use

   A.   D.

   B.   E.

   C.   F.

STRETCHING EXERCISE

Choose a folktale to read to a group of children. Read it first yourself and then to the children. Help them generate a plot web, character web, or K-W-L Plus sheet. Help them retell the story with the aid of the web or sheet.

• • • • •

Encouraging Independent Reading

Promoting independent reading helps develop lifelong readers who love to read. Your reading program should include independent reading that is meaningful and special for each child. Initially, to encourage this, you should know children's reading interests and approximate reading levels so that you can help them find appropriate books. Second, the classroom environment needs to be filled with materials that heighten interests but also let children explore new areas. Third, you need to promote children's ownership of reading by immersing them in books and making reading an important part of each day.

A Print-Rich Environment

Talking with individual children gives you information about interests, but when you deal with an entire class, it is often difficult to remember individual interests. Administer the survey in Chapter 4 regularly to provide a written record of changes in student interests. Then you can keep your classroom library stocked with books your students will want to read.

If, for instance, one of a sixth-grader's current interests is computers, but not reading, it may be that a book such as *Finders Keepers* by Noela Young (1993), about a boy who reads a message on a computer screen in an electronics store and finds himself propelled into another universe, might nudge this child to read. Other books, such as *To Space and Back* by Sally Ride and Susan Okie (1989) and *Star Walk* by Seymour Simon (1995), are nonfictional explorations of other worlds and may entice reluctant readers.

The classroom library is not the only way to add print to children's environment. Magazines, newspapers, cereal boxes, recipes, posters, cartoons, mail fliers, ads, and any number of other materials can also provide interesting and relevant print for children to read in the classroom. Your arrangement and use of bulletin boards invites or discourages reading, as well. Children like to read each other's stories and poetry, so displaying their original written work can foster reading. Bulletin board displays on a particular author or illustrator provide information about a professional's work and pique interest in reading particular books. Most publishers will send you a picture, a short biographical sketch, and book jackets to use in a display such as this.

Some teachers feel that reading is more inviting for children if it is occasionally done away from their desks and chairs in another part of the room. Often, the class library is located in one corner, where soft floor pillows, a small couch, an overstuffed chair, or carpet remnants make the area comfortable for reading. Other print and media such as magazines, pamphlets, brochures, filmstrips, videos, and directions for activities and games should also be in your reading center.

Computers in your classroom can also contribute to a print-rich environment. When children use software to compose and publish their own stories, they read and reread as they write. Children must also read to use other special programs on the computer. The computer is like a magnet that draws children who are otherwise not interested in reading. More about how computers can be used in the classroom will be discussed later in this chapter.

You can help English learners become proficient readers by making sure that the classroom is not only print rich but also language rich. Students who have a native language that is not English need to use language in context, see print used in the classroom environment, and be exposed to language activities that integrate listening, speaking, reading, and writing. Their involvement in interactive language environments that build their experiential background may well be more profitable for them than pull-out remedial programs.

Ownership of Reading

Once you identify interests and provide children with a choice of materials to read, you need to promote ownership in reading. Ownership means that children make decisions about their own reading—the topic to explore, the kinds of books to read, where to obtain them, their purposes for reading, reading rate, when to stop reading, and what to do with what they have learned.

To promote ownership, build in time each day for reading personally chosen materials. When children read what they are interested in and what they want to read, then reading is important and rewarding and they own it. One way to make time for personal reading is to ask children to complete only those workbook pages and activity sheets that involve skills in which they need independent practice and that transfer to real reading. Omit pages that involve practice of fragmented skills with little transfer value or that reinforce known skills. Use this time instead to have children read and write personally interesting and relevant material.

Another way to promote ownership is to use student librarians and a computer database of books (Brooks, 1995). First, students separate and alphabetize classroom books by genre. Next, write the first three letters of the author's name on a small sticker and place it on the lower spine of each book. Then, have students enter each book into a software database program. Use a spiral notebook to record checked-out books and have each student leave a cardboard marker with his name and the book's title on the shelf in place of the book he borrows. This project builds ownership for reading, exposes students to the computer, gives them responsibility for classroom management, and provides a real-world experience.

Use your classroom library or other books to begin Sustained Silent Reading (SSR) or Uninterrupted Sustained Silent Reading (USSR) (Gutkin, 1990). (This technique is also known by various other names: High Intensity Practice [HIP], Free Reading Every Day [FRED], Drop Everything And Read [DEAR], Super Quiet Uninterrupted Reading Time [SQUIRT], and Daily Independent Reading Time [DIRT].) SSR allots short periods of time for silent reading of self-selected materials. It often occurs in entire schools. SSR lets children practice reading and it provides for the growth of interests and skills through personal choice of reading materials. It promotes reading through teacher modeling and peer imitation and is even used with kindergartners who cannot yet read but can look at books and read the pictures.

Keeping a record of books read is another way to promote independent reading. Atwell (1987) suggests students keep response journals to maintain a list of books read and to record their personal reactions to them. With young children, you may want to encourage them to draw pictures as a response and add print if they are able. Topics explored, titles, authors, dates, and summaries of books provide important information for both you and your students on their progress.

Response journals are a good way to develop ownership because they provide children with a sense of what they have accomplished. The entries children write can be shared during literature discussion groups. Hansen and Graves (1986) report that one poor reader in second grade read 23 books between December 10 and January 17 and was able to discuss most of them successfully with the aid of his reading journal.

Another way to promote ownership in reading is to integrate the basal with children's literature. Some teachers use the basal three days a week and literature two days a week. Others use the basal for a month and then literature for a month. Some teachers use appropriate selections from the basal and literature to coordinate with a content area unit. Some use a reading workshop of 45 minutes or so a day for independent reading of self-selected literature, writing in response journals, and sharing during discussion time at the end of the workshop. One third-grade teacher promoted ownership and kept parents in touch with what their children were doing in reading by videotaping her class's reading lessons and activities. Children with VCRs at home could then share the tape with their families. Another third-grade teacher sends his students' response journals home each Friday for parents to read, write in, sign, and return on Monday. Children enjoy making their reading real for parents and siblings in ways such as these.

Modeling reading for children is another way to develop ownership, because it helps children understand the entire reading process, thus making it their own. Shared reading with enlarged texts or big books that are predictable allows an entire group of children to follow along with you as you read aloud. They can experience both spoken

• • • • •
Shared reading of a predictable text allows this first-grader with special needs to succeed.

and written language as they match words with sounds. With enlarged texts, seeing as well as hearing written language used in a meaningful context, children can better imitate your reading behavior.

Of course, seeing you read, talking about what you have read, and demonstrating an appreciation of reading inspires children and gives them an appreciation for reading. No matter how you formulate your program, let the literature response ideas suggested in Chapter 7 and here guide you in replacing busywork with meaningful activities.

Reading Role Models in Literature

Several books for younger children include main characters who read for the sake of reading because they appreciate and enjoy it (see Children's Books about Reading at the end of this chapter). These books, such as *The Wednesday Surprise* by Eve Bunting (1989), in which a young girl teaches her grandmother to read, offer role models with whom children can identify. Books such as Patricia Polacco's *Aunt Chip and the Triple Creek Dam Affair* (1996) and *The Bee Tree* (1993) focus on the excitement and satisfaction of reading.

Books for older children also provide similar reading role models. In *Amber on the Mountain* by T. Johnston (1994), Amber's friend, Anna, teaches her to read. Reading is central to the lives of the main characters in *Abraham Lincoln* by the D'Aulaires (1957) and in *Nightjohn* by Gary Paulsen (1993). *Mrs. Frisbie and the Rats of NIMH* by Robert O'Brien (1971) is a fantasy older readers enjoy about a group of rats given experimental steroids that allow them to learn to read. Its sequel, *Racso and the Rats of NIMH* is written by O'Brien's daughter, Jane Leslie Conly (1986).

Several books provide role models for children who speak other languages but who are learning English. *The Two Uncles of Pablo* by Harry Behn (1959) and *Waiting for Mama* by Marietta Moskin (1974) present the acquisition of reading as necessary and satisfying for children whose first languages are Spanish and Russian, respectively.

For nonreaders or children with reading problems, *The Flunking of Joshua T. Bates* by Susan Shreve (1984) and *The Girl Who Knew It All* by Patricia Reilly Giff (1979) present reading as an attainable goal once children face their reading problems and try to do something about them. *My Mom Can't Read*, written by Muriel Stanek (1986), shows how Tina, who is learning to read at school, helps her mother overcome her problem.

As well as providing role models for children, these and other books like them help children develop an appreciation of reading, in general. These books are appropriate for reading aloud, illustrate the function of reading, demonstrate the value of reading, show a learner's desire to read or pride in reading, and even teach children about the library. By encouraging independent reading and individualizing your program with some of the titles suggested here, you develop the affective dimension of children's reading.

To see how teachers modify the basal, read "Book Club: An Alternative Framework for Reading Instruction" by Taffy Raphael and Susan McMahon in *The Reading Teacher*, Volume 48, Number 2, pages 102–116. Why do you think the project was a success? How else could you modify the basal to promote independent reading?

STRETCHING EXERCISE

Using Computers

Teachers use computers in a variety of ways to augment their reading instruction. Software programs and electronic mail will be discussed here; Chapter 13 will focus more on technology. Computer-assisted instruction (CAI) is a process in which the learner interacts directly with lessons that are displayed on a computer screen. CAI programs use a variety of formats (e.g., drill-and-practice exercises, simulations, games, and tutorials). Children receive a stimulus to which they respond at their own rates. CAI is motivating for many children because it involves interactive technology that responds immediately.

Although many older CAI programs did not provide opportunities to read or write complete sentences, paragraphs, or stories, there are many software programs today that require reading and writing. This software includes games, computer magazines, and stories in which the user must participate. Other new software packages accompany individual pieces of children's literature and are written from a more wholistic perspective (Wepner, 1990). The following programs allow children to construct their own semantic webs or maps:

> *Inspiration 4.0: The Easiest Way to Brainstorm and Write*. Portland, OR: Inspiration Software.
> *Kid Pix II*. San Rafael, CA: Broderbund Software.
> *The Literary Mapper* and *The Semantic Mapper*. Gainesville, FL: Teacher Support Software.

Wepner (1990) discusses how six different teachers use computers in a wholistic way with literature-based lessons to complement their students' literacy development. This CAI seems to be effective as a supplement to teacher-led reading instruction. However, Wepner wisely reminds you to consider your educational goals when selecting and using software.

Word-processing software holds rich promise for enhancing language arts and promoting reading and writing. As children use word processors to create, revise, edit, and publish their own written work, they read and write in purposeful ways. Many of these programs contain a dictionary and thesaurus with a spell-checker that scans text

FIGURE 8.10 This poem shows the need for accurate spelling, even when using the spell-checker provided in most word-processing programs.

Spell Checker

Aye has uh spelling checker;
It came with my PC
It plainly marx four my revue
Miss takes I can knot sea;
I've ran this poem threw it,
I'm sure yore pleas too no
Its letter perfect in it's weigh;
My checker tolled me sew.

—Source unknown

• • • • •

and provides correct spelling for incorrectly spelled words. A spell-checker is no substitute for the ability to spell accurately, however (see Figure 8.10).

There are a variety of other software packages that provide children with exciting avenues to literacy. Programs for creating data files for comparison and analysis are useful in science and social studies (Newman, 1986). Graphics programs allow children to create pictures that can accompany text. The computer programs and activities that allow children to demonstrate the natural purposes of reading and writing are the most useful.

The potential of CAI for helping ESL learners as well as children with reading problems, learning disabilities, and physical handicaps is encouraging. *Hypertext* is computer technology that provides electronically supported text that is enhanced to increase comprehension and the use of metacognitive reading strategies (Anderson-Inman, Horney, Chen, & Lewin, 1994). Hypertext enhances print by accessing connected information and providing graphics and sound embellishments that allow students to interact directly with text in a variety of ways, such as the following:

- If a child reads a story and does not know the pronunciation or meaning of a word, he can use the "mouse" to highlight the word and see a definition, a digitized drawing, and/or hear the word pronounced.
- If a child questions his comprehension of the story, he can ask himself the self-monitoring questions available on the screen and check his answers against the computer's answers.
- As a child searches for elements in a story—for example, foreshadowing or literary elements—he can create a list or graphic organizer and print it to review later.

Hypertext may help some students as they read and it may hinder other students who are distracted by it or come to rely on it too heavily. It certainly has potential for enriching the language arts and building literacy for some students, however. In a three-year longitudinal study of 300 K–3 students, Boone (1993) provided reading lessons in a hypermedia format that was supplemental to the basal reader. He found children of low ability achieved significantly higher than did control children.

•••••
Computers are motivating for many students because they involve interactive technology that responds immediately.

However, much existing CAI material fragments reading and uses primarily drill and practice, and, as such, is not much different from an automated workbook. Much of the material has been prepared by people who do not understand reading comprehension; thus, the most pressing need is for the development of adequate software.

Computer-managed instruction (CMI) is the use of the computer as a record keeper, diagnostic tester, test scorer, and prescriber of what to study next. CMI programs keep records of student progress, administer diagnostic tests, score and analyze these tests, suggest objectives that need to be mastered, and provide prescriptions and suggestions for remedial materials. Aside from these basic uses, CMI programs offer simulations of the informal reading inventory, test generation forms and item banks, and translations of print into braille (Blanchard, Mason, & Daniel, 1987). CMI, however, also tends to fragment reading into a hierarchy of subskills and is only as effective as the designers who create the programs and the teachers who use them.

Critiques of computer software appear in many professional journals. *Only the Best* is a journal that publishes reviews of the best software reviewed in 10 other journals. Along with reading the opinions of others, you can learn some important questions to ask when considering a software program for purchase and use. One format for evaluating software appears in Figure 8.11.

STRETCHING EXERCISE	Evaluate a software program used by upper-elementary students (grades 3–6). Use the program yourself and answer the questions on the checklist in Figure 8.11, adding your own observations. Then talk with a child who has used the program and discuss what the child likes or dislikes about it. Talk to the teacher about why he has his students use the program.

• • • • •

Computers have much potential for promoting reading independence. When computers expose children to real texts that are written to be read, and not written to teach fragmented skills, and when children use computer software to solve problems, think critically, and create and manipulate real texts, then computers have a positive influence on the teaching of reading. There is also a hidden benefit with computers that you should not overlook: children's magnetic attraction to them. Computers can "sell" reading to children, even those who have special needs. Dunkeld and Denny (1986) tell the story of a fifth-grade boy who was a nonreader until his family purchased a computer. The child soon began to use it to communicate with other people through the modem, and finally became an avid reader and writer.

Assessing the Reader

Systematically analyzing and monitoring children's strengths, needs, and progress is a necessary component of any teacher's reading program. One way for you to accomplish this is to observe children as they read in group situations and in individual conferences, and then assess their responses, enjoyment, comprehension, and fluency.

As you observe silent reading, for example, note behaviors that might indicate problems, such as when children finger point, lose their place, or hold the book ex-

FIGURE 8.11   A checklist for evaluating software.

269
· · · · ·
Reading

Software Evaluation

Title _____   Publisher/Date _____

Instructional Level(s) _____   Subject Area(s) _____

Average Completion Time _____

Objectives/Purpose

	High	Medium	Low
Content			
1. Clearly stated objectives/purpose			
2. Match between stated purpose and content			
3. Match with curricular needs			
4. Interesting and accurate content			
5. Appropriate reading level for users			
Operation			
1. Clearly stated directions			
2. User friendly/"bug" free			
3. Appropriate pacing			
4. Feedback with remediation			
5. Interactive			
6. Wholistic vs. fragmented language			
7. Accomplishes objectives/purpose			
9. Includes record keeping			
10. Effective graphics, sound, and color			

Strengths

Weaknesses

Recommendation _____

Reviewer _____

tremely close or at an angle. Informally check word recognition by having children read orally to share a favorite part, prove or disprove a point, answer a question, or fulfill some other relevant purpose. Listen to oral reading and note when material is too difficult, which is evident when children read haltingly or word by word, pause often, omit or insert words, substitute words, use a word analysis strategy, read with expression, and observe punctuation.

You may want to keep a running record of a child's oral reading of a story or long selection by recording everything the child says or does as he tries to read the story or book (Clay, 1985). You will have a good idea of how to help the child become a proficient reader by observing and recording patterns in his miscues (the words he omits, self-corrects, substitutes, inserts); his use of context, phonics, and word structure; and the specific strategies (rereading, predicting, self-questioning, surveying, etc.) he uses to make sense of print. Observing reading behavior in the context of a real situation reveals much that a score on a standardized test cannot.

STRETCHING EXERCISE   Read Lynn Rhodes and Nancy Shanklin's "Miscue Analysis in the Classroom" in *The Reading Teacher*, Volume 44, Number 3, pages 252–255. Listen to a child read orally, then use the child's modified miscue analysis to analyze the oral reading. Share your findings with the child.

• • • • •

You may want to use an informal reading inventory (IRI) composed of graded word lists to determine a child's approximate oral reading level, graded selections for children to read, and questions to ask following reading to determine comprehension. A child reads the graded selections orally and you record miscues that you can examine for meaning, grammar, and graphic similarity to text. Many basal readers contain an IRI to help the teacher find children's reading levels and to determine which basal is appropriate for a child.

Record keeping is an important part of evaluation and should not be overlooked. Encourage children to keep records because records can tell them where they are going and where they came from. Keeping careful records of strengths and needs allows you determine progress or lack of progress. It lets you identify those children who should be brought together in a group for discussion of a story or for teaching or reteaching particular strategies or skills. Record keeping provides you with important information for parent conferences, as well. You will want to keep anecdotal notes in your own notebook on the reading behaviors and proficiency of individual children. Some teachers put tabs on every 8 to 10 pages in a spiral-bound notebook, earmarking each section with one child's name so that as they observe a child and write a comment, each observation is dated and occurs in the same section of the notebook.

Checklists of reading behaviors are also helpful. If you administer them regularly, they can give you information on children's growth (see Figure 8.12). Use various means of recording on a checklist, such as: G = good, F = fair, P = poor; B = beginning, D = developing, I = independent; or + = mastery, / = partial mastery, − = nonmastery. Modify this checklist or create your own list of behaviors appropriate to the age or grade level you teach.

Attitude inventories, such as the Elementary Reading Attitude Survey (McKenna & Kear, 1990), use the comic-strip character, Garfield, and have empirically documented reliability and validity. They provide an informal measure of children's attitudes toward reading, which is critical in their literacy development. Self-evaluation checklists

FIGURE 8.12 A checklist for assessing reading behavior.

Reading Behavior Checklist

Student _____

Date
Uses prior knowledge
Makes reasonable predictions
Uses sounds to construct meaning
Uses context to construct meaning
Uses pictures to construct meaning
Uses word structure to construct meaning
Monitors comprehension:
  ■ Knows reading should make sense
  ■ Recognizes meaning disruptions
  ■ Rereads
  ■ Summarizes
  ■ Questions
  ■ Continues reading/suspends judgment
Responds personally
Sees self as a reader
Remembers what is read
Reads critically
Interprets what is read
Applies what is read to a broader context
Enjoys reading
Chooses books at an appropriate level
Reads a variety of genres
Chooses to read independently

Comments

Date:
Date:
Date:
Date:

FIGURE 8.13 A self-evaluation inventory to measure feelings and involvement in reading.

Reading Inventory

Student _____ Date _____

	No	Yes	Maybe
1. I like to read.			
2. I like to listen to the teacher read.			
3. I like to read out loud.			
4. I like to act out what I read.			
5. I like to write about what I read.			
6. I like to draw about what I read.			
7. I like to talk about what I read.			
8. I read at home.			
9. I read with my parents or family.			
10. I enjoy picture books.			
11. I enjoy stories about people's lives.			
12. I like poems.			
13. I like folktales and fairy tales.			
14. I like true stories of nonfiction.			
15. I enjoy stories about the past.			
16. I like stories about make-believe things.			
17. I like stories about life today.			
18. I enjoy magazines.			
19. Sometimes I can figure out hard words.			
20. I can predict what will happen in a story.			
21. I look at pictures for clues.			
22. I understand what I read most of the time.			
23. I like to go to the library.			
24. I borrow books and read them.			
25. I read the newspaper.			

like the one in Figure 8.13 involve students in assessing their own performance, which helps children take ownership of their reading progress and learning.

One way to determine progress in reading is to collect and place samples of a student's reading performance in a portfolio. Portfolios are also helpful in planning for instruction and grouping. Valencia (1990) suggests an expandable file folder that holds samples of a student's work selected by teacher and student, the teacher's observational notes, the student's own periodic self-evaluations, and notes on progress. A portfolio can include written responses to reading, reading logs, lists of books read, selected daily work, classroom tests, standardized tests, checklists, interest inventories, attitude inventories, and audio- or videotapes. Portfolios capture reading behaviors, strengths, and needs in several ways and thus are useful in conferencing with parents and/or students about progress. For the most effective use of portfolios, students should evaluate their own work and set goals for themselves.

Summary

The long-range goal of reading instruction is to develop proficient readers who are fluent, strategic, engaged, and independent. No matter what strategies you use to guide reading and build comprehension (e.g., DRA, DRTA, webbing, K-W-L Plus, read-a-book-in-an-hour, or others) and whether you use the basal reader and/or children's literature, children need to set their own purposes and construct meaning as they read.

R•••••eflections

1. What components of Denise's Reader's Choice program described at the beginning of this chapter would you change to make it more child centered and less teacher directed? Why?

2. Look carefully at one story from a basal reader that is a children's book. Compare it to the original children's book. Has the book been adapted? How much original art is included in the basal? Examine the teacher's manual to see how the publisher suggests teaching the story. Do you agree? What are some alternative ways to share the story to develop children's interests and comprehension?

Professional Resources

Browzer → Book link (1997). Newark, DE: Touchstone Applied Science Associates/IRA. This software (versions for Mac or PC) contains summary annotations of over 5,000 titles of both classic and contemporary children's books for elementary and middle-school readers. It lets you select from 15 interest categories and sort by author, title, or difficulty level.

Fox, B. J. (1996). *Strategies for word identification: Phonics from a new perspective.* Englewood Cliffs, NJ: Prentice Hall. This book provides ways to teach students the word identification strategies of pictures, single-code cues, familiar words, letter sounds, and chunking.

Griffin, P., Smith, P. G., & Burrill, L. (1996). *The American literacy profile scales.* Portsmouth, NH: Heinemann. This book contains normed scales for reading, writing, listening, speaking and viewing.

McGee, L., & Richgels, D. (1996). *Literacy's beginnings: Supporting young readers and writers* (2nd ed.). Boston: Allyn and Bacon. This book discusses an integrated approach to reading and writing instruction keyed to the developmental stages through which most children pass.

Rhodes, L. K., & Dudley-Marling, C. (1996). *Readers and writers with a difference: A holistic approach to teaching struggling readers and writers* (2nd ed.). Portsmouth, NH: Heinemann. This book offers myriad suggestions for supporting students with remedial and learning disabilities as they learn a range of literate practice.

Roller, C. M. (1996). *Variability not disability: Struggling readers in a workshop classroom*. Newark, DE: International Reading Association. This book is about 8- to 12-year-old readers with disabilities in a summer reading program operated like a workshop and with an approach that emphasizes these students' abilities.

References

Adams, M. J. (1990). *Beginning to read: Thinking and learning about print*. Cambridge, MA: MIT Press.

Anderson, R. C., Hiebert, E. H., Scott, J. A., & Wilkinson, I. A. (1985). *Becoming a nation of readers*. Champaign, IL: Center for the Study of Reading.

Anderson-Inman, L., Horney, M. A., Chen, D., & Lewin, L. (1994). Hypertext literacy: Observations from the ElectroText project. *Language Arts, 71* (4), 279–287.

Atwell, N. (1987). *In the middle: Writing, reading and learning with adolescents*. Portsmouth, NH: Heinemann.

Bear, D. R., Invernizzi, M., Templeton, S., & Johnston, F. (1996). *Words their way: Word study for phonics, vocabulary and spelling*. Saddle River, NJ: Merrill.

Blanchard, J. S., Mason, G. E., & Daniel, D. (1987). *Computer applications in reading* (3rd ed.). Newark, DE: International Reading Association.

Boone, R. (1993). Hypermedia basal readers: Three years of school-based research. *Journal of Special Education Technology, 12* (2), 86–106.

Bromley, K., Irwin-DeVitis, L., & Modlo, M. (1995). *Graphic organizers: Visual strategies for active learning*. New York: Scholastic.

Brooks, H. (1995). "I know that book's here somewhere!" How to organize your classroom library. *The Reading Teacher, 48* (7), 638–639.

Butler, D., & Clay, M. (1982). *Reading begins at home*. Exeter, NH: Heinemann.

Carr, E., & Ogle, D. (1987). KWL Plus: A strategy for comprehension and summarization. *The Journal of Reading, 30* (6), 626–631.

Childrey, J. (1980). Read a book in an hour. *Reading Horizons*, Spring, 174–176.

Clay, M. M. (1985). *The early detection of reading difficulties*. Portsmouth, NH: Heinemann.

Come, B., & Fredericks, A. D. (1995). Family literacy in the urban schools: Meeting the needs of at risk children. *The Reading Teacher, 48* (7), 566–571.

Cunningham, P. M., & Cunningham, J. W. (1992). Making words: Enhancing the invented spelling-decoding connection. *The Reading Teacher, 46* (3), 106–107.

Dooley, C. (1993). The challenge: Meeting the needs of gifted readers. *The Reading Teacher, 46* (7), 46–51.

Dunkeld, C., & Denny, P. N. (1986). Tom's way: Dialogue with an electronic twist. *Journal of Reading, 29* (8), 710–716.

Ehri, L. C., & Wilce, L. S. (1980). Do beginners learn to read function words better in sentences or lists? *Reading Research Quarterly, 15* (4), 451–476.

Erickson, K. A., & Koppenhaver, D. A. (1995). Developing a literacy program for children with severe disabilities. *The Reading Teacher, 48* (8), 676–684.

Flood, J., & Lapp, D. (1986). Types of texts: The match between what students read in basals and what they encounter in tests. *Reading Research Quarterly, 21* (3), 284–297.

Freedman, G., & Reynolds, E. G. (1980). Enriching basal reader lessons with semantic webbing. *The Reading Teacher, 33* (6), 677–684.

Freeman, D. E., & Freeman, Y. S. (1993). Strategies for promoting the primary languages of all students. *The Reading Teacher, 46* (97), 552–558.

Goodman, K. (1988). Look what they've done to Judy Blume: The basalization of children's literature. *The New Advocate, 1*, 29–41.

Goodman, K. S. (1986). Basal readers: A call for action. *Language Arts*, 63 (4), 358–363.

Griffith, P. L., & Olson, M. W. (1992). Phonemic awareness helps beginning readers break the code. *The Reading Teacher*, 45 (7), 516–523.

Gutkin, R. J. (1990). Sustained _____ reading. *Language Arts*, 67, 490–491.

Haack, P. (1993). *Strengthening your third grade program using outstanding whole-language, literature-based strategies resource handbook.* Washington, DC: Bureau of Education and Research.

Hansen, J., & Graves, D. H. (1986). Do you know what backstrung means? *The Reading Teacher*, 38 (8), 807–812.

Heimlich, J. E., & Pittelman, S. D. (1986). *Semantic mapping: Classroom applications.* Newark, DE: International Reading Association.

Koskinen, P. S., Wilson, R. M., Gambrell, L. B., & Neuman, S. B. (1993). Captioned video and vocabulary learning: An innovative practice in literacy instruction. *The Reading Teacher*, 47 (1), 36–43.

Lyons, C. A., Pinnell, G. S., & DeFord, D. E. (1993). *Partners in learning: Teachers and children in reading recovery.* New York: Teachers College Press.

Madden, N. (1986). *Reading instruction in the mainstream: A cooperative learning approach.* Report No. 5. Baltimore: Center for Research on Elementary and Middle Schoools.

McCallum, R. D. (1988). Don't throw the basals out with the bath water. *The Reading Teacher, 42,* 204–207.

McCarthey, S. J., & Hoffman, J. V. (1995). The new basals: How are they different? *The Reading Teacher*, 49 (1), 72–75.

McKenna, M. C., & Kear, D. (1990). Measuring attitude toward reading: A new tool for teachers. *The Reading Teacher*, 43, 626–639.

Morris, D., Ervin, C., & Conrad, K. (1996). A case study of middle school reading disability. *The Reading Teacher*, 49 (5), 368–377.

Morrow, L. M. (1997). *Literacy development in the early years: Helping children read and write* (3rd ed.). Boston: Allyn and Bacon.

Newman, J. (1986). Online: Using a database in the classroom. *Language Arts*, 63 (3), 315–319.

Norton, D. E. (1992). *The impact of literature-based reading.* New York: Merrill.

Ogle, D. M. (1986). K-W-L: A teaching model that develops active reading of expository text. *The Reading Teacher*, 39, 564–570.

Pikulski, J. (1994). Preventing reading failure: A review of five effective programs. *The Reading Teacher*, 48 (1), 30–39.

Porter, E. (1988). Read a book in an hour. *The Reading Teacher*, 41, 615–616.

Purcell-Gates, V., L'Allier, S., & Smith, D. (1995). Literacy at the Harts' and the Larsons': Diversity among poor, innercity families. *The Reading Teacher*, 48 (7), 572–578.

Rhodes, L. K., & Shanklin, N. L. (1990). Miscue analysis in the classsroom. *The Reading Teacher*, 44 (3), 252–255.

Routman, R., & Butler, A. (1995). Why talk about phonics? *School Talk: Ideas for the Classroom, 1* (2), 1–6.

Schickedanz, J. (1990). The jury is still out on the effects of whole-language and language experience approaches for beginning reading: A critique of Stahl and Miller's study. *Review of Educational Research*, 60, 127–131.

Sears, S., Carpenter, C., & Burstein, N. (1994). Meaningful reading instruction for learners with special needs. *The Reading Teacher*, 47 (8), 632–638.

Spiegel, D. L. (1995). A comparison of traditional remedial programs and Reading Recovery: Guidelines for success for all programs. *The Reading Teacher*, 49 (2), 86–96.

Spiegel, D. L. (1981). Six alternatives to the directed reading activity. *The Reading Teacher*, 34 (8), 914–920.

Stahl, S., & Fairbanks, M. (1986). The effects of vocabulary instruction: A model-based meta-analysis. *Review of Educational Research*, 56 (1), 72–110.

Stahl, S. A., & Miller, P. D. (1989). Whole-language and language experience approaches for beginning reading: A quantitative research synthesis. *Review of Educational Research*, 59, 87–116.

Stanovitch, K. E. (1994). Romance and reason. *The Reading Teacher*, 47 (4), 280–291.

Sweet, A. P., & Guthrie, J. T. (1996). How children's motivations relate to literacy development and instruction. *The Reading Teacher*, 49 (8), 660–662.

Teale, W. H., & Sulzby, E. (1989). Emergent literacy: New perspectives. In D. S. Strickland & L. M. Morrow (Eds.), *Emerging literacy: Young children learn to read and write* (pp. 1–15). Newark, DE: International Reading Association.

Tunnell, M. O., & Jacobs, J. S. (1989). Using "real" books: Research findings on literature based reading instruction. *The Reading Teacher*, 43, 470–477.

Valencia, S. (1990). A portfolio approach to classroom reading assessment: The whys, whats, and hows. *The Reading Teacher, 43*, 338–340.

Weaver, C. (1994). *Reading process and practice: From socio-linguistics to whole-language* (2nd ed.). Portsmouth, NH: Heinemann.

Wells, G. (1986). *The meaning makers: Children learning language and using language to learn.* Portsmouth, NH: Heinemann.

Wepner, S. B. (1990). Holistic computer applications in literature-based classrooms. *The Reading Teacher, 44*, 12–19.

Yopp, H. K. (1995). A test for assessing phonemic awareness in young children. *The Reading Teacher, 49* (1), 20–29.

Yopp, H. K. (1992). Developing phonemic awareness in young children. *The Reading Teacher, 45* (9), 696–707.

Zarillo, J. (1989). Teachers' interpretations of literature-based reading. *The Reading Teacher, 43* (1), 22–28.

Children's Book References

Armstrong, W. (1969). *Sounder.* New York: Harper and Row.

Barrett, J. (1983). *A snake is totally tail.* New York: Atheneum.

Clifton, L. (1992). *Everett Anderson's year.* New York: Holt.

DeFelice, C. (1989). *Weasel.* New York: Avon.

Dewey, A. (1995). *Naming colors.* New York: Harper-Collins.

Gardiner, J. (1980). *Stone fox.* New York: Harper and Row.

Kraus, R. (1971). *Leo the late bloomer.* New York: Dutton.

Lear, E. (1995). *The pelican chorus and other nonsense.* New York: HarperCollins.

L'Engle, M. (1962). *A wrinkle in time.* New York: Farrar.

Merriam, E. (1996). *The inner city mother goose.* New York: Simon & Schuster.

Merriam, E. (1960). *A gaggle of geese.* New York: Knopf.

Moskin, M. (1974). *Waiting for mama.* New York: Coward-McCann.

Nikola-Lisa (1994). *Bein' with you this way.* New York: Lee & Low.

Numeroff, L. (1986). *If you give a mouse a cookie.* New York: Scholastic.

Oppel, K. (1985). *Colin's fantastic video adventure.* New York: Dutton.

Pearson, S. (1977). *That's enough for one day.* New York: Dial.

Ride, S., & Okie, S. (1989). *To space and back.* New York: Beech Tree.

Scarry, R. (1963). *The fables of LaFontaine.* Garden City, NY: Doubleday.

Shannon, G. (1996). *Spring: A haiku story.* New York: Greenwillow.

Simon, S. (1995). *Star walk.* New York: Morrow.

Wilson, G. (1994). *Prowlpuss.* New York: Candlewick.

Young, N. (1993). *Finders keepers.* New York: Beech Tree.

Children's Books about Reading

Aliki (1982). *We are best friends.* New York: Greenwillow. (Gr. K–3). A small boy named Peter, angry that his best friend has moved away, reads a letter from him and feels better.

Armstrong, W. H. (1969). *Sounder.* New York: Harper and Row. (Gr. 4–6). A poor African American family suffers tragedy and the son who is determined to learn to read must leave home to do so.

Bauer, C. F. (1986). *Too many books.* New York: Viking. (Gr. K–3). A young girl decides she has too many books in her collection and gives some away. She pleases many people in doing so.

Behn, H. (1959). *The two uncles of Pablo.* New York: Harcourt Brace Jovanovich. (Gr. 3). Pablo goes to the city to learn to read an important letter his mother received.

Bradby, M. (1995). *More than anything else.* New York: Orchard. (Gr. 1–3). Nine-year old Booker T. Washington works from sunup to sundown packing salt in barrels but wants to learn to read.

Bunting, E. (1989). *The Wednesday surprise.* New York: Clarion. (Gr. K–3). A young girl teaches her grandmother to read every Wednesday night to prepare a birthday surprise for Dad.

Cleary, B. (1967). *Mitch and Amy.* New York: Morrow. (Gr. 3–6). Fourth-grade twins, Amy, a good reader, and Mitch, with a reading problem, help each other out.

Conly, J. L. (1986). *Racso and the rats of NIMH.* New York: Harper and Row. (Gr. 3–6). In this sequel to *Mrs. Frisbie at the Rats of NIMH* (O'Brien, 1971), Racso, a city mouse, brings new ideas to the country. He can read and he shares his knowledge of dancing, candy, the lyrics to rock songs and reprogramming computers with Mrs. Frisbie's children.

Cummins, J. (1996). *The inside-outside book of libraries.* New York: Dutton. (Gr. 2–4). Illustrations and brief text present all kinds of libraries from book mobiles and home libraries to the New York Public Library and the Library of Congress.

d'Aulaire, I., & d'Aulaire, E. P. (1957). *Abraham Lincoln.* New York: Doubleday. (Gr. 3–6). (Caldecott Medal). This biography of Abraham Lincoln discusses his strong desire to learn to read and how his stepmother helped.

Davidson, M. (1985). *Helen Keller.* New York: Scholastic. (Gr. K–3). The inspiring story of Helen Keller, who is blind and deaf yet learns to read, write, and communicate, is told.

Davidson, M. (1985). *Louis Braille: The boy who invented books for the blind.* New York: Scholastic. (Gr. K–3). This is the story of a blind 15-year-old who invented an important system of reading.

Duvoisin, R. A. (1950). *Petunia.* New York: Knopf. (Gr. K–3). A goose named Petunia learns that merely carrying a book under her wing does not make her wise.

Furtado, J. (1988). *Sorry, Miss Folio!* Brooklyn, NY: Kane/Miller. (Gr. K–3). A boy loves his library book read to him, so he conveniently forgets to return it to the library and creates outlandish excuses for the librarian, Miss Folio.

Giff, P. R. (1980). *Today was a terrible day.* New York: Viking. (Gr. K–2). A nonreader surprises himself when he can read a note from the teacher.

Giff, P. R. (1979). *The girl who knew it all.* New York: Yearling. (Gr. 3–6). Tracy, who appears to be a know-it-all, secretly is unable to read. When her pen-pal comes for a visit, she can't hide her secret any longer.

Gilson, J. (1980). *Do bananas chew gum?* New York: Lothrop, Lee & Shepard. (Gr. 4–6). Able to read on a second-grade level, a sixth-grader thinks he is dumb until he cooperates and overcomes his reading problem.

Greenwald, S. (1986). *The Mariah Delany Lending Library disaster.* New York: Yearling. (Gr. 3–6). An 11-year-old sets up her own library in competition with the New York Public Library and has some problems.

Hoban, L. (1978). *Arthur's prize reader.* New York: Harper and Row. (Gr. K–3). Arthur, the chimp, learns that he must not only be able to "read" hard words but also understand them.

Hoban, T. (1984). *I walk and read.* New York: Greenwillow. (Gr. K–2). Excellent color photos of city signs give children practice in learning to read what is in their environment.

Hoban, T. (1983). *I read signs.* New York: Greenwillow. (Gr. K–3). This book introduces signs and symbols usually seen along the street.

Johnson, D. (1994). *Papa's stories.* New York: Macmillan. (Gr. K–3). Kari loves the way her father "reads" stories to her but she learns that he can't read. They discuss the importance of reading and how her mother is teaching him to read.

Johnston, T. (1994). *Amber on the mountain.* New York: Dial. (Gr. 1–4). A young girl named Amber lives with her family in the mountains. She has no teacher and has not learned to read until Anna moves nearby. The two girls form a strong friendship and Anna teaches Amber to read.

King-Smith, D. (1995). *The school mouse.* New York: Hyperion. (Gr. K–2). Flora, a mouse born in a kindergarten classroom on the first day of school, learns how to read and eventually saves her parents' lives because of it.

Kline, S. (1985). *Herbie Jones.* New York: Putnam. (Gr. 2–4). Herbie deals with his feelings as he becomes a proficient reader and moves through stratified reading groups.

Marek, M. (1985). *Different, not dumb.* New York: Watts. (Gr. 2–4). A boy in the bottom reading group in his class learns to read better and helps a good reader.

Marshall, J. (1986). *Wings: A tale of two chickens.* New York: Viking. (Gr. K–3). Harriet reads often and Winnie doesn't read at all. Because Winnie doesn't know how to read, she doesn't know what a fox is and she gets into many dangerous situations.

McPhail, D. (1984). *Fix-it*. New York: Dutton. (Gr. K–3). Emma finds that she enjoys reading while her television set is not working.

Moskin, M. (1974). *Waiting for Mama*. New York: Coward-McCann. (Gr. K–3). In this story about the reuniting of a Russian immigrant family, the young daughter learns to read her mother's handwritten letters saying that she will rejoin the family.

O'Brien, R. (1971). *Mrs. Frisbie and the rats of NIMH*. New York: Atheneum. (Gr. 3–6). Experimental rats receive steroids and escape from a laboratory to a farm where Mrs. Frisbie and her children live. The rats, who can read, finally leave to establish their own society free of dependence on humans and the farm.

Ormondroyd, E. (1969). *Broderick*. Berkeley, CA: Parnassus. (Gr. K–3). A mouse who is an avid reader learns from a book how to surf and becomes so good at it that he makes it his career.

Paulsen, G. (1993). *Nightjohn*. New York: Delacorte. (Gr. 5–8). Twelve-year-old Sarny's brutal life as a slave in the South in the 1850s becomes even more dangerous when a newly arrived slave named Nightjohn offers to teach her to read.

Pearson, S. (1977). *That's enough for one day*! New York: Dial. (Gr. K–3). Philip won't stop reading, so his mother orders him outdoors to play. He gets into trouble and is sent back to his room where he happily settles down to enjoy reading again.

Polacco, P. (1996). *Aunt Chip and the Triple Creek Dam affair*. New York: Philomel. (Gr. 1–5). The people in the town of Triple Creek have become so involved with their televisions that they have forgotten how to read. Thanks to the will of a young boy and his Aunt Chip, the people of Triple Creek rediscover the importance and joy of reading books.

Polacco, P. (1993). *The bee tree*. New York: Philomel. (Gr. 1–4). Mary Ellen complains to her grandfather that she is tired of reading. Together, they set out on an adventure, chasing after bees to find their honey tree. Mary Ellen learns that reading can be as exciting and sweet as the honey from a bee tree.

Purdy, C. (1987). *Least of all*. New York: McElderry. (Gr. 1–4). The youngest girl in a big farm family helps with the chores by doing the churning, a very tedious task. To relieve the tedium, she uses the Bible to teach herself to read.

Seuss, T. G. (1978). *I can read with my eyes shut*. New York: Random House. (Gr. K–3). Cat in the Hat shows Young Cat how to read with both eyes open.

Shreve, S. (1984). *The flunking of Joshua T. Bates*. New York: Knopf. (Gr. 3–6). Joshua repeats third grade because he cannot read, but with the help of a surprising teacher, he finally learns how and is promoted.

Speare, E. G. (1958). *The witch of Blackbird Pond*. Boston: Houghton Mifflin. (Gr. 4–7). (Newbery Medal). Kit Tyler, leaving Barbados in the 1770s after her parents die, goes to live in Connecticut with Puritan relatives, where reading and writing are quite different from what she was used to.

Spinelli, J. (1997). *The library card*. New York: Scholastic. (Gr. 3–6). Four funny stories are told of the life-changing effects of a little blue library card on four young people who discover it.

Stanek, M. (1986). *My mom can't read*. New York: Whitman. (Gr. K–3). Tina, a beginning reader in school, finds that her mother makes many excuses for not helping her read at home. Tina's mother finally admits her problem, and they both learn to read together.

Thompson, C. (1996). *How to live forever*. New York: Knopf. (Gr. 2–4). Every night for two years, Peter searches in the library for the lost book on how to live forever, and when he finds it he makes an important decision.

West, D. (1988). *The day the TV blew up*. Niles, IL: Whitman. (Gr. 1–3) Ralph's favorite activity is watching television, until it explodes one day and he finds out about the library.

White E. B. (1952). *Charlotte's web*. New York: Harper and Row. (Gr. 2–4). Charlotte, an intelligent spider who can read and write, weaves messages in her web. Being able to read the writing in the web finally saves the life of Wilbur the pig.

Connections:
Speaking and
Writing

9

W·····indow on Teaching

In *Nightjohn* by Gary Paulsen, Sarny uses a stick to scratch each letter in the dirt as a slave named John teaches her how to read and write. He was called Nightjohn because he had escaped from his owner, but instead of running away, he came back each night to teach the slaves how to read and write.

> "*Bee*," he said. "It be *B*."
> "That sounds crazy . . . "
> "That's how you say the letter. *B*. It's for "*behh* or *be* or *buh* or *boo*. That's how a *B* looks and how you make the sound."
> I made it sound in my mouth, whispering. "So where's the bottom to it?"

"I swear—you always want to know the bottom to things. Here, here it is. It sits on itself this way, facing so the two round places push to the front." (Paulsen, 1993, pp. 52–53)

For John, talk was vital to teaching Sarny. He explained what he was doing and clarified ideas for her. For Sarny, talk was vital to learning. She questioned John and processed what he told her in order to make sense of it. Talk, both John's and her own, supported and guided Sarny's literacy learning as she made letters and formed words in the dirt.

What drove John to place himself in perilous danger with the White slave owners for his teaching? When an older slave woman named Mammy discovers what Nightjohn is doing, she asks him about his intentions. He tells her he came back to teach reading and writing.

"They have to be able to write," John said. . . . "They have to read and write so we can write about this—what they doing to us. It has to be written." (Paulsen, 1993, pp. 56–58)

This powerful story, probably most appropriate for fifth-grade and up because of its sensitive content, shows how Nightjohn used oral language as a key to unlock written language for his people. Nightjohn believed knowledge and literacy bring power and independence. He was passionate about bettering his people's lives, no matter what the consequences. He used talk in the same way classroom teachers use it to support and guide learning. As you continue reading, you will discover other connections between speaking and writing.

•••••

O•••••verview

Speaking and writing are processes that use expressive language in the construction of meaning. In both processes, students demonstrate and develop comprehension. This chapter discusses the similarities and differences between spoken and written composition and explores strategies for developing students' composing skills. The background information and understandings in this chapter prepare you for Chapters 10 and 11.

Composition is the process of constructing meaning with language. *Speaking* is composition that produces oral output, and *writing* is composition that produces written output. Just as oral language begins with cooing and babbling, written language begins with scribbling and drawing as young children begin to express themselves (see Figure 9.1). From the time children begin to talk, they create oral compositions. In fact, oral language is considered the "rooting system" for the development of written language (Dyson, 1981). As young children begin to write, they build from their oral compositions to their written ones.

"Mom, Jon's talkin' scribbles again."

FIGURE 9.1 Babbling and scribbling share a similar purpose in the composing process.

· · · · ·

Functions of Speaking and Writing

Research has just begun to explore the connections between spoken and written discourses that might make writing instruction and learning more fruitful for the diverse students in today's classrooms (Sperling, 1996). Because most people learn to speak fluently, whereas only some people learn to write well, the relationship of writing to speaking is of special interest. In a review of the research on writing/speaking relationships, Sperling (1996) concludes that speaking and writing are similar and different. She says that writing and speaking are both conversational acts and that writers and speakers have much to learn from each other.

Oral language and social interaction both affect literacy and learning (Hiebert, 1990). Children acquire expressive language, both oral and written, as they interact with others. Halliday (1985) believes that childern learn language to manipulate and control their environment. They learn and use language to get things done. Vygotsky (1978) believes that children's cognition and ability to learn grow through verbal interactions with others. In other words, he sees verbal and nonverbal interactions with others as the raw material of thought. To put it more formally, composing functions for children in several ways. Children use language to do the following:

- Identify wants and needs.
- Change and/or control behavior.
- Facilitate cognitive growth.
- Interact more fully with others.
- Express their individual uniqueness.

To perform these functions, children need to be immersed in rich and varied language environments. They need support and encouragement from adults and peers who provide interaction, reinforcement, and standard language models. Good teachers know that speech and writing develop naturally, as children need to use them in authentic situations. For example, a child asks for a toy or writes to a company for a free poster. A child tells a friend about a fire truck she has just seen or about a new game she just learned. A child writes a letter to tell someone about a trip to the zoo or a favorite birthday present. A child tries to convince her parent that it is too early to go to bed. A child writes an essay to persuade her classmates to vote for her for school president.

Both spoken and written language involve thinking and learning. Only a few moments spent observing in a classroom will show you that children think before, during, and after speaking and writing. In turn, spoken and written language can be a springboard for thinking. As a proficient listener and reader, you know that myriad ideas occur to you as you listen and read. Researchers know that both spoken and written language result in learning. Therefore, children who talk as they write and think, or who think and talk together in purposeful situations, can develop cognitively during the composition process. When children use speech and writing to explore what they know, clarify their ideas, and link new knowledge with known understanding, they learn. You can promote learning by encouraging your students to explore what they know by asking questions and seeking answers.

Although there are many similarities, there are also many differences between the two modes of expression. Writing is sometimes characterized as "speech written down." This definition is not totally accurate, however. Writing is not simply speech written down, even though it is clear that children learn to read and write using their own oral language as a base (Purcell-Gates, 1989).

On one hand, writing is actually *less* than speech written down. Speech allows a listener a range of ways to understand and interpret a message that writing only approximates but cannot duplicate. When speaking, we can suggest emphasis, clarify relationships, and increase understanding with intonation, juncture, stress, gestures, and facial expressions. We can use italics, punctuation, spacing, and so forth when we write, but these do not communicate the same depth of meaning as the elements we use when we speak. Children can learn how to use italics to indicate emphasis as they read aloud sentences (e.g., The house is on *fire!* The *house* is on fire! or The house *is* on fire!). As a teacher, you can show children how to use other written symbols to make writing more closely approximate speech.

On the other hand, writing is *more* than speech written down. The vocabulary, syntax, and language patterns we use in written language are often more complex than those we use in speech. In writing, we use more subordinate clauses, elaborations, abstractions, sentence combining, transformations, embeddings, and passive verb forms than we do in speech (Sperling, 1996). Writing also gives the author time to choose the precise word. Unless it is a prepared speech, we rarely have the time or inclination to mull over a word while we are speaking. Mark Twain's analogy comes to mind here. He said that the difference between *a word* and *the right word* is like the difference between a lightning bug and lightning. Also, in writing, we eliminate the *uhhh*s and *ummm*s so the written message is presented clearly without the distractions often found in speech. The speaker who constantly says, "That is . . . I really mean to say . . . " or "What I mean is . . . " detracts from the message and its effect. The writer controls the message more than the speaker because the writer can revise it many times if necessary, before it is presented.

For example, if you were to have a conversation with your mother, the *register,* or the language forms and patterns you might use, would probably be quite different from the register you might use if you were to write to her. Your mother's collaboration in the conversation is one aspect of the difference. The time factor and richness of the extra clues in spoken language also account for differences between your letter and a conversation.

Speaking and Writing to Compose

Written compositions are the result of simultaneous interaction between children's oral language and written language. There are two kinds of talk that affect writing: talk to others and self-talk. Talking is an integral part of planning and drafting because it provides both meaning and, for some children, the systematic means for getting that meaning on paper. Children talk to each other about their topics, and the content and form of what they write. So, a quiet classroom may inhibit writing.

Children also engage in self-talk; they talk to themselves as they write; they write what they say; they ask themselves questions about the meaning of what they write; they talk to explain the meaning of their graphics and fill in where there are omissions; they sound out the spellings of words; they make comments about how their writing looks; and they often reread their writing aloud to themselves or others.

Talk and discussion can feed good writing. Of course, *too* much talk and noise can inhibit writing, since writing requires thinking and some of us think best without distractions. In fact, Calkins and Harwayne (1991) talk about a teacher, Antoinette, who includes silent time in her writing workshop (discussed in Chapter 11). Antoinette begins with 30 minues of "the hustle and laughter of interactive study groups" and then moves into 30 to 40 minutes of writing in "a bubble of silence" in which the whole classroom thinks and writes (p. 119). This silent writing time creates a space for solitude and stillness "so that writers can listen to themselves." It makes sense to let self-talk or inner-speech inform children's writing in this way.

Of course, children also often interact in conferences with the teacher as they write. Many children know they have deleted information from their written compositions, and can supply facts and details when you ask them to. Often, when you ask questions about a written composition, the child will elaborate and clarify her story, making changes in both content and form.

Marissa, a first-grader, produced the story in Figure 9.2 in October after a directed writing activity (discussed later in this chapter). In this lesson, children wrote a story that included a character, a problem, and a resolution. When questioned in a conference about her story, Marissa explained to her teacher that the problem was the bubble gum caught in the little girl's hair, which was the reason for "First the girl gets a pair of scissors." The solution to the problem was for the little girl to cut her hair: "Then she cuts her hair" and "Then she was bald." Marissa said that the bubble gum was the problem and that she would tell her classmates that when she read the story aloud. (Children often fill in their stories when they retell them.) She elaborated the story even further, saying that the girl's parents would be angry if they found the gum in her hair.

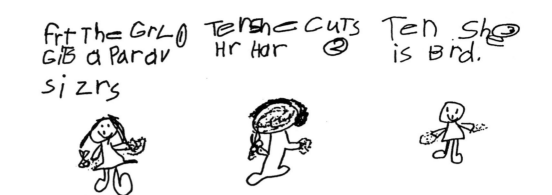

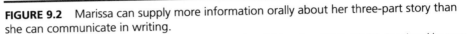

FIGURE 9.2 Marissa can supply more information orally about her three-part story than she can communicate in writing.

Source: SSW: Sustained Spontaneous Writing. *Childhood Education, 62*(1), 23–29. Reprinted by permission of Karen Bromley and the Association for Childhood Education International, 17904 Georgia Ave., Ste. 215, Onley, MD. Copyright © 1985 by the Association.

When children share their written work by reading it and answering peer questions about it, they validate their stories and refine their thinking (Calkins, 1994). Whole-class sharing sessions based on children's written texts, which Hubbard (1985) calls Write-and-Tell and Hansen and Graves (1983) call Author's Chair, allow children to develop simultaneously their speaking and writing. Questioning children about what they mean encourages them to elaborate and clarify the content of their spoken messages, as well.

Show and Tell or Share and Tell is a type of oral composition in which children engage in elementary school. In these oral compositions, children frequently omit details, wander from the main point, and require the listener to make many inferences. The teacher and other children often ask the speaker to elaborate on one point or another so that the message is clearer. Questioning to clarify meaning, then, is a natural part of revising an oral or written piece and an important tool that peers and a good teacher use.

Peer conferences allow for interaction among children as they write. Research with beginning writers shows that peers provide models, assistance, and encouragement to the writer (Dyson & Genishi, 1982). Children tell others about what they have written; they ask questions about how their writing sounds and looks; they request help with spelling; they receive feedback on the meaning and quality of what they have read; and they read their writing orally for others to hear.

STRETCHING EXERCISE

Before you read this section, make a web of the factors that affect spoken and written compositions. Use *Purpose, Audience,* and *Form* as your strand concepts and list information to support each. Then read this next section and compare it with your list. What other factors did you identify?

•••••

In any kind of composition, whether oral or written, three elements contribute to effective communication. The elements of purpose, audience, and form continually interact to shape the message communicated through talk or writing. When one of the three elements changes in any way, this change affects the other two.

Purpose

Purpose is a marriage between the intent and content of a message. Intent is the reason for sharing. It may be to inform, entertain, or persuade the listener or reader, or it may be a personal venting of emotions or reactions intended only for oneself. Content is what the message is about. Content may include anything from whales or how to create an origami bird to a significant personal experience or political statement. Children talk and write about many impersonal and personal subjects. When children talk during sharing time, they often select their content but many times do not seem sure of their intent. This may account for why some children ramble during sharing. When children write, especially when they write about teacher-chosen topics, they are often unsure of content and uncertain of any intention other than to please the teacher or finish the assignment.

Purpose, then, is critical to every composing activity in which children engage. Unless both intent and content are personally meaningful for children and they receive appropriate reinforcement or feedback, the activity may lack a relevant purpose for them. When this happens there is a good chance that effective communication won't occur.

You can prepare your students for oral sharing or writing by helping them establish a purpose. First, have the children talk or write about personally chosen topics that have meaning and relevancy for them. When children are sure of content, then intent is more easily established. You can then ask questions such as Why will you share this message? and What do you want people to know when they hear or read it?

When children learn a specific written form, such as letter writing, be sure there is a real reason for the letter—for example, to obtain free or inexpensive materials, to persuade or influence someone's opinion, to praise or question someone or something, or to request travel information. When there is a purpose for the letter writing, then learning to write a letter makes sense. It is also easier, and there is a greater likelihood that children will transfer the skills involved to other real-life situations.

When children learn a specific oral form, such as persuasive speaking, have them talk about a topic they choose and feel strongly about. This will affect purpose. In one elementary school, each class was asked to contribute three objects that told about the students' lives, to include in a time capsule buried at the site of a new community building. Nancy, a fifth-grade teacher, found this an excellent opportunity to engage her class in persuasive speaking. She asked each child to choose objects and then present short speeches, telling the class why a specific object should be included in the capsule. The class then voted for its top three choices. Some children worked alone and some in pairs to plan, write, and present the reasons for including their particular choice.

Both the letter writing and persuasive speaking examples demonstrate the importance of personal relevance in establishing purpose. You can help your students prepare for speaking and writing by having them talk and write about things that are real to them and in which they are interested. When you do this, both intent and content come into focus.

Audience

Purpose is also clarified when children consider to whom they are speaking or for whom they are writing. Children often address their written or spoken messages to someone, either themselves (as in journal writing) or someone else (as in letter writing or buddy journals) (Bromley, 1989). Typically, however, the message is directed to others. When children address one another, as in conversation on the playground or with notes passed in the classroom, they have little difficulty identifying the audience for whom their message is meant. However, when message sending becomes more formalized, as in oral and written reports, for example, audience awareness becomes less distinct.

Lack of a sense of audience characterizes much of what young children write. One reason is *egocentrism,* Piaget's (1962) term for thinking that is centered on one's own point of view (and that subsides at age 7 or 8). Another reason for children's insensitivity to their audience is the fact that many spoken and written assignments are exercises in demonstrating a skill for the teacher.

Why is it important for children to possess a sense of audience? When children know why and to whom they write, they are more apt to present their information cogently. They begin to eliminate irrelevant details, repetitions, lack of transitions, and inappropriate punctuation. Problems with spelling, handwriting, and form also are minimized. When a teacher identifies for children, or they decide themselves who the potential audience is for a spoken or written composition, the purpose of the activity is further clarified. An audience should, as often as possible, be real and audience feedback should be an important part of composing.

Children and adults adjust their speaking to their audience. When we talk to ESL students or students with hearing difficulties, we often slow our speech and enunciate more clearly and loudly. If you listen to children speak to adults, peers, or younger children, you will note that they do, indeed, adjust for audience when they speak about something they know. No matter how well children adjust to an audience when speaking, they will still need help adjusting their writing to an audience.

Most children have a built-in sense about different audiences when they talk. You can help them transfer this knowledge to writing by having them choose an experience or concern they have and then draft written compositions for different audiences. For example, when Nancy's students presented short speeches to persuade the class that their object should be included in the time capsule, they could also have written brief persuasive compositions to at least two different audiences: the committee who makes the final decision and their own classmates. Comparing these drafts could reveal that the audience one writes for helps determines the language one uses.

One way to attune children to audience is by giving them real audiences to whom they can speak and write. Have your students write and send letters to real people for real reasons. Have them write directions for games or science experiments for each other or younger children. Have them write stories and reports for each other. Have them prepare materials or presentations for their peers or younger children in the school. Then be sure to have them read and interact with the audiences about these written pieces. Results of research support the idea that children can learn to write with a sense of audience and that this improves the effectiveness of their writing (Hansen, Newkirk, & Graves, 1985; Short, Harste, & Burke, 1995).

Form

The form of a composition is what the final message looks or sounds like. Some messages are informative, such as an explanatory report, a brochure, a how-to demonstration, or a description of certain objects and their functions. Some messages are persuasive, such as a letter-to-the-editor, a speech, a petition, or an essay. Still other messages are meant to entertain, such as poetry, a dramatized story, riddles, or creative writing like a mystery, fantasy, or science fiction story. There are many forms for spoken and written messages, some of which appear in the list in Figure 9.3.

Children are not innately aware of these forms. In fact, when teachers do engage children in composing experiences, the forms are likely to be story writing and share-and-tell. But children need experiences with all these forms. Hearing them read and reading them themselves, as well as being taught the components of various forms, will be good exposure.

Children usually do very well when they write stories. This, no doubt, is related to their experiences with stories. As young children, they were read stories. They read books themselves by telling stories from the pictures and they were encouraged to relate events they experienced. Children internalize story grammar elements so that when you ask them to compose a story, they are working from existing knowledge.

Other spoken and written froms are just as easily mastered when children have the opportunity to become familiar with them. When you ask children to abandon their fa-

FIGURE 9.3 Spoken and written composition forms.

acknowledgments	definitions	lyrics	recipes
addresses	diaries	magazines	remedies
advertisements	directions	menus	reports
allegories	directories	mysteries	requests
analogies	dramas	myths	requisitions
announcements	editorials	newscasts	résumés
autobiographies	encyclopedia entries	newspapers	reviews
awards	epitaphs	notes	riddles
billboards	essays	obituaries	sales pitches
biographies	fables	observational notes	schedules
book jackets	folktales	pamphlets	self-descriptions
book reviews	game rules	parodies	sequels
books	good news–bad news	persuasive letters	skits
brochures	graffiti	plays	slogans
bulletins	grocery lists	poems	speeches
bumper stickers	headlines	posters	stories
campaign speeches	how-to-do-it speeches	product descriptions	summaries
captions	impromptu speeches	propaganda	TV commercials
cartoons	interviews	puppet shows	telegrams
certificates	job applications	puzzles	travel folders
character sketches	journals	questionnaires	tributes
comic strips	laboratory notes	questions	vignettes
contracts	letters	quizzes	want ads
conversations	lists	quotations	wanted posters
critiques	logs	real estate notices	wills

miliar story grammar and move to another form, such as poetry, advertisements, or reports, you need to show them examples that include the form's elements and model composing for them. Harwayne (1992) gives innumerable examples of how children's books can be models for children's writing. She says if we want children to write with style, they must read that style and internalize it first.

When students understand the elements of a particular form, give them practice in orally composing that form before expecting them to compose it in writing. For example, teach children how to orally construct paragraphs consisting of a topic sentence and several supporting details without extraneous matter before having them write paragraphs. If children are to succeed in doing this, you need to speak in complete thoughts or paragraphs, thus providing them with a good model.

Form also includes such mechanical aspects of written composition as spelling, legibility, handwriting, punctuation, capitalization, and indentation. In spoken composition, form includes aspects of voice such as intonation, juncture, and stress, as well as nonverbal communication that includes gestures, facial expressions, and eye contact, among other things. In general, however, these aspects of spoken and written form are secondary to the content and meaning of the message.

How Purpose, Audience, and Form Interact

Purpose, audience, and form interact together to determine the message of a composition. Suppose you receive a traffic ticket for going through a familiar intersection in your neighborhood where a new stop sign was just erected. Your purpose for relating the event will vary with your audience. You will probably defend your action and try to persuade the judge to void the ticket. You may tell your friend the story to entertain her or to persuade her to support you. You will relate the event to your 7-year-old nephew to inform him of the consequences of failing to be observant.

The audience you speak to also determines the form you use in telling about the experience. The language you use to describe the incident to the judge, a friend, or your nephew will vary. You will probably use formal language, more multisyllabic words, and fewer slang terms and contractions with the judge. You might use slang, contractions, and questions like "You know?" with your friend, and you will probably use simpler vocabulary and fewer words when talking to your nephew.

Intonation, juncture, stress, and nonverbal language will also differ with purpose and audience. Specifically, the tone of your explanation to the judge will be conciliatory, reflecting your respect for that position. To your friend, your tone could be joking, disbelieving, or indignant. To your nephew, your tone may be didactic. You might say something like "You see? You must always look carefully at all road signs."

In both spoken and written composition, it is nearly impossible to change either purpose, audience, or form without affecting the other elements. Purpose, the intent and content, influences who the message is directed to as well as how the message is formed. If one wants to describe a marshmallow, for example, the vocabulary and analogies chosen will differ, depending on the audience and the form of the message. Helping children simultaneously juggle considerations of purpose, audience, and form is not an easy task. Since children seem to adjust for these three elements in their speech, it makes sense to build from the oral base.

One way to help children tie spoken language to written language is through the use of audience. Children naturally interact with an audience when they speak. They rephrase, repeat, answer questions, and ask questions. They use these interactions to help shape the meaning and form of what they say. You can build on this awareness and use of audience in spoken language and help children transfer it to written language. You can do this by responding to children's writing the way you respond to their conversation. Either orally or in notes jotted to them in the margins of their drafts, respond first in a personal way to their message. Tell them how it makes you feel, what it reminds you of, whether it makes sense or is clear, and if you enjoyed reading it. Praise well-crafted language. Ask questions about points that are unclear. Suggest places where children can elaborate. Respond to content first, and you will see how form begins to take care of itself.

One specific type of interactive writing that demonstrates the interaction of purpose, audience, and form is buddy journal writing (Bromley, 1995, 1989). *Buddy journals,* an outgrowth of the dialogue journal in which the student and teacher converse in writing (Kreeft, 1984), are bound notebooks in which students converse as they write messages back and forth to each other (see Figure 9.4) Buddy journals allow students to transfer their strengths in oral conversation to writing and provide a legitimate way for students to write notes to each other. Students can describe feelings and activities, ask questions, make requests, share ideas, and build relationships with each other. Also, buddy journals support further talk between buddies.

The buddy journal has wide application in the classroom. It can be used by students who have read the same book and want to share their responses. It can also be a

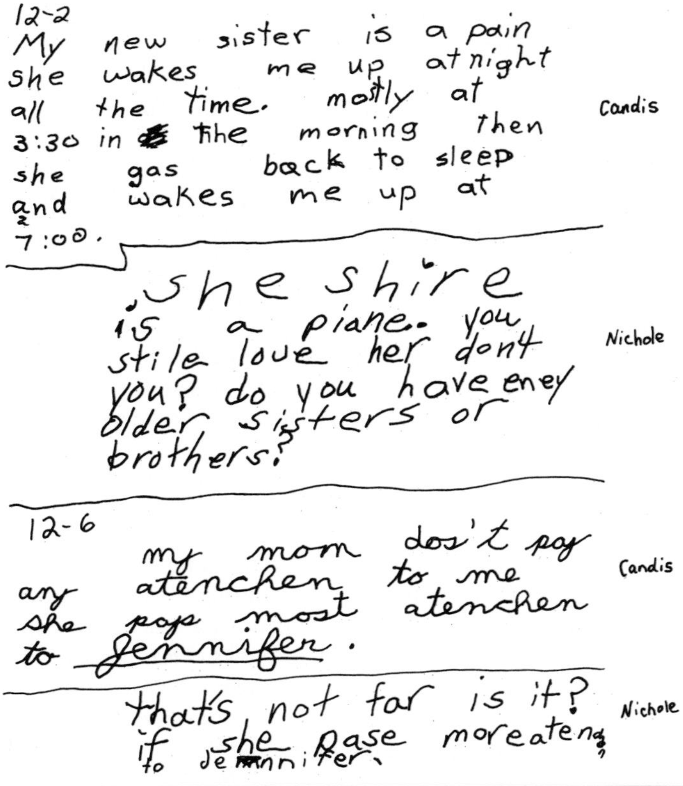

FIGURE 9.4 Nichole gave Candis support and sympathy in their buddy journal entries (12/2 and 12/6).

vehicle for integrating learning across the curriculum. Students can observe, summarize, and/or question what they have learned in science or social studies.

As you can see, it makes sense to connect speaking and writing in your teaching because of the important similarities that purpose, audience, and form possess. As you connect speaking and writing, keep the following things in mind:

- Focus on purpose, the intent and content, of the spoken or written messages and encourage children to elaborate and clarify their ideas.
- Direct speaking and writing activities or assignments to real audiences that are relevant to the learner.
- Give children opportunities to speak and write a variety of forms for a variety of audiences.
- View the mechanics of form in spoken and written language as a contributor to meaning, not as the most important aspect.

Aspects of Composing

The composing process has four generally recognized aspects: planning, drafting, revising, and sharing. These aspects are the same whether children are learning to speak or write. The term *aspects,* rather than *stages,* best describes what happens when children compose, since there are actually no discrete stages that composers move through sequentially. Speakers and writers do not first plan, then speak or write, and then revise. Rather, speakers and writers move back and forth among the aspects as they compose, much like listeners and speakers do. Composing requires speakers and writers to plan, begin drafting, go back to plan some more, revise, continue drafting, and so on. At the same time, they are considering their purpose and their audience. The composing process is a recursive process, not a sequential one.

Although speaking and writing possess similiar aspects, one basic difference separates them. Writing is a more deliberate and exact form of communication than speaking. Since written compositions stay put, they undergo analysis and revision more easily than does oral language. Writers reread texts and make changes to clarify their meaning, whereas memory limits speakers and restricts what they change or rephrase. Oral compositions tend to fade away and be forgotten, and so are more difficult to analyze and revise. Of course, tape recorders or video recorders help make an oral report or sharing more permanent and available for analysis and revision. Another possibility is to have children work from note cards. This structures the oral presentation and keeps it nearly the same in later presentations.

Planning

Planning includes preparatory activities that precede drafting. It takes into consideration the purpose, the audience, and the form of a composition. It is during planning that formal oral and written compositions most resemble one another. Whether the draft is spoken or written, children use planning time to learn about their topics. They discuss their topics with others and search their sources to gain more information. This is also the time they spend thinking about their topics and fusing their own knowledge with new knowledge. And last, planning involves deciding on the intent and the content, how the information will be organized, and what the form of the draft will be.

· · · · ·
*Creating a web or concept map of
literary elements helps students
prepare for retelling or writing a
story summary.*

Children, even young ones, can brainstorm, collect, and organize information, interact with others on a topic, draw a picture, or make notes as part of planning a spoken or written composition. Figure 9.5 shows the picture drawn by a first-grade child as she planned her contribution to her class's sharing time. Figure 9.6 shows a web two first-grade children made before they wrote, on the computer, the story in Figure 9.7, called "Frog and Toad Met." Figure 9.8 shows webs of information about the Olympics made by a fifth-grader in preparation for doing an oral report.

This is a fairy She
on the Cloud and with
The roinbow u buv her

FIGURE 9.5 Preparing for Share and Tell, this first-grader planned what to write by first drawing a picture.

· · · · ·

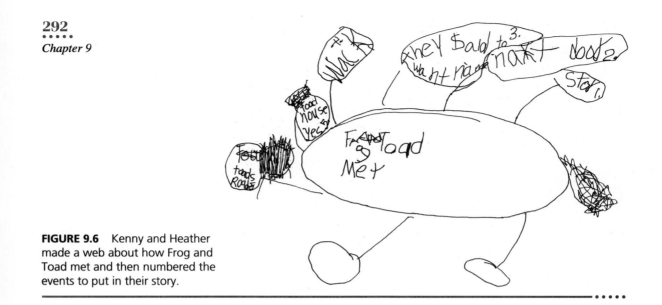

FIGURE 9.6 Kenny and Heather made a web about how Frog and Toad met and then numbered the events to put in their story.

FIGURE 9.7 The final copy of Kenny and Heather's story became a book with a page and picture for each sentence.

FROG AND TOAD MET

by

Kenny and Heather

One day Frog and Toad went to the same store and met each other.

They went home and Frog went next door and it was Toad's house.

"What is your name?" said Frog.

"Toad. What is your name?" said Toad.

"Frog. Do you want to go for a walk?" said Frog.

"Yes," said Toad. They saw a turtle on their walk.

"Do you want to go to my house?" said Toad.

"Yes," Frog said.

They went to Toad's house. When they got there, Toad asked, "Do you want to play a game?"

"O.K." said Frog. "What game do you have?"

"Toad's Road," said Toad.

Frog and Toad fought about winning. They both won because they got to the finish line at the same time.

"Are we friends now?" said Toad.

"Of course," laughed Frog.

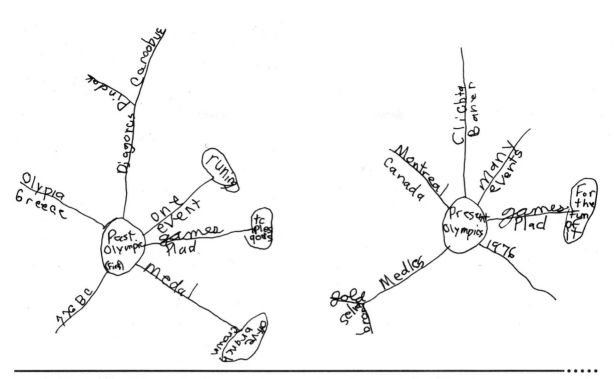

FIGURE 9.8 A fifth-grader created these webs to prepare his oral report on the Olympics.

Drafting

Drafting both oral and written compositions consists of actually elaborating the ideas chosen during planning. In this part of the composing process, children create the words, phrases, and sentences of the composition either orally or in writing. During drafting, it is important that the speaker or writer continue to keep in mind purpose, audience, and form; otherwise, the draft loses its effectiveness.

Drafting does not always happen smoothly and steadily, especially for children. They pause, reword, repeat, think, speak, and monitor what they say as they draft oral language. Children write, add, delete, and generally draft their compositions unevenly, with words coming quickly at times and not at all at other times.

If you have taken a college course in public speaking, you probably practiced your speech before giving it formally, perhaps talking to yourself in the mirror or presenting it to a friend. This kind of oral drafting provides an opportunity to:

- Know whether you composed a piece in which the parts fit together.
- See how your facial expressions and gestures influence content.
- Get a feel for the smooth and rough parts of the presentation.
- Know what to change or learn better.

The same process occurs when you draft on paper. Ideas do not come easily. Some paragraphs are difficult to write and some are easy. Certain sentences or paragraphs do not fit where you first placed them. Spelling and/or punctuation could be a problem. You monitor what you write and often go back and plan some parts of the piece over again. Throughout the writing of this book, for example, drafting occurred in these very same ways and happened concurrently with replanning and revising.

Children who learn to monitor as they draft become effective composers. They learn to listen to their oral drafts unfold and reread their written drafts as they create them to monitor both for problems. So, self-monitoring during talk and writing is as important as it is during listening and reading. Asking questions like Does this make sense? What else do I know? and How does this sound or look to the audience? will help children know how to revise and monitor as they draft.

Of course, children need opportunities to draft a composition without any expectations that they will revise or even share the composition. Practice in writing, such as in journal writing, just for the sake of writing, helps children become fluent composers. Similarly, when children engage in sharing time, brainstorming sessions, conversations, or group discussions, there is generally no formal revision of these oral products.

Drafting a composition is similar to practicing a musical instrument. Children who learn to play an instrument must practice daily so that the fingering and sound of a particular piece of music become automatic. The music teacher does not attend these practice sessions because every note a child plays need not be commented on and observed. In fact, such constant analysis might interfere with learning. Comments made by the teacher at weekly intervals and the opportunity to perform at special recitals seem to be sufficient feedback when children are motivated to learn. Children who learn to speak or write must practice daily to become fluent at drafting. The teacher need not hear, read, respond to, or evaluate every draft; in fact, such constant analysis may have a negative effect.

Revising

Revising, or refining the content and form of a draft, often occurs in a limited way as children draft. As children speak, they use the feedback from listeners and monitor their own oral language to reword, elaborate, and clarify the original drafts. When children write, they reread, add, delete, cross out, and change what they first wrote.

Most children's informal oral language is not formally revised. Children revise by rephrasing and adding, based on their interactions with others and the feedback they receive from what they say. In terms of formal oral compositions, do encourage children to revise. When they give oral reports, tape recording a practice draft and then revising it before the final presentation is a good idea.

Many teachers think that every piece of writing a child does must be revised and perfected. What these teachers are unaware of or have forgotten is that drafting for the sake of drafting is necessary practice. It is like becoming a good tennis player who practices serves and volleys for hours without ever playing a real game. Teachers also forget that not all compositions are worth revision. When a child is excited about a particular draft and feels good about it, that is the draft to have the child revise and polish for sharing with a real audience.

The most important way to help children revise is to have them again think about purpose, audience, and form. As they ask questions like Does this make sense? What else do I know? and How does this sound or look to the audience? their revisions will greatly improve the form and content of their compositions.

One way to extend speakers' or writers' audience awareness is to have them listen to each other's oral reports and read each other's drafts and then provide feedback. This feedback from a real audience is one of the most useful aids to revising. Have the children respond to each other's formal oral and written drafts in peer conferences using a written Response Guide such as the ones in Figures 9.9 and 9.10. Notice that each requires students to sign their responses, which helps some students respond more gently. Both guides first focus on positive apsects of a draft or report. Then, they elecit helpful suggestions from the responder. The format of "Praise, Question, Suggest" can be further simplified to "Tell, Ask, Give" for young children.

When initially teaching children how to use the guide, it is a good idea to model appropriate responses yourself as you and they look at a written draft using copies of it on the overhead projector. You can then give children practice using the guide in the same kind of group situation. Anonymous drafts, or examples written specifically for helping children learn how to react, are best used so that an individual's work is the focus of the entire group.

FIGURE 9.9 Feedback from a real audience is an excellent way to help writers and speaker revise.

Response Guide

Title _____

Author/Speaker _____

Date _____   Responder _____

1. Does the draft/report make sense?

2. What do you like about it?

3. What questions do you have?

4. How can it be improved?

5. Check the things the author/speaker does well:

_____ grammar	_____ spelling
_____ voice	_____ punctuation
_____ pitch	_____ precise words
_____ pauses	_____ paragraphs
_____ stress	_____ organization
_____ gestures	_____ clarity
_____ eye contact	_____ neatness/legibility
_____ facial expressions	_____ consistency

```
┌────────────────────────────────────────────────────────────┐
│  Title _____  │
│                                                              │
│  Author/Speaker _____    │
│                                                              │
│  P (Praise):                                                 │
│                                                              │
│                                                              │
│                                                              │
│                                                              │
│  Q (Question):                                               │
│                                                              │
│                                                              │
│                                                              │
│  S (Suggest):                                                │
│                                                              │
│                                                              │
│                                                              │
│                                                              │
│  Signed _____    │
└────────────────────────────────────────────────────────────┘
```

FIGURE 9.10 Students can use the PQS Guide to respond to either a spoken or written composition.

You can also help children revise their oral drafts. Use these Response Guides, or ones like them, with children to help them respond to their tape-recorded oral compositions. The tape can even be stopped and insertions or deletions made, and the person reviewing the speech can request more information or clarification of ideas.

STRETCHING EXERCISE

Find a child who is preparing to give an oral report. Tape record the child's practice draft of the oral report and use the Reaction Guide with the child to provide feedback about revising. Tape record the actual report and talk with the child about how the guide helped. Revise the guide according to the child's input.

• • • • •

Sharing

Sharing the composition in final form with others is a critical part of speaking and writing because it provides feedback from a real audience. It may not seem important for a child to share a composition with others if they have already reacted to it and helped the child revise, but it is well documented that children are eager to share their written works with others (Hansen & Graves, 1983; Short, Harste, & Burke, 1995).

Encourage children to engage in voluntary sharing and avoid required sharing, since both oral and written compositions are sometimes quite personal. If the atmosphere in the classroom is positive and supportive, children will feel comfortable and volunteer to share their work. At first, it may be easier for a shy child to prepare a tape recording for others to listen to individually or in groups. Once the child gains confidence, the tape recorder is no longer necessary.

Just as you respond to something your friend says or writes, so children respond to each other's oral and written work. This natural feedback is a tangible result of communicating with an audience. Additionally, when a book of original poetry is bound and placed on the library shelf for others to borrow and read or when an oral presentation of the life cycle of a butterfly is taped and included in a learning center for others to listen to and enjoy, children look at the completed project with pride and a better understanding of all that goes into producing written or spoken work.

Sharing oral compositions adds dignity to children's work and highlights their accomplishments, as well (Wolsch & Wolsch, 1982). Children enjoy performing or presenting their best oral compositions to small groups, the class, assembly programs for several classes, and for parents. Outside school, there are retirement homes, senior citizens' centers, hospitals, and even shopping malls that are often eager to have children perform. These audiences are very appreciative.

Share children's work through display as well as performance. You can put written compositions in the classroom on bulletin boards, walls, window shades, window panes, wires or string, or folding screens. Tastefully arranged displays—with stories or poems mounted on colored paper, for example—give children the message that their work is valued and deserving of special care and notice. Don't overlook displaying work throughout the school on hall bulletin boards or in special showcases, as well as in the cafeteria, principal's office, library, and faculty room. Displays outside school in a library, store, hospital, shopping mall, retirement home, or senior citizens' center are also possibilities.

· · · · ·
*An Author of the Week display recognizes the writing
of a second-grade student.*

Sharing written compositions as gifts for others also motivates children. Special-occasion cards, poetry, stories made into books, and other such things are inexpensive but highly valued gifts. Personalized writing, composed especially for or about a certain person, is a great experience for the composer as well as the recipient. One student made a keepsake album to show her appreciation for her foster father (Wolsch & Wolsch, 1982). She interviewed her father and compiled his life story. She collected old family photographs, newspaper clippings, and copies of legal documents and alternated them with chapters or passages about his life, creating an heirloom as well as a gift.

Guiding Composition

You can guide children's development of specific speaking and writing skills both directly and indirectly in a number of ways. An especially important way is to read aloud regularly to children and make all kinds of written forms available in the classroom for them to read. Before they do formal spoken presentations or written pieces, expose them to books, stories, and other literary forms that are good models. Allow time for children to read these forms, so they develop a sense of how the forms should look and sound. You can develop background, supply children with vocabulary they might use, and show them how to approach the activity. Activities that precede speaking and writing are similar to what you do before children listen or read to aid comprehension.

For example, Harwayne (1992) describes a visit to an early childhood classroom where the children were studying Dr. Seuss and Eric Carle. She noticed a huge papier-maché dinosaur and incubator of hatching eggs as she joined a small group. She talked with the children about their study and then asked, "If Dr. Seuss were to visit this classroom and write about that dinosaur, how might his writing go?" This type of conversation before writing is a rehearsal for the actual writing. Some teachers jot down the vocabulary and ideas children share during these free discussions to give children a ready reference when they begin writing. Beforehand then, you can help build background for composing through talk.

During composing, you can show children the process you go through as you compose. You can actively listen to and read what they say and write. You can guide the composing process along by asking questions and encouraging children to ask questions that help them link what they planned to do with what they are actually doing. Remind them to keep in mind why they are composing, who will hear or see the composition, and how it should sound or look.

After a speaking and writing composition lesson, you can also encourage response from others. Spoken and written pieces can be shared and responses promoted so that communication transpires between speaker and/or writer and audience. Author's Chair, mentioned earlier, and Author Share, a time for voluntary sharing, gives purpose and provides an audience for writing. Some specific ideas for writing conferences follow, which you can adapt for spoken compositions.

Writing Conferences

While the rest of the class is writing, you can conduct a conference or brief discussion with individual children about their writing (Calkins, 1994; Graves, 1983). A conference can occur at a child's desk, as you move quietly around the room, at the writing center, or at your desk. The purpose of a writing conference is to provide you and the child with some uninterrupted one-on-one time that focuses on a child's particular needs at that point in the composing process.

You should conference regularly with children. In fact, it's a good idea to let children know when their conference will be so they can prepare for it. Of course, you won't be able to meet with every child every time writing occurs in the classroom, but you can see each child at least once a week. Joan, a first-grade teacher frustrated by her inability to conference with children often enough, began occasionally to conference with small groups of children who were at the same place in their writing and needed similar help. She found this was a good way to model drafting and revising for them and to teach mini-lessons. The small group conferences provided an opportunity for children to begin peer conferencing with each other, as well.

To begin a conference, ask a question such as, "How is your writing going, Kim?" and then wait for the child's response. Graves (1994), too, believes much can be learned about children if teachers listen to them and give them the opportunity to share. To help a child talk, follow the child's train of thought, ask questions she can answer, and help her focus her thoughts. Here is an example of a conference:

Ms. Garcia:	How is your writing going, Kim?
Kim:	OK.
Ms. Garcia:	Tell me what you are writing about.
Kim:	My parrot.
Ms. Garcia:	Your parrot?
Kim:	Yes.
Ms. Garcia:	What about your parrot?
Kim:	Toby gets out of his cage and flies all over the house and my mother doesn't like it.
Ms. Garcia:	He must be a pretty smart parrot to get out of his cage. How does he do it?
Kim:	He hangs on the door and bites the hook with his beak.
Ms. Garcia:	What are you going to do about it?
Kim:	Nothing. My brother and me think it's OK.
Ms. Garcia:	Have you been writing about this?
Kim:	I got a start.
Ms. Garcia:	Well, keep up the writing. It sounds like you'll have a good story.

In later conferences, as Kim's writing progresses, Ms. Garcia continues to listen and respond to what she says, and Kim, in turn, responds with more information. Ms. Garcia asks questions Kim can answer with the knowledge she has, and she tries to help Kim clarify her thoughts and put them down on paper. Here are some other possible questions Ms. Garcia could ask Kim to help her focus on content:

What does your parrot do when he flies around?
How does he get back into his cage?
Why doesn't your mother like it?
Does your parrot do any other tricks?
How did he learn to do them?

As Ms. Garcia talks with Kim and reads her written work, she encourages Kim to reread her piece silently and to read it aloud. Often, when children reread their own work, they discover problems with clarity, spelling, punctuation, and capitalization, and will self-correct.

Here are several more questions Ms. Garcia could ask. These questions focus on the actual writing process.

If you were going to put in new information, how would you do it?

When you can't spell a word, how do you figure it out?

How do you figure out where one sentence ends and another begins?

So you think your story is mixed up. How will you change it?

What will you be doing next with this story?

Do you think this is ready to be published?

Will you circle the words you know are spelled right and put a line under the ones you'd like me to help you spell?

Will you read your story out loud, so I can help you put in periods and capitals? This will help us know what you want to go together.

It is impossible, of course, to prescribe a set of questions that is appropriate for every child and every conference. The perceptive teacher realizes that each child and each story are unique; each has different strengths and weaknesses. But if you remember that the questions you ask teach you a lot about what a child knows and help a child learn what she knows, then you will strengthen the composing process for that child.

To initiate peer conferences, first model the performance you expect. Let the group function independently once you feel confident they will be constructive. The following sequence suggests one approach:

1. Respond personally to content first. Then ask questions and make a suggestion. Do most of the responding.
2. Be with the group, observing and modeling, but encourage the children to respond, question, and suggest. Do less responding.
3. Be near the group, observing the group on its own as the children respond, question, and make suggestions. Do not respond.

Your biggest job is to help children give and receive relevant and tactful information about the written product. Another way to do this is to use something you have written or to select an anonymous sample paper to share on an overhead projector as a focus for class discussion on unsolved issues or ways to revise. Deb Pease often shares entries from her own journal, using the overhead projector to demonstrate particular skills and revision possibilities. Her fifth-graders are usually very attentive during these minilessons.

Research suggests that even elementary-grade students can evaluate writing and respond to both content and how content is communicated (e.g., run-on sentences, repetitions, inappropriate punctuation, misspellings, etc.) (Crowhurst, 1979; Hansen & Graves, 1983).

Crowhurst (1979) reports that children themselves act as valuable assets in the evaluation process when you teach them to respond appropriately to each other's written work. She found that in a writing workshop environment, third- and fifth-grade students made constructively critical comments about the content and form of each other's work. These children were taught to encourage each other with praise and positive comments, to request clarification, and to make suggestions for improvement. Also, reading the writing of others in order to comment usefully was valuable practice in critical reading for a real purpose.

As children are alternately readers and writers, they learn more about the composing process and become more sophisticated communicators. They learn to share common problems; they find out that they are not alone in misspelling words or in having trouble forming paragraphs. Peer conferences have rich potential not only for developing writers and readers but also for teaching interpersonal relations skills—an extra bonus (see Figures 9.11 and 9.12).

Directed Speaking/Writing Activity

Once you decide that your students have had sufficient exposure to a specific spoken or written form through listening and reading, they are ready to compose this form themselves. You can use a plan called the *Directed Speaking/Writing Activity (DSA)* (or *DWA*) (Moore & Moore, 1991) that helps develop oral or written language use in specific formats.

1. What did you like about your partner's story?

2. Did the story take place in Endicott?

3. Were there characters?

4. Was there a plot?

5. Was there a setting?

6. Draw a picture to show your favorite part of the story.

Your Name _____ Date _____

FIGURE 9.11 Third-graders respond to the content of each other's writing with these questions.

Source: Reprinted by permission of Jo Anbro.

STORY CHECKLIST

1. Does the story make sense?

2. What do you like about it?

3. Did the writer use capitals?

4. Are there endmarks?

5. Are there words that tell how things look, feel, smell, sound, and taste?

6. Does the story have 10 sentences?

FIGURE 9.12 Fourth-graders respond to content and form with this story checklist.

Your Name _____

Author's _____

••••

If you teach the lesson individually, then the child determines the purpose, audience, and form. If you use the lesson as a demonstration for a group, you can determine these elements or help the group make a decision about them. The model lesson in Figure 9.13 shows how you might show middle- or upper-grade children how to write a report on an animal.

You can evaluate your teaching of a DSA/DWA such as this one by not only examining the content and form of the children's final compositions but also by reviewing each part of the lesson you taught. Did you include each of the steps and in the order suggested? Were the children ready for the lesson or could they benefit from more exposure to models? How would you change your next lesson?

In a lesson such as this, through modeling the process and outcome, you teach children how to gather and organize information for a particular form. When you react to the content of a final report in the lesson, you should also examine how well children integrated information from a variety of sources. You can see evidence of the planning process and determine if that or something else causes a composition to ineffectively communicate meaning.

Note the amount of time in the lesson in Figure 9.13 devoted to planning. Do you think this is appropriate? Why or why not? As a teacher, what might you do during drafting to be most helpful to children?

• • • • •

A DWA will probably take several days to complete. You can spend a lesson or two just motivating and developing background. Several lessons can be spent modeling the process and outcome and generating and organizing information. As you can see,

FIGURE 9.13 This is an example of a DWA.

DWA for Teaching Report Writing

I. *Plan*

   A. *Identify purpose, audience, and form:*
     —To describe where an animal lives, what it eats, and what dangers it faces.
     —Peers (third-graders).
     —A four-paragraph report (oral or written).

   B. *Motivate and develop background:*
     —Show books and pictures of animal.
     —Brainstorm what children already know. Record this information.
     —Read books, discuss new information, and add to existing record or make new record.

   C. *Model process and outcome:*
     —Read or show a report on another animal, using four paragraphs, one for each of the three questions and one as the summary.
     —Show children a completed grid with 3 columns (one for each of the questions) and 3 or 4 rows (on which information is entered from several sources).

   D. *Generate and organize information:*
     —Give children a blank grid or have them make one on a sheet of paper and have them write in the three questions.
     —Show children how to search a source for answers to the first question. Enter information and source on the grid using key words and phrases.
     —Have children find and enter information to answer the next two questions.

II. *Draft*

   A. *Direct children to draft composition:*
     —Write four-paragraph report using information from grid.

III. *Revise*

   A. *Have children reread or tape record and listen to their own compositions:*
     —Use Reaction Guide to help with revision.

   B. *Have peers orally read and react to each other's compositions:*
     —Use Reaction Guide to help with revision.

IV. *Share*

   A. *Have volunteers share final reports:*
     —Read orally or display for others to read.

• • • • •

each aspect of the composing process is quite involved, and children need time to effectively complete each one. The revision aspect may not be one that you engage children in each time they write, since you probably will want children to revise only those compositions they are eager to share or feel are worth revising.

If you use the plan to develop spoken language with a DSA, you may or may not want to encourage children to revise their oral compositions and share them again. Revision in a DSA might occur only occasionally, so that children do not become overly concerned with how they sound rather than with what they are saying. When children revise a speech or report, they can tape record and listen to their own compositions first. Then they might have a friend listen to the tape recording and react to it. Use the the Reaction Guide included earlier in the chapter during this aspect of composition.

The DSA/DWA is flexible enough to accommodate a variety of composition forms, both oral and written. The format of a DSA/DWA allows you to plan lessons that help children become better speakers and writers because it involves them in setting a purpose and planning before composing begins.

Speaking/Writing Transfer Lesson

Although speaking and writing differ in many ways, they also have several similarities. One similarity is that the learner composes meaning in both processes. Generally, a child in elementary school can construct meaning orally more easily than in writing because her listening and speaking vocabularies are larger than her reading and writing vocabularies. Remember, too, that writing involves physical coordination and spelling ability, among other things.

To direct and develop children's composing, it makes sense to begin from an area of strength. A speaking/writing transfer lesson, based on Cunningham and Allington's (1994) listening/reading transfer lesson, is one way to promote the composition process with children. In a speaking/writing transfer lesson, children learn that the kinds of things they do before and during speaking are the same as the kinds of things they do before and during writing to construct meaning.

To teach a transfer lesson, you need to plan two parallel activities. In the first, have the children speak and respond, and in the second, have the children write and respond. Responses might involve reasons for liking or disliking a story or movie or analysis of a science experiment. Or the children can identify advantages and disadvantages or the pros and cons of an issue such as the use of the cotton gin in the economy of the South or the erection of taller smoke stacks as a way to control pollution.

After children orally describe, you should make it clear, by identifying or comparing ideas, that what they do as they speak is exactly the same as what they will do in writing. Remember three essentials to the successful transfer lesson (based on Cunningham, 1975):

1. Tell the students they will do the same thing in talk and writing.
2. Set specific purposes for speaking and writing.
3. As the children talk, have them explain their responses.

Descriptions of two speaking/writing transfer lessons follow.

Pam's Lesson. Pam taught a speaking/writing transfer lesson to a group of third-grade students with disabilities in writing. Her objective was to help students write a humorous account from the first person using consistent grammar. She decided to use a book written from the *I* perspective, *How I Spent My Summer Vacation* by Mark Teague (1995). It is a tall tale in the form of an essay written by a boy for his teacher about how he was sent by train to visit his aunt and was captured by a gang of cowboys who invited him to join them. Pam chose this story because of the immediacy of the writing and its potential to inspire her students' imaginations. First, Pam read the book to them and they discussed Wallace's adventure and his imagination. Pam noted the strong voice and narrative style for them.

Then, Pam had students work in pairs to tell each other of a journey in their lives that had a funny or unexpected ending or one they could invent, as had Wallace. After creating the trip orally, each student then drew a map of the trip and wrote a brief adventure story from the *I* perspective to accompany it. Pam thought the map might prompt writing because of its concrete nature. The students were taken with Wallace's adventure and spent several days writing and revising their stories, which they first told each other orally. Pam felt this speaking/writing transfer lesson achieved her goals well and she soon found other journey books to use with her students:

Sophie and Auntie Pearl by Jeanne Titherington (New York: Greenwillow, 1995).
  A girl and her aunt can fly.
The Wretched Stone by Chris VanAllsburg (New York: Houghton Mifflin, 1991). A
  strange stone is picked up on a sea voyage by a shop's crew.
Suddenly! by Collin McNaughton (San Diego: Harcourt, 1994). A pig is followed
  to the store by a wolf.
Summer on Wheels by Gary Soto (New York: Scholastic, 1995). Two Mexican
  American boys take a bicycle trip between Los Angeles and Santa Monica.
Song Lee and the Leech Man by Suzy Kline (New York: Penguin, 1995). This
  first-person story is about Ronald Morgan and his friends who visit Camp
  Echo lake.

Matt's Lesson. As part of a unit on local history, Matt Gallagher's fourth-graders decided to create a brochure about local tourist attractions. They were reading *The Cricket in Times Square* by George Seldon, and had just finished the chapter in which Tucker and Harry take Chester Cricket to visit Times Square. Chester was unaccustomed to city crowds and sounds, but he was curious and interested to see what the city had to offer. First, Matt explained the speaking/writing transfer lesson to his class, telling the children they would compose their brochure entries orally and then write them. Next, he asked the students to remember how Chester felt and to put themselves in the place of a long-lost relative or visitor who has just come to the area. They talked about how the person would travel, where he would go, what special places he might see, who he might want to meet, and whether he might want to come back for a visit. With the aid of area maps and telephone books, the class made a list of area attractions:

Veteran's Memorial Arena	Nanticoke Historical Museum
Binghamton Mets Stadium	Roberson Museum
Kopernic Observatory	Discovery Center
Ross Park Zoo	Carousels (6)

Oakdale Mall
Binghamton University
Cider Mill Playhouse
Chenango Valley State Park
Otsiningo Park
Hiawatha Island
Spiedie Fest
Binghamton Music Festival

Town Square Mall
Broome Community College
The Forum
Enjoie Golf Course
Finch Hollow Nature Center
Waterman Conservation Center
BC Open Golf Tournament
Two Rivers Craft Festival

Then, pairs of students chose one attraction to present orally to the class in 3 minutes. The categories they decided to include in their "3-Minute Ads" were *Where, Attractions,* and *Dates and Times.* Over a weekend they did their research and made notes. In school on Monday, the children prepared their ads and then presented them to their peers, who gave constructive feedback. With this preparation, the students then wrote their brochure entries, which Matt checked for accuracy before they used computer graphics and a word processor to put them in final form for the brochure (see Figure 9.14).

When students engage in the same activities during and before writing that they use during and before speaking, they have a better chance of realizing how the two are similar. Of course, your observations about this similarity are important to reinforce the idea. When you set specific purposes for speaking and writing, then children have a reason to speak and write, and you direct their compositions more effectively. When you have children explain and elaborate on their responses, then you provide them with opportunities to share the way they think so that the rest of the class can observe the cogni-

Nanticoke Valley Historical Museum

Where: Take Route 26N past Maine Memorial Elementary School.
The road will split; stay left.
The museum is on your left. It is yellow.

Attractions: This is a museum with old artifacts and ways of life of the people who many, many years ago lived in this area. We went on a field trip there this year and it was fun. There is even an outhouse there.

Dates and Monday through Saturday, except holidays.
Times: 9:00 a.m. to 5:00 p.m.
Tour groups please call ahead
for information.

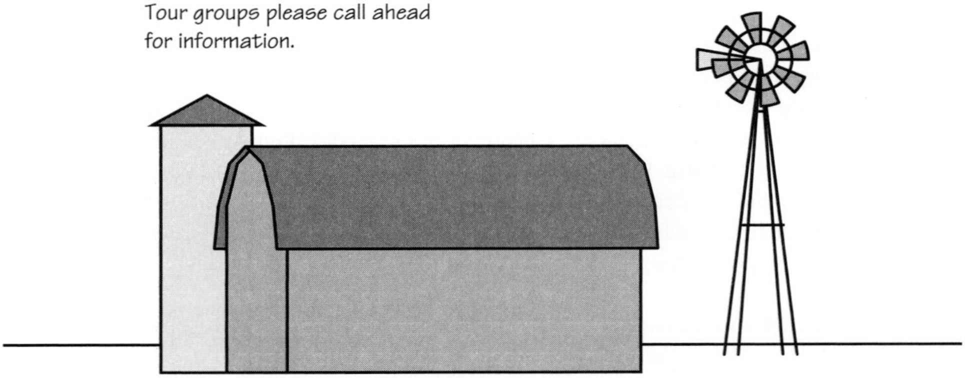

FIGURE 9.14 The written brochure entry that grew out of an oral 3-Minute Ad.

tive processing of those who can successfully construct meaning. In this way, children model for each other how they compose both oral and written text and you model for them, too, as a member of the group.

Create a speaking/writing transfer lesson. Teach this lesson to a group of children. Have a friend observe you and help you evaluate how it went. Could children make the transfer? What could you do differently in another similar lesson?

● ● ● ● ●

STRETCHING EXERCISE

Summary

Both oral and written language develop as children use expressive language. The common elements of purpose, audience, and form must be considered in order for effective expressive communication to occur. Interactions with others and exposure to appropriate models promote the development of talk and writing. Oral and written compositions progress recursively through the aspects of planning, drafting, revising, and final sharing. The Directed Speaking/Writing Activity is a structure for teaching children either spoken or written language forms.

R·····eflections

1. Your third-graders need a model for writing a letter requesting information or a product. Design a bulletin board that includes the elements of purpose, audience, and form and the four aspects of composing. How is an oral request similar to a written letter?

2. Look at your school's curriculum guides for speaking and writing. What similarities or differences do you see in the coverage of composition? How do you explain what you found?

3. Observe a group of children as they engage in a focused discussion in the classroom. Make some guesses about the kind of writer each child might be and look at samples of written work to check your predictions.

Professional Resources

Roser, N. L., & Martinez, M. G. (Eds.) (1995). *Book talk and beyond: Children and teachers respond to literature*. Newark, DE: International Reading Association. This collection of work by teachers and researchers is about classrooms where literature is talked about and what happens as a result of these rich discussions.

Short, K., Harste, J. C., & Burke, C. (1995). *Creating classrooms for authors and inquirers*. Portsmouth, NH: Heinemann. A collection of chapters by these authors and contributing teachers link oral and written language. The book contains classroom-tested ideas for organizing the curriculum around the authoring cycle.

Van Tassel-Baska, J., Johnson, D. T., & Boyce, L. N. (1996). *Developing verbal talent: Ideas and strategies for teachers of elementary and middle school students*. Boston: Allyn and Bacon. In this book, practitioners provide classroom-tested ideas for developing the writing and oral skills of high-ability learners in inclusive classrooms and challenging all readers.

Watson, D. J. (Ed.) (1988). *Ideas and insights: Language arts in the elementary school.* Urbana, IL: National Council of Teachers of English. This book contains over 100 teacher-tested classroom activities based on the link between oral and written language.

References

Bromley, K. (1995). Buddy journals for ESL and Native-English-speaking students. *TESOL Journal, 4* (3), 7–11.

Bromley, K. D. (1989). Buddy journals make the reading-writing connection. *The Reading Teacher, 43,* 122–129.

Calkins, L. M. (1994). *The art of teaching writing.* Portsmouth, NH: Heinemann.

Calkins, L. M., & Harwayne, S., (1991). *Living between the lines.* Portsmouth, NH: Heinemann.

Crowhurst, M. (1979). The writing workshop: An experiement in peer response to writing. *Language Arts, 56* (5), 757–762.

Cunningham, P. M. (1975). Transferring comprehension from listening to reading. *The Reading Teacher, 29* (2), 169–172.

Cunningham, P. M., & Allington, R. L. (1994). *Classrooms that work: They can all read and write.* New York: HarperCollins.

Dyson, A. H. (1981). Oral language: The rooting system for learning to write. *Language Arts, 58* (7), 776–784.

Dyson, A. H., & Genishi, C. (1982). "Whatta ya tryin' to write?" Writing as an interactive process. *Language Arts, 59* (2), 126–132.

Graves, D. (1994). *A fresh look at writing.* Portsmouth, NH: Heinemann.

Graves, D. (1983). *Writing: Teachers and children at work.* Portsmouth, NH: Heinemann.

Halliday, M. A. K. (1985). Spoken and written modes of meaning. In R. Horowitz & S. J. Samuels (Eds.), *Comprehending oral and written language* (pp. 55–82). San Diego: Academic.

Hansen, J., & Graves, D. H. (1983). The author's chair. *Language Arts 60* (2), 176–183.

Hansen, J., Newkirk, T., & Graves, D. M. (Eds.) (1985). *Breaking ground: Teachers relate reading and writing in the elementary school.* Portsmouth, NH: Heinemann.

Harwayne, S. (1992). *Lasting impressions.* Portsmouth, NH: Heinemann.

Hiebert, E. H. (1990). Starting with oral language. *Language Arts, 67,* 502–506.

Hubbard, R. (1985). Write-and-tell. *Language Arts, 62* (6), 624–630.

Kreeft, J. (1984). Dialogue writing: Bridge from talk to essay writing. *Language Arts, 61* (2), 141–150.

Moore, S., & Moore, D. (1991). *Directed writing/speaking activity: Lesson plan format.* Phoenix, AZ: Arizona State University West.

Piaget, J. (1962). *The language and thought of the child.* New York: Humanities Press.

Purcell-Gates, V. (1989). What oral/written language differences can tell us about beginning instruction. *The Reading Teacher, 42,* 290–295.

Short, K. G., Harste, J. C., & Burke, C. (1995). *Creating classrooms for authors and inquirers.* Portsmouth, NH: Heinemann.

Sperling, M. (1996). Revisiting the writing-speaking connection: Challenges for research on writing and writing instruction. *Review of Educational Research, 66* (1), 53–86.

Vygotsky, L. S. (1962). *Thought and language.* Cambridge, MA: MIT Press.

Watson, K., & Young, B. (1986). Discourse for learning in the classroom. *Language Arts, 63* (2), 126–133.

Wolsch, R. A., & Wolsch, L. A. (1982). *From speaking to writing to reading: Relating the arts of communication.* New York: Teachers College Press.

Children's Book References

Paulsen, G. (1993). *Nightjohn.* New York: Delacorte.

Seldon, G. (1960). *The cricket in Times Square.* New York: Farrar.

Teague, M. (1995). *How I spent my summer vacation.* New York: Crown.

Speaking
to Learn

10

W•••••indow on Teaching

Arline Drann, a fifth-grade teacher, talks about *jackdaws*.

> *I first heard of jackdaws in my children's literature class. We were required to read a piece of historical fiction or a biography and create a jackdaw to introduce the book. Then we shared them with the class and everyone tried to guess the title of the book. They were a great way to stimulate interest in a book and bring litera- ture to life. I remember the professor saying, "Jackdaws help bring kids to the historical moment." Because kids often avoid historical fiction, jackdaws can help bring them back to it by making that time period visual and concrete. We had fun*

in that class putting each clue together and trying to guess the identity of the book or person.

What is a *jackdaw?* It is a bird, similar to the grackle, that collects bright objects. A jackdaw for the classroom is a collection of artifacts (made and written) that extend and explore a historical time period within a book. The items, including the table of contents of the book, are put in a container that reflects the historical period and the book.

My jackdaw for that class included several objects in a small wooden picnic basket: a bag of cranberries; a horseshoe; a bag of cornmeal; a hatchet; a diary entry about pioneer life, signed "Sara"; a suede moaccasin; a pair of pantaloons; a bonnet that ties under the chin; a map of Connecticut; and the book's table of contents. They represented The Courage of Sarah Noble *by Alice Dalgliesh (1954), which one person guessed. But that was because I told a little about each object and gave the class enough clues to help them guess it. It turned out that we all really got into the guessing, and the jackdaw artifacts became concrete objects to support our storytelling!*

Arline uses the jackdaw idea with her students for book sharing or reporting. She says,

After I shared my jackdaw with my students as a way of introducing The Courage of Sarah Noble, *they asked if they could each read their own book and make a jackdaw to share with the class. They're a great way to link social studies with the language arts. They help get my kids into reading historical fiction and they make for focused oral presentations that don't ramble. We looked up* artifact *in the dictionary and now the kids know it is "an object made by human work." The process of thinking about the range of artifacts that might fit and then collecting them for the book has resulted in my kids doing independent research and writing, too.*

I require them to include at least one piece of their own writing. One girl wrote a fictitious interview with her main character. One boy created a typical menu from the book's time period. Someone wrote an obituary. Another student wrote a letter to herself from the main character. I encourage students to use their artistic and dramatic talents, too. One boy painted a mural depicting an important scene in his book. A girl whose hobby is dance brought in a cassette of music from the time period and danced for us. Some of the container ideas were authentic, too, such as an old tin lunchbox, a small toy covered wagon, an old suitcase, a cigar box, and a milk pail.

Arline's observations about her students' jackdaw presentations suggest how jackdaws promote speaking. She continues,

When my kids share their jackdaws, it's amazing to see how easily they talk and how focused they are. Having the concrete object to hold as they talk seems to give the shyer ones confidence. Without my telling them, they learned some effective oral presentation techniques, too. From initially sharing objects at random, they learned that order can affect the message. They learned to set the stage first by describing artifacts about the setting and then showing evidence of story conflict or insight into the character, or they learned to begin with a dramatic artifact to get everyone's attention and then unveil the supporting artifacts. The concrete objects were usually so interesting that they helped keep our attention on what the presenter was saying, too.

Arline has questions about jackdaws, however. She asks,

I always wonder: Am I using class time effectively when we do jackdaws? Am I seeing long-lasting benefits in student interest, literacy, oral language, and engagement with books? My students are becoming better storytellers, but does this really make them better presenters?

Her questions are valid to ask about any oral language activity in which the teacher engages students. As you read this chapter, consider possible answers to Arline's questions.

Overview

Speaking is a composing process requiring the speaker to use expressive language to construct meaning. Effective oral language develops with a classroom environment and instruction that encourages opportunities for a variety of purposeful interactions among children. Listening and speaking are interactive processes. Listeners are the audience that helps determine the purpose, content, and form of what speakers say.

Speaking is an expressive language skill in which the speaker uses verbal symbols to construct meaning and to communicate. Speaking allows us to voice and explore our thoughts. It allows us to create ideas and develop new thoughts. Speech progresses from the cooing and babbling of a baby to the relatively sophisticated talk of the typical 6-year-old who knows most of the rules of syntax and has a large speaking vocabulary.

Role of Talk in Learning

About two-thirds of a typical school day is taken up with speech, and teachers produce two-thirds of that speech (Wells & Chang-Wells, 1992). This statistic is troubling, in view of what is known about the role of student talk in learning. However, these figures are changing. As teachers begin to view learning as the construction and coconstruction of meaning, they realize the importance of different types of student talk for different purposes and in different contexts. Wells and Chang-Wells's research (1992) shows, "In sum, it is the talk through which tasks are defined, negotiated and evaluated, and by means of which the students' participation is monitored and assisted, that students and teacher engage in the dialogic co-construction of meaning, which is the essence of education" (p. 33).

The notion that dialogue, or talk, is at the heart of learning is based on a sociocultural perspective. Dewey's (1915) theory that learning results from active exploration and "doing" and Vygotsky's (1978) theory that thought and knowledge emerge from social interaction are central to this constructivist perspective. Loban's (1976) seminal study of K–12 students established the firm relationship between oral language development and success in reading and writing. Writing about Loban's work, Buckley (1992) reiterates, "Oral language is primary, it contains the secrets of verbal thinking, social communication and the intricacies of reading and writing" (p. 625).

Three oral language events, all rooted in a constructivist perspective, are a good place to begin to explore speaking:

▬ In a kindergarten, a small group of children finish a shared retelling of the wordless picture book *Re-zoom* by Istvan Banyai (1995), in which each page "zooms" away from the previous one, creating an increasingly complex story. The children choose partners and a new wordless picture book for which they enthusiastically take turns telling each other the story. They help each other by supplying words and adding overlooked details. Pairs talk quietly together as the teacher listens.

▬ In a third-grade class, the children finish a science unit on the solar system and brainstorm key ideas. The teacher listens and writes their ideas on the chalkboard, often erasing and rewriting what they dictate as they read, discuss, and reword their transcribed statements. Children talk to decide the importance of different things they have learned.

▬ In a fifth-grade class, the children work in groups, using a Venn diagram to focus their discussion on comparing two books, *Everglades* by Jean Craighead George (1995), a story about five children who take a dugout canoe ride through the Everglades and learn about its evolution, and *Lostman's River* by Cynthia DeFelice (1994), a story about a boy and his family who live in a Florida swamp in 1906. The students have read the stories over the past three weeks as part of a study of ecosystems. One student in each group is the discussion leader who directs the talking, and one child is the scribe who writes the group's ideas on the Venn diagram. The room is comfortably noisy, with children talking in controlled voices. The teacher moves among groups and occasionally asks a question or makes a comment.

Second-Language Learners and Language Variation

In each of these situations, children with language variations (e.g., English learners and ESL students) engage in purposeful composing with oral language guided by a teacher who carefully plans and sets the stage but is involved minimally in the interactions. The children who are bilingual or nonstandard speakers of English have opportunities to hear and use English to learn. In two of the classrooms, the use of oral language is naturally interwoven with content learning, and in the kindergarten class, it is a natural way of building the literacy of emergent readers and reinforcing their vocabulary. In two of the classrooms, groups engage in discussions, one specific to a task and one to a topic, and in the third classroom, pairs of children, or dyads, engage in storytelling, a form of creative dramatics. In all these situations, second-language learners and students with diverse language abilities are involved together in listening, reading, speaking, and thinking. They have specific tasks and topics to guide their talking. They talk to:

retell	refine	review	analyze
identify	interpret	enjoy	request
compare	describe	define	predict
paraphrase	inquire	speculate	reflect
entertain	create	remember	contrast
persuade	summarize	specify	explore
elaborate	share	clarify	synthesize
explain	inform	evaluate	justify

Through this kind of purposeful talk, children learn how to use language to compose meaning and gain knowledge appropriate to the content of the activity. So, two kinds of learning occur naturally: one involving language and one involving knowledge. This type of integration provides exciting and interesting ways to make the best use of classroom time.

Does research support a relationship between speaking and learning? Yes. Research shows that children's talk is a significant factor in learning subject content. In fact, engaging in discussion about text results in deeper understanding, higher-level thinking, and improved communication skills (Gambrell, 1997). Small-group discussions allow students more oppportunities to speak, interact, interpret, clarify, and exchange points of view than other types of talk allow. Additionally, students' communication skills improve naturally as they become more experienced in small-group discussions (Almasi, 1995).

Schifini (1997) cautions that for second-language speakers, discussion and problem solving in the native language support cognitive growth and learning new abstract material. However, in situations where there are small numbers of English learners or where many languages are spoken, this may not be possible. Schifini notes, however, that classroom teachers of second-language learners can

- Celebrate approximations and use sensitive strategies for correcting errors while modeling correct responses.
- Encourage students to use English, even if it is nonstandard, by showing them that *what* they say is more important than *how* they say it.
- Integrate language and content instruction, using all the language arts to make language input more understandable.

Second-language speakers have rich native language resources that can help them bridge the language gap. When classroom activities involve real communication that uses language to carry out interesting, relevant tasks, the teacher is supporting English language development.

Austin (1989) also relates how the writing of Brian, a sixth-grader, developed after dialogue with her as his teacher. Both theory and research suggest children learn more when teachers listen more. In fact, Mikkelson (1990) urges teachers of "nonmainstream," low-achieving students who come from differing backgrounds to listen to these students' talk and story making. Engagement in oral meaning making allows these children to grow "more as themselves" and not be transformed into what teachers want them to be.

As well as influencing learning, speaking influences others' perceptions of the speaker. Many important decisions about a person made by friends, colleagues, or prospective employers are made on the basis of spoken language. Speaking is a person's most often used method of communicating with others. Consequently, the way individuals present themselves verbally affects how they are viewed by others.

It is important to remember, though, that oral language is not necessarily equivalent to what a child thinks or knows. One can't infer cognitive development and intellectual ability from speaking, since talk is only one part of a child's total development. The oral language that children compose depends on a number of factors. It depends on what they want to say, how much they want to say, how secure they are with themselves and others, their level of intellectual development, the level of language use they have obtained, how much they trust the teacher, how well they understand what is going on, and how supportive the environment is in which they are speaking. This understanding is especially critical with ESL students or students with speech or dialect differences. The observable aspects of phonology, morphology, semantics, and syntax a child uses when he speaks shouldn't guide the teacher in making decisions about personality, character, or ability.

STRETCHING EXERCISE

Tape record a science or social studies lesson in a classroom and a small group working on a specific task. Notice the amount and type of teacher talk and child talk in both. What are the functions of each kind of talk?

• • • • •

Although people often make fun of those who talk to themselves, Smith (1982) believes inner speech has important implications for the cognitive, emotional, and social growth of children. All the functions of spoken language previously discussed hold true for the kind of talk people do in their own heads. Self-talk helps a person clarify, plan, decide, vent anger or frustration, feel less lonely, relieve stress, and a number of other things. Smith surmises that people probably don't talk to themselves in the same way they speak to others. There is probably wide variation in the amount and type of inner speech that goes on. Steiner's (1985) interviews of highly intelligent and successful people in a variety of fields suggest they use their minds as notebooks where, using inner speech, they think, solve problems, brainstorm, and grapple with ideas. So, recognize the potential functions of self-talk and don't embarrass children when they do talk to themselves.

Effective Speaking

Because children have learned to talk before they come to school and they continue to talk in school does not mean they are necessarily effective speakers. What factors separate talkers from effective speakers? There are several characteristics of effective speaking:

▬ *Fluency.* The ease of speech flow in social situations is one way to measure effective speaking. Children should be able to produce words and phrases easily and smoothly to communicate their ideas or feelings. Firsthand experiences and confidence probably contribute to fluency. Children who stutter (i.e., repeat sounds and syllables) and pause often may be tense and lack confidence.

■ *Clarity.* The accuracy of speech is important. Children should be able to convey ideas that are understandable and properly articulated. Clarity refers to both content (organization and conciseness) and voice (changing rate of delivery, tone, pitch, loudness, stress, juncture, and diction).

■ *Sensitivity.* Effective speaking is tied to the awareness of the audience and situation, and the use of appropriate verbal and nonverbal language. Children should be able to use nonverbal language to enhance their messages and "read" an audience's posture, eye contact, and facial expressions.

How much of a message is communicated by nonverbal means? Good speakers use nonverbal language, or body language, to hold listeners' attention. Eye contact, facial expressions, gestures with hands, and body movement are all aspects of speaking that add action and force to delivery and that can help persuade an audience. Walking, pointing, shrugging, turning, holding up a hand, counting on one's fingers, and pantomiming are examples of body language that many good speakers seem to use naturally. Since nonverbal language can either enhance or contradict a spoken message, we need to help children use and interpret nonverbal language.

Your role as a teacher is to provide a relaxed environment that models, encourages, and supports effective speaking. This is especially true for ESL students, English learners, and students with language delays and difficulties who often struggle to be fluent and clear in their speech. One type of language variation called *code switching,* moving back and forth between one's native language or dialect and standard English, is a positive signal that language learning is occurring, and it should not be discouraged. In your classroom, the meaning and content of a child's spoken message need to be honored by you and a child's peers, above all. Children need to feel unafraid to use both languages until they can use one consistently and accurately, and they need to be able to make mistakes without being ridiculed as they become effective speakers. Think about learning standard English as similar to the crawling a baby does before walking or the uncertainty and shakiness you might experience as you learn to roller skate or ice skate for the first time.

Oral Language Models

Just as with listening, reading, and writing, children learn to speak, in part, by imitating what others say and, of course, through interactions with others. Parents or caregivers, especially those who spend a majority of time with a child, are early models of spoken language for children. As a child's world grows and relationships with others are established both in and out of school, other models become even more critical, however.

Teacher and Peers

As a teacher, you and a child's peers are important models for oral language learning. You have only to listen to a group of children during recess or free time while they are playing school to recognize the importance of the teacher as a model. The pitch, stress, juncture, pronunciation, and vocabulary used by the child playing the teacher are usually surprisingly similar to the teacher's actual voice patterns and word choices. But after peer models are established for children, parent and teacher models often wane in their importance. If you have listened to children's oral language on the playground or when they engage in activities with peers, you have probably heard a different kind of oral language than they might use in more formal situations.

As well as being a model, you are a weaver of classroom talk. You will need to be skilled at keeping your students "engaged in substantive and extended conversation, weaving individual particapants' comments into a larger tapestry of meaning" (Goldenberg, 1993, p. 318). How do you do this? Goldenberg suggests that you keep talk focused, activate students' background knowledge, invite students to elaborate, directly teach a skill or concept, ask students to prove their assertions, pose questions with multiple answers, respond to and connect student contributions, maintain a nonthreatening classsroom atmosphere, and encourage everyone's participation. As you model this type of supportive, knowledge-building talk, your students will also begin to use it.

Speaking Role Models in Literature

Children's literature also provides children with important models for language learning. Books mentioned throughout this chapter that have speaking as a theme or activity in which main characters engage are found in the annotated bibliography called Children's Books about Speaking at the end of the chapter.

In these books, students can identify with and learn from the oral language experiences of fictional contemporaries. For example, in *Grandfather Tang's Story* by Ann Tompert (1990), a Chinese girl and her grandfather use tangram puzzle pieces to tell a story. In *Officer Buckle and Gloria* by Peggy Rathman (Caldecott Medal, 1995), a police officer's speeches are aided by a police dog. You can develop listening skills with the cumulative tale *Oh, What a Noisy Farm!* by Harriet Ziefert (1995).

For older children, Lee Bennett Hopkins's (1981) *Mama and Her Boys* is about a boy who interviews a custodian for his school newspaper and starts a special friendship. Joan Detz's (1986) *You Mean I Have to Stand Up and Say Something?* deals with the fear of speaking to a large group. *The Gift of the Girl Who Couldn't Hear* by Susan Shreve (1993) is about a girl who teaches her deaf friend to sing. In *How to Speak Chimpanzee: The Phrasebook No Human Should Be Without*, Richard Brassey (1995) combines body language, facial expressions, and sounds to help the reader learn to communicate without oral speech but "speak" chimpanzee.

Creating a Classroom Context

Children learn when they talk. They learn about language and its uses and they learn subject matter. So how can you promote talk in your classroom? Two approaches provide children with a talk-rich environment.

An environment that nurtures effective speakers is relaxed and positive. There are no corrections or reprisals for the use of nonstandard English or talk that is ungrammatical. Children must first feel free to speak and confident that they will be accepted without criticism before they use oral language. Since children learn language by using it, they need lots of opportunities that encourage self-expression and that don't restrict their use of language.

The environment that nurtures effective speaking is also an interactive one. Good listening reinforces good speaking when listeners and talkers operate together in a situa-

• • • • •
Children need lots of opportunities that encourage self-expression and that do not restrict their use of language.

tion. As children talk to and with each other and you, listening and speaking are intricately related, like the warp and woof of threads in woven fabric. Both are needed and neither works well without the other.

Oral language interactions occur not just between teacher and child but also, and more often, among children. It is important that you build on these child-to-child language interactions. One way to do this is to work together with children in collaborative efforts that require you to be a team member, as opposed to a team leader. This lets children collaborate, interact, and learn how to be leaders as they learn from each other.

Providing Spoken Language Experiences

A variety of oral language activities help to develop effective speakers. As you read, remember that the place for exciting and meaningful language use is within content studies, such as in science, social studies, math, art, and literature.

Conversation: Talking Informally Together

Peter:	I'm going on a trip this summer to Canada when my mom gets off work.
Susan:	Where are you going?
Peter:	Toronto. It's in Canada, and we're gonna see Niagara Falls on the way.
Susan:	That's where they have Mounties, isn't it?
Peter:	I think so. It's where my grandmother lives. But I never saw any Mounties.
Susan:	My brother's got a Mountie doll. It's a kind of soldier with a red jacket on, and he's riding a horse, and it says "Canada" on it.
Peter:	Are you going on any trips this summer?

Carrying on successful conversations lets children learn to open and close dialogue, keep a listener's attention, and seek clarification from the speaker. Casual conversations like the one between fourth-graders Peter and Susan, which occurred in the cafeteria, are important in helping children learn to use language in these ways and in promoting their social and emotional growth. Chances to talk together like this also help children build friendships.

The ability to talk to another person by responding appropriately, staying on topic, offering personal information, expressing feelings, requesting information, and moving to new subjects, as Peter and Susan demonstrate, are all critical social skills they will use throughout life.

Don't overlook the importance of conversations you have with children, whether a 30-second chat while waiting for the bus, a 2-minute exchange before school, or a 10-minute conversation during lunch. Children reveal much about themselves as they talk, just as adults do—their interests, fears, beliefs, and ways of looking at the world. There is no better way to tell children that you value them and are genuinely interested in them than by making yourself available whenever possible to talk with them. Many teachers find that time before and after school and on the playground is valuable conversation time. It is important, too, to understand that every child's dialect is worthy of respect as a valid system for communication. As a teacher, you need to treat young children as though they are conversationalists, even if they are not yet talking.

Informal conversation is a skill used throughout one's life and it is the basis for more formal speech that children engage in academically in school. As well as encouraging conversation at other times, you may want to provide a special time and place for conversation in your classroom. Some teachers designate a Conversation Corner or a place where children can go in pairs or a small group for the purpose of chatting together. Children can choose their topic, share objects brought from home, or discuss pictures or objects the teacher has put there. Help your class set rules for good conversation and post them as a reminder.

Some teachers also form conversation groups at various times and encourage children to talk together about whatever they choose. In *The Conversation Club* by Diane Stanley (1993), a book for primary-grade children, Peter Fieldmouse learns how important good listening is in a group where everyone talks at once. Conversation etiquette is something that children can imitate. You model courtesy when you introduce a visitor to the class or use words such as, "Excuse me for the interruption . . . ," "Thank you very much for . . . ," or "Would you please . . . ."

Telephoning.   Telephone skills, giving and taking telephone messages, and talking on the telephone are activities young children enjoy. They also need to learn telephone skills for possible emergency situations and as lifetime skills. Many telephone companies loan telephones and supply telephone books, message pads, and other materials for the classroom. Set things up in a Telephone Center so children can talk on the telephones and practice writing messages.

Interviewing.   An *interview* is a conversation with a question and answer format that probes a person about his life or about a topic. Interviews include a person's special knowledge, opinions, experiences, or feelings elicited through a blend of planned and spontaneous questions.

Planning before an actual interview occurs makes a huge difference in what emerges from an interview. You can use a K-W-L chart to help children think about and write down the things they know and want to know about a person they will interview (see Figure 10.1). During an interview, older children can make notes or tape record the conversation for transcription later. Or, younger children can retell their interviews for older children to transcribe.

Have the children conduct interviews with each other, teachers, the principal, or members of the community for the class or school newspaper or in regard to a unit in science or social studies. In *The Kidnapping of Aunt Elizabeth* by Barbara Parte (1985), a girl collects material for a social studies report by interviewing her aunt about her youth. Children can even role-play a favorite author or historical figure in interviews that are tape recorded for others to listen to at a later time.

Mary's third-grade class interviewed residents of a retirement home near their school as part of their study of the local community. Before the interviews, they prepared questions and practiced with each other. After the interviews, they informally reported to the class about what they learned from the interviewed person and then wrote a summary of their interview (see Figure 10.2). A parent typed each interview on a word processor and printed off copies of all the interviews for each child. Children then shared their interviews with the person they had interviewed. There were other visits back and forth between the retirement home and school during the year. Several retirees came to the third grade to help with class projects and to see a class play. The children returned to the retirement home to perform folk dances they learned and to share books they had written. Mary said it was an enjoyable language experience for everyone involved, especially the retirees.

THINGS WE WANT TO KNOW ABOUT <u>HOMER</u>

History	Schools	Natural Resources	Pollution
— What is our population? — Who were the first settlers? — Who named Homer and why? — Who named Clinton Ave.? — When and why did the bike helmet law go into effect?	— Why is our school built on a swamp? — Why is the elementary school built on a Native American graveyard? — What were the first schools like?	— Why is Little York Lake named that name? — Where are the forests and parks? — Where are the good fishing streams? — Is hunting allowed?	— What companies pollute us? — Why do we dump garbage here?

FIGURE 10.1 Elizabeth's students created this K-W-L chart to plan their interviews of village leaders.

Source: Reprinted by permission of Elizabeth Pylypciw, sixth-grade Resource Room teacher.

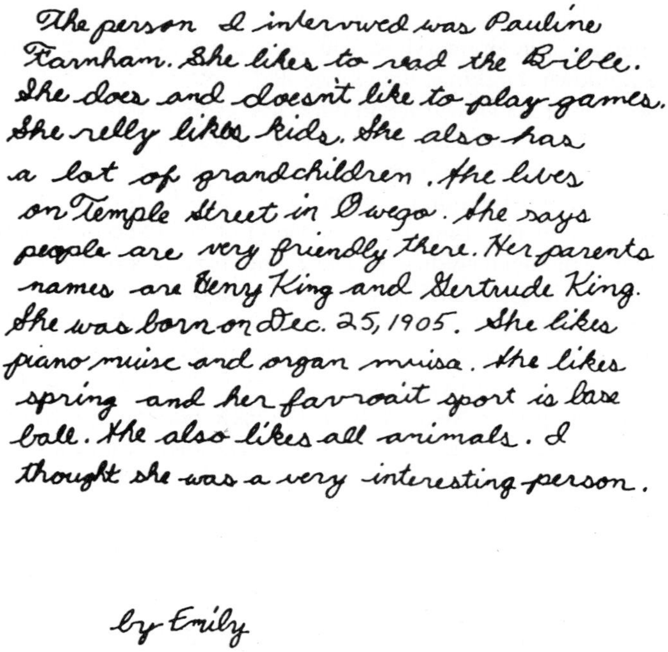

The person I intervwed was Pauline Farnham. She likes to read the Bible. She does and doesn't like to play games. She relly likes kids. She also has a lot of grandchildren. She lives on Temple Street in Owego. She says people are very friendly there. Her parents names are Henry King and Gertrude King. She was born on Dec. 25, 1905. She likes piano muise and organ muisa. She likes spring and her favroait sport is base ball. She also likes all animals. I thought she was a very interesting person.

by Emily

FIGURE 10.2 A third-grader's written report of an interview she conducted with an adult living in a retirement home.

Discussion: Interacting in Cooperative Groups

Discussion is formal conversation that usually centers on a topic and has a purpose. Discussion provides opportunities to hear other children's points of view and to develop new understanding as students talk and listen (Gambrell & Almasi, 1997; Alvermann, Dillon, & O'Brien, 1987). Discussion plays an important role in helping students comprehend what they have read because it results in the sharing of ideas and the coconstruction of new knowledge.

For a good discussion, rules are often necessary so that students will listen, take turns, remain on the topic, be courteous, and use a moderate voice and appropriate vocabulary. Listening to a tape recording of one of their group discussions can help children identify the elements of a good discussion. A fifth-grade class established these criteria:

Listen to each other.
Think before you talk.
Talk in a normal voice.
Stick to the subject.
Be polite.
Take turns.

Use discussion to tap preknowledge before a lesson or to recap and extend the learning that occurred as a result of the lesson. Form discussion groups to plan or talk about such things as a science or social studies project, vacation activities, a classroom or schoolwide problem, an assembly program, or an upcoming classroom activity such as a storytelling festival.

How do you, as a classroom teacher, perhaps with no knowledge of a second language yourself or expertise in second language development, help ESL students learn English? What kinds of instructional conversations help second-language learners learn English? Conversations focused on concepts and content related to curriculum are probably most helpful for elementary-age students acquiring English (Perez, 1996). ESL students need lots of opportunities in group situations to practice taking turns, interrupting, and listening (Ernst, 1994). Discussion activities like the ones mentioned previously that center on academic conversations, rather than conversational drills in which students practice rote responses, foster English language learning. So, even without special training, you can do much to develop your ESL students' spoken language by including them in purposeful discussions with English speakers.

Brainstorming. *Brainstorming* is a way of fostering creativity and obtaining many ideas from a group on a particular topic or problem. You can use brainstorming with a whole class or with small groups. It is based on four simple rules that should be followed for good results:

1. Ideas are not criticized.
2. All ideas are accepted.
3. Emphasis is on quantity.
4. Ideas can be combined.

The overhead projector is a good tool for brainstorming, since you can face the class and write each idea for everyone to see. You can then reproduce the transparency and give it to your students to examine if need be.

Task and Topic Groups. *Cooperative learning* is the instructional use of small heterogeneous groups of students working together to accomplish a common purpose and maximize learning. It requires purposeful talk in the form of discussion as children use language to learn and learn to use language to accomplish a task or discuss a topic.

Kagan's (1994) approach to cooperative learning is based on the use of structures or ways of organizing social interaction in the classroom. A *structure* is a content-free strategy that uses group work. Definitions follow of some popular cooperative learning structures that work well, regardless of the content of the lesson:

▪ *Numbered Heads Together.* In small groups, each student takes a number (e.g., 1–5) and finds answers to questions such as "Why are leaves called the 'food factories' of a plant?" When the teacher calls one of the numbers (e.g., 3), all the 3s give their group's response. This makes everyone responsible for learning the material because numbers are called at random.

▪ *Roundtable.* A small group of students sits in a circle with one piece of paper and one pen or pencil and collaborates to answer a question or solve a problem that has multiple answers, such as "What are the functions of the stem?" Each student makes an oral contribution, which he writes down, and then passes the paper around the table for everyone to add their response.

▪ *Revolving Roundtable.* Each group's solution is passed on to the next roundtable group to read and check or to add an answer. This builds cumulative lists and reinforces understandings.

■ *Simultaneous Roundtable.* Several questions or topics, each on a different piece of paper, circulate around the table (e.g., a roundtable on Food Groups might have four pieces of paper, one for grains and pasta, meat, vegetables and fruit, and dairy products). Each student writes an answer and passes the paper on to the next student, who adds an answer and passes the paper on.

■ *Think-Pair-Share.* Children have a question or task to think about. First, they reflect individually and then they share their ideas with a partner and then the class. Use this at the beginning of a lesson to activate prior knowledge or during a lesson to give students a chance to process information actively (e.g., "Think-Pair-Share your definition of *photosynthesis*").

■ *Think-Pair-Square.* This is Think-Pair-Share, first with a partner but then two partners share with two other partners. This allows for a wider sharing of opinions.

■ *Think-Write-Pair-Share.* Students write their responses to a question or problem and then share them with a partner. This adds writing to the oral language activity.

■ *Inside-Outside Circles.* Students are in two concentric circles with the inside circle facing out and the outside circle facing in. Each student faces another student. The teacher tells them how many people to rotate before they face the person who becomes their partner with whom to do something (e.g., read their haiku poems about the class visit to a wetland, discuss a topic or answer a question, etc.).

■ *Jigsaw.* A task is divided into as many parts as there are groups, and each small group works on a separate part of the problem. There are many forms of Jigsaw that divide the work within a group or among class members. If children are studying a country, for example, it can be divided into geography, industry, transportation, government, and so on, with each serving as a topic for one group. Or perhaps Jigsaw groups can study the Middle Ages with small groups exploring such topics as knights, serfs, royalty, religion, and castles. First, groups work together until they are experts on their topics. Then, one person from each group meets with one person from every other group to form a Jigsaw group in which everyone has unique expertise and teaches it to the new group.

Cooperative learning structures require small groups of two to six students to work together with a purpose, either to accomplish some sort of task or to discuss a topic for a reason. Often, groups have leaders who guide them by keeping the discussion moving and who help the group summarize and evaluate. Many groups also have scribes who take notes or record ideas covered by the group. These small groups form as one-time-only groups or they function for longer, depending on how well they work.

Tasks that groups can discuss include such things as making up directions (to get from one place to another for a game, or how to construct something); comparing main characters in two books (settings, plots, themes, styles, etc.); comparing the handling of a topic by their social studies text and a more current book; generating questions for an interview; planning a field trip; deciding on a moral for a fable or the theme of a book; brainstorming a list; and any number of other goal-related activities. Problems to be solved—for example, planning a field trip or suggesting improvements of a community's waste-management program—make excellent tasks for cooperative groups. Other topics that groups can discuss are readily drawn from units of study in science, social studies, and math.

The discussion web (Alvermann, 1991; Duthie, 1986) is a graphic organizer that students can create during discussion. It helps them consider more than one point of view after reading a text or viewing a video before drawing a conclusion (see Figure 10.3). Any question in the center that has no right or wrong answer and involves multiple viewpoints or opinions works best.

One way to use the discussion web is to have each student first think about the question and then pair with another student to take turns filling the web by listing ideas on both sides of the question. Think-Pair-Share-Square works well to help students refine their thinking and work toward consensus. The four can then decide which ideas best support their conclusion and choose a spokesperson to share with the class. Or students can individually write their answer to the question that includes the reasons from the discussion web they view as most important.

The discussion web prevents a small number of vocal students or the teacher from dominating discussion. All students have the opportunity to contribute opinions. It also allows students to give an opinion in a relatively risk-free environment with a peer first and then in a small group. The discussion web helps develop tolerance for different points of view and can be used before or after reading or before writing. Some teachers have students write their opinions as well or write an essay based on the conclusion and opinions shared in their group.

You can use small groups successfully even with young children if you build in supports. Have group members sit around a table or in a circle, perhaps in a corner or on the carpet, but away from any distractions. A specific visual stimulus, such as a picture or object or the task written on a card or the chalkboard nearby, helps focus children.

Cooperative learning groups are motivating and effective for students who have special needs. For example, Johnson (1988) suggests one way to develop English for ESL learners is to have them teach their peers. When teachers "nudge" children to use language in functional ways such as this, and set up conditions that foster success, then children's oral language grows. Palinscar (1992) has found that students with learning disabilities benefit from reciprocal teaching in which they teach each other metecognitive strategies for improving reading comprehension. Reciprocal teaching was designed with middle-school students in mind, and the research evidence in support of it as a way to improve reading comprehension is positive (Rosenshine, 1994).

Choose an appropriate task or topic for a group of children to discuss, either a subject-related concept or a book they have just read. Talk with them about what makes a good discussion and list some rules together. Guide them in discussion using their rules. What would you do differently next time?

● ● ● ● ●

STRETCHING EXERCISE

Literature Discussion Groups.   One type of cooperative group many teachers use to develop students' comprehension and to stimulate learning is the literature discussion group (Keegan & Shrake, 1991; Leal, 1993). These groups are not necessarily focused on tasks, but are organized to discuss a book, its literary elements, and topics arising from the book. Peterson and Eeds (1990) believe that good children's literature that is read "intensively" naturally produces "grand conversations" among students.

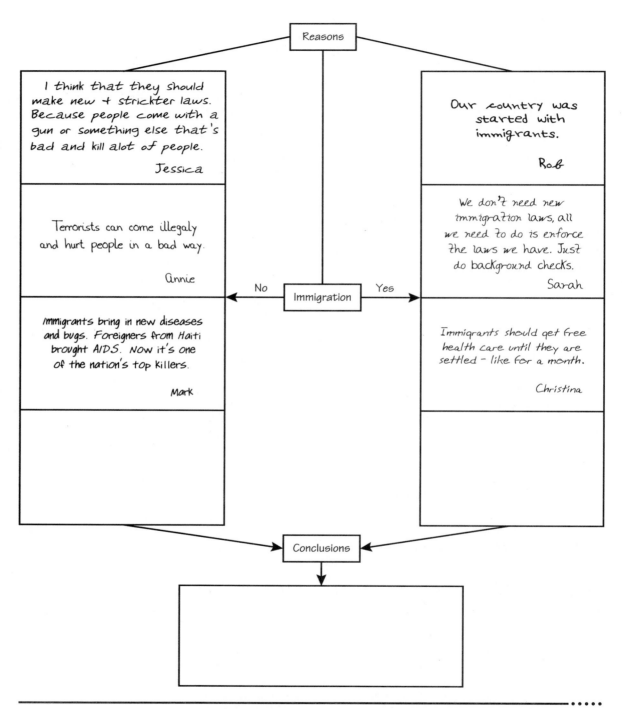

FIGURE 10.3 Fifth-graders debated both sides of the immigration issue and documented their debate on this discussion web.

Jan Minetola's fifth-grade students read *Who Comes with Cannons?* by Patricia Beatty (1992), the story of a Quaker family living in North Carolina during the Civil War. The family does not believe in slavery or the use of arms, and their home is a station on the Underground Railroad. Jan chose this book to initiate literature discussion groups because her students were studying the Civil War, and the story raises many complex issues concerning slavery, war, tolerance, and family loyalties. To encourage intensive, thoughtful reading, Jan had the students keep character journals at different points in the story (Hancock, 1993). Each student became a character, had a conversation with himself or herself, and wrote it in a journal as that character might have said it. Examples of their journal entries follow, with the student's own name in parentheses:

I am so mad today. Truth came to live with us. We're poor as it is, and now she comes! It's one more mouth to feed. She is a kettle-cousin. She should have to lick the pot after we're done eating. Oh, I just hate her so much.

—Robert (Amber)

I was waiting for a long time to hear about my father. Then a letter came to the Bardwell's house, and I knew it wasn't my father's handwriting. I was afraid to open the letter, but I had to know. When I opened it and read it, it said my dad had died. I felt really bad, but I'm going on with my life. I thought I was going to go back to Indiana to live there, but I will be happy to live here now that my father died.

—Truth (Frankie)

I know that slaves are here. Squire did it before. I didn't find him because he is hidden real well. I don't like you, Quakers. You take our good workers. If I catch you with one of our slaves, we will send you to jail.

—Mr. Fields (Chris)

Writing these entries helped the students relate to the characters' feelings and emotions and prompted meaningful talk in their literature discussion groups. Students brought the journals to their discussion group and read their entries orally. The discussions that resulted were substantive because the students were personally involved in the issues related to the story. Jan found that when students directed the discussion to issues they raised themselves, she became a group member rather than a group leader, and the students became leaders.

Barbara Masi, a third-grade teacher also uses literature discussion groups to encourage purposeful talk and promote shared meaning construction. As they read *Stone Fox* by John Gardner (1960), the story of a boy who enters a dogsled race to win money to pay the taxes on his grandfather's farm, Barbara's students responded several times in their journals to the following prompts:

How did the story make you feel?
Did anything in the story remind you of your own life?
I was wondering . . .
Make a prediction about how the conflict will end.
What was your favorite part? Why?

Then the children brought their journals to literature group and the journal entries prompted discussions of the book. An excerpt from Tyler's journal and some of the discussion that followed his oral reading of it show the nature of these third-graders' talk and comprehension:

> Tyler's journal entry: *"I was wondering why grandfather didn't pay the taxes. I wonder why the tax guy had a gun."*

Matthew:	The idea I had was that he was too old to farm the land and grow a crop to sell and so he didn't have enough money.
Jennifer:	But probably he could pay them at first, but then his taxes kept going up and pretty soon he couldn't afford it.
Kaylie:	That's sort of like my grandfather, who says all the retired people are getting a raw deal. They get social security but it doesn't ever go up and everything else keeps going up.
Jennifer:	Yeah. That's like my great aunt who is sort of poor and every month her daughter gives her money.
Matthew:	But let's get back to the gun. I think the tax guy packed a gun because he carried money and he could protect himself in case anyone tried to hold him up.
Tyler:	Yeah! Or maybe everybody carried a gun in the mountains.
Kaylie:	They might have had to protect themselves from bears and snakes and things.
Matthew:	The sheriff probably had a lot of territory to cover and people needed their own protection.
Tyler:	The tax man might have used the gun to get people to pay their taxes—to scare them.
Kaylie:	I bet it scared some of those retired people too and then they paid.

Tyler's "wonderings" in his written journal entry prompted his group to talk together and perhaps arrive at richer understandings of the story than they might have come to individually. Both Kaylie and Jennifer relate personally to the story when they talk about a grandfather and great aunt who suffer economically because of their fixed incomes. Matthew helps Tyler recognize the role firearms can play in intimidation and coercion, while Kaylie's comment reminds them that the historical setting of the story may dictate the carrying of a gun and Matthew exhibits his knowledge of vast expanses of the west.

In their literature discussion group, these students clearly made connections to real life and deepened their understandings of the story together through talk. Barbara believes her students clarify, notice the author at work, make personal connections, and make connections to real life. Figure 10.4 shows a teacher-created form to assess participation of students.

Daniels (1994) believes that *literature circles* support strategic readers and a process approach to reading. He suggests giving each student in a group a different role to help facilitate intensive and thoughtful reading and student-led discussions. The eight roles he proposes appear in Figure 10. 5. With groups of fewer than eight children, some students can take on more than one role (e.g., Connector and Investigator can be assigned together to one student, as can Vocabulary Enricher and Travel Tracer, since their roles are somewhat similar). Or every student might have two roles—Illustrator, since that is one that everyone can probably do easily, and another role. Or everyone might be a Literary Luminary and take on another role, as well. Figure 10. 6 shows how a student feels about literature circles.

Literature circles work equally well with fiction and nonfiction. Daniels (1994) suggests that providing students with role sheets on which they can write their particular assignment are temporary devices until groups are capable of lively, text-centered discussions. Daniels feels they initiate "genuine, kid-led, self-sustaining discussion" (p. 75), and the many examples he includes of teachers who use literature circles give evidence of this.

FIGURE 10.4 Lisa Rieger created this assessment tool to record her fourth-graders' participation in literature discussion groups.

Literature Group Checklist/Assessment

Date: _____

Name	Prepared	Participation	Oral Reading	Comments

Source: Reprinted by permission of Lisa Rieger.

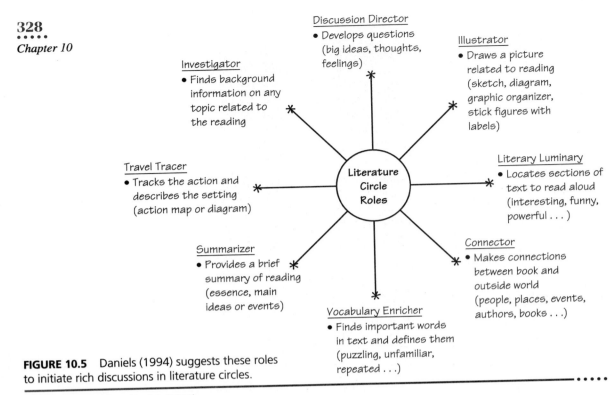

FIGURE 10.5 Daniels (1994) suggests these roles to initiate rich discussions in literature circles.

Source: Adapted from Daniels (1994).

I thought that the group was really neat because we got to be the teachers. And also we got to be in charge. The jobs were neat my favorite job was the discussion director. I liked how we made folders and how we kept track of things by writing down things in the folder. I also liked the notepad we could write things on them and then stick them in the books. The group made a very successfull ending by doing the play for the book. I enjoyed being in the group.

Allyson

FIGURE 10.6 Allyson, a fourth-grader, explains why she enjoys literature circles.

• • • • •
*A panel discussion makes an
excellent concluding activity
for a unit.*

Panel Discussions. *Panel discussions* are more formal than task and topic groups and require an audience. Each member becomes an authority on a subject or part of a topic. When the global topic is discussed, each child makes a contribution. The audience asks questions and participates at the conclusion of the presentation.

This form of discussion is more appropriate for older students because it calls for self-direction. A panel discussion makes an excellent concluding activity for a unit of study within a particular subject. You can invite other classes and parents to participate, but give the children who will be on the panel a chance to practice before they discuss their topic in front of an audience.

Debates. *Debates* are formal discussions of a topic, question, or issue with opposing sides of an argument presented. Two children or two teams of children usually prepare their reasons or arguments and then take turns presenting them to an audience. The discussion web (discussed previously) is a format your students can use to prepare for a debate. In formal debates, there is a moderator who introduces and concludes the debate. The audience judges and decides on the winning team. For children in the upper-elementary grades, this format is challenging and fun for the entire class, who must also know the topic being debated to be able to accurately judge the debaters. Debates provide impetus for children to do library research and thoroughly investigate a topic.

Reports: Presenting to a Group

An *oral report* is a formal sharing or presentation of information to a group. Reporting begins informally in kindergarten and the early elementary grades as children first talk in front of a group, and extends to the upper grades when they present results of their research and study. Some special types of reports follow.

Share and Tell. Share and Tell is a voluntary reporting that many teachers of young children consider a critical part of each day because it fosters self-expression. Some teachers find that sharing an important event with the class (excluding toys and clothing as topics) broadens the range of content. Share and Tell gives each child time in which he is the center of attention. You can occasionally have children in groups of four share together to practice speaking to a smaller audience and use less class time.

Newstime. Newstime is also a voluntary sharing activity teachers use to encourage more general, less personal, speaking opportunities. In many middle- and upper-grade classrooms, teachers begin the year by including children's reports of local events and community news as well as their own personal news. They share national and world news, along with personal news, later in the year. Even though this reporting is not on a personal topic, it should still be relevant to the students. Children can put their initials on the chalkboard if they have news to share.

Roth (1986) supports this practical use of language in the classroom when the focus of Share and Tell or Newstime is on the speaker, the content of what is said, and whether the children are saying and hearing the message. She feels that this opportunity for the practical use of language should have a planned place in each day's agenda, with enough time for every child who wants to participate to do so.

Announcements. Announcements require clear and concise use of oral language, and don't usually depend on audience feedback. Children of all ages can make announcements that ask Who? What? When? Where? Why? and If? Children learn the importance of brevity and clarity and develop confidence in themselves when they make announcements to the class about such real events as an upcoming television show related to a unit of study, lost or found items, scout or club meetings, and community events.

To promote natural language learning, it is important that students make real announcements of actual events. Deb Pease's fifth-grade class took responsibility for their school's daily announcements that were videotaped and viewed by students on the TV monitor in each classroom. A microphone and tape recorder or a TV set made from a cardboard box are props that can also make announcing more realistic and fun. Children can share current events and news effectively with these props.

Formal Reports. *Formal reports* are organized accounts by an individual to a group and are usually the result of research and study. A good report requires the child to ask himself some questions: What is my purpose? Who is the audience? How long should it be? Do content and form of delivery fit the audience? To give a good report, children must select and organize information as they use the appropriate reading and study strategies of researching, notetaking, outlining, organizing, and summarizing. The ability to give a report is an important life skill.

Especially helpful for second-language learners, ESL students, and students with language difficulties, appropriate visuals can highlight and reinforce the content of their reports. When children give reports, note cards or visual aids (see Figure 10.7) help avoid memorizing and make delivery more natural. Creating a drawing, chart, graphic organizer, web, or map, or using photos, artifacts, or the overhead projector help clarify what the speaker has to say and gives him the added support of a visual aid. Including a prop or something that illustrates content builds confidence in an uncertain speaker and adds audience interest.

Help the children select topics that pertain to research and study in which they are genuinely interested. Interest and enthusiasm for a topic build confidence and make de-

> ① What is a rocket?
>
> Purpose — launch satellites, interplanetary probes, and manned spaceflights
>
> ② Who Invented the Rocket?
>
> Sir William Congreve — advanced gunpowder rockets
>
> Tsiolkovsky — improved liquid fuel

> Rocket facts
>
> Names, stages, heights, take off thrust, payload. Refer to chart
>
> Conclusions
>
> Rockets are important, teach us solar system, possibilities could be done, it could help build space station
>
> Picture refer to Outline

> Goddard — Invented liquid & solid prop rockets. Missed discovery of hypergolic fuels
>
> Parts
>
> ① fell — nose cone must be aerodynamic 3 types, friction burns rocket if not. stabilizer keep rocket from spinning
>
> ② fuel — refer to chart

> There is a rocket I made, that has stages (Saturn V)
>
> Pass graph around

FIGURE 10.7 Note cards for a report presented by a fifth-grader show how he planned and organized before speaking.

livery easier, and the end result is more effective. Then, help the children establish criteria for giving a good report, which they can review before and after giving it. The criteria should focus on content and meaning first. Have the children practice their reports beforehand.

You and your students can use the PQS (Praise, Question, Suggest) format introduced in Chapter 9 to give the reporter feedback. This format focuses on the positive aspects. When you share your own feedback first, children will take your lead. The positive remarks you make will set the tone for their comments. This supportive environment is critical for building the confidence of a shy or uncertain child.

Creative Dramatics: Role-Playing through Drama

Creative drama is the representation of feelings and actions in situations, scenes, or plays. It may or may not include an audience. Creative drama has many forms, including both informal, spontaneous drama and formal, scripted drama. Sometimes speech is improvised and sometimes writing is read interpretively.

Drama evokes higher-order thinking, problem solving, feelings, and language as students demonstrate their knowledge orally (Heller, 1996). Studies of the effects of creative dramatics on elementary children's skills in reading, writing, and oral communication show a moderate positive effect on achievement in all areas (Kardash & Wright, 1987). Research shows that kindergartners' dramatic play and written fluency have a high correlation, and fourth- and eighth-graders who engage in role-playing write significantly better persuasive letters than after a lecture or no instruction at all (Wagner, 1988).

Language performs a dual function in drama (Verriour, 1986). It accompanies the acting and is used to discuss, plan, implement, and evaluate the drama. Drama involves the improvisation or creation of language, which is basic to language development. It allows for many different levels or styles of language use and exploration by children. Dramatic story reenactments build kindergartners' sense of story and literacy (Martinez, 1993). Drama reinforces and builds reading and writing skills and is particularly useful with remedial readers (Hoyt, 1992). When children transform a story into a play, they use reading and writing as well as oral language (Bromley, 1995) (see Figure 10.8). Descriptions of some special types of creative drama follow.

Pantomime.   Pantomime uses gestures and actions without words to communicate meaning. Although it does not use oral language during the enactment, pantomime or mime does require purposeful talk about the task and/or topic to plan and carry out the drama. Mime builds awareness of the importance of nonverbal language and facial expressions to communicate feelings and thoughts. Children see how gestures and the face can reflect meaning.

A good way to introduce pantomime to young children is to have them imagine and act out situations in which they walk together in a circle and pretend they are

---

FIGURE 10.8   A story can easily become a play.

Eight Steps for Turning a Story into a Play

1. *Choose a story with many characters, lots of action, and much dialogue.* You can include more characters if necessary (e.g., five trees rather than one), but every student should have at least two or three lines of dialogue.
2. *Read the story several times until everyone is familiar with it.* You can even analyze characters and role-play so everyone understands the story.
3. *Write down the dialogue.* If you divide the story into sections, jigsaw groups or individuals can transcribe different parts of the story and the job is easier.
4. *List or make a sequence web of the main events of the story.* Each event can become a scene in the show or events can be combined into acts.
5. *Try it and edit.* Aim for a 15- to 30-minute play, depending on the age of your students. Omit scenes or events that are redundant and action or dialogue that is not important.
6. *Cast the show.* Ask for volunteers and have students try out by reading parts. You and a committee of students can make decisions. Don't forget to cast a narrator, who will provide transitions.
7. *Rehearse the play.* Practice so students learn to speak loudly and clearly as they face the audience.
8. *Keep props and costumes simple.* Your students and art teacher will have creative ideas for costumes and props that are not elaborate. The suggestion of a character's physical attributes using color, or a special hat, or object to carry will often suffice.

• • • • •

Snowflakes swirling to the ground
Leaves dancing in the wind
Walking barefoot in squishy mud
Frogs jumping from toadstool to toadstool
Hungry foxes following field mice
Trying to walk through a thickly cobwebbed cave

Once children feel comfortable and uninhibited in using their bodies to act out scenes, small groups can explore simple characterizations and role-play various everyday situations such as

Eating an ice-cream cone on a hot day
Watching a favorite team win or lose
Seeing lightning strike an old barn and set it on fire
Threading a needle and sewing a button
Setting the table
Opening and closing an umbrella

Children enjoy making up their own situations and pantomiming them for others to guess. One fifth-grade class identified all the activities related to an early American household they had studied. They then held a Colonial Mime Fest in which they acted out—individually, in pairs, or in small groups—life in colonial America, pantomiming everyday tasks such as making candles or shoeing a horse. Using slow motion to mime each action in a series of acts in a careful and exaggerated way helped these children be effective mime artists. They asked their fourth-grade audience to guess each mime from a list they provided at the Fest.

From individual action mimes, children can begin to pantomime stories. Without props or words, children can establish roles, discuss and plan actions, carry out mimes, change roles, and revise actions to do mimes in different ways.

Use some of the ideas just explored or think of your own and try pantomime with a group of children. Be sure to participate with them. When they are comfortable, have them work in pairs to pantomime activities two people might do together (e.g., eat a spaghetti dinner, ride a tandem bicycle, lift a heavy box from the floor to a table, etc.).

STRETCHING EXERCISE

● ● ● ● ●

Charades.   Charades is a game where the audience guesses the title, quotation, or name that an actor dramatizes. Charades promotes precision in communication by requiring the actor to use appropriate movements and gestures and asking the audience to suggest words until the actor lets them know, through body language, that they have found the right word. Titles of children's favorite books, television shows, movies, songs, and names of famous people and favorite authors are possible topics for charades. The following suggestions will help you use charades successfully:

- Divide the students into small groups. Have them take turns acting out a message for their group, or the group can act out a message for the rest of the class to guess.
- Establish common signals to indicate what is being acted out (e.g., designate a certain signal for a book title, a TV show, a famous person, etc.).
- Show the number of words by holding up that many fingers and show the number of syllables in a word by placing that many fingers against the inner arm.
- The student or group to perform next is the one who guesses correctly.

Improvisation. Improvisation is drama with dialogue but without a script. For younger children, material can come from a folktale or other story that children know or have just heard. For older students, situations from content—such as Henry Ford's invention of the first car, the discovery of gold at Sutter's Mine in California, or the first artificial heart implantation—as well as stories with several characters, are appropriate material. Stories are best rehearsed and acted out several times until participants are satisfied with the entire drama and the enactment itself holds together. When the improvisation is ready, children often enjoy performing for an audience.

Children get to know a piece of literature or situation more intimately through improvisation than they might normally know it. They can understand and appreciate the characters better. Their comprehension of what took place and the feelings the story evokes are also heightened. Fennessey (1995) describes a full-length play on the life of Langston Hughes, created by fifth-graders, that focused on history and grew out of several improvised scenes and included poetry, storytelling, music, dance, costumes, and a minimum of scenery. Even simple role-playing in sixth grade (Bigelow, 1989) after reading from the letters and log entries of Columbus helps students write more effectively as they put themselves in a different place and time and relive history to gain a new feeling and understanding for the past. A play planned and performed by fourth-grade students based on *The Day They Parachuted Cats on Borneo: A Drama of Ecology* by Charlotte Pomerantz (1971) helped solidify their understanding of the food chain and ecology. The book is based on an actual happening reported in the *New York Times* (November 13, 1969), when the rat population was overtaking the island and a natural predator, rather than DDT, was introduced to destroy them.

Improvisation stimulates students' use of purposeful and natural language. Deciding on characters, planning the action, improvising dialogue, trying out what they have planned, and revising or changing ideas are all language activities that have a clear purpose. Students can stick closely to the original work or they can enlarge the part of one character, add characters, or omit certain parts from the drama. In this way, they naturally create language. Dialogue is ad-libbed, not memorized, and does not need to be said in exactly the same way each time the drama unfolds.

Successful improvisations lead children to perform more formal plays in which they deliver lines they have learned, wear costumes, make or collect props, and generally take part in all the other tasks that are part of a formal dramatic production. Rather than expecting children in elementary grades to memorize parts, improvised dialogue is not stilted nor is it forgotten at the first sight of an audience.

Children can easily identify with the main characters in the following books about the pitfalls and satisfactions of dramatic performances. Sara, a fourth-grader in *Stage Fright*, written by Ann Martin (1984), learns that her shyness and fear of the stage can sometimes be healthy. In Joanne Oppenheim's (1984) *Mrs. Peloki's Class Play*, a second-grade class has a disastrous dress play rehearsal but a successful performance. *Arthur's Thanksgiving Play* by Marc Brown (1983) relates Arthur's difficult role as director of a play in which no one wants to be the turkey. He finally solves his problem.

Readers Theater. "Readers theater is a presentation of text that is expressively and dramatically read aloud by two or more readers" (Young & Vardell, 1993, p. 398). It lets the audience create its own images through the performance of the readers. All genres of literature can be used effectively—from history, biography, realistic fiction, and poetry to letters or documentary materials. Readers theater is a way of enjoying literature while developing clear and expressive oral reading.

Readers theater avoids the burden of acting out a play in which children memorize parts and are anxious about costumes, props, and remembering lines. Although usually used by middle- and upper-grade students, readers theater can be used as early as second grade, as long as children can read the literature or script. Even second-graders can write and present their own readers theater (Forsythe, 1995). As well, there are numerous benefits for at-risk readers who can become experts in interpretation, direction, set design, and costuming (Wolf, 1993).

Performers create images of characters, actions, and feelings with their voices, facial expressions, and gestures. They learn how to use their voices—change rate of delivery, pitch, tone, and loudness to transmit meaning—and how to use nonverbal language and gestures to enhance meaning. Performances are given with (or without) a narrator, who supplies the setting and action. Costumes and settings can be suggested but are not required and do not need to be complete. Platforms, stools, chairs, ladders, benches, and readers can hold the scripts or books from which the children read. The objective of readers theater is the sharing and enjoyment of literature.

Students can prepare their own script from a text for readers theater by (1) reading the story; (2) transforming the story into a script (through retelling, listing characters, discussing the role of the narrator, changing narrative into dialogue or vice-versa, and dictating and transcribing the script); (3) practicing the script; and (4) performing the script for an audience.

• • • • •
Improvisation stimulates students to use language in purposeful and natural ways as they dramatize a scene, situation, or story.

You can use almost any piece of literature for readers theater, but keep two things in mind. First, students should be able to read the material independently, without help on unknown words. Second, the material should offer action, excitement, and the potential for dramatic interpretation. The more characters there are, the more parts there are to be played by students. Teachers of older students use radio and television scripts they obtain by writing to television shows. In addition, Readers Theater Script Service, established by the Institute for Readers Theater (P.O. Box 178333, San Diego CA 92177) is a good source. Step-by-step instructions accompany packets for such stories as "The Tale of Peter Rabbit," "The Emperor's New Clothes," and "The Pancake and the Poor Old Lady" for early elementary grades and "Uncle Remus Tales," "The Ballad of the Oysterman," and "A Gift for Mr. Lincoln," among many others, for upper-elementary grades.

Choral Speaking.   Choral speaking is the oral reading of poetry or rhymed prose by several voices together. The entire class can present material together or the class may be divided in half, with halves responding to each other. There may be solos, duets, quartets, or other types of groupings that seem appropriate. The four types of choral speaking are:

1. *Refrain.* The leader speaks most of the lines while the group repeats the refrain.
2. *Line-a-child or line-a-group.* A child or small group speaks a line or couplet, then another individual or small group speaks a line or couplet, and so on.
3. *Antiphonal.* Two or more groups of speakers alternate. Sometimes male and females read together or voices are grouped according to pitch. Groups alternate or are combined for effect.
4. *Unison.* An entire group speaks lines together.

McCaslin (1990) lists several advantages of choral speaking. It can be successful regardless of space or class size. It improves speech, requires cooperation, and works with any age level. As well, it teaches children to recognize and use intonation, stress, and duration and it focuses on reading with expression, thus contributing to oral reading fluency.

Any or all of the four types of choral speaking can be incorporated into an improvisational drama. For example, one third-grade class enacting parts of *Ramona Quimby, Age 8* by Beverly Cleary (1981) decided to add poems about school, teachers, and homework. A different group of three children spoke each poem at various points during the improvisation.

Movies, Films, and Television Shows.   Movies, films, and television shows are forms of creative drama that include video and audio. Video improves children's visual and verbal skills and encourages self-awareness, spontaneity, and creativity. The making of a movie, film, or show is a great motivator for children to take part in creative dramatics and oral language activities in general. Using a video camera, you or a parent can record an interview, report, pantomime, or charades; film a TV show, a current events special, a panel discussion, or a report; or make a movie of an improvisational play such as the one performed by the third-grade class mentioned earlier. Videos are a sure way to stimulate interest, reinforce concepts, and foster oral language growth. Student-created video projects don't have to be expensive ventures (Valmont, 1995). Many schools or school districts have video equipment that you can borrow.

Videotaping an oral language experience has several benefits. Video cameras give children opportunities to see themselves on a television screen and see and hear how they sound. When practice sessions or rehearsals are recorded, children can study their performances, evaluate themselves, and make changes in content or style of delivery. Kim videotaped the dramatization a group of her fourth-graders created in science to show pollination and fertilization. Although the students had practiced before the video-taping, it did not go as smoothly as they had hoped and they wanted to repeat the drama-tization. Caught on the video, which was never turned off between dramatizations, one boy observed that the first taping was "sort of like a rough draft in writing." Clearly, he had made the connection between speaking and writing.

Videotaping an oral language event and showing it to parents as part of a parents' night program is an enjoyable way for them to learn more about their children. The tape can also be borrowed by children and taken home, so parents and siblings can view the activity, too.

Puppets.   Puppets can help dramatize scenes, situations, or stories. Their use with ele-mentary-age children to develop effective oral language has long been recognized. When children use puppets, they tend to imitate the standard English that the puppet would use, thus improving their own speech. As with many of the other oral language experiences discussed here, puppets yield opportunities for informal and formal lan-guage use when children plan, discuss, and perform their show. Puppets are discussed in Chapter 5, where several suggestions are made for their use as aids in improvisation and storytelling.

Storytelling: Relating Stories to Others

Storytelling is the oral account of a happening. It occurs naturally and informally at the dinner table when a child tells about his class trip to a sugaring house, or a mother tells about a traffic accident she witnessed on her way home from work, or a grandmother talks about an incident from her childhood, or a father is reminded of a long ago camp-ing trip and tells about his unexpected encounter with a bear. In recounting everyday events, recalling past events, and creating fictional events that people share orally, they take part daily in storytelling.

Barton and Booth (1990) explore the power of stories and storying in the class-room, reminding readers how important listening and responding are to storytelling. Most everyone has heard an excellent and spellbinding storyteller at one time or another and probably felt a bit intimidated while wishing for those skills. If you can think of sto-rytelling as a natural way of communicating with others, as in a comfortable dinner table conversation, you can realize that it is a tool everyone uses easily everyday.

From kindergarten through elementary school and beyond, children develop their own personal, expressive language when they tell a story. Telling stories stimulates the imagination, inspires creativity, and helps develop a sense of humor. It gives children an opportunity to improvise and compose with language both informally and formally. Sto-rytelling develops vocabulary, heightens comprehension, and fosters social and emo-tional growth.

In several books, main characters take part in pleasurable storytelling. *Four on the Shore and Three by the Sea* by Edward Marshall (1985) is an example for younger stu-dents of the satisfactions of storytelling. In *Knots on a Counting Rope* by Bill Martin and John Archambault (1990), a blind Native American boy listens to his grandfather tell the story of his birth and life.

Chapter 5 includes some suggestions for developing storytelling and retelling. Additional ideas are given here.

■ *Personal experiences.* Personal experiences are the best place to start teaching children about storytelling. Everyone usually has a contribution to make. *Tell Me Again about the Night I Was Born* by Jamie Lee Curtis (1996), in which a girl recounts the comforting tale about the time she was born, invites family tales. Children can relate short accounts of things that have happened to them, such as the funniest thing, the most embarrassing thing, the thing that made them happiest, saddest, wisest, and so on. When children realize that they each have something to share and that it is easy to tell a story, they willingly take part in storytelling.

■ *Wordless picture books.* Wordless picture books are perfect for launching children into storytelling and writing. The children merely need to recount what they see in the pictures. It is interesting to watch the development of a story when a group of children take turns telling it together several times. A group of second-grade students tape-recorded their retelling of *The Ring* by Lisa Maizlish (1996), about a boy who floats over New York City and has an amazing adventure when he puts on a magic ring he finds in the park. They listened to their retelling and then each wrote his own version of what might happen if he put the ring on his finger.

■ *Plot completion.* Plot completion is another way to foster storytelling. Read or tell a story almost to the end, leaving the conclusion for children to tell themselves. Perhaps in pairs or small groups, children can decide on and relate the conclusion. True stories, with several possible endings, that challenge students to think of options work well to inspire storytelling (e.g., *The Blizzard (Survive!)* by Jim O'Connor [1994] and *The Hurricane (Survive!)* by J. B Watson [1994]).

■ *Chain stories.* A chain story begins when someone starts a story by perhaps introducing setting or characters, and then each person (sometimes including the teacher) takes a turn adding to it. Many story starters, such as the ones listed here can be adapted to any age and ability level:

—Every night at midnight, strange music is heard in the park.
—Third-graders find their pencils missing and replaced with spaghetti.
—A big black rabbit knocks on Mrs. Joslin's back door every night at five o'clock.
—The dragon and the knight had a problem.
—Justin awoke far away from his own home. He was on an unknown planet in a distant time in the future.

Don't overlook the possibility of relating chain stories to content learning. Chain stories about fictional characters living in places the children are studying about in social studies give the children opportunities to tell stories using facts and information they have learned.

■ *Dial-a-story.* Dial-a-story is a way of recording a number of children's stories and making them available for everyone to listen to. When children learn to tell stories and are comfortable with this type of oral language experience, this activity can promote both good storytelling and good listening. A commercially purchased telephone answering service can be set up so that each child's story is recorded to play back when a certain telephone number is dialed. A telephone book arranged by storytellers or story titles

and corresponding numbers can be compiled and the book and telephone located in a
listening center or conversation corner. The dial-a-story anthologies can be borrowed for
use in another classroom or two teachers can swap dial-a-story anthologies.

339
•••••
Speaking

Dial-a-story has possibilities for promoting other oral language experiences. Identify
a group of children and think of three other ways you could use this idea to develop
their speaking skills. Share your ideas with a peer.

• • • • •

**STRETCHING
EXERCISE**

Puppets and other props can enhance storytelling. These aids not only provide you
with support as you tell stories to children but they can also help children feel comfortable and make the stories they tell more vivid and exciting. Effective storytellers often
use puppets, props, and other objects to add interest and to focus attention—all of which
reinforce their oral language.

Evaluating Speaking

If you were the teacher in the classrooms where the three different oral language experiences described at the beginning of this chapter took place, how would you evaluate
your students' language competence? When assessing spoken language skills, you need
to ask and answer several questions:

> What objectives or goals have I set for these children?
> What means of assessing match these goals?
> What do I want to know about children's progress?
> How often do I want to measure growth?

Informal assessment scales created together by the teacher and the children, and
used by both consistently throughout the school year, probably have the best potential
for effective evaluation. Children grow in their language competence when they are involved in determining objectives, know what is expected of them, and become active in
monitoring their own behavior and progress.

Scales or checklists like those shown in Figures 10.9, 10.10, and 10.11 can be
adapted to fit your objectives. Figures 10.9 and 10.10 are self-evaluation tools that students can use; Figure 10.11 is a rating scale for the teacher to use.

When using the rating scale, keep in mind that the evaluation of children's informal (spontaneous) and formal (prepared) language should include vocal, verbal, and
nonverbal language factors. If you recall the characteristics of effective speaking discussed at the beginning of this chapter, you will remember that they encompass vocal,
verbal, and nonverbal factors. *Fluency* refers to proper word choice and smoothness of
delivery. *Clarity* refers to the ease with which spoken language can be understood. Both
the *vocal* factors of rate, tone, pitch, loudness, stress, juncture, diction, and so on, as
well as the *content* factors related to meaning, such as organization and conciseness, determine clarity. *Sensitivity* refers to the awareness and use of appropriate verbal and nonverbal language to enhance a message's meaning.

FIGURE 10.9 Help children become actively involved in improving their oral language with checklists such as this.

My Speaking Checklist

	Sept.	Dec.	Mar.	June

When I speak in a group:
- I stick to the subject.
- I speak clearly.
- I take turns and wait for my turn to talk.
- I talk so others in the group can hear me.
- I speak smoothly.
- I use courteous language.

When I speak to a group:
- I stay on the subject.
- My talk is organized and interesting.
- I speak clearly.
- I talk so everyone can hear me.
- I speak smoothly.
- I use courteous language.
- I answer questions about my talk.

A = Always, S = Sometimes, N = Never

•••••

FIGURE 10.10 Students can use checklists such as this to self-evaluate their group participation.

Group Work Checklist

Name: _____

Group: _____ Date: _____

	Yes	?	No
We had a clear goal(s).			
We made progress toward our goal(s).			
We accomplished our goal(s).			
We stayed on task.			
We took turns talking.			
We listened to each other.			
Everyone contributed.			
We respected each other's opinions.			
We asked questions.			
We helped each other.			
We negotiated solutions.			
We gave each other positive feedback.			

•••••

FIGURE 10.11 Adapt this checklist to meet your students' needs.

341
·····
Speaking

Rating Scale: Oral Language Experiences

Experiences	Fluency	Clarity	Sensitivity
Conversation			
Telephoning			
Interviewing			
Discussion			
Brainstorming			
Large Group			
Small Group			
Panel			
Debate			
Reports			
Share and Tell			
Newstime			
Announcements			
Formal Reports			
Creative Dramatics			
Pantomime			
Charades			
Improvisation			
Readers Theater			
Choral Speaking			
Shows			
Puppets			
Storytelling			
Personal Experiences			
Books			
Plot Completion			
Chain Stories			
Other			

(*Excellent, + Acceptable, – Needs Improvement)

Assessment by both you and your students that takes place in natural situations where students produce purposeful language yields the most useful information about students' oral language progress. Sampling students' talk often, in a variety of situations and for a variety of purposes, provides a realistic assessment of speaking.

Summary

To be effective speakers, children need structured and unstructured opportunities to talk purposefully in real situations. Children gain knowledge through talk and they use language to construct meaning. Interactions and collaboration with peers promote fluency, clarity, and sensitivity. Meaningful experiences with conversation, discussion, reports, creative dramatics, and storytelling promote natural oral language in informal and formal situations and help promote verbal and nonverbal language that is important throughout children's lives.

R•••••eflections

1. Watch a television news show and a popular "sitcom" and identify an effective speaker in each show. Discuss with a group of students the characteristics that make the individuals good oral language models.

2. Prepare a letter to parents, identifying the goals of your classroom speaking program and providing ideas for things they can do at home to strengthen their child's spoken language.

3. Interview a speech teacher. Explore a definition of *speech problem,* discuss the students he or she sees daily, and talk about how he or she works with these students and the teacher's philosophy of teaching language. Decide what you and your children might do in the classroom to help a child who stutters.

Professional Resources

Bauer, C. F. (1993). *New handbook for storytellers.* Chicago: American Library Association. This book is full of ideas about how to stimulate storytelling with technology, puppets, storyboards and story aprons, magic, music, dramatics, jokes and riddles, television, and radio.

Cecil, N. L., & Lauritzen, P. (1994). *Literacy and the arts for the integrated classroom.* New York: Longman. This book promotes an innovative, integrated program of drama, song, dance, photography, art, and poetry to promote children's literacy development.

Gambrell, L. B., & Alamasi, J. F. (Eds.) (1996). *Lively discussions! Fostering engaged reading.* Each chapter by a well-known educator emphasizes why classroom discussion is important and offers

"how-to" advice with examples for adapting strategies to diverse classrooms.

Pierce, K. M. (Ed.) (1993). *Cycles of meaning: Exploring the potential of talk in learning communities.* Portsmouth, NH: Heinemann. Contributors examine talk in classrooms as it enables students to create new meanings and sustain learning communities in classrooms that use literature.

Roser, N. L., & Martinez, M. G. (Eds.) (1995). *Booktalk and beyond: Children and teachers respond to literature.* Newark, DE: International Reading Association. These practical essays focus on classroom talk about book-related topics in literature discussion groups, book clubs, literature circles, and other strategies currently used in classrooms.

References

Almasi, J. F. (1995). The nature of fourth graders' sociocognitive conflicts in peer-led and teacher-led discussions of literature. *Reading Research Quarterly, 30*, 314–351.

Alvermann, D. E. (1991). The discussion web: A graphic aid for learning across the curriculum. *The Reading Teacher, 45* (2), 92–99.

Alvermann, D. E., Dillon, D. R., & O'Brien, D. G. (1987). *Using discussion to promote reading comprehension.* Newark, DE: International Reading Association.

Austin, P. (1989). Brian's story: Implications for learning through dialogue. *Language Arts, 66*, 184–191.

Barton, B., & Booth, D. (1990). *Stories in the classroom.* Portsmouth, NH: Heinemann.

Bigelow, B. (1989). Discovering Columbus: Rereading the past. *Language Arts, 66*, 635–641.

Bromley, K. (1995). *Webbing with literature: Creating story maps with children's books.* Boston: Allyn and Bacon.

Buckley, M. H. (1992). We listen a book a day; we speak a book a week: Learning from Walter Loban. *Language Arts, 69* (8), 622–626.

Daniels, H. (1994). *Literature circles: Voice and choice in the student-centered classroom.* York, ME: Stenhouse.

Dewey, J. (1915). *Democracy and education.* New York: Macmillan.

Duthie, J. (1986). The web: A powerful tool for the teaching and evaluation of the expository essay. *The History and Social Science Teacher, 21* (3), 232–236.

Ernst, G. (1994). "Talking circle": Conversation and negotiation in the ESL classroom. *TESOL Quarterly, 28* (2), 293–322.

Fennessey, S. (1995). Living history through drama and literature. *The Reading Teacher, 49* (1), 16–19.

Forsythe, S. J. (1995). It worked! Readers theater in second grade. *The Reading Teacher, 49* (3), 264–265.

Gambrell, L. B. (1997). What research reveals about discussion. In L. B. Gambrell & J. F. Almasi (Eds.), *Lively discussions: Fostering engaged reading* (pp. 25–38). Newark, DE: International Reading Association.

Gambrell, L. B., & Almasi, J. F. (Eds.) (1997). *Lively discussions: Fostering engaged reading.* Newark, DE: International Reading Association.

Goldenberg, C. (1993). Instructional conversations: Promoting comprehension through discussion. *The Reading Teacher, 46* (4), 316–326.

Hancock, M. R. (1993). Character journals: Initiating involvement and identification through literature. *Journal of Reading, 37,* (1), 42–53.

Heller, P. G. (1996). *Drama as a way of knowing.* York, ME: Stenhouse.

Hoyt, L. (1992). Many ways of knowing: Using drama, oral interactions, and the visual arts to enhance reading comprehension. *The Reading Teacher, 45* (8), 580–584.

Johnson, D. M. (1988). ESL children as teachers: A social view of second language use. *Language Arts, 65*, 154–163.

Kagan, S. (1994). *Cooperative learning.* San Juan Capistrano, CA: Resources for Teacher.

Kardash, C. A., & Wright, L. (1987). Does creative drama benefit elementary school students?: A meta-analysis. *Youth Theater Journal, 1*, 11–18.

Keegan, S., & Shrake, K. (1991). Literature study groups: An alternative to ability grouping. *The Reading Teacher, 44* (8), 542–547.

Leal, D. (1993). The power of literary peer-group discussions: How children collaboratively negotiate meaning. *The Reading Teacher, 47* (2), 114–120.

Loban, W. (1976). *Language development: Kindergarten through grade twelve.* NCTE Research report No. 18. Urbana, IL: National Council of Teachers of English.

Martinez, M. ((1993). Motivating dramatic story reenactments. *The Reading Teacher, 46* (8), 682–688.

McCaslin, N. (1990). *Creative drama in the classroom* (5th ed.). New York: Longman.

Mikkelson, N. (1990). Toward greater equity in literacy education: Storymaking and nonmainstream students. *Language Arts, 67*, 556–566.

Palinscar, A. M. (1992). Fostering literacy learning in supportive contexts. *Journal of Learning Disabilities, 25* (4), 211–225.

Perez, B. (1996). Instructional conversations as opportunities for English language acquisition for culturally and linguistically diverse students. *Language Arts, 73* (3), 173–183.

Peterson, R., & Eeds, M. (1990). *Grand conversations: Literature groups in action.* New York: Scholastic.

Rosenshine, B. (1994). Reciprocal teaching: A review of the research. *Review of Educational Research, 64* (4), 479–530.

Roth, R. (1986). Practical use of language in school. *Language Arts, 63* (2), 134–142.

Schifini, A. (1997). Discussion in multilingual, multicultural classrooms. In L. B. Gambrell & J. F. Almasi (Eds.), *Lively discussions: Fostering engaged reading* (pp. 39–51). Newark, DE: International Reading Association.

Smith, F. (1982). The unspeakable habit. *Language Arts, 59* (6), 550–554.

Steiner, V. J. (1985). *Notebooks of the mind: Explorations of thinking.* New York: Harper.

Stewig, J. W. (1979). Nonverbal communication: I see what you say. *Language Arts, 56* (2), 150–155.

Tudge, J. (1988). Cooperative problem solving in the classroom: Enhancing young children's cognitive development. *Young Children, 44,* 46–52.

Valmont, W. J. (1995). *Creating videos for school use.* Boston: Allyn and Bacon.

Verriour, P. (1986). Creating worlds of dramatic discourse. *Language Arts, 63* (3), 253–263.

Vygotsky, L. (1978). *Mind in society.* Cambridge, MA: Harvard University Press.

Wagner, B. J. (1988). Research currents: Does classroom drama affect the arts of language? *Language Arts, 65,* 46–55.

Wells, G., & Chang-Wells, G. L. (1992). *Constructing knowledge together: Classrooms as centers of inquiry.* Portsmouth, NH: Heinemann.

Wolf, S. A. (1993). What's in a name? Labels and literacy in Readers Theater. *The Reading Teacher, 46* (7), 540–545.

Young, T. A., & Vardell, S. (1993). Weaving Readers Theater and nonfiction into the curriculum. *The Reading Teacher, 46* (5), 398–406.

Children's Book References

Banyai, I. (1995). *Re-zoom.* New York: Viking.

Beatty, P. (1992). *Who comes with cannons?* New York: Morrow.

Cleary, B. (1981). *Ramona Quimby, age 8.* New York: Dell.

Dalgliesh, A. (1954). *The courage of Sarah Noble.* New York: Scribners.

DeFelice, C. (1994). *Lostman's river.* New York: Macmillan.

Gardner, J. (1960). *Stone fox.* New York: Harper.

George, J. C. (1995). *Everglades.* New York: HarperCollins.

Maizlish, L. (1996). *The ring.* New York: Greenwillow.

O'Connor, J. (1994). *The blizzard (Survive!).* New York: Grosset & Dunlap.

Pomerantz, C. (1971). *The day they parachuted cats on Borneo: A drama of ecology.* Reading, MA: Addison-Wesley.

Watson, J. B. (1994). *The hurricane (Survive!).* New York: Grosset & Dunlap.

Children's Books about Speaking

Alexander, S. (1982). *Witch, goblin, and ghost's book of things to do.* New York: Pantheon. (Gr. 1–3). This book contains stories that tell how to put on a play and create a secret code.

Aliki (1993). *Communication.* New York: Greenwillow. (Gr. 1–4). This book describes the importance of communication and the many ways people share knowledge and express themselves.

Betancourt, J. (1982). *Smile! How to cope with braces.* New York: Knopf. (Gr. 4–6). Dental problems, orthodontic hardware, and the problems that braces sometimes create for wearers are discussed.

Brandenberg, F. (1984). *Aunt Nina's visit.* New York: Greenwillow. (Gr. 1–3). Alex, Alexandria, their cousins, and their kittens put on an improvised puppet show for their aunt, who makes a rainy day fun.

Brassey, R. (1995). *How to speak chimpanzee: The phrasebook no human should be without.* New York: Crown. (Gr. 1–6). In this humorus book, with a combinaton of body language, facial expressions and sound, the reader learns to speak chimpanzee.

Brown, M. (1996). *Arthur writes a story.* Boston: Little, Brown. (Gr. 1–3). Arthur has to write a story as a homework assignment and he keeps changing his ideas of what to write as he talks to friends.

Brown, M. T. (1983). *Arthur's Thanksgiving play.* Boston: Atlantic-Little, Brown. (Gr. 1–3). Arthur finds his role as director of the Thanksgiving play a difficult one, especially since no one will agree to play the turkey.

Cohen, M. (1985). *Starring first grade*. New York: Greenwillow. (Gr. 1–3). Even though he doesn't like his part in the first-grade play, Jimmy saves the performance when one of the key players gets stage fright.

Coy, J. (1996). *Night driving*. New York: Holt. (Gr. 1–3). A father and son drive through the night, talking and singing songs to stay awake.

Curtis, J. L. (1996). *Tell me again about the night I was born*. New York: HarperCollins. (Gr. K–2). A young girl asks for the story of her birth and shows that it is a cherished tale she knows by heart.

Curtis, R. (1984). *The story of Elsie and Jane*. Bodley Head-Merrimack. (Gr. 1–3). Both Elsie and Jane enjoy reciting poetry.

Demuth, R. B. (1986). *Max, the bad-talking parrot*. New York: Dodd, Mead. (Gr. K–3). A parrot, who talks in rhymes, saves the day with his language abilities.

Detz, J. (1986). *You mean I have to stand up and say something?* New York: Atheneum. (Gr. 4–6). The prospective speaker is guided through each step of the preparation and delivery of a public speech in this simply written and organized book.

Fain, K. (1993). *Handsigns: A sign language alphabet*. San Francisco: Chronicle Books. (Gr. K–2). This short history of sign language is followed by the American Manual Alphabet, illustrated with animals from A to Z.

Fleishman, P. (1988). *Joyful noise: Poems for two voices*. New York: Harper and Row. (all grades). This companion to *I Am Phoenix* contains poems about insects that can be read alone, in a duet, or in chorus.

Fleishman, P. (1985). *I am Phoenix*. New York: Harper and Row. (all grades). This collection of verbal, visual, musical, and imaginative poems celebrate birds and can be read alone, in duet, or in chorus.

Gackenbach, D. G. (1986). *Timothy's tongue twisters*. New York: Holiday House. (Gr. K–3). This is a collection of a 5-year-old's favorite tongue twisters.

Giff, P. R. (1984). *The almost awful play*. New York: Viking. (Gr. 1–3). Second-grader Ronald Morgan is Winkey the Cat in a humorous story about a class play that does not go as planned.

Hopkins, L. B. (1981). *Mama and her boys*. New York: Harper and Row. (Gr. 3–6). A boy interviews a custodian for his school newspaper, a friendship develops, and the family gains a father.

Hubbard, P. (1996). *My crayons talk*. New York: Holt. (Gr. K–2). Brown crayon sings, "Play, mud-pie day" and Blue crayon calls, "Sky, swing so high" in this story about talking crayons.

Klass, S. S. (1986). *Page four*. New York: Scribner. (Gr. 7–8). When David Smith learns his father is moving to Alaska, he is devastated. His only refuge is talking to his best friend, Bean, who helps David turn his life around.

Levine, E. (1989). *I hate English!* New York: Scholastic. (Gr. K–6). Mei Mei, a new immigrant from China, is afraid to speak English because she feels she will lose her Chinese culture. A teacher from the learning center helps Mei Mei become more comfortable with her new country and its language.

MacDonald, A. (1990). *Little beaver and the echo*. New York: Putnam. (Gr. 1–3). Little Beaver is unaware that the voice from across the pond telling him he is lonely is his echo. In trying to make friends with the voice, Little Beaver makes real friends along the way.

MacLachlin, P. (1982). *Mama one, Mama two*. New York: HarperCollins. (Gr. 1–4). A young girl named Maudie goes to live with a foster family while her mother is away. Maudie's foster mother helps her cope as the two of them tell the story of why Maudie's mama went away and how they hope she will be home in the spring.

Marshall, E. (1985). *Four on the shore and three by the sea*. New York: Dial. (Gr. K–3). Lolly, Spider, and Sam try to scare Willie with their repertoire of ghost stories. They don't succeed and then Willie tells his ghost story.

Martin, A. M. (1984). *Stage fright*. New York: Holiday House. (Gr. 3–6). Shy Sara panics when her fourth-grade teacher announces that her class is to perform a play before the entire school. But she eventually learns that stage fright can sometimes be healthy.

Martin, B., & Archambault, J. (1990). *Knots on a counting rope*. New York: Trumpet (Gr. 2–6). A blind Native American boy listens to his grandfather tell the story of his life and they put another knot on a rope to mark another telling of the story.

McCully, E. A. (1989). *Zaza's big break*. New York: Harper and Row. (Gr. K–3). Little Zaza bear is an actress in her family's theater. After an audition for a TV show in Hollywood, she finds TV acting is very different from theater acting.

McGuire, R. (1994). *Night becomes day*. New York: Viking. (Gr. 1–3). This book of objects that are transformed into other things (e.g., "paper becomes news") can prompt round-robin storytelling.

Oppenheim, J. (1984). *Mrs. Peloki's class play*. New York: Dodd, Mead. (Gr. 1–4). After a disastrous dress rehearsal of "Cinderella," the second-grade play is a great success but has an unexpected ending.

Parte, B. A. (1985). *The kidnapping of Aunt Elizabeth*. New York: Greenwillow. (Gr. 3–6). A young girl collects material for a social studies report by interviewing her relatives and listening to tales of their youth.

Patterson, F. (1987). *Koko's story*. New York: Scholastic. (Gr. K & up). A step-by-step depiction of how a gorilla and his mate learn American Sign Language. Dr. Patterson hoped that the two would produce a baby gorilla and eventually teach their young to use sign language.

Rathman, P. (1995). *Officer Buckle and Gloria*. New York: Putnam. (Gr. 1–3). The children at Napville Elementary School always ignore Officer Buckle's safety tips until a police dog named Gloria accompanies him when he gives his safety speeches.

Scott, E. (1988). *Ramona: Behind the scenes of a television show*. New York: Morrow. (Gr. 3–7). A book about the making of a TV show using the "Ramona" series (Beverly Cleary's Quimby family) as an example; includes black and white photos.

Shreve, S. (1993). *The gift of the girl who couldn't hear*. New York: Beech Tree. (Gr. 3–6). Two girls learn about courage and friendship when one teaches the other how to sing.

Stanley, D. (1993). *The conversation club*. New York: Macmillan. (Gr. 1–3). Peter Fieldmouse joins the neighborhood Conversation Club, but since he feels he has little speaking expertise, he becomes a listening expert and establishes his own club.

Tompert, A. (1990). *Grandfather Tang's story*. New York: Crown. (Gr. 1–4). A young Chinese girl named Soo and her Grandfather Tang tell a story as they arrange their tangram puzzle pieces into animal shapes.

Yolen, J. (1981). *The boy who spoke chimp*. New York: Knopf. (Gr. 3–6). This is the story of a boy who learns to speak to a chimp who has been taught to communicate.

Ziefert, H. (1995). *Oh, what a noisy farm!* New York: Tambourine. (Gr. K–2). Full of animal sounds, this cumulative tale can build listening and speaking skills.

Writing
to Learn

11

Jan Mason believes her fourth-grade students are capable of becoming accomplished writers. She uses modeling and conversation about writing to help them develop as writers. Jan says,

At the beginning of the year, revision is difficult for my students. They often write just enough to fulfill the bare-bones requirements and are reluctant to revise. So, I share my own writing as a basis for discussion of the writing process. I model composing, thinking aloud, revising, and reworking a rough draft. First, at breakfast, I write an entry in my journal. It might be a quick description of the weather, or what

I plan to acccomplish that day, or a summary of a book I've just read, or a description of how I feel about something I did. At school, I make a transparency of the entry and share it with my class on the overhead projector. We look at the piece as an example of quickly crafted prose, with an eye to clarifying and expanding it to make it clearer and more desriptive. Together, we reread it, add words and phrases, use arrows to reorder sentences, and do all the things that typically occur during revision. This has made a huge difference in my students' understanding of what revision means and their ability to sharpen and expand their own writing.

This attention on revision has caused Maria to slow down as a writer so that her first drafts are now more thoughtful and complete. Austin reorganizes and sequences his ideas now. Tricia now indents to signal a change in ideas and at the beginning of a new paragraph. In addition to adding words to extend his writing, Shawn also uses punctuation appropriately. So, as well as better writing that comes from revision, I've seen this type of modeling improve my students' understanding of form and mechanics.

Jan also knows the value of conversation as a prewriting tool. Through talk, Jan helps her fourth-graders orally rehearse what they will later write. Jan says,

I want my students to be able to write an objective news article, which is one of our grade-level's four writing outcomes. So, after the class returned from a field trip to the Farmer's Museum in Cooperstown, which was part of our social studies unit on state history, we talked about taking a reporter's perspective and how a newspaper account of our visit might sound. I invited the children to retell the field trip as if they were news reporters, and we did this in cooperative groups. In each group, students passed a microphone, created from an ice-cream cone and styrofoam ball, and each student took a turn retelling a part of the visit. With this oral practice as rehearsal for writing, they then wrote their objective accounts. Next, using their knowledge of revision, they created objective accounts that were full and descriptive.

Jan has found that modeling and conversation are excellent ways to help her students become accomplished writers. She continues,

When we talk about writing and I show them how I go about writing something, I think it makes the writing process more personal and attainable for them. It seems to "hook" them and once they have some success, they're willing to try more and they feel they are capable writers.

• • • • •

Overview

Writing requires the use of expressive language to construct meaning graphically. This chapter discusses writing as a composition process that includes planning, drafting, revising, and publishing. Reading and writing are interactive processes, with each dependent on the other; writers read their work as they compose and readers are the final consumers of the written message. Writing instruction needs to balance process and product.

349
• • • • •
Writing

Writing is traditionally viewed as the last phase of language development. In the natural order of things, children first learn to listen and speak, and then they learn to read and write. The definition of *writing* in *Webster's II New College Dictionary* (1995) is "to form (e.g., letters) on a surface with a tool, as a pen or pencil" (p. 1274). *Compose* means "to make up the constituent parts of" or "to create by putting together" (p. 230). Writing is, of course, more than the first definition, which suggests only the mechanical aspects of handwriting. *Writing* is the complicated interaction of cognitive as well as physical factors. When one writes, one also composes or creates meaning with words.

Technology, discussed in more detail later in this chapter and in Chapter 13, has redefined aspects of writing. Software programs—including word processors with spell-checkers, grammar-checkers, graphics, and desktop publishing capabilities—make the writing process easier and written products visually more pleasing and professional. Computers with speech-to-print capabilities allow students with physical handicaps to dictate writing. CD-ROMs, with color graphics and sound, make the creation of hypertext a possibility for students. Clearly, technology has made writing more than the creation of meaning with words. For most young children, however, making meaning with words is where writing begins.

Research shows that young children who cannot yet read are ready to write, almost from their first day of school, and many write before they start school. Graves (1983) found that about 90 percent of the children entering first grade believe they can write, but only about 15 percent believe they can read. One reason for this is that children probably learn to anticipate problems with reading but they have different expectations for writing. Young children also may define writing more liberally than adults. In order to write, children who have some letter and word knowledge can express ideas and communicate meaning in as sophisticated or unsophisticated a manner as they choose. They are independent of others. In order to read, however, children with some letter and word knowledge need help to extract meaning from the code the writer uses. At age 3, Emily proudly says she can write (see Figure 11.1). Her depiction of a storm shows that she is capable of composing to communicate meaning.

When we write, we produce thoughts, ideas, and feelings in written symbols. It is one way of communicating with other people the many things already existing in one's head. It may be a note to a friend, a letter to a relative, or a paper for a professor. Smith (1982) states that writing can also occur without the intention to communicate with others but rather to transcribe one's thoughts. Making a list for yourself, writing in a journal, or writing a letter that no one else reads serves this purpose. Therefore, you might write to communicate with others or for the introspection it affords.

Writing is much more than the communication of meaning already existing in one's head. Writing also results in the generation of new knowledge. By writing, we learn what we know. We come to new understandings, and we create new knowledge. Smith (1982) believes that writing does more than reflect underlying thought; it liberates and develops it. Writing allows us to transfer our imaginations to paper while over-

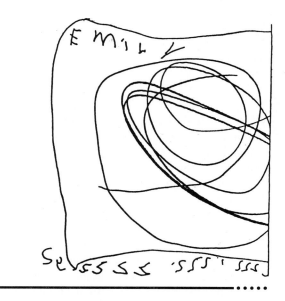

FIGURE 11.1 Three-year-old Emily's depiction of a storm.

····

coming the limiting factors of memory and attention. We remember more of what we imagine when we write it because we can refer to it over and over again. Remembering and attending to spoken thoughts is more difficult than remembering and attending to written statements.

Writing Workshop

Writer's workshop, or the writing workshop, is a popular teaching technique, partly because the writing process does not always lend itself to whole-class, teacher-led methods (Calkins, 1994; Graves, 1994). In a writing workshop, time is set aside each day for writing by each student on a topic of the student's choice. Atwell (1987) spent an hour a day in writing workshop, about one-third of which was comprised of brief lessons focused on a demonstrated need of a group of students. She also spent time hearing, discussing, and sharing a well-written piece of literature at the end of the workshop to help students improve their writing and learn to respond to each other's work.

Tonya Dauphin has used writing workshop for several years. Like other teachers, Tonya experiments with the organization and delivery of writing workshop. She listens to her students and reflects on what works and doesn't work, and her approach continues to develop and change each year (Sudol & Sudol, 1995; Zaragoza & Vaughn, 1995). This year, Tonya uses writing workshop for three days each week with her third-graders. She begins each workshop with a mini-lesson on a skill she has noticed the class or several students need. Then, students write for 30 minutes and there is a 10-minute sharing time when a student sits in the Author's Chair and reads her work to the class. Tonya has a wall calendar on which students sign up in advance to share a finished story. She requires that students share at least twice a month.

Tonya's room is striking in that there is evidence of her commitment to writing. Posters about each aspect of the writing process adorn the walls and the students' writing is posted on bulletin boards. For Tonya's students, writing workshop was a new idea. One of the things she did early in the year to help the children develop good habits was to have a discussion about what a writing workshop is. Tonya and her students created the following *T-chart,* which she posted in the classroom as a reminder:

A Successful Writer's Workshop

Looks Like	*Sounds Like*
▪ People being polite	▪ Quiet but not silent
▪ Working not talking	▪ No put-downs
▪ Sharing ideas quietly	▪ Clean language
▪ Cooperation	▪ No unpleasant noises
▪ People writing	▪ Listening during sharing time
▪ People reading	

Some teachers, like Tonya, encourage students to read literature during writing workshop so that they are reading good models as they compose. In an integrated curriculum, encouraging students also to write on topics they are studying about in content areas such as science and/or social studies seems logical. Then students can use concepts and information they have learned as a basis for some of their writing.

During a typical writing workshop, students work at their own rates and are at different points in the writing process. Some students may be drafting, while others may be reading their works to a peer or group of peers who, in turn, respond to their work. Others may conference with the teacher, revise, use the computer, gather information, read, draw, create webs, or in some way plan a new piece or edit and create a finished piece, perhaps a book. Students keep their writing in a folder or envelope, even stories they have stopped working on and left unfinished, so they can see their progress and return to what they have written for ideas.

Lisa Rieger and a colleague, both fourth-grade teachers, have been using writing workshop for several years and report that it is one of the most exciting things they do. Their students love to write. Even children who were reluctant writers and previously bored with school have been transformed and are eager and prolific writers. The children are openly disappointed and distressed when there is no time for writing workshop.

In a writing workshop, composition and transcription are usually separate, with students' attention focused first on content and message as they compose and second on the aspects of transcription that are associated with form and mechanics. Experiences in writing workshop allow children to read, react, listen, think, and talk as they give and accept helpful feedback and evaluate their own writing as well as that of others. Thus, they become independent and more effective writers.

Three cautions should be considered before you proceed. This chapter deals with the writing process and within this context gives you a background for developing effective writers in your classroom, but not every piece of writing a student does should proceed through the entire process. Some writing is done just for the sake of writing. A good teacher of writing knows how to balance process and product and helps students decide which of their pieces to take through the entire process to publication. Some writing—for example, in response journals, buddy journals, and learning logs—will probably not be revised and rewritten. If every piece of student writing is perfected, the children will soon lose their eagerness to revise and publish. The purpose of the piece and the student's wishes should help decide whether a piece is published.

The second caution is that writers need direct and systematic instruction in writing as well as time to write (Routman, 1996). Writers are not born; they are created. All students can become capable of sharing their ideas and thoughts in writing if they are taught how. Good teachers of writing have learned to strike a balance between the writing process and the written product, honoring each in their writing programs. Good writing teachers

- Grow and change in their pedagogy and so their classrooms and approaches to writing look and sound different from one year to the next.
- Encourage and celebrate individuality, creativity, standard form, and the conventions of language in student writing.

The third caution involves students who are learning to speak English and those with difficulties in learning to write either because of a language difference or delay, a learning disability, or a physical difference. Writing may be the most difficult language art for these students because composing involves both thinking and reading, coupled with the physical aspect of transcribing. These students may write less and seem less creative and motivated. English learners especially want to spell correctly, use proper punctuation, and use standard English, which is doubly difficult if they do not yet use standard spoken English. These reluctant writers need more support or scaffolding than other students. So, provide them with models to imitate, guidelines to follow, direct instruction, and guided practice that support their English language learning. And don't overlook the potential of technology, cooperative learning, shared writing, and authentic learning to provide the extra support and reinforcement they need.

Planning

As with any creative process, before children's pens or pencils touch paper or their fingers touch the keyboard of a typewriter, a certain amount of thinking, planning, brainstorming, and organizing usually occurs. Prewriting activities consist of thinking about a topic, experience, or idea; discussing it; perhaps drawing a picture; and possibly reading about the topic or reading the similar work of others. Talking is a critical precursor, especially for the young child. For the older child, prewriting includes these activities and may include imaging, webbing or mapping, notetaking, listing, generating questions, studying a model, or creating an outline of content (see Figure 11.2). Figure 11.3 shows a picture drawn by a first-grader as she planned the sentence she later wrote underneath it. Figure 11.4 shows what a second-grade child was thinking about as he planned the composition he wrote on the first day of school. Figure 11.5 shows the journal a fifth-

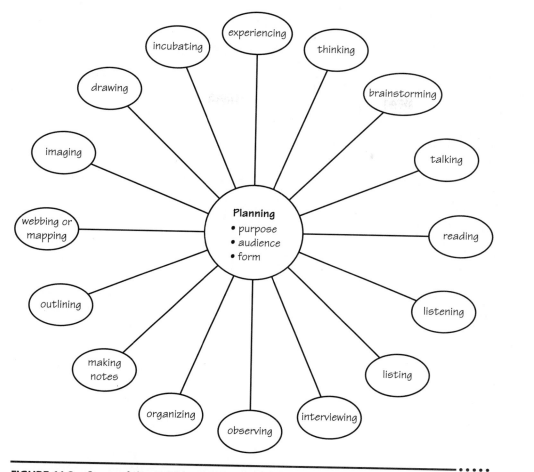

FIGURE 11.2 Some of the activities that may occur during planning.

grader wrote after he read about Sacagawea's life as she accompanied the Lewis and Clark expedition.

Whatever the activities, students may spend up to two-thirds of their entire writing time planning and prewriting. If this part of the process is overlooked, the quality of the written product will suffer. Planning allows students an important incubation time to crystallize their thoughts. Many adult writers say that the quality of their work is directly related to the amount of time allowed for thinking about and playing with ideas.

Forms of Writing

It is during prewriting that children consider the purpose, audience, and form of the piece they will write. The following discussion outlines four kinds of writing done for a variety of reasons, for different audiences, and in different formats.

This is a donkey on his tippy toz.

FIGURE 11.3 A first-grade child planned before drafting by drawing this picture first.

Source: "SSW: Sustained Spontaneous Writing." *Childhood Education, 62*(1), 23–29. Reprinted by permission of Karen Bromley and the Association for Childhood Education International, 17904 Georgia Ave., Ste. 215, Olney, MD. Copyright © 1985 by the Association.

1. NoTes & k 2
2. PepE i l s
3. ma t p
4.

The first day of school I think of writing in my notebook and sharpining pencils

The EnD

FIGURE 11.4 Before drafting, this second-grade child planned ahead by making a list.

Daniel   4/7
                        Sacagawea Journal

April 7, 1805 I just met two white men. My husband, Toussaint Charbonneau, a frenchman, want me to guide them through. I am glad to help them.

May 15, 1805 We explored the river that feeds into the Platte River I am surprised that the white men had enough gradatude to name the river after me, The Sacagawea River.

June 15, 1805 I feel so sick my stomach hurts. I have a bad fever, but my worst fear is Jean Baptiste. he has trouble with his teeth. Thank goodness that Captain Lewis gave us both medicine.

FIGURE 11.5 Reading and talking were part of the prewriting this fifth-grader did before he wrote these journal entries.

354

Writing to Convey Feelings. Writing to convey feelings or express inner thoughts and the self is a type of writing that can take many forms, one of which for young children is drawing pictures. As children gain facility with written language, their pictures are accompanied by scribbles, letterlike shapes, words, and later sentences. Often, in order to convey feelings, children need the stimulus of drawing a concrete picture. Other ways to convey feelings in writing are through personal journals, response journals, dialogue journals, and buddy journals. Of course, you can encourage students to express themselves by writing in a variety of other formats as well, such as letters, poems (see Figure 11.6), first-person accounts, and essays.

STRETCHING EXERCISE

If you don't already keep a personal journal, purchase or make one and write in it every day for a week. Write about memorable sights, sounds, events, issues, feelings, questions, challenges, thoughts, or anything that enters your mind. Reread your entries. Does your writing surprise you? How?

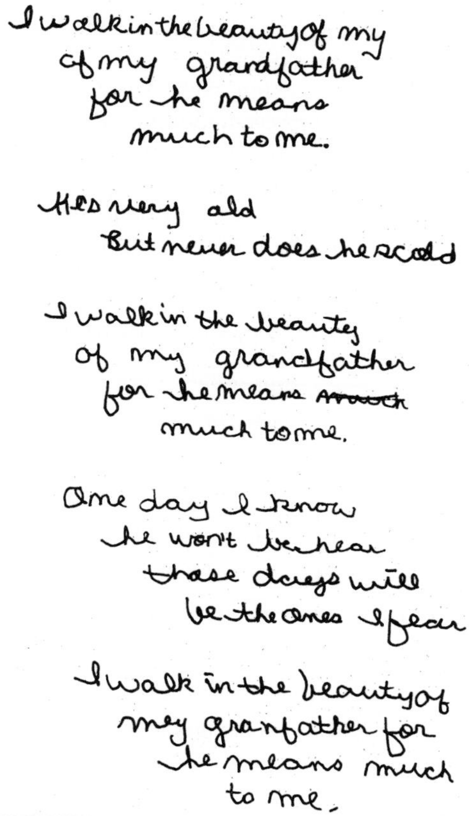

• • • • •

I walk in the beauty of my
of my grandfather
for he means
much to me.

Hes very old
But never does he scold

I walk in the beauty
of my grandfather
for he means ~~much~~
much to me.

One day I know
he won't be hear
these days will
be the ones I fear

I walk in the beauty of
mey granfather for
he means much
to me.

FIGURE 11.6 A poem that conveys a sixth-grader's feelings after she read *Knots on a Counting Rope* by Bill Martin and John Archambault (1990).

Writing to Narrate. Another type of writing is writing to narrate, in which students give a fictional account of events or tell a story. This kind of writing may mean retelling in a student's own words a story just read or heard (see Figure 11.7), creating a new version of a story or sequel, or concocting a totally new story. As students write to narrate, they need to be able to write an introduction and conclusion and maintain an appropriate sequence of events. They may use personification by giving human traits to animals or inanimate objects and using dialogue, or they may read historical accounts and write their own narrative stories. Again, you can engage your students in using many written forms—such as newscasts, skits, obituaries, biographies, short stories, and sequels—to develop their skills in narrative writing.

Writing to Explain. Writing to explain, inform, or make factual information clear and understandable is a third type of writing. Writing notes, messages, reports, and letters of complaint or requests for information are examples of expository writing in which students need to possess skill.

The ability to take notes from a lecture or textbook, compose an outline to organize thoughts, or write a report or research paper are important expository skills for students who hope to be academically successful. Research skills—such as using the library, referring to reference and information books, and composing written representations of important information read—are critical student skills. Writing a summary or précis (an abstract) is also a sophisticated academic skill children need to learn. Composing an essay to inform others of opinions or personal beliefs that states ideas but does not necessarily try to persuade someone is another important skill.

Often, creating illustrative material such as a simple drawing, web, concept map, or Venn diagram aids this type of writing since a graphic representation of ideas provides organization and structure. For struggling writers and ESL students, drawing and illustrating aid writing because they provide a visual stimulus to prompt and support writing. In Figure 11.8, Lisa Rieger encouraged her fourth-graders to draw their Journey Vehicles before describing them in writing. In Figure 11.9, Maria Moy's fourth-graders

FIGURE 11.7   A folktale created in response to *The People Could Fly* by Virginia Hamilton (1985).

There once was a man by the name of Harry and he was a slave owner. He owned fifty slaves and was recievin more

One day Harry was ridin on his favorite horse and saw Mr. Wilson (another slave owner) whippin one of his slaves. The blood was pourin off of him. Harry felt so bad.

He said to himself, "This isn't right to'be whippin the dickens out of that black slave."

From then on Harry was a part of the Underground Railroad. He was one of the biggest conductors of the whole Underground Railroad system. He freed over one thousand slaves.

We will always remember Harry for opening up his eyes to the big problem of slavery.

NOTE: This tale was told by all the village slaves throughout the country to the other side. Tales like this gave hope that someday freedom would be theirs.

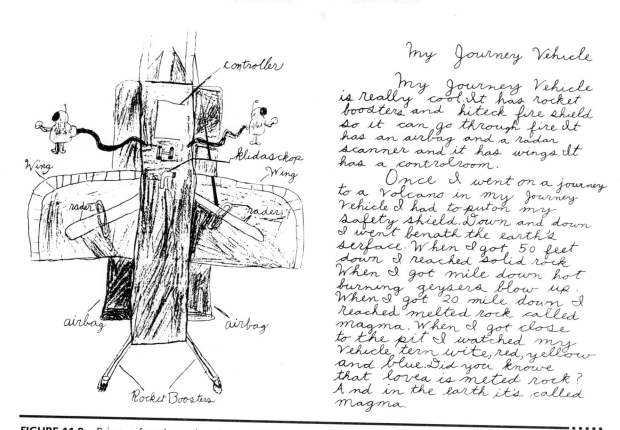

My Journey Vehicle

My Journey Vehicle is really cool. It has rocket boosters and hiteck fire shield so it can go through fire. It has an airbag and a radar scanner and it has wings. It has a controlroom.

Once I went on a journey to a volcano in my Journey Vehicle. I had to put on my safety shield. Down and down I went benath the earth's serface. When I got 50 feet down I reached solid rock. When I got mile down hot burning geysers blow up. When I got 20 mile down I reached melted rock called magma. When I got close to the pit I watched my Vehicle tern wite, red, yellow and blue. Did you knowe that lovea is meted rock? And in the earth it's called magma.

FIGURE 11.8 Brian, a fourth-grader, drew an illustration of his Special Journey Vehicle before writing a description of it.

used Venn diagrams to compare characters in two different books, *Beezus and Ramona* by Beverly Cleary (1979) and *Tales of a Fourth Grade Nothing* by Judy Blume (1972), before writing character descriptions.

Answering the five Ws and I (Who? What? Why? When? Where? and If?) also guides students in writing news articles and other forms of exposition. Writing in journals and learning logs and writing directions are further examples of writing to explain. Students also enjoy writing lists, telephone messages, telegrams, interviews, sketches, and poetic song lyrics that explain or clarify.

Writing to Persuade. A fourth type of writing is that done to persuade or convince. In this kind of writing, students try to change the opinion of others or influence the actions of the audience. Typically, students in grade 3 and beyond enjoy this kind of writing and do it with success. In writing that persuades, students often need to state an opinion and support it with evidence, use vivid and specific vocabulary, and use language and tone appropriate for a specific audience (see Figure 11.10). Letters, essays, book reviews, advertisements, product descriptions, sales pitches, tributes, travel folders, and remedies are a few of the many forms you can teach your students to use so that they can become proficient, persuasive writers.

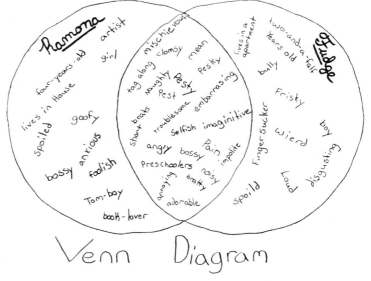

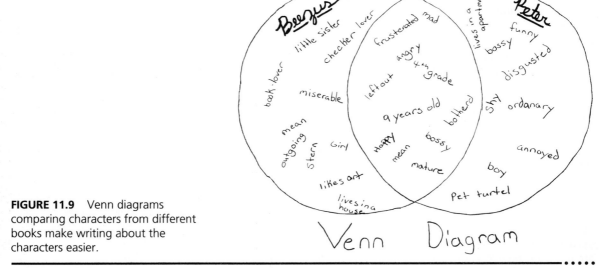

FIGURE 11.9 Venn diagrams comparing characters from different books make writing about the characters easier.

East Middle School
167 East Frederick Street
Binghamton, New York 13904
October 2

Binghamton Press Co.
Vestal Parkway East
Binghamton, New York 13902

Dear Editor:

   Recently, there was an issue before the Supreme Court about flag burning that we feel was resolved in an upsetting manner. We think it is important that we speak out on this matter, as we feel it is unpatriotic to burn the flag in protest. Though it allows our freedoms as a democratic society to prevail, it promotes trampling versus cherishing. The flag was flown for years over schoolhouses and public buildings as a symbol of the unity of our nation. Are we now going to allow someone the freedom to damage something that they teach us, as students, to pledge our lives and allegiance to everyday? We feel there should be an amendment to the Constitution that would protect our flag from such disfigurement. This amendment is needed to make the particular act of flag burning punishable by law and to ensure the freedom of our flag to stand in its proper place. May our flag always remind us of the love and lives that allow us our freedoms today. Join us in writing to our Congresspeople for an amendment.

                         Sincerely,

                         Gabe Guy
                         Gabe Guy

                         Marcia Hayes
                         Marcie Hayes

                         Robert Oakley
                         Robert Oakley

                         Melissa Rollins
                         Melissa Rollins

FIGURE 11.10 A persuasive letter written by sixth-graders to gain support for an amendment to ban flag burning.

Graves (1983) suggests that especially when children first learn how to write, they should choose their own topics for writing. If the teacher supplies a topic, children may not have anything to say about it nor want to try to find anything to say. For this reason, writing is best done if it involves a subject or idea about which a child has some knowledge or possesses some feeling. So do allow children to choose their own topics, but also be ready to help them identify what they do know about or to suggest possible topics for them. You can give children who are stuck an example of what you might include in a topic and how you might write something.

STRETCHING EXERCISE	Brainstorm a list of examples for each of the different types of writing in which you have engaged during the last month. Did you do any writing that is not discussed here? What was it and under which category does it fit?
	• • • • •

Writing Role Models in Literature

In many children's books for younger and older students, writing is a main theme, a critical aspect, or related in some important way to plot or characterization. When read aloud by you or chosen as independent reading, these books provide writing role models for students. (See Children's Books about Writing at the end of this chapter for descriptions of such books.)

Books such as *Lives of the Writers: Comedies, Tragedies (and What the Neighbors Thought)* by Kathleen Krull (1994), which contains brief biographies of 19 writers, provide adult models with whom children can identify. Robert Quackenbush's (1984) *Mark Twain? What Kind of Name Is That?* gives the young reader a glimpse into the life of one of America's finest humorous writers. These books show the enjoyment and satisfaction writing brings to writers and help students understand the difficulties of writing.

Main characters write for a variety of purposes. There are several books in which main characters write to convey their feelings. In *Dear Mr. Henshaw* by Beverly Cleary (Newbery Medal, 1984), a boy writes in a diary and sends letters to his favorite author as he adjusts to a new school (see Figure 11.11). In *Zlata's Diary—A Child's Life in Sarajevo* by Zlata Filipovic (1994), the young author relates her feelings about life in war-torn Bosnia, as does G. Bowen's (1994) young male character in *Stranded at Plimouth Plantation, 1626.*

In other diaries, main characters narrate trips. Boys tell accounts of their travel in E. Woodruff's (1994) *Dear Levi: Letters from the Overland Trail* and Loretta Krupinski's (1995) *Bluewater Journal: The Voyage of the Sea Tiger.* A young African American girl, Latoya Hunter (1992), tells of another kind of travel from middle school to high school in *The Diary of Latoya Hunter.* Vera Williams's (1981) *Three Days on a River in a Red Canoe,* the story of a young boy, his mother, aunt, and cousin who take a long camping and canoeing trip, is a good model for students to use to write and illustrate an account of a trip they have made.

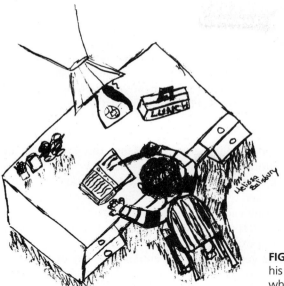

FIGURE 11.11   Eleven-year-old Leigh Botts writes letters to his favorite author and keeps a diary as he tries to figure out who the "lunchbox thief" is.

Source: Courtesy of Melissa Salisbury.

Writing to explain or inform is found in *Cherries and Cherry Pits* by Vera Williams (1986), in which an African American girl named Bidemmi draws pictures and writes stories about eating cherries and growing cherry trees. In *Angel Child, Dragon Child* by Michele Surat (1983), a Vietnamese girl and Euro-American boy write the story of her immigration and thus become friends. There are many books written in letter format or that include letter writing by main characters, such as Ezra Keats's (1968) *A Letter to Amy,* Martina Selway's (1992) *Don't Forget to Write,* and Uri Shulevitz's (1990) *Toddle Creek Post Office.*

There are also examples of books that persuade or convince the reader of the value of writing. In Patricia MacLachlan's (1994) *Skylark,* writing ties a family together in difficult times. In Nellie Toll's (1993) *Behind the Secret Window: A Memoir of a Hidden Childhood during World War II*, the reader sees how important writing and drawing were to Nellie while she hid from the Nazis. Randall Jarrell's (1964) *The Bat Poet* is about a brown bat who entertains himself by writing poems about various animal friends.

In addition, many books that deal with writing in novel ways may provide students with the impetus to write. For example, Janet and Allan Ahlberg's *The Jolly Postman* (1986) and *The Jolly Pocket Postman* (1995) contain actual envelopes and letters that a mail carrier delivers to storybook characters such as Goldilocks, Cinderella, and others. Some sixth-graders used the format of this book and created their own book, *Letters from Grandmother's Attic*, which included letters their main character found in a trunk that had been written by people living in the historical time they were studying in social studies. Vera Williams's (1988) *Stringbean's Trip to the Shining Sea* uses postcards to tell the story of a young boy's trip to the ocean. It, too, is a novel idea for writing a documentary or expository account.

Classroom Climate

Creating a climate that nurtures authors and the composing process is important (Graves, 1994; Short, Harste, & Burke, 1995). A classroom environment can either inspire and aid or discourage and thwart the composing process. The time invested in turning a classroom into a stimulating and accepting environment will galvanize children into becoming independent and proficient writers. Following are just some of the ideas you can use in your classroom:

- Create a writing center where books, magazines, and other forms of print are available as well as all types of writing tools and paper.
- Set up a message board or bank of mailboxes where students can post or "mail" the messages they write to each other.
- Encourage journal writing by giving each child a spiral notebook. Guide them to vary the way they use journals to respond to stories, write to a buddy, or keep a learning log in science or math, for example.
- Keep a journal yourself and share your own journal entries as a way of modeling how you learn about yourself by writing. Occasionally put your entries on transparencies and use the overhead projector to teach mini-lessons on particular skills.
- Make a special Author's Chair where students sit to read their work to a group or the class and receive their responses.
- Invite adults to come to the classroom to read their writing and discuss its creation (e.g., letters to the editor, poetry, journals, reports, personal letters, articles, books, etc.).
- Help the children formulate guidelines, hints, tips, and rubrics for each writing activity, and post them on a bulletin board or provide the children with copies to guide their writing.
- Display each aspect of the composing process (prewriting, drafting, revising, and publishing) on a poster with a brief description or list of things that can occur during each stage. Then the children can see where they are in the process and have ready access for ideas of what to do at each stage.
- Brainstorm special vocabulary needed to complete a certain composing activity and make it available to the children so they can more easily spell and use the words.
- Make dictionaries and thesauruses appropriate to the children's reading levels available in the classroom or have the childen make and keep their own individual dictionaries.
- Keep books such as *Free Stuff for Kids*, edited by Bruce Lansky (1997), in your classroom so the children have ready access to them. This book provides addresses for over 350 free and up-to-a-dollar things students can send for by mail. It also provides models of a business letter, postcards, and a properly addressed envelope.
- Make a regular time for the children to keep word banks or dictionaries with words they often use that are hard to spell.
- Place upper- and lowercase alphabet letters on the walls of the classroom, leaving space for taping word cards below. Place frequently used words and other words of interest to the children under the appropriate alphabet letter.

Just like tennis players, writers need practice to develop independence. You can provide time to practice writing in a nonthreatening and enjoyable way with *Sustained Spontaneous Writing (SSW)* at any grade level. SSW allots short periods of time to *both* children and teachers for writing on personally chosen topics. This not only gives children a regular routine of writing but it also gives them a model as they see you using this time to write. SSW requires little time or planning, and it complements any writing program. This strategy is called many things by different teachers: Dear Diary, Journal Time, Day Books, Log Jam, Write-In, Can't Stop Writing, Five-Minute Writing, Free Writing, Friday Writing, and so on.

SSW is especially important for second-language learners and students with writing difficulties for three main reasons:

1. It provides time for the growth of new thoughts and ideas.
2. It allows freedom to express thoughts and feelings in a risk-free context.
3. It provides handwriting practice and the growth of fluency.

The three elements of SSW are discussed next.

S—Sustained. Depending on the students' ages and attention, 5 to 15 minutes is spent in continuous uninterrupted writing. Everyone participates, including the teacher, who models writing. To avoid interruptions, tell the children to spell unknown words as best they can and encourage invented or temporary spellings.

S—Spontaneous. Encourage the children to write on topics they choose that are personally meaningful, or give them a choice of "starters." Their writing need not be read by anyone, unless a child asks you or a peer to read it. However, regular sharing by volunteers to a small group or the class increases interest and pride. Written work is not graded or evaluated. In this way, you encourage writing for the pleasure and sake of writing, and you provide a safe outlet for a child's thoughts and ideas.

W—Writing. Composing is usually done in a personal notebook, journal, log, or diary, with each entry dated. Sharon, a kindergarten teacher, has her children stamp each entry with the current date. This gives Sharon and her students a record of their progress. The writing tool (pencil, pen, or crayon) is one of individual choice. Writing with a pen or colored pencils, when this is not the usual tool for class work, is motivating for some children. Maureen, a fourth-grade teacher, encourages her students to make drawings that inspire them to write.

Even kindergarten and first-grade children like to spend short periods of uninterrupted time drawing or experimenting with graphics on paper or in a notebook. Some teachers of young children use the Draw and Tell journal (Bromley, 1993) in which children draw a picture, an adult transcribes a sentence onto the page, and then children tell their classmates about the entry. Hipple (1985) describes kindergartners who saw themselves as writers and wrote in their journals for the first 30 minutes of each day. The writing consisted of making drawings accompanied by scribbles, random letters, numerals, or even words. The word *drawing* was never used in connection with the journals; rather, children "wrote" and then later dictated what they had written to an adult. Other media such as paint, clay, or blocks can also be used as forms of composition.

As writing proficiency develops, children can write for longer periods of time. Some teachers of young children use SSW at the beginning of every day and report that children remain enthusiastic. Some teachers of older students use SSW for longer periods of time twice or three times a week, since older writers are capable of spending more time expressing their thoughts.

There are several techniques teachers use to get students started. Something as simple as practicing handwriting may be enough. For younger children who have trouble thinking of a topic to write about, you can furnish "starters" in the form of a phrase, such as *My favorite thing to do on Saturday is . . .* or you can give them a picture to describe. Children can occasionally write notes to peers. For older students, some teachers suggest varying the content of their journals, encouraging them to make different types of entries, such as lists, poetry, handwriting practice, calligraphy, short stories, or letters.

Content journals or learning logs are another variation of SSW. When students learn to write a summary, they can write summaries of the material they read in science or social studies class. Children can also write questions, reactions, or summaries to demonstrate knowledge of subject matter in science, social studies, or math. Teachers typically write comments or dialogue in content journals to help students clarify and elaborate information. Finally, have children use their learning logs during science or social studies to write responses to a question you or other children pose. In this way, children see writing as a regular and functional part of subject matter learning.

Dialogue journals, response journals, and buddy journals are other ways to use SSW time to emphasize meaning in writing and to provide natural experiences in both reading and writing. In dialogue journal writing, both student and teacher converse in writing (Gambrell, 1985). In response journals, students write their personal reactions and responses to literature they are reading (Atwell, 1987). In buddy journals, students write back and forth to each other, conversing on topics they choose.

Regardless of the age group, children must write something. You can make quick assessments of the amount of writing students are doing by circulating among the children about midway and at the end of the SSW period. But remember: To be successful with any form of sustained writing, you must participate and model expected student behavior. Determine an appropriate time but don't overuse the strategy. Vary the topics, tools, or process to maintain interest in a strategy that builds children's competence and independence in the composing process.

Word Processing

The computer and word processor are fast becoming valuable tools for teaching writing. A variety of word-processing programs are available for students to use as they create text on the screen, revise it, and finally publish it. Some of these programs have graphics capabilities, so a child can choose a picture to write about or to accompany a story she has written (see Figure 11.15). There is also increased availability of word-processing programs with voice-synthesized speech (Anderson-Inman, 1990). A talking word processor provides immediate access to what a student has written. With the eventual addition of voice recognition and speech-to-text capabilities, the computer will become an even more powerful tool for young children, ESL students, and those with language and learning difficulties.

However, Kahn and Freyd (1990) report results of research that cautions against an undue focus on keyboarding instruction. In contrast to popular notions about the need for

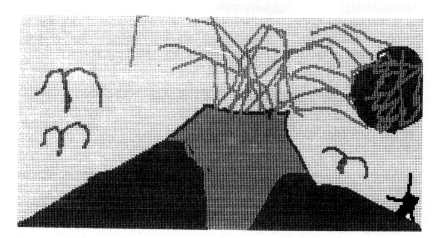

My stoy is adout a valcano it uhruptid.
It was mad and it was unhappy. It solvd
it by a boy. He had a feather he ticled
the valcano and it lafed.

THE END

BY CHRIS

FIGURE 11.15 Seven-year-old Chris uses computer graphics to choose a picture and then write a story to accompany it.
.....

traditional instruction in keyboarding skills, they found that time spent using the computer for writing and occasional games actually helped children develop a sense of the "home row" of keys and enough familiarity with the keyboard to develop their own "hunt and peck" systems. These systems were at least as effective as their handwriting and, in many cases, quicker and less tedious. In addition, children wrote longer and more meaningful pieces earlier than they previously had with paper and pencil. Drafting on the computer is doubly helpful for ESL children since they see correct letter formation as well as top-to-bottom and left-to-right progression modeled for them as they write.

Computers give children control over their learning. Children can experiment with language, learn to work out an argument or story, and play with the structure and tone of a piece (Newman, 1984). In one study, the use of a word-processing program with first-grade children had several significant effects on writing behavior (Phenix & Hannan, 1984). These children had written daily since September, had conferenced frequently with the teacher, were encouraged to use invented spellings, and kept writing folders. In November, they were introduced to the computer, and each had an opportunity to compose daily at the screen. Each day, the previous day's story was loaded onto the screen, so children could reread what they had written. Rather than begin a new piece of writing as they had been doing, the children generally chose to revise or continue writing. Drafting, it seems, was not such an odious task. Use of the computer not only resulted in longer compositions but also in more revisions. Each child's daily work was printed out, so she could compare successive drafts to see how her work had changed. Even when the computer was no longer available to the children, they seemed to have acquired the habit of revising. They continued to insert, delete, rewrite, and concerned themselves with spelling and punctuation only after composing was complete.

The writing of sixth-grade students was also dramatically affected when they used a word processor to transcribe their critical reviews of a show performed by various classes in the school (first written on paper) onto the computer (Bruce, Michaels, & Watson-Grego, 1985). As they waited for a turn on the computer, they read each other's writing, offering positive criticism that affected both the content and form of their compositions. The benefits for students of collaborative writing via the computer are many, as well (Vibert, 1988).

Writing Folders

Keeping written work in a manila pocket-folder or even a large manila envelope saves time and eliminates lost papers. Many teachers staple a sheet of paper in each child's folder on which children can brainstorm and keep a list of possible topics about which they want to write. These folders represent the collected fruits of the children's labors— a tangible result of their efforts. When all the work done during planning, writing, and revising on the current piece is kept together, children get a feeling for the writing process, as well as a sense of pride in what they have produced.

These writing folders are working tools children can use during writing workshop or free time. Jan, a first-grade teacher, has cut out and laminated large construction paper circles in green, yellow, and red. Each child has a set in her writing folder. Depending on the stage the child is in at the end of each writing workshop, she clips one of the circles on the outside of her folder. Green means she is planning and drafting, yellow signifies she is ready for a conference with the teacher, and red means she is revising and editing. Now, Jan can see at a glance where everyone is in the writing process and who is ready for a conference. Jan has a worktable with chairs at the back of her room and she often holds conferences with a small group of children all at once so they can learn from each other.

Writing Center

A designated writing center can serve several practical purposes, as well as give children the message that you value writing. Some ideas for creating and using a corner or a part of the classroom devoted to writing follow:

- Allow children to use the writing center whenever they have time.
- Keep writing folders, envelopes, or portfolios there.
- Keep supplies available, such as paper (various types, colors, and sizes), pens, pencils, crayons, dictionary, thesaurus, word bank, magazines, newspapers, glue, scissors, tape, stapler, and a box of story starters or pictures (see Figure 11.16).
- Display on the walls some of the models and guidelines discussed previously.
- Keep a chalkboard or lined paper on an easel for children who want to write on these materials.
- Keep journals or diaries in this area.
- Put a computer and printer or a typewriter in this area and set up a schedule so each student (or pair) has her own time slot, so good use is made of this equipment.

FIGURE 11.16 A list of some of the things to keep in a Writing Center.

369
Writing

Pencil sharpener	Scotch tape
Pencils (regular and colored)	Stapler
Erasers (including white correction fluid)	Dictionary
Pens (ink, ballpoint, felt tip, erasable, calligraphy)	Thesaurus
	Bulletin board
Paper (lined, unlined, white, colored, construction)	Calligraphy set
	Crayons
Notebooks	Paints (finger, water, oil)
Diary/journal	Chalkboard (chalk)
Stationery	Magnetic letters
Postcards	Magic slate
Stamps	Scrabble (Junior)
Letter opener	Lamp
Ruler	Desk
Scissors	Typewriter
Rubber cement	Computer/word processor

- Make mailboxes for children to encourage them to correspond with each other. Use round cardboard cylinders (e.g., glue empty potato chip containers together), adding a child's name to each.
- Provide comfortable seating for pairs of children to use while discussing compositions in peer conferences.

Revising

During revision, a writer may cross out, erase, insert ideas in the margins or on separate sheets of paper, or move sections around (see Figure 11.17). Revision happens during drafting, but it also occurs after drafting when a writer rereads the final version of what she has written and realizes that it can be said more cogently or aesthetically. Calkins (1994) reinforces the importance of rereading during revising when she reports that one 6-year-old reread a sentence 27 times before he finished writing it to his satisfaction. As he reread, he was able to decide how to make his written work say exactly what he meant and read more smoothly. Traditionally, the teacher has made corrections or suggested ways to revise students' work. But children's own responses to their work are as important to revision as feedback from others. Children as writers are their own best critics when they use self-revising and self-editing checklists to find and correct many of their own errors. Children can use these checklists to make their own revisions for clarity and form as they gain the experience and confidence needed to write well.

Research shows that feedback from peers is effective and feedback from peers and teachers together has an advantage over teacher feedback alone (Hansen, 1983; Hillocks, 1986). When children personally respond to meaning in each other's work, ask questions that help the writer clarify in peer revising conferences, and read each other's work to check for and help with proper mechanics in peer editing conferences, they provide special insight as they actively try to comprehend each other's text (see Figure 11.18).

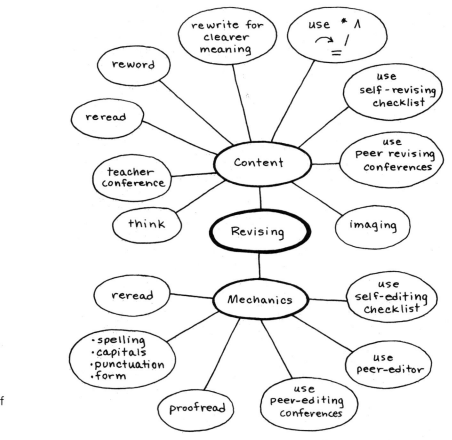

FIGURE 11.17 Elements of composing that may occur during revising.

There are two parts to revision—revising to improve content and organization, and editing to correct the mechanics of spelling, punctuation, and grammar. Each should be undertaken separately. It is usually overwhelming, even for the adult writer, to consider both at once. Not only is this easier to handle but it also encourages children to revise a written piece several times, thus making it more likely they will be happy with their work and their work will be of better quality.

One of the simplest ways to promote revising is to allow time between drafts. Leaving a day or several days between composing a draft and revising it allows children to reread their work with fresh and objective minds. Rereading a piece that one has been away from for a time seems to make revising for clarity and meaning easier. As Chris, a fifth-grader, said after rereading something he had written previously, "I can't believe I said that. It doesn't even make sense and I spelled two words wrong!" And he promptly revised his own first draft.

A computer and a word-processing program, of course, make revision even easier because, by touching a few keys, whole segments of text are replaced, added to, or moved around. Children learn the valuable lesson that writing does not have to come out right the first time and that they can manipulate it until it reads the way they want it to read.

Peer Response Sheet

1. What do you particularly like about this piece?

   _____

   _____

2. What part of it brings back a special memory for you?

   _____

   _____

3. What special words or phrases make the writing "talk" to you?

   _____

   _____

4. What advice or suggestions do you have for the writer?

   _____

   _____

   Author's Name   Partner's Name

   _____   _____

FIGURE 11.18 Students can provide feedback to each other on their writing.

Conduct a conference with a child regarding the content or form of a piece of the child's writing. Note the changes the child makes as a result of the conference. Then conference again in the revised work. Note the differences between the first draft and the third draft.

STRETCHING EXERCISE

• • • • •

Editing

When students edit, they put the finishing touches on a composition. They proofread for misspellings, errors in grammar and punctuation, legibility, and so on. You can teach editing in mini-lessons or during a writing conference. Following are several aspects of content and form children can look for as they edit:

Content	*Form*
Word clarity	Punctuation
Sentence sense	Capitalization
Coherence	Misspelled words
Organization and order	Margins
Topic and/or final sentences	Legibility

Using a checklist or guide helps students learn to edit. One way to illustrate how editing works is to project on the wall or make copies of an anonymous draft and then go through the process with the class or a small group, as Lisa did with her fourth-graders. Figures 11.19, 11.20, and 11.21 contain ideas for involving students in editing their work.

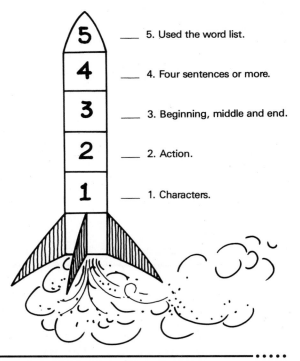

_____ 5. Used the word list.

_____ 4. Four sentences or more.

_____ 3. Beginning, middle and end.

_____ 2. Action.

_____ 1. Characters.

FIGURE 11.19 "Blast-Off" checklist created by first-graders.

FIGURE 11.20 A proofreading checklist helps students edit their work.

Proofreading Checklist

Did I remember . . . ?

_____ 1. Punctuation (. , ? ! ' ")   _____ 4. Margins

_____ 2. Capitals   _____ 5. Indenting

_____ 3. Spelling   _____ 6. Neatness

Do I have . . . ?

_____ 7. Complete sentences

_____ 8. A good beginning and ending

Watch out for . . .

_____ 9. Did I use the best word?

_____ 10. Are all my sentences important?

_____ 11. Are my sentences in order?

Children can also learn to use simple proofreading symbols. The list of proofreading symbols and sample of text in Figure 11.21 shows how the symbols indicate where this fifth-grader should make changes on his draft. With these tools, you or a classroom editing team can help children with the conventions they are capable of dealing with, and then you can make other suggestions before final revision and publication.

In conclusion, revising is a difficult part of the writing process for students. Fitzgerald (1988) suggests several reasons: Children may have trouble establishing clear

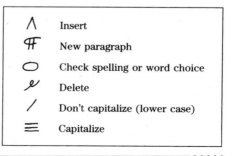

FIGURE 11.21   Proofreading symbols and a sample of text.

goals for their writing, juggling presentation and content can be too much for them as they attempt to revise, and they may not know where or how to make changes. At any rate, it seems clear that children need considerable support from peers and teachers in activities such as Author's Chair, conferences, writing workshops, mini-lessons, and modeling to accomplish effective revisions.

Mini-Lessons and Conferences

In Lisa Rieger and her colleague's writing workshop, their fourth-graders were writing *journey stories* when Lisa noticed an overuse of the words *nice* and *good.* So Lisa planned and taught a brief mini-lesson in which the students brainstormed a list of other descriptive words to use in place of the overused terms. They came up with words such as *stupendous, splendid, great, awesome, spectacular, wonderful, spontaneous,* and so on. The lesson offered opportunities to discuss word meanings and broaden vocabularies.

Next, Lisa shared a story written by Heather, who had volunteered to get some help from the class. Lisa had put the story on chart paper before school that day. She read it to the children and they offered suggestions to help Heather make her story more interesting. As each student made a suggestion, Lisa used colored markers to make proposed changes so the revision process was clearly different from the first draft. To signal the differences between the two, Lisa used blue for the changes that affected meaning and red for the punctuation and format changes. Then Lisa asked the students to use colored pens or pencils to revise their own drafts.

As the students revised and conferred with each other, Lisa and her colleague moved around the room, holding brief conferences with those students who wanted or needed further help. Many times, the conference lasted only two or three minutes and most consisted of Lisa and the other teacher first listening to the child's response to What seems to be your problem? or What are you stuck on? and then asking a pointed question or two, such as What sounds might someone hear as this happened? Which thing happened first? What were your feelings about the event? (Writing conferences are discussed in more detail in Chapter 9.)

Publishing

Publishing, which means "to make publicly known," motivates many students. The chance to share one's work in its finished form for others to see, touch, hear, read, and reread has a special appeal and provides the incentive for many students to write. It helps students focus on the communication of meaning to a real audience, thus legitimizing their writing efforts and providing a boost for self-esteem (see Figure 11.22).

Some students may be interested in publishing beyond their classroom and school in a children's magazine (Bromley & Mannix, 1993). There are nearly 40 children's magazines that publish children's work and you may want to encourage your young writers to send a piece in for review and possible publication (e.g., poetry, puzzles, brainteasers, letters, character sketches, riddles, songs, interviews, recipes, questions, games, limericks, crafts, cartoons, plays, true stories, fiction, projects, opinions, hobby and sports hints, and book reviews). Many magazines feature contests that specifically

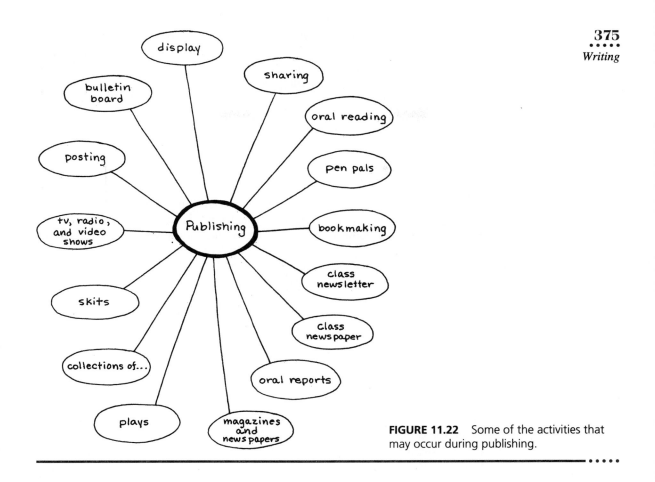

FIGURE 11.22 Some of the activities that may occur during publishing.

· · · · ·

encourage student participation, and many publish children's drawings, artwork, and photographs, as well.

What happens to the finished piece after a draft is revised, edited, and proofread is critical. Before they write, writers should consider if a piece will be displayed on a bulletin board, become a book, or be part of a class newsletter or newspaper. How will the piece be shared and with whom? Is it good enough to publish for others to read, to read orally, or post on a bulletin board? These questions help shape the composition and determine what the finished product will look like. A clear idea of how the audience will read the written product is important to the entire composing process. If the piece is for public consumption, the final form it takes may be quite different from the final form of an entry in a journal that only the author will read. Through publishing, children learn that spelling, legibility, punctuation, indenting, and capitalization are indeed an important courtesy to the reader.

Don't overlook the possibility of having student work published in other ways. Over 400 daily newspapers in the United States publish youth features (*Survey of News-*

papers in Education Programs, 1989). In addition, there are books such as *The National Written and Illustrated by . . . Awards for Students,* published yearly by Landmark Editions (1420 Kansas Avenue, Kansas City MO 64127). Entries of children's work must be submitted by a teacher or librarian. Guidelines for writing in magazines, newspapers, or the Landmark Edition can be obtained by sending a stamped, self-addressed envelope to those publishers.

Display and Bookmaking

Children thrive on recognition and are intensely curious about what their peers' work looks like. Displaying written work is a way to recognize and motivate children. You can post each child's story on a bulletin board in the classroom, in the hall outside your room, or on cafeteria walls, for instance, or you can help children make their own books.

Many teachers have publishing centers in their classrooms or have materials available so that children can make their own books. Books can be simply pieces of folded paper stapled together, or hardcover, sewn books can be made with a dry-mount press. Graves (1994) suggests that all children, not just the best writers, choose one high-quality piece to publish out of every few pieces they write.

Besides books that contain creative compositions and the various forms discussed earlier in this chapter, some other types of children's publications include:

Alphabet books	Idioms
Number books	Poetry
Color books	Reports or information books
Concept books	*Dinosaurs*
Red Is . . .	*The Space Shuttle*
Terrific Is . . .	*How to Make a Robot*
Favorite riddles	Recipes or cookbooks
Brainteasers	Special holidays
Jokes	Valentine's Day
Slang expressions	Yom Kippur
Songs	Autobiography

Each of these publications can represent the work of one child, or several children can publish work together in a collection. Older children enjoy publishing a class newsletter or magazine to share with other classes and parents. Class yearbooks including pictures and stories about each child are also a possibility. Of course, you should explore all kinds of books, according to the age and interests of your students: *shape books* (e.g., stories about Halloween put together in a book shaped like a pumpkin); *sewn books* with wallpaper covers; *big books* that an entire class has contributed to and can read; *information books* that use photographs a child has taken; and perhaps even collections of postcards about which a text is written.

There are many ways to make books. Folded books that are stapled with wallpaper covers are the easiest. Many schools have binding tools that punch holes on pages and affix plastic spines to make class books or an individual student book. Many teachers enlist the aid of volunteer parents or the school parent/teacher organization to organize and operate bookbinding projects. They make cloth-covered or other types of blank

•••••
Curiosity about each other's work makes student-created books eagerly anticipated and read by classmates.

books to hold children's final products. With proper direction, older students can make books for themselves or for younger children. Often, these child-created books are some of the most popular in the room. So don't overlook the possibility of including them in the classroom library, where each can receive a pocket and "library" card and then be checked out by children and taken home to read.

Children's drawings and illustrations, pictures cut out of magazines, or actual photographs can accompany text. Creating pop-up illustrations for books or about which stories can be written is an extremely motivating activity for some young writers. Evans and Moore (1985) suggest several ways that folded and cut paper can enhance any story. Children can illustrate with felt pens, colored pencils, paints, crayons, vegetable prints, wood cuts, or other media. Children who are not comfortable with their own artwork can have other children illustrate for them. They can print text by hand in manuscript, cursive, or calligraphy, or type it on a typewriter or word processor.

Oral Reading

Set aside a regular time for children to read some of their work aloud to the class. In some classrooms, this occurs regularly each day at the end of writing workshop, or when a student sits in the Author's Chair to share her work, or in peer conferences as children confer with each other, or in conferences with you. Children should be encouraged to take their finished work home, where they can read it to family members, as well.

Children also enjoy the opportunity to read their work to each other in paired reading situations. Another enjoyable experience for children is reading to other classes or adults, perhaps those in hospitals or at a center for senior citizens. Even those children who have difficulties in reading can often read their own writing more easily than someone else's. This practice develops fluency and builds confidence.

When children tape record their oral reading of a book they have written, a collection of these stories can be made available to the entire class in the listening corner as a Dial-a-Story Center (see Chapter 10). When children record their oral reading and play it back, they gain a sensitivity not only to what they say but also to how they say it. Oral reading in this context can help improve both reading comprehension and fluency.

Writing Assessment

One goal of writing instruction should be to help students gain an awareness of standards for good writing so they can become strong and fluent writers. To begin self-evaluation, Anne Gardner and Elaine Pytel ask their first-graders to use the checklist in Fig-

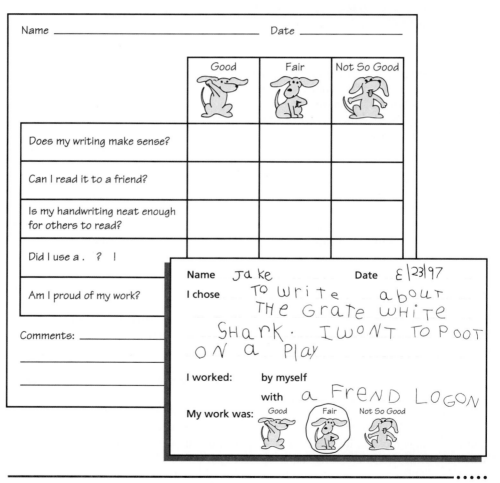

FIGURE 11.23   A self-assessment tool for first-graders.

Source: Reprinted by permission of Anne Gardner and Elaine Pytel.

FIGURE 11.24   Middle-grade students created this 12-question checklist for their research papers.

Checklist for Research Papers

Name:_____   Date: _____

Partner: _____

	You	Partner
1. Do I have a topic sentence that tells what each paragraph is about?	_____	_____
2. Did I add details to tell more about the main ideas?	_____	_____
3. Did I choose interesting verbs (action words) and adjectives (word to describe)?	_____	_____
4. Did I use the correct form of verbs to show past, present, and future?	_____	_____
5. Did I indent the first word of each paragraph?	_____	_____
6. Is each sentence a complete thought?	_____	_____
7. Did I use capitals at the beginning of sentences?	_____	_____
8. Did I use capitals for names (proper nouns)?	_____	_____
9. Did I use endmarks?	_____	_____
10. Did I check spelling and correct it?	_____	_____
11. Is it neatly written?	_____	_____
12. Did I include all the information and answer all the questions that were required?	_____	_____

ure 11.23 to assess their story writing. Chris Howe has her middle-school students use the Checklist for Research Papers in Figure 11.24 first themselves. Then each student makes revisions on her first draft before a partner uses the checklist to check it.

Rubrics

Another way to develop standards for good writing is to involve students at the very beginning of the writing task in creating standards or guidelines for a good finished product. Tonya Dauphin discovered in conferences with her third-graders that "they tend to give themselves high marks for long stories, even if the stories don't make sense." So, the idea of engaging children in discussions that lead to creating criteria for good pieces of writing *before* they write makes sense to Tonya.

What is a rubric? A *rubric* is a set of criteria for a piece of student work that describes the quality of the piece. A rubric can be a teaching tool if you create it with a group of students who then use it to guide their writing and to assess the finished product. Tricia Engineri says, "In some ways, making a rubric reminds me of when students create classroom rules. It empowers them. It gives them a say and they are more likely to follow the rules they have made themselves. I think students are more willing to work up to the expectations of the rubric if they helped create it. Then the requirements are not just coming from me—the authority."

How does a teacher create a rubric with a group of students? *Before* students begin to plan and draft, talk together about what an excellent finished piece looks like. The following steps may serve as a guide:

1. Think of a piece of writing in its *best* form.
2. Brainstorm and list its key elements.
3. Group elements into categories and label each.
4. Check elements against the *best* form.
5. Revise if needed.

Both Tonya and Tricia realize the importance of class discussion and debate of issues and ideas during shared rubric creation to understand why something is important. For example, Tricia discovered that although "students usually know what is important in writing, it is not always easy to make a rubric with a class. Problems arise when students disagree, but it teaches them about negotiation." Tonya says, "It is difficult for them to describe the qualities of good writing clearly, so I often revise the first rubric we make. And, of course, they leave things out that I believe are important. But I am part of the discussion, too, and I add aspects of good writing that I believe are important. I also have the option of giving things more weight in the rubric than students might." To create a rubric, students may discuss, for example, how setting or characters are important, how descriptive words communicate meaning, or how indenting and spelling help the reader, and then use these ideas as they write.

To culminate a fourth-grade unit called *The Earth's Great Balancing Act,* Doreen Layton and her students talked about a story they could write to demonstrate what they had learned. In the story, each student would become an "Ecobird" and fly around the world, viewing the six ecosystems they studied. The class discussed criteria for the story before writing it and listed characteristics which, with Doreen's help, became the rubric in Figure 11.25. Over several days, students used the rubric and the writing process, finally evaluating their finished work with the rubric. Doreen used the rubric to evaluate the stories and conferenced with each student about the two evaluations.

Doreen said, "While developing a guide to show how well they could relay information to others, my students were enthusiastic and eager to contribute. Even though I had an outline of expectations, the class went well beyond what I felt was important and came up with more specific ideas. In the end, the rubric was collaborative and comprehensive." Tonya, Tricia, and Doreen realize the power of rubrics to develop good writing but they also know that rubrics need not be created for everything students write.

STRETCHING EXERCISE	Work with a child to create a rubric for a piece of writing the student must do. Use the five steps provided in this chapter. Help the child use the rubric to evaluate her finished piece.

•••••

FIGURE 11.25 With their teacher, a third-grade class decided on criteria for their written report and presentation.

"Ecobird" Story Rubric

	? 1	Needs Work 2	Almost 3	Great! 4
1. Story Content				
A. Story tells of Ecobird's travel.				
B. Story describes an ecosystem & its wonders.				
C. Story describes a polluted area & gives at least 1 suggestion for fixing the problem.				
D. Story has a setting, plot, at least 2 characters & an ending.				
E. Story makes sense.				
2. Story Mechanics				
A. Capitals				
B. Punctuation				
C. Sentences				
D. Paragraphs				
E. Spelling				
3. Appearance				
A. Neatness				
Total Points (44)				

Source: Courtesy of Doreen Layton.

Audience Response

Audience response is important during the writing process and when writing is finished. The best responses are those that are personal and sincere, not necessarily educational, positive, supportive, or kind (Graves, 1991; Hunt, 1987). When one responds personally to content, one communicates directly with the writer to help her evaluate her work. As children receive both written and verbal responses from their peers and from their teachers during the composing process, they learn to value thoughtful feedback from others.

There are several things to keep in mind as you respond to and help children with composing. In both verbal and written responses to a draft, react to the content first. This

•••••
When you conference with a student about a piece of writing, respond first in a positive way to the content of the writing and then ask a question to clarify the intended meaning.

reaction should communicate personal feelings about the ideas a child is trying to express and may include praise. You might also ask for clarification of content and elaboration of a point that is not clear. When responding to form, the same reaction, clarification, and elaboration are appropriate. Additionally, you can make suggestions about both content and form. The story by Billy G. and the responses his teacher made (see Figure 11.26) are examples of these three types of evaluative responses. Research on the comparative effects of praise and criticism on children's written compositions indicates

Why do cows have horns

Once there was 50 cow in a feld they are had horns and were blowing them every day and farmer was tring to stop them but all a sudden a fairy came to the farmer and fairy said, you have one wish what would it be. The farmer said, I wish cows have on horns there herd. So the fairy did it and that why cows have horns on there heads

By Billy G.

Some Possible Responses to Billy's Story

Content

Reaction: "I felt like I was reading a Rudyard Kipling story! It's great!"

Clarification: "Where did the fairy come from?"

Elaboration: "Why was the farmer trying to stop the cows? "

Form

Reaction: "Your story has good form. You indented and kept margins."

Clarification: "Can you add apostrophes when the fairy and farmer speak?"

Suggestion: "Read your story and add commas and periods where they are needed. Your first sentence needs a comma and a period."

FIGURE 11.26 Some possible responses to a third-grader's how-and-why story.

that positive comments appear to be more effective than negative comments (Hillocks, 1986). It may be that children who receive responses to content and whose work is not corrected write more, have more creative ideas, experience more enjoyment from writing, and make fewer mechanical errors.

Be sure to limit your reaction to those areas where you have a genuine response or where you believe a child needs help. Especially for a young child or a novice writer, too many responses to too many problems with content and form is overwhelming. It is probably better to focus responses on one or two things at first to help a child evaluate and revise a draft.

Evaluation needs to be ongoing, then, occurring both verbally and in writing, as the child's writing skills develop. It should not occur once a week or with each piece of written work. In fact, in preparation for assigning a grade, evaluate the best example of a child's finished work periodically. This should represent what the child has learned.

Analyzing and evaluating writing involves both the process and the product (see Figure 11.27). In order to evaluate the process, you need to examine each aspect of the child's writing performance. By observing children as they compose, conferencing with them and reading their written work, you can assess their writing with the checklist in Figure 11.28. This checklist is a guide; revise it to fit your needs. Use it periodically during a writing conference to evaluate children's involvement in composing. Older children can keep their own checklists, regularly filling them out and charting their progress.

To evaluate a composition, you and a student can ask several questions concerning the purpose of the writing task. These questions will guide your writing conferences with children as you look at drafts or finished products together. The first and most important question is: Does the writing communicate the meaning I want it to communicate? A second question is: How well does my writing communicate? A third question is: What aspects of my writing promote or inhibit its meaningful communication? By re-

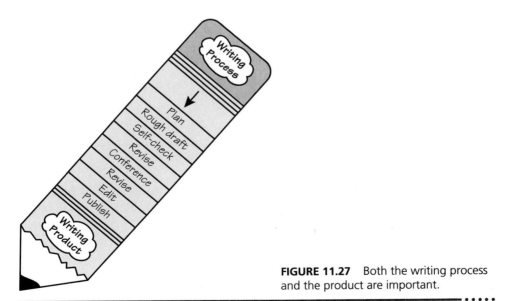

FIGURE 11.27 Both the writing process and the product are important.

FIGURE 11.28   Teachers can use an evaluation checklist to give constructive criticism that is appropriate to each child.

Writing Evaluation Checklist

B   D   I   *When planning, the child:*
☐ ☐ ☐   Thinks and talks about the topic.
☐ ☐ ☐   Considers the purpose of the piece.
☐ ☐ ☐   Reads about the topic or reads similar products.
☐ ☐ ☐   Brainstorms and organizes ideas.
☐ ☐ ☐   Generates questions and makes notes, lists, webs, or an outline.
☐ ☐ ☐   Considers audience and aspects of form.

When drafting, the child:
☐ ☐ ☐   Focuses on communicating meaning first.
☐ ☐ ☐   Uses invented spelling or attempts to spell unknown words.
☐ ☐ ☐   Attends to the conventions appropriately.
☐ ☐ ☐   Pauses, rereads, and thinks as writing occurs.
☐ ☐ ☐   Revises as he or she is writing.
☐ ☐ ☐   Consults peers, teacher, dictionary, thesaurus, or other resource when needed.

When revising, the child:
☐ ☐ ☐   Inserts, deletes, changes, or reorganizes to clarify writing.
☐ ☐ ☐   Pauses, rereads, and thinks as revision occurs.
☐ ☐ ☐   Edits and proofreads to include appropriate conventions.
☐ ☐ ☐   Consults peers, teacher, dictionary, thesaurus, or other resource when needed.

When publishing, the child:
☐ ☐ ☐   Takes work to completion.
☐ ☐ ☐   Reads orally the finished piece.
☐ ☐ ☐   Exchanges the written piece with peers for silent reading.
☐ ☐ ☐   Writes legibly.

(B = Beginning, D = Developing, I = Independent)

sponding to the work in this way, you and the child focus on the meaning of the composition, rather than on the conventions of the transcription, which are a secondary but related concern.

Portfolios

The *portfolio,* a collection of works representing a range of abilities and accomplishments, traditionally was used by artists to represent their work. Today, many teachers use the portfolio as a means of documenting and assessing student growth. If you decide to use portfolios in your classroom, the most important first step is to decide on your purpose(s) for the portfolio. Once you have established a purpose—for example, to monitor and assess your students' reading and writing growth and plan for instruction—your portfolios should consist of a variety of materials that will help you achieve your purposes.

Valencia (1990) provides these four principles to guide your use of portfolios in the classroom:

1. *Reliable assessment is based on authentic tasks.* When you have students read and write a variety of texts for a range of purposes that reflect real-life situations, you are providing authentic tasks. Student performance on these tasks needs to be included in portfolios.

How to do it. When you plan a unit, always ask the all-important question Why? before you include any lesson or activity. Your answer should relate to learning that makes sense and, as much as possible, translate to the real world. In a unit on *Nature's Great Balancing Act: Relationships between Predators and Prey,* having students take the perspective of predators and prey and write letters to each other about their roles in nature makes more sense than writing letters to a fictitious person, for example. But writing letters to wildlife organizations, zoos, zoologists, or a representative in Congress to obtain information or influence legislation may be an even more authentic task. These authentic tasks, as well as teacher-made tests, should be part of portfolios.

You should be able to articulate to your students why they are doing something and how it will help them perform better. Students should read all genres of literature and have opportunities to learn from all types of texts (e.g., audiotapes, videotapes, magazines, newspapers, etc.). They should also write for themselves, you, their peers, and real audiences outside the classroom for a variety of purposes.

2. *Assessment should be a continuous process.* Evidence of student work should be included regularly in the portfolio so that growth or lack of it can be identified. The usefulness of the portfolio is not as an end-of-the-year exhibit, but rather as a working exhibit of your students' accomplishments that reflect their learning in process throughout the year.

· · · · ·
A child may choose to put a copy of a student-made book in her portfolio as evidence of her writing progress.

How to do it. Some teachers have their students select pieces to include in their portfolios at the end of each week. Other teachers evaluate portfolios at natural breaks in the curriculum, such as when one unit ends and another begins, or on a regular basis, such as the first week of an 8- or 12-week period. Perhaps you will find some other regular time that makes sense to assess your portfolios. At these times, a 10-minute conference with each of five or six students a day lets you complete an assessment of your entire class in a week.

3. *Literacy assesments should be multidimensional.* Reading and writing include a wide range of behaviors and performances that should be represented in the portfolio. Both your students and you should decide what to include in portfolios.

How to do it. Teachers use large manila envelopes, accordian folders, or file boxes in which to keep portfolio artifacts such as

Reading logs	Creative writing
Journal pages	Responses to reading
End-of-unit tests	Letters
Tapes of oral reading	Poetry
Videos	Classroom tests
Checklists of skills	Reports
Teacher observations	

What other kinds of things can be included in portfolios? Suggestions include anecdotal records, interest inventories, attitude inventories, checklists of skills, self-evaluations (see Figure 11.29), and writing samples displaying a range of types of writing and the components of writing from planning to finished product. Portfolios help you evaluate the process of writing as well as student products, and they involve students more directly in learning how to become better writers by providing them a record of their progress to examine and on which to reflect.

4. *An evaluation tool must assist in cooperative reflection between teacher and student.* Periodically, a student's portfolio should be evaluated by both you and the student. When you include your students in choosing artifacts to include in their portfolios and invite them to be part of the assessment process in conferences, you give students responsibility for their own learning.

How to do it. Kelly Hawley combines self-selection and goal setting by her first-graders in their literacy portfolios. She asks them to complete the form in Figure 11.30 and staple it to each piece they choose to include in their portfolio. Kelly does the same with pieces she includes in each child's portfolio. When samples of a student's work representing each aspect of the writing process are kept in a portfolio from the beginning of the year, there is good documentation of the child's growth as a writer.

Another way to help your students take ownership of the conference is to ask them to select artifacts and then write a brief self-evaluation to prepare for the conference. Students become honest and critical observers of their own learning with directions like those given in Figure 11.31.

Goal setting with students is a critical component of successful portfolios. After examining a student's literacy portfolio together, Kelly can help the student establish reading and writing goals for herself. Kelly can also identify her goals as the teacher and goals for the parents, which she can share in writing or in a parent/teacher conference.

FIGURE 11.29 A self-evaluation inventory to measure feelings and involvement in writings.

387
• • • • •
Writing

Self-Evaluation Inventory

Student: _____ Date: _____

Directions: Draw a long arrow to the YES if the sentence is true or a shorter arrow if it is only sometimes true.

		No	**Yes**
1.	I like to write.	•	•
2.	There are a lot of things I can write about.	•	•
3.	I enjoy drawing pictures to go with my writing.	•	•
4.	I am growing and improving as a writer.	•	•
5.	I think about and plan my story writing before I write.	•	•
6.	I use invented spelling when I don't know how to spell a word.	•	•
7.	I revise to make my writing clearer and more interesting.	•	•
8.	I listen in peer conferences to what others have to say about my writing.	•	•
9.	I ask for help from others when my writing gets stuck.	•	•
10.	I read books to help me become a better writer.	•	•
11.	I use legible handwriting so that others can easily read my writing.	•	•
12.	I use descriptive words in my writing.	•	•
13.	I use punctuation marks when I should.	•	•
14.	I use complete sentences in my work.	•	•
15.	I use paragraphs in my work.	•	•
16.	I like to use the computer to write.	•	•
17.	I publish my writing.	•	•
18.	I like to read my work for others to hear.	•	•
19.	I enjoy writing in my journal.	•	•
20.	I can write in many different forms (letters, plays, poems, reports, stories).	•	•

Student-led conferences grow from portfolio use (Norwick, 1996). Four times a year, Lisa Norwick has her second-graders set goals for themselves, after reflection and examination of their portfolios, and then lead the parent/teacher conference. This shifts the reponsibility for learning from the teacher to the student and puts the student in charge of deciding on the direction of her education.

Of course, portfolios have their disadvantages. They are time consuming and, without a clear purpose, can become just collections of work. They are claimed by some to be unreliable because they include a degree of human interpretation and judgment (Wolf, 1989). However, keep in mind that every standardized test contains a standard error of measurement—unrecognized by many parents, teachers, and administrators—

that contributes to the unreliability of scores. When the portfolio is mandated and standardized with minimal teacher input as a districtwide assessment tool and becomes "a collection of student work produced to meet preset categories that does not provide meaningful oppportunities for student input, reflection and choice," some teachers question its usefulness (Irwin-DeVitis, 1996, p. 230).

My Portfolio

1. I chose this for my portfolio because. . .

____

2. I know how to. . . ____________________

3. My goal is to learn. . . ____________________

Date__________ Signed____________________

FIGURE 11.30 Kelly Hawley's first-graders complete this form for each piece they put in their portfolio.

Source: Reprinted by permission of Kelley A. Hawley, primary teacher, Johnson City, NY.

FIGURE 11.31 Older students can use this form to be more critical in evaluating their own writing.

My Portfolio Self-Evaluation

1. The piece I am proudest of is ____________________.

   The reason is ____________________.

2. Two pieces that show the most growth in my learning are

   a. ____________________.

   b. ____________________.

   They show that I have learned ____________________.

   ____________________.

3. What I need to learn next is ____________________.

   The piece that shows this is ____________________.

Portfolios have many uses. They can help you track and communicate student progress with parents, other teachers, and administrators. They allow you to easily demonstrate student strengths and needs in conferences with parents. They can be used to determine groups for mini-lessons, as an explanation and documentation of curriculum and instruction, and for collective problem solving with colleagues about individual students. Wolf (1989) also points out the benefits for students when they are involved in evaluating the work appearing in their portfolios. He suggests that students periodically look at and evaluate the progress of their own work. He believes the portfolio should not only be used in conferences with parents but also with students so that they can see their own strengths and needs and begin to take ownership for their own learning.

Summary

Writing is the construction of meaning that requires both cognitive and physical skills. It is a process as well as a product in which the writer usually focuses first on meaning or content and second on conventions. Children compose to convey feelings, narrate, explain, and persuade as they fulfill their personal needs and communicate with others. Writing assessment should consider both the process and the product in an ongoing examination of children's growth, needs, and goals.

R·····eflections

1. Call your local newspaper to inquire about a class visit to the newspaper or a visit by a news reporter to your school to learn about journalism and the production of the newspaper. Request free teaching materials the newspaper may have available for your elementary classroom.

2. Conduct a writing conference with a child. What are the child's strengths and what are the child's problems? What questions did you ask to help the child clarify, organize, and focus her writing?

3. Prepare a brief description of your writing program in the form of a letter to go home to parents. Describe your goals for the children and how you will achieve them. Include concrete ways parents can help develop children's writing abilities at home.

Professional Resources

Chancer, J., & Rester-Zodrow, G. (1997). *Moon journals: Writing, art, and inquiry through focused nature study.* Portsmouth, NH: Heinemann. Two teachers show how their students' journal writing to record and illustrate their observations of the moon evolves into prose, poetry, and art. The book includes 28 Writing Invitations and 28 Art Invitations, mini-lessons that can be adapted for other areas of inquiry.

Hamilton, M., & Weiss, M. (1996). *Stories in my pocket: Tales kids can tell.* Golden, CO: Fulcrum. This handbook contains 30 stories chiefly from folk literature, helpful tips for storytelling, and an overview for teachers.

Rhodes, L. K., & Dudley-Marling, C. (1996). *Readers and writers with a difference: A wholistic approach to teaching struggling readers and writers* (2nd ed.). Portsmouth, NH: Heinemann. With new sections on literacy theory, instruction, and assessment and literacy as social practice, this book supports the wholistic methods it describes, such as writing workshop, for building the literacy of at-risk learners.

Short, K. G., Harste, J., & Burke, C. (1995). *Creating classrooms for authors and inquirers* (2nd ed.). Portsmouth, NH: Heinemann. This book shows how to set up supportive classrooms in which children move from reading and writing to in-

quiry. Many strategies are given for including the authoring cycle within the curriculum.

Tompkins, G. E. (1994). *Teaching writing: Balancing process and product* (2nd ed.). New York: Macmillan. This text gives practical strategies for teaching writing, emphasizing writers' workshop and thematic writing. Individual chapters focus on seven written forms: journal, letter, descriptive, biographical, expository, narrative, and persuasive writing.

References

Anderson-Inman, L. (1990). Enhancing the reading-writing connection: Classroom applications. *The Writing Notebook*, 7, 6–8.

Atwell, N. (1987). *In the middle: Writing, reading, and learning with adolescents*. Portsmouth, NH: Heinemann.

Bromley, K. (1993). *Journaling: Engagements in reading, writing and thinking*. New York: Scholastic.

Bromley, K., & Mannix, D. (1993). Beyond the classroom: Publishing student work in magazines. *The Reading Teacher*, 47 (1), 72–77.

Bruce, B., Michaels, S., & Watson-Grego, K. (1985). How computers can change the writing process. *Language Arts*, 62 (2), 143–149.

Calkins, L. M. (1994). *The art of teaching writing*. Portsmouth, NH: Heinemann.

Calkins, L. M., & Harwayne, S., (1991). *Living between the lines*. Portsmouth, NH: Heinemann.

Evans, J., & Moore, J. E. (1985). *How to make books with children*. Monterey, CA: Evan-Moore.

Fitzgerald, J. (1988). Helping young writers revise: A brief review for teachers. *The Reading Teacher*, 42, 124–129.

Gambrell, L. B. (1985). Dialogue journals: Reading-writing interaction. *The Reading Teacher*, 38 (6), 512–515.

Graves, D. (1994). *A fresh look at writing*. Portsmouth, NH: Heinemann.

Graves, D. (1991). *Build a literate classroom*. Portsmouth, NH: Heinemann.

Graves, D. (1983). *Writing: Teachers and children at work*. Exeter, NH: Heinemann.

Graves, D. (1979). Research update: Handwriting is for writing. *Language Arts*, 55 (3), 393–399.

Hansen, J. (1983). Authors respond to authors. *Language Arts*, 60 (8), 970–976.

Hillocks, G. (1986). *Research on written composition*. Urbana, IL: ERIC Clearinghouse.

Hipple, M. L. (1985). Journal writing in kindergarten. *Language Arts*, 62 (3), 255–261.

Hunt, R. A. (1987). "Could you put lots of holes?" Modes of response to writing. *Language Arts*, 64 (2), 229–232.

Irwin-DeVitis, L. (1996). Teachers' voices: Literacy portfolios in the classroom and beyond. *Reading Research and Instruction*, 35 (3), 223–236.

Kahn, J., & Freyd, P. (1990). Online: A whole language perspective on keyboarding. *Language Arts*, 67, 84–90.

Newman, J. (1984). Language learning and computers. *Language Arts*, 61 (5), 494–497.

Norwick, L. (1996). Student-led parent conferences. *Instructor*, October, 100–101.

Phenix, J., & Hannan, E. (1984). Word processing in the grade one classroom. *Language Arts*, 61 (8), 804–812.

Routman, R. (1996). *Literacy at the crossroads: Crucial talk about reading, writing and other teaching dilemmas*. Portsmouth, NH: Heinemann.

Short, K. G., Harste, J., & Burke, C. (1995). *Creating classrooms for authors and inquirers* (2nd ed.). Portsmouth, NH: Heinemann.

Smith, F. (1982). *Writing and the writer*. New York: Holt.

Sudol, D., & Sudol, P. (1995). Yet another story: Writers' workshop revisited. *Language Arts*, 72 (3), 171–178.

Survey of Newspapers in Education Programs. (1989). Washington, DC: American Newspaper Publishers Association Foundation and International Newspaper Marketing Association.

Valencia, S. (1990). A portfolio approach to classroom reading assessment: The whys, whats and hows. *The Reading Teacher, 43* (4), 338–341.

Vibert, A. (1988). Collaborative writing: *Language Arts, 65,* 74–76.

Webster's II new college dictionary. (1995). Boston: Houghton Mifflin.

Wolf, D. P. (1989). Portfolio assessment: Sampling student work. *Educational Leadership, 46,* 35–39.

Zaragoza, N., & Vaughn, S. (1995). Children teach us to teach writing. *The Reading Teacher, 49* (1), 42–49.

Children's Book References

Blume, J. (1972). *Tales of a fourth grade nothing.* New York: Dutton.

Cleary, B. (1979). *Beezus and Ramona.* New York: Dell.

Hamilton, V. (1985). *The people could fly.* New York: Knopf.

Lansky, B. (1997). *Free stuff for kids.* Deephaven, MN: Meadowbrook.

Martin, B., & Archambault, J. (1990). *Knots on a counting rope.* New York: Trumpet.

Children's Books about Writing

Ahlberg, J., & Ahlberg, A. (1995). *The jolly pocket postman.* Boston: Little, Brown. (Gr. 1–4). Pages crafted like envelopes and letters from storybook characters show a mail carrier delivering the letters.

Ahlberg, J., & Ahlberg, A. (1986). *The jolly postman.* New York: Little, Brown. (Gr. 1–4). The same format as *The Jolly Pocket Postman* with letters addressed to various fairy-tale characters.

Aliki. (1986). *How a book is made.* New York: Crowell. (Gr. 2–5). Text and cartoon characters in this book explain writing, illustrating, editing, and publishing a picture book.

Axworthy, A. (1995). *Anni's diary of France.* Boston: Whispering Coyote Press. (Gr. 4–6). In her diary, a preteen records her family's travel through France and includes some French vocabulary.

Blos, J. (1976). *A gathering of days.* New York: Scribner. (Gr. 4–9). (Newbery Medal). Written as a journal, this book relates Catherine Hall's thoughts and feelings about her life in New England in the 1880s.

Bowen, G. (1994). *Stranded at Plimouth plantation, 1626.* New York: HarperCollins. (Gr. 3–6). In brief journal entries accompanied by lovely woodcuts, Christopher, a 13-year-old orphan, chronicles his first month in the New World as he awaits passage to Jamestown.

Brookfield, K. (1993). *Book.* New York: Knopf. (Gr. 5–12). This book contains a history of writing systems, printing, and books. Photographs are included.

Carlson, J. (1989). *"Nothing is impossible," said Nellie Bly.* Milwaukee, WI: Raintree. (Gr. 3–6). This story of Nellie Bly's life describes her as a successful reporter at age 17, who traveled around the world in 72 days.

Caselley, J. (1991). *Dear Annie.* New York: Greenwillow. (Gr. 1–3). For Show and Tell at school, Annie takes over 100 letters from Grandpa, who has been her pen pal since birth.

Cleary, B. (1984). *Dear Mr. Henshaw.* New York: Morrow. (Gr. 3–6). Leigh Botts writes letters to his favorite author and begins his own diary, where he shows how he copes with his parents' divorce and difficulties at school.

Conrad, P. (1991). *Pedro's journal.* Honesdale, PA: Caroline House. (Gr. 3–6). This is the story of Christopher Columbus, told from the perspective of Pedro, a cabin boy aboard the *Santa Maria,* whose sketches and journal entries chronicle Columbus's first voyage.

Cooney, B. (1994). *Only Opal: The diary of a young girl.* New York: Philomel. (Gr. 2–6). In the early 1900s, an orphaned 5-year-old girl keeps a diary of life with a family that thinks she's a nuisance. Opal finds peace by making friends with kind neighbors and animals.

Cushman, K. (1994). *Catherine called Birdy.* New York: Clarion. (Gr. 5–8). Catherine, a young woman in the thirteenth century, keeps a diary of her life as her father tries to find her a wealthy husband. She has hopes of her own and uses clever tricks to get rid of unwanted suitors.

Dupasquier, P. (1985). *Dear Daddy . . . .* New York: Bradbury. (Gr. 1–3). Young Sophie writes letters to her father who is away on a long sea voyage.

Epstein, S., & Epstein, B. (1975). *The first book of printing.* New York: Watts. (Gr. 3–6). This book contains a history of printing from the seals of ancient kings to the production of the Gutenberg Bible. It explains the many methods of printing text and pictures and includes a glossary of printing terms.

Ets, M. H. (1967). *Bad boy, good boy.* New York: Crowell. (Gr. 2–4). Roberto's Spanish-speaking family moves to the United States from Mexico and has difficulties until his ability to read and write helps them adjust.

Filipovic, Z. (1994). *Zlata's diary: A child's life in Sarajevo.* New York: Viking. (Gr. 4–8). Zlata, an 11-year-old, begins her diary with entries written by a happy, bright, and care-free girl in peaceful Sarajevo. As war encroaches, the tone of her diary changes as she describes the violence and horror of war.

Galate, L. (1980). *A beginner's guide to calligraphy.* New York: Dell. (Gr. 3–8). This book provides suggestions about style, techniques, materials, and equipment, as well as exercises for beginners.

Gallicich, A. (1987). *Samantha Smith: A journey for peace.* Minneapolis: Dillon. (Gr. 2–6). This is the story of an 11-year-old, Samantha Smith, who traveled to the Soviet Union after writing a letter to a Russian leader about world peace. She later died tragically in a plane crash.

George, J. C. (1993). *Dear Rebecca, winter is here.* New York: HarperCollins. (Gr. 2–5). A grandmother writes her granddaughter a poetic letter about the changes that happen in the Northern Hemisphere as the earth tilts on its axis and winter occurs.

Gregory, K. (1997). *Across the wide and lonesome prairie: The Oregon trail diary of Hattie Campbell, 1847.* New York: Scholastic/Dear America. (Gr. 4–6). A young pioneer girl chronicles her family's rigorous and brave journey westward as they pave the way for the thousands of Americans who will follow.

Hahn, M. D. (1983). *Daphne's book.* New York: Clarion. (Gr. 4–6). A friendship develops when two girls collaborate on the writing of a picture book.

Heide, F. P., & Gilliland, J. H. (1990). *The day of Ahmed's secret.* New York: Lothrop. (Gr. 2–4). This is the story of a boy in Cairo, Egypt, who learns to write his own name.

Hesse, K. (1992). *Letters from Rifka.* New York: Holt. (Gr. 5–8). In this journal, a young girl writes to her cousin, describing her family's flight from Russia to America in 1919 and her experiences when she is left behind in Belgium.

Hoban, L. (1976). *Arthur's pen pal.* New York: Harper and Row. (Gr. K–3). Arthur would rather play with his pen pal than his sister and is surprised to receive a letter from his pen pal.

Holl, K. D. (1996). *Perfect or not, here I come.* New York: Atheneum. (Gr. 3–6). Tara Brown wants to be a playwright and she is thrilled when one of her plays is chosen as the production for Sixth Grade Drama Night. She learns much about herself as she copes with several crises that threaten to spoil the production.

Holmes, B. W. (1988). *Charlotte the starlet.* New York: Harper and Row. (Gr. 3–6). When Charlotte decides to stop telling tall tales and start writing a book, she gains instant popularity at school but almost loses her best friend.

Hunter, L. (1992). *The diary of Latoya Hunter.* New York: Crown. (Gr. 6–8). In this true story of a 12-year-old African American girl's first year in a Bronx junior high school, Latoya writes about friendships, boys, television, and conflicts with her mother.

Jarrell, R. (1964). *The bat poet.* New York: Macmillan. (Gr. 3–6). This is the story of a brown bat who makes up poems about his various animal friends.

Kaye, M. (1987). *Daphne.* Orlando: Harcourt Brace Jovanovich. (Gr. 3–6). Twelve-year-old Daphne is content writing poetry, and even wants to join the Creative Writing Club, but her older sisters think she should pursue other interests.

Keats, E. J. (1968). *A letter to Amy.* New York: Harper and Row. (Gr. K–3). Peter writes a special letter to his friend, Amy, inviting her to his party. Through a misunderstanding, she is hurt by Peter but she comes to the party and all is well.

Krull, K. (1994). *Lives of the writers: Comedies, tragedies (and what the neighbors thought).* New York: Harcourt. (Gr. 3–8), Brief biographies of 19 writers create memorable images and reveal the authors as real people with quirks, failures, and successes.

Krupinski, L. (1995). *Bluewater journal: The voyage of the sea tiger.* New York: HarperCollins. (Gr.

3–6). Twelve-year-old Benjamin's journal entries describe the adventures and hardships of travel with his family from Boston to Hong Kong on a clipper ship in 1860.

Lowry, L. (1984). *Anastasia, ask your analyst.* Boston: Houghton Mifflin. (Gr. 3–6). Anastasia keeps a science project notebook of humorous observations about her gerbils and her personal problems.

MacLachlan, P. (1994). *Skylark.* New York: HarperCollins. (Gr. 3–6). In this sequel to *Sarah Plain and Tall*, letters from Sarah's aunts in Maine and Anna's journal entries help weave this story together and show how writing ties the family together during a difficult time.

MacLachlan, P. (1980). *Arthur, for the very first time.* New York: Harper and Row (Gr. 3–6). Uncle Wrisby and Aunt Elda introduce 10-year-old Arthur to new worlds when he comes for a visit.

Marshall, J. (1983). *Rapscallion Jones.* New York: Viking. (Gr. K–3). An unemployed fox decides to become a writer and finds the career harder then he anticipated.

Mazer, N. (1971). *I, Trissi.* New York: Delacorte. (Gr. 3–6). Printed as if 11-year-old Trissi typed it on her typewriter, this book includes stories, a play, letters, poetry, reports, a multiple-choice test, and a will.

McKissock, P. (1997). *A picture of freedom: The diary of Clotee, a slave girl, Belmont plantation, Virginia, 1859.* New York: Scholastic/Dear America. (Gr. 4–6). A slave girl's secret writings reveal that hope and strength can prevail even in the face of unspeakable hardships.

Merriam, E. (1986). *The birthday door.* New York: Morrow. (Gr. 1–3). Helen follows a treasure hunt of notes written in rhyme that directs her to a series of doors (the mailbox, bird feeder, refrigerator) and finally to her birthday cake and a present in a box.

Merriam, E. (1966). *Miss Tibbett's typewriter.* New York: Knopf. (Gr. 3–6). Miss Tibbett has funny experiences because she loves to type notes to people but some of the keys on her typewriter are broken, making the notes difficult to interpret.

Mills, C. (1986). *The one and only Cynthia Jane Thornton.* New York: Macmillan. (Gr. 3–6). A fifth-grade poet discovers that although she loves to write and writes well, this doesn't guarantee status or friendship.

Mitgutsch, A. (1985). *From graphite to pencil.* Minneapolis: Carolrhoda. (Gr. K–3). Easy-to-follow text and colorful illustrations describe how graphite is made, encased in cedar, and finally topped with an eraser to become a pencil.

Moss, M. (1995). *Amelia's notebook.* Berkeley, CA: Tricycle Press. (Gr. 2–5). Nine-year-old Amelia moves to a new town with her family. In her own handwriting and with pictures, she records her thoughts and feelings about these new experiences.

Pfeffer, S. B. (1989). *Dear Dad, love Laurie.* New York: Scholastic. (Gr. 3–6). Written in the form of letters to her divorced dad, Laurie tells of her year in sixth grade and her efforts to enter her school's gifted program.

Quackenbush, R. (1984). *Mark Twain? What kind of name is that? A story of Samuel Langhorne Clemens.* Englewood Cliffs, NJ: Prentice-Hall. (Gr. 3–5). The life of one of America's best-loved authors, from his birth to his death, is told in a humorous style befitting this writer.

Rocklin, J. (1997). *For your eyes only!* New York: Scholastic. (Gr. 4–6). This humorous story is about a journal-writing project that helps sixth-grade students, Lucy and Andy, find their voices.

Ross, L. H. (1991). *Buba Leah and her paper children.* Philadelphia: The Jewish Publication Society. (Gr. 2–6). In an Eastern European village, a small girl visits her great-aunt every day and learns that "paper children" are the aunt's children who live in the United States and write her letters. The story explores immigration, emigration, separation, and love between generations.

Selway, M. (1992). *Don't forget to write.* Nashville: Ideals. (Gr. 1–3). Rosie writes a page a day in a letter home, telling how she changes her opinion of the farm she is visiting.

Shulevitz, U. (1990). *Toddle Creek post office.* New York: Farrar. (Gr. 3–6). This story is about the role of the post office in the life of a community.

Speare, E. G. (1958). *The witch of Blackbird Pond.* Boston: Houghton Mifflin. (Gr. 5–9). (Newbery Medal). Kit Tyler leaves Barbados in the 1770s and goes to live in Connecticut with Puritan relatives, where the roles of reading and writing are different from what she was used to.

Stanek, L. W. (1994). *Thinking like a writer.* New York: Random House. (Gr. 3–6). This manual of ideas and exercises helps students improve their writing, from keeping a notebook and what to put in it, to turning an idea into a story with well-developed characters, an intriguing plot, and a unique storytelling voice.

Surat, M. (1983). *Angel child, dragon child.* New York: Scholastic (Gr. 1–3). A Vietnamese girl and a Euro-American boy settle their differences by writing the story of her immigration together.

Talbott, H. (1996). *Amazon diary.* New York: Putnam. (Gr. 2–6). Alex Winters's journal documents the most amazing adventure of his life in which he visits the land of the Yanomami people in Brazil, who are a Stone Age tribe living in harmony and simplicity.

Taylor, E. J. (1986). *Rag doll press.* New York: Knopf. (Gr. K–3). A girl dreams of a career as a writer and has an adventure starting her own newspaper.

Tchudi, S., & Tchudi, S. (1984). *The young writer's handbook.* New York: Scribner. (Gr. 3–6). This book presents clear guidelines for writing journals, letters, notes, stories, poems, and school papers.

Toll, N. (1993). *Behind the secret window: A memoir of a hidden childhood during World War II.* New York: Dial. (Gr. 5–8). Eight year-old Nellie's diary and vivid watercolor paintings (produced while in hiding from the Nazis in Poland) inspired her to write this powerful memoir of her childhood.

Turner, A. (1987). *Nettie's trip south.* New York: Macmillan. (Gr. 2–6). Based on the real diary of the author's great-grandmother, this is an account of one girl's reaction to slavery on her trip from Albany to Richmond.

Van Allsburg, C. (1991). *The wretched stone.* Boston: Houghton Mifflin. (Gr. 3–6). Excerpts from the log of a ship's captain tell the story of a strange glowing stone picked up on a sea voyage that transforms the ship's crew.

Van Leeuwen, J. (1989). *Dear Mom, you're ruining my life.* New York: Fitzhenry & Whiteside. (Gr. 3–7). An 11-year-old struggles through adolescence, and communication with her family often takes the form of written letters.

White, E. B. (1970). *The trumpet of the swan.* New York: Harper and Row. (Gr. 2–4). Louis, a voiceless trumpeter swan, learns to read, write, and play the trumpet, which brings him fame, fortune, and fatherhood.

Wild, M. (1991). *Thank you, Santa.* New York: Scholastic. (Gr. 1–3). Sick in bed after Christmas, Samantha is Santa's pen pal for a year. Through her letters, the reader learns about several polar animals.

Williams, V. B. (1988). *Stringbean's trip to the shining sea.* New York: Scholastic. (Gr. 3–6) This book contains a collection of postcards and snapshots Stringbean and his brother sent home to their family during a summer trip.

Williams, V. B. (1986). *Cherries and cherry pits.* New York: Greenwillow. (Gr. 1–3). An African American girl draws stories about growing cherries for her family and neighborhood.

Williams, V. B. (1981). *Three days on a river in a red canoe.* New York: Mulberry (Gr. 3–6). An account of a three-day camping trip by canoe taken by a boy, his cousin, mother, and aunt. Drawn pictures and diagrams are included.

Woodruff, E. (1994). *Dear Levi: Letters from the Overland Trail.* New York: Knopf. (Gr. 4–6). A young boy writes back to his brother in Pennsylvania about his trip West.

Language Tools: Spelling, Grammar, and Handwriting

12

W•••••indow on Teaching

Parents often question elementary school teachers about how and what will be taught to their children. Many parents do not understand what *invented spelling* is, nor do they understand that children progress developmentally in their ability to spell. Many parents want grammar and handwriting taught to their children the way they learned it. So, most teachers communicate with parents both on curriculum nights and through regular letters home about the curriculum, in general, and in particular about how they teach such things as spelling, grammar, and writing.

Jane Bonner and Lisa France sent the following letter home to the parents of their first-graders. The year before, a group of disgruntled parents questioned how spelling was taught and so these teachers decided to educate their parents right away.

September 29

Dear Parents,

We would like to explain how we will teach spelling to your child. Spelling is a skill that is developmental, like crawling and walking. Until a child is at the appropriate developmental stage, he or she is not ready for a formal spelling program.

We have assessed each child to determine his or her developmental stage and we will continue to retest each month. If your child is ready to spell, he or she will be tested on a list of words at the end of each month. If he or she is not ready, your child will take a test that consists of filling in a few letters for each word, usually the beginning and ending sounds. We will send home a list of 20 words each month. Our first goal with these words is for your child to be able to read them quickly, so they become part of his or her sight vocabulary. Until that occurs, please do not worry about spelling these words. If your child is developmentally ready, then you can practice spelling these words.

We will work with these words in class throughout the month in our spelling center. The ultimate goal of our spelling program is to make these words part of your child's everyday writing—to transfer the ability to spell these words on the test to what he or she writes in his or her journal or uses in writing workshop.

We appreciate your cooperation at home in helping with spelling. We hope you can make it part of your daily routine, as opposed to waiting until the night before the test to look at the words. If you have any questions or concerns, please call us at 555-1243.

Sincerely,

Jane Bonner and Lisa France

Page 2 of this letter consists of the following:

_____ is currently in the _____ stage of spelling.

The stages of spelling development follow:

Precommunicative. If your child is in this stage, read to him or her every day, pointing to words as you read. Don't worry about spelling yet.

Semiphonetic: If your child is in this stage, focus on making the monthly words part of your child's sight vocabulary.

Phonetic: If your child is in this stage, practice reading the monthly words and focus on beginning and ending sounds of the words.

Transitional. If your child is in this stage, practice the correct spelling of the monthly words. Use the Super Seven Spelling Steps that follow.

Super Seven Spelling Steps: Word Study

1. *Look.*   Look at the word and form a visual image.
   Look for tricky parts.
   Look for little words within the word.
   Look for memory helps (a "fri*end* to the end").
2. *Say.*   Say the word softly several times as you look at it.
   Stretch out the sounds, if it helps.
3. *Cover.*   Cover the word with your hand or a piece of paper.
4. *Write.*   Write the word from memory.
   Sound it out as you write, if it helps.
5. *Check.*   Uncover the word and check each letter.
   Touch under each letter with a pencil as you check.
6. *Correct.*   Immediately rewrite the word with correct spelling.
7. *Repeat.*   If you don't get it the first time, repeat the steps.
   If you don't get it the second time, give it a rest and come back to it later.

Often, a letter like this one sent home by Jane and Lisa is enough to answer questions parents may have and gives parents ideas for working at home in ways that will help their child at school. Some schools go one step further, though, and hold a Parents' Day, where parents are invited to visit and observe in their child's classroom. When this school holds a Parents' Day, parents come in the morning and first attend a brief session in which they learn about district philosophy and what constitutes a good learning environment. After parents observe in classrooms, they come back together to discuss what they saw or didn't see and to have their questions answered. This format has been very successful in building parent understanding and support for curriculum and instruction in the district.

•••••

Overview

This chapter explores the tools, or conventions, of written language that students master as effective language users. Using the tools of language in standard ways is a courtesy people extend to those with whom they communicate to clarify and sharpen the messages they send. The individual who uses the tools of language properly demonstrates one aspect of the fully literate person.

*C*onventions are accepted ways of doing things. They are customs, practices, or rules that can also be viewed as tools, since they help us get things done. Sometimes, conventions may seem to have little logic or consistency. For instance, people in England drive cars on the left side of the road. In the United States and Canada, we drive on the right side. The side of the road on which you drive is a convention that, if deviated from in certain places, can cause unfortunate outcomes. Written language has several conventions or tools—spelling, grammar, handwriting, punctuation, capitalization, and indenting—that, if deviated from, can cause problems, as well. What are some of these problems?

- Comprehension may be disrupted when a message contains misspellings or inappropriate grammar.
- Grades may be adversely affected if written work is illegibile and a teacher cannot read it.
- One's perception by others may be influenced by errors (e.g., inaccurate spelling or lack of punctuation) even if the message's content makes sense.

In simple terms, communication with others suffers when the learner does not master the conventions or tools of language.

Composition and Transcription

Writing is both composition and transcription. *Composition* is the mental act of creating ideas, through apppropriate word selection and grammar. *Transcription* is the physical act of creation that involves spelling, handwriting, grammar, punctuation, capitalization, and indenting. Composition and transcription sometimes conflict since they occur concurrently; and one often impedes the progress of the other. For instance, if children are too concerned about proper spelling and punctuation, they may be unable to transcribe or communicate their ideas. Or children sometimes misspell or omit words because their ideas flow faster than their ability to transcribe what they are thinking. Problems with transcription may stifle creativity.

Today, many experts believe that the teaching of writing ought to separate composition and transcription, with attention to the aspects of composition coming first. When children concentrate on handwriting, spelling, capitalization, and punctuation, as they try to create and express ideas, composing is often hindered. For this reason, it makes sense to focus on transcription second. When meaning comes first, transcription often falls into place naturally. For example, when a child wants to communicate excitement or a sense of danger in a composition, spelling words accurately so that others can read the story and using exclamation signs appropriately become important and relevant for that child. However, for many ESL and other English language learners who are often quite concerned with transcription, compositon suffers as they make sure their letter formation and spelling are correct.

The focus of research in writing has shifted from evaluation of the written product to investigation of the composing process, from examination of the writings of older students to that of younger children, and from handwriting to writing as a way of communicating. The teaching of writing in the past often meant providing children with a topic or topics, paper and pencils, and time to write. There was excessive initial attention to neatness, spelling, punctuation, and capitalization. The written product was corrected by the teacher, and the children received grades based on aspects of transcription. The composing process received little attention.

Recent research, however, offers a better understanding of the written composition process. This process includes what happens before children write, what occurs as they write and revise, and what happens when the finished product is complete. Two important trends in teaching writing are the integration of reading and writing instruction and the use of children's literature as models. Teachers are helping students read and look at written products with new eyes—the eyes of writers—and teachers are helping students write with an audience in mind—as the reader would read the piece. Teachers are introducing students to authors of children's books and helping students see how authors use the writing process in their own composing (Calkins, 1994; Harwayne, 1992). Today, the composing and transcribing processes are being informed more and more by the reading of real books.

As children are alternately readers and writers, they learn more about the composing process and become more sophisticated communicators. As they become more competent writers and are able to focus on transcription as well as composition, they begin to observe conventions. Upon refelection, one can see that these conventions are courtesies to the reader. They provide meaning, they help the reader pronounce what is written, and they give clues about where to pause and how to read a composition. As a writer rereads his work to revise it, the importance of conventions becomes apparent. He sees that ideas should be separated, or that there are places where the reader needs to pause, or that he has omitted an article such as *a* or a word ending such as *ing,* for example.

However, the importance of composition—that is, creating ideas and selecting words—should not be forgotten. Once children have their ideas down, they can then attend to the conventions of spelling, grammar, and handwriting. Children need to build confidence in expressing themselves before they tackle the technicalities of composition. A cake analogy fits here: The conventions of language are like the frosting that is more easily spread on the cake once it is mixed, baked, and cooled, just as the conventions of language are more easily attended to after meaning is constructed. This may be especially true for young children who have both composition and transcription to master and for ESL students, English learners, and students with language difficulties.

Of course, considering both composition and transcription together makes for a more effficiently prepared, quality product. If you consider the flavor and type of frosting before preparing the cake, you can mix the frosting as the cake bakes or cools, just as using standard conventions during drafting can cut down your revision and editing time after drafting. Ultimately, the goal is to be good at transcribing and composing concurrently.

Spelling: To Teach or Not?

The first convention, and perhaps the most troublesome for both teachers and students, is word structure, or orthography, commonly called *spelling*. It is troublesome for teachers because, despite decades of research, teachers still do not know how best to teach spelling. It is troublesome for students because the English language is variable and the development and teaching of spelling has not been approached in sensible ways. Current research, theory, and practice do suggest some important things about spelling and spelling instruction.

Key Ideas about Spelling

Here are some key ideas for you to consider about spelling:

1. *Spelling is a tool for writing.* Students should understand that the primary reason for learning how to spell is to make writing easier and quicker. You can help them recognize that, as readers, standard spelling is important for them. Not only is it a courtesy to the reader but it is also important for accurate communication of ideas. Some would argue that with word processors and spell-checkers, accurate spelling is not necessary today. But this reasoning holds true only in situations where written language is created on a computer. Think about how difficult it would be for a poor speller to access information from the World Wide Web or Internet, a telephone book, an encyclopedia, or a dictionary, not to mention all the opportunities for on-the-spot spelling that occur in a day, whether at work or at home.

2. *Spelling is developmental.* An awareness and understanding of developmental spelling enables you to make modifications for faster or slower students and to provide instruction that is appropriate for a child's stage of development. Gentry (1987) identifies stages of spelling development and his research shows that children progress naturally through these stages (see Table 12.1). In the precommunicative stage, children show an awareness of letters but no awareness that certain letters represent certain sounds (see Figure 12.1). In the semiphonetic stage, children are beginning to represent some of the letters in words (see Figure 12.2). In the phonetic stage, they begin to spell

TABLE 12.1 These stages of spelling development usually occur between the ages of 5 to 7 or 8.

Stage	*Characteristics*	*Examples*
Precommunicative	Random ordering of letters.	*IEOOS, FISOS, MSOOE* (for foods on a grocery list)
Semiphonetic	One-, two-, or three-letter spellings that represent some sounds in words.	*crts* (for *carats*), *lbrte* (for *liberty*), *camr* (for *camera*)
Phonetic	Spellings include all the sound features of words.	*shuts* (for *shoots*), *ses* (for *says*), *oll* (for *oil*)
Transitional	Spelling words as they sound and as they look. Vowels appear in every syllable.	*whair* (for *where*), *clime* (for *climb*), *billdings* (for *buildings*), *tiyerd* (for *tired*)
Mature	Spelling is accurate.	

Source: Reprinted by permission of J. Richard Gentry.

words the way they sound (see Figure 12.3). When children reach the transitional stage, they begin to spell words the way they look, including a vowel in every syllable (see Figure 12.4). It is at this stage that Gentry says children are ready for formal instruction in spelling, since they possess relatively sophisticated phonemic awareness.

FIGURE 12.1 A child's precommunicative use of letters.

FIGURE 12.2 Four-year-old Erin's semiphonetic representation of *a table and pitcher and saucer and cup and sugar and cream.*

FIGURE 12.3 Phonetic spelling in a page from a 6-year-old's journal.

FIGURE 12.4 Transitional spelling in a 7-year-old's story about an astronaut.

STRETCHING EXERCISE

At what developmental spelling stage is the child who spells *Africa* as *afrak*, *Europe* as *Eourup*, *Pacific Ocean* as *pisifik ocen*? Is this child ready for formal spelling instruction?

• • • • •

There is further research evidence that spelling accuracy improves with age. Jongsma (1990) discusses a study of 28,000 essays written by students from grade 2 through college that shows how spelling improves over time. The study shows that most students spell better than the general public thinks and spelling becomes more accurate as students grow older. The following grade levels and percentages show the developmental nature of spelling found in essays written in response to prompts on standardized tests:

Grade Level	Words Spelled Correctly
2	87%
3	90%
5	94%
7	95%
High School	97%
College	98%

3. *Good spellers write a lot, invent spellings, learn through use, and imitate models.* Spelling development is similar to the development of speech. Just as children learn to manipulate spoken sounds to form words orally, they learn to spell by manipulating written letters to form words. Think about how babies progress from cooing and babbling (e.g., *buh, buh, buh*) to single words (e.g., *dog, horsee*) to telegraphic speech (e.g., *allgone milk*) to mispronunciations (e.g., *buh bull* for *belly button*) to nongrammatical creations (e.g., *Why you give me two watches?*) to standard and accurate speech patterns. Children invent spellings by spelling words the way they sound and by trial and error. These invented, or temporary, spellings are windows on a child's spelling level and development.

One of the most effective ways to help children develop accurate spelling is to encourage creative writing and allow them to manipulate and acquire written language naturally. Using new words and practicing the spelling of known words while composing are critical experiences. Writing gives children a reason to learn how to spell.

4. *Good spellers read a lot and write about what they read.* Learning to spell is integrally related to learning underlying concepts about words that become more sophisticated as students have more interactions with written language. Spelling expertise evolves, then, from an initial awareness of print as a form of language to progressively greater understandings of relationships between spoken and written language, which come from reading.

Reading provides students with opportunities to see standard spelling in print and, as a natural consequence, to develop visual memories for words. Visual memory plays a big part in spelling accuracy. Children who read a lot often have huge stores of words they recognize on sight and can reproduce in writing. As well, when children write about what they are reading, they often use the author's vocabulary and language patterns in their own writing. This reinforcement may be quite helpful in learning standard spelling.

5. *Good spellers often have a sense of audience.* As children learn to read and begin to develop as writers, their concepts of orthography, or spelling, gradually change. Children who read, more so than those who do not, are likely to realize the importance of accurate spelling by the writer to understand the writer's message. Children who write to communicate with a real audience often pay attention to standard spelling because they know it affects those who read their work. When children read each other's writing, this also focuses their attention on correct spelling, since inaccuracies disrupt meaning. In fact, peers often deliver important messages to each other about spelling that may be more meaningful for some students than the messages teachers send.

Teaching Spelling

In many school systems today, a basal spelling program is adopted and each child receives a single, grade-level speller. Formal instruction follows the directions given in the teacher's manual and occurs for about 15 minutes every day, with much of the work carried out independently by children. Many teachers give a pretest on Monday, a posttest on Friday, and assigned activities during the week.

In some classrooms, teachers use strategies to individualize spelling instruction (Gentry & Gillett, 1993; Henderson, 1990; Opitz & Cooper, 1993). One way to ease into individualized instruction is first to teach spelling in several instructional groups. When you are comfortable with this, you can fully individualize spelling instruction by providing each child with his own special list of words to learn. Teachers who use this approach give each child a placement test before they decide on a word list. Then each child proceeds at his own rate, using a peer or a tape recorder for the pre- and posttest dictations. An individualized spelling program requires that teachers have good organization and management skills. Teachers must make sure that appropriate word lists are compiled and assigned to individual children, that children study these words regularly, and that they teach spelling principles and phonics generalizations as the need arises.

Some teachers, frustrated with the disadvantages of both basal and individualized programs, use modifications of one or the other program or a combination of each. Some use a spelling workshop approach that includes self-selection, ownership, self-monitoring feedback, and individualized instruction (Opitz & Cooper, 1993). Some teachers individualize the basal program somewhat by assigning basals according to children's spelling abilities. This may require having from three to six (or more) different levels of basals in one classroom. Other teachers assign additional words to individual children to learn each week or assign fewer than the required number of words in the basal, depending on the children's abilities.

•••••
Many teachers reinforce standard spelling by pointing out word patterns and spelling irregularities as they teach reading and writing.

Since the purpose of word knowledge is to serve readers as they read and writers as they write, many teachers integrate spelling into reading and writing instruction. These teachers teach spelling rules and phonic generalizations as the need arises. For example, errors in spelling unstressed vowels (the *schwa*) are the most numerous types of errors that middle- to upper-grade children make (Henderson, 1990). One way to help children with this problem is to point out the meaning relationship between words such as *confide* and *confident,* and *resign* and *resignation.* When they understand that the root word and its derivation share a common meaning, the children can easily understand that the two share a similar spelling pattern. As you can see, any form of spelling instruction, and especially any individualized form, requires close attention on your part to ensure that it transfers to the children's own writing.

Examine several samples of a child's writing, perhaps creative stories, informative reports, and journal entries. Look at the child's invented spellings and use Table 12.1 to identify the child's stage of spelling development. Is this child ready for formal spelling instruction?

• • • • •

STRETCHING EXERCISE

Key Ideas about Spelling Instruction

Templeton (1992) says that the differences among teachers regarding formal spelling instruction seems to hinge in part on what they consider spelling to be and whether direct examination of words in isolation is necessary for advancing spelling in writing and fluency of word identification in reading. Templeton reminds readers of Henderson's (1985) concise and elegant advice:

> *Those who set out to remember every letter of every word will never make it. Those who try to spell by sound alone will be defeated. Those who learn how to "walk through" words with sensible expectations, noting sound, pattern and meaning relationships will know what to remember, and they will learn to spell English.* (p. 67)

1. *Spelling instruction is a necessity.* At least half the letters in the alphabet possess more than one distinct sound, and many possess several more sounds when coupled with other letters. Many children, including some who are good readers, do not acquire standard spelling naturally and they need specific instruction in letter patterns and word families to become good spellers.

A study of good and poor spellers' perceptions of the spelling strategies they use provides some useful information (Radenich, 1985). When good and poor readers were asked how they were able to spell *easy words*, both reported that they memorized them. When asked how they spelled *difficult words*, good spellers most often said that they broke the difficult words into parts and then tried to spell each part correctly. Many good spellers also reported sounding the word out and using visual images, either visualizing the setting for the word or the word itself. After some probing, several of the good spellers mentioned visual images of the printed word. One child said that she spelled *squirrel* correctly by visualizing it as she had written it on her crayon box earlier in the year. None of the poor spellers reported using this strategy. It may be that since good spellers typically are good readers and read more, they see more repetitions of standard spelling in print and associate meanings with these words. Good spellers also said they tried to hear smaller words in a larger one, used spelling rules, and just "knew [they] could do it" (p. 534).

On the other hand, poor spellers reported many fewer strategies for spelling difficult words, and a large number of their responses involved sounding out or using letter-by-letter strategies. The poor spellers never reported using visual images to aid their spelling. Further research is needed, however, to determine how best to help poor spellers. Although it seems reasonable that teachers should teach poor spellers the good spellers' strategies, it may be that there are other underlying reasons for spelling ability.

Your knowledge of the stages of spelling development will allow you to provide instruction that is appropriate to each child, whether a good speller or a poor speller. But you should hold off introducing a formal spelling program until children are in the transitional stage of spelling development. It is in this stage that children hear vowels in each syllable of a word and can begin to learn standard spelling.

2. *Do not omit phonics and spelling rules.* Researchers generally agree that phonics should be part of spelling instruction but that it should not be the entire program (Gentry, 1996). Because of the variability of the English language, most attempts to teach spelling solely by phonic generalizations are questionable. Developing sight vocabulary is more appropriate for young children because a child with a strong sight vocabulary has a fund of words to generalize to and from once phonics instruction begins. Phonics can be an *aid* to correct spelling, but it must not be the only *tool*. Reading and writing may be the best tools.

Research on the teaching of spelling rules provides similar insights. Time spent on memorizing rules that do not consistently apply to words, especially if children already know how to spell the words, is wasted. Hillerich (1977) found that a computer programmed to use 203 rules was able to spell correctly only 49 percent of 17,000 words. A group of fifth-grade students did better than this when they were asked to complete the same activity. It seems that only rules with few or no exceptions should be taught and only taught when there is a need for them.

3. *Select words with similar patterns.* Research on word lists is perhaps not so discouraging. Gentry and Gillett (1993) report that presenting words in list form initially is a more successful method than presenting spelling words in sentences or paragraphs. It makes sense to choose words from the same word family that have a similar pattern or to choose words that have similar derivations. It also makes sense to teach children the meanings of words they are learning to spell. Knowing meaning helps a child visualize the concept a word stands for and perhaps visualize how the word looks, which is one of the characteristics of good spellers. There is evidence that children learn how to spell the words they use daily or at least frequently, which is an argument for drawing word lists primarily from their writing.

4. *Select words from students' writing.* When one thinks of the thousands of words contained in children's listening, speaking, and reading vocabularies, one gets an idea of the huge number of words children might potentially need to accumulate in their writing vocabularies and know how to spell. Tricia Enginiri, a third-grade teacher, uses the list from the spelling basal and encourages her students to choose their own words from their writing and other sources (e.g., science and social studies, books they are reading,

seasonal words, or high-frequency word lists). With her guidance, each child chooses his own words to add to the basal list—a few or several words, depending on the child's ability. Tricia believes this personalized approach to spelling instruction is most effective because it allows each child to make decisions about the level and rate of his own learning.

Gill and Scharar's (1996) work with 15 elementary teachers makes an important point about selecting words for spelling lists. Words that students misspell in their writing are perhaps more developmentally appropriate than those they meet in reading, science, or social studies. It is more important to let students make their own choices, however. Research says that children's self-selected words are usually longer and more complex than those chosen by the teacher and are retained to at least the same degree (Michael, 1986). Remember: Most students need and like a challenge, so don't discourage them from choosing words to learn to spell from sources other than their writing.

5. *Use the test-study-test method with a self-corrected pretest.* When you begin a formal spelling program, the test-study-test technique (DiStefano & Hagerty, 1985) requires a high degree of individual student responsibility and produces good results. This technique is outlined in Figure 12.5. If you give grades for spelling, you should also examine everyday classroom writing for evidence of the application of spelling skills.

In Tricia's third-grade class, everyone takes the pretest and posttest on the basal list that Tricia provides. She has the children work in pairs to test each other both at the beginning and end of the week on their individually chosen words, and she oversees this. Tricia reports that her students are rigorous in correcting their own pretests and they work hard during the week to master the words they missed initially. After many years of teaching, she feels that placing responsibility with students for their own individual spelling improvement makes the best sense.

FIGURE 12.5   The test-study-test method is an effective tool for learning to spell.

Test-Study-Test Method

- Day 1   Give the pretest. With your supervision, students can correct a partner's test or their own test.

- Day 2   Students study the words they missed. They:
    1. Look at the word and say it.
    2. Close their eyes, visualize the word, and spell it correctly.
    3. Check to see if their oral spelling is correct.
    4. Cover the word and write it.
    5. Check their spelling against the model.
    If the word is misspelled, the child goes back to Step 1.

- Day 3   Give a midweek test. Let the students self-correct or practice their words.

- Day 4   Do activities (allow 12 to 15 minutes each): placing words in configuration boxes, filling in letters in incomplete words, completing word-search puzzles, and so on. Use all spelling words so correct spellings are reinforced.

- Day 5   Give the posttest. Each student takes all the words on the posttest, regardless of the words misspelled on the pretest. Correct and return the tests so students can see the results and record them.

Maria Pellicciotti, a third-grade teacher, also reports success with the test-study-test method. She found that her children's scores increased by an average of 20 percent, as compared with the study-test method. Maria uses a variety of study techniques to keep interest high, some of which were suggested by the children themselves. One idea her children particularly enjoy is the creation of Super-Silly-Strange-Sci-Fi-Spelling-Stories. Each child can use his own list of spelling words to write a creative science-fiction story set in the future. Maria accepts invented spelling for words students want to use that are not on their spelling lists, but only correct spelling for the words on their lists. Children write the stories one day and then reread them the next day before reading them orally to a buddy.

STRETCHING EXERCISE
Use the test-study-test method with a child for three weeks. Compare the child's test scores with scores from the previous three weeks. Talk with the child about whether the method is helpful and why or why not.
• • • • •

6. *Select comparison/contrast activities for young children.* Young children's phonemic awareness is a precursor to their acquisition of spelling and reading expertise. Richgels, Poremba, and McGee (1996) suggest that within the context of shared story reading, you can encourage young children to look carefully at print and talk about what they see. Invite the children to pay conscious attention to phonemes and letters and then ask them What can you tell us? This allows the children to demonstrate their knowledge to the class. This is a functional, contextualized, social literacy activity that lets children learn from one another using material that is relevant to other classroom events.

Word Sorts is an activity that also involves comparing and contrasting words to build children's orthographic knowledge (Barnes, 1989; Schlagal & Schlagal, 1992). Pat Kuenecke uses this activity with her second-graders because it promotes fluency and accuracy in identifying recurring patterns and different features in groups of words. Word Sorts reinforces spelling and vocabulary. To model this activity for her students, Pat begins with several words in a pocket chart, which she sorts into groups that share similar characteristics. She then asks the children to figure out why she sorted the way she did. Some of the ways she groups words are:

—Number of syllables
—Consonant or vowel sounds
—Consonant clusters or blends
—Vowel/consonant patterns
—Silent *e*
—Parts of speech
—Words from a common root
—Names or proper nouns
—Word families
—Vocabulary from a theme or topic

Pat has four pocket charts, one on each wall of her classroom, that she uses daily with her students. The children group and regroup the words in as many ways as they can and then share what they did with others. Pat uses spelling words, words from stu-

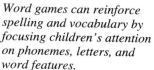

• • • • •
Word games can reinforce spelling and vocabulary by focusing children's attention on phonemes, letters, and word features.

dent writing, seasonal words, and content area vocabulary. She often has the children choose the words to use in sorting because it increases their ownership and involvement. She says that her students see relationships that surprise her, and that all her students participate, even struggling readers who may not recognize a word at first but can focus on word parts and compare word structures. The activity involves reading the words several times after they are in groups, which benefits poorer readers who need this reinforcement.

Pat accepts any grouping of words for which her students can give reasons. She says that the children not only sort words according to similarities in how they look but they also often group words based on similar meanings or relationships. Pat encourages buddies and small groups of children to work on sorting whenever they have time. She has used this activity for several years and believes it does more for developing visual memory for words and spelling consciousness than anything else she has tried. She says, "It is only when words are taken out of context and arranged in groups that the patterns emerge and the children can compare and contrast them."

David, a second-grade teacher, uses an activity called Making Words (Cunningham & Cunningham, 1992) to help his students discover how the alphabetic system works. During this 15-minute activity, children are given letters that they use to make words, beginning with two-letter words and continuing with three-, four-, or five-letter (or more) words. David gives each group of students a set of letters that spells a different word. For example, he puts each letter of the word *earthquakes* on a 3″ × 5″ card. The students make as many one- and two-syllable words as they can (e.g., *use, heat, rake, take, shake, quart, earth, reuse,* etc.), and in the process they usually discover what the big word is. David often chooses multisyllabic words from science or social studies, but this activity is just as successful with younger children using one-syllable words (e.g., *scratch* from which they can make *car, cat, cart, art, scar, star, cash, trash,* etc.). The words children create can then be sorted into groups that have a commonality. Making Words is a quick, manipulative activity that provides practice for problem spellers in comparing and contrasting words and challenges everyone.

7. *Select meaningful spelling activities.* Tricia uses a variety of study techniques to keep interest high, some of which are her children's suggestions. She assigns Spelling Buddies and invites her children to choose the activities they will complete each week. She matches students who have similar lists or those who are at about the same level. Children check each other's work and each buddy initials the completed activity. Examples of Tricia's activities for students follow:

—Write your words in alphabetical order. Trade and check.
—Write each spelling word in a sentence. Box your spelling words. Trade and check.
—Write your words in order from shortest to longest. Trade and check.
—Use two different colors to write your words. Use one color for vowels and another color for consonants. Make a key to the colors. Trade and check.
—Draw a picture for each word in your list. Have your buddy label your pictures with the correct words.
—Do a practice test with your buddy. Write five times any words you miss.
—Use your spelling words to make a crossword puzzle for your buddy. Check it yourself.
—Create your own Spelling Buddy activity to do with your spelling words.

Many teachers use a combination of reading, writing, and saying each spelling word for effective practice (see Figure 12.6).

8. *Teach a strategy for independence.* Students' self-selection of words for their spelling lists has gained in popularity. So, too, has the notion that children can identify their own best ways to remember how words are spelled. Topping (1995) suggests *cued spelling*, a technique complementary to regular teacher-directed classroom spelling instruction. It is meant for two individuals (e.g., two classmates, a child and a parent, etc.) who work together. Cued spelling follows a sequence. One child (the tutee) chooses the words to be learned. Both (tutor and tutee) check the spelling and put the words in a diary. They read the words aloud together and the tutee reads them alone. Then the tutee chooses cues (prompts or reminders) that will help him remember the written structure of the word, such as the following:

—A rule (e.g., *i before e . . .*)
—A word within a word (e.g., *hearse* in *rehearse*)
—A word family (e.g., *-amp, -ill, -other*)
—A meaning (e.g., *creation—create* means "make")
—A picture (e.g., *caterpiller*—a cat playing with a furry worm)
—A mnemonic (e.g., *b/e/c/a/u/s/e*—*b*ig *e*lephants *c*an *a*lways *u*se *s*ome *e*nergy)
—A beginning or end (e.g., *pre-* or *sta-* and *-tion* or *-ate*)

Then the tutor and tutee alternate saying the cues and writing the words before the tutee writes the words himself and reads them aloud. Topping (1995) suggests that children choose their own idiosyncratic prompts because the cues that appeal to one person do not necessarily appeal to another. This method highlights the individual nature of word learning, depends on a supportive model, and is socially interactive—three good reasons to use it.

Kelly Hawley, a first-grade teacher, and her students created the four section Flip-Folder in Figure 12.7 to help them learn their words. The children chose the words to describe each step and made their own folders. Kelly provides blank lined sheets to fit

FIGURE 12.6 Children can use their own word lists with these spelling activities.

inside each folder in which the child write his words. She believes this strategy is beneficial because it includes visualizing and it combines several modalities to reinforce correct spelling. Kelly also encourages her students to work in pairs to learn their spelling words, but she believes this individual activity best develops independence, which is one of her spelling goals.

9. *Teach students to edit for spelling errors.* One way to develop spelling accuracy is to encourage children to reread and edit their own work at least once before they go to a peer or you for help. Often, many of the errors children make result from lack of attention to letter order and from writing quickly to get ideas down. So, in rereading, children often see misspellings and can correct them immediately or circle words they can't spell.

Some teachers use the Three Before Me rule to help students become independently capable of dealing with misspellings. When one of her second-graders cannot spell a word, Kris suggests they first consult three other sources before coming to her. Kris encourages her students to use environmental print, books, and words they know

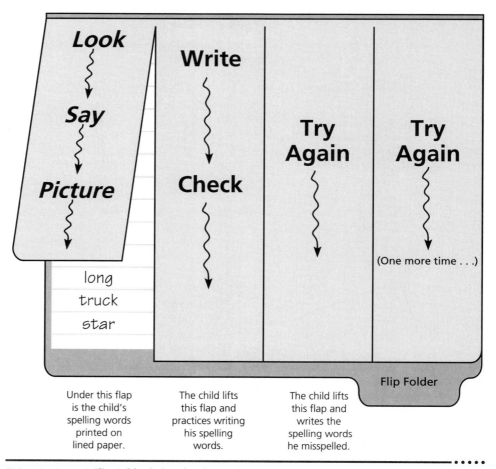

Look

Say

Picture

long
truck
star

Write

Check

Try Again

Try Again

(One more time . . .)

| Under this flap is the child's spelling words printed on lined paper. | The child lifts this flap and practices writing his spelling words. | The child lifts this flap and writes the spelling words he misspelled. |

Flip Folder

FIGURE 12.7 A Flip-Folder helps develop independence in learning to spell.
Source: Reprinted by permission of Kelly A. Hawley, primary teacher, Johnson City, NY.

that sound the same. Shawn, who at first misspelled *nocturnal* in his story about bats, came close to figuring out how to spell it by himself. Kris asked him to share his thinking with the class:

> First, I saw I spelled it wrong and then I began to think if I could see anything around the room to help. And I spotted "October" that helped me get started if I put a "n" before it. Then, I said it again and thought about taking turns. I looked at our list of rules and there it was—"turn." The last was easy—I just added an "l" and showed Miss Lamarre. She put an "a" before the "l" and I got "nocturnal."

Kris encourages her students to model their spelling processes for each other. She says this has a positive impact on the children's abilities to figure out the spelling of unknown words.

10. *Explain "temporary spelling" to parents.* Educating parents about the nature of spelling development, as Jane and Lisa did in their letter at the beginning of this chapter, will help parents understand how temporary spelling leads to standard spelling. Through

regular letters home, a class newsletter, and curriculum nights, you can inform parents about your spelling and writing program. Gentry's two books, *My Kid Can't Spell* (1996) and *Spel . . . Is a Four-Letter Word* (1987), are both intended for parents who want to play a more active role in their child's literacy learning, so you might lend these books to your parents.

Another way to involve parents in their children's spelling and writing development is through the use of a writing backpack (Reutzel, 1990). Fill it with all sorts of writing materials (e.g., paper, blank books, felt-tip markers, colored pencils, glu-stick, white-out, paints, etc.) that children take home for shared writing with parents, caregivers, and siblings. Both at home and in school, children need to have as much support as possible to reinforce their writing and their attempts at invented spelling.

Computers and Spelling

For many children, a video display terminal and computer present a novel and challenging way to learn how to spell. An article called "What Works in Spelling" (*Learning*, Volume 24, Number 2, pages 47–53) describes computer spelling programs that take the emphasis off memorization and provide creative ideas for helping students remember their spelling words. As well, the computer has the potential to generate various types of word searches, puzzles, word scrambles, and other gametype activities to accompany any word list. Discouraged learners are often more interested in overcoming their spelling problems when they use a computer. Often, ESL students are drawn to the computer and can use it to support their learning of English orthography. Tricia Engineri realizes the potential of the computer to support her spelling program and encourages her third-grade students to do at least one activity a week on the computer. Tricia's students also use the spell-checker feature of their word processor to correct final copies of their other writing.

In conclusion, getting children to write and take risks with their writing is the single-best technique for teaching spelling. Gentry and Gillett (1993) suggest these strategies to help create an effective spelling program:

- Teach spelling as part of the whole curriculum.
- Have the children write frequently.
- Encourage the children to invent spellings for words they may not have learned to spell.
- Deemphasize correctness, memorization, and writing mechanics.
- Respond to the children's writing in ways that help them discover more about spelling.

In the context of formal spelling instruction, Gentry and Gillett (1993) suggest the following research-supported procedures:

- Allot 60 to 75 minutes per week to formal spelling instruction.
- Present words to be studied in a list or a column form.
- Give a pretest to determine which words are unknown. Have the children study the unknown words, then give a posttest.
- Have the children correct their own spelling tests under your direction.
- Teach a systematic technique for studying unknown words.
- Use spelling games to make spelling lessons more fun.

Grammar: Why, How Much, and When?

After reading current literature on grammar instruction, four teachers—Diane Connors, Melissa Spierling, Elizabeth Pylypciw, and Michele Cahill—created a *reaction guide* to introduce a presentation on the topic to their fellow teachers (see Figure 12.8). Follow the directions for the reaction guide independently or with a partner. Use a pen to fill in each line. Then read the rest of this section on grammar and reread the statements in the reaction guide. This time, use a pencil or pen of a different color to make any changes to your first responses. Be ready to talk with your classmates about your answers.

In the discussion that followed the presentation on grammar, the teachers carefully analyzed each statement, supplying reasons for the answers they marked. Here are some of the reasons for the group's collective responses. Do you agree or disagree? What other ideas can you think of to support your opinions?

1. *Grammar is the study of the way a language works. It includes morphology (meaningful forms), syntax (sentence structure), and phonology (sounds).*   Answer: Agree.

Grammar is the rules of language—its form and order. *Usage* is the conventions of language that are appropriate in certain situations. Newkirk (1978) says, "Grammar is the rationale of language; usage is its etiquette" (p. 47). Grammar deals with the form and structure of words (*morphology*) and their function and arrangement in phrases and sentences (*syntax*). *Phonology* is the pronunciation and semantics is the meaning of language. Usage is a smaller list of forms that are socially preferred within a dialect and de-

---

FIGURE 12.8   Complete this reaction guide first, before reading the accompanying text.

Grammar Instruction: A Reaction Guide

Directions: Discuss each statement with a partner. Put an *A* on the line if you agree or a *D* if you disagree with the statement. Be ready to support your opinions.

_____ 1. Grammar is the study of the way a language works. It includes morphology (meaningful forms), syntax (sentence structure), and phonology (sounds).

_____ 2. In order for students to become productive and efficient writers, they must know all grammar rules.

_____ 3. Grammar is best taught in a series of mini-lessons based on common student errors.

_____ 4. Grammatical knowledge is best gained when it is related to reading and writing.

_____ 5. To prepare students for standardized tests, grammar should be taught in isolated units.

_____ 6. Basic grammar skills should be taught because they have always been taught and the public expects it.

_____ 7. Grammar is best taught by having students memorize rules and examples of rules.

_____ 8. Worksheets are useful for grammar instruction.

_____ 9. Student writing is important, even if it contains nonstandard grammar.

_____ 10. A mini-lesson on punctuation might take about three weeks.

• • • • •

pend on content and situation. A teenager's response of "Yup. No problem" to a friend's request demonstrates a usage pattern. The same teenager's response to an adult, "Yes, I can take care of that for you," demonstrates knowledge of both usage and grammar. When people speak, both the situation and the audience dictate their usage and/or grammar.

Listen to children's language on the playground or with peers in the lunchroom. What slang and usage patterns do you hear that are different from those they might use if they were talking about the same topic to the principal or a teacher?

•••••

2. *In order for students to become productive and efficient writers, they must know all grammar rules.* Answer: Disagree.

Three types of grammar have affected language teaching in the classroom over the years: traditional, structural, and transformational-generative grammar.

Traditional grammar is the rules of language taught by teachers for generations. Included are parts of speech, functions of parts of speech, terms, explanations of larger units, sentence expansion, diagraming, and parsing. It is basically a prescriptive approach to teaching children. In other words, this type of grammar teaches how language ought to be spoken.

Structural grammar is the analysis of the structure and features of language. Included are phonemes (sounds of language), morphemes (smallest units of meaning), form (what one sees or hears), function, and sentence patterns. It is descriptive in that it defines how language is used for communication rather than how it ought to be used.

Transformational-generative grammar is the analysis of the relationship between surface structure (form) and deep structure (meaning). Meaning is generated by transforming surface structure into deep structure. This grammar is concerned with semantics and the generating of sentences. It is also descriptive rather than prescriptive.

Disagreement exists as to which type of grammar to teach children or even whether formal grammar should be taught at all in school. Traditionally, grammar has been taught because it was thought to improve the ability to write and speak and to strengthen mental discipline. Research, however, does not support these assumptions; little relationship is seen between grammar and written composition. Additionally, Petrosky (1977), Western (1978), and Hillocks (1986) conclude that neither research nor experience provide convincing evidence that the study of grammar or mechanics helps students significantly with the quality of their writing. In fact, the correlation between grammar knowledge and writing ability is .23 and that between grammar knowledge and math ability is .48 (Hillocks, 1986). This means that grammar knowledge and math ability actually share greater commonality (23 percent) than writing and grammar ability (5 percent). So, the teaching of grammar as a way of improving writing skills is questionable.

3. *Grammar is best taught in a series of mini-lessons based on common student errors.* Answer: Both Agree and Disagree.

There is probably no *best* way to teach grammar. But there is value in providing plenty of opportunities to use language in relevant and purposeful contexts. This happens when teachers encourage learners to practice what they know about langauge by talking and writing often about things that are meaningful to them.

Many teachers, however, do use daily mini-lessons with their classes to examine a sentence that contains errors (e.g., nonstandard grammar or inappropriate use of the conventions such as capitalization and pucntuation). In this way, learners make linguistic discoveries for themselves about grammar as they focus attention on the importance of standard grammar for effective communication with an audience.

4. *Grammatical knowledge is best gained when it is related to reading and writing.* Answer: Both Agree and Disagree.

By the age of 5 or 6, children have already developed considerable understanding of the grammatical system of English. By the time they leave third grade, students know the system as well as they will ever know it (Devine, 1989). In the past, teachers have mistakenly thought that dialect speakers did not have knowledge of grammar. But today, teachers know that children who speak a nonstandard dialect such as Ebonics use its grammar as a guide to produce and comprehend discourse.

Grammar and usage are learned through immersion in language, interaction with others, and imitation of language users. Typically, oral language is learned first and written language begins to develop later. So, it makes sense for teachers to build on young children's oral grammatical knowledge and extend it through authentic reading and writing activities in school.

Many studies report that time spent teaching grammar does not have the positive effect on writing that actual time spent in composing has. When children learn to use the rules of English as they write, you can teach specific aspects of grammar and usage as the need arises with a particular aspect of composition. When usage and the accepted conventions of language are the focus, rather than formal grammar instruction, improved writing results (Hillocks, 1986). Knowledge of the forms and structures of words and their arrangement in phrases and sentences does not necessarily lead to their accurate use in the composing process. Elbow (1981) teaches students not to think about grammar while they compose, but rather to consider it a matter of editorial correction at the end of the process.

5. *To prepare students for standardized tests, grammar should be taught in isolated units.* Answer: Disagree.

Perhaps one should question the appropriateness of testing discrete skills out of context rather than teach these skills so that students can do well on tests. A more authentic assessment of grammar and usage might be to examine a piece of writing a student has created and look at the student's use of grammar and usage in each step of the writing process.

Sperling (1996) notes that children from schools characterized by sociocultural diversity and poor standardized test scores are often taught specific skills of grammar, spelling, and punctuation but not in extended writing. Bilingual and ESL students are likely to receive little instruction in composing; rather, their classes are heavily grammar oriented. Both these populations clearly need opportunities to learn grammar within the natural context of creating their own written compositions. Teachers must continue to examine the kinds of writing instruction these students receive as it relates to their lives.

6. *Basic grammar skills should be taught because they have always been taught and the public expects it.* Answer: Disagree.

Traditions die hard and change comes slowly. In addition, there is a gap between what theory and research show and what teachers practice. Grammarians themselves advise that the teaching of formal grammar be delayed until high school, when students have had many experiences using spoken and written language and can understand the principles of grammar.

This does not mean that elementary school teachers have no responsibilities in terms of grammar. Rudimentary grammar instruction can and should occur in the elementary school. Why is a knowledge of basic grammatical terms important in K–6? Being able to use these terms allows children to talk more easily about their writing during revision and editing. As well, knowledge of the parts of speech can help children know where to punctuate and use capital letters.

What grammar should be taught in the elementary school? Children in grades 1 and 2 can and should learn to use words such as *noun* and *adjective* and know what these words do in sentences. By third grade, the terms *verb, pronoun,* and *adverb* are often taught. *Preposition* and *conjunction* can be taught early in fourth grade. Certainly, by the end of fourth grade, students should know the names for parts of speech and be able to use them naturally in discussions with each other about their own reading and writing.

7. *Grammar is best taught by having students memorize rules and examples of rules.* Answer: Disagree.

Memorizing rules and examples of rules may not appreciably help students use standard grammar in their speaking and writing. Unless discussion and application of the rules occur in the natural context of reading and writing, students may just learn the isolated rules and carryover may not occur.

Grammar is probably best taught when the need for it arises naturally. For example, when a writer wants to paint a vivid picture with words, it is time for that student to become familiar with the terms *adjective* and *adverb* and examples of them.

8. *Worksheets are useful for grammar instruction.* Answer: Both Agree and Disagree.

In general, grammar can be improved by implementing meaningful writing and editing activities in the classroom rather than assigning decontextualized worksheets. Renwick (1994) says, "English is a skill to be developed, not a content to be taught, and is learned best through active and purposeful use" (p. 32). However, worksheets can be helpful with specific skills and individuals or small groups of students when you believe

• • • • •
Grammar is probably best taught when the need for it arises naturally during reading and writing so students can discuss rules and usage together.

reinforcement and practice are necessary. Worksheets can be appropriate and useful for these mini-lessons, but not as the only means of grammar instruction.

9. *Student writing is important, even if it contains nonstandard grammar.* Answer: Agree.

Just as a child's first oral language contains nonstandard grammar, so does the child's first writing contain nonstandard grammar. By the end of first grade, most sound substitutions and overgeneralized grammar rules disappear from children's speech (Fields & Lee, 1987). This is not due to lessons or drills, but to immersion in language environments and to language interactions with others who demonstrate and model language for children to use, imitate, and create on their own. The same applies in writing. Children must be given many opportunities to undertake a range of writing tasks where they use different syntactic structures (Wray & Medwell, 1994). For example, children use different syntactic structures and voices when they write journals, letters, reports, creative stories, poetry, debates, and many of the other forms.

10. *A mini-lesson on punctuation might take about three weeks.* Answer: Disagree.

A mini-lesson, true to its name, typically takes only a few minutes and is aimed at a specific skill or understanding. You could teach a brief mini-lesson to students who are using dialogue in their stories but are not yet using quotation marks appropriately. As an example of standard use, you could show the students pages from several recent pieces of children's literature they had read or are reading. Then have your students find the places where characters talk and ask them how the author shows the reader that the characters are talking. Briefly teaching the skill and using real examples from the children's own reading materials, which they can then transfer to their own writing, have good results.

Key Ideas about Grammar

As the teachers discussed the research and theory presented to them and talked about their own beliefs and classroom experiences about the teaching of grammar, the following key ideas emerged.

1. *Knowledge of grammar enriches the reading experience.* Knowing the basics of grammar gives learners a tool for reading and allows them to relate to an author's use of language. For example, Diane Connors wanted to develop her students' appreciation for the descriptive language used in *Georgia Music* by Helen Griffith (1988). So she used the term *adjective* with her second-graders as she talked about why Helen Griffith used *Georgia* rather than *chirpy* or *buzzy* to describe the music the little girl's grandfather made on his harmonica. Then, as the children talked about Griffith's language, they used the word *adjective* in their own discussions as they examined the rich nuances of meaning in Griffith's "summer sounds" and "noisy songs."

2. *Knowing grammar terms gives learners a common vocabulary to discuss their writing.* Knowing the names of the parts of speech and the parts of a sentence, and using these terms to discuss their own written work, makes it easier for students to work on their writing. Terban's (1993) book for students, *Checking Your Grammar*, is an easy-to-use reference book for grades 3 through 6 that helps students understand such grammatical concepts as parts of speech, the parts of a sentence, noun-verb agreement, capitalization, and punctuation (see Figures 12.9 and 12.10). Weaver (1996) also suggests teaching the concepts of subject, verb, clause, sentence, and related editing concepts.

Parts of Speech

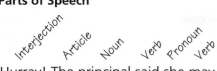

Interjection Article Noun Verb Pronoun Verb

Hurray! The principal said she may

Verb Article Noun Preposition Article Noun Preposition

open the school on the weekend for

Article Noun Conjunction Adverb Adjective

a "Read-In" because so many

Noun Verb Verb Pronoun

students have requested it.

FIGURE 12.9 By fourth grade, students
should know the parts of speech.
•••••

Parts of a Sentence

Hurray! The principal said she may
└── Subject──┘
└·········· Main Clause··········
└·-Predicate·─

open the school on the weekend for
···
└── Phrase ──┘

a "Read-In" because so many
··············┘
└─────── Subordinate

students have requested it.
Clause──────────────────┘

Subject	———————
Predicate	—·—·—·—
Main clause	············
Phrase	———————
Subordinate clause	———————

FIGURE 12.10 Learning the parts of speech and sentences gives students a vocabulary
for discussing and improving their writing.

Sophia saw changes in some of her fourth-graders' writing after she taught them to identify examples in their reading of *noun, verb, subject, predicate, phrase clause, singular,* and *plural.* From there, Spohia said it was easier to help her students see instances of noun-verb disagreement (e.g., *The boy and girl* was *looking into the telescope*) in their own writing and eventually correct them. As well, learning about the parts of a sentence gave her students the tools to write with more varied and interesting sentence structure.

3. *Writing conferences are for teaching grammar to individual students.* Weaver (1996) believes teaching grammar in isolation is less than effective and believes grammar should be taught in the context of writing conferences. She urges teachers to guide students in applying grammatical concepts as they write, revise sentences, and edit pieces for publication.

When you talk individually with a child about the piece of writing he is currently working on, having a common vocabulary to use makes the conversation about grammatical concepts easier. For example, when Elizabeth Pylypciw talked to a student who was ready for editing her letter to a local newspaper, Elizabeth helped the student see that capital letters are important because they signal the reader that the person, place, or thing being written about is special. Elizabeth often points out to her students during writing conferences that grammar, punctuation, capitalization, spelling, and legibility in handwriting exist as courtesies to the reader. Just as *Please* and *Thank you* are standard spoken courtesies, good grammar usage is like extending good manners to the reader.

4. *Mini-lessons are for teaching grammar to groups of students with similar needs.* In conferences with individual students, you may notice that several are at the same point in their writing and are ready for direct instruction in a specific aspect of grammar. For example, it made sense to Melissa Spierling to call four students together for a brief lesson on quotation marks when she noted that each of them was attempting to use dialogue in their stories but were not using appropriate punctuation. Melissa first focused these students' attention on the way Mem Fox, author of *Wilfred Gordon McDonald Partridge* (1985), a book they were currently reading, used quotation marks when Wilfred spoke to Miss Nancy and the other people who lived in the old people's home next door. Then Melissa had the children compare their own use of dialogue with Fox's and helped them generalize some rules about punctuating conversations to use in their own writing.

5. *Knowledge of grammar makes foreign language learning easier.* In the English language, word order is a huge clue to word and sentence meaning. For example, adjectives precede nouns in English and help us understand the special meanings the author intended for the nouns they modify. We know that conjunctions such as *and* connect objects and equivalent clauses. But in other languages—German, for example—adjectives follow subjects and verbs. Knowing the terminology and being able to discuss and identify this difference can make learning German that much easier for students. Although every language has its own grammar, knowing the grammar and structure of one language makes it easier to master the grammar and structure of another language.

As an elementary school language arts teacher, you can teach grammar both indirectly and directly. You can develop children's spoken and written language effectiveness by providing plenty of opportunities to use language in relevant and purposeful contexts. Let the children practice what they know about language by talking and writing often about things that are meaningful to them. Teach children grammar and usage in mini-lessons when there is a need to clarify a specific problem with a particular composition. For example, if you notice in several children's writings that they are omitting articles such as *the* and *a* or *an* or endings such as *ed* or *ing,* it is time for specific instruction to teach those skills.

Handwriting: Legibility or Neatness?

In some schools and communities, controversy surrounds handwriting instruction (Farris, 1991). There are three main reasons for this. First, many teachers ignore handwriting instruction because they lack training in handwriting and they assume their students will develop the skill on their own. Second, in the 1980s, the emphasis on writing as a process rather than a product and whole-language theories freed many teachers from handwriting instruction, which they and their students may have been bored with and considered a waste of time. Third, the advent of word processors in K–12 classrooms is seen by some teachers as negating the need to teach handwriting. A decreased emphasis on handwriting in some elementary programs has angered both parents and junior and senior high school teachers who simply can't read their students' writing.

So why is it important to teach handwriting in the elementary school? Most significant, perhaps, is so students can communicate effectively in writing—so their handwriting can be read easily by others. Illigible or poor handwriting by students can result in lower grades from teachers who lose their objectivity in trying to decipher poor penmanship. Markham (1976) found that the quality of students' handwriting influences how teachers evaluate papers. The quality of a paper's content made no difference in the grade, but students with better handwriting got higher grades than those with poorer handwriting.

As an adult, legible handwriting can make life easier and can make the difference between life and death. You can undoubtedly think of many examples, but one from the March 16, 1995, issue of *USA Today* makes the point well. Pharmacists were asked about the results of doctors' illegible handwriting. Their responses follow:

- Ninety-three percent said illegible handwriting results in loss of time.
- Eighty-five percent said illegible handwriting results in errors or safety problems.
- Seventy-six percent said illegible handwriting results in loss of money.

Suffice it to say that legible handwriting in teachers' lives and in students' lives is necessary and important.

Key Ideas about Handwriting

Here are six key ideas for you to consider about handwriting before you read the remainder of this chapter, where they are discussed in greater depth:

1. *Handwriting instruction is a necessity.* Children need systematic instruction in penmanship because effective written communication is important both in and out of school.

2. *Stress legibility and fluency.* Children need to write neatly, easily, and rapidly enough so they can transcribe their thoughts and others can read what they have written.

3. *Teach manuscript or cursive according to students' needs.* It is important to look carefully at individual students to determine their needs and preferences before deciding on a handwriting program or encouraging variations that best suit individual needs.

4. *Set standards for legibility with students.* When children know the components of legible and neat handwriting, they can self-evaluate and improve their form.

5. *Teach handwriting and spelling together.* Children can analyze the structure of a word and learn to spell it by seeing, saying, and picturing it as they learn to write it legibly.

6. *Teach the mechanics related to form and appearance.* Children can naturally learn punctuation, capitalization, indenting, spacing, margins, and special formats as they use them in their own writing.

Teaching Handwriting

The major objectives of handwriting instruction in the elementary school should be legibility and fluency. *Legibility* is the quality of being easily deciphered. This differs from *neatness,* which is a subjective term meaning trim, tidy, and well proportioned. A child's writing may be legible but not neat, whereas neat writing is usually legible. Legibility and neatness are reasonable objectives for most children, but neatness may not be possible for some. What a child with a physical handicap or delayed muscular coordination writes may not necessarily be considered neat, but according to his physical capabilities, it may be the best he can do. If his writing is legible, then he has met the first standard for communicating through handwriting. An important contributing factor to legibility is fluency or adequate speed in writing. A child needs to be able to write easily and rapidly enough that his thoughts and ideas are not lost as he forms letters and words.

Until the 1920s, when manuscript (printing) was introduced, cursive (writing) handwriting was the only type of handwriting taught in classrooms in the United States. Then for many years, children were taught manuscript in first and second grade and cursive in third grade, although there was no research evidence to support this practice. A large portion of the time spent on writing was spent in the teaching of handwriting until the late 1970s. Today, many school systems use any one of a number of popular handwriting programs in the early grades (e.g., the D'Nealian Model, the Palmer Method, and the Zaner-Bloser Model). Research does not support the superiority of a single manuscript or cursive handwriting method (Koenke, 1986). Handwriting instruction often occurs daily, usually through repetitive activities where children copy a model or sample.

Before formal handwriting begins, children need many opportunities to explore space, whether through artwork, cutting and pasting, puzzles, movement activities, or observation of writing. Drawing and writing development are closely related. For instance, 2- and 3-year-olds do not differentiate between the two, but as children mature, picture drawing becomes something distinctly different from writing. Writing then becomes scribbles across a page.

Beginning in kindergarten and throughout first grade, many teachers use crayons and pencils with a larger than normal diameter when teaching handwriting because they think these big crayons and beginner pencils are easier to hold and maneuver than regular crayons and pencils. There is no research evidence to support this practice. In English, French, and other European schools, children begin to write and draw with pencils and crayons of regular size. In fact, research indicates that children prefer adult pencils and do not write better with the beginner pencil (Koenke, 1986). In addition, manuscript programs in the United States usually call for the use of larger paper with half lines supplied and larger spaces between lines than traditional lined paper. Again, there is no evidence that this type of paper or unlined paper provides any added advantage to the young child who is ready to learn how to write. However, second- and third-graders who are introduced to cursive handwriting perform better when they use special paper (Koenke, 1986).

Manuscript versus Cursive

Generally, manuscript is taught before cursive probably because the stand-alone letters of manuscript seem easier to read and write than the connected letters of cursive. Also, it is felt that young children's muscular coordination makes cursive difficult and manuscript easier to learn. Most teachers of young children provide direct instruction in manuscript. The transition to cursive is usually made in second or third grade.

There is some evidence, however, to support the reverse in certain cases (Kaufman & Biren, 1979). Teaching cursive to children with physical disabilities may be better because cursive is continuous writing without repeated stops and starts. In cursive, commonly confused letters such as *b* and *d* and *p* and *q* no longer look alike and are not so apt to be mixed up. Letter and word reversals are thus eliminated. Additionally, cursive is highly motivating. So it may well be that there are sufficient reasons to forego the teaching of manuscript in certain instances and with certain children and teach cursive immediately.

The fluidity of cursive may mean the difference between illegible handwriting with poor spelling and legible handwriting with good spelling for children with physical disabilities, in which case cursive should be taught to some children. The only disadvantage to learning cursive before manuscript or in place of manuscript by very young children is that they may have a difficult time reading typeset materials. But a careful look at several books, newspapers, magazines, and signs shows the range of representations the manuscript letter *a* possesses. Young children, whether learning to write in manuscript or cursive, must and do adjust to reading print in several different forms anyway.

There is some evidence that intermediate-grade children who write in manuscript write faster and just as legibly as children who write in cursive (Peck, Askov, & Fairchild, 1980). For some students, writing in uppercase manuscript is "symbolic and distinctive," helping some students separate themselves as being unique individuals from their classmates (Farris, 1991). A teacher, then, must look carefully at a student's needs and preferences before deciding on a handwriting program or encouraging variations that best suit individual students.

Legibility

There are several elements of legible handwriting to discuss with children. When children know what the components of legibility are and have a chance to evaluate their own handwriting, their legibility improves. It also improves as children read each other's writing and peers make requests for clarity. Also, you can teach children the components of legible manuscript: shape, size and proportion, slant, spacing, steadiness of line, and styling. Copying a model and practicing proper letter formation can improve legibility (see Figure 12.11).

FIGURE 12.11 Practicing with a handwriting model can improve legibility.

Source: Used with permission from Zaner-Bloser, Inc.

Supplying children with a short evaluative checklist of questions such as the following motivates them to improve the legibility of their manuscript. These questions are meant as examples and you can modify them for cursive:

- Are my letters straight up and down?
- Do they sit on the line?
- Do they fill the whole space?
- Do they fill the half-space?
- Are my spaces even?
- Is my paper legible?

This self-evaluation checklist could be used regularly by children to plot their progress. In this way, they can begin to see where their strengths and needs are. In addition, periodic checks of children's handwriting help them identify letters that still need practice.

Children can also teach legible handwriting to each other. You can assign a letter of the alphabet to each child so that each becomes an expert on the assigned letter and assumes responsibility for teaching that letter to other children. Children often learn much more from each other in indirect ways than teachers realize, as the page from a third-grade student's buddy journal indicates (see Figure 12.12).

You can teach both handwriting and spelling with a five-step approach that is similar to the plan for Day 2 of the test-study-test technique. When children are learning to spell words or write manuscript or cursive, teach them to follow these steps:

1. *Look and say*. Look at the model (word/letter) and say it out loud. Spell it out loud or tell how it is formed. Take a picture of it with your eyes.
2. *Picture*. Close your eyes and make a picture in your mind of the word (or letter). Spell it out loud or tell how it is formed.
3. *Study*. Look at the word (or letter) and compare it to the picture you made in your mind. Does it look the same or different?
4. *Write*. Look at the word (or letter) again. Cover the model and write it.
5. *Compare*. Compare what you wrote with the word (or letter). Does it match? If not, where is it different?

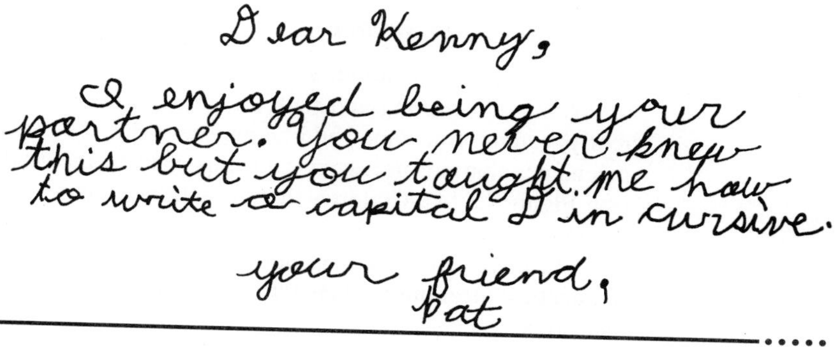
Dear Kenny,
I enjoyed being your partner. You never knew this but you taught me how to write a capital D in cursive.
your friend,
Pat

FIGURE 12.12 Children can teach handwriting to each other.

Children should repeat these steps as often as necessary, so they can write the word or letter accurately at least three times in succession. The picture step of this approach is critical because visualization involves children in active cognitive processing. Through visualization or the construction of mental images, children become active rather than passive learners and what they learn more easily transfers to everyday use.

Encourage older students in upper-elementary grades to analyze the structure of a word they are learning to spell. Have them look for familiar prefixes, suffixes, or root words, or associate the meaning, appearance, and pronunciation of known words with the new word to more easily learn to spell it. For example, if the word to learn is *amusement*, then *amuse* may be a known word and *ment* a known suffix, which, if recalled, makes learning the new word easier.

STRETCHING EXERCISE

Here are several commonly misspelled words: *pronunciation, accommodate, achieve, connoisseur, indispensable, definitely, dilettante, occurrence, recommendation, prerogative, perseverance, argument.* Try the five-step approach on page 425 to help you learn the standard spelling of at least three of these words.

• • • • •

Calligraphy

For interested students, calligraphy is a creative art form that helps develop neatness, legibility, and uniqueness in handwriting. Teachers who use calligraphy with their students say that the results are positive and the students are enthusiastic. Since calligraphy involves correct letter formation to match an unusual model, the focus of attention is on form and legibility. Practicing the alphabet in this way results in pride in penmanship and neatness. Nanette's spelling paper (see Figure 12.13) gives an idea of how calligraphy can even be used within a subject area.

Calligraphy also helps children and teachers understand that everyone's handwriting is not the same and that individuality is to be respected. Calligraphy provides children with opportunities for the development of a legible and uniquely distinctive handwriting style. It provides opportunities for children to practice their handwriting in an enjoyable way and has a positive effect on everyday handwriting.

Form and Appearance

Punctuation, capitalization, and indenting are taught most naturally within the context of writing and reading and with material children have written themselves or are currently reading. But some children may need direct as well as indirect instruction in these mechanics that are necessary and important to the readability of the finished product (see Figure 12.14). Children should view mechanics as courtesies to the reader, not as the most important aspect of composing. Since the communication of meaning is the first objective of composing, only when children are comfortable and capable of communicating meaning in their written work should they begin to be aware of form and appearance.

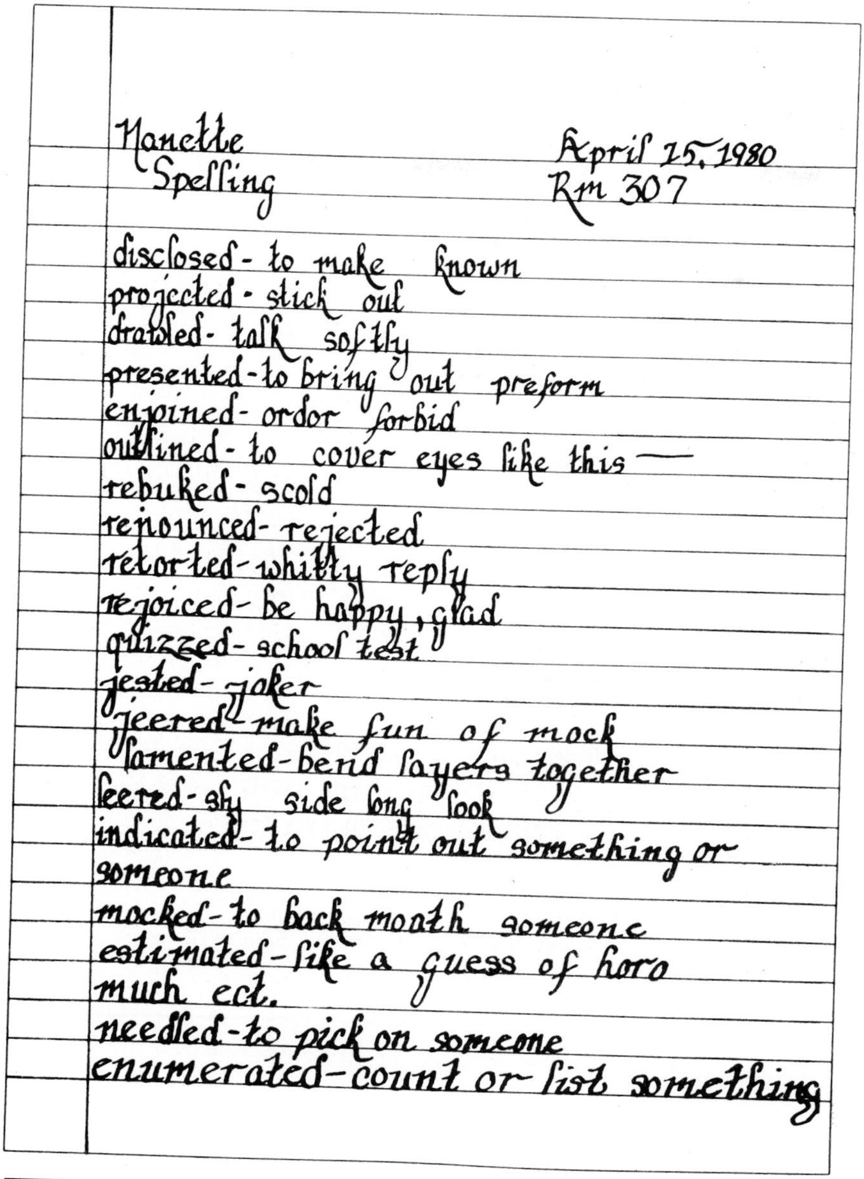

Nanette   April 15, 1980
  Spelling   Rm 307

disclosed - to make known
projected - stick out
drawled - talk softly
presented - to bring out preform
enjoined - ordor forbid
outlined - to cover eyes like this —
rebuked - scold
renounced - rejected
retorted - whitty reply
rejoiced - be happy, glad
quizzed - school test
jested - joker
jeered - make fun of mock
lamented - bend layers together
leered - sly side long look
indicated - to point out something or
someone
mocked - to back month someone
estimated - like a guess of horo
much ect.
needled - to pick on someone
enumerated - count or list something

FIGURE 12.13 Nanette's interest in calligraphy transferred and her spelling improved.

Source: D'Angelo, K. (1982). Handwriting with Calligraphy. *Language Arts, 59*(1), 23–27. © 1982 by the National Council of Teachers of English. Reprinted with permission.

Each mechanical aspect serves several purposes. Punctuation is a way of clarifying meaning; it serves to alert the reader to how written language might be read—where to pause, whether or not to read with inflection, when to stop, and when to read dialogue. Capitalization serves some of these same functions and also alerts the reader to proper names, places, and things. Together with punctuation, capitalization helps the

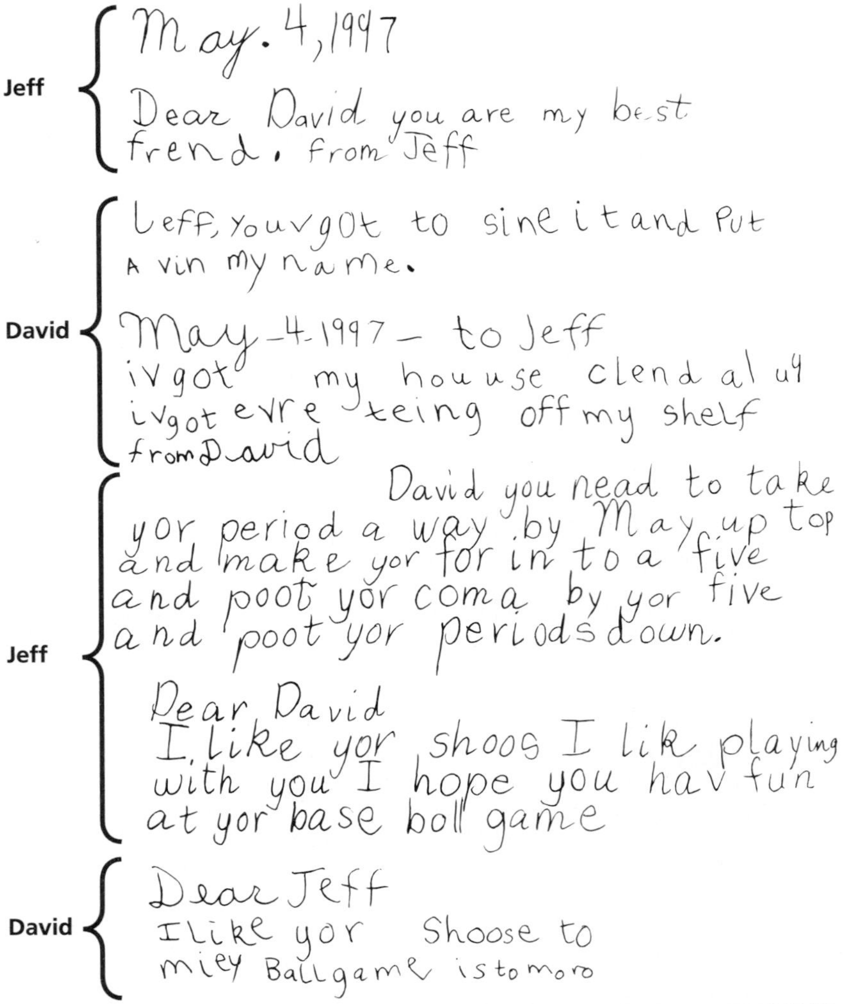

Jeff {

May. 4, 1997

Dear David you are my best
frend. From Jeff

David {

Leff, you v got to sine it and Put
A v in my name.

May _ 4. 1997 _ to Jeff
iv got my houuse clend al uy
iv got evre teing off my shelf
from David

Jeff {

David you nead to take
yor period a way by May up top
and make yor for in to a five
and poot yor coma by yor five
and poot yor periods down.

Dear David
I like yor shoos I lik playing
with you I hope you hav fun
at yor base boll game

David {

Dear Jeff
I Like yor Shoose to
miey Ballgame is to moro

FIGURE 12.14 When children write to each other, punctuation becomes important.

reader know when to finish and begin a sentence. Indentation signals the end of a group of ideas that have something in common and the start of another group of ideas. Margins, spacing, and proper form also indicate a particular type of written expression (e.g., a letter is much different in these respects than a research paper).

Summary

The conventions of spelling, grammar, handwriting, form, and appearance are like dessert that complements a balanced meal. The conventions complement a language event. They are not absolutely necessary but serve as a courtesy that facilitates proficient reading, writing, and speech.

1. Prepare for parents a brief overview of the spelling program you will use as an elementary teacher. Use both a narrative format and a graphic organizer to explain your rationale and the components of your program, including both the direct and indirect instruction your students will receive.

2. Work with a group of students to create their own editing checklist for writing that includes spelling, grammar, handwriting, and form/appearance. Help them use it on a piece of writing and then see if they have suggestions for revising the checklist.

Professional Resources

Bear, D. R., Invernizzi, M., Templeton, S., & Johnston, F. (1996). *Words their way: Word study for phonics, vocabulary, and spelling instruction.* Upper Saddle River, NJ: Prentice Hall. Based on research on invented spelling and the five stages of developmental spelling, this book provides 300+ word-study activities and mini-lessons that draw on student learning in reading and language arts.

Cunningham, P. M. (1991). *Phonics they use: Words for reading and writing.* New York: Harper-Collins. This book is full of classroom-tested methods for helping children develop language skills. Activities cover many styles and modalities of learning and each begins with a warm-up and ends with a challenge.

Gentry, J. R. (1996). *My kid can't spell! Understanding and assisting your child's literacy development.* Portsmouth, NH: Heinemann. This is an excellent resource to recommend to parents since it provides guidelines, tools, and strategies for parents who want to play an active role in helping their child become a good speller.

Hall, N., & Robinson, A. (Eds.) (1996). *Learning about punctuation.* Portsmouth, NH: Heinemann. Issues and research about how young children use and understand punctuation as early writers are discussed. Research on punctuation knowledge and development is included.

References

Barnes, W. (1989). Word sorting: The cultivation of rules for spelling and English. *Reading Psychology, 10* (3), 293–307.

Calkins, L. M. (1994). *The art of teaching writing.* Portsmouth, NH: Heinemann.

Cunningham, P. M., & Cunningham, J. W. (1992). Making words: Enhancing the invented spelling-decoding connection. *The Reading Teacher, 46* (2), 106–113.

D'Angelo, K. (1982). Handwriting with calligraphy. *Language Arts, 59* (1), 23–27.

Devine, T. (1989). *Teaching reading in the elementary school: From theory to practice* (pp. 133–134). Boston: Allyn and Bacon.

DiStefano, P. D., & Hagerty, P. J. (1985). Teaching spelling at the elementary level: A realistic perspective. *The Reading Teacher, 38* (4), 373–377.

Elbow, P. (1981). *Writing with power.* New York: Oxford University Press.

Farris, P. J. (1991). Handwriting instruction should not become extinct. *Language Arts, 68* (4), 312–314.

Fields, M., & Lee, D. (1987). *Let's begin reading right* (pp. 24–26). Columbus, OH: Merrill.

Gentry, J. R. (1996). *My kid can't spell: Understanding and assisting your child's literacy development.* Portsmouth, NH: Heinemann.

Gentry, J. R. (1987). *Spel . . . is a four-letter word.* Portsmouth, NH: Heinemann.

Gentry, J. R., & Gillett, J. W. (1993). *Teaching kids to spell.* Portsmouth, NH: Heinemann.

Gill, C. H., & Scharer, P. L. (1996). "Why do they get it on Friday and misspell it on Monday?": Teachers inquiring about their students as spellers. *Language Arts, 73* (2), 89–96.

Harwayne, S. (1992). *Lasting impressions.* Portsmouth, NH: Heinemann.

Henderson, E. H. (1990). *Teaching spelling* (2nd ed.). Boston: Houghton Mifflin.

Henderson, E. H. (1985). *Teaching spelling.* Boston: Houghton Mifflin.

Hillerich, R. L. (1977). Let's teach spelling—Not phonetic misspelling. *Language Arts, 54* (2), 301–307.

Hillocks, G. (1986). *Research on written composition.* Urbana, IL: National Council of Teachers of English.

Jongsma, K. S. (1990). Reading-spelling links. *The Reading Teacher 43* (8), 608–609.

Kaufman, H. S., & Biren, P. L. (1979). Cursive writing: An aid to reading and spelling. *Academic Therapy, 15,* 201–219.

Koenke, K. (1986). Handwriting instruction: What do we know? *The Reading Teacher,* 40 (2), 214–216.

Markham, L. R. (1976). Influences of handwriting quality on teacher evaluation of written work. *American Educational Research Journal, 13,* 277–283.

Michael, J. (1986). Self-selected spelling. *Academic Therapy, 21,* 557–563.

Newkirk, T. (1978). Grammar instruction and writing: What we don't know. *English Journal, 67,* 46–54.

Optiz, M. F., & Cooper, D. (1993). Adapting the spelling basal for spelling workshop. *The Reading Teacher, 47* (2), 106–120.

Peck, M., Askov, E. N., & Fairchild, S. H. (1980). Another decade of research in handwriting: Progress and prospect in the 1970s. *Journal of Educational Research, 73,* 283–298.

Petrosky, A. R. (1977). Grammar instruction: What we know. *English Journal, 66,* 86–88.

Radenich, M. R. (1985). Children's perceptions of their spelling strategies. *The Reading Teacher, 38* (6), 532–536.

Renwick, M. (1994). Real research into the real problems of grammar and usage instruction. *English Journal, 83* (6), 29–32.

Reutzel, D. R. (1990). Traveling tales: Connecting parents and children through writing. *The Reading Teacher, 44,* 222–228.

Richgels, D. J., Poremba, K. L., & McGee, L. M. (1996). Kindergartners talk about print: Phonemic awareness in meaningful contexts. *The Reading Teacher, 49* (8), 632–645.

Schlagal, R. C., & Schlagal, J. H. (1992). The integral character of spelling: Teaching strategies for multiple purposes. *Language Arts, 69* (6), 418–424.

Sperling, M. (1996). Revisiting the writing-speaking connection: Challenges for research on writing and writing instruction. *Review of Educational Research, 66* (1), 53–86.

Templeton, S. (1992). Old story, new resolution—Sound and meaning in spelling. *Language Arts, 69* (6), 444–453.

Topping, K. J. (1995). Cued spelling: A powerful technnique for parent and peer tutoring. *The Reading Teacher, 48* (5), 374–383.

Weaver, C. (1996). *Teaching grammar in context.* Portsmouth, NH: Heinemann.

Western, R. D. (1978). Grammar and composition: Why people disagree about their relation to each other. *The Elementary School Journal, 78,* 284–289.

What works in spelling (1995). *Learning, 24* (2), 47–53.

Wray, D., & Medwell, J. (1994). *Teaching primary english: The state of the art.* New York: Routledge.

Children's Book References

Fox, M. (1985). *Wilfred Gordon McDonald Partridge.* New York: Kane/Miller.

Griffith, H. V. (1988). *Georgia music.* New York: Mulberry.

Terban, M. (1993). *Checking your grammar.* New York: Scholastic.

Connections
among the
Language Arts

W••••• indow on Teaching

The use of archival records in the classroom is not a new idea. Individual teachers acting on their own for many years have had classes study selected documents.

With this introduction, fourth-grade teachers Pat Chaney, Gail Kovac, and Nadine Towne began their Archival Records Workshop about learning local history with archival records. At a summer conference for teachers, these teachers presented their year-long exploration and use of historical records and original documents, called *primary sources,* to teach local history.

Why use primary sources? Primary sources personalize history, are interesting for both students and teachers, encourage high-level thinking skills, introduce students to the "tools" of historians, make interdisciplinary connections, are modifiable to different learning abilities and levels, can be used in cooperative settings, supplement standard social studies texts and resources, and are a natural way to establish the support of community and parents.

These teachers were part of a grant written by their school district and funded by the state of New York to locate appropriate historical documents and to plan interdisciplinary instruction to incorporate New York state's *Learning Standards for Social Studies* (1996). The teachers spent several weeks of one summer finding documents, planning lessons, and creating units.

First, the teachers examined the Standards for Social Studies in New York State to determine the skills and processes the standards identify for their students. They decided that some of the types of skills to consider were locating, organizing, and evaluating information; acquiring information through reading, listening, and observing; communicating orally and in writing; interpreting media such as pictures, graphs, tables, charts, maps, and globes; understanding time and chronology; and problem solving.

Next, they obtained documents at the county clerk's office, the town clerk's office, local historical societies, the main office of their school district, local university libraries, and local museums. They gathered census records, land deeds, journals, photos, maps, newspapers, business records, military records, and school lunch menus, to name a few.

Then, with guidelines from the National Archives in Washington, DC, they determined how to use each document (Chaney, Kovac, & Towne, 1996):

- Determine what is usable in the document.
- Decide how the document can be used in the curriculum.
- Relate the document to larger issues or concepts.
- Determine the personal application the document has for a student.
- Establish the context of the document.
- Work directly with the document.
- Use documents to raise questions for further research.
- Use documents when longer reading assignments would be too much for available time.
- Allow the student to become the historian and to examine the document as a historian's tool.

Using these guidelines, the teachers chose documents they felt were appropriate for developing specific skills in interpreting a document: gathering, using, and presenting information. They worked cooperatively to create lessons based on these documents and put together a model booklet containing documents and lessons for other teachers to use (Chaney, Kovac, & Towne, 1996). One of Gail's lessons to develop students' ability to draw inferences and make comparisons follows:

TOPIC: *Interpreting a Document—1943 School Menu*
- *Objectives:* At the end of this lesson, students will be able to:
    1. Draw inferences from a primary source.
    2. Make generalizations from evidence presented.
    3. Identify social/cultural differences within two time periods that span 50 years.

- *Materials:* (Sources)
    1. Vestal School Menu from week of January 4, 1943
    2. Current school menu
    3. Document analysis worksheet
- *Procedure:*
    1. In small groups, read and discuss information in 1943 menu, comparing it to current menu for similarities and differences.
    2. Complete document analysis worksheet by identifying appropriate information from the primary sources.
    3. Using sources and worksheet, decide three broad conclusions drawn from comparisons. Share with class.
- *Evaluation:* (Student and teacher)
    1. Completed document analysis worksheet.
    2. Discussion of completed worksheet.
    3. Presentations and explanations of conclusions.

Gail's document analysis worksheet directed students to list and compare the similarities and differences in the two menus, read the notices at the bottom of each, speculate about what a "shortage" is, and figure the cost of a typical lunch for one day and one week in 1943 and today.

To obtain other documents with relevance and interest for students, these teachers sent a letter home to parents, describing their unit and requesting the loan of appropriate documents. Families produced old journals, yearbooks, travel brochures, family histories, recipes, immigration papers, maps, newspapers, books, and birth certificates that personalized their students' study of local history.

Pat, Gail, and Nadine believe strongly in the power of historical records and original documents for connecting young learners with history. They have found that in inviting students to become historians by examining a document as a historian's tool, their students not only become literate but they also use their literacy to learn.

───────────────────────────── • • • • •

Overview

The interrelatedness of the langage arts makes them best developed together in the context of learning that is meaningful. This chapter discusses strategies for using spoken language to develop written language and strategies for translating print into meaningful spoken language. As you read, remember that meaning construction and language development occur as students learn about the world through studies in science, social studies, and mathematics.

At this point, you know the connections within the receptive language arts, listening and reading, and the expressive arts, speaking and writing. But what about the connections between receptive and expressive language? Certainly, you have seen evidence of these relationships throughout this book. What are the explicit connections between listening and speaking, reading and writing, and spoken and written language? This chapter addresses these issues and examines instruction to promote the simultaneous development of the language arts.

A Language Arts Quilt

In Chapter 1, you read about a pieced quilt as a metaphor for language arts teaching. Different ways of making quilts were compared to different ways of teaching integrated language arts. A pieced quilt such as "Fence and Rail" or "Corn and Beans" uses a specifically chosen pattern, colors, shapes, and textures to create a symbolic and pleasing overall design or motif. The materials used in a pieced quilt (e.g., the fabric, thread, and batting) are integral and necessary to the overall design or motif. Think of these materials as representing language, literature, and content. In integrated language arts teaching, language is the thread in a quilt that holds the individual pieces of fabric together. Literature is the varied shapes, colors, and textures of fabric in the quilt that come in many forms and genres, all of which add to the richness of learning. Content is the batting of the quilt that provides substance, weight, and warmth. In quilt making, all three components—fabric, thread, and batting—are key elements, just as language, literature, and content are key elements of integrated language arts learning and teaching.

Literacy Connections

Meaning construction is basic to both the spoken and written language arts. Both reception and expression involve "literate thinking" (Wells & Chang-Wells, 1992) in which the learner uses the symbols of language to think. This is a broader view of literacy than the way it was defined in the past. Wells and Chang-Wells (1992) believe literacy is more than the ability to read and write print; rather, it is a "way of using language for particular intellectual and communicative purposes" (p. 121). They believe literate thinking is the development of mental muscles that allow us to effectively tackle intellectual tasks that would otherwise be beyond our grasp. It is through our use of the interrelated language arts, then, that we are able to employ existing knowledge to create and acquire new knowledge and solve problems. The literate person is a competent user of language to function and better her life and the lives of others.

How does literacy work for a young child? The child who listens to another child talk about a monarch butterfly in a glass jar associates her own knowledge with what she hears as she constructs new meaning. The child who talks about how the butterfly emerges from the chrysalis makes sense from what she observes and what she knows. The predictions one child makes about when and where the butterfly will eventually go and her response to a question or challenge by another child are demonstrations of literate thinking at work. When these children read Eric Carle's *The Very Hungry Caterpillar* (1969) and draw pictures to represent the life cycle of the butterfly or write a story about it, they also use their literacy to construct meaning. Children's literacy—their use of spoken and written language to think—involves the construction of meaning, which is different for each child, depending on factors such as background, culture, perceptions, attitudes, learning style, and opportunites for social interaction.

Loban's (1976) longitudinal research has been a cornerstone of understanding literacy and language arts teaching. He followed the language development of a group of over 200 children from the ages of 5 to 18 years old. Results indicated there are, indeed, important connections between spoken and written language. Children who are effective listeners and speakers with large vocabularies and sophisticated oral composition skills are also often fluent and proficient readers and writers. Loban found positive correlations among the listening, speaking, reading, and writing abilities of these children. Implications of this research suggest that children's spoken language development and ability directly influence their written language and ability.

For children, literature is a critical bridge between spoken and written language learning. In fact, Lauritzen and Jaeger (1997) propose that children's literature should be at the heart of curriculum. They suggest using a children's book with a "rich, compelling story with a universal theme" to contain and organize curriculum. They recount a week-long unit from *Very Last First Time* by J. Andrews (1985) that they developed with and for elementary students that initiated "questions we would normally encounter in social studies, science, mathematics, art, technology, music, and other areas."

Some other titles suggest similar potential:

Who Belongs Here? by M. B. Knight (New York: Tilbury, 1993). A young boy flees Cambodia for the United States where he finds problems and intolerance.
Billy by A. French (New York: Viking, 1995). A young boy is the victim of racism and is convicted and executed of murdering a girl in Mississippi in 1937.
There's an Owl in the Shower by J. C. George (New York: HarperCollins, 1995). Environmental concerns and the ecosystem are at the heart of a family's experience with an owlet.
A Very Important Day by M. R. Herold (New York: Morrow, 1995). Told from the perspective of several characters living in New York City, all from another culture, this book examines immigration and citizenship.

Not only can curriculum arise from literature, but literature can support and enrich curriculum. Hearing stories read, reading stories themselves, talking about literature, and writing about it result in children who are literate language users. Through literature, listening and speaking connect for children, as do reading and writing. Children learn the language of literature by hearing parents and teachers read it to them or by reading it themselves. They learn how to use language by talking, reading, and writing about their responses to literature.

Listening/Speaking Relationship

Listening and speaking are interactive processes. Each requires the occurrence of the other for effective communication. Because listening and speaking develop simultaneously, children alternate their roles as listeners and speakers, moving back and forth easily between the two. Interestingly, Walter Loban has said that teachers and their students *listen* to the equivalent of a book a day and *talk* the equivalent of a book a week (Buckley, 1992).

The listening/speaking interaction is probably the most basic form of human communication. Most people spend a good deal of time in oral interactions with others and may not recognize the power of this interaction. A good listener who knows when to switch roles and become a speaker who responds perceptively to what is said can foster a productive and satisfying interchange. Effective listening/speaking interactions are a critical communication skill.

Reading/Writing Relationship

Reading and writing are also interactive processes. Readers read what writers write. Writers are usually readers, at least of their own work as they compose, make revisions, and read their finished compositions. But readers are not necessarily writers; readers can comprehend without composing. For the reader, the reading/writing interaction involves constructing the writer's message. For the writer, the reading/writing interaction involves alternating roles as writer and reader. Walter Loban has said we *read* the equivalent of a book a month and *write* the equivalent of a book a year (Buckley, 1992).

In reality, communication and language use are not this simple. Learners continually alternate roles as listeners, speakers, readers, and writers and use language in complicated interchanges. They move from one role to another and back and forth without established routines or patterns. Children who understand how their language roles change and know that listening and speaking are complementary processes realize that each role represents language in a slightly different disguise. Children who understand these connections more easily transfer what they know or can do in one area to another area.

Language Differences

For children whose first language is not English or who have dialects, language delays or difficulties, or communication disorders, the connections you make for them between spoken and written language are critical. These children need to understand early on that when they construct meaning orally, it can be represented in writing also. For them, understanding and effectively using spoken language are essential to becoming literate.

Children with language and cultural differences are learning to read and write from textbooks written in an unfamiliar language about topics that may not be relevant for them. The same is often true for children whose language is slow to develop and for those with difficulties in processing or expressing language. It is more likely that these children will learn to write if they can first attain some facility with oral language and then use this facility to support their written language growth.

In schools where ESL teachers work with immigrant children or where speech and language specialists work with those who have language problems, remedial instruction that occurs outside the classroom is not enough to help children develop effective language skills. As the classroom teacher of these children, you play an important role in their acquisition of literacy. Your beliefs, your language program, the type of social interaction in which the children participate, and how you make the connections between oral and written language are critical.

It is important that you view potential bilingualism and the language abilities of children for whom English is not their first language as strengths and resources for your classroom. Nonnative speakers of English should experience the same language arts environments as English-speaking children because it is through the social aspects of interacting and responding in meaningful situations that children become successful language learners. Perez (1996) reports that regular classroom settings allow children to acquire language as they interact with peers and the teacher. In fact, Perez says that instructional conversations in which learners focus on concepts and content allow children to acquire English language proficiency. She says children acquire English as their second language when they build on each other's ideas, pose alternatives, agree or disagree, and focus "intensely" together on shared development of their oral text.

Interest is another important factor. Children learning English as a second language need to understand and use language in the context of meaningful communication about things of interest to them (Wong Fillmore, 1986). In fact, teaching English through the learning of interesting subject matter content is advocated as a way of promoting educated, lifelong language growth for ESL students. Early (1990) suggests guidelines for effective second-language learning through integrated English and content instruction. She believes that ESL students' learnings should build on the educational and personal experiences they bring to school. In this regard, she suggests the use of thematic units that involve the interactive use of language for real purposes. For these reasons, this approach seems appropriate not only for second-language learners but also for students with language delays and difficulties.

So, don't feel that as a classroom teacher you lack the time or skills to help children with second-language development. You can provide these children with the climate and oral langauge interactions that will build their English language proficiency. These children need an environment that helps them draw meaning from the context in which they are working, activities that provide a range of opportunities to use language in a variety of ways, an input of predictable and repetitive language on which to draw, and opportunities to practice language in purposeful ways.

Connections That Build Literacy

Since most children develop oral language first and possess fairly large listening and speaking vocabularies when they come to school, it is not surprising that many kindergarten and first-grade teachers build on these strengths to develop reading and writing abilities. As well, the development of oral English language conversational skills for ESL children is a precursor to acquiring knowledge and learning to read and write. Children who can talk about what they see, hear, and experience can easily learn to read their own spoken language when it is written down for them. The same is true for children with language differences and difficulties. The following discussion provides you with practical ideas for implementing some strategies that are particularly appropriate for these children.

Speaking is a natural springboard for generating writing and it leads to more sophisticated oral language. There are many ways you can set this process in motion, but the basic method is to encourage children to speak, then write down what they have said, and then read. Pueblo children, who orally shared many stories from their culture and heard trickster tales from around the world read to them, used elements of both the oral stories and the written narratives when they wrote their own tales (Van Dongen, 1987).

The importance of story and the oral basis for writing personal stories is well established for students from diverse cultures (Dyson & Genishi, 1994).

At the beginning of this chapter, *literacy* was defined as the use of language to think and communicate in purposeful ways. The rest of the chapter discusses ways to build literacy by connecting the language arts.

Technology, Literacy, and Learning

The computer has radically changed the way we live. Even for those of us who do not own personal computers, our lives are touched daily by computers. For example, restaurants, hotels, telephone companies, grocery stores, and libraries rely on computers to do business. Computer chips are found nearly everywhere—in thermostats, talking greeting cards, watches, games, cameras, elevators, and gas pumps, to name a few. Most experts say that technology is just beginning to change.

Gates (1995), founder and chairman of Microsoft, one of the most successful companies in the world, believes we are on the brink of a new revolution. He contends that we are crossing a technology threshold that will forever change the way we learn, work, buy, and communicate with each other. He says that the tools of the information age will not dehumanize but rather "humanize the educational environment" (p. 184) and facilitate collaborative learning both in classrooms and across continents. Technology will not replace teachers, but it will require them to be facilitators who will guide, monitor, and evaluate students as students access and analyze unlimited information. Gates believes that multimedia documents and easy-to-use authoring tools will allow teachers to customize curriculum and provide diverse students with opportunities to make the most of their individual talents.

Gates makes one startling omission in his predictions about the role of teachers, however. He says,

> *The good teachers of the future will be doing much more than showing kids where to find information on the highway. They will still have to understand when to probe, observe, stimulate or agitate. They'll still have to build kids' skills in written and oral communications, and will use technology as a starting point or aid. Successful teachers will act as coaches, partners, creative outlets, and communications bridges to the world.* (p. 198)

Gates highlights written and oral communications but ignores reading. He overlooks the fact that teaching students to read and read well is the most basic skill necessary for successful information processing and learning. Teachers are integral to developing learners who can read and write and thus can become technologically literate. To build your own technological literacy, see how many of the terms in Figure 13.1 you can define before reading the definitions that follow.

Reasons for Using Technology. Peck and Dorricott (1994) cite these 10 reasons for using technology in the classroom:

1. Students develop and learn at different rates and technology supports this.
2. Graduates must be proficient at accessing, evaluating, and communicating information.

FIGURE 13.1 Some computer and Internet terms you should know to be technologically literate.

BBS   A computerized message board or bulletin board system.

Browser   A special software application that lets the user access and navigate the Internet (e.g., Netscape, Yahoo, Altavista).

CD-ROM   A compact disk (CD) with read-only memory (ROM) that cannot be erased. It is used in place of a floppy disk and disk drive because it has a much larger capacity for sound, graphics, video, and computer programs. A CD-ROM disk requires a CD-ROM reader called a drive or player.

Chat mode   Interactive communication on the Internet that is instantaneous. It is similar to a telephone conversation, but participants use the computer keyboard rather their voices.

Cyberspace   Electronic communications among computer users who roam the Internet.

Database   A large collection of computerized data organized so information can be retrieved rapidly.

Disk   A 3- or 5-inch plastic square that stores information and is sometimes called a floppy.

E-mail   Personal messages or electronic mail sent via computer through a network. An ID number and password are required to send and receive e-mail.

Hard drive   The "file cabinet" of the computer that stores information.

Hardware   The physical equipment of a computer (e.g., keyboard, monitor (screen), printer, disk drive, diskettes, mouse, and modem).

Home page   The first web page a user sees when visiting a site, similar to the table of contents in a book.

Hypertext   A system of writing and displaying text that enables the text to contain links to related documents. Hypertext includes graphics and sounds as well as text.

Internet   A global computer network connecting more than 50 million people and organizations in 160 countries who send and receive e-mail, browse databases of information, and interact with each other.

Laser disk   A disk on which large amounts of video and audio are stored. The image is read by a laser beam and displayed on a television screen or a computer monitor.

Listserv   A group with common interests or concerns who communicate and have discussions through electronic mail.

Menu   A list of options for computer operations displayed on the monitor.

Modem   A device that connects the computer and a telephone line to send and receive information from a remote computer.

Mouse   A device that allows a user to get to a certain place on the screen or in a menu.

Multimedia   The integration of different pieces of technology for a presentation (e.g., computer, laser disk, television, music, graphics, and software).

Network   A system of interconnected computers sometimes called a Local Area Network (LAN) or bank (when the computers are in the same room).

Online   The electronic connection between one computer and another.

Software   Computer programs that instruct the computer to perform certain tasks. Software is written in a language (such as basic or logo) that the CPU (central processing unit) understands.

Word processing   Composing written text on a computer that allows for shifting of words or paragraphs that can be easily edited for spelling and grammar before printing.

WWW (World Wide Web)   An Internet navigation system that connects users and provides access to information on a variety of subjects. Named for its spiderweblike interconnections of millions of pieces of information located on computers around the world.

3. Technology can foster an increase in the quantity and quality of students' thinking and writing.
4. Graduates must solve complex problems.
5. Technology can nurture artistic expression.
6. Graduates must be globally aware and able to use resources that exist outside school.
7. Technology creates opportunities for students to do meaningful work.
8. All students need access to high-level and high-interest courses.
9. Students must feel comfortable with tools of the information age.
10. Schools must increase their productivity and efficiency.

Technology's interactive nature makes it interesting and motivating as a tool for learning language. For ESL students and students with language difficulties, the allure of technology and the social interactions that often involve its use can create natural situations for English language use.

This 10-item list suggests technology's potential as a motivating and challenging learning tool in the classroom. It also reminds us of our responsibility to prepare students for the world beyond school. Despite this knowledge, however, the technology many U.S. students are exposed to in school is still limited to using a tape recorder, watching a teacher use an overhead projector, or perhaps working once a week in a computer lab with drill-and-practice software. Even schools that want to update their technology are increasingly challenged by budgetary constraints. In some schools that lack technology, students are exposed to it when a teacher purchases his own computer and uses the Internet or a desktop publishing program to create documents for his classroom. Even in schools with money to purchase computers and install networks, systems are soon outdated and many teachers are intimidated or feel they do not have the time needed to learn and use the technology.

Regardless of these problems, many schools provide students and teachers with rich opportunities to join the information age. Nearly every school in the Netherlands has computers, and in Britain, Japan, China, and France, information technology is being incorporated into national curricula (Gates, 1995). In the Unites States, according to Goals 2000, a plan for improving U.S. education, by the year 2000, every classroom will have at least one computer connected to the Internet. In many counties and states across the country, schools and school districts are responding. In Horry County, South Carolina, for example, every elementary and high school is connected to each other and the Internet with fiber-optic cable installed by the Horry Telephone Cooperative. In this county, which is the size of Rhode Island, each school has its own World Wide Web page.

STRETCHING EXERCISE

Read "Strategies for Gaining Access to the Information Superhighway: Off the Side Street and on to the Main Road" by Diane Lapp, James Flood, and Linda Lundgren in *The Reading Teacher*, Volume 48, Number 5, pages 432–436. Then visit an elementary or middle school to see how the Information Superhighway is used there. Interview the library media specialist or the computer coordinator.

•••••

Some school districts establish a Technology Planning Committee to identify the district's vision and goals for technology, assess the current technology status, and propose a multiyear strategy for future purchases, curriculum integration, staff development, and funding. Vestal, New York, plans to use 1 percent of its budget to install cable in all buildings and computer clusters in classrooms connected via a local network and the Internet (Information Technology Plan, 1995). Other districts establish Budget Advisory Committees, made up of school personnel and community members, to provide feedback and advice to schools about how taxpayer dollars should be spent not only with regard to technology but also with regard to the overall budget. Both planning and advisory committees make sense in that they allow a broader mix of people with a range of expertise to provide input into important educational decisions.

Technology in an Elementary School. Another school district in Endicott, New York, is further along in its multiyear plan for technology partly because it received grants of hardware from IBM to supplement its own hardware purchases. Students in several elementary schools are immersed in technology and the information age. Observations in classrooms and conversations with faculty and students give an idea of some of the possibilities. These elementary schools use a large, instructional, management and assessment computer system called *Integrated Learning System (ILS).*

Jackie Visser, K–6 Curriculum Coordinator, says the availablity of computers has significantly changed the way teachers deliver curriculum and instruction. She believes technology has made learning more interactive, individualized, and exciting for students and, in some cases, has helped combat teacher burnout. Technology is part of the fiber of every school in the district and a topic that district committees explore when they interview prospective teachers. Jackie believes that attitudes, awareness, knowledge, and experiences with computers and technology are a plus for those in search of an elementary teaching job today.

Katie Bertrand, Library Media Specialist, exposes students to a variety of electronic reference sources. Books in the school's library media center are catalogued on the computer, enabling students to do an online search for books. Katie monitors and tracks library circulation, as well. Students access a laser disk with *Compton's Multimedia Encyclopedia* and other CD-ROM laser disks that contain information, color pictures, and narration on diverse subjects such as the rain forest, animals, and the history of the West. This popular tool expands students' research opportunities for reports, as well. When studying archaeology, for example, students can search the Internet to find information on current "digs" and pictures of the artifacts archaeologists are discovering. Students can even talk online to an archaeologist. Katie says students still use the books and magazines the library provides, but they are very excited by the interactive nature of computer software and its multmedia presentations.

Susan Hallenbeck, second-grade teacher, uses computer-assisted instruction in reading with her students. Susan's classroom has a cluster of six computers, where students work on software that contains a sequenced literature collection and track their own progress. Each story has three forms: a computer version that allows students to manipulate the graphics, a storybook for independent reading, and an audiotaped reading by a narrator. The program allows students to interact with literature in different ways and at their own individual levels and rates.

Barbara Bose, fifth-grade teacher, also has a cluster of six networked computers in her classroom and her students use the *Josten's Writing Program* and *Compton's Multi-*

media Encyclopedia. Barbara believes these tools connect reading and writing naturally for her students. The computers are one of the centers set up in Barbara's classroom that students use in small groups. Barbara's students draft, revise, edit, and publish their written work with these computers. They also search the Internet for primary source documents, just as they do from the computers in the school's library, and the students make their own multimedia presentation on subjects they are studying.

Judy Rowe, Computer Coordinator, uses *Write Time!* and *Storymaker*, graphics-based writing tools for grades K–4, in the learning lab. Groups of students come to the lab with their teacher and use these programs to write stories and then add graphics or create and print scenes that illustrate their stories (off line). Judy says the chance to write creatively with a computer makes learning the language arts dynamic, interactive, and motivating. Keyboarding skills are not emphasized until third grade, when most students' hands can better accommodate the keyboard. Judy says younger students do quite well with the two-hand hunt-and-peck method for short writing assignments. Teachers accompany their students to the lab, where writing is often an extension of what the children are studying in the classroom. Carol Gendle's grades 1, 2, 3 "family" of students use an integrated language arts software program to research information and write reports on desert animals. In this way, technology supports the class's integrated thematic unit on the Southwest.

There are many other possibilities for labs like this one. For example, students learning Spanish can exchange letters via e-mail with students in Spain. Or U.S. students from the Southwest can exchange letters on e-mail with students in the Northeast to learn about each other and the similarities and differences between their regions. Another popular idea is for students in one class to e-mail their written stories to an art class, which then illustrates the stories.

Karen Guzyk, third-grade teacher, has a bank of computers in her classroom and a large-screen monitor connected to them for whole-class use. Karen has creatively integrated this technology into her math program. Her students individually create and save word problems on a word processor that require reasoning and computation skills the class is working to learn. Then each student's problem is presented to the whole class via the large-screen monitor. In groups of four or five, students use a small chalkboard to diagram and solve the problem and then demonstrate their process and answer on the large screen. Karen says this use of technology helps her students learn from each other as well as her. She is surprised and pleased at how usually shy and quiet children blossom and become leaders using this venue.

Many teachers in this district are using the Information Super-Highway. Some teachers use the computer for e-mail to send and receive messages from others who are connected to the system. Others use the Internet and subscribe to listserves or electronic discussion groups that focus on a topic of common interest or concern. For a list of listserves and subscription directions, e-mail to this address: LISTSERV@Bitnic.educom. edu. For example, CHILDLIT-L or KIDLIT-L are two listserves that connect librarians, teachers, and anyone interested in children's literature and related issues.

Of course, the successful use of technology hinges on proper teacher training. Fiber-optic connections to the Internet, expensive hardware, and a wide array of software are often left unused to gather dust in a corner or at best are underused when teachers do not take part in adequate training. Proper instruction and opportunities to use a school's technology are necessary in order to best foster your learning and student learning about communications and new technology. Technology's possibilities for enhancing learning are numerous and exciting. One way to quickly become computer-literate or technology-literate is to turn your students loose and learn from them.

Unleashing Students.   Even when school districts provide adequate teacher training initially, technology is changing so quickly that teachers must stretch to keep up. Tricia Engineri, a third-grade teacher, wanted to extend her knowledge beyond the computer training she received a few years earlier from her school district. First, Tricia spent time with her computer coordinator to update her own computer literacy. Then she decided to unleash her students' curiosity and energy to develop everyone's computer literacy.

Tricia's outcomes, objectives, and performance-based activities for a year-long technology unit appear in Figure 13.2. She began the unit by reading her students *A River Ran Wild* (1992) by Lynne Cherry, the story of the history, pollution, and cleanup of the Nashua River in New Hampshire. They discussed the border art on each page of the book and how it represented the change and conflict that occurred over the river's history. They talked about technology and how the environment was changed by it and how people could have been more careful. Tricia's students decided to read more about technology and share their learning with other third-grade classes.

To organize their inquiry, Tricia and her students created a K-W-H-L chart to assess the knowledge they already possessed and to direct their inquiry in areas where they wanted to learn more (Ogle, 1987). On chart paper divided into four columns, Tricia listed what the students knew under *K—Know,* the things they wanted to learn and the questions they had under *W—Want to Know,* and how they planned to find answers to their questions under *H—How to Find Answers.* They left the *L—Learned* column blank so they could add this information as they acquired it. Tricia kept this chart on a bulletin board and periodically her students filled in the *L* section as they learned new information and completed various projects. They also added questions to the *W* section and resources and activities to the *H* section as they continued with their investigation.

The students read many books on technology and computers and even evaluated various software programs available in the school's library-media collection. One of the projects the students did was to create *The Important Computer Information Book,* a collection of current vocabulary, concepts, and pictures about computers. The Table of Contents and a sample page (see Figure 13.3) give an idea of how this helped students learn some of the vocabulary and concepts related to computers. Tricia will repeat many of the projects these third-grade students were involved in with next year's class because they were so popular and effective.

Distance Learning.   An example of technology that links schools to provide enhanced educational opportunities is the use of fiber-optic networks for distance learning. In the southern tier of New York, *Luminet* is a network of 21 linked sites: 15 school districts, a university, a community college, a health-services organization, a museum-science center, a TV-radio station, and a cooperative educational facility (Basler, 1994). The network allows full video and audio classroom interaction among the sites, with up to three sites interacting at one time. It serves both schools and the communities and businesses of the region. Teleconferencing (discussed in Chapter 7), credit and noncredit courses, continuing education, and inservice and teacher education programs are some of the possibilities.

Luminet offers exciting possibilities to students and teachers in participating schools. Through collaboration, teachers in one school can offer courses for students in their own and two other schools. For smaller schools that cannot afford to offer specialized or advanced placement courses, Luminet is a boon. For example, a course in Russ-

FIGURE 13.2 Tricia's year-long plan for a third-grade technology unit.

Technology Unit

Length of Unit: Entire Year

Outcomes:

1. Students will become familiar with the use of various components of technology.
2. Students will gain a reasonable comfort and confidence level with working with computer, CD-ROM, and software.
3. Students will have opportunities to utilize other technology available to them.
   a. Overhead projector
   b. Tape recorder
   c. Opaque machine

Objectives:

1. Students will become familiar with the various components that are part of a personal computer system.
2. Students will be knowledgeable in the use of the various computer components that they use.
3. Students will be comfortable using the computers for a variety of purposes .
4. Students will have experience with the various available software.
5. Students will understand the use of the overhead for presentations. As desired, students will have the opportunity to use this machine throughout the year.
6. Students will use the tape recorder for listening and speaking activities.
7. Students will access the opaque machine to assist them with projects.

Performance-Based Activities

1. Big Book of Knowledge—computer components
2. Bulletin board
3. Book of current information on computers
4. Software review
5. Online—Students will generate questions to ask for a session in one of the Chat Rooms
6. Computer-generated maps, writing, and drawings
7. Other—Student-generated projects (to be determined at a later time)

Assessment

1. Student-generated work samples
2. Informal assessment based on student interest and participation
   a. Student-generated behaviors for using the computer
      —What would the activity time look like?
      —What would the activity time sound like?
      —What would the activity time feel like?

· · · · ·

Source: Reprinted by permission of Tricia A. Engineri.

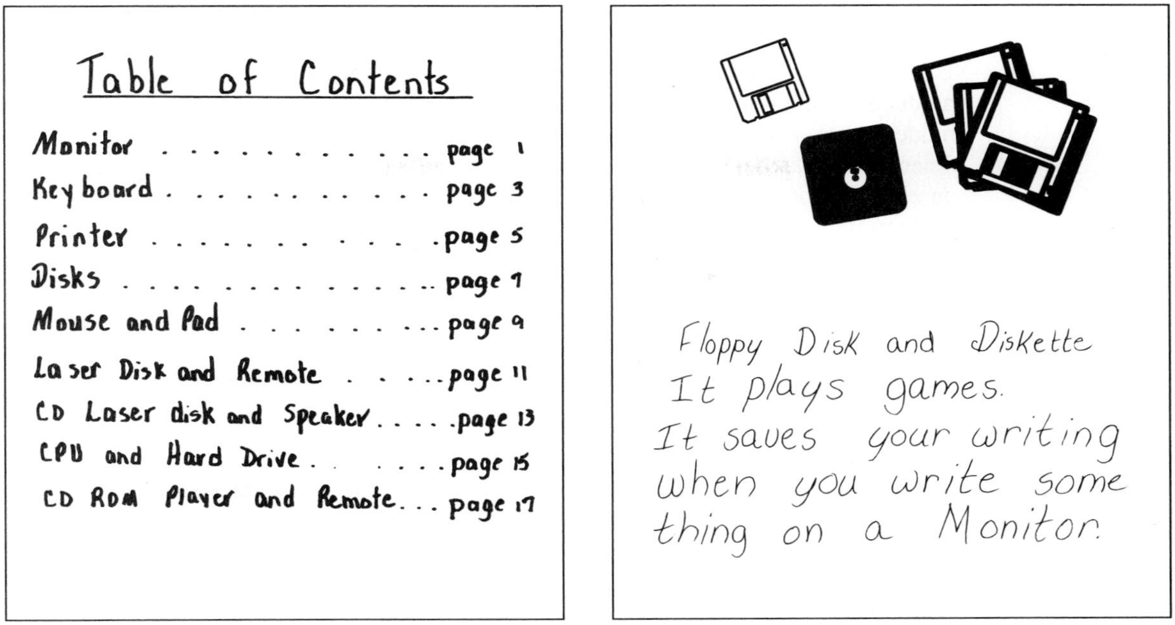

Table of Contents

Floppy Disk and Diskette
It plays games.
It saves your writing
when you write some
thing on a Monitor.

FIGURE 13.3 Table of Contents and a sample page from *The Important Computer Book*, created by third-graders to teach their peers about technology.

ian is now available to students in schools where it might otherwise not be offered. Special multimedia classrooms are outfitted at each site and include large-scale monitors, teacher and student cameras, VCRs, videodisk players, computers with CD-ROM capabilities, sophisticated projection systems, slide projectors, microphones, and fax machines. At any site, classrooms hold up to 21 students, and live video and audio is transmitted to remote sites. Area elementary schools are not yet part of this network, but they will be soon.

> Think of one creative way to use a Luminet hook-up to support and enrich the study of a specific topic by a group of fifth- or sixth-grade students in a participating school district. What other possibilities do you see for enhanced educational opportunities through networks like Luminet?
>
> **STRETCHING EXERCISE**

Electronic Fieldtrips. "Children who participate in electronic fieldtrips are on the cutting edge of learning. They explore topics that the texts don't address very well yet—topics like the new concept of 'biozoo' the careers of female pilots and astronauts, and the mysterious way the Federal Reserve Board functions" (Scherer, 1994, p. 38). An electronic fieldtrip is similar to a typical fieldtrip except it is accomplished through a local telephone or cable company, a television service, or a videotape. Access to a satellite dish and a modem is necessary for video-conferencing.

Electronic fieldtrips are offered free to schools throughout the nation. They are produced by the Fairfax County Public Schools Network in collaboration with outside funders such as the National Air and Space Administration (NASA) and the National Science Foundation (NSF). Teachers receive a packet of material with suggested hands-on class activities to use before the fieldtrip. A 30-minute pretaped program presents background in preparation for the live event, which is an hour-long interactive teleconference with experts. Students can call in questions on an 800 number. These distance-learning fieldtrips—mostly for elementary, middle and high school students—allow interactions between students and expert adults such as anthropologists, historians, and zoologists. These electronic fieldtrips give students opportunities to explore realms and careers far afield of their own locale and can be an exciting stimulus to learning.

| **STRETCHING EXERCISE** | Research has not yet established the impact of technology on learning. What are some of the limitations or disadvantages of technology over more traditional forms of instruction? Read "The Ill-Considered Dash to Technology" by R. P. Lookatch in the April 1996 issue of *The School Administrator*, pages 28–31, or another article that is cautious of technology as a panacea for education. |

••••••

Experience Stories

Using experience stories, or the Language Experience Approach (LEA), is a way of teaching reading and writing that uses the connections between oral and written language (Stauffer, 1969). The learner's own language and thinking are the foundation for instruction. The children describe their experiences to create stories that they can then

•••••
Oral and written language connections are made when children's oral language is transcribed to create text that they can then read.

learn to read. It is a highly motivating and personal approach with much potential for flexibility and creativity. Several steps are usually followed:

1. *Experience.* Some type of shared activity or experience (of interest to children) to observe, participate in, and comprehend
2. *Language.* Interaction with others and use of oral language to discuss activity or experience
3. *Dictation.* Transcription of oral language by teacher
4. *Reading-rereading.* With the teacher as model, then chorally, then individually
5. *Skill development.* Vocabulary, word analysis, comprehension, and revision/rewriting as appropriate

The critical aspect of any experience story is the language children generate as they think and talk about the experience and activity. The type of experience, patterns of language composed, and ways of using the experience story vary. Four second-graders who listened to a story about cacti and examined a prickly pear cactus plant as part of their study of the desert dictated these sentences about cacti:

Only use a little water on cactus plants.
                                    —*Theresa*

Most cacti have prickery things.
                                    —*Theresa*

Cacti are very pretty in spring.
                                    —*Connie*

The leaves store the water.
                                    —*Craig*

If you pull the prickery things off, the cactus will suffocate.
                                    —*Craig*

Cacti are found in the desert.
                                    —*Nanette*

If you plant the leaves, they will probably grow.
                                    —*Craig*

Cacti can grow very big.
                                    —*Connie*

Cacti have flowers.
                                    —*Nanette*

Cacti are round and some have weird shapes.
                                    —*Nanette*

Some have white stuff on the bottom like a beard.
                                    —*Craig*

Two third-grade students with learning disabilities who read Mercer Mayer's wordless picture book *Frog Goes to Dinner* (1974) made a list of vocabulary from the

The frog hid in the boy's jacket. The boy, the boy's family and the frog went to the fancy restaurant. The frog jumped in the saxophone. Then he jumped into the salad. He jumped in the man's drink. The lady who found the frog in her salad told the manager off. The manager caught the frog and started to throw him out the fire exit. The boy told the manager, "that is my frog!" The manager told the family, "Get out of my restaurant." The family got in the car and they went home mad. Father told the boy to go to his room. When the boy went to his room he was laughing and giggling and glad to get out of the restaurant.

FIGURE 13.4 A third-grader's experience story based on a book.

pictures and dictated the story in Figure 13.4. A fifth-grade class began to plan for a fieldtrip to a city zoo and museum by brainstorming questions about the upcoming trip:

Where are we going to eat?

Who will drive the bus?

What should we bring?

What should we wear?

How should we behave?

What do we do if an animal gets loose?

What do we do if we get lost?

Where do we sit on the bus and who do we sit with?

Should we bring cameras?

Do we need permission?

What and how children dictate varies, depending on the particular experience, your objectives, the children's facility with language, and the size of the group. How you transcribe children's oral compositions varies, also, depending on the material and equipment available. Many teachers of young children use an easel and write on lined chart paper with a magic marker, some teachers prefer the chalkboard, some use the overhead projector, and some use a typewriter or a computer. The most important thing is that children see their spoken words become written language they can read.

Some teachers duplicate copies of a dictated story they have handwritten or print multiple copies of the text using a computer and printer. Children can show parents and peers their work and, if it is kept, they can compare with their later work or publish it.

You can use dictated text in a variety of ways, depending on your objectives. For example, with the sentences about cacti, the teacher helped her students reorganize and revise their sentences. She asked them to identify the sentences that told about what the cacti look like (form) and what the cacti do (function). Then she had them reorder the two groups of sentences into a logical sequence and they added, changed, or deleted words to make the story more interesting and easier to understand. Each child read orally with her dictated sentence, then each read her sentence alone, then everyone read the story together, and finally individuals read the story alone.

You can use dictated text to develop vocabulary. Each child should have a copy of the story and be familiar with it. With *Frog Goes to Dinner* (Mayer, 1974), the teacher gave each child a copy and helped each circle the verbs and put boxes around nouns (see Figure 13.4). To teach a sequence of events, the teacher cut one copy into individual sentences and had the children put the sentences back together again in the correct order, using their memories and the book as a reference. Both teachers and children chose several words they learned from the dictated text to add to their personal dictionaries or word banks, where children wrote each word in isolation and then in the context of a sentence. Children can either keep their own dictionary in a notebook with several pages for each alphabet letter or as a word bank in a file box containing alphabetized 3×5 cards (see Figure 13.5). These files give children visual evidence of how their vocabularies are growing and serve as references during writing when children do not know how to spell a word.

As well as using a shared experience or a literary work as a basis for writing experience stories, LEA can be used to promote problem solving. You and your students can explore a problem, topic, or issue through discussion and dictated text. A fifth-grade class's brainstorming session about a trip they were planning to a zoo and a museum in New York City is a good example of how this can work. Their teacher helped them orga-

FIGURE 13.5 A word bank or personal dictionary helps build vocabulary.

Source: Reprinted by permission of Valerie M. White.

nize their questions into categories. They then formed small groups to find answers or ways to answer the questions. One group composed a letter to parents, requesting permission to go on the trip and inviting those interested to accompany them. One group developed rules for dress and behavior. One group developed "Disaster Plans" to deal with lost children and loose zoo animals. Another group contacted the bus driver, and, using a map, planned the itinerary, including which routes to take and where to stop for meals. To prepare those children who had never been to a museum, during her regular oral reading time the teacher read Elizabeth Konigsburg's *From the Mixed-Up Files of Mrs. Basil E. Frankweiler* (1967), a humorous story about two children who get to know what's inside the Metropolitan Museum of Modern Art in New York City when they spend a weekend locked inside it.

As you can see, experience stories allow children to learn to read and write as they use listening and speaking to explore real and highly motivating activities together. LEA is successful in kindergarten and first grade as a precursor to the basal or a literature-based program, or as an introduction to process writing. It is used to teach reading and writing in the subject areas at all grade levels. When science and social studies texts are too difficult for children to read, *experience story charts,* as they are sometimes called, provide a comprehensive way for children to create their own text, and they personalize a core curriculum. With older ESL students, LEA is effective as a group problem-solving strategy that promotes questioning, discussion, and suggestions for solutions or alternatives. When problem posing begins with issues in students' lives and, through dialogue, helps them become critical observers, they learn to act in ways that enhance their self-esteem and improve their lives.

Are LEA and process writing compatible? If you believe in the value of individual writing, does LEA rob children of rich opportunities to use and manipulate language firsthand since *you* transcribe the stories? On the contrary, both approaches actively involve the learner in creating real, relevant print—one in collaborative, group writing and the other in individual writing. Both approaches are compatible, since children need to see the teacher model reading and writing behaviors as well as experiment with both processes on their own. If you use LEA, remember that children need to have pencils in their hands as often as you do so they can experience writing and manipulate language. On the other hand, don't ignore LEA if you use process writing, because LEA lets you model the writing process for students and lets them see standard spelling, punctuation, and form.

LEA lets the teacher use materials that match children's varied backgrounds and language patterns. Children who are struggling readers learn to write and develop proficiency with both reading and writing. LEA allows for foreign-language-speaking children and children with language difficulties—such as dialects, impairments, and delays—to work together with children who are proficient English-language users. LEA also is effective with adolescents and adults who are learning English. In diverse classrooms, both English learners and English speakers are invaluable models for each other.

Inquiry and Research

Since much of children's learning, both in and outside school, involves constructing meaning, interpreting and analyzing the language of others, remembering what is important when someone speaks (or when they read), and making personal judgments,

•••••
Making decisions about what to include in a class publication allows students to use the research skills of collecting, analyzing, and interpreting data.

children need opportunities to learn to do these things well. Many adults never learned strategies for collecting, analyzing, and interpreting information, and those who did probably did not learn them in the elementary school. But it is in elementary school that this kind of instruction needs to begin.

Calkins (1994) says she thinks best with a pencil in her hand. When she is talking with another person, she jots down key words and ideas that help her listen as she structures what she hears. All people probably do more of this than they realize; it is a way of physically responding, aiding memories, and generating new ideas. Many people who listen to a speech or read either take notes or create some type of graphic to show the information and ideas in the text. Children can be taught to collect, analyze, and interpret data by learning to take notes, draw visual representations, outline, summarize, and use charts. Learners who have a system for taking notes, drawing a graphic organizer, or writing about what they hear or read can then more easily think about, talk about, or write in depth about, it later.

Since most young children's experiences with print include picture books from the library, stories in a basal reader, and their own dictated language, they have little to prepare them for the expository writing of content materials. Children who use newer basal readers read a range of genres that typically contain many nonfiction expository selections. However, when students write expository reports, they often copy verbatim from sources and often don't understand what they write.

Expository writing includes content-specific technical vocabulary and organizational patterns not found in narrative stories. Consequently, children need to be taught special vocabularies and helped to identify such patterns as cause/effect, comparison/contrast, simple listing, and analogies. One way to do this is to preteach, before reading, any vocabulary, structural, or organizational concepts that may give children problems. Another way is to follow the reading with a discussion in which the students together create a graphic organizer—a semantic web, diagram, or picture representation of important information. From this informal structure, you can show children how to use a more formal outline or summary strategy to write a report.

Manning, Manning, and Long (1994) and Short, Harste, and Burke (1995) suggest you teach children the process of inquiry and how to do research by first inviting them to explore topics of their own choosing. When they have identified topics, encourage them to pose questions for which they want to find answers. Then, help them identify all the different kinds of sources they can use to collect information to answer their questions. By using books, newspapers, magazines, the Internet, CD-ROM disks, interviews with people, and collecting data themselves, your students will engage in reading, writing, listening, and talking that is part of doing research. When students engage in inquiry-driven research, their use of language and construction of meaning is authentic.

STRETCHING EXERCISE

For a description of a personal approach to reseach that you can easily adapt for elementary and middle-school learners, read "Reflections on the I-Search Project" by M. Kaszyca and A. M. Krueger (1994), *The English Journal*, Volume 83, Number 1, pages 62–65.

• • • • •

The following sections describe how to teach students the process of researching. The strategies described here give students ways to begin to research and organize information so they can present it orally, or in a written report, or both.

Notetaking.   *Notetaking* involves reading or listening and writing words or phrases to represent the most important information that is read or heard. Good notes trigger the remembering of information and ideas. The trick is to put in one's notes the most memorable words, or *key words*. Learning to take key-word notes is one way young learners begin to record information for later use. You can show children how to take key-word notes by reading sentences or a short selection to them and writing key words on a piece of chart paper that you divide into two sections. As they occur, list the key words in the narrow section on the left side of the page. Use the rest of the page to elaborate on the key words and expand them into phrases or sentences. You can model this on the overhead projector or chalkboard so everyone sees the process. Help the children determine that

- Key words carry the "big" ideas or meaning.
- Key words help paraphrase information.
- Key words may be different for each person.

When the children can identify key words, help them paraphrase or retell the ideas they represent. First, model for the children by using synonyms to paraphrase in your own words. Once the children can do this, they have mastered a strategy that can help them remember important information to retell a story, write a report about what they heard in a lecture, or study information for a test. In Figure 13.6, a sixth-grader listened to a selection read aloud and took notes, which he expanded into fuller thoughts on the right.

Encouraging children to jot down key words and phrases to help them structure what they hear into a visual graphic aids both memory and learning. With older students, you may want to view a video, stopping it occasionally to model notetaking for them on the overhead projector or chart paper. Then review the notes at the end of the video for

Maria Tallchief (1925 –)   Notes from the book:

Key words	Sentences
Oklahoma	Maria was born in Oklahoma.
Scot-Irish and Osage Indian	Her mother was Scotch + Irish and her father was American Indian
4 yrs. old dance + piano	She started lessons in piano + dance when she was 4
12 yrs. old — concert	She gave a concert at age 12 — ½ was piano and ½ was dance.
after hs — NYC ballerina	After high school she went to New York City where she became a ballerina
"Firebird" "Swan Lake" "The Nutcracker" — George Balanchine	George Balanchine was a choreographer who designed her dances and put them to music. These are three of her most famous —
prima — 35 yrs.	At 35 she was the Prima — first ballerina for the American Ballet Theater
retired — 41 yrs.	She retired or "hung up her shoes" at age 41

* From TV — I learned that   in 1996 she was celebrated at the Kennedy Center in Washington for her artistic contributions by President + Mrs. Clinton

•••••

FIGURE 13.6   Key-word notes expanded to sentences.

the key points mentioned. The active involvement in processing information is as important a factor as the key words that students read later to remember what they saw, heard, or read.

Organizing. A *graphic organizer* is a visual representation of knowledge or a way of structuring information that arranges important aspects of a concept or topic into a pattern using labels (Bromley, Irwin-DeVitis, Modlo, 1995). Graphic organizers go by many names (e.g., semantic maps, webs, story maps, diagrams, and structured overviews). All types of visual graphics, drawing, or sketches that represent ideas and information and their relationships fit the definition (see Figures 13.7 through 13.10).

A review of research on the use of graphic organizers shows that they aid comprehension of content area texts (Dunston, 1992). When graphic organizers are presented

FIGURE 13.7 A picture map by Valerie Myers-White for *Today Was a Terrible Day* by Patricia Reilly Giff (1984).

Source: Reprinted by permission of Valerie M. White.

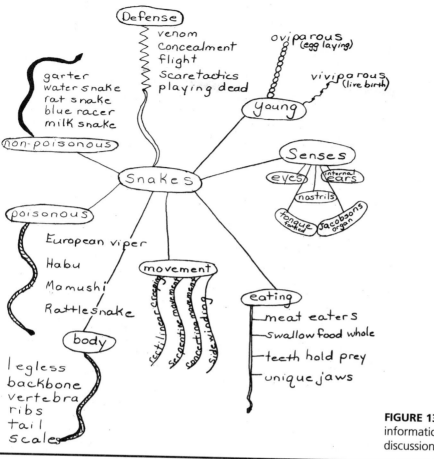

FIGURE 13.8 A web or map of information resulting from a science discussion of a book on snakes.

Source: Reprinted by permission of Suzanne French.

before reading, they aid comprehension and recall of information, and when students construct their own graphic organizers after reading, elementary students' recall improves and secondary students' scores on vocabulary and comprehension improve. The effects of graphic organizers may be greatest when students have in-depth instruction and training in their use and when students construct graphic organizers themselves. The students' active manipulation and processing of information to arrange and rearrange information into a complex relationship may be the key to learning it.

It is a good idea to use the chalkboard or overhead projector, rather than chart paper, to make a diagram, web, or map. These media allow you to revise and make changes as the story, selection, or discussion unfolds, whereas a chart is less flexible. Children need to see that creating a graphic organizer, like drafting, is a process of modifying and changing information and organization. The resulting graphic aids discussion of content, provides material for oral retellings, and supports the writing of summaries or other compositions. You can help prewriters create graphic organizers with either pictures or words by transcribing their ideas for them, whereas older learners can gain much by creating their own.

Graphic organizers seem especially appropriate for ESL learners and students with language differences or difficulties because these visual organizers help children

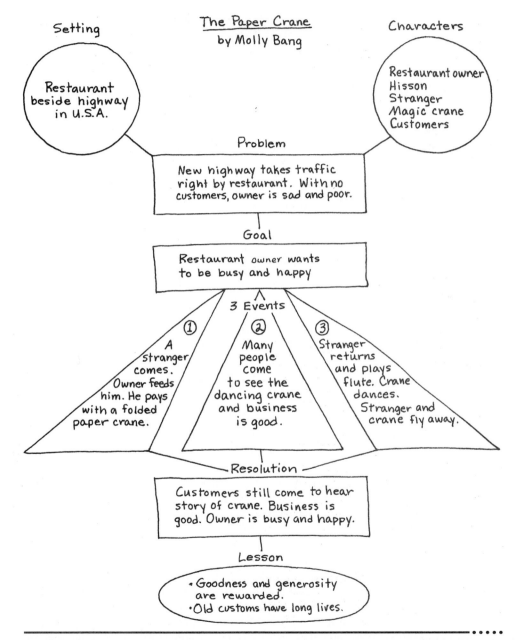

FIGURE 13.9 A web or map of the story elements in *The Paper Crane* by Molly Bang (1985).

structure and label information with key vocabulary. An organizer provides a meaning-ful context within which students can produce language. Graphic organizers allow for the connection of visual and verbal language as well—an important reinforcement for language learners.

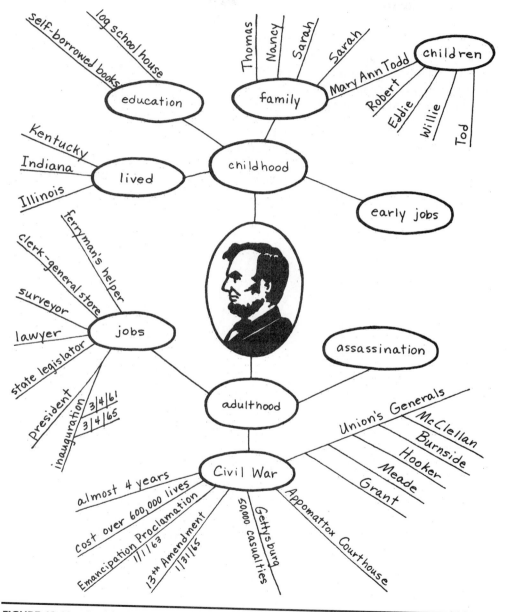

FIGURE 13.10 A web or map of information found in *Lincoln: A Photobiography* by Russell Freedman (1987).

Read a story to a child or a group of children. Discuss personal responses to the story. Then explain the purpose of notetaking and graphic organizers before you collaboratively create key-word notes or a graphic organizer based on the story. Last, encourage a retelling of the story from the notes or organizer. What did you learn?

• • • • •

As children learn to read and rely on their abilities to comprehend text to learn, especially as they engage in content reading and writing, there are several things you can do to help them construct meaning from the written language they read. You can help them discuss and extend their comprehension of content, and its organization or structure, before you ask them to write. You can help them learn to identify and summarize important information. You can help them compose written language in a variety of formats. First reading, then talking to create a web, and last writing (see Figure 13.11), make an effective sequence because students use a full range of language to process content and solidify their learning.

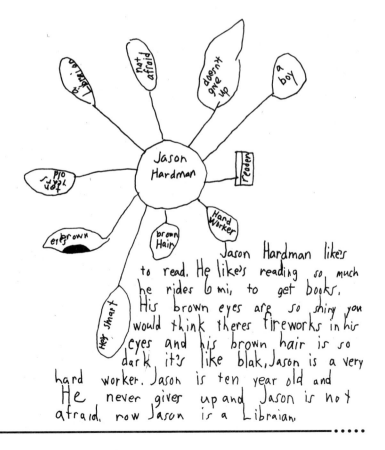

FIGURE 13.11 Webbing provides the support some students need to write.

458

Outlining.   *Outlining* is using a specified written format for the identification of main ideas and supporting details. It can help students recall specific facts and improve test taking. Although there is little research at the elementary level, one study of fifth-grade children suggests that outlining is an effective way to help them gain information from print (Bromley, 1985).

Outlining is perhaps best taught by modeling. After reading and discussion, use chart paper, a chalkboard, or an overhead projector to outline the content by transcribing the students' dictated ideas. This spoken rehearsal gives children a chance to learn from you and each other as they try out their ideas. Begin by showing the children how to rephrase headings and subheadings into questions. These questions then become the main ideas in an outline. The answers to the questions are the subtopics and details. You can supply the children with an outline format like the one given here or you can give them a partially filled in outline. For example, you can supply the main ideas and the children can supply the subtopics and details.

Topic Outline Format
I. Main idea (more important or general topic)
  A. Subtopic (important idea about general topic)
    1. Detail (fact to support subtopic)
    2. Detail
  B. Subtopic (second important idea)
    1. Detail
    2. Detail
II. Another main idea (main ideas begin with Roman numerals)
  A. Subtopic (subtopics are indented and need capital letters)
  B. Subtopic
    1. Detail (details are indented again and need numerals)
    2. Detail

To teach outlining, help students brainstorm questions or types of information they want to learn from reading a chapter, for example. Then these questions become the main outline ideas. For instance, some third-grade children first decided before reading that they wanted to know a number of things about spiders. They categorized their questions, which became main ideas in their outlines. The outlines became bare-bones versions of longer segments of text. Students can retell content from good outlines, write summaries of important information, or just review them as a way of studying for tests.

Summarizing.   When children write summaries or précis (a paraphrased summary or abstract of an original composition), their comprehension and content learning are enhanced. Middle-grade students who learn to write summaries after reading social studies and science material have better recall and comprehension of important information. As well, when students write summaries, often their spelling of content vocabulary improves as they write and reread their own summaries. Both précis writing and outlining can have the same positive effect on learning content material.

Summary writing requires students to locate the main ideas in a passage. A main idea states the central thought and is supported by the other information contained in the selection. It is often expressed in a topic sentence that may appear anywhere in a paragraph. Burmeister (1974) suggests using five graphic shapes to illustrate possible locations of topic sentences in paragraphs:

▽ Topic sentence at beginning of paragraph

△ Topic sentence at end of paragraph

✕ Topic sentence at beginning and end

▣ Topic sentence within paragraph

⬤ Topic sentence not stated

Again, as with outlining, demonstrating how to summarize or write a précis through class discussion and collaboration is a good way to model for children. Once children can identify topic sentences, they can paraphrase or restate these ideas in their own words. Identifying key words and supplying synonyms for them helps children learn paraphrasing. Older children can use a thesaurus—a tool many of them enjoy using as they try to say something another way. Identifying topic sentences or key words in paragraphs and paraphrasing them stimulates vocabulary growth as children learn to use synonyms, practice purposeful spoken language, and try out their ideas before they write them. Keeping summaries or précis in a folder, journal, or binder notebook gives children a record of what they are learning and material to review and study for tests. Précis of material from different sources can be combined to write reports.

A number of other ideas may help you successfully teach children to summarize. First, spend several lessons working together to build children's confidence before you ask them to proceed alone. Second, after group lessons, groups of children can work together, with stronger students sometimes paired with less able students. Third, children can also write summaries, make outlines, or take notes on cards and then use the summaries or outlines or organize the cards into a logical order before composing a report.

Charting. Charts help students see how a report differs from a summary. They also help students summarize material from several sources and organize it for analysis and writing. Feature matrices and data charts are a type of graphic organizer that helps even very young students organize information and show types of relationships (Cunningham & Allington, 1994). They consist of worksheets divided by horizontal and vertical lines into a calendarlike grid of 9, 12, or more cells.

A feature matrix holds information about several members of a category or group (see Figure 13.12). Before introducing the children to a matrix like the one shown here, discuss cats and their characteristics so that the children are familiar with the animal. Next have the children describe their cats or a neighbor's cat and then complete the matrix.

A data chart is a way of organizing information that compares and contrasts members of the same category or group. With help, even first-grade children, after listening or reading, can dictate information for you to transcribe on a data chart. Children can reread or retell the recorded information and dictate or write a report or summary. When a content text is too difficult for children to read, you may want to read it to them. Then help them construct a data chart from which they can compose an experience story about the content.

Even older children who can read and understand a text often need support when writing a report that blends information from several sources and includes one paragraph on each of several questions or subtopics. You can help students decide what they want to know about a topic, show them how to put these headings in the row across the top of a chart, and supply them with specific sources to enter in the left column, which they can use to obtain the identified information.

Students can record key words and phrases or short sentences in each cell. Those who are familiar with the idea of paragraph organization and topic sentences may have an easier time finding the specific information they need from longer sources, so you may want to teach paragraph shapes and identification of topic sentences first. When data charts are filled in, help the children find the common information in each column and write a sentence to summarize it. These sentences can then serve as the topic sentences of each paragraph in a written report.

As students become comfortable with the basic procedure, you can add complexity. One way is to provide students with sources that contain conflicting information. This will teach them to include in their reports phrases such as *Most sources agree. . .* and *However, some . . . .* Another way is to work with more elaborate comparison charts to cover more complex subjects. For example, each child can report on one aspect of a

Our Cats													
Names	Long Hair	Claws	Male	Female	Black	Brown	Orange	Grey	White	Green Eyes	Yellow Eyes	Purrs	Plays
Coco	☺	☹	☺	☹	☺	☺	☹	☹	☺	☹	☺	☺	☺
Skippy	☺	☹	☹	☺	☺	☺	☹	☹	☺	☺	☹	☺	☺
Squirt	☹	☺	☺	☹	☹	☹	☺	☹	☹	☹	☺	☺	☺
Misty													
Robert													
Ebony													
Desi													

FIGURE 13.12 The skeleton for a feature matrix on cats.

topic—perhaps a geographical region—then each report is compared and contrasted with the others. Each child can gather information on one country in the region. Then each country's geography, climate, products, language, economy, and so on, are compared to get a picture of the entire region. Or students can compare and contrast two versions of the same story (see Figure 13.13).

	Cinderella illus., Galdone	Indian Cinderella
1. What was the young girl wearing when she first met her future husband?	She was wearing a beautiful dress	Rags patched with bark of tree
2. What kind of person was the young girl?	Kind ebcauiful pretty face.	truthful nice to others pretty but scared
3. What was the position of the future husband?	prince	warrior he had a powerful friend
4. What changed the girl?	fairy	Strong winds sister gave her a bath
5. What happened to the two sisters?	they were married and given a palace	they were punished and turned into trees
6. What type of person was the young man?	Prince nice charming	invisble magical, smart truthful stern.
7. Which Cinderella was the happiest in the end? Why?	Cinderella married a rich man	husban magical she felt safe ☆

I think Indian cinderella was more happyer because she felt safe.

FIGURE 13.13 With a data chart, this fourth-grader compared two versions of the Cinderella story.

As with outlining and summarizing, you should demonstrate and model charting for children several times, inviting them to participate and contribute. Children can work in teams to complete data charts and compose reports before they work independently. Whether together or alone, be sure to have children talk, summarize, and compose oral reports before they write, because this oral practice is part of planning for writing. Cunningham and Cunningham (1987) confirm the importance of connecting reading and writing and suggest how it can be done in the content areas. They suggest using an organizational device in a reading/writing lesson that includes the components of good reading lessons that help children access prior knowledge, set purposes, read actively, see what they have learned, and deal with comprehension problems. The device also offers the components of good writing lessons: modeling, guided practice, and feedback about success. Two of the organizational devices Cunningham and Cunningham suggest are webs and outlines, but they also suggest feature matrices and time lines as ways of helping children collect, analyze, and interpret information.

Literature Models

Reading is critical to becoming a writer. It makes sense that reading quality literature provides students with models of good language that can affect their writing. Children assimilate aspects of the literature they read and incorporate these features into their own writing (Harwayne, 1992). Children use words, content, and structure from their reading in their own writing. They are influenced as well by the conversations they have with you and their peers about literature, the purposes and audiences for whom they write, and by your interpretations and observations about the literature you read to them. Learning to write stories, poems, plays, obituaries, journals, letters, and songs—to name only a few of the genres and composition forms presented in Chapters 4 and 9—is enhanced with exposure and interactions around these literature models.

Exposure to good models has particular benefits for English learners and students with language differences or difficulties who need to hear good models. They profit from having a structure on which to base their composing and especially the need to hear, read, analyze, and orally compose before they write. The following sections suggest several models that lend themselves to both oral storytelling and writing.

Songs and Musical Lyrics. Through picture books with musical themes, children can explore the world of music and you can enrich your curriculum (Lamme, 1990). Music is an integral part of children's lives as they sing, chant, play instruments, and enjoy being an audience for other people's musical performances. Music is a unique way to expose children to vocabulary, syntax, semantics, and the rhythm of language.

Picture books based on song lyrics hold special appeal for children of all ages because of its potential for involvement. These books connect oral language to written language and to build children's listening and speaking vocabularies as you promote reading and writing. Even using musical lyrics without the benefit of picture books stimulates vocabulary growth, comprehension, and written language production.

Most children love music. They enjoy listening to the lyrics of songs and imitating what they hear. Imitation, although not always accurate or representative of language comprehension, is one of the ways language develops naturally. All children, regardless of the stage of their language development—delayed or advanced oral language—use imitation to develop linguistic competence. This is especially true of children with limited English proficiency who need a steady flow of predictable and repetitive language on which to draw. You can use song picture books in several ways to encourage children to connect oral and written language. Many books include records that children enjoy listening to as they follow along visually in the book, or you can accompany lyrics on the piano or autoharp. Another possibility is to have the music teacher play the song and make a tape for the children to use. You can also write the lyrics on chart paper or duplicate them so each child has a copy. Perhaps you can make a large picture-song chart by writing lyrics on pages of chart paper or have children write the lyrics and then draw accompanying pictures. This big book is easily used by a group or pair of children who want to read and sing together. These ideas promote repetitive listening, singing, and seeing lyrics in print, which help children recognize the relationship between spoken and written words. Some popular song-picture books follow:

> *Shake My Sillies Out* by D. Allender (New York: Crown, 1987).
> *Old MacDonald Had a Farm* by H. Berry (New York: Morrow, 1994).
> *Twinkle, Twinkle Little Star* by M. Hague (New York: Morrow, 1992).
> *Mary Had a Little Lamb* by S. J. Hale (New York: Orchard, 1995).
> *I Know an Old Lady Who Swallowed a Fly* by G. Rounds (New York: Holiday House, 1990).
> *The Itsy, Bitsy Spider* by I. Trapani (Boston: Whispering Coyote, 1994).
> *What a Wonderful World* by N. Weiss & B. Thiele (New York: Atheneum, 1995).
> *If You're Happy and You Know It* by N. Weiss (New York: Greenwillow, 1987).

Once the children know lyrics, you can help them see patterns of rhyming words and draw their attention to the number of syllables in words, so they can create new lyrics that are syntactically similar to the original song. Children enjoy using a song they know, choosing a new topic, and supplying appropriate rhyming words to create an original song parody. For example, four lines from *Hush Little Baby* (Long, 1997) became a new song for some second graders:

Original
Hush little baby, don't say a word
Mama's going to show you a hummingbird.
If that hummingbird should fly
Mama's going to show you the evening sky.

Model
Hush little (noun)², *don't you* (verb)¹

Mama's going to show you a (adjective)² (noun)¹.

If that (adjective)² (noun)¹ (verb)¹ (verb)¹

Mama's going to show you a (adjective)² (noun)¹.

New Lyrics
Hush little chicken, don't say a peep
Mama's going to show you a wooly sheep.
If that wooly sheep runs away
Mama's going to show you a little blue jay.

Song-picture books and activities like those discussed here are appropriate for older students, as well. Older children enjoy music and spend quite a bit of their leisure time listening to the radio and taped songs. Several children's magazines print the words to popular music, and older children enjoy using them to learn lyrics. Some sixth-graders created a song-picture book for a recent popular song and used reference sources to find out more about the artist. They wrote a profile of Christopher Cross, developed a slide show to accompany his award-winning song "Sailing," and wrote original compositions on their own favorite form of recreation.

Musical lyrics without the benefit of picture books also stimulate and connect reading and writing. A fifth-grade student asked his teacher the meaning of some of the lyrics from Billy Joel's "I Didn't Start the Fire," which prompted the teacher to use the song lyrics as a means of helping the class learn about history as well as popular idioms. Chilcoat and Vocke (1990) advocate supplementing textbook reading with song lyrics to enhance the learning of history. Through song lyrics, they show their social studies classes how popular music depicted the antiwar sentiment during the Vietnam era and how country and western music defended government action. The ballad can be a medium for reliving historic events, and students can research these events to write their own song lyrics. Creating original songs and "raps" that use current slang and are performed rhythmically are also popular and foster language use and learning.

Song-picture books and musical lyrics offer children opportunities to develop vocabulary and accompanying concepts, understand proper word order and function, experience the rhythm of language, and use expressive and receptive language in meaningful ways. In addition, they are excellent tools for developing the language of children with linguistic differences.

Fables.   One way to involve children in composing after they have heard, read, or studied models is to help them identify elements specific to the model. This gives them criteria for their own writing and can form the basis for a rubric. For instance, second-grade children decided to make their own books of modern-day fables as Mother's Day gifts. First, they listened to their teacher read several fables (e.g., Ed Young's [1995] *Donkey Trouble* and Mem Fox's [1996] *Feathers and Fools*). They also read a fable in their basal. Then they discussed what they heard and read and what they liked or disliked in each selection. Finally, they studied one fable carefully and identified its characteristics, which they listed:

- It is short.
- It has talking animals as characters.
- It has an easy plot with not too many things happening.
- It tells at the end what the lesson is.

In a teacher-guided, group-writing activity, children brainstormed a list of animals and chose two they wanted to write about. In their discussion, they identified the special characteristics of each animal and began to create some possible oral stories about them. The teacher encouraged them to build on each other's suggestions, as in a chain story, and provided an environment in the classroom that encouraged creativity. Next, the children chose a moral from a list the teacher provided that they thought fit their animals' characteristics:

- The high and mighty fall the hardest.
- Once in a while change can be good.
- All's well that ends well.
- Too much of anything can be dangerous.
- What works in one case may not work in another.
- Two are sometimes better than one.
- Actions speak louder than words.
- Look before you leap.

Together, they talked through a fable, making many changes, adding and deleting until they had a plot with which they were happy. They dictated the fable to the teacher, who wrote it on chart paper so the children could see the story unfold. Silent rereading and oral reading gave them opportunities to revise the fable until it was exactly the way they wanted it. Because children had a strong model to work from, they were more easily able to write their own fables later in a form like the traditional fable format. Peers read and evaluated each other's fables using a short checklist that included the elements of a fable and good writing. Then the teacher had children repeat the process as they independently composed their own fable using a rubric.

Jason's three drafts (see Figure 13.14) show how he added quotation marks to denote dialogue and changed spelling (*Hary–Harry, burbed–burped, gobbed–gobbled*) in his fable about Porky (the pig) and Harry (the monkey). These changes were the result of the feedback he received from a peer reader. He made his final revisions and draft on a word processor.

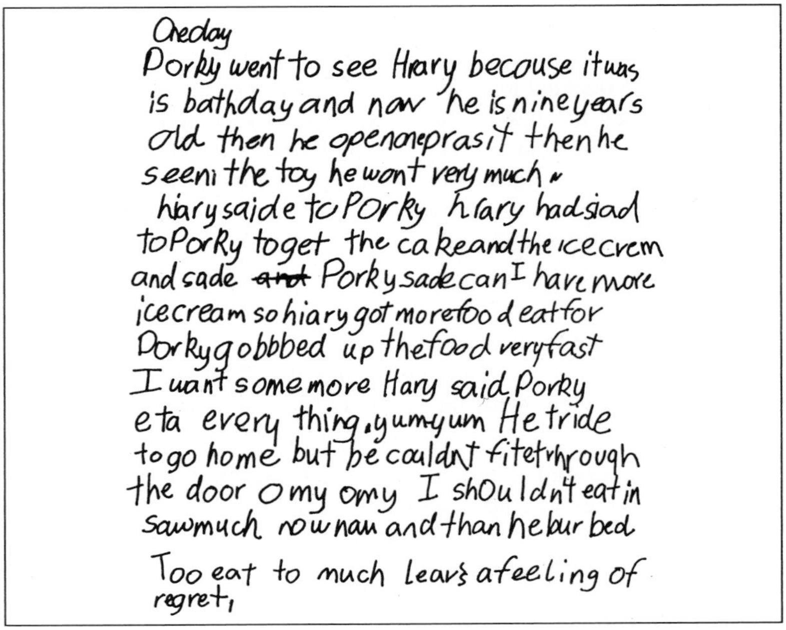
Oneday
Porky went to see Hrary becouse itwas
is bathday and naw he is nineyears
old then he openoneprasit then he
seeni the toy he wont very much.
hiary saide to Porky hiary hadsiad
toPorky toget the cakeandthe icecrem
and sade ~~and~~ Porky sade can I have more
icecream so hiary got morefood eat for
Porkygobbbed up thefood veryfast
I want some more Hary said Porky
eta every thing. yumyum He tride
togo home but he couldnt fitetrhrough
the door O my omy I shouldnt eatin
sawmuch now naw and than heburbed
Too eat to much leavs a feeling of
regret,

FIGURE 13.14 The evolution of Jason's fable.

Notice the differences between Jason's second draft and final computer version in Figure 13.14. What is missing from the third version? Can you speculate about why? Does this suggest any cautions to you about the writing process and computers?

STRETCHING
EXERCISE

• • • • •

The Birthday Party

One day Porky went to see Harry because it was his birthday and he is nine year's Old. ~~Then~~ He oppend his present. He got the toy he wanted very much.

→ Harry said to Porky, "Go get the cake, the ice cream, and the soda." Porky said "Can I have more ice cream." Harry got more food to eat for Porky He gobbled up the food very fast "Yum, Yum!

→ He tried to go home, but he couldn't fit through the door "Oh my, Oh my! I shouldn't have eaten so much." Now and then he burped.

Too much of anything often Leaves one with a feeling of regret.

The Birthday Party

   One day Porky went to see Harry because it was his birthday. He is nine years old. Porky handed a present to him. Harry said "Thank you Porky."

   Harry said "Let's eat ok?"

   They had cake, ice cream, soda, and pie. "This is not enough. I want some more ice cream, soda, and cake." said Porky. Harry go more to eat.

   He ate everything. "Yum, Yum" he said.

   Porky tried to go home but he could not get through the door.

   "Oh my, Oh my. I shouldn't have had so much" said Porky. He burped now and then too.

   To eat to much leaves a feeling of regret.

FIGURE 13.14   Continued

Exposure to and interaction with a model before they write their own composition helps children move more easily from print to oral language and back to print. Similar types of exposure to other kinds of literature models promote children's abilities to compose in those formats, as well.

How-and-Why Tales. Rudyard Kipling originally wrote how-and-why tales that explain the characteristics of particular animals. These stories are similar to fables in that Kipling used personification by giving human traits to animals and inanimate objects. Children enjoy these tales perhaps because they are about animals and involve an element of fantasy.

Hearing how-and-why tales, such as the Nigerian tale *Tiger Soup* by Frances Temple (1994) and *How the Ostrich Got Its Long Neck* by Verna Aardema (1995), prepares children to tell their own tales and write these stories. Again, help children identify the characteristics of these tales and then brainstorm possible titles for them. Teacher-guided oral storytelling and group writing can precede independent writing. Peer evaluation with a checklist helps children structure rereading and revision. Bookmaking projects might be a final activity.

Pattern Stories. Hearing or reading stories that follow a pattern and are predictable provide children with models on which to base their own oral language and writing (e.g., *Crocodile Beat* by Gail Jorgenson [1989], *Possum Come a-Knockin'* by Nancy Van Laan [1990] and *The Very Lonely Firefly* by Eric Carle [1995]). *Bein' with You This Way* by W. Nikola-Lisa (1994) contains the playground "rap" of a girl who notices and celebrates the differences in her friends. Because of their rhyme, repetition, and cadence, these books often make English more easily learned by ESL students, learners with English variations, and students with language difficulties. Again, as with fables and how-and-why tales, oral story composing and group story writing strengthen independent writing.

STRETCHING EXERCISE How can you use story grammar as a model to build the writing skills of a group of struggling fourth-grade writers? What elements of a story will you help them identify and how will you do this?

• • • • •

Poetry. Exposure to poetry models promotes successful writing experiences for many children. Syllable poetry and arranged verse are written according to predetermined formats. When children read and analyze these forms and use them as models, they learn to use synonyms, adjectives, nouns, and verbs to describe a specific topic and fit a certain pattern. Some examples of syllable poetry follow:

Haiku (hi-ku) (3 lines)
5 syllables
7 syllables
5 syllables

Lanterne (written in shape of a Japanese lantern) (5 lines)
  1 syllable
  2 syllables
  3 syllables
  4 syllables
  1 syllable

Cinquain (sin-cane) (5 lines)
  2 syllables (1 word, giving title)
  4 syllables (2 words describing title)
  6 syllables (3 words expressing actions)
  8 syllables (4 words expressing feelings)
  2 syllables (1 word synonym for title)

You can easily link writing with the content areas and integrate writing across the curriculum with poetry. First, use a topic that children are currently studying in science or social studies. Next, help students brainstorm and list as many words or phrases as they can think of about the topic. Then children can choose one of those words or phrases and brainstorm another list of words and phrases in the prescribed format of cinquain (2–4–6–8–2 syllables per line) to compose their own poem (see Figure 13.15). Brainstorming and listing words to describe a topic has many advantages for almost all writing, since it provides children with a variety of ideas and correctly spelled vocabulary to use as they write.

Remember that when you use models to encourage writing, your main objective is to have children begin with a model and use it as a basis for their own writing. Tonya Dauphin shared her "bio-poem" (adapted from Abromitis, 1994) for Jess Aarons, a main

Haiku

Fall

The smell of apples
and cider   and burning leaves,
and frost on pumpkins.

Lanterne

Ghosts
Making
Shrieks, screams, howls.
Rustling, silence.
Boo!

Cinquain

Spooky
dark and eerie
running, screaming, darting
frightened, scared, and yet excited
Creepy

FIGURE 13.15 Japanese poetry follows patterns.

character in *Bridge to Terabithia* by Katherine Paterson (1977), and then gave her students the following model to use in creating poems about themselves. Later, Tonya's third-graders used the bio-poem format to create poems about other characters from books they were reading.

Bio-Poem
Line 1	Your first name
Line 2	Four traits that describe you
Line 3	Sibling of . . . , son/daughter of . . . , friend of . . .
Line 4	Who loves (3 people, things, or ideas)
Line 5	Who feels (3 things)
Line 6	Who needs (3 things)
Line 7	Who gives (3 things)
Line 8	Who fears (3 things)
Line 9	Who would like to see (3 things)
Line 10	Who lives in (city, state)
Line 11	Your last name

Children's writing does not necessarily need to follow the form of a model, however. For some children, the security of a standard form helps them in writing poetry, but it may stifle other children who may not need it and may move easily to their own personal style or freer forms of unrhymed poetry. If children enjoy what they are doing and can create new forms of poetry, you have accomplished your goal and more (see Figures 13.16 through 13.20).

FIGURE 13.16 A concrete poem that uses words to look like an object.

FIGURE 13.17 An acrostic poem Jason wrote for social studies.

There once was a ghost named Larry,
Who thought he was extremely scary,
But instead of a "Boo",
He let out an "Achoo!",
And the people laughed and were merry!

FIGURE 13.18
A limerick.
•••••

Owl Moon
Cold, late, quiet,
Walking, watching, waiting.
Hope, anticipation, then awe!
HOOOOOT!

FIGURE 13.19 A poem by Ann
Clune based on Jane Yolen's
(1990) *Owl Moon* that is both
concrete (visual) and auditory.
•••••

Source: Reprinted by permission of Ann D'Agostino Clune.

FIGURE 13.20 A bio-poem by Tonya Dauphin for Jess from *A Bridge to Terabithia* by Katherine Peterson (1977).

Jess
Runner, artist, dreamer, king
Friend of Leslie
Who loves racing, drawing, learning
Who feels scared, alone, loyal
Who needs his dad, experiences, space
Who give smiles, gifts, comfort
Who fears dark, water, himself
Who would like to see Leslie, a museum, his father
Who lives in Lark Creek, Virginia
Aarons

Source: Reprinted by permission of Tonya Dauphin.

You promote meaning construction for all learners when you help children read and analyze models, generate characteristics, orally compose, and revise before they write independently in a specific form. From exposure to and interaction with models, children learn content as well as form. When children move from reading print to creating oral and written compositions, they need reasons or relevant purposes and they need organizational structures and models to support their compositions. They also need to know who their audience is. If children have a good idea of the purpose, audience, and form of their writing, they not only enjoy writing and speaking but they produce better compositions.

Summary

Listening and speaking are naturally tied to one another, as are reading and writing. When you imbed the language arts in content, you help children develop literacy as they learn subject area content. Making these connections is especially important for English learners and students with language differences and difficulties who struggle to learn.

Reflections

1. Begin a collection of model letters, reports, poems, stories, diagrams, outlines, summaries, notes, and other writing done by children. Begin a list of books that you can use with children as models of particular written language forms.

2. Plan a bookmaking project for young learners that includes transcribing oral language into experience stories. Use an appealing theme that lends itself to individual chapters. Teach children the parts of a book, have them illustrate their stories and design covers, endpapers, table of contents, indexes, and author profiles.

3. Write a letter to the parents of the children in your class, explaining why and how you connect oral and written language in your instruction. Use two specific examples of upcoming topics or projects and include your reasons for making language connections within them.

4. How do you think Pat, Gail, and Nadine (the teachers mentioned at the beginning of the chapter) could use technology to access primary source documents to teach local history?

Professional Resources

Flood, J., Heath, S. B., & Lapp, D. (1996). *Handbook on teaching the communicative and visual arts.* New York: Macmillan. This comprehensive reference includes overviews of recent research and practices in the field of language arts.

Graves, D. H. (1992). *The reading/writing teacher's companion series.* Portsmouth, NH: Heinemann. This series of five brief paperback volumes provides "actions" or experiments that help you explore the reading and writing processes for yourself and develop a literate classroom.

Leu, D. J., & Leu, D. D. (1997). *Teaching with the internet: Lessons from the classroom.* Norwood, MA: Christopher Gordon. This book tells how to systematically integrate the Internet into the curriculum and use it wisely in the classroom while explaining technical terms within the context of current instructional practices.

Rogers, L. K. (1997). *Geographic literacy through children's literature.* Englewood, CO: Libraries Unlimited/Teachers Ideas Press. Combining practical student-centered activities with an annotated bibliography of 160+ books, this guide models ways to teach geography in science, math, and social studies using children's books.

Routman, R. (1996). *Literacy at the crossroads: Crucial talk about reading, writing, and other teaching dilemmas.* Portsmouth, NH: Heinemann. A classroom teacher discusses controversies and dilemmas in education, whole language, back to basics, grammar, and spelling, and says teachers need to be clear about their goals and beliefs.

References

Abromitis, B. S. (1994). Bringing lives to life: Biographies in reading and the content areas. *Reading Today, 11* (26).

Basler, G. (1994). Luminet gets highmarks in the classroom. *Press & Sun Bulletin* (Binghamton, NY), October 16.

Bromley, K. D. (1996). *Webbing with literature: Creating story maps with children's literature* (2nd ed.). Boston: Allyn and Bacon.

Bromley, K. (1985). Precis writing and outlining enhance content learning. *The Reading Teacher, 38* (4), 406–411.

Bromley, K., Irwin-DeVitis, L. & Modlo, M. (1995). *Graphic organizers: Visual strategies for active learning.* New York: Scholastic.

Buckley, M. H. (1992). We listen a book a day; We speak a book a week: Learning from Walter Loban. *Language Arts, 69* (8), 622–626.

Burmeister, L. (1974). *Reading strategies for secondary school teachers.* Reading, MA: Addison-Wesley.

Calkins, L. M. (1994). *The art of teaching writing.* Portsmouth, NH: Heinemann.

Chaney, P., Kovac, G., & Towne, N. (1996). *Archival records workshop: Vestal central schools.* Endwell, NY: Twin Rivers Whole Language Conference.

Chilcoat, G., & Vocke, D. E. (1990). Music in the social studies: Resources from the Vietnam era. *Social Studies Texan, 5,* 45–48.

Cunningham, P. M., & Allington, R. L. (1994). *Classrooms that work: They can all read and write.* New York: HarperCollins.

Cunningham, P. M., & Cunningham, J. W. (1987). Content area reading-writing lessons. *The Reading Teacher, 40* (6), 506–513.

Dunston, P. J. (1992). A critique of graphic organizer research. *Reading Research and Instruction, 31* (2), 57–65.

Dyson, A. H., & Genishi, C. (Eds.) (1994). *The need for story: Cultural diversity in classroom and community.* Urbana, IL: National Council of Teachers of English.

Gates, B. (1995). *The road ahead.* New York: Viking.

Harwayne, S. (1992). *Lasting impressions: Weaving literature into the writing workshop.* Portsmouth, NH: Heinemann.

Information technology plan (1995). Vestal Central School District. New York: Vestal.

Kaszyca, M., & Krueger, A. M. (1994). Reflections on the I-Search Project. *The English Journal, 83* (1), 62–65.

Lamme, L. L. (1990). Exploring the world of music through picture books. *The Reading Tecaher, 44,* 294–301.

Lauritzen, C., & Jaeger, M. (1997). *Integrating learning through story: The narrative curriculum.* Albany, NY: Delmar.

Learning standards for social studies (1996). Albany, NY: State Education Department.

Loban, W. (1976). *Language development: Kindergarten through grade twelve.* Urbana, IL: National Council of Teachers of English.

Lookatch, R. P. (1996). The ill-considered dash to technology. *The School Administrator,* April, 28–31.

Manning, M., Manning, G., & Long, R. (1994). *Theme immersion: Inquiry-based curriculum in elementary school.* Portsmouth, NH: Heinemann.

Ogle, D. (1987). K-W-L Plus: A strategy for comprehension and summarization. *Journal of Reading, 30* (97), 626–631.

Peck, K. L., & Dorricott, D. (1994). Why use technology? *Educational Leadership, 51* (7), 11–14.

Perez, B. (1996). Instructional conversations as opportunities for English language acquisition for culturally and linguistically diverse students. *Language Arts, 73* (3), 173–181.

Scherer, M. (1994). Electronic fieldtrips. *Educational Leadership, 51* (7), 38.

Short, K. G., Harste, J. C., & Burke, C. (1995). *Creating classrooms for authors and inquirers* (2nd ed.). Portsmouth, NH: Heinemann.

Stauffer, R. (1969). *Teaching reading as a thinking process.* New York: Harper and Row.

Van Dongen, R. (1987). Children's narrative thought, at home and at school. *Language Arts, 64* (1), 79–89.

Wells, G., & Chang-Wells, G. L. (1992). *Constructing knowledge together: Classrooms as centers of inquiry and literacy.* Portsmouth, NH: Heinemann.

Wong Fillmore, L. (1986). Research currents: Equity or excellence? *Language Arts, 63* (5), 474–481.

Children's Book References

Aardema, V. (1995). *How the ostrich got its long neck.* New York Scholastic.

Andrews, J. (1985). *Very last first time.* New York: Atheneum.

Bang, M. (1985). *The paper crane.* New York: Greenwillow.

Carle, E. (1995). *The very lonely firefly.* New York: Philomel.

Carle, E. (1969). *The very hungry caterpillar.* New York: Philomel.

Cherry, L. (1992). *A river ran wild.* San Diego: Harcourt.

Fox, M. (1996). *Feathers and fools.* San Diego: Harcourt.

Freedman, R. (1987). *Lincoln: A photobiography.* New York: Clarion.

Galdone, P. (1978). *Cinderella.* New York: McGraw-Hill.

Giff, P. R. (1984). *Today was a terrible day.* New York: Puffin.

Haviland, V. (Ed.) (1979). *North American legends.* New York: Putnam.

Jorgenson, G. (1989). *Crocodile beat.* New York: Bradbury.

Kipling, R. (1980). *Just so stories.* Mahwah, NJ: Watermill.

Konigsburg, E. L. (1967). *From the mixed-up files of Mrs. Basil E. Frankweiler.* New York: Atheneum.

Lavies, B. (1993). *A gathering of garter snakes.* New York: Dutton.

Lobel, A. (1980). *Fables.* New York: Harper and Row.

Long, S. (1997). *Hush little baby.* San Francisco: Chronicle.

Marzollo, J. (1994). *My first book of biographies.* New York: Scholastic.

Mayer, M. (1974). *Frog goes to dinner.* New York: Dial.

Nikola-Lisa, W. (1994). *Bein' with you this way.* New York: Lee & Low.

Paterson, K. (1977). *Bridge to Terabithia.* New York: Crowell.

Temple, F. (1994). *Tiger soup.* New York: Orchard.

Van Laan, N. (1990). *Possum come a-knockin'.* New York: Knopf.

Yolen, J. (1990). *Owl moon.* New York: Scholastic.

Young, E. (1995). *Donkey trouble.* New York: Simon & Schuster.

Managing an Integrated Language Arts Program

W. . . . .indow on Teaching

To an observer visiting Doreen McSain's sixth-grade classroom on a Monday morning, her management of a language arts program that is integrated with social studies is clearly evident. In a lesson that interweaves reading and writing as it moves from whole-group instruction to small-group and individual work, Doreen actively involves all 27 students in using their literacy to learn.

Desks are arranged in clusters of five, with proficient readers, struggling readers, students with learning disabilities and ESL students in each group. Doreen begins by asking for volunteers to review last week's learning. She sets the stage for today's lesson and shows how it fits into last week's learning and the present unit. In this lesson, Doreen's objectives are for students to use a variety of strategies as they construct meaning from print to form an opinion (e.g., using listening, reading, writing, and discussion in groups).

Doreen begins by assessing students' prior knowledge about hunting. She develops background for the lesson by establishing reasons people hunt animals. Students make predictions about a newspaper article from its title, "Beluga Whale Hunt." Doreen reads the first paragraph aloud to the students and then they read, silently or orally with a partner, the rest of the action-filled, graphic account of a Beluga whale killing. After reading, Doreen puts three questions on the chalkboard and has students respond in their journals before sharing their entries orally in small groups:

How did it make you feel?
What do you remember?
Is what the men did right or wrong? Why?

Doreen wants her students to respond personally, visualize what they read about, form an opinion, share it with their small group, and identify the majority opinion. After each small group forms an opinion and shares it with the class, the majority opinion is: Hunting is wrong. Then Doreen gives the students the remainder of the article to read in which they discover the whale hunters belong to a Native American tribe that, according to the Constitution, has the right to hunt whales. Next, Doreen asks students in their small groups to agree or disagree and write justifications for these statements:

Rules and laws should be the same for everyone.
The rights of animals are as important as the rights of people.
Because some whales are endangered, we should work to protect all of them.
It is important to allow groups of people to follow their old customs and traditions.

Each small group forms a majority opinion and shares it with the class and the class identifies its majority opinion. Then, students compare their original opinions with their final opinions. They talk about how their opinions changed and what caused the changes. Doreen shares with her students the process she observed as some of them rethought their original opinions. The class also discussed the validity of holding an unpopular opinion and the importance of being able to justify that opinion with evidence and reasoned thinking.

Doreen concludes the lesson by asking students to respond briefly in writing to a self-evaluation:

What did I learn?
How hard was it to arrive at a majority opinion?

Doreen planned her hour-long lesson to include listening, reading, writing, and discussion to extend knowledge and thinking. Her sequencing and pacing required students to use their literacy to learn to think critically. Her objectives were clear and she knew why she was using journals and cooperative groups. Doreen assessed student learning and involvement by moving among groups to listen and work with them. She also read journals and wrote responses to entries, and read students' written justifications and self-evaluations. Only two students seemed off task occasionally and Doreen gently redirected them when they needed it. By her own high standards, Doreen felt the lesson was a success and her students were engaged and learning.

O..... verview

This chapter discusses management of language arts programs through planning, organization, and evaluation. Some keys to good planning include the learners, curriculum, instructional time, and resources. In organizing your program, it is important to consider various ways of grouping students to enhance instruction and learning. In evaluating your program, consider both curriculum and learning. Program management requires knowledge and flexibility in all three areas.

Management is the way a teacher uses various activities and strategies to maintain order in the classroom. Maintaining order in a classroom involves examining the academic learning that takes place and establishing structure, routines, rules, and procedures that allow the learning to occur. Research shows that teachers' managerial abilities relate positively to student achievement. Good teachers are good managers whose students achieve well.

The responsibility of managing language arts instruction in your classroom is yours, but you may find different schools or districts have different general approaches to language arts. You may teach in a school where there is little direction from administrators or curriculum supervisors, or you may find that curriculum and its implementation is carefully orchestrated and that the teaching of language is closely monitored. You may teach in a school where you team with other teachers or are totally on your own. In any case, understanding the aspects of managing a language arts program—how to plan, organize, and assess it—will help you create an orderly classroom, where students can be effective listeners, speakers, readers, and writers.

Planning an Integrated Program

Whether giving a party for someone or going on a fieldtrip, success depends on how well you and your students planned. Careful planning is also the key to implementing an integrated and exciting language arts program that engages learners in exploring and using language to learn.

Diverse Learners

The first consideration in developing plans is the diverse learners in your classroom. To get a fuller picture of your students, ask yourself several questions:

- What strengths does each student have?
- Are there physical or emotional problems that may affect the students' work?
- What languages do students speak? Who are the English learners? Which students have language difficulties?
- Who are the students with learning difficulties?
- What family backgrounds, ethnic heritages, and cultural groups do students represent?
- Do the learners' homes include rich language experiences? What kind of language is valued at home?
- What is the climate for learning at home? Does the family value education?
- What are the students' interests, hobbies, and areas of expertise?
- What views do students have of themselves? Do they see themselves as effective learners, listeners, speakers, readers, and writers?
- Where are the students functioning as listeners, speakers, readers, and writers?
- What are the students' abilities? Potentials?
- What kind of school experiences have they had?
- What experiences have learners had working independently? In small groups? In large groups?

Often, you can obtain answers to these and other questions, at least in part, by looking at students' permanent records or files. Some teachers look carefully at files and, with open minds, make curriculum and grouping decisions. Many teachers prefer not to read comments made by previous teachers or to look at standardized test or IQ scores until they are acquainted with students and can make their own decisions about students' strengths and needs. These teachers do not want to prejudice themselves or perpetuate someone else's assumptions. They learn about students by observing and interacting with them as they function in the classroom with a variety of different tasks and situations. These teachers look carefully at portfolios of student work and evidence of progress to see what students have done and are capable of doing so they know where to begin teaching them. These teachers often determine their own language arts curriculum and ways of grouping, rather than maintaining intact groups formed by previous teachers.

Whatever avenue you choose to follow to answer your questions about the students you teach, you should briefly examine permanent files to see if there are health problems and then be prepared to deal with them. At the same time, you can often determine quite a bit about background experiences, family values, and home environment from the students themselves, which will then help you decide how to teach them. Individual conferences with students is one of the best ways to learn about them. Brief work-related conferences with a few students every day pays dividends in understanding how they learn and who they are. At the same time, you build strong relationships with them.

Because today's classrooms are often composed of students from diverse backgrounds with widely different strengths and needs, it is important to ensure that your classroom functions smoothly. Willis (1996) says that classroom management "poses bigger challenges today than in the past" and traditional approaches are less effective today. For further guidance on classroom management issues, see Curwin and Mendler (1996) and Porro (1996). Briefly, here are several ideas to help you have a smoothly functioning classsroom:

■ *Plan, plan, and overplan so you are well organized and prepared each day.* When there is confusion or "down time" during lessons, activities, or tasks, you invite off-task behavior. To combat this, have a plan and be prepared. Know what you will do and have materials and resources at your fingertips to use.

■ *Establish a spirit of community and common ground.* Invite students to decide the classroom rules they will follow. When students create the rules, they are more apt to follow them than if you impose them yourself. Engage students in group projects and cooperative learning tasks to help them get to know each other as they develop team spirit and camaraderie.

■ *Hold class discussions often.* Class discussions help build a spirit of community and develop student thinking and oral speaking skills. Have students make group decisions (e.g., discuss and decide on the consequences for breaking class rules or how to implement a class trip). Discussing a problem together and finding solutions encourages creative thinking and positive social interactions.

■ *Focus on learning with an engaging curriculum.* Share decisions with the students about the content to study. Give them choices and let them make decisions about how they will learn and demonstrate that learning. When curriculum is relevant for students, learning is interesting and students are engaged rather than involved in off-task behavior.

■ *Remember to be consistent.* When students break classroom rules that have established consequences, enforce those consequences. However, give students choices so that they do not feel powerless in a potentially highly charged situation.

■ *Use appropriate prompting for off-task behavior.* One effective way to deal with off-task behavior is to focus on on-task behavior (e.g., use comments such as "Maria has her hand up," "I need to be able to hear John's answer," "Tanisha listened to the directions," and "Ahmed is really thinking about this problem"). T-charts also work wonders in shaping behavior when students decide what goes under the Looks Like and Sounds Like headings. Posting the chart for later reference gives the class a guide to follow.

One way to enlist student help in planning is to ask students to set their own goals for learning (Carroll & Christenson, 1995). When a fifth-grade teacher and curriculum coordinator collaborated to create a classroom where this happened, they found that students acquired a sense of ownership for their learning. They also found that students needed help in establishing realistic goals and assessing them, but goal setting helped focus both students and teachers on learning.

Curriculum

Think again about the party and fieldtrip mentioned earlier. The purpose of either one is usually to provide a special experience. Purpose is also an important element in your language arts program. One purpose of an integrated language arts program is to provide learners with opportunities to become effective language users.

How do you achieve this? How do you help children become effective language users? The components of a special experience and an integrated program share many things. A birthday party might include gathering friends, sharing favorite games or food, and giving gifts. A fieldtrip might include observing something, listening to a speaker, taking part in a process, and interacting with people. An integrated language arts program includes curriculum specific to listening, speaking, reading, and writing, interrelated with content curriculum such as science, social studies, mathematics, and children's literature.

Who decides what the curriculum will be? Some teachers make these decisions unilaterally, whereas other teachers invite students to be part of curriculum decisions, realizing that student-directed learning makes for committed and on-task students (Manning, Manning, & Long, 1994). Shared decisions about what will be learned and how it will be demonstrated give learners a voice and ownership in their own learning that can yield motivation and commitment. So, inviting students to be part of the curriculum-making process and sharing these decisions can be a positive experience.

You can view curriculum as a course of study or outline of content or, more broadly, a plan for providing learning opportunities to achieve various goals and objectives (Miller & Seller, 1985). Differences in the definition of *curriculum* are evident when you examine various curriculum guides. Some are lists of content and/or skills and some include goals, objectives, concepts, content, skills, teaching strategies, materials, and resources.

The Language Arts.   When planning your program, you will want to read and study the national *Standards for the English Language Arts* (1996) created by the National Council of Teachers of English and the International Reading Association (discussed in

•••••
Teachers often find it stimulating to share curriculum planning with each other and, of course, with their students.

Chapter 1). You can also consult published language arts curriculum guides that are available from at least three sources: state education departments, local school districts, and the publishers of language texts for children.

Departments of education in many states publish a recommended language arts curriculum to guide teachers in program planning. Copies of these curriculum guides are available for every classroom teacher, or at least one copy is available in each school. Many of these guides include content, strategies, and ideas for using the standards to plan curriculum and assess learning and performance.

Committees of teachers in school districts often write their own curriculum guides to help in teaching the content, skills, and understandings they feel their students need. Curriculum guides written by local school districts often incorporate special regional topics or concerns not included in guides created by educators at the state level.

Language texts for children are another source of help if you are looking for a guide to help you plan your program. Publishers usually include in the teacher's manual a chart of the content and skills they suggest should be taught at each grade level. These *scope and sequence charts* provide teachers with a hierarchically ordered list of language skills organized by grade level.

Subject Areas.   The three sources of information about language arts curriculum just discussed also provide curriculum guides for science, social studies, and mathematics. State education departments, local school districts, and some textbook publishers all publish some form of curriculum guide or scope and sequence chart. These guides, available for each grade level, contain content objectives and instructional suggestions.

Children's Literature.   Curriculum guides for teaching children's literature are usually published by state education departments, local school districts, and publishers of basal readers. State and local reading guides also include children's literature and suggestions for their use at each grade level. Educators often design their own curriculum that incorporates reading and writing, includes a management system, and provides a list of recommended books for various grade levels to accompany the state department's guide.

Teachers' manuals from basal readers usually include titles of appropriate children's books and suggestions for using these books as enrichment for the selections and/or skills taught. These are often listed as Suggested Activities or Enrichment Activities. Although these book titles and ideas, and those included in science or social studies curriculum guides, do not constitute a curriculum guide for children's literature, they do provide a resource to use as you integrate your curriculum.

Obtain copies of your state or local school district's curriculum guides for language arts and science or social studies. Look at the scope and sequence chart from those guides from a published language arts series. What do they include? How are they similar and different? To what extent do these guides integrate content, children's literature, and language learning? How helpful are they to you as a teacher?

STRETCHING EXERCISE

·····

As you make decisions or invite students to help decide what their integrated curriculum will include, it is a good idea to consult available guides and resources. These guides are prepared by educators and experts who have studied children and subject area content carefully. For this reason, using one or a combination of published curriculum guides to plan your integrated program makes sense. Teachers in upper-elementary grades often look at content guides and integrate language arts and literature within content. Teachers of early-elementary grades often identify suggested language arts curriculum, integrating both content and literature within it.

Time and Schedules

To integrate the teaching of language arts, content, and children's literature, it is critical to allocate large blocks of time each day for instruction. A teaching day in which individual subjects are covered, each in their own 20- or 30-minute time slot, is not always conducive to an integrated program in which real learning occurs. Small blocks of time do not allow children to interact with each other or for guided whole-language learning to occur. For example, a writing lesson that focuses on process and the composition of meaningful, coherent text takes more time than a lesson that focuses on capitalization skills and requires children to capitalize appropriate words in a list of phrases.

Lessons planned for extended amounts of time are quite useful to both teachers and children. See Figure 14.1 for Karen Wassell's Food and Nutrition unit plan and web for kindergarten and Figure 14.2 for sample lesson plans in that unit. Yvonne Caravaglia's lesson plan in social studies for fifth-graders in Figure 14.3 also shows how more time is needed when small groups work together to create individual reports on different biome areas than when group work and oral reports are not objectives. A lesson that involves teacher dissemination of facts and ideas or the use of workbooks or skill sheets to reinforce isolated skills allows for little student involvement or oral rehearsal. Although it takes less time to complete, it often results in questionable learning.

Realize, of course, that the optimal lesson length for children who are diverse in age, facility with English, learning style or ability to learn is shorter than for older children or children who do not exhibit learning difficulties. This is primarily because of differences in attention spans. Younger children may be less able to concentrate for long periods of time than older children because they are not ready developmentally. Children with language or learning problems are often easily frustrated and need instruction in shorter blocks of time. Keep in mind, though, that when young children or those with language and learning difficulties engage in challenging tasks and learning that is relevant and meaningful for them, their attention spans are often longer than one might expect.

When you integrate language, literature, and content and teach them together in one time block rather than separately, you can spend three times as long as what you would spend individually. Examples of three teachers' daily and weekly schedules in Figure 14.4 give you an idea of some ways to configure a school day and week to include extended time periods for implementing an integrated program.

Resources

For many teachers, the first resource they turn to is the school library media specialist. This person knows the books, magazines, newspapers, reference materials, films, filmstrips, CD-ROMs, audiotapes, videotapes, cassettes, pamphlets, prints, slides, film

FIGURE 14.1 Karen Wassell's unit plan and web.

Integrated Kindergarten Unit

Theme: Food and Nutrition
Organizing Idea: Eat Smart, Be Smart

Rationale and Goals

This unit is designed to meet the educational needs of a kindergarten class, but could be adapted to first or second grade. Because the typical kindergarten class can have children from diverse backgrounds and of various abilities and ages, it is important to create activities that will accommodate this diversity. According to Piaget, children at this age level tend to be egocentric, thus requiring learning experiences that meet their own personal concerns and interests. They learn by doing, exploring, and playing, therefore activities require the children's active engagement. To meet these needs, I have integrated the curriculum around the theme *Food and Nutrition* since food is a fundamental need of all people and is naturally relevant to their interests. To keep children actively engaged in learning, the children will be involved in a language-rich environment to allow for literacy development as well as content learning. They will have ample time for hands-on learning experiences in learning centers, class activities, small-group activities, pairs, and individual activities. The organizing idea of this unit, Eat Smart, Be Smart, has a dual message. First, when we eat well and take care of our bodies, our minds can concentrate on the job of learning. Second, by integrating the curriculum around the theme *Food and Nutrition,* the children are actually becoming smart not only in body facts but in their literacy, mathematical, and social development, as well.

Objectives

Content Area: Food and Nutrition

1. Explore the question *Why do we eat?*
   —Learn that we need to eat food to give us energy, to help our brains think, and to grow and heal.
   —We like to eat because food tastes good.
   —We all have different likes and dislikes.
2. Explore the question *What should we eat?*
   —Learn that we need to eat a variety of foods found on the food pyramid and we need to eat more foods that are high in nutrition than those that are not.
3. Explore the question *Where does food come from?*
   —Learn that food comes from a variety of plants and animals.
   —Plant and care for seeds and observe and record their growth.
   —Learn about baking and the mixing of ingredients that is important for the recipe to turn out right.
   —Visit a farm (dairy, apple, pumpkin, etc.) or a store or food-processing plant to learn about some of the places that our food comes from (if fieldtrips are in the budget).

Language Arts

1. Develop the following literacy concepts:
   —Books are pleasurable.
   —Books are handled in particular ways.
   —Pictures in books support the story.
   —Words in books tell the story.
   —Stories can be talked about and interpreted by readers and listeners.
   —We all have stories to tell.
   —Our stories and thoughts can be expressed by symbols (pictures and words).
   —Words, sentences, and stories have structure and meaning.
   —Spoken words are made up of sounds (phonemes).
   —Sounds can be represented by written letters (phonetics).
   —Written letters can form written words, sentences, stories, etc.
   —We can read what we write.

Mathematics: Children will have experiences with counting, sorting, classifying, measuring, and the concept of more and less.

(continued)

Source: Reprinted by permission of Karen Wassell.

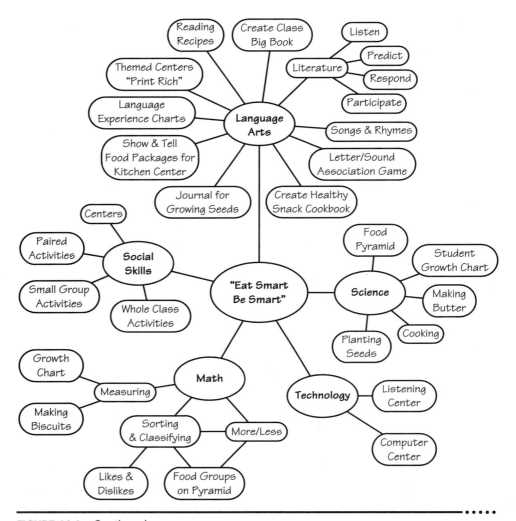

FIGURE 14.1 Continued

loops, records, microfilms, models, realia, and other materials often housed in a library media center. This person can be a wonderful ally as you plan and implement your program. If you give enough advance notice about a particular topic or unit your class will study, the specialist can collect a wide array of materials to make your teaching easier and to enhance student learning.

Other professionals in your school can also assist you. You should consult your reading specialist, special education teacher, and ESL teacher for ideas and materials to use in adapting your curriculum and teaching to students who have difficulties with literacy and learning. The art teacher, music teacher, and physical education teacher can also be valuable resources. Every unit or theme you teach is enriched when you invite these people with their special expertise to extend your students' learning within their

FIGURE 14.2   Sample lesson plans from Karen Wassell's unit.

485
•••••
Integrated Program

Lesson Plans for Food and Nutrition

Growing Vegetable Soup: Five Lesson Plans

Rationale: The following activities are part of a larger unit about food and nutrition in which we have been exploring the questions Why do we eat? What should we eat? and Where does our food come from? Today, we will be exploring where the vegetables we eat come from and this will guide our activities for the day.

Overall Goals: Children will develop an understanding of where vegetables come from by participating in a variety of related activities. These activities will integrate reading, writing, listening, and speaking development during active participation in singing, children's literature, gross-motor activity, and hands-on experiences with seeds and beans.

Lesson 1: "Hello Everybody" Song

Goals/Objectives:

1. To provide participation in a musical experience
2. To develop ability in listening and responding to directions
3. To create interest and curiosity about today's topic

Procedures:

1. Sing song to children and encourage participation:

   > Hello everybody, how do you do
   > How do you do, how do you do
   > Hello everybody, how do you do
   > How do you do today?
   > If you like broccoli, stand up
   > If you like carrots, stand up
   > If you like green beans, stand up
   > If you like corn, stand up

   (Repeat, trying different vegetables until all children are standing. End with *sit down* instead of *stand up*.)

Lesson 2: Shared Book Experience:
Growing Vegetable Soup by Lois Ehlert

Goals/Objectives:

1. To promote enjoyment of children's literature
2. To engage children in the reading process by encouraging listening, thinking, predicting, and responding to the story
3. To develop children's understanding of plant growth and where our vegetables come from

Materials:

1. *Growing Vegetable Soup* by Lois Ehlert
2. A can of vegetable soup

(continued)
•••••

Source: Reprinted by permission of Karen Wassell.

FIGURE 14.2   Continued

Procedures:

1. Introduce story (title, author, illustrator) and encourage discussion and prediction (show children can of vegetable soup to prompt discussion).
2. Read story. Encourage participation, questions, prediction.
3. Repeat story without discussion. Encourage children to complete the phrases.
4. Afterwards: Questions to encourage thought:
   —*Who likes vegetable soup?*
   —*Has anyone ever helped make vegetable soup?*
   —*Has anyone ever helped plant seeds?*
5. Introduce next activity: "Now we're going to pretend we're planting seeds."

Lesson 3: Action Chant: "Dig a Little Hole"

Goals/Objectives:

1. To provide gross-motor activity
2. To provide experience with listening, following directions, and reciting a poem
3. To reinforce concepts learned about growing seeds

Procedures:

1. Model and encourage participation in the following action chant:

   Dig a little hole
   Plant a little seed
   Pour a little water
   Pull a little weed
   Up, up, up
   The green stem climbs
   Open wide, it's blossom time!

Lesson 4: "Green Beans"

Goals/Objectives:

1. To activate prior knowledge about green beans prior to planting activity
2. To explore print concepts while reading bean packages
3. To compare similarities and differences between green beans in different forms

Materials:

1. Green bag with a can of green beans, a package of frozen green beans, a bag of fresh green beans, and a package of green bean seeds

Procedures:

1. Show children green bag and ask them to think of green vegetables that might be in it.
2. When they guess green beans, have them close their eyes and think about green beans.
3. Have them open their eyes and ask them to describe what they pictured in their minds.
4. Open bag and take out one package of beans at a time, read packages, encourage discussion of similarities and differences between them.
5. Give each child a green bean, encourage them to snap it open and look for the seeds.
6. Discuss where bean seeds come from.
7. Invite children to taste the fresh green beans.
8. Introduce next activity.

FIGURE 14.2 Continued

487
• • • • •
*Integrated
Program*

Lesson 5: Our Bean Journal: A Planting, Observing, Recording Experience

This activity may be modified as needed to accommodate children's abilities.

Goals/Objectives:

1. To participate in the actual planting and care of seeds
2. To observe the changes and growth in our bean plants
3. To promote development of written expression by recording observations and predictions of plant growth using drawing and/or writing

Materials:

1. Empty clear soda bottles cut for containers
2. Potting soil
3. Green bean seeds
4. Spoons or scoops for filling containers with soil
5. Watering can
6. Bean Journals for each group (or one for class, if doing as class project)
7. Scientist for the Day chart to keep track of whose turn it is to care for plants and record observations

Procedures:

1. Explain to children that they will be called to the science center in small groups to plant bean seeds. Show them the containers, seeds, and Bean Journal that they will be using.
2. During center time, call groups one at a time for more explicit instructions and guidance through the planting and recording process.
3. As project progresses, children will be encouraged to share their journal entries with the class. This will be an ongoing project as we watch and learn about our bean plants. With any luck, they will mature and actually grow real beans!

Clear plastic soda
bottle planter to
watch for root
development

Chart for taking care of plant
and keeping journal

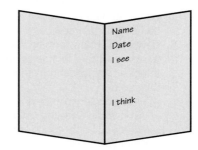

Children draw and/or write their
observations and thoughts

Lesson Assessment:

Children will be observed throughout the unit and participation may be noted in anecdotal records or the children's checklists. I will note what stage of writing development each child is in by observing journal entries (drawing and/or writing). Copies of their writing can be put in children's portfolios.

• • • • •

FIGURE 14.3   Yvonne Caravaglia's oral language lesson on biomes for fifth-graders.

Oral Language Lesson on Biomes

No. children: 20   **Grade Level:** 5

Lesson: Description of Biomes

Previous Learning Assumed: Students have basic knowledge of the geography of the Western Hemisphere and have read material on the six biome areas. They have had no formal oral reporting experience in this class.

Objectives

1. To use social studies content as a base for developing oral language
2. To work effectively in pairs
3. To orally contribute appropriate ideas to a larger group
4. To stabilize descriptions of biomes by distinguishing their individual characteristics
5. To compose and present descriptive oral reports that will be the basis for the next lesson involving writing

Materials

1. Index cards with different biome areas written on each one
2. Charts devised in previous lesson to be used as reference
3. Textbook reading selection and display of library books in reading center

Procedure

1. Explain lesson by overviewing objectives and what students will do.
2. Have students self-select pairs in which to work.
3. Have students pick a biome card and keep the name written on it secret.
4. Have students imagine that as partners they are walking through the biome area on their card. Ask: What are some of the things you could tell a person who is not with you about what this place is like? How could you describe it without telling them the name of the biome?
5. Develop by brainstorming with the whole class the items they might describe to characterize a particular biome as one is walking through it. Help students identify such things as the following and make a list on the board so they can refer to it when in their pairs:
   —What you see (plants, animals)
   —What you are feeling (cold, hot, wet)
   —What you might touch and how it would feel (insects, plants, ground)
   —What you smell
   —What you are wearing (parka, raincoat, shorts)
   —What you can find to eat
   —What you might hear (birds, wind)
   —What you are thinking
   —If there are other people there and what they are like
6. Using these and any other ideas students may come up with as guidelines, give pairs 10 minutes to develop a description of what they might experience as they walk through their areas. Have pairs work together to develop a statement that includes at least four different characteristics that each student in a pair can present orally.

•••••

Source: Reprinted by permission of Yvonne Caravaglia.

FIGURE 14.3 Continued

489
• • • •
*Integrated
Program*

7. Give each pair an opportunity to present their oral descriptions without telling the name of their biome. Have students guess what area is described. *Evaluation:* All students were able to use social studies content as a base for developing oral language. The whole group brainstormed ideas initially and then pairs discussed, made notes, and orally composed their descriptive reports which they then presented. Three pairs needed teacher help to come up with appropriate characteristics. All pairs presented their descriptive reports and each biome area was guessed accurately. A few of the reports were clever, using a lot of descriptive words and phrases, and one was humorous.

Reactions: I was worried at first because pairs did not focus and conversed off the topic, but when I reminded them that there was a strict time limit, they focused. At first, they called out guesses before pairs had finished reporting, but with direction, they were able to wait to guess biome names until pairs were done. We made rules for courteous listening together on the board that helped. The lesson went well and students enjoyed working together as content learning and effective language use were developed. I felt good about the way my objectives were met and how I dealt with problems. The lesson was a good lead-in to the written reports we'll do tomorrow.

• • • • •

special areas. Also, the children's librarian at your public library can help you supplement the books in your school. If this librarian knows you are a teacher, you may be able to borrow more books, tapes, or other resources and keep them longer than normal.

Parents and other community individuals are also rich resources. At the beginning of the year, many teachers send home questionnaires that ask parents information about their particular areas of interest, hobbies, careers or professions, recent travels, and so on. Parents can serve as resource people who share their knowledge to enrich your curriculum. This is also a good opportunity to inform parents about the science and social studies you will teach during the year. Of course, there are many other ways to encourage parents to become active in your classroom and school (see Figure 14.5).

You can also tap institutions and businesses in or near your community to provide students with real-life examples of what they are learning. A visit to a local newspaper, bakery, factory, museum, farm, library, or courthouse can greatly augment a science or social studies unit. Preparation for the visit, and the learning that follows it, will increase competence and offer practice in a variety of listening, speaking, reading, and writing tasks.

One second-grade teacher in an inner-city school arranged to take her class to the neighborhood public library as a first step in initiating a sustained silent reading (SSR) period in her classroom. She found that of her 24 children, 1 had a library card and only 2 others had ever visited the library before. As part of the visit, every child received a card. Several months later, more than half of the children reported visiting the library often and borrowing books. In this case, an easily planned trip to a nearby institution made a difference in the reading habits and learning of some children.

Fourth-grade teachers Lisa Rieger and her colleague collaborated with their city museum to carry out a long-term partnership that involved students in learning more about their ancestors and families, the community, and the museum's holdings and function. At the end of the year, the students created museum displays and planned an

FIGURE 14.4   These schedules illustrate different ways to configure a school day.

Daily Schedules of Three Teachers

First-Grade Teacher

8:45–9:00	Sharing time
9:00–10:30	Reading/writing/language (group & independent work)
10:30–11:00	Math
11:00–11:15	Journal writing
11:15–12:15	Lunch & recess
12:15–12:30	Read aloud
12:30–1:15	Special classes (physical education, art, music, computers, library-media)
1:15–2:30	Science/social studies/language
2:30–3:15	Groups & independent integrated work time

Third-Grade Teacher

9:00–9:15	Newstime
9:15–9:45	Math
9:45–11:30	Reading/language/journals
11:30–12:30	Lunch & recess
12:30–12:45	Read aloud
12:45–1:30	Special classes
1:30–2:45	Science/social studies/language (whole class & groups)
2:45–3:30	Independent work/Computer Learning Lab

Fifth-Grade Teacher

9:00–10:30	Science/social studies/language (whole class & groups)
10:30–11:00	Read aloud
11:00–12:00	Reading (groups & independent work related to content)
12:00–1:00	Lunch & recess
1:00–1:15	Sustained Silent reading (SSR)
1:15–2:00	Math
2:00–2:45	Focus time (groups & independent work; math, spelling, etc.)
2:45–3:30	Special classes

evening when they invited families to visit the museum and view their work. The initial partnership continued into a second year and the teachers are pursuing funding to expand it because it was so successful.

Local businesses are also often eager to "partner" with schools, whether to mentor or tutor students in the school or to provide opportunities for students to see and experience the workplace. Businesses are often sources of free or inexpensive materials. A visit to a local newspaper showed fifth-graders how important computers and word processors have become and provided students with new knowledge about how the news is made. They interacted with a reporter and an editor who spoke with them about careers in journalism. Each student received a complimentary copy of the day's paper and the teacher received a package of learning activities and bulletin board materials to use in the classroom.

FIGURE 14.5 Parent involvement in school can take many forms.

491
......

Integrated Program

20 Ideas for Building Parent Awareness, Knowledge, and Involvement

1. *Letters home.* Send home letters written by you and/or your students to inform parents about unit activities and to invite them to participate.
2. *Parent Visitation Day.* Organize a morning or afternoon in which parents come to visit your classroom. It can begin with a mini-workshop to orient parents to your rationale for curriculum and/or instruction before they observe. Then host a get together to answer questions and provide explanations after the visit.
3. *PTO meetings.* At Parent-Teacher Organization meetings, invite your students to share some aspect of their unit, perhaps by reading or performing.
4. *Newsletters.* Publish biweekly or monthly newsletters with text and drawings created by your students and you. Share class activities and include a calendar of events.
5. *Information Night/Family Night/Open House.* Plan presentations to explain your philosophy, curriculum, instruction, expectations, and so on, and to request parent support.
6. *Traveling Backpack.* Include books, a journal, stuffed animal, games, paper, colored pens, and activities related to a unit that invites parents and children to interact around reading and writing.
7. *Conferences.* Invite both the child and his or her parents to discuss progress, future goals, and so forth.
8. *Notes and telephone calls.* Call or write a certain number of parents per week so you reach all parents in a month's time.
9. *Friday Folder.* Send home a folder with the week's work and a letter to parents.
10. *Reenactment parade.* Have the children dress as people, animals, or things they are studying and parade around school/into community to appropriate music with improvisation or creative drama to reenact events from unit.
11. *Make & Take Workshop.* Invite parent volunteers to create games, blank books, or other materials to support a unit. For each one they make for your classroom, they make one to take home to use with their own children.
12. *Communication committee.* Organize a group of volunteer students from the class to communicate with parents and the community about their curriculum and learning.
13. *Directory of School Volunteers.* Have a group of older student volunteers create one for the school.
14. *Home visits.* Visit the home of each student to meet parents and talk to them about their goals for their child, the curriculum, ways to be involved, and so on. Home visitors can also function in similar ways.
15. *Classroom celebration.* Organize a special celebration at the end of a unit to conclude study and share products. Committees of children can plan it, organize it, write invitations to parents, and so forth.
16. *Parents as reading partners.* Encourage parents to read at least 10 minutes each night with their child. Send home a list of books related to topics the class is studying.
17. *Handbook for First Grade.* (Or for any grade). Ask for parent volunteers in the spring of the year to prepare a handbook for next fall's parents.
18. *Contracts.* Create written agreements to be signed by student, parent, and teacher about what will be done, how, and when.
19. *Home/School journal.* On every Friday, have students write a letter home to their family about school. On the weekend, family members can write a letter back to the student in the journal and they can read it together. You can also include a note home in this journal.
20. *Letter from the principal.* Ask your principal to write a one-page letter to parents explaining Goals 2000, Title I, Standards, or other topics of schoolwide or broader community interest.

For many teachers, manuals that accompany children's language arts texts and basal readers are a rich source of teaching materials and suggestions. Selected portions, specific lessons, and suggested materials from these texts can help meet the needs of diverse students. Even when you use only selected portions of a text in teaching, as has been suggested at different points in this book, it is helpful if the text is based on wholistic language activities and if the text connects the language arts and develops them in relevant contexts. For these reasons, look carefully at the components of several published texts and use them selectively on a trial basis before making a decision about which text to adopt.

As you teach, a number of professional journals can inform you of recent research and current practices. A few of these are:

Language Arts	*Reading Research and Instruction*
Educational Leadership	*Teaching Exceptional Children*
English Journal	*Young Children*
Research in the Teaching of English	*Early Years*
The New Advocate	*Childhood Education*
The Reading Teacher	*The Hornbook Magazine*
Journal of Reading	*Children's Literature in Education*
Reading Research Quarterly	*School Library Journal*

Although they are not refereed journals, but have an editorial board that often does most of the writing, teacher magazines such as *Teaching Prek–8* and *Instructor* also offer excellent ideas for classroom teaching. Journals, magazines, and newsletters provide current knowledge in the field, a better understanding of theory and research-based instructional practices, and ideas for being a more effective teacher.

There are several professional organizations, three of them listed here, that publish journals (in parentheses) and other professional materials and hold local, regional, or national conferences where you can also learn about new materials, resources, teaching strategies, and research. The journals include teaching ideas, reports of research, and reviews of instructional materials and resources that are invaluable for the teacher who wants to stay abreast of current practices. To become a member, write or call:

International Reading Association (IRA) (*The Reading Teacher*)
800 Barksdale Road
Box 8139
Newark, DE 19714-8139
302-731-1600

National Council of Teachers of English (NCTE) (*Language Arts*)
1111 Kenyon Road
Urbana, IL 61801
217-328-3870

The Council for Exceptional Children (CEC) (*Teaching Exceptional Children*)
1920 Association Drive
Reston, VA 22091-1589
800-232-7323

In summary, when you consider each of the four aspects of planning—the learners, the curriculum, the instructional time, and the materials and resources—you have begun to manage and implement a successful program. Failing to consider one of these aspects and being inflexible can have negative effects on your program. Think about the success of a birthday party if people are not invited or the success of a too brief trip to the zoo. Each aspect of planning a party, trip, or language arts program needs appropriate consideration so that the event or program is well managed and learners are constantly challenged to develop more effective communication.

Organizing for Instruction

Organizing a birthday party or fieldtrip involves creating order so each event occurs successfully. Organizing for instruction involves arranging, composing, and creating purposeful order in the classroom and among the learners to enhance their potential for learning. You will find that instruction is more effective, and you will more easily meet student needs when you plan for and vary the way in which students work. For some lessons, large groups may be the most advantageous way to work with students. For other types of learning, small groups work best or partners/dyads make the most sense. Your classroom should also encourage students to become independent learners and provide opportunities for individuals to work alone. Varied ways of grouping help you give proper attention to students with special needs such as language differences or difficulties, or learning problems.

Flexible Grouping

Two terms often used in discussions of grouping are *heterogeneous* and *homogeneous*. Heterogeneous groups contain learners with varying abilities and homogeneous groups contain learners with similar abilities. Reviews of research indicate that when students are "tracked," or placed in homogeneous groups by ability, they do not necessarily achieve better than students who are placed in heterogeneous groups but receive some instruction in homogeneous groups (Slavin, 1990). In fact, a combination of cooperative learning and within-class ability grouping is effective (e.g., in the Joplin Plan, students are assigned to a graded heterogenous homeroom for most of the day but regroup across grade lines for reading). Slavin (1990) explains that ability grouping is most effective when it is done for very small groups of students with specific skill strengths or needs and when students remain in heterogeneous groups for most of the day, with group assignments assessed and changed frequently, so that level and pace of instruction vary according to student needs.

There is some evidence that the exclusive use of ability grouping for language arts instruction has a negative effect on student learning, particularly for those students assigned to the lowest groups (Flood, Lapp, Flood, & Nagle, 1992). Often, these students do more drill work in skill materials, are asked lower-level questions, do more word-level than text-level work, read more orally than silently, and have more behavior problems than students in higher-achieving groups. In addition, teacher expectations for these students are lower and the students do not have opportunities to work with more able peers who can model learning for them and actually teach them.

Identify three possible reasons for the differences in achievement between heterogeneous and homogeneous groups and discuss them with a friend. How might the length of time a group works together affect achievement?

● ● ● ● ●

You may teach in a school that uses either heterogeneous grouping or homogeneous ability grouping for the entire day or for specific content subjects. Whichever method your school uses, keep in mind that there are other ways to define groups within your own classroom.

Why group children for instruction rather than teach them as a whole class? Grouping should exist in the classroom to facilitate teaching and learning (Johnson & Johnson, 1992; Johnson, Johnson, & Holubec, 1994; Kagan, 1992, 1990). It can be highly motivating and an effective instructional technique for several reasons.

■ Grouping enhances peer interaction. When children work together in small groups, they have more opportunities to learn from each other than when they work in a large group where dialogue is often between teacher and student.

■ Grouping encourages and allows students who are highly motivated and interested in a certain topic to explore it together. When a few students are free of those who may be more interested in other topics, possibilities for everyone's learning increase.

■ Grouping permits selective teaching and helps ensure that all students in a class do not have to sit through lessons targeted on what they already know or what they are not yet ready for. Grouping allows children with similar abilities or skills to be instructed together in relation to their specific areas of strength or need.

■ Grouping provides opportunities for friends to work together and for new friendships to develop. This kind of peer support enhances learning.

■ When students work together cooperatively in teams, their achievement improves (Slavin, 1990). Learning is heightened when students are accountable for their performances and when groups are rewarded for their work. The benefits to self-esteem also cannot be overlooked. As students work with others, build positive peer relationships, have success, and develop positive attitudes toward school, their feelings of self-worth and esteem are strengthened.

The key word to remember as you consider classroom grouping for effective instruction is *flexibility*. Flexibility means that groups are fluid and mobile, not static. The purposes and composition of groups change as students grow and learn, and as your objectives and ways for achieving these objectives change. Consider using the different kinds of groups described next at various times in your classroom.

Interest Groups.   One way to arrange your class for learning is to form groups of learners who share common interests and meet together for a common purpose. Research topics or themes provide natural reasons for groups. For example, as students in a fourth-grade classroom study wind power, some may be interested in exploring the causes of lift and thrust and reporting their findings to the class, while others may want to find out what makes a jet engine work, and yet others may want to study windmills.

Students may want to group themselves according to interest in a particular kind of activity. For example, in another fourth-grade class, one group of students wanted to write and perform a play about Hiawatha as part of their social studies learning, another group wanted to make an illustrated book about life among the early settlers, and yet another group wanted to plan and organize a trip to the local museum.

Naturally, there will be differences and changes in learner interest on a topic. Using flexible interest groups means giving each learner opportunities to work with a number of different students, depending on topic, idea, or task. It may be that groups are assigned based on the teacher's knowledge of interests or children choose groups they want to work in.

Interest groups offer some disadvantages and some advantages. One disadvantage of interest groups is that it is not easy to meet the needs of certain students within each group who are at different points in learning. Interest grouping also may not allow friends to work together, unless, of course, friends share the same interests. On the other hand, since motivation, enthusiasm, and commitment are usually higher in these groups, it makes sense to capitalize on this.

Teacher-Selected Groups.

A second way to arrange learners for instruction is to determine individual strengths and needs. For example, in conferencing with students who are writing, you may discover that several understand and use topic sentences when they write reports or that several use quotation marks appropriately when they write dialogue. Knowing this, you can go a step further and organize these students into groups. The children who have mastered topic sentences can go on to learn about comparison/contrast. The students who understand quotations can be grouped together to learn about the use of personification. At the same time, you may want to group students who do not understand main ideas and topic sentences or the use of conversation in a story and work with them to develop these understandings. Groups learning specific areas of knowledge or skills are usually formed for brief periods of time until learners master a particular task, or until you determine their readiness to master that task.

Teacher-selected groups based on skills also have both disadvantages and advantages. One potential disadvantage is that if these groups work together over long periods of time, the students in them miss the opportunity of learning from other students not in the group. An obvious advantage of teacher-selected groups is that students who know how to do something are able to pursue new learning and need not be bored when you teach or reteach something to members of the group who have not yet mastered it.

There are several other possibilities for teacher-selected groups (Flood, Lapp, Flood, & Nagel, 1992). You may want to group students according to their work habits so you can partner one student with another who can be a model. You can group students by their knowledge of content by putting them all together in the same group or spreading them as experts among several groups. Knowledge of strategies can also help you decide where to put certain children (e.g., you would spread among groups those whom you want to model certain problem-solving strategies). You may decide that certain students are leaders and distribute them accordingly in groups.

Social Groups.

Another way to arrange learners for instruction is based on friendship or choice. When social grouping is used, students choose their buddies and best friends with whom to work and study. Choice grouping allows students to choose among a list of topics or tasks and, at the same time, choose a group that a friend or friends has chosen.

One advantage to this type of grouping is the potential it has for encouraging behavior problems. If students enjoy each other's company and are not challenged by the group's work, they may become disruptive or unproductive. However, if they enjoy each other and share a genuine interest in the topic, their friendship can be a wonderful catalyst to learning. Social groups have the benefits of comfortableness and friendship among group members, and this in itself can encourage positive attitudes toward learning.

Random Groups. Random selection is a fourth way to arrange students in groups. Have students draw names from a hat, number off (e.g., all the 1s make one group, 2s another, etc.), or use a characteristic such as birthday or eye color to decide group membership. This type of grouping is effective at the beginning of the year when you don't know students and they don't know each other. Random groups have the advantage of being viewed by students as fair because it is chance rather than the teacher that assigns group membership.

Flood, Lapp, Flood, and Nagle (1992) have other good ideas for grouping. They believe the most often used sizes of groups are individuals, dyads or pairs, small groups of 3 or 4, large groups of 6 to 10, half-class groups, and whole-class groups. They suggest that materials for groups can differ in four ways:

1. Use the same material for all groups.
2. Use different levels or kinds of similar material so the students can learn the same concepts but benefit from reading easier or more challenging material or material in their own language.
3. Use different areas or themes within a topic, as in jigsaw groups, when each group focuses on a specific item (e.g., a different character in a story or a different stage in a person's life).
4. Use different topics when students group themselves according to interests.

STRETCHING EXERCISE   How can flexible groups support ESL students, bilingual students, and students with special needs?

• • • • •

In summary, flexibility in grouping is important. As you use groups in your classroom, remember that learners need guidance and practice in working together if they are to be successful. Guidance includes careful planning, identification, and explanation of the tasks or topics involved, as well as close supervision. This is especially important at first. Many teachers find that by continually circulating among groups to provide help and to monitor activity, students seem to stay on track better. You may also want to ask your students to establish some rules to help foster cooperation as they work in groups. A fourth-grade class listed the following:

Nine Rules for Cooperative Groups
1. Get into groups quickly and quietly.
2. Stay with your group.
3. Use quiet voices.

4. Encourage everyone to participate.
5. Keep hands and feet to yourself.
6. One person talks at a time.
7. Listen to/look at the speaker.
8. Use the person's name when talking.
9. NO PUT-DOWNS.

Another important factor in the success of group work is time. When a group realizes there is only a certain amount of time in which to accomplish its task, this helps maintain group momentum. It is also critical to build in time for group members to share their work. When the fruits of a group's labor are shared with others, students soon see how important the group's contribution is to the learning of the whole class.

Research supports the notion that grouping for instruction is motivating, rewarding, and promotes learning (Johnson & Johnson, 1992; Kagan, 1990, 1992). In many instances, children learn as much, if not more, from each other than they learn from teachers. At first, there may be some awkwardness and confusion, but once groups are instituted and become part of your class's regular routine, you'll find that they are productive methods for learning.

Classroom Arrangement

The key word in arranging your classroom for effective instruction is, again, *flexibility*. That does not mean that you move desks and change the furniture arrangement weekly. It means that you are aware of the importance of varying your room arrangement and that you make regular changes in furniture or student groups to best facilitate student learning and meet your instructional goals.

There are a number of ways to arrange a room to facilitate group and independent work. Figure 14.6 shows three possibilities. One arrangement includes seating students in twos and threes and leaving space in the corners of the room for special areas and learning centers. Another arrangement clusters desks in groups of five or six. Both these plans allow for whole-group instruction, since all students sit so they can see the chalkboard. A third arrangement leaves the center of the room open and encourages oral interaction, since it allows for eye contact among all students.

Often, teachers find that some experimentation is necessary to discover the most comfortable and usable arrangements. If you have found a workable desk or table arrangement and do not want to change it, then consider making regular changes in student seating. This gives a student opportunities to work near and with different students, rather than in close proximity with the same students continually. Many teachers find that regular monthly or bimonthly furniture rearrangement or seating changes keep interest high and promote interactions and learning.

Regular changes in seating allow learners to serve as models for each other. If a student in your class does not finish work and tends to be disruptive, besides talking to him about why this is happening and making whatever instructional modifications seem appropriate, you can seat the student between two students who do finish their work and are not disruptive. Often, the effect of two models and peer pressure is enough to change behavior. If there is a persistent behavior problem or an unpopular student, change the children's seats and groups regularly so that the same students do not continually suffer.

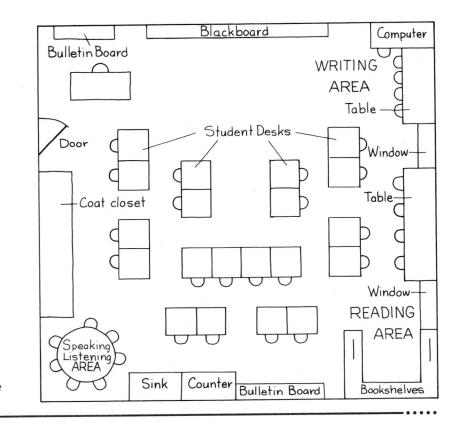

FIGURE 14.6 Three possible
room arrangements.

Independent Learning

Since one of your overall goals for students is to help them become independent learners, it is important to plan individual work. One way to do this is to create different areas, perhaps in corners of the classroom, where students can work alone on focused tasks.

Earlier chapters suggest the creation of special corners or areas where students work independently or with a partner on a task or topic related to listening, talking, reading, or writing. As well as providing a place where students can work, these areas hold appropriate equipment and materials for this work. For instance, in a listening corner, students use headsets and cassettes or records; in a talking area, they use a telephone or a tape recorder; in a reading area, they use books, magazines, and other print; and in a writing area, a word processor and a computer or typewriter are used (see Figure 14.6).

Learning Centers or Stations. Students can direct much of their own learning in learning centers or stations. More specifically, the materials in a learning center are organized to offer students a set of structured activities or tasks that focus on accomplishing specific goals. Teacher-created learning centers are used to teach new skills and concepts, reinforce or follow up what has already been taught, and enrich the curricula.

Centers or stations can effectively connect language arts learning and also integrate this learning into subjects areas. For example, literature centers that feature a par-

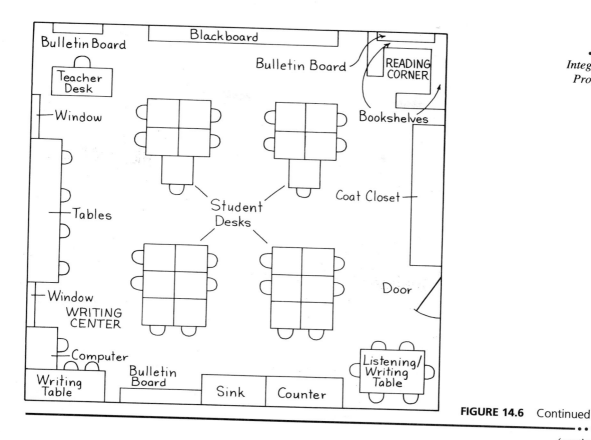

FIGURE 14.6   Continued

· · · · ·

(continued)

ticular author, topic, or genre of literature can provide opportunities for both oral and written book-sharing activities. With this kind of learning, students use listening, speaking, reading, and writing together in relevant ways. Writing centers and publishing centers also offer opportunities for students to connect expressive and receptive language as they write, read, and hear each other's work and help each other make and illustrate books. Literature centers or writing centers organized around a specific science or social studies unit not only offer students opportunities to learn concepts in these subject areas but they also connect this content learning to language learning.

Many teachers find that students in their classrooms are not literate in reading and using everyday materials such as newspapers, menus, guides for TV viewing, telephone books, job applications, maps, instructions, product guarantees, recipes, and coupons. Developing a learning center that uses these materials makes sense, since students need to read and understand this kind of everyday print and because these materials reinforce and enrich learning in language arts, science, and social studies. For example, you can develop a learning center that focuses on reading and using the menu from a local restaurant. Students might choose from a number of activities of graduated difficulty that reinforce nutritional concepts taught in science, computation, and problem solving taught in mathematics, and in consumerism and community awareness taught in social studies. These activities involve students in using language in meaningful and relevant ways to read, write, reason, listen, talk with a friend, and play a game, among other activities.

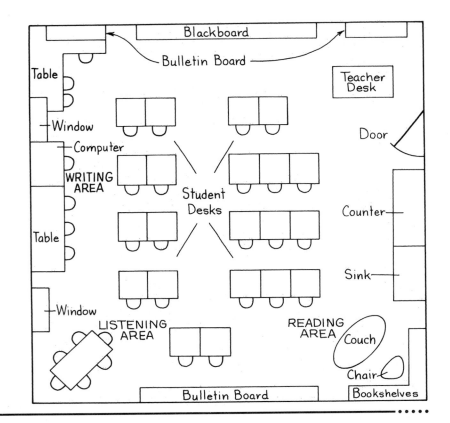

FIGURE 14.6   Continued

STRETCHING
EXERCISE

Identify a grade level and an everyday material that students at that grade level should be able to read and understand. In what ways could the material be used to create a number of multilevel activities to teach, reinforce, or enrich the classroom mathematics, science, and social studies curriculum?

• • • • •

Learning centers or stations have several benefits. They promote independence because students choose the tasks they wish to do (you can also direct students to specific tasks that are appropriate for them) and then complete them alone or with a friend without teacher guidance. Learning centers meet individual needs because they include a number of multilevel activities from which students choose, ranging from easy to difficult. Learning centers are motivating and fun and students often return to them to repeat activities over and over again. They ensure success by allowing students to choose activities and follow directions to complete them, and since most centers provide answer keys or teachers make answers available somewhere in the room, students can evaluate their own or a partner's work.

Many learning centers contain clearly stated objectives, sequential and clear directions, and choices among multilevel activities (Waynant, 1977). They actively involve children by including manipulative as well as paper-and-pencil activities and they often provide opportunities for students to work together in pairs or small groups. Because stations are continually used, materials may become worn, scattered, and unusable if they are not made durable and storable. Here are some ideas for creating a learning center or station:

1. Identify the purpose or reason for creating the center and selecting the skill(s), concept(s), or unit.
2. Identify the objectives.
3. Choose materials and activities at various levels of difficulty to meet the objectives.
4. Choose the method of presenting or packaging (folder, box, notebook, etc.).
5. Decide on the technique for evaluation (correction by teacher, self, or peer).
6. Prepare the directions (include objectives).
7. Choose the system of record keeping and evaluation (contract, log, ditto sheet).
8. Put it all together.

Here are some questions to ask yourself when you have finished:

Does the Learning Center Possess . . .
Interest and appeal?
Legible and permanent graphics?
Briefly and clearly stated objectives?
Easy-to-follow directions?
Activity alternatives?
Means of evaluation?
Durable and protected surfaces and materials?
Adaptability to meet various needs?
Storability and easy identification?

.....
*Students can evaluate each other's
or their own learning center work
when you provide an answer key.*

Boardgames. You can also include various kinds of boardgames in your learning areas, centers, or stations for listening, talking, reading, or writing (see Figure 14.7). Boardgames are included here because they are great motivators, students of all abilities and ages enjoy them, and they promote interactions among students. When gameboards are designed as cooperative ventures in which the game is not finished until all players reach the terminal goal, they encourage positive interactions among children of varying academic and social levels (Salend, 1981). There is a wide variety of possibilities for learning with boardgames. Just as with learning centers, boardgames teach new concepts, reinforce previously taught information, and enrich the curriculum (Macwilliam, 1978; Bruni & Silverman, 1980). Boardgames develop sight-word vocabulary, reading comprehension, spoken language, social skills, and listening and reasoning, as well as concepts and information specific to particular content areas.

When designing a gameboard, first choose a theme or topic. Space exploration, dinosaurs, maps, nutrition, sports events, popular movies or television shows, favorite car-

---

Directions
(on separate card—not on back of gameboard)
1. Clearly state objective of game.
2. List parts of game needed to play.
3. Make steps simple and concise by numbering.
4. Underline or use color to emphasize key words.
5. Use illustrations or pictures as substitutes for difficult vocabulary.
6. If game is complex, give examples.

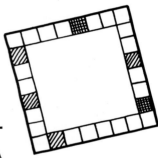

Gameboards
1. Size of board should fit your storage area and space where students will use it.
2. Make it colorful with stickers, colored tape, pictures, or colored dots for tracks. Choose a content theme and incorporate this into all aspects of game.
3. Use an adequate number of spaces (20–40 for younger children, 40–60 for older children).
4. Include container for storing game parts.
5. Identify direction of play with arrows or "Start" and "Finish."
6. Use water-base markers (clear Contact will cause permanent marker ink to bleed).
7. Make board adaptable to reinforcing different skills and using various task cards.
8. Make durable with clear Contact or lamination (plastic coated restaurant menus or pizza rounds make sturdy boards).

• • • • •

FIGURE 14.7 Tips for making boardgames.

toons or book characters, or any other idea of interest to the students you teach is appropriate. If the game has a common goal that all members strive toward—such as arriving on Mars safely, avoiding dangers that result in the extinction of a group of dinosaurs, or traveling to a common destination—then winning is not accomplished by the player who gets to the end first, but rather when both or all players arrive there. A common goal is a cooperative game strategy that promotes peer support, help, and positive interactions (Salend, 1981).

Gameboards made on the inside of manila folders are easily portable and storable. These folder games can be made colorful with pictures you draw or cut from magazines, menus, comics, advertisements, or whatever materials contain pictures of graphics that accompany the theme. For example, a book jacket from a new book written by a popular author and obtained from the publisher can be cut up and used creatively to enhance a boardgame using the book's title as its name and, perhaps, main characters as movers/markers. Menus and placemats are ready-made "boards" on which to make games, since

---

Task Cards

1. Keep cards clear, brief, and attractive.
2. Include Bonus Cards that are fun or Bonus Spaces on board that allow students to choose another task card. (Avoid too many penalty cards.)
3. Size of cards and print should depend on age and reading ability of students (larger print and cards for younger students).
4. Build versatility into task cards (so that students can practice vocabulary, spelling, math facts, etc.)
5. Match cards to gameboard and by color or pictures so loose cards are easily put with appropriate game.
6. Make cards durable with clear Contact or lamination.

Actual Play

1. Play the game as "dry-run" simulation with small group of students. (This can help work out "bugs" and these students can teach others.)
2. Use "quiet" game parts (eraser, sponge, or foam rubber dice).
3. Use everyday objects as markers (1" × 1" squares cut from plastic placements, soap bottle tops, spools, buttons, golf tees, marker pen tops).
4. Coordinate highest number on spinner or dice to number of spaces on board so game takes at least 10 turns.
5. Include enough task cards to take students completely around gameboard (or have students shuffle cards and use again).
6. Add interest by adding variation in spaces on board so landing on certain space means moving ahead a few extra spaces.
7. For short games, flip a coin or button for 1 or 2 moves.

Challenge kids to make their own games, including directions, gameboards, and task and bonus cards!

•••••

FIGURE 14.7 Continued

they are usually heavy and often laminated. The size of these games makes them easily usable, and their novelty gives them interest and appeal.

Games designed to be played on a board have spaces marked in a sequential pattern so players can move from Start to Finish. Usually, a die or spinner determines the number of spaces a player moves after correctly completing a task card. Task cards consist of problems to solve, sight vocabulary to use in sentences, arithmetic facts to practice, content vocabulary to define, questions to answer, words to spell, or a variety of other activities. The type and complexity of task cards can vary, depending on the individuals playing the game.

If your gameboard is designed around a theme with a few task cards related to the theme and all bonus cards related to the theme, students can use their own individual vocabulary or spelling words as task cards. For example, you can create a gameboard from a plastic-coated restaurant menu. Make space for play with stick-on file labels and task cards such as Which pizza costs more: a large pepperoni or a large sausage? or How many different beverages are on the menu? Students can intermix their own vocabulary words with the game's task cards. Game directions can instruct children to move one space each time they supply a correct answer. (Answers to task cards related to the theme of the gameboard can be written on the card and another player can read task cards and check answers.) You can also supply task cards that focus on specific content or concepts from a science or social studies unit and change them periodically to accompany a new unit of study. A less elaborate gameboard to reinforce content learning is made from a plain file folder and includes no task cards, but rather content vocabulary cards and bonus cards.

Bonus cards keyed to the theme of the game add interest (e.g., It's your birthday and the waitress tells you to take an extra turn, or Triceratops says to try another task card. If you get it right, move 3 extra spaces). If bonus cards are positive rather than negative, they enhance play and reinforce learning rather than impede a player's progress.

Just as learning centers promote independence, so can boardgames. Initially, you can teach students how to read the directions and play the game, and then as they play it independently, they can refer to the directions for help. Although not usually designed to be played alone, keep in mind that some children enjoy solitary play. As well as promoting independence, boardgames also provide for individual needs, motivate learning, and ensure success. For these reasons, many teachers find that time invested in making several boardgames that are placed in various special areas or corners of the room is time well spent because of the many benefits to student learning. Some teachers make one boardgame as a model and have interested students or parent volunteers make more for the classroom.

As you organize for instruction, remember that grouping, classroom arrangement, and independent learning are critical to the success of your program. Your success will also depend on the flexibility of your organization. Don't be afraid to experiment with all three until you find what is comfortable for you and your students and what best facilitates their learning.

STRETCHING EXERCISE Make a file folder game that could be used to help students practice their math facts or extend their vocabulary.
• • • • •

Assessing the Program

Just as you might ask yourself after a birthday party or fieldtrip how successful it was, you should also ask yourself how effective your language arts program is in accomplishing your goals and objectives. There are some general principles to consider as you assess language and subject area learning. As well as being relevant to learners, your language arts program should be based on student needs to communicate effectively. When deciding what to teach, you should consider how frequently, critically, or universally the learning will be used, and whether the student is ready to learn.

Curriculum

Evaluation of a language arts program involves examining the curriculum you use and the instruction that implements the curriculum. The National Council of Teachers of English publishes *Standards for the Assessment of Reading and Writing* (1994), which includes 11 standards that are illustrated with case studies and guidelines for assessment methods. As well, the *English Language Arts Standards Exemplar Series* (Myers & Spalding, 1996) is a good resource for those interested in creating a system for assessing student performance. The four-volume series (grades K–2, 3–5, 6–8, and 9–12) includes samples of student performance, rubrics, and teacher commentary on various types and levels of student performance. It illustrates the range of work across classrooms and includes selections from individual student portfolios.

Teaching

As you evaluate your program, keep in mind the two common themes that emerged from a comprehensive review of research on teaching behaviors and student achievement (Brophy & Good, 1986):

1. Academic learning is influenced by the amount of time children spend engaged in appropriate academic tasks.
2. Children learn more efficiently when teachers structure new information for them, help them relate it to what they already know, then monitor their performances and provide corrective feedback.

These findings can be interpreted in several ways. The order (structure), routines, rules, and procedures you establish in your classroom as mechanisms for getting children involved in learning are critical. As you decrease the amount of transition time and off-task time children spend in learning, you increase the time available for active involvement in learning. Your ability to organize and tie new learning into children's existing knowledge affects what and how easily they will learn. In addition, the guidance and reinforcement you provide children as they work influences their learning.

In what other ways do these research findings translate to teaching? Make a list of questions to evaluate a program's effectiveness in implementing the two themes identified by Brophy and Good (1986).

**STRETCHING
EXERCISE**

• • • • •

Of course, self-assessment is extremely important. As you are teaching a lesson, as well as after you finish teaching a lesson, you should ask yourself: What worked? What didn't work? Why? and How can I change my practice so I am more effective next time? Continual reflection, self-examination, and appropriate modifications in your teaching will help to make you a better teacher.

Some teachers also involve students in evaluating their teaching. Lynne Calvey periodically asks her students to fill out a report card on her. In a class discussion, Lynne's students decided on the five categories for the report card (see Figure 14.8). Feedback from Kyle and several other students told Lynne she was unfair in recently disciplining the entire class for one group's breaking of the rules. Reflecting on this, Lynne listened to student suggestions for what makes appropriate punishments. She also discovered that she needs to make her explanations clearer and more explicit for Kyle. She decided to ask students to explain concepts in their own words and paraphrase directions more often. In other areas, she discovered she was achieving her goals. James

MRS. CALVEY'S REPORT CARD:

DATE: March 11

USE LETTER GRADES A+, A, B+, B, C+, C, OR N

CATEGORY	MARK	COMMENTS
FRIENDLINESS	A+	your always nice
FAIRNESS	B–	you go with who every body ses
TEACHING ABILITY	A+	you teach me a lot
LISTENING	A+	you listen to what every body has to say
EXPLAINING	B–	sometimes I have trouble understanding what you mean

SIGNED Kyle   ☺

FIGURE 14.8 Students can give teachers valuable feedback on their teaching.
Source: Reprinted by permission of Lynn Calvey.

gave Lynne a B for *teaching ability* and noted "She is very smarte. I've leard to treat uther peple whit respect." Abby gave Lynne an A for *teaching ability* and commented "Pretty good. You'd get more things done if you found a way to make us quiet." And Abby had a specific suggestion for classroom management, which Lynne adopted, "I think after you read after play ground, if we could have freetime. And if we're noisy in the morning we'll get it tookin away from us." From these brief examples, it seems clear that students also can play an important role in assessing our teaching.

Learning

You will also want to assess your program in terms of student learning. You can determine learning, in part, by evaluating the specific objectives you establish for each lesson and unit you teach. Do students demonstrate behaviors to show they have achieved the objectives? As you teach, your assessment should be ongoing. Invite your students to continually self-assess their strengths and needs in terms of their performance of everyday tasks. Then you can make decisions about modifying instruction and materials based on these performances. Figure 14.9 gives 10 guiding principles of sound assessment. The decisions you make based on your assessments are important because they have an impact on self-esteem, motivation, performance, placement, and learning.

Assessment based on instruction and student performance is "responsive evaluation" (Cambourne & Turbill, 1990). To be responsive, you gather information, talk to students, observe them in action, and collect "artifacts" or outcomes from the various situations you observe. Assessment of this type naturally occurs alongside instruction, both during and following whole- and small-group lessons and independent work. This naturalistic assessment might also take the form of interviews, questionnaires dealing

FIGURE 14.9   Ten guiding principles of sound assessment.

Assessment should:

1. Guide and be an integral part of instruction and teaching.
2. Determine student growth, strengths, and achievement.
3. Identify student needs and goals.
4. Help students help themselves take responsibility for learning.
5. Reflect a developmental perspective of the individual.
6. Focus on the performance of real outcomes valued in the curriculum: writing, research, reading, experiments, speaking, problem solving, creating, and so on.
7. Inform parents/caregivers and students.
8. Be practical and systematic.
9. Be ongoing, formative, and summative.
10. Be comprehensive and multistrategic.
    —Kidwatching/Anecdotal records
    —Checklists
    —Interviews/Conferences
    —Portfolios/Work samples
    —Performance assessment
    —Classroom tests

· · · · ·

with attitudes, teacher-made tests of content knowledge, samples of student writing, running records of student reading, and logs of voluntary reading.

Au, Scheu, Kawakami, and Herman (1990) describe an assessment and accountability model designed for a literacy curriculum that serves cultural minority students and includes several of these components. They also see assessment as closely tied to instruction and suggest that assessment be linked to information gleaned from portfolios of student work. Their assessment model grew from dissatisfaction with standardized tests. To be accountable, they anchored their portfolio assessment to grade-level benchmarks that reflect expectations for the hypothetical average student.

But should standardized tests be avoided altogether? Pikulski (1990) believes the greatest misuse of standardized tests may be their overuse. Instead of testing every student in state assessment programs, he suggests that only students at selected grade levels be tested, preferably not before third or fourth grade. He further believes that sampling from the total school population, rather than testing every student, makes more sense, since the results of large-scale testing are rarely meaningful for interpreting the performance of individual students. Pikulski reminds readers that, by definition, only 50 percent of those who take a standardized test can be expected to score above the mean and 50 percent to score below, and expecting everyone to score above is an impossible goal. He cites evidence that current reading tests are improving, with some including measures of free recall, conceptual knowledge related to literacy, and the use of testing materials that look like short paperback books with color illustrations. Moreover, Pikulski challenges teachers to find alternative assessment procedures and suggests the portfolio as a way to supplement and place in better perspective the results of standardized tests.

Each of the preceding chapters has included specific suggestions for informally assessing student learning and involving students in self-evaluation. These questionnaires and checklists—as well as anecdotal records, finished work products, test results, records of communications with parents, and more—can all be kept in portfolios that serve as funds of information from which patterns of growth and progress can be identified.

Assessment is perhaps most effective when you involve the learners themselves, as did Doreen, the teacher you read about at the beginning of this chapter. By asking students to evaluate their learning, set goals for themselves, and create rubrics together, you directly involve students in learning and in creating standards for their finished products. By having students self-evaluate—providing them with notebooks, file folders, manila envelopes, or loose-leaf binders in which to keep their own records—you give them opportunities to look critically at their own work and progress. By providing students with checklists of behaviors or criteria to use in judging themselves and their work, you help them monitor their progress and learning. Students who record and evaluate their work begin to take responsibility for their learning.

In conclusion, as you plan, organize, and assess your language arts program, remember the vital link that parents play in student success. Building a bridge between your classroom and the home of each learner you teach can have a profoundly positive influence—not only on the learner's attitude and achievement but also on parental perceptions of school and your role as their child's teacher. Parental support and involvement can help you teach for understanding that emphasizes students as lifelong learners, future citizens, and future professionals and workers.

Summary

Managing an integrated language arts program involves flexible planning, organization, and assessment so that learners are challenged to develop effective communication. It means planning that includes reflection on the learners, curriculum, instructional time, and resources; organizing your classroom to optimally meet the needs of all students through appropriate grouping and opportunities for independent learning; and continually assessing student learning, your own teaching, and your program.

R•••••eflections

1. Interview an elementary school teacher to find out how he or she plans, organizes, and assesses his or her language arts program. What do daily, weekly, and yearly lesson plans look like? How are students grouped? Does the current classroom arrangement change or is it constant? What assessment tools and report cards are used? What new ideas about effective planning, organization, and assessment do you have after this interview?

2. The components of an effective language arts program that were discussed in Chapter 1 are:

- Curricular integration
- Children's literature
- Learner interaction and involvement
- Direct instruction and authentic experiences
- An environment that fosters integrated learning
- Teachers with values and children who feel valued

After finishing this book, what is your philosophy of teaching? What other important features of a language arts program would you add to this list? Why?

Professional Resources

Allington, R. L., & Cunningham, P. M. (1996). *Schools that work: Where all children read and write.* New York: HarperCollins. This book gives ideas and explains features of K–6 schools (school organization plans, professional roles, organization of time, curriculum, student assessment, professional development, and parental involvement) that foster the kinds of classrooms where all children become readers and writers.

Campbell, P., & Siperstein, G. M. (1994). *Improving social competence: A resource for elementary school teachers.* Boston: Allyn and Bacon. This is a resource of helpful classroom-tested activities for working with students to develop social skills, cooperation, and friendship. It is especially relevant for students with social problems and at-risk for school failure.

Edwards, C. (1997). *Classroom discipline and management* (2nd ed.). Columbus, OH: Merrill. Through narratives and case studies of students and classrooms, several discipline models are presented with strategies and application ideas.

Kohn, A. (1996). *Beyond discipline: From compliance to community.* Alexandria, VA: Association for Supervision and Curriculum Development. In this book, the author discusses many ideas for developing a spirit of relatedness or community, rather than isolation in the classroom.

References

Au, K. H., Scheu, J. A., Kawakami, A. J., & Herman, P. A. (1990). Assessment and accountability in a whole literacy curriculum. *The Reading Teacher, 43*, 574–578.

Brophy, J., & Good, T. L. (1986). Teacher behavior and student achievement. In M. Wittrock (Ed.), *Handbook of research on teaching* (4th ed.). New York: Macmillan.

Bruni, J. V., & Silverman, H. (1980). Making and using board games. *The Arithmetic Teacher,* March, 172–179.

Cambourne, B., & Turbill, J. (1990). Assessment in whole-language classrooms: Theory into practice. *The Elementary School Journal, 90*, 337–431.

Carroll, J. H., & Christenson, C. N. (1995). Teaching and learning about student goal setting in a fifth-grade classroom. *Language Arts, 72* (1), 42–49.

Curwin, R., & Mendler, A. N. (1996). *Discipline with dignity.* Alexandria, VA: Association for Supervision and Curriculum development.

Flood, J., Lapp, D., Flood, S., & Nagel, G. (1992). Am I allowed to group? Using flexible patterns for effective instruction. *The Reading Teacher, 45* (8), 608–617.

Good, T. L. (1996). Teaching effects and teacher evaluation. In J. Sikula, T. J. Buttery, & E. Guyton (Eds.), *Handbook of research on teacher education* (2nd ed.). New York: Simon & Schuster.

Good, T. L. (1979). Teacher effectiveness in the elementary school. *Journal of Teacher Education, 30* (2), 52–64.

Johnson, D. W., & Johnson, R. T. (1992). Implementing cooperative learning. *Contemporary Education, 63* (3), 173–180.

Johnson, D. W., Johnson, R. T., & Holubec, E. J. (1994). *The new circles of learning: Cooperation in the classroom and school.* Alexandria, VA: Association of Supervision and Curriculum Development.

Kagan, S. (1992). *Cooperative learning.* San Juan Capistrano, CA: Resources for Teachers.

Kagan, S. (1990). The structural approach to cooperative learning. *Educational Leadership, 47* (4), 12–15.

Learning standards for English language arts (1996). Albany, NY: State Education Department.

Learning standards for social studies (1996). Albany, NY: State Education Department.

Macwilliam, L. J. (1978). Mobility boardgames: Not only for rainy days. *Teaching Exceptional Children, 11* (1), 22–25.

Manning, M., Manning, G., & Long, R. (1994). *Theme immersion: Inquiry-based curriculum in elementary and middle school.* Portsmouth, NH: Heinemann.

Miller, J. P., & Seller, W. (1985). *Curriculum: Perspectives and practices.* New York: Longman.

Myers, M., & Spalding, L. (1996). *English language arts standards exemplar series: Assessment of student performance, grades K–2, 3–5, 6–8, and 7–12.* Urbana, IL: National Council of Teachers of English.

Pikulski, J. J. (1990). The role of tests in a literacy assessment program. *The Reading Teacher, 43*, 686–689.

Porro, B. (1996). *Talk it out: Conflict resolution in the elementary classroom.* Alexandria, VA: Association for Supervision and Curriculum Development.

Salend, S. (1981). Active academic games: The aim of the game is mainstreaming. *Teaching Exceptional Children,* Fall, 3–6.

Slavin, R. E. (1990). Research on cooperative learning: Consensus and controversy. *Educational Leadership, 47* (4), 52–54.

Standards for the assessment of reading and writing (1994). Urbana, IL: National Council of Teachers of English.

Standards for the English language arts (1996). Newark, DE: International Reading Association.

Waynant, L. F. (1977). *Learning centers 2: Practical ideas for you.* Paoli, PA: Instructo.

Willis, S. (1996). Managing today's classroom: Finding alternatives to control and compliance. *Education Update, 38* (6), 1, 3–7.

Annotated Bibliography of Children's Books

Children with Various Heritages

African Americans

Aardema, V. (1981). *Bringing the rain to Kapiti Plain*. New York: Scholastic. (Gr. 1–3). Using the rhythm of "The House That Jack Built," this cumulative tale tells how Ki-pat, a Kenyan herdsman, helped end the drought on Kapiti Plain to save his cattle.

Feelings, T. (1993). *Soul looks back in wonder*. New York: Dial. (Gr. 3–6). This collection of illustrated poems touches on aspects of the African American experience.

Grimes, N. (1994). *Meet Danitra Brown*. New York: Lathrop. (Gr. K–3). The friendship experiences between two young city girls are told through this collection of poems.

Hamilton, V. (1996). *When birds could talk and bats could sing*. (Gr. K–6). Seven rare trickster stories are retold and illustrated.

Hamilton, V. (1985). *The people could fly*. New York: Knopf. (Gr. 3–6). A retelling of Afro-American folktales of animals, fantasy, the supernatural, and the desire for freedom.

Haskins, J. (1997). *Colin Powell: A biography*. New York: Scholastic. (Gr. 3–6). A biography of the first African American to achieve the highest military position in the United States: Chairman of the Joint Chiefs of Staff.

Hoffman, M. (1991). *Amazing Grace*. New York: Dial. (Gr. 1–3). Grace wants to be Peter Pan in the class play but is told she can't because she is Black.

Lester, J. (1996). *Sam and the tigers*. New York: Dial. (Gr. 1–4). A new version of "Sambo" is told in the southern Black storyteller's voice.

Lester, J. (1993). *Long journey home: Stories from Black history*. New York: Dial. (Gr. 4–6). Six stories tell about the impact of escaping from slavery on these people's lives and families.

Medlicott, M. (Ed.) (1994). *The river that went to the sky: Twelve tales by African storytellers*. San Francisco: Children's Book Press. (Gr. 3–6). This story book tells humorous and wise tales from across

Africa. (Smithsonian's Notable Children's Books, 1995).

Miller, W. (1994). *Frederick Douglass: The last day of slavery*. New York: Lee & Low. (Gr. 3–6). An account of this activist's bravery and years in the Maryland fields is told. (Smithsonian's Notable Children's Books, 1995).

Pinkney, G. J. (1994). *Sunday outing*. New York: Dial. (Gr. 1–4). A young girl named Ernestine listens to her aunt's stories of relatives in North Carolina while watching the trains at the railroad station on Sundays. She longs to make the trip herself, and with her family's support, she realizes this dream.

Polacco, P. (1994). *Pink and say*. New York: Putnam. (Gr. 3 and up). A Black Civil War soldier finds and helps an injured White soldier. They share a brief yet strong friendship in this powerful story.

Sisulu, E. B. (1995). *The day Gogo went to vote*. Boston: Little, Brown. (Gr. 1–4). In 1994, a 6-year-old South African girl and her 100-year-old grandmother go to the polls and make history. (Smithsonian's Notable Children's Books, 1996).

Steptoe, J. (1987). *Mufaro's beautiful daughters: An African tale*. New York: Lothrop, Lee & Shepard. (Gr. K–3). This Caldecott Honor Book tells a Cinderella tale from Africa.

Taylor, M. (1995). *The well*. New York: Dial. (Gr. 3–6). When the wells dry up, David Logan (Cassie's father) deals with pride, racism, and generosity.

Taylor, M. (1987). *The gold Cadillac*. New York: Dial. (Gr. 3–6). A Black family travels from Ohio to Mississippi and finds ignorance and prejudice on their way. Two daughters discover what it is like to be afraid because of their race.

Taylor, M. (1976). *Roll of thunder, hear my cry*. New York: Dial. (Gr. 3–6). The theme of this second book in a trilogy is the injustice of White society in contrast to the strength and moral fortitude of a southern Black family.

Asian Americans

Atkins, J. (1994). *Aani and the tree huggers*. New York: Lee & Low. (Gr. 3–6). In the 1970s, when developers came to cut down the forests of India, a village girl inspires the village women to stop the destruction. (Smithsonian's Notable Children's Book, 1995).

Bash, B. (1991). *In the heart of the village*. San Francisco: Sierra Club. (Gr. 3–6). The sacred banyan tree is at the heart of many an Indian hamlet. (Smithsonian's Notable Children's Book, 1996).

Coerr, E. (1977). *Sadako and the thousand paper cranes*. Pine Brook, NJ: Dell. (Gr. 3–8). A Japanese girl and her classmates fold 644 paper cranes, trying to rid her of leukemia caused by radiation from the bombing of Hiroshima.

Demi (1997). *One grain of rice*. New York: Scholastic. (Gr. K–3). A clever girl outwits a selfish man and turns her reward of one grain of rice into billions of grains.

Garrigue, S. (1985). *The eternal spring of Mr. Ito*. New York: Bradbury. (Gr. 4–6). This is the story of a young girl who helps a Canadian family understand and change their feelings toward their Japanese gardener and his family during World War II.

Haugaard, E. C. (1984). *The Samurai's tale*. Boston: Houghton Mifflin. (Gr. 3–6). After his family is slaughtered, Taro becomes a Samurai warrior. As he grows and learns, he realizes the tragedy of war.

Heo, Y. (1995). *Father's rubber shoes*. New York: Orchard. (Gr. K–3). This is the story of Yungsu, a young boy who has moved with his family from Korea to America. He misses his friends in Korea, but begins making new ones in his new neighborhood.

Lewin, T. (1995). *Sacred river*. New York: Clarion. (Gr. 3–6). This is the story of the Ganges River in India and the pilgrims who go to this holy river.

Mochizuki, K. (1994). *Heroes*. New York: Lee & Low. (Gr. 3–6). The valor of Americans of Asian and Pacific Island descent in World War II runs through this tale. (Smithsonian's Notable Children's Book, 1995).

Nunes, S. M. (1994). *The last dragon*. New York: Clarion. (Gr. 2–6). In San Francisco's Chinatown, a boy finds his ancient culture and rescues a faded silk dragon from a shop. (Smithsonian's Notable Children's Book, 1995).

Quayle, E. (1989). *The shining princess and other Japanese legends*. New York: Arcade. (Gr. 3–6). This is a collection of 10 Japanese folktales about demons and dragons, heroes and villains, and greed and bad manners.

Say, A. (1993). *Grandfather's journey*. Boston: Houghton Mifflin. (Gr. 1–4). Say tells the story of his grandfather's journey to and life in America as a young man and how he, too, made the journey and came to love both countries.

Say, A. (1982). *The bicycle man*. Berkeley, CA: Parnassus. (Gr. K–4). This is a gentle story of the author's childhood during the American occupation of Japan, including a visit by bicycle-riding American soldiers.

Schmidt, J., & Wood, T. (1994). *Two lands, one heart: An American boy's journey to his mother's Vietnam*. New York: Walker. (Gr. 4–6). This is the story of a Vietnamese girl and her siblings who come to the United States after being separated from their parents at the end of the Vietnam War. After 16 years, she goes back with her son for a reunion with her family. (Smithsonian's Notable Books for Children, 1995).

Snyder, D. (1988). *The boy of the three-year nap*. Boston: Houghton Mifflin. (Gr. K–3). This Caldecott Medal Book depicts Japanese homes and ways of living, as well as the relationship between a mother and her lazy boy.

Staples, S. F. (1989). *Shabanu: Daughter of the wind*. New York: Knopf. (Gr. 3–6). This is the story of an 11-year-old girl named Shabanu who must face life in a traditional nomadic society and an unwanted marriage. This 1990 Newbery Medal Book is set in the Cholistan Desert along the India-Pakistan border.

Uchida, Y. (1993). *The bracelet*. New York: Philomel. (Gr. 1–4). In an internment camp during World War II, Emi loses her friend's bracelet but realizes this doesn't mean she has lost her friend.

Uchida, Y. (1979). *Journey home*. New York: Atheneum. (Gr. 4–6). This sequel to *Journey to Topaz* tells of the hardships a Japanese-American family encounters upon their return home from an internment camp.

Vuong, L. D. (1993). *The golden carp and other tales from Vietnam*. New York: Lothrop. (Gr. 3–6). Folktales are shared from ancient Vietnam about bravery, courage and honesty.

Yee, R. (1989). *Tales from Gold Mountain*. New York: Macmillan. (Gr. 2–5). This collection of tales about the Chinese migration to the New World includes the author's memories of gambling halls, railroad building, gold mines, and hard labor.

Yep, L. (1997). *The Khan's daughter*. New York: Scholastic. (Gr. 1–3). A shepherd boy defeats 7 demons, drives away an army, and meets the mighty "Bagatur," the Khan's daughter, who is his match.

Yep, L. (1995). *Hiroshima*. New York: Scholastic. (Gr. 4–8). This is the story of two sisters who lived in Hiroshima at the time of its bombing and the life of the one sister who survives.

Young, E. (1989). *Lon Po Po: A red riding hood story from China*. New York: Philomel. (Gr. K–3). This 1990 Caldecott Medal Book is the Chinese retelling of the well-known American tale of a wolf who pretends to be Grandmother.

European Americans

Feder, P. K. (1994). *The feather-bed journey*. New York: Whitman. (Gr. 3–6). On Hanukkah, a girl and her mother remember how some Poles saved Jewish children. (Smithsonian's Notable Children's Book, 1995).

Gilman, P. (1997). *The gypsy princess*. New York: Scholastic (Gr. K–3). A gypsy girl yearns for the life of a princess but once she finds it, she discovers her simple life is much happier.

Matthews, W. (1994). *The gift of a traveler*. Morgan, CA: Bridgewater. (Gr. 2–4). In turn-of-the-century Romania, a wolf offers a paw of friendship to gypsies in this Christmas tale. (Smithsonian's Notable Children's Book, 1995).

Morpurgo, M. (1994). *Arthur: High king of Britain*. San Diego: Harcourt. (Gr. 3–6). Tales are told of the days of King Arthur. (Smithsonian's Notable Children's Book, 1995).

Murphy, J. (1993). *Across America on an emigrant train*. New York: Scholastic. (Gr. 4–9). This is the true story of Robert Louis Stevenson's experiences as he goes from Scotland to the United States and then across America.

Oberman, S. (1994). *The always prayer shawl*. Honesdale, PA: Boyds Mills Press. (Gr. 2–6). A Russian Jewish boy comes to the United States with his family and grows up with one constant in his life.

Polacco, P. (1992). *Mrs. Katz and Tush*. New York: Dell. (Gr. 2–5). This is a story of friendship between a Jewish widow from Poland and a young African American boy.

Polacco, P. (1988). *Rechenka's eggs*. New York: Philomel. (Gr. K–3). At the Easter Festival, Babushka's eggs always win first prize, but an injured goose she is caring for knocks over her precious eggs. The festivals of Old Moscow are described in this story.

Polacco, P. (1989). *Uncle Vova's tree*. New York: Philomel. (Gr. K–3). This is a Christmas story about an American family that celebrates a traditional Russian Orthodox Epiphany each year at their Great Uncle Vova's farm. Uncle Vova dies and all his farm animals gather around one of his trees on the Christmas following his death.

Pryor, B. (1995). *The dream jar*. New York: Morrow. (Gr. 3–6). For Valechka, a Russian immigrant, learning to read makes the New York City of 100 years ago more livable. (Smithsonian's Notable Children's Book, 1996).

Sachs, M. (1982). *Call me Ruth*. Garden City, NY: Doubleday. (Gr. 4–6). Ruth and her family emigrate from Russia to New York City and Ruth adjusts to American life in the early twentieth century.

Sandin, J. (1981). *The long way to a new land*. New York: Harper and Row. (Gr. K–4). This is a story about the emigration of a Swedish family to America in the last half of the nineteenth century.

Vestley, A. (1974). *Hello Aurora*. New York: Crowell. (Gr. 2–5). This is a story about a Norwegian family in which the mother is a lawyer and the father stays home to care for the family.

Watson, M. (1994). *The butterfly seeds*. New York: Tambourine. (Gr. 1–3). Seeds given by his grandfather to a British boy bound for America in 1908 tie the two across time and distance. (Smithsonian's Notable Children's Book, 1995).

Hispanic Americans

Altman, L. J. (1996). *Amelia's road*. New York: Lothrop & Lee. (Gr. K–3). A girl from a migrant worker family overcomes the hardship of moving by creating a special place for herself.

Anderson, J. (1989). *Spanish pioneers of the southwest*. New York: Lodestar. (Gr. 3–7). This book depicts life in the mid-1700s near Santa Fe and tells about the life of a young boy and early Mexican American settlers.

Borton de Trevino, E. (1989). *El Guero: A true adventure story*. New York: Farrar. (Gr. 3–6). Set in Baja, California, in the mid-1800s, this is the story of a boy who is exiled when Porfirio Diaz seized power in Mexico in 1876.

Bragg, B. (1989). *The very first Thanksgiving: Pioneers on the Rio Grande*. Tucson, AZ: Harbinger House. (Gr. 2–6). Two Spanish brothers who are orphans escape a life of work in a silver mine and join the expedition of Don Juan de Onate and have a Thanksgiving feast 24 years before the first one.

Bunting, E. (1996). *Going home*. New York: Harper-Collins. (Gr. 1–3). A Mexican family that lives in California, where their children have "more opportunities," return to Mexico for Christmas and realize it is still their home.

Castaneda, O. S. (1996). *Abuela's weave*. New York: Lee & Low. (Gr. K–3). A girl in Guatemala learns about family traditions and trust from her grandmother.

de Mariscal, B. L. (1994). *The harvest birds/los pajaros de la cosecha*. San Francisco: Children's Book Press. (Gr. 2–4). This Mexican folktale is about a young man who learns the secrets of nature and grows a garden. (Smithsonian's Notable Children's Book, 1995).

Dorros, A. (1995). *Isla*. New York: Dutton. (Gr. K–3). Rosalba and Abuela travel to la Isla, the island where Abuela grew up. Rosalba learns about the land and culture of her relatives.

Dorros, A. (1991). *Abuela*. New York: Dutton. (Gr. K–3). Rosalba and her grandmother take an imaginary flying trip over Manhatten Island. Abuela speaks Spanish and Rosalba speaks English while together they share an adventure in the city.

Gollub, M. (1994). *The moon was at a fiesta*. New York: Tambourine. (Gr. K–3). This Mexican folktale explains why the moon lights the night and the sun lights the day, but sometimes they both appear in the sky at dawn.

Gonzalez, L. M. (1997). *Senor Cat's romance and other favirite stories from Latin America*. New York Scholastic. (Gr. K–3). Favorite stories form South America include silly Juan Bobo, a beautiful cockroach Martina, and flamboyant Senor Sir Cat.

Herrera, F. (1994). *Calling the doves/Elcanto de las palomas*. San Francisco: Children's Book Press. (Gr. 2–4). Fond memories are told of the author's life as a young migrant worker on California backroads with his family. (Smithsonian's Notable Children's Book, 1995).

Hewett, J. (1990). *Hector lives in the United States now: The story of a Mexican-American child*. New York: Lippincott. (Gr. 2–5). This is the story of a 10-year-old Mexican boy who now lives in Los Angeles with his family. The photographic essay describes two special events in Hector's life: his first communion and his parents' decision to apply for amnesty under the new migration law.

Johnston, T. (1996). *The magic maguey*. San Diego: Harcourt. (Gr. 2–4). A young hero saves the great, spiky agave plant that grows in the center of the village in Mexico. (Smithsonian's Notable Children's Book, 1996).

Keister, D. (1994). *Fernando's gift/El regalo de fernando*. San Fransisco: Sierra Club. (Gr. 2–4). Photos and English and Spanish text tell the story of a family in Costa Rica that is trying to save the jungle. (Smithsonian's Notable Children's Book, 1995).

Marrin, A. (1990). *Inca and Spaniard: Pizarro and the conquest of Peru*. New York: Atheneum. (Gr. 6–8). This book describes the rise of the Inca Empire and its fall to the Spanish conqueror, Hernando Pizarro. It lends itself to the discussion of cultural clashes, colonialism, war, and conquest.

Soto, G. (1993). *Too many tamales*. New York: Putnam. (Gr. 1–4). Maria, a young Mexican American girl, loses her mother's wedding ring while making tamales for Christmas dinner so she and her cousins try to find it by eating the tamales.

Soto, G. (1990). *Baseball in April and other stories*. San Diego: Harcourt. (Gr. 4–6). This is a collection of short stories about growing up as a Mexican American in Fresno, California.

Spanish: Hablo Espanola (1989). New York: Berlitz-Macmillan. (Gr. 1–3). Teddy Berlitz introduces basic phrases, the alphabet, numbers, and colors in Spanish, accompanied by a cassette that incorporates music, sound effects, and the voices of native speakers.

Tompert, A. (1988). *The silver whistle*. New York: Macmillan. (Gr. K–3). At the Christmas Eve Procession of Gifts, Miguel's generous gift to the infant is given the place of honor.

Vivas, J. (1997). *Let's eat/ana zamorano*. New York: Scholastic. (Gr. K–2). In Spanish and English, a family prepares food and eats together.

Native Americans

Bruchac, J. (1993). *The first strawberries*. New York: Dial. (Gr. 1–3). This Cherokee legend is about the first strawberries and how they came to symbolize friendship and respect among people.

Bruchac, J. (1993). *Fox song*. New York: Philomel. (Gr. 1–3). This is the story of a young girl's memories of the special relationship, Abanaki traditions, and stories she shared with her grandmother.

Bruchac, J., & London, J. (1992). *Thirteen moons on turtle's back: A Native American year of moons*. New York: Trumpet. (Gr. 3–6). This collection of stories from 13 different Native American tribal nations relate to the 13 cycles of the moon.

dePaola, T. (1988). *The legend of the Indian paintbrush*. New York: Putnam. (Gr. K–3). Little Gopher records his people's history on painted animal skins. However, his Dream-Vision is to capture the colors of the sunset on canvas.

dePaola, T. (1983). *The legend of Bluebonnet*. New York: Putnam. (Gr. K–4). This Comanche tale describes the life of an orphaned girl who sacrifices what she loves best to save her tribe.

George, J. C. (1972). *Julie of the wolves*. New York: Harper and Row. (Gr. 5–6). This Newbery Medal Book is about a 13-year-old Eskimo who runs away and becomes lost on the tundra where she must learn to survive.

Goble, P. (1985). *Buffalo woman*. New York: Bradbury. (Gr. 2–6). This is a beautifully illustrated story of a Native American legend from the South Dakota area.

Manitonquat (1994). *The children of the morning light: Wampanoag tales*. New York: Macmillan. (Gr. 2–5). This is a collection of tales and legends of the Wampanoag, a Native American tribe from southeastern Massachusetts. The stories are retold by Manitonquat (Medicine Story), a Wampanoag elder.

Mayo, G. W. (1989). *Earthmaker's tales: North American Indian stories about earth happenings*. New York: Walker. (Gr. 3–6). This is a collection of 17 North American folklore tales that explain natural phenomena such as floods, volcanoes, and snow.

Savageau, C. (1994). *Muskrat will be swimming*. Boon, MI: Northland. (Gr. 3–6). A Seneca girl learns from her grandfather's stories that these legends can help her in this world. (Smithsonian's Notable Childrens' Book, 1996).

Stroud, V. A. (1994). *A walk to the great mystery*. New York: Dial. (Gr. 1–3). A Cherokee medicine woman, a kindred spirit of hummingbirds and pine trees, takes a walk. (Smithsonian Notable Children's Book, 1995).

Taylor, H. P. (1993). *Coyote places the stars*. New York: Macmillan. This story is based on a Wasco Indian legend about the clever coyote and the origin of the constellations.

Van Laan, N. (1994). *In a circle long ago: A treasury of native lore from North America*. New York: Knopf. (Gr. 2–6). From how the beaver stole fire to the tale of two mice, this is a sharing of legends, songs, and poems of 20 tribes from Inuit and Lenape to Nez Perce and Pueblo. (Smithsonian's Notable Children's Book, 1994).

Watkins, S. (1994). *White bead ceremony*. Tulsa, OK: Council Oaks Books. (Gr. 1–5). A girl is torn between her traditional Shawnee heritage and the American culture.

Wolfson, E. (1988). *From Abenaki to Zuni: A dictionary of Native American tribes*. New York: Walker. (Gr. 3–6). This reference work includes information on 68 Native American tribes, such as tribal customs, food, clothing, and means of travel.

Yue, C., & Yue, D. (1988). *The igloo*. Boston: Houghton Mifflin. (Gr. 3–6). This book describes the construction of an igloo and the role igloos play in the lives of Eskimos, as well as Eskimo culture and challenges.

Various Backgrounds and Heritages

Archambault, J. (1997). *Grandmother's garden*. Parsippany, NJ: Silver Press. (Gr. 1–3). Grandmother's rose garden provides a place for children of different backgrounds to meet and become friends.

Dooley, N. (1991). *Everybody cooks rice*. Minneapolis: Carolrhoda. (Gr. 1–3). A girl visits many families at dinnertime and discovers rice is cooked differently by families from different cultures.

Jenness, A. (1990). *Families: A celebration of diversity, commitment and love*. New York: Houghton Mifflin. (Gr. 2–6). Photos and text introduce 17 different kinds of families, such as divorced, step, gay, foster siblings, and extended families.

Latkin, P. (1995). *Families around the world*. Black Birch Press. (Gr. 2–6). Fourteen families from around the world take care of their children and teach them cultural traditions and family history.

Morris, A. (1992). *Houses and homes*. New York: Lothrop. (Gr. 1–4). The range of houses around the world in which people live are shown through photos and text.

Nye, N. S. (Ed.) (1992). *This same sky: A collection of poems from around the world*. New York: Four Winds Press. (Gr. 3–6). In poems by 129 poets, the world's various forms of life—human, animal, and nature—are noted.

Children with Special Needs

Ausch, M. J. (1990). *Kidnapping Kevin Kowalski*. (Gr. 4–6). Friends kidnap Kevin, who has physical and mental injuries from an accident, and he performs a feat of bravery.

Banks, J. T. (1995). *Egg-drop blues*. New York: Houghton Mifflin. (Gr. 3–6). A boy with dyslexia and his brother try to win a science competition.

Betancourt, J. (1993). *My name is Brian*. New York: Scholastic. (Gr. 4–6). A boy with dyslexia writes his name as "Brain" and changes his attitude toward school and his father.

Booth, B. D. (1991). *Mandy*. New York: Lothrop. (Gr. 1–3). This story shares the thoughts and fears of a girl with a hearing loss.

Bunting, E. (1988). *A sudden silence*. New York: Harcourt (Gr. 3–6). Jesse and Chloe find the hit-and-run driver who killed Jesse's deaf brother, and two families deal with guilt.

Byars, B. (1971). *Summer of the swans*. New York: Viking. (Gr. 4–9). Fourteen-year-old Betsy is concerned for her missing brother, who has brain damage, and accepts help from a supposed enemy.

Condra, E. (1994). *See the ocean*. Nashville: Ideals. (Gr. 1–3). This is the story of a girl who is blind but is the first to "see" the ocean as her family travels to the beach.

Conly, J. L. (1993). *Crazy lady!* New York: HarperCollins. (Gr. 4–6). A boy befriends the neighborhood "crazy lady" and helps her care for her teenage son who is disabled.

Drimmer, F. (1988). *Born different: Amazing stories of very special people*. New York: Atheneum. (Gr. 3–6). This collection of stories is about people who have overcome physical disabilities to become famous. Some of these people were exploited because of their disability.

Dwyer, K. M. (1991). *What do you mean I have a learning disability?* New York: Walker. (Gr. 3–6). In photos, this story explores the self-esteem and challenges of a boy with a learning disability.

Fleming, V. (1993). *Be good to Eddie Lee*. New York: Philomel. (Gr. 1–4). A boy with Down Syndrome helps a girl learn about what is inside a person.

Gehret, J. (1990). *Learning disabilities and the don't give up kid*. Fairport, NY: Verbal Images Press. (Gr. K–3). Placement in a special class for LD students helps Alex shine and be creative.

Haldane, S. (1991). *Helping hands: How monkeys assist people who are disabled*. (Gr. 4–6). A teenager who is a quadriplegic is helped by a monkey named Willie.

Krementz, J. (1989). *How it feels to fight for your life*. Boston: Little, Brown. (Gr. 4–6). This collection of stories is about children with cancer, diabetes, spina bifida, epilepsy, severe burns, and cystic fibrosis and their relationships with people around them.

Little, J. (1987). *Little by little: A writer's education*. New York: Viking. (Gr. 4–6). In this autobiography, the author tells how her "bad eyes" caused her to be ridiculed as a child, which led to her use of her imagination to write.

McMahon, P. (1995). *Listen for the bus*. Honesdale, PA: Boyds Mills. (Gr. 1–3). Photos and text show how a blind boy learns about the world.

Miller, M. B., & Ancona, G. (1991). *Handtalk school*. New York: Four Winds. (Gr. 1–6). A day at a residential school for the deaf shows how children communicate through American Sign Language (ASL) and with Telephone Device for the Deaf (TDD).

Philbrick, R. (1993). *Freak the mighty*. New York: Blue Sky/Scholastic. (Gr. 4–6). Together, a boy with physical strength and size and a boy with high intelligence become "Freak the Mighty."

Pollock, P. (1982). *Keeping it secret*. New York: Putnam. (Gr. 4–6). A sixth-grader moves to a new town and tries to keep her hearing difficulty from classmates, but changes her attitude and makes friends.

Rankin, L. (1991). *The handicap alphabet*. New York: Dial. (Gr. 1–6). Sign language letters are depicted alphabetically with pictures.

Roby, C. (1993). *When learning is tough: Kids talk about their learning disabilities*. Morton Grove, IL: Albert Whitman. (Gr. 4–6). Eight students talk about the difference between having a learning disability and being stupid.

Rosenberg, M. B. (1988). *Finding a way: Living with exceptional brothers and sisters*. New York: Lothrop. (Gr. 2–4). Children describe what it is like to live with siblings who have spina bifida, diabetes, and severe asthma.

Slepian, J. (1990). *Risk'n'roses*. New York: Philomel. (Gr. 4–6). A girl's developmentally disabled sister becomes the brunt of neighborhood kids' ill will.

Author Index

517

Subject Index

Cognition, 281
cognitive deficit, 63
cognitive development and intellectual ability, 314
cognitive elements, 130
Collaboration:
among teachers, 15, 23, 363
in writing, 291–292, 368
Communication, definition, 3, 34–35, 37
Community, classroom, 69, 132, 479
Comparison charts, 461
Composition:
aspects of, 290–307
guiding, 280, 298–307
and transcription, 351, 398–399
processes, 3–4, 362, 398
Comprehensible language input, 42, 46
Comprehension, 113, 129, 137, 140, 146, 156, 159, 172–177, 207, 229, 249–250, 323, 398, 454, 458–459, 463, 502
difficulties/problems, 187–195
factors affecting, 177–178
inviting and extending, 179–200
monitoring strategies, 179–186, 187–189, 240
reading 236–237, 239, 244, 252, 258–259, 267, 270
self-assessment checklist, 215
strategies, 179–200
types of, 176–177, 180, 192
Compton's Multimedia Encyclopedia, 441–442
Computer-assisted instruction (CAI), 266
Computer-managed instruction (CMI), 268
Computers:
and Internet terms, 438–439
literacy, 443
programs and software, 26, 117, 266–268, 291, 306, 370
and reading, 263, 266–268
word processors, 363
and writing process, 467
Conferences, 478
student-led, 67, 38
writing, 283, 380, 382, 386
Connections:
among language arts, 2–3, 66, 69, 78, 241
language and content, 472

listening and reading, 161, 169–200, 205
speaking and writing, 280
Construction of meaning, 3–4, 7, 169–200, 249–250
Constructivist philosophy/perspective, 49, 312
Content area learning, 3–4, 14, 16, 19, 21, 26, 69, 94–95
Content areas, 141, 151–153, 196, 216–219, 221–222, 224, 227–228, 236, 267, 290
Content texts, 178
Context, 250
Conventions, 384, 397–398
Conversation, 317–318, 323
Conversation Corner, 318
Cooperative groups, 9
rules for, 496–497
Cooperative learning, 26, 69, 71–74, 235–238
groups, 216, 320–329, 348, 475–477, 508
strategies, 261
structures, 320–329
teams, 494
Creative writing, 403
Crossword puzzles, 164
Cuing systems, 173–176, 250
Cumulative tales, 155
Curriculum (*see also* Integration, curriculum):
decisions, 15–16
guides (syllabuses), 15, 81–82, 200, 481
models, 14–19
Cursive, 422–428

Data chart, 460–463
Database of books, 263
Deaf, 7 (*see also* Hearing difficulties/deaf [impairments])
Debates, 329
Deep structure, 415
Desktop publishing, 29
Dial-a-story, 338–339, 378
Dialects, 38–39, 48, 177, 436
differences in, 5, 41
of speakers, 46, 64–65, 416
Dialogue, 69, 31
Dictionary:
personal, 449
usage, 252–253
Diorama, 163

Direct instruction:
explicit, 12–13, 24, 206, 246, 252–254,
systematic, 215, 352, 428
Directed Listening Activity (DLA), 180
Directed Listening/Reading Activity (DL/RA), 179–180
Directed Listening/Reading-Thinking Activity (DL/RTA), 180–186
Directed Listening/Thinking Activity (DL/TA), 180–188
Directed Reading Activity (DRA), 180, 185–186
Directed Reading-Thinking Activity (DRTA), 180–188
Directed Speaking/Writing Activity (DSA/DWA), 301–304
Directed Writing Activity (DWA), 283
Discussion, 312–314, 320–329
panels, 329
webs, 323–324, 329
Display and bookmaking, 376–377
Distance learning, 443–446
Diverse learners, 1–2, 9, 13, 18, 26, 57–59, 235–238, 246, 248, 257–261, 267, 478–479
teaching, 68–88
Diversity:
bilingual and ESL students, 416
cognitive and physical, 59–63, 88
cultural and linguistic, 22, 63–68, 69–70
gap, bridging, 85–88
self-assessment, 86
statistics, 63
Drafting, 293–294, 363–369, 455, 466–467
web for, 364
Dramatic play, 240
Dramatics, creative, 155, 331–337
Draw-and-Tell Stories, 225–226

Early intervention programs, 243–244
Early reading programs, effective, 243–244
Ebonics, 39, 64, 416 (*see also* Black English)
Editing, 371–374, 417, 420
proofreading, checklists, 363, 372, 429
for spelling errors, 411

UNIVERSITY OF RHODE ISLAND

3 1222 00986 760 0

CML PROF. RES. LB 1576 .B76
Bromley, Karen D'Angelo,
1944-
Language arts

DISCARDED
URI LIBRARY